DOWNHILL ALL THE WAY
AN AUTOBIOGRAPHY
OF THE YEARS
1919 to 1939

BY THE SAME AUTHOR

The author and Sally

DOWNHILL ALL THE WAY

AN AUTOBIOGRAPHY
OF THE YEARS 1919–1939

By
LEONARD WOOLF

1967
THE HOGARTH PRESS
LONDON

Published by
The Hogarth Press Ltd
42 William IV Street
London WC2

*

Clarke, Irwin & Co. Ltd
Toronto

Printed in Great Britain by
T. & A. Constable Ltd
Hopetoun Street, Edinburgh

The herd ran violently down a steep place
into the lake, and were choked.

St Luke, Chapter 8

CONTENTS

ILLUSTRATIONS

Chapter One

PEACE IN OUR TIME, O LORD

AT THE end of the third volume of my autobiography the great war of 1914 to 1918 had just ended, having in its four years killed 10 million men and caused 36 million casualties. It has been estimated that the direct cost of the war was about £60,000 million and its indirect cost about £50,000 million. It destroyed, I think, the bases of European civilization. We, like everyone who lived through those years, had been profoundly influenced by them. When the maroons boomed on November 11, 1918, we were no longer the same people who, on August 4, 1914, heard with amazed despair that the guns had begun to boom. In 1914 in the background of one's life and one's mind there were light and hope; by 1918 one had unconsciously accepted a perpetual public menace and darkness and had admitted into the privacy of one's mind or soul an iron fatalistic acquiescence in insecurity and barbarism. There was nothing to be done about it, and so, as I recorded, Virginia and I celebrated the end of a civilization and the beginning of peace by sitting in the lovely, panelled room in Hogarth House, Richmond, which had been built almost exactly 200 years before as the country house of Lord Suffield, and eating, almost sacramentally, some small bars of chocolate cream.

The last sentence seduces me into a digression, though what I am about to say is not really irrelevant on the first page of a volume of autobiography, for it is concerned with the impossibility of telling the truth, the extraordinary difficulty of unearthing facts. The moment one begins to investigate the truth of the simplest facts which one has accepted

9

as true—about one's own life, for instance—it is as though one had stepped off a firm narrow path into a bog or quicksand—every step one takes one sinks deeper into the bog of uncertainty.

For instance, the above statement about Hogarth House is not true, though for years I believed it to be true. When in 1915 we took a lease of Hogarth House, it was part of a large eighteenth-century mansion which belonged to a lady living in Bushey. The mansion had been very ingeniously divided into two houses, one called Suffield House and the other Hogarth House. We were told at the time that the whole house had been built originally in 1720 as a country house for Lord Suffield and had been converted into two houses with two front doors in the nineteenth century. That it was built in 1720 was, I think, almost certainly true. That was, it seems to me, about the best moment for English architecture, at any rate for the medium-sized, aristocratic country house like the one which Lord Suffield did not build in Richmond in 1720. The interior of the original undivided house must have been perfect. All the rooms were panelled, the ones on the ground floor with a certain amount of chaste ornamentation; in the others the panels became progressively plainer as one went up from floor to floor. Every room was beautifully proportioned. Most houses and gardens are, like most of the people who make them or live in them, featureless, amorphous; the houses are closed boxes in which people live, the gardens open boxes in which people grow flowers or vegetables. Occasionally one comes across a house upon which those who built it or lived in it have imposed a character and form markedly and specifically its own, as though it were a person or a work of art. Hogarth House was one of these. All the rooms, even when we first saw them in the dirty, dusty desolation of an empty house, had beauty, repose, peace, and yet life. One felt at once that each of them only needed a table and chair, a bed or a bookcase to become the perfect cell in which a human being might eat and sleep, talk, read, or work. Perhaps the people who for 200 years had been doing just that in these rooms had left the aura of their lives in them, but more prosaically it was matter— bricks and mortar and wood—and the way in which they had been used 200 years before which gave to Hogarth House its extraordinary character of being the perfect envelope for everyday life. It was partly its combination of immense solidity with grace, lightness, and beauty. The electrician who had to take a wire through the inside wall of the drawing-room, told us that in all his experience he had never seen as thick an inside wall in a house. In the room itself one felt the security from anything like a hostile world, the peace and quiet, in this tremendous solidity of walls, doors, and windows, and yet nothing could have been more light and graceful, more delicately and beautifully proportioned than the room itself, its fireplace and great windows, its panelling and carved woodwork.

In the house before it was divided there was a great hall and a very beautiful staircase, and on the first floor a tremendously broad corridor. We lived in this house from 1915 to 1924. After the war, in 1920, the owner refused to renew our lease, but offered to sell us the whole property, i.e. both Suffield and Hogarth House. We bought it for £2,000, and at one moment we thought we might restore the two houses to their original condition as one great country house and live for the remainder of our lives in this magnificent Suffield House. But it was a project half serious and half a day dream. By 1924 we had abandoned it, for the house would have been much too large for us and we had decided that it was time to move back into London. So we sold what had once been Suffield House and moved to Tavistock Square.

But had it ever been Suffield House? Had it ever belonged to Lord Suffield? It is impossible to know, but what is quite certain is that no Lord Suffield built it as his country house in 1720, because the barony of Suffield was created in 1786. So much for the truth about the genealogy of a house. I recently discovered that when I bought Monks House, Rodmell, in 1919, what I was then told about its name and its genealogy was also quite untrue. As I recorded in a previous volume of my autobiography,[1] it was said to have been called Monks House, because in the fifteenth century it belonged to Lewes Priory and the monks used it for their 'retreats'. I said that I hoped the story was true, but I rather doubted such legends about houses when there is no documentary evidence for them. Since writing that, I have examined the deeds for Monks House and find that the story is entirely untrue. The deeds go back to 1707 and record the names of everyone who lived in it (together usually with the names of all their sons and daughters) from 1707 to 1919, when I bought it from the heirs of Jacob Verrall. From 1707 to 1919 only three families owned and lived in it. In 1707 John Cleere or Clear, carpenter of Rottingdean, acquired it from James de la Chambre. From 1707 to 1796 it remained in the Clear family, passing from father to son. In 1779 John Clear, carpenter, great-grandson of the original John Clear, carpenter, inherited it, and left it, when he died in 1782, to his son James. (He left five guineas to each of his two sons, Edward and Thomas, and a guinea to his granddaughter Charity.) In 1796 James Clear sold it to John Glazebrook. All this time, from 1707 to 1796, the house was called Clear's.

From 1796 to 1877 the house was in the Glazebrook family, 33 years in the hands of John Glazebrook and 48 years in those of his widow, Mercy, and his son William,

---

[1] *Beginning Again*, p. 61.

except for a short interval in 1829 when it was sold for
£300 to Matthew Lower, publican, of Rodmell, who resold
it for £300 back to William Glazebrook. The Glazebrooks
must have been connected with the Clears and with the
house already 30 years before they actually acquired it, for
in a mortgage deed of 1765 the property is described as a
messuage in the tenure of John Clear and John Glazebrook.
The Glazebrooks were millers; John Glazebrook in 1749
bought the mill which was up on the down above Rodmell,
and it remained in the family for 128 years, when the executors of William Glazebrook sold it to Jacob Verrall in 1877.

At the same time, in the same year, the executors also sold
what is now called Monks House to Jacob Verrall. From
1796 to 1877 the house was called Glazebrook's except for
a short interval when it was called Lower's. The first time
that it was ever called Monks House in any document was
when it was advertised for sale in 1919 on Jacob Verrall's
death. The story that Monks House belonged to the Lewes
monks in the fifteenth century is therefore just as false as
the story that Suffield House was built by Lord Suffield in
1720.

It is rather depressing for an autobiographer starting on
a fourth volume to find in this way that most of his facts are
will-o'-the-wisps and that it is almost impossible to tell the
truth. Facts about the houses in which one lives during the
whole journey from the womb to the grave are not unimportant. The house—in which I include its material and spiritual
environment—has an immense influence upon its inhabitants.
Looking back over one's life, one sees it divided by events
into compartments or chronological sections, e.g. I was at
St Paul's School 1894 to 1899, I was in the Ceylon Civil
Service 1904 to 1911, I lived through the war of 1914 to
1918 and the war of 1939 to 1945, I was married in 1912.
All such momentous or catastrophic events moulded the

13

form of one's life, disrupted or distorted its movement. But what has the deepest and most permanent effect upon oneself and one's way of living is the house in which one lives. The house determines the day-to-day, hour-to-hour, minute-to-minute quality, colour, atmosphere, pace of one's life; it is the framework of what one does, of. what one can do, and of one's relations with people. The Leonard and Virginia who lived in Hogarth House, Richmond, from 1915 to 1924 were not the same people who lived in 52 Tavistock Square from 1924 to 1939; the Leonard and Virginia who lived in Asham House from 1912 to 1919 were not the same people who lived in Monks House from 1919 to 1941. In each case the most powerful moulder of them and of their lives was the house in which they lived. That is why looking back over my life I tend to see it divided into sections which are determined by the houses in which I lived, not by school, university, work, marriage, death, division, or war.

When I bought Monks House in 1919 there was an auction of all its contents. It took place in the garden on a marvellous sunny summer day. All the village attended, including descendants of the long line of Glazebrooks who had already been moving about in the house and garden 155 years before. 1919 was a great fruit year in Sussex; the trees were laden with plums and pears and apples. The branches of an enormous apple-tree heavy with great red apples hung over the yew hedge along which we stood bidding or just watching the auction; and every now and again someone would pull a great red apple off the tree and eat it. There is nearly always something sad and sinister in the auction of the contents of a house, a kind of indecent exposure of the lives of dead men, women, and children. This is particularly the case when the auctioneer reaches those cold and comfortess attics in which in distant days servants slept on iron bedsteads. As the auctioneer's men carried the furniture, glass, and china, ornaments, pictures, and the accumulated odds and ends of a family's possessions on to the Monks House lawn, it seemed at moments as though one were watching the disembowelling, not merely of a house, but of time. Old Jacob Verrall's[1] wife Lydia was, I think, a connection of the Glazebrooks and much of the furniture etc. must have belonged to them and to have been in the house for a century and more. Some of the old furniture and china was beautiful and was bought up at quite high prices by dealers. I bought three pictures painted on wood by a Glazebrook in the middle of the nineteenth century or perhaps a little earlier. They were painted in that curious stiff uncompromising style of the inn signboard of a hundred years ago. One was of a middle-aged man, very dark and bewhiskered, and another of a man holding a horse. The third was of four children heavily swaddled in hats and coats standing stiffly in a line in front of the house. They were, I am sure, the Glazebrook children of a hundred years ago. Their spirits, I almost felt and feel, walk in the house, clattering up and down the narrow stairs, now deeply worn by the countless comings and goings of Clears, Glazebrooks, and Verralls. At the top of the stairs you can see the place where they had once put a small gate to prevent the children plunging downstairs. And once when a floorboard was taken up by a workman we found a tiny little wooden eighteenth-century shoe; another time I found in the cellar a George III fourpenny piece which appeared to have been charred in a fire.

These little facts are not, I think, either unimportant or irrelevant. In the atmosphere of both houses, Monks House in Rodmell and Hogarth House in Richmond, there was something similar. In both one felt a quiet continuity of

[1] I gave some facts about old Verrall and his wife in *Beginning Again*, pp. 63 and 64.

people living. Unconsciously one was absorbed into this procession of men, women, and children who since 1600 or 1700 sat in the panelled rooms, clattered up and down stairs, and had planted the great Blenheim apple-tree or the ancient fig-tree. One became a part of history and of a civilization by continuing in the line of all their lives. And there was something curiously stable and peaceful in the civilization of these two houses. In 1919 when we bought Monks House, Virginia was only just recovered or recovering from the mental breakdown which I have described in *Beginning Again*; in 1919 we still had six years of life in Hogarth House before we moved into London. Those six years were, I am sure, crucial for the stabilizing of her mind and health and for her work, and I am quite sure that the tranquil atmosphere of these two houses, which was in their walls and windows and gardens and orchard, but also in the soothing, chastening feeling of that long line of quiet people who century after century had lived and died in them—I am sure that this tranquil atmosphere helped to tranquillize her mind.

At the end of 1919, then, we were the owners of two houses. Our expenses during the previous twelve months had been £845. We had been printing and publishing books in the Hogarth Press for two years, but the Press was still a hobby which we practised in our spare time. The three books which we published in 1919 were Virginia's *Kew Gardens*, T. S. Eliot's *Poems*, and J. Middleton Murry's *Critic in Judgment* —on which we made a net profit of £26, 3s. 10d. Virginia had just begun her 'career' of a novelist. Her first novel, *The Voyage Out*, had been published by Duckworth four years ago in 1915. Her second novel, *Night and Day*, had just been published, also by Duckworth, in October 1919. *The Voyage Out* had received high praise, and so did *Night and Day*, but to a less degree. Neither book was a success financially either for the author or publishers, for, as I have recorded elsewhere, nine years after it was published Duckworth had sold only 2,238 copies of *Night and Day*. Virginia's only other publications by the end of 1919 were *The Mark on the Wall*, which the Hogarth Press published in 1917, and *Kew Gardens*, which we published in May 1919. She did not begin to write her third novel, *Jacob's Room*, until April 1920, but she wrote some short pieces like *An Unwritten Novel* and did a certain amount of reviewing in the *Times Literary Supplement* and *Athenaeum*. Her earnings in 1919 from her writing, at the age of 37, were £153, 17s. 0d. Virginia was 40 years old before she earned a living wage by writing; if she had had to earn her living during those years, it is highly improbable that she would ever have written a novel.

By 1920 I had accumulated a considerable number of paid and unpaid occupations. I was editor of the *International Review* on a salary of £250. I did a good deal of freelance ournalism, mostly for the *New Statesman*, but a certain amount for the *Nation* and the *Athenaeum*. I earned in 1919 £578, £262 by freelance journalism, £250 from my editorship, and £66 from my books. The *International Review* was a monthly financed by the Rowntrees; I had an office in Red Lion Court, Fleet Street, in which sat Miss Matthaei, Assistant Editor, and Miss Green, Secretary. I went to the office three or four days a week. We did a great deal of work. My idea was that the *Review* should cover the whole field of foreign affairs, international relations, and the problem of preventing war which centred in the inchoate League of Nations. My main object was to try to put before readers the facts without a knowledge of which it was impossible even to begin to understand the intricate problems of the international chaos created by the war. I therefore had two features in the paper which I thought of great importance. The first, which I wrote myself, was an 'international diary'; in it I dealt with the chief international events of the previous month. In order to produce this diary Miss Matthaei and I read French, German, Austrian, Italian, and Spanish daily papers. The second feature was, I think, something quite new in this kind of journalism. I had a section called 'The World of Nations: Facts and Documents'. It ran to 30 or 40 pages and it contained all kinds of documents, most of which were unobtainable elsewhere. We took any amount of trouble to obtain documents, and the kind of thing we published is shown by the contents of a single number, November 1919: (1) Message of Admiral Kilchak to the peoples of Siberia and instructions to military officers; (2) Declaration of the Ukrainian Government regarding Denikin; (3) The text of an Anglo-Persian Treaty; (4) The text of an alleged treaty between Germany and Japan which had been published in America but not in Britain; (5) A translation of the full text of the new German Constitution.

In my search for documents I had some curious experiences; the following was one of the most interesting. I do not remember how or when I first got to know Theodore Rothstein, a Russian Jew living in London. He is frequently mentioned in the diaries of Wilfrid Scawen Blunt, for in 1907 he was London Correspondent of the *Egyptian Standard* and worked closely with Blunt and Brailsford for Egyptian independence. When I knew him in 1919 he was unofficial ambassador of the unrecognized Bolshevik Government. He told me that, when the Bolsheviks first seized power, the London police arrested him and put him on a ship lying in the Pool just below London Bridge, meaning to deport him in it to Russia. Rothstein knew Lloyd George and had had 'off the record' communication with him on behalf of Lenin. He succeeded in getting a letter to the Prime Minister smuggled out of the ship, and orders were immediately given to the police to release the Russian 'ambassador'.

Rothstein was a short, stumpy, bearded, bespectacled

revolutionary who looked like Karl Marx. He was the first of
the many hundred per cent. dyed in the wool, dedicated
communists that I have had the misfortune to come across
in the last 45 years of my life. Communists, Roman Catholics,
Rosicrucians, Adventists, and all those sects which fero-
ciously maintain as divine or absolute truth, monopolistically
revealed to them, an elaborate abracadabra of dogmas and
fantasies, fill me with melancholic misery. The ruthlessness
and the absurdity of the believers' beliefs reduce me to despair. What is the point, one feels, of any political, social,
scientific, or intellectual activity if civilized people in the
twentieth century not only accept as divine truth the myths
dreamed by Palestinian Jews two or three thousand years
ago or by German Jews a hundred years ago, but also condemn to Hell, death, or Siberia those who disagree with them?

Rothstein, as I said, was the first of these modern civilized
savages, these communist fanatics, that I came across. Outside the circle of his Marxist religion he seemed to me a nice
man and highly intelligent; inside the magic circle he was a
cross between a schoolman and a dancing dervish. He would
expound the gospel of Marxism-Leninism to me at great
length in that dreadful jargon of meaningless abstractions
which has become the language of communism and the
excuse for the torture or killing of hundreds of thousands of
human beings. Some time in 1919 he came to me and said
that he had the full text of a number of speeches made by
Lenin since his return to Russia. None of these very important speeches and statements of policy had been reported
in the British or American press, and he was willing to give
me translations of them if I would publish them in the
International Review. I said that I would, and then I had my
first experience of the behaviour of the real underground
revolutionary.

The question was how the typescript of the translation of

Lenin's speeches should be physically handed over by Rothstein, his agent, to me, the editor. Having had no experience of revolutionaries, secret agents, or spies, I naturally thought that it would be sent to me in the ordinary way through the post. Rothstein was horrified at such a crude and naïve idea. There was, he said, and in this he was correct, still operating a censorship, which was a legacy from the war, and if the authorities knew of the existence of verbatim translations of Lenin's speeches, they would refuse to allow publication; we must on no account allow the police to know that he was going to give them to me. The only way to defeat the police was for me to follow his instructions meticulously. On Wednesday afternoon I was to walk down the Strand towards Fleet Street, timing it so that I should pass under the clock at the Law Courts precisely at 2.30. I must walk on the inside of the pavement and precisely at 2.30 I would meet Rothstein under the clock walking from Fleet Street to Trafalgar Square on the outside of the pavement. He would be carrying in his right hand an envelope containing Lenin's speeches, and, as we passed, without speaking or looking at each other, he would transfer the envelope from his right hand to mine.

This elaborate procedure was carried out and I sent the speeches to the printer to be printed in the next issue of the *International Review*. I do not know how the police discovered that we were going to publish these documents or why the authorities thought that it would be dangerous for the British people to know what Lenin was saying—it seems rather fantastic to believe that a Secret Service man was always trailing Rothstein and saw him hand over the envelope to me outside the Law Courts. At any rate a few days later the police went to the printers, seized the documents and, I think, some type which had already been set, and forbade publication.

The British public were thus prevented from knowing what Lenin was saying in Russia at the historical moment when that knowledge was most interesting and politically important. This is one of the many instances of congenital stupidity in secret services and censorship which I have come across in my life and which, however often I come across them, fill me with innocent surprise. No intelligent person who went about his business in London in 1918 and 1919, who talked to the common man and knew what is called the climate of opinion, could possibly have thought that the number of people who would have been politically influenced by reading Lenin's speeches in the *International Review* would have exceeded the number of righteous men whom Abraham and the Lord found in Sodom. But once one begins to try to suppress some knowledge or some opinions, one loses all sense of proportion and relevance in one's obsession with the danger of ideas. In the end the only safe course for the worried, nervous policeman and the cloistered censor, sitting aloof in his office with the blue pencil in his hand, is to try to suppress all knowledge and all thought.

I do not think that I saw Theodore Rothstein many times after the fiasco with Lenin's speeches. It was not very long before he went back to Russia. I was told—I do not remember by whom or know with what truth—that he became a Commissar in Samarkand or some other remote province of the Soviet Empire. He was such a ruthless dogmatist and such a dedicated Leninist-Marxist that he must, I think, sooner or later have been liquidated in one of the great purges by some equally dedicated and ruthless comrade.

To someone like myself born in the comparative civilization of the nineteenth century one of the horrors of life since 1920 is its senseless savagery. If one shuts one's eyes or one's mind, it is just possible to ignore the millions of Jews slaughtered in Hitler's gas chambers and the millions of unstigmatized persons killed in concentration camps and 'on the field of battle' during the 1939 war. But somehow or other the crowning point of barbarism seems to have been reached in the kind of doctrinal or racial cannibalism that has swept over the earth. The merciless savagery with which Spaniard treated Spaniard in the civil war, or Italian treated Italian under Mussolini, or German treated German under Hitler, or African is now treating African in the Congo, makes such outbreaks as the Armenian atrocities, which horrified Gladstonian liberals towards the end of the nineteenth century, appear insignificant. 'Dog does not eat dog' and 'a wolf does not make war on a wolf' are such ancient truths that they are proverbial, but in the twentieth century large-scale fratricide has been common among patriots, monarchists, republicans, fascists, nazis, socialists, anarchists in Germany, Italy, Spain, and Africa. But the doctrinal cannibalism of communists since 1917, particularly in Russia, has been even more repulsive if only because of its scale. The liquidation in 1930 of the Russian kulaks— peasants numbering with their families five million persons —is one of the most dreadful stories in the whole of history.[1] And no one will ever know how many hundreds of thousands of Russians have been liquidated by Russians in the last 40 years—in forced-labour camps, prisons, judicial murders, purges. When one reads that a million kulaks have been ruined or done to death because they were rather prosperous peasants, or 500,000 Russian communists have been killed by Russian communists because they were either right deviationists or left deviationists, or six million German Jews

[1] Sir John Maynard in *The Russian Peasant* says that 'it can only be compared for ruthlessness with the wholesale removals of population by the ancient monarchies, or the expulsion of the Moors from Spain or the Jews from Germany'.

have been killed by German Christians because they were Jews, one cannot feel that each one of these persons was an individual like oneself, that every one of a million Russian peasants when he was suddenly driven out of his house and off his land to starve and die with his family in the snow, and each one of those hundreds of thousands of Russian communists when he felt himself rotting to death in the Siberian labour camp, and each of those six million Jews when he found himself being driven naked by the nazi guards into the gas chamber, suffered, before the final annihilation of death, the same agony which you or I would suffer if it happened to us.

I do not think that to say this is sentimental or here irrelevant. At any rate it has, I know, to me personally a peculiar and profound relevance. I have known as individuals and friends in London two Russians who went back to Russia and put their heads into the noose of Stalinist communism. I feel pretty certain that in each case the noose was pulled sooner or later and my friends were liquidated. If you had searched the world, you could not anywhere have found two men more unlike each other than Theodore Rothstein and Prince Mirsky, the Russian Jew and the Russian aristocrat. Rothstein was, as I have said, a mediaeval schoolman born into the twentieth century, a pedant and fanatic where the gospel of Karl Marx was concerned. He was, I think, by nature a gentle and civilized man, who loved talk and the intellectual pleasure to be derived from the intricate working of good brains. But he had been caught in the cruel inhuman machinery of communism. If he were not ruthlessly liquidated, he would himself have been a ruthless liquidator.

Let me leave Rothstein for the moment being shot by a comrade or shooting a comrade in one of those purges by which behind the iron curtain men build the perfect society. Let me turn to Prince Mirsky. Mirsky was a stranger man than Rothstein. I always felt that he was fundamentally one

of those unpredictable nineteenth-century Russian aristocrats whom one meets in Aksakov, Tolstoy, and Turgenev.
Sometimes when one caught in a certain light the vision of
his mouth and jaw, it gave one that tiny little clutch of fear
in the heart. It made one think of Turgenev's mother flogg-
ing the servant to death. I have known only a very few
people with this kind of mouth; its sinister shape comes, I
think, from the form of the jaw and arrangement of the
teeth. There is always the shadow of a smile in it, but it is
the baleful smile of the shark or crocodile.[1] Mirsky had this
kind of smile. It may have had no psychological significance
and he may well have had nothing cruel or sharklike in his
character. In all our relations with him he seemed an un-
usually courteous and even gentle man, highly intelligent,
cultivated, devoted to the arts, and a good literary critic.
He had, at the same time, that air of profound pessimism
which seemed to be characteristic of intellectual Russians,
both within and without the pages of Dostoevsky. Certainly
Prince Mirsky would have found himself spiritually at home
in *The Possessed* or *The Idiot*.

One day Mirsky came to us in Tavistock Square and told
us that he was going back to Russia. This must have been
in 1931. By that time one knew something of the kind of
life (or death) that an intellectual might expect in the Russia
of Stalin. It seemed madness, if not suicide, for a man like
Mirsky voluntarily to return to Russia and put himself in the

[1] One day when I was travelling by train along the south coast of
Ceylon from Matara to Galle, on the platform of one of the stations
through which we passed there were dozens of dead sharks. I had
never seen anything like it in Ceylon and I do not know why they
were there. On each dead face there was this sinister grin. Talking to
Mirsky in a London sitting-room, as he suddenly turned his head to say
something and there was a glint of teeth and smile, I was back in Ceylon
twelve years ago in the railway carriage looking at the rows of dead,
smiling sharks.

power of the ferocious fanatics who could not possibly have the slightest sympathy with or for him. We knew Mirsky well enough to say so. He was extremely reticent, shrugging it all off with some platitude, but he left us with the impression of an unhappy man who, with his eyes open, was going not half, but the whole, way to meet a nasty fate. We never saw him again.

The fate of Mirsky and of Rothstein seems to me terribly typical of our time. Both of them, as I said, were almost certainly liquidated, which means that they were in some horrible way put to death, murdered. Even if they were not, they must have escaped by some accident, for thousands of men like them have been liquidated in Russia. Contemplating this and them, I feel the horror of the savagery of contemporary man in a way in which I do not feel it when I hear of the more horrible stories of the massacre of millions. I knew them as individuals, and it is as an individual that I feel their fate, this liquidation, this senseless torture and killing of two harmless individual human beings. For what after all could be more harmless than the slightly ridiculous bespectacled Rothstein spinning the endless web of the Marxian abracadabra or Mirsky endlessly discussing the magnificent absurdity of Tolstoy or the niceties in the torrential style of Dostoevsky? That Theodore Rothstein may have been himself potentially as cold-blooded a murderer as his cold-blooded murderers, or that Prince Mirsky may have been potentially as inhumanly cruel as so many other Russian aristocrats, does not contradict or make nonsense of what I have just written; it only underlines the senseless political and social stupidity of contemporary Europe. I have sat talking in Richmond with Rothstein and in Paris and Tavistock Square with Mirsky, and I know that what interested them and what gave them pleasure were things of the intellect and the arts, painting, music, and literature.

In a world which had the slightest claim to civilization, they would have lived and died civilized men, doing or suffering no public evil. As it was, their lives became hopelessly entangled in the wheels of an idiotic, barbarous social and political system, and the misery and death which they suffered (or which perhaps they caused) were inflicted on pretexts or for reasons which have no sense, no reality, no importance for the vast majority of the human race. Power and the struggle for power are of course realities involved in the machinery of communism and Soviet Russia in which Rothstein and Mirsky became fatally involved; but power is always the concern of a tiny minority. The Rothsteins and Mirskys and the thousands of anonymous victims of communism are sacrificed for words and phrases, tales 'told by an idiot, full of sound and fury, signifying nothing'.

I know that I am prejudiced against communism, which seems to me in some ways worse than nazism and fascism. *Corruptio optimi pessima*—the greatest evil is the good corrupted. The Hitlers and Mussolinis are just thugs or psychopaths, savages who in all ages have formed the scum of society; their imitators like Oswald Mosley rouse in me no emotion more serious than contempt. But communism has its roots in some of the finest of human political motives and social aspirations and its corruption is repulsive. The first time I met Mirsky was in Paris, in Jane Harrison's flat. Jane Harrison, the brilliant Newnham classical scholar, was one of the most civilized persons I have ever known. She was also the most charming, humorous, witty, individual human being. When I knew her she was old and frail physically, but she had a mind which remained eternally young. She liked Mirsky and enjoyed talking to him, and he, I felt, sat at her feet. That from that environment he should have been drawn into the spider web of Soviet Russia to be destroyed there fills one with despair, despair that communism, by *corruptio*

26

optimi, again and again and again has 'lighted fools the way to dusty death'.[1]

I have reached the period in my autobiography in which our lives and the lives of everyone have become penetrated, dominated by politics. Happy the country and era—if there can ever have been one—which has no politics. Ever since 1914 in the background of our lives and thoughts has loomed the menace of politics, the canker of public events. (One has ceased to believe that a public event can be anything other than a horror or disaster.) Virginia was the least political animal that has lived since Aristotle invented the definition, though she was not a bit like the Virginia Woolf who appears in many books written by literary critics or autobiographers who did not know her, a frail invalidish lady living in an ivory tower in Bloomsbury and worshipped by a little clique of aesthetes. She was intensely interested in things, people, and events, and, as her new books show, highly sensitive to the atmosphere which surrounded her, whether it was personal, social, or historical. She was therefore the last person who could ignore the political menaces under which we all lived. *A Room of One's Own* and *Three Guineas* are political pamphlets belonging to a long line stretching back to *Vindication of the Rights of Women* by Mary Wollstonecraft, and she took part in the pedestrian operations of the Labour Party and Co-operative Movement. And by 'pedestrian' I mean the grass roots of Labour politics, for she had a branch of the Women's Co-operative Guild meeting regularly in our house in Richmond and we had the Rodmell Labour Party meeting regularly in Monks House, Rodmell.

[1] Since writing the above, I have been told by Malcolm Muggeridge, who saw a good deal of Mirsky in Moscow in 1932-33, that Mirsky just before the war was sent to a camp for ten years and either died or was shot there.

The theme of politics and public events must therefore
become more important and more persistent in this autobiography from 1919 onwards. It was not merely that I
became more and more actively immersed in them. We lived
our daily life and ate our daily bread in the shadow of recurring crises and catastrophes. When peace at last came in
1918, it was, of course, like the break in the appalling sky
which must have covered poor Noah's ark, a gleam of sun
'after the end of the hundred and fifty days' when 'the
fountains of the deep and the windows of heaven were stopped
and the rain from heaven was restrained'. Of course we welcomed the dove with the olive leaf in her beak. We put out
a few flags and a few hopes hesitantly, apprehensively.
Almost immediately the flags drooped, the olive leaf withered,
the hopes faded. In the years 1918 to 1939 one impotently
watched a series of events leading step by step to barbarism
and war: the Versailles Treaty and the canker of reparations;
the creation of Stalin's Russia, the iron curtain, and the cold
war; the rise of fascism and nazism; the failure of the League
of Nations; the menace of nuclear war; the Hitlerian
Götterdämmerung.

In all this gloom the darkest spot seemed to me and to
many other people, at any rate until Hitler came to power
in 1933, Stalin's Russia. I have described in *Beginning Again*
(pp. 207-215) how, when the Tsarist regime fell, we welcomed the 1917 revolution with the same kind of relief and
elation which Wordsworth felt in 1789 in the first days of
the French revolution. The disillusionment was all the
greater. At first one was puzzled by the senselessness of the
iron curtain—the shutting off of millions of civilized persons
in the twentieth century from the rest of the world and from
truth. Then gradually it became clear that the communist
rulers of Russia were determined not only to keep their
subjects in darkness and ignorance, but also, if possible, to

keep the rest of the world in a state of fluid chaos. The foreign policy of the Soviet Government was always simple and consistent: they fished in troubled waters, but they were also continually trying to make the waters troubled so that they could fish. Hence the cold war.

Then still more gradually one became aware of the sense-less barbarism of communist society behind the iron curtain. Here again, so far as I was concerned, a realization of the truth only came gradually by personal experience, by know-ing some insignificant individual caught and crushed in the inhuman machinery of the Soviet state—which according to Theodore Rothstein and Karl Marx ought to have withered away. I remember the shock of the first time when I caught a glimpse of this monstrous juggernaut crushing a little individual (and innocent) fly. I knew a young woman, whom I will call Jane, who married, in the early years of the Soviet regime, a Russian scientist employed in Russia. They lived in Leningrad and she was allowed to come for a few weeks every year and visit her mother in England. She always came to see me. I knew her well and she used to tell me about her life and her views with the greatest frankness. Jane was intel-ligent and had that spontaneous, generous political enthus-iasm often characteristic of the young, and particularly the female young. She was a communist before she married her Russian, for she was one of the many intelligent young people on the political Left who in the early 1920s were depressed by the dreary record of German social democracy and were carried away by the promises of communists and commun-ism. Every year for a year or two after her marriage the day used to come when Jane would burst into my room in the highest spirits and tell me of all that the communist regime was doing and was going to do for the 'toiling masses'. Even-tually when a year had gone round and the day came for her visit, things had changed. She was depressed and worried, and admitted that she was anxious about the way things were going in Russia. According to her account, the idealistic asceticism which Lenin had imposed upon the party was breaking up. What had attracted her in communism and what she had found in Lenin's Russia was the selfless dedication of the leaders to the task of transforming Russia into a society 'in which the free development of each is the condition of the free development of all'. Lenin was a ruthless man, and he created a ruthless party; but he was ruthless with himself and he insisted upon communists being ruthless with themselves. Their aim was socialism pure and undefiled, both in theory and in practice. Nearly all communists whom I have known have been very callow or very cunning. (Some of the most hoary old Marxists, like Rothstein, were really both at the same time.) Jane was as politically callow, when a young woman, as an unfledged sparrow. She married and went to Russia believing that the communists and she with them were out to build Utopia—the New Jerusalem and Cloud-Cuckoo-Land. After Lenin's death and the struggle for power which followed it, even Jane could see that idealism and a good deal of freedom were dying out of communism and the Soviet Republic. Something new had come in with Stalin and Stalin's men. Any clouds or cuckoos faded away, for the new rulers were tough and realists. They drove about in big cars and you had to be careful of what you said about them. Jane went back to Russia depressed and uneasy.

It must have been in 1936 that Jane returned to England from Russia for good and came to see me. She was in tears when she told me her wretched story. Her husband, she said, was a scientist, and a devoted scientist who took no part in politics. He was an extremely cautious man and, whatever he may have thought about the regime, never criticized it. One day he did not return home from his laboratory; he just disappeared. Some time later she received an official notification directing her to take some of his clothes and personal possessions to a certain government building. When she got there, she found a series of what looked like ticket offices each labelled with letters of the alphabet. She was told to hand in her husband's possessions at the ticket office labelled with the initial letter of his name. There were long queues of people, like herself, waiting to hand in bundles and suitcases at the various ticket offices. She was given a receipt for her husband's possessions. She never saw him again; eventually she received a letter from him from a labour camp in the Far East. When the time came for her annual visit to England, she was given her permit. In London she went to see Mirsky and consulted him as to what she should do; he strongly advised her not to return to Russia, and she took his advice.

Thus the enormous machinery of the Soviet state was used to disrupt the lives of these two little innocuous insects, Jane and her husband. And senselessly this two-handed engine at the door smote, and smote no more, so far as these two insects were concerned. It is this streak of senselessness in the savagery of communist, and indeed all authoritarian, states which repels and puzzles one. I am quite sure that Jane was speaking the truth when she said that her husband was entirely non-political and that the only possible reason for his liquidation was that one of his fellow-scientists, working in the same laboratory, who was arrested at the same time, was notoriously indiscreet in his criticism of the regime.

I got from Jane another glimpse of the grotesque nightmare of mutual fear in which, under the shadow of the secret police, both rulers and ruled lived in Russia. 1937 was the centenary of the great Russian poet Pushkin's death. Jane gave me a manuscript translation of a short book by

Pushkin which had not been translated into English before, I think, or at any rate was not in print; as far as I can remember, it was autobiographical and extremely interesting. The translation, which was excellent, was by a Russian woman, a friend of Jane's. The suggestion was that the Hogarth Press should publish it in the centenary year. I was eager to do so, but instantly the menacing spectre of the Soviet Government and the secret police and Siberia rose up out of the manuscript to make us pause in Tavistock Square, London, W.C. 1, in the year 1936. Jane explained the difficulty to me. Whether in fact to publish was a nice question, the nicety being for her friend the thinnest partition between life and death. For it to be known that someone in Russia was the translator of a book written by Pushkin over 100 years ago and now published in London might or might not be extremely dangerous for the translator. Whether it would lead to the liquidation of the translator or not would depend upon the amount of terror and fear obtaining at any particular moment among the rulers, secret police, and the ruled in Leningrad and Moscow. Jane had therefore arranged with her friend that, if I decided that the Hogarth Press would like to publish, I should send her a telegram saying simply: 'Many happy returns'. If it was safe to publish, she would reply: 'Many thanks for good wishes'; if it was not safe, she would not reply. I sent off my wire and got no reply, and so the book was never published. It is interesting to compare this incident with the action of the London police with regard to Lenin's speeches which I have related above. The idea that the publication of a translation of a book by Pushkin in London could have harmed in any way the Russian state or people was as fantastic as the idea that the publication of Lenin's speeches in the *International Review* could have done the slightest damage to the British state or people. But, as I said before, censorship of thought and opinion in the hands of a government and its police is a malignant canker which grows and grows, gradually destroying its environment, the mind of society. If there are dangerous thoughts, all thought may be dangerous; it is safer therefore to suppress as much as you can whether it be Lenin or Pushkin.[1]

The insistent pressure of politics, increasing rapidly as soon as war ended, caused me to stand rather halfheartedly for Parliament. It began in 1920. In those days there was a Combined English University Constituency which included all the English universities other than Cambridge and Oxford; they elected two M.P.s. After the khaki election of December 1918, the Seven Universities' Democratic Association asked me whether I would consider becoming a candidate at the next election. It was not a prospect which filled me with any enthusiasm. As a secretary of the Labour Party Advisory Committees on International and Imperial Affairs, which after a time took to meeting in a Committee Room in the House of Commons, I got to know a good many Labour M.P.s who were members of my committees, and I saw from the inside the kind of life they had to lead. The hour-to-hour and day-to-day life of professional and business men in their offices and at their 'work' consists largely or time wasted in a vicious circle of unnecessary inaction or futile conversations. Nearly all important business is done effectively and expeditiously outside the office, which can be reserved mainly as a place in which one dictates and signs letters. (That is why during the last 50 years, whether as editor or publisher, I have always stipulated that I would spend the minimum amount of time 'in the office'.) The business life of a backbench M.P. in the 1920s seemed to me the acme of futility and boredom. He was, no doubt, a member of what was said to be the best club in London,

[1] I suppose that the secret police were not merely afraid of Pushkin, but afraid that a Soviet citizen should know a British citizen.

but he had to be perpetually in it, endlessly doing nothing as he waited to record his vote at the next division.

This prospect of joining the melancholy procession of backbenchers through the lobbies of the House of Commons, as I said, did not appeal to me, and for some time I hesitated to become a candidate. However, eventually I agreed, and in May 1920 was adopted as a candidate. I agreed partly, and rather pusillanimously, because there was really no chance of my being elected. The sitting members were the Conservative Sir Martin Conway and the Liberal Herbert Fisher. I must admit that a second reason which induced me to stand was the prospect of standing against Herbert Fisher. Herbert was a first cousin of Virginia's, a man of great charm, both physical and mental, but also the kind of man whom in those days I thought it to be almost a public duty to oppose in public life. For he was the kind of respectable Liberal who made respectable liberalism stink in the nostrils of so many of my generation who began their political lives as liberals. Winchester and New College, Oxford; Trustee of the British Museum; Vice-Chancellor of Sheffield University; Warden of New College Oxford; he was chosen by Lloyd George, with his unerring instinct for political window-dressing, to be in 1916 Minister for Education (in those days called President of the Board of Education). I may have been prejudiced and unfair, but I thought the Fisher Education Act, which Herbert was responsible for, to be the sort of cowardly compromise which seemed to save the face of its author at the expense of his principles. When he was a Minister, we used to see him fairly often. He would come to us in Richmond, but he also sometimes stayed with Sir Amherst Selby-Bigge, Permanent Secretary at the Board of Education, at Kingston, which was three miles from us at Rodmell, and then he would walk over to see us. His conversation fascinated us; he was so nice, so distinguished,

34

and so ridiculous that he might have walked straight into
Crotchet Castle. His face and his mind had the gentle, pale,
ivory glow, the patina which Oxford culture and innumerable
meals at College high-tables give to Oxford dons. So quiet
flows the life of the don that there is nearly always something
innocent and childlike in his mind. Herbert, with all this
academic innocence, suddenly found himself projected into
the very centre of the world of action, the House of Commons,
Downing Street, the Cabinet. L. G. and the Cabinet went
to his head, and he was intoxicated by this 'life of action',
though his intoxication, like everything else in him and the
Fisher family, was a muted, genteel intoxication. He was
obsessed by L. G., who was to him a cross between the
superman and a siren, and by Downing Street, sitting in
which he felt himself to be sitting bang on the hub of the
universe.

About all this poor Herbert discoursed to us lyrically, but
with just that touch of humour and restraint required by the
good taste which with him was a characteristic both inherited from nineteenth-century ladies and gentlemen and
acquired all over again in Oxford. He was never tired of
telling us that we and everyone else who did not sit in Downing Street knew nothing about anything. He gave us a
vision of the Prime Minister and the President of the Board
of Education sitting in the Cabinet Room in Downing
Street and receiving an unending stream of secret, momentous messages from every quarter of the earth, if not the
remotest galaxies of the outer universe. When the Lloyd
George government fell and Herbert went back to New College, he still continued to tell and retell nostalgically the
fairy story of his days in Downing Street. And before I leave
him in New College I cannot refrain from telling another
little absurd story which Adrian Stephen, Herbert's cousin,
once told me. Adrian went to stay for a week-end with the

Fishers at New College. The Fisher household was run on extremely economic (to put it euphemistically) lines, which extended to the blankets. It was a bitter cold winter night and Adrian, who was six foot five inches in height, was given a very short bed with a single thin blanket. In the middle of the night he could stand it no longer; he managed to get the whole carpet up and put it over instead of under the bed, and then crept in under it. Unfortunately in the morning he found it impossible to get the carpet properly back in its place and he left his room in a state of chaos. He was not again invited to spend a week-end in New College.

I must return to the election of 1922 and my candidature. I propose to quote from my election address, because it shows where I stood politically a few years after the first great war ended, and also because, I think, my attitude was also that of those who at the time were considered to be on the Left in the Labour Party: we stood between the Labour Party Centre and the Communists and their Fellow Travellers, who were called the Extreme Left. (It has always seemed to me to be curious and confusing that communists are accepted, on their own classification, as Extreme Left; their political outlook and organization is more like that of the Catholic clerical parties on the Continent, the old Centre Party in Germany, and the Present Christian Democrats in Italy, and of the deceased Fascists and Nazis, i.e. their correct classification is slightly to the Right of the Extreme Right.) Here then is my declaration of political faith in October 1922:

I am asking for your votes as a candidate adopted by the Seven Universities' Democratic Association. . . . The Association is affiliated to the Labour Party, of which I have been a member for some considerable time. . . . We have in this country two alternatives before us at this

36

election: we can once more entrust the government of the country to one of the two political parties which, for the better part of a century, have separately or in coalition been in power, and which, therefore, are jointly and severally responsible for the social, political, economic, and international conditions in which we find ourselves today; on the other hand, we have an opportunity of making a break with the past and of entrusting the government to a party of new principles and of new men. I confess that one reason why I am a member of the Labour Party, and why ... I ask you to support that Party with your vote, is this: that, looking round upon the political and economic conditions in London and Manchester, in Dublin, India, and Egypt, and remembering the graves in France and Gallipoli which were to be the price of a new world, I feel that this is no time for a mere reshuffle of the ancient Conservative and Liberal Pack and for entrusting power to one or other of the two parties whose political principles and practice are directly responsible for the disastrous situation in which the country finds itself today. A century of Conservative and Liberal Governments brought us war and a peace which has proved hardly better than war. There will be no change if the old men and the old methods are reinstated in Westminster, and if we want a change we must try a party with new principles and new men. I have no illusions with regard to governments and political parties, and I do not ask you to vote for me and for Labour on any promise that we will hang the Kaiser, or make Germany pay, or take five shillings off the income tax, or make everyone peaceful and prosperous. If the Labour Party is returned to power, it will make many mistakes; it will not succeed in carrying out all its principles or all its promises; it will disappoint very many of its supporters. But the Party has this great advantage over the two older parties: unlike them it has ideals and principles which are real and alive, based not upon the possessions and privileges of classes or upon political doctrines which were dead before our grandfathers were born, but upon the generous hopes and vital needs of millions of ordinary men and women. It is these ideals, hopes, and needs which, if I were elected, I should endeavour to help the Labour Party to translate into details of the following practical policy. . . .

There can be no economic recovery in this country, no beginning to build up an educated and prosperous community, unless there is a complete break with the dangerous and extravagant foreign policy which has been pursued equally by Conservative and Liberal Governments. This country must stand out in Europe and the world as a sincere supporter of a policy of peace and international co-operation. The pivot of its programme must therefore be (1) a real League of Nations, inclusive of all nations, the members of which undertake a definite obligation not to go to war; (2) disarmament, beginning with drastic limitation of naval and military armaments, coupled with a general guarantee against aggression; (3) an equitable settlement of the reparation problem and the promotion of good relations between France, Germany, and this country, as the first step towards economic recovery in Europe. This third point is urgent, and it is practicable. The policy which I would support is an offer by this country to France to relieve her of her debt to us in return for her consent (a) to fix reparation payments at a figure which Germany can reasonably be expected to pay, to confine such payments strictly to restoration of the devastated areas, and to grant a sufficiently long moratorium to enable German credit to be restored; (b) to revise the Treaty of Versailles and withdraw the armies of occupation.

I went on to say that I believed 'that the only hope for Europe consists in the gradual building up of a close understanding and co-operation between Britain, France, and Germany in a League of Nations', and that the policy outlined above was the first step towards such an understanding. I added four other steps which I considered essential: (1) recognition of the Russian Government and promotion of trade with Russia; (2) close co-operation with the U.S.A.; (3) 'complete abandonment of the policy of imperialism and economic penetration and exploration which has been pursued by us from time to time in the Near East, Mesopotamia, Persia, and China'; (4) 'It is essential that the promises of self-government made to India and Ceylon, and of independence to Egypt, should immediately be carried out with scrupulous honesty, and, further, that those methods in our government of the so-called backward races of Africa which are leading to their subjection and exploitation should be fundamentally revised'.

In home affairs I said that education was the subject of greatest importance and I set out an educational policy which would 'assure to all classes a complete equality of opportunity to obtain elementary, secondary, and university education' and which would produce 'an adequate staff of trained and certified teachers'. I pledged myself to a policy of economy on unproductive expenditure, a more equitable system of taxation, and 'a special graduated levy upon fortunes exceeding £5,000'. I ended my manifesto thus:

In this statement I have confined myself to the immediate and practical problems which will have to be faced by the next House of Commons. I believe in socialism and co-operation, but not in violent revolution; I believe that the resources of the community should be controlled by and in the interests of the whole community rather than

39

small groups and classes. But the work of the next Parliament ought to consist neither in bolstering up the vested interests of the present economic system nor in immediately destroying it, but in laying the foundations of a real peace in Europe and of an educated democracy in this country.

I have given at some length this declaration of my political faith in October 1922 both for general, historical, and also for personal reasons. If a man has the temerity to write the story of his life, he should have a double aim: first, to show it and his little ego in relation to the time and place in which he lived his life, to the procession of historical events, even to the absurd metaphysics of the universe; secondly to describe, as simply and clearly as he can, his personal life, his relation, not to history and the universe, but to persons and to himself, his record in the trivial, difficult, fascinating art of living from day to day, hour to hour, minute to minute. I have reached the years in the story of my life which make the first aspect of my autobiography more and more insistent. I have been alive from November 1880 until November 1965; no period in the world's history has been more full of what are called great events, bringing disruption, disaster, cataclysms to the human race, than those 84 years. In the 1914 war there was a nasty poster the object of which was to shame the reluctant citizen into joining the army; it was of a cherubic child asking: 'What did you do in the great war, Daddy?' The question soon lost its meaning—its sting. But 'What did you do in the years between the two great wars?' is a vital question which anyone who took any part in public affairs must answer. The policy for which I declared in the election address was not popular in 1922; it was, and still often is, misrepresented. Looking back over what has happened since, I think that it was the only policy which might have saved Europe from fascism and nazism and from the horror and disaster which they brought upon the world.

I still have to deal with all this later in my passage through the years from 1919 to 1939; now I must return to the election. I rather enjoyed the election campaign, such as it was. The procedure for this peculiar constituency was that candidates made, at most, only one visit to each of the seven universities and made a speech in each. As far as I can remember I visited only Liverpool, Manchester, Durham, and Newcastle. In each I made a speech to what seemed to me a semi-public meeting of already convinced supporters. I do not think that I made a very good impression, partly because I did not always succeed in concealing the fact that I was not really very eager to be an M.P. In March 1921, when I went to Manchester, Virginia came with me. It is many years since I have been in that city, and in 1965 it may be a very different place from what it was when I knew it in the 1920s. In 1921, from the moment when I arrived at its grimy station to the moment when I departed from it, it filled me with a kind of exasperated despair. It was the City of Dreadful Night—'the street lamps burn amidst the baleful glooms'; a drizzle of sooty raindrops dripped remorselessly from the dirty yellow sky upon the blackened buildings and the grey crowds of melancholy men scurrying perpetually, like ants, this way and that way through the foggy streets. Through these streets an unending string of trams ground their way one behind the other; everywhere all the time one's ears were battered by the scraping and grating of their wheels and the striking of their bells. We stayed at the Queen's Hotel, as Virginia recorded in her diary, paying 18s. each for a bed, 'in a large square, but what's a square when the trams meet there? Then there's Queen Victoria like a large tea-cosy, and Wellington, sleek as a mastiff with paw extended.'

My spirits, depressed by the streets and sky, by Queen Victoria and the Duke of Wellington, were not raised by my constituents. I made two speeches to them, one before and one after dinner. They were extremely nice and extremely good people, many of them professors or lecturers, who had been conscientious objectors or had been arrested for keeping the flag of liberty flying in Manchester during the war. But, like Queen Victoria and the Duke, they were somewhat grey, depressed, low in tone. 'Old Mrs Hereford and Professor Findlay', Virginia noted, 'sat patiently looking at the tablecloth with nothing to say, like two old horses who have been working in the fields all day together.' When Mrs Findlay asked Virginia whether she was a politician and whether she did much organizing work, Virginia said she listened. 'Mrs Findlay shook her head. Why was I there then?' There was, it must be admitted, no satisfactory answer to that question.

When I find myself in a strange city, at a loose end, waiting as one does eternally in strange cities for a boat, a plane, or an interview—when time seems to stop and the universe seems to have dwindled to an unending series of hotel corridors, lavatories, and lounges—I tend to go to the zoo. I am ambivalent about zoos: I have an uneasy feeling that one should not keep animals in cages, but I never get tired of watching animals anywhere. You can learn a great deal about the character of a country or city by going to its zoo and studying its arrangement and the behaviour of the animals. The London Zoo is an animal microcosm of London, and even the lions, as a rule, behave as if they had been born in South Kensington. I once saw a curious incident there when one of them did not. It was a warm summer day and the lions were in their outdoor cages. A stout, middle-aged, middle-class lady was standing near the bars looking at a magnificent lion who was standing on the other side of the bars gazing over her head, as lions seem to do, into eternity.

Suddenly he turned round, presented his backside to her, and pissed on her through the bars. 'Oh the dirty beast,' she said, 'Oh, the dirty beast,' wiping her face and blouse, half angry, half amused, and the tone of her voice was exactly as if some nasty little boy had done some dirty trick in the Earls Court Road.

I recall vividly two other zoos. When I was in Jerusalem in 1957, I had to go to the Foreign Office which seemed to me a long weary way out from the centre of the city. I started to walk back; it was hot and dusty, and I seemed to have got into a ramshackle suburb frequented by those unshaven, long-haired orthodox Jews, young men whose self-conscious, self-righteous hair and orthodoxy fill me with despair. When I saw a signpost directing me to the zoo, I made off for it at once. But I did not, as I had hoped, escape from the melancholy of the dreary streets and the moth-eaten anachronism of those ridiculous young men. I have never seen anywhere else so melancholy a collection of animals. The architecture of the zoo seemed to be a ramshackle replica of the surrounding streets, and long-haired monkeys gazed at one, it seemed to me, with the self-satisfaction of all the orthodox who have learned eternal truth from the primeval monkey, all the scribes and pharisees who spend their lives making mountains of pernicious stupidity out of molehills of nonsense.

I should add that the long-haired monkeys in the Jerusalem Zoo and the long-haired orthodox Israelis in the neighbouring streets are characteristic of only one side of contemporary Israel. When you enter Israel by Tel Aviv, buzzing with business as though it were a gigantic human hive, drive up the road to Jerusalem, or visit Haifa and Tiberias, you are exhilarated by the energetic exhilaration of the people who are everywhere living dangerously and happily wresting from the rocky earth and a ring of implacable enemies a new way of life in a strange land. These people, who form the immense majority of the population, are the exact opposite of the orthodox Jews in Jerusalem. It makes it the more lamentable that they should allow politics and therefore life in Israel to be continually influenced by orthodox Judaism. Again and again one has in life to say, with Lucretius, '*tantum religio potuit suadere malorum*'—how much evil religion has induced human beings to do! One is accustomed to see throughout history down to today the absurd delusions of savages promoted to divine truths and their morality and rules of conduct maintained for two or three thousand years as an excuse for protecting the vested interests of ignorance and injustice. To see this process once more repeated in modern Israel is horrifying. After all, the austere, bare monotheism which the ancient Hebrews developed made it comparatively easy for their Jewish descendants in modern times to shed the primitive beliefs and rituals and morality of the Pentateuch. Already two thousand years ago the writers of the books which we call *Job*, *Ecclesiastes*, and *Micah* had laid the foundations of a civilized morality and a sceptical, rational theism, from which by the process of time might come 'the religion of all sensible men'—agnosticism or atheism. It is deplorable to find the builders of the modern state in Israel making its laws conform to the belief that the creator of the universe, with its suns, planets, galaxies, atoms—old bearded Jehovah sitting up there on Mount Sinai amid the thunder and lightning and once in three thousand years showing his backside to a favoured Moses—that this omnipotent deity has enacted an eternal law, revealed to a handful of rabbis and ignorant men in Jerusalem, regulating the shaving and haircutting of males, the eating of pork and the slaughtering of sheep, and the use of trains and taxis on days which some people happen to call Saturday and others Samedi.

PEACE IN OUR TIME, O LORD

The other zoo which I vividly recall is in Colombo. Colombo is as different from Jerusalem as the Sinhalese are from the Israelis. My likes and dislikes are catholic, and I have remarked before in this autobiography that I see no reason why, because one likes claret, one should not also like burgundy; I like both, and I like both Israel, with its fierce sun, fiery rocks, its furnace of human activity, and Ceylon, with its tropical 'lilies and languors', the gaily coloured kaleidoscope of flowers, trees, and cheerful, drifting crowds. Three years after I visited the Jerusalem Zoo I visited Ceylon. The plane which was to take me back to England was delayed somewhere in eastern Asia and I found myself in one of those exasperating predicaments in which one has nothing to do but wait indefinitely for someone to ring you up and say that you need wait no longer. I waited from 8 in the morning, when my plane should have left, until 12 midnight, when it did. Half-way through the morning I went to the Colombo Zoo. It was a microcosm of Colombo, of the Sinhalese low country, of the Sinhalese way of life. It was 'full of trees and waving leaves', amid which, in the humid languorous heat, elephants, lions, leopards, bears lived their happy natural lives. I was watching a family of lions, father, mother, and three cubs, who were in a large open-air enclosure. The male was lying asleep up in one corner and the female was drowsing down in the other corner; the cubs were playing about. Suddenly one of the cubs went over and began to play with his father's tail. There was a low growl; the tail flapped angrily on the ground; the cub made another dart at it. The lion lifted his great head just off the ground and let out a blood-curdling snarl. The lioness rose up and slowly, threateningly went over to the lion and quite silently stood over him between him and the cub. The lion got up and slowly, sullenly walked over to the farthest corner where he flopped down

45

to sleep again. The lioness shooed the cub back to her corner. It seemed to me what I might have been watching a domestic scene in a compound in one of those Sinhalese villages, a Sinhalese mother slowly, firmly shooing her child away from mischief and danger.

I must unfortunately return once more from the Colombo Zoo in 1960 to Manchester, Durham, and the election in 1922. When I went to meet my constituents and make a speech to them in Durham, the meeting was held in the room of a graduate. The audience was extremely small; indeed, in each of the universities the number of people who came to my meetings was very small. I was told by the chairman of the Durham meeting that many who would support and might vote Labour would not do anything openly which might connect them with the Labour Party, because that connection would be viewed with disapproval by the university authorities and would jeopardize their prospects of a good job after they had taken a degree. He said that this was to some extent due to political prejudice, but what was more important was the fact that the university relied for financial and other support in part upon the local wealthy Conservatives, often 'big business', and had to be careful not to offend or antagonize them. Theoretically and on the surface your religion, politics, or economics were as unimportant as the colour of your hair, but if you wanted to do well for yourself academically it was safer to conceal the fact that you were left of centre. I was told that this was more or less true of all the provincial universities in those bad old days.

I came, as was expected, at the bottom of the poll, Sir Martin Conway, Conservative, and the Right Honourable Herbert Fisher, Liberal, being elected. Conway was a curious man. He had been mountaineer and explorer and a Slade Professor, and in 1922 he was Director General of the Imperial War Museum. Shortly after the election I received the following letter from him:

> It was only two days ago that I learned who you are—the author of *A Village in the Jungle*. That is a book which I read with extraordinary delight and which I treasure alongside of the *Soul of a People*. I am really sorry to have been put in opposition to a writer I so heartily admire. Of one thing, however, I am certain: the writer of such a book would have found the H. of C. a most unattractive place and would have been very unhappy there, especially if he had been obliged to associate intimately with the rank and file of the Labour Party—tho', of course, among them are some delightful simple souls, very lovable, but the bulk are not such.
>
> I am venturing to send you a book of mine in kindly remembrance of our contest. Your late father-in-law was an honoured friend of mine, as you may guess.
>
> Yours faithfully
Martin Conway

Sir Martin asked me to lunch with him in the House of Commons and I found him to be a pleasant, not very interesting man. His letter—and the attitude towards the Labour Party in the Universities—show clearly the social and political snobbery of those days. It amused me that the Slade Professor of Fine Arts should think that I must be such a sensitive plant that I would wilt unhappily in the company of the rough trade unionists of the Labour Party. As a matter of fact I knew a good many Labour M.P.s as Secretary of the Labour Party Advisory Committees and because for a time I was Parliamentary Correspondent of the *Labour Leader*. Of course, some of them were pretty tough, but I never found any difficulty in getting on with them.

In the period of my life of which I am now trying to tell

the story—and indeed in the whole of my life after the year 1919—it has, as I have said, been dominated by politics and public events which are living and lived history. As I look back over the mental and physical chaos and kaleidoscope which has been my individual life from 1919 to 1965, I see that history ruthlessly divided it into four periods: (1) 1919 to 1933, the fourteen years of struggle for civilization which ended with Hitler's rise to power; (2) 1933 to 1939, the six years in which civilization was finally destroyed and which ended with war; (3) 1939 to 1945, the six years of war; (4) the post-war world. If I am to continue with the story of my life, I shall have to deal with the events of each of these four periods, the effect of each upon me and my life, and my reaction to each of them. But even in our cruel, mechanized, barbarous age, we have not yet become completely robots, puppets jerked through life by history, governments, and computers. We still have, at any rate in Britain, some shreds of private life, which we can preserve unaffected by public events. It is to our private lives that I must now turn—to return later to politics in the kind of seesaw which must inevitably continue through the fourth volume of my autobiography. What dominates or moulds our private lives privately is, as I have said, the house in which we live. In each period of our living we are profoundly influenced, therefore, by both history and geography, by time and place. In my own case, war and peace and Stalin, Mussolini, and Hitler divided the twenty years of my life from 1919 to 1939 into the two periods 1919-1933 and 1933-1939, and the same twenty years were deeply divided for us into two other periods by two houses, Hogarth House in Richmond from 1919 to 1924 and Tavistock Square in Bloomsbury from 1924 to 1939. I must now deal with the period of six years in Richmond.

One must begin with Virginia's illness and her slow

recovery from it, for we continued to live in Richmond mainly to protect her from London and the devastating disorientation which would threaten her from social life if we returned to live there. It was a perpetual struggle to find the precarious balance of health for her among the strains and stresses of writing and society. The routine of everyday life had to be regular and rather rigid. Everything had to be rationed, from work and walking to people and parties. Despite all our precautions, her diary shows how often in the first few years after the war she was ill or threatened with illness. The threat was almost always a headache, which was the warning signal of mental strain; the 'illness', if it came to that, was the first stage towards breakdown. We knew exactly what the treatment should be; the moment the headache came, she had to go to bed, and remain there comatose, eating and sleeping, until the symptoms began to abate. That was the cure; the difficulty was always to perform the actions which the cure required: unfortunately one does not sleep—or even eat—because one knows that sleeping or eating is the one thing which will cure one of a shadow across one's brain.

In 1921 and 1922 Virginia was continually beset with these attacks. For instance, in the 1921 diary there is an entry for June 7 describing how Tom Eliot came to tea and joined us in lamenting the Pecksniffian character of John Middleton Murry. The next entry in the diary is August 8 and I will quote it, because it shows so clearly what Virginia actually suffered in one of these threatening attacks:

What a gap! How it would have astounded me to be told when I wrote the last word here, on June 7th, that within a week I should be in bed, and not entirely out of it till the 6th of August—two whole months rubbed out— These, this morning, the first words I have written—to

call writing—for 60 days; and those days spent in weari-
some headache, jumping pulse, aching back, frets,
fidgets, lying awake, sleeping draughts, sedatives, digita-
lis, going for a little walk, and plunging back into bed
again—all the horrors of the dark cupboard of illness
once more displayed for my diversion. Let me make a
vow that this shall never, never, happen again; and *then*
confess that there are some compensations. To be tired
and authorized to lie in bed is pleasant; then scribbling
365 days of the year as I do, merely to receive without
agitation of my right hand in giving out is salutary. I feel
that I can take stock of things in a leisurely way. Then the
dark underworld has its fascinations as well as its terrors;
and then sometimes I compare the fundamental security
of my life in all (here Mrs Dedman interrupts for 15
minutes) storms (perhaps I meant) with its old fearfully
random condition. Later I had my visitors, one every day,
so that I saw more people than normally even. Perhaps, in
future I shall adopt this method more than I have done.
Roger, Lytton, Nessa, Duncan, Dorothy Bussy, Pippa,
Carrington, James and Alix—all these came; and were
as detached portraits—cut out, emphatic, seen thus
separately compared with the usual way of seeing them in
crowds. Lytton, I note, is more than ever affectionate.
One must be, I think, if one is famous. One must say to
one's old friends 'Ah my celebrity is nothing—nothing—
compared with this'.

This was, of course, a severe bout, and in the autumn and
winter of 1921 she had recovered to her normal equilibrium
which allowed her safely—but within limits—to work and
live a social life. But during the first seven months of 1922
she was off and on continually unwell or threatened with
headaches. In March she started a temperature which the

doctors took seriously and sent us on a fairly long odyssey through Harley Street and Wimpole Street which gave us a curious view of medical science and the tiptop Harley Street specialists. We had at the time an extremely nice, sensible G.P., Dr Ferguson. He sent us first to a lung specialist who said that Virginia's symptoms were due to her lungs, which were in a serious state. When this was reported to Ferguson, he said it was nonsense; he had examined her lungs frequently and there was nothing wrong with them; we should ignore the diagnosis. He sent us off to a heart specialist, who said that Virginia's symptoms were due to her heart, which was in a serious state. We returned sadly to Richmond and Ferguson. I was told by him that the great man had diagnosed inflammation of the heart, a disease from which some famous man—I think it was the great Alfred Harmsworth, Lord Northcliffe—had just died. The disease was incurable and death imminent and inevitable. In his opinion, he said, this was nonsense; he had frequently examined her heart and there was nothing seriously wrong with it; we should ignore the diagnosis. We did so. We went, I think, to one more specialist, a distinguished pathologist who discovered that Virginia was suffering from the disease in which he specialized. He was wrong; we ignored his diagnosis and decided to forget about it and about Harley Street. She not only recovered from the three fatal and incurable diseases; the disquieting symptoms gradually disappeared.

At our last interview with the last famous Harley Street specialist to whom we paid our three guineas, the great Dr Saintsbury, as he shook Virginia's hand, said to her: 'Equanimity—equanimity—practise equanimity, Mrs Woolf'. It was, no doubt, excellent advice and worth the three guineas, but, as the door closed behind us, I felt that he might just as usefully have said: 'A normal temperature—ninety-eight point four—practise a normal temperature, Mrs Woolf'.

With regard to her writing, Virginia certainly never learned to practise equanimity. Like most professional writers, if she was well, she went into her room and sat down to write her novel with the daily regularity of a stock-broker who commutes every day between his house in the suburbs and his office in the neighbourhood of Throg-morton Street. Her room was very different from a stock-broker's office. She was an untidy writer, indeed an untidy liver, an accumulator of what Lytton Strachey used to call 'filth packets', those pockets of old nibs, bits of string, used matches, rusty paper-clips, crumpled envelopes, broken cigarette-holders, etc., which accumulate malignantly on some people's tables and mantelpieces. In Virginia's work-room there was always a very large, solid, plain wooden table covered with filth packets, papers, letters, manuscripts, and large bottles of ink. She very rarely sat at this table, cer-tainly never when she was writing a novel in the morning. To write her novel of a morning she sat in a very low arm-chair, which always appeared to be suffering from prolapsus uteri; on her knees was a large board made of plywood which had an inkstand glued to it, and on the board was a large quarto notebook of plain paper which she had bound up for her and covered herself in (usually) some gaily-coloured paper. The first draft of all her novels was written in one of these notebooks with pen and ink in the mornings. Later in the morning or in the afternoon, or sometimes at the beginning of the next morning, she typed out what she had written in the notebook, revising it as she typed, and all subsequent revisions were made on the typewriter. A curious thing about her was that, although she was extremely sensitive to noise and was one of those people who 'jumped out of her skin' at a sudden noise or unexpected confrontation, she seemed usually, when writing, to acquire a protective skin or integument which insulated her from her surroundings. Her room tended to become not merely untidy but squalid. She reached the final stage of organized disorganization and discomfort when we moved from Richmond to 52 Tavistock Square in Bloomsbury. At the back of the house was what had once been an immense billiard room. We used it as a storeroom for the Hogarth Press and there embedded among the pyramids and mountains of parcels, books, and brown paper sat Virginia with her disembowelled chair, her table, and her gas fire.

In the regularity of this routine of writing and in her disregard of her surroundings when writing one might not unreasonably have seen a measure of equanimity. Up to a point this was true; in some ways her attitude in writing and to her writing was extraordinarily controlled, dispassionate, coldly critical. In the process of her writing—of her artistic creation—there were long periods of, first, quiet and intense dreamlike rumination when she drifted through London streets or walked across the Sussex water-meadows or merely sat silent by the fire, and secondly of intense, analytical, critical revision of what she had written. No writer could possibly have given more time and intensive thought to the preparation for writing and to the revision of what she had written. Both these periods required and got from her dispassionate equanimity. But there were also for her two periods of passion and excitement. The first was in the moment of creation, in the whole process of actual writing. I think that, when writing, Virginia was almost the whole time writing with concentrated passion. The long strenuous intellectual process was over and would be called in again for revision; now emotion and imagination took control. And at moments, as I pointed out in *Beginning Again*,[1] genius or inspiration seemed to take control, and then, as she described how she wrote the last pages of *The Waves*, 'having

[1] Page 31.

reeled across the last ten pages with some moments of such intensity and intoxication that I seemed to stumble after my own voice, or almost after some sort of speaker (as when I was mad) I was almost afraid, remembering the voices that used to fly ahead'.[1] There was, of course, no place or possibility for Dr Saintsbury's 'equanimity' in this kind of emotional and imaginative volcanic eruption, the moment of artistic creation. But I think that whenever Virginia was actually writing a novel—or rather the first draft of a novel—her psychological state was in a modified degree that described above. The tension was great and unremitting; it was emotionally volcanic; the conscious mind, though intent, seemed to follow a hair's breadth behind the voice, or the 'thought', which flew ahead.[2] It was this terrific, persistent tension which, because it naturally produced mental exhaustion, made her writing a perpetual menace to her mental stability. And the moment that the symptoms of mental exhaustion began, she was unable to write.

In what I have written above, I have distinguished two markedly different—indeed almost antithetical—phases in Virginia's creative process. This swing of the pendulum in the mind between conscious, rational, analytic, controlled thought and an undirected intuitive or emotional process almost always takes place where the mind produces something original or creative. It happens with creative thinkers, scientists, or philosophers, no less than with artists. Perhaps the most famous instance was recorded over two thousand

[1] *A Writer's Diary*, p. 169.

[2] I think that when she was revising and rewriting on a typewriter what she had written with pen and ink in the morning, her psychological state and her method were quite different. The conscious, critical intellect was in control and the tension was less. It was largely the same when she was writing criticism. I used to say that, when she came in to lunch after a morning's work, I could tell by the depth of the flush on her face whether she had been writing fiction or criticism.

years ago in Sicily when the problem in hydrostatics which Archimedes had unsuccessfully worked upon for days suddenly solved itself in his drowsing mind as he lay in his bath and he dashed out naked into the streets of Syracuse shouting: 'I have found it, I have found it!' Virginia, too, often 'found it' by the same kind of mental process and with the same excitement.

It was this excitement which was the sign and symptom of the mental strain of her writing and which was a perpetual menace to her stability. But there was also, as I have said above, a second period of passion and excitement through which she almost always had to pass in the process of writing a novel. This came upon her almost invariably as soon as she had finished writing a book and the moment arrived for it to be sent to the printer. It was a kind of passion of despair, and it was emotionally so violent and exhausting that each time she became ill with the symptoms threatening a breakdown. In fact, the mental breakdown which I described in *Beginning Again* occurred immediately after she had finished writing *The Voyage Out*, and the breakdown in 1941 which ended in her suicide occurred immediately after she had finished *Between the Acts*. And in 1936, when she had finished *The Years* and she had to begin correcting the proofs, she came desperately near a mental breakdown. On April 19 she wrote in her diary:

> The horror is that tomorrow, after this one windy day of respite—oh the cold north wind that has blown ravaging daily since we came, but I've had no ears, eyes, or nose: only making my quick transits from house to room, often in despair—after this one day's respite, I say, I must begin at the beginning and go through 600 pages of cold proof. Why, oh why? Never again, never again.[1]

[1] *A Writer's Diary*, p. 268.

The psychology of the artist in the final stages of creation and production is very interesting. Many writers have I think felt, but have not, like Virginia, recorded, the horror of facing those pages of 'cold proof' and, even more, the cold breath of criticism in the first days after publication. In *Beginning Again* I said that, in my opinion, one reason why Desmond MacCarthy never wrote the novel which, when he was a young man, we thought he would write and which he intended to write, was that he could not face the responsibility of publication, the horror of the final day when the book and the author are handed over to the icy judgment of the reviewers and the public. However sensitive the serious author may be, the moment comes when he has to be ruthless with himself. He must coldly go through the weary waste of cold proof, put the last comma into the last sentence, deliver himself artistically naked to the public, take the icy plunge of publication. At that point he must have the courage to say to himself: 'Literary editors, reviewers, my friends, the great public—they can say what they like about the book and about me. Hippokleides doesn't care.'[1] Virginia was terribly —even morbidly—sensitive to criticism of any kind and from anyone. Her writing was to her the most serious thing in life, and, as with so many serious writers, her books were

[1] I have the greatest admiration for Hippokleides—his story is in Herodotus. He became engaged to Kleisthenes's daughter, and at the feast to celebrate the engagement he got rather above himself and danced on his head on the table. When Kleisthenes, who was very grand, being Dictator of Sikuon, saw the legs waving in the air, he was outraged and said: 'O son of Tisandros, you have danced away your marriage'. To which Hippokleides replied: 'Hippokleides doesn't care'. His reply became a Greek wisecrack. How surprised Kleisthenes and, indeed, Hippokleides would be at the vagaries of immortality if they knew that the Dictator and hundreds of other 'great' men of his time are completely forgotten while Hippokleides, with his legs waving in the air above his head and his wisecrack, are still, 2,400 years later, recalled with approval and affection.

to her part of herself and felt to be part of herself somewhat in the same way as a mother often seems all her life to feel that her child remains still part of herself. And just as the mother feels acutely the slightest criticism of her child, so any criticism of her book even by the most negligible nitwit gave Virginia acute pain. It is therefore hardly an exaggeration to say that the publication of a book meant something very like torture to her.

The torture began as soon as she had written the last word of the first draft of her book; it continued off and on until the last reviewer, critic, friend, or acquaintance had said his say. And yet, despite her terrifying hypersensitivity, there was in Virginia an intellectual and spiritual toughness which Desmond lacked. It came out in the dogged persistence with which she worked at every word, sentence, paragraph of everything she wrote, from a major novel to a trumpery— or what to almost any other writer would have seemed a trumpery—review. The consequence was that the moment always came when she stiffened against the critics, against herself, and against the world; ultimately she had the courage of her convictions and published, saying—not with much conviction—'Virginia doesn't care'. And that was why, unlike Desmond, she had published, when she died, seventeen books.

The psychology of human misery is curious and complicated. Several critics have expressed surprise and disapproval at the spectacle of Virginia's misery over blame or even the lack of praise. Max Beerbohm, for instance, 'had reservations' about her and disliked her diary. 'I have never understood,' he said, 'why people write diaries. I never had the slightest desire to do so—one has to be so very self-conscious.' (It is significant that Max thought that his not wanting to do something was a good reason or an excuse for his not understanding why other people wanted to do it and did it.) 'It was deplorable,' he said, 'to mind hostile criticism as much as Virginia Woolf did.'[1] It was no doubt highly deplorable both ethically and from the point of view of her own happiness. But it and the writing of diaries is surely a little less difficult to understand than Max found them. The mother's instinct to resent criticism of her children is irrational and deplorable, but common and not entirely unnatural. Vanity explains part of it, but not, I think, all. Oddly enough there is mixed in with the vanity something which is almost the opposite of vanity in these cases, a kind of objective ideal. The mother wants the child to be perfect for its own sake, and Virginia, whose attitude towards her books was, as with so many serious writers, maternal, wanted her books to be perfect for their own sake. She was also abnormally sensitive, both physically and mentally, and it was this which helped her both to produce her novels and to be miserable when Mrs Jones or Max Beerbohm didn't like them. And I rather think it helped her once to hear the sparrows talking Greek outside her bedroom window.

When I remember how, owing to her health, Virginia always had to restrict her daily writing to a few hours and often had to give up writing for weeks or even months, how slowly she wrote and how persistently she revised and worked over what she had written before she published it, I am amazed that she had written and published seventeen books before she died. There are today (in 1965) 21 volumes in the list of her publications. This is the more surprising because none of these books had been written by her before the age of 30, and all her major works, except *The Voyage Out* and *Night and Day*, were written in the last 21 years of her life. In the period with which I am now concerned, our years at Richmond from 1919 to 1924, her writing was strictly rationed and often interrupted. They were years of

[1] See *Max*, by Lord David Cecil, pp. 483-484.

crucial importance in her development as a novelist, for during them she revolted against the methods and form of contemporary fiction—pre-eminently the fiction of Galsworthy, Wells, and Bennett—and created the first versions of her own form and methods which ultimately and logically developed into those of *The Waves* and *Between the Acts*.

The process began with the 'short stories' which she collected and published in March 1921 in *Monday or Tuesday*. They were all written between the years 1917 and 1921 and were a kind of prelude or preliminary canter to *Jacob's Room* which was published in October 1922. *The Mark on the Wall* was the first sign of the mutation in method which was leading to *Jacob's Room*; it was published in July 1917, forming part of *Two Stories*, our first Hogarth Press publication, and was written at the end of 1916 or the beginning of 1917. It has been said by some critics that Virginia derived her method, which they call the stream of consciousness, from Joyce and Dorothy Richardson. The idea that no one in the arts has ever invented anything or indeed has ever had an original thought, since everything is always 'derived' from something else in an unending artistic House that Jack Built, is extremely common and has always seemed to me untrue—and if not untrue, unimportant. The merits or defects of *The Waves* remain unaffected whether they were or were not 'influenced' by Joyce's *Ulysses* or Dorothy Richardson's *The Tunnel*. But it is perhaps just worth while to point out that *The Mark on the Wall* had been written at latest in the first part of 1917, while it was not until April 1918 that Virginia read *Ulysses* in manuscript and January 1919 that she read *The Tunnel*.

In May 1919 we published in the Hogarth Press *Kew Gardens*. As I recorded in *Beginning Again* (p. 241), this thin little volume, which we had printed ourselves, had great importance for us, for its immediate success was the first of many unforeseen happenings which led us, unintentionally and often reluctantly, to turn the Hogarth Press into a commercial publishing business. But it was also a decisive step in Virginia's development as a writer. It is in its own small way and within its own limits perfect; in its rhythms, movement, imagery, method, it could have been written by no one but Virginia. It is a microcosm of all her then unwritten novels, from *Jacob's Room* to *Between the Acts*; for instance, Simon's silent soliloquy is a characteristic produced by the same artistic gene or chromosome which was to produce 12 years later Bernard's soliloquy in *The Waves* and 22 years later the silent murmurings of Isa in *Between the Acts*.

Virginia began to write *Jacob's Room* in April 1920; the period of eleven months between that date and May 1919, when *Kew Gardens* was published, had been one of rumination and preparation. She wrote little, and what she did write was journalism. It was for her a disturbed period, partly because of warning headaches and partly because of the publication of *Night and Day* in October. It is clear from the diary that 'the creative power' which, Virginia said, 'bubbles so pleasantly in beginning a new book' was simmering throughout those eleven months. By April 1920 the content, characters, form of *Jacob's Room* must have been in her mind in some detail, for she had already given the book its significant name. And she was conscious that the method of her experimental short stories, *The Mark on the Wall*, *Kew Gardens*, and *An Unwritten Novel*, must be adapted to produce a full-length novel. This is what she wrote in her diary on January 26, 1920 (*A Writer's Diary*, p. 23):

> Suppose one thing should open out of another—as in an unwritten novel—only not for 10 pages but 200 or so —doesn't that give the looseness and lightness I want; doesn't that get closer and yet keep form and speed, and

enclose everything, everything? My doubt is how far it will enclose the human heart—Am I sufficiently mistress of my dialogue to net it there? For I figure that the approach will be entirely different this time: no scaffolding; scarcely a brick to be seen; all crepuscular, but the heart, passion, humour, everything, as bright as fire in the mist. Then I'll find room for so much—a gaiety—an inconsequence— a light spirited stepping at my sweet will. Whether I'm sufficiently mistress of things—that's the doubt; but conceive *Mark on the Wall, K. G.*, and *Unwritten Novel* taking hands and dancing in unity.

On November 6, 1921, she wrote the last words of *Jacob's Room*; it was published in October 1922. The writing of this novel was the beginning of a period of great fertility. In the three years 1921 to 1924 she wrote *Mr Bennett and Mrs Brown* (published in 1924), and prepared or wrote the material included in *Monday or Tuesday* (published in 1921) and *The Common Reader* (published in 1925). In 1922 she began *Mrs Dalloway* and was writing it all through 1923 and 1924. She began it as a short story and for a short time hesitated whether to expand it into a full-length novel. Early in 1923 she had decided upon its being a novel; she called it at first *The Hours*, but finally went back to the original title *Mrs Dalloway*.

Throughout these six years, 1919 to 1924, she was also writing a considerable amount of journalism, if one remembers how much work she was giving to her books and how limited was the total time she could devote to writing. Most of her journalism consisted of reviews in the *Times Literary Supplement* and, after 1923, in the *Nation*. Her attitude to her reviewing was not consistent. She looked upon it usually as a method of making money—at this time, indeed, it was almost her only way. As such she resented it and occasionally decided to give it up altogether. The following entry in her diary on September 15, 1920, shows this:

> I should have made more of my release from reviewing. When I sent my letter to Richmond,[1] I felt like someone turned out into the open air. Now I've written another in the same sense to Murry,[2] returning Mallock; and I believe this is the last book any editor will ever send me. To have broken free at the age of 38 seems a great piece of good fortune—coming at the nick of time, and due of course to L., without whose journalism I couldn't quit mine. But I quiet my conscience with the belief that a foreign article once a week is of greater worth, less labour and better paid than my work; and with luck, if I can get my books done, we shall profit in moneymaking eventually. And, when one faces it, the book public is more of an ordeal than the newspaper public, so that I'm not shirking responsibility. Now, of course, I can scarcely believe that I ever wrote reviews weekly; and literary papers have lost all interest for me. Thank God, I've stepped clear of that *Athenaeum* world, with its reviews, editions, lunches, and tittle tattle—I should like never to meet a writer again. The proximity of Mr Allison,[3] reputed editor of the *Field*, is enough for me. I should like to know masses of sensitive, imaginative, unselfconscious, unliterary people, who have never read a book. Now, in the rain, up to Dean, to talk about the door of the coal cellar.

But Virginia did not always hold this uncompromising view of her journalism and reviewing. She found that she

[1] Bruce Richmond, editor of the *Times Literary Supplement*.
[2] J. Middleton Murry, editor of the *Athenaeum*.
[3] Wrongly reputed. He was advertisement manager of *The Times* and owner of the *London Mercury*. He had just bought a large house and farm in Rodmell.

could not go on for long periods uninterruptedly writing fiction and she relieved the strain by doing something which used another part of her brain or literary imagination. As the years went on, she discovered that reviewing performed this function admirably; it gave her the relief which some thinkers or writers find in chess or crossword puzzles.

I give below the figures of Virginia's earnings by her pen or typewriter in the years 1919 to 1924. They are interesting, I think, from a particular point of view, from the light which they throw on her work as a novelist and journalist, but also from a general point of view, the economics of the literary profession in the 1920s.

	Journalism			*Books*			*Total*		
1919	£153	17	0	nil			£153	17	0
1920	234	6	10	£106	5	10	340	12	8
1921	47	15	1	10	10	8	58	5	9
1922	69	5	0	33	13	0	102	18	0
1923	158	3	9	40	0	5	198	4	2
1924	128	0	0	37	0	0	165	0	0

Virginia was 42 years old in 1924. Jane Austen died at the age of 42, George Eliot at the age of 41, Charlotte Brontë at the age of 39; all three were famous novelists and had written best-sellers at the time of their deaths. By the age of 42 Virginia had already published three major novels: *The Voyage Out, Night and Day,* and *Jacob's Room.* All three had been widely recognized as novels of great merit, and even genius; they had been published in America as well as in Britain; but their sales were small in both countries. Thus the total which she earned from her books, including the American editions, in the six years, ending with 1924 was £228, or £38 per annum; indeed her total earnings, from books and journalism, during the period were only £1,019, or £170 per annum.

Many people, including even many writers and publishers, will be surprised at these miserable figures. Having for 50 years observed, as writer, editor, and publisher, the rise and fall of many literary reputations and incomes, I know that there is nothing particularly unusual in them. Nothing can be more erratic and fickle than literary reputations and earnings. In 1963, i.e. 40 years after 1924, these three novels earned in royalties in Britain alone £251—£22 more than all Virginia's books, including the three novels, had earned in Britain and America during the six years. There must be many best-sellers of the year 1924 which did not sell a copy or earn their authors a penny in the year 1963. I shall later on give from time to time the figures of Virginia's sales and earnings; here I will give only one other fact to show how sudden and unpredictable are the movements in the market where writers sell their wares. Five years after 1924, the year in which Virginia earned £38 by her books, she earned £2,063 by her books. This astronomical increase after the six years of complete stagnation was due partly to *Mrs Dalloway*, published in 1925, and *To the Lighthouse*, published in 1927, but still more to *Orlando*, which was published in 1928.

The development of the Hogarth Press was bound up with the development of Virginia as a writer and with her literary or creative psychology. When we moved from Hogarth House, Richmond, to 52 Tavistock Square on March 13, 1924, the Hogarth Press had published 32 books in the seven years of its existence. I give below the complete list of books published in each of these seven years, for it shows the scale and quality of the development. I have marked with an asterisk the books which we printed with our own hands.

1917 *Two Stories* by Leonard and Virginia Woolf
1918 *Prelude* by Katherine Mansfield

1919 *Poems* by T. S. Eliot
     Kew Gardens by Virginia Woolf
     Critic in Judgment by J. Middleton Murry
1920 *Story of the Siren* by E. M. Forster
     Paris by Hope Mirrlees
     Gorky's *Reminiscences of Tolstoi*
     Stories from the Old Testament by Logan Pearsall Smith
1921 *Monday or Tuesday* by Virginia Woolf
     Stories from the East by Leonard Woolf
     Poems by Clive Bell
     Tchekhov's Notebooks
1922 *Jacob's Room* by Virginia Woolf
     Stavrogin's Confession by Dostoevsky
     The Gentleman from San Francisco by Bunin
     Autobiography of Countess Tolstoi
     Daybreak by Fredegond Shove
     Karn by Ruth Manning-Sanders
1923 *Pharos and Pharillon* by E. M. Forster
     Woodcuts by Roger Fry
     Sampler of Castile by Roger Fry
     The Waste Land by T. S. Eliot
     The Feather Bed by Robert Graves
     Mutations of the Phoenix by Herbert Read
     Legend of Monte della Sibilla by Clive Bell
     Poems by Ena Limebeer
     Tolstoi's Love Letters
     Talks with Tolstoi by A. V. Goldenveiser
     Letters of Stephen Reynolds
     The Dark by Leonid Andreev
     When it was June by Mrs Lowther

The above list shows that, though we started the Hogarth Press in 1917, it was only in 1920 that we began—with Gorky's *Reminiscences of Tolstoi* and Logan Pearsall Smith's

Stories from the Old Testament—to have books printed for us by commercial printers and so to become ourselves commercial publishers. The four books published by us in 1917, 1918, and 1919 were all printed and bound by ourselves,[1] and the production, such as it was, was entirely that of the hands of Leonard and Virginia Woolf. Until 1920 the idea of seriously becoming professional publishers never occurred to us. The Hogarth Press was a hobby, and the hobby consisted in the printing which we did in our spare time in the afternoons. A second object, which developed from the first, was to produce and publish short works which commercial publishers could not or would not publish, like T. S. Eliot's poems, Virginia's *Kew Gardens*, and Katherine Mansfield's *Prelude*. We were able to do this without financial loss, because we printed and bound the books ourselves in the dining-room or basement of Hogarth House and had no 'overheads'. Our first step up or down into professional publishing was the result of the sudden success of *Kew Gardens*. As I explained in *Beginning Again* (p. 241), when we were suddenly overwhelmed with orders for the book from booksellers, we decided to have a second edition printed for us commercially. This brought us into contact with all the big and many of the small booksellers, both wholesale and retail, and it was not difficult to learn the not very complicated customs and structure of the book trade. *Kew Gardens* showed me that we could, if we wished, publish a book commercially and successfully.

When, therefore, Koteliansky brought us Gorky's

[1] On the title-page of our first book, *Two Stories*, we put 'Written and printed by Virginia Woolf and L. S. Woolf' and the imprint was Hogarth Press, Richmond. Later on our usual imprint on books printed by ourselves was 'Printed and published by Leonard and Virginia Woolf at The Hogarth Press' and on books printed for us by a commercial printer 'published by Leonard and Virginia Woolf at The Hogarth Press'.

Reminiscences of Tolstoi and suggested that we should publish it, we were faced with a difficult decision. He translated some of it to us and we saw at once that it was a masterpiece. If we published it, we should have to print at least 1,000 copies, a number which we could not possibly manage ourselves. We took the plunge and had 1,000 copies printed for us by the Pelican Press for £73. It was our first commercial venture.[1] It was an immediate success and we had to reprint another 1,000 copies before the end of the year. Kot and I translated it and I do not think that I have ever got more aesthetic pleasure from anything than from doing that translation. It is one of the most remarkable biographical pieces ever written. It makes one hear, see, feel Tolstoy and his character as if one were sitting in the same room—his greatness and his littleness, his entrancing and enfuriating complexity, his titanic and poetic personality, his superb humour. The writing is beautiful; every word and every sentence are perfect, and there is not one superfluous word or sentence in the book. I got immense pleasure from trying to translate this ravishing Russian into adequate English.

The success of Gorky's book was really the turning point for the future of the Press and for our future. Neither of us wanted to be professional, full-time publishers; what we wanted to do primarily was to write books, not print and publish them. On the other hand, our three years' experience of printing and publishing had given us great pleasure and whetted our appetite for more. In 1920 I felt in my bones that the Hogarth Press, like the universe and so many things in it, must either expand or explode or dwindle and die; it was too young and too vigorous to be able just to sit

[1] In 1919 we had had Middleton Murry's *Critic in Judgment* printed for us by a small printer, my friend McDermott, but he and I had really printed it together, and we printed only 200 copies. Virginia and I bound it.

still and survive. And we were impelled by another very powerful motive for keeping the Press in existence. Publishing our *Two Stories* and Virginia's *Kew Gardens* had shown us, and particularly Virginia, how pleasant it is for a writer to be able to publish his own books. As I have said more than once, Virginia suffered abnormally from the normal occupational disease of writers—indeed of artists—hypersensitiveness to criticism. The publisher of her first two novels was her own half-brother, Gerald Duckworth, a kindly, uncensorious man who had considerable affection for Virginia. His reader, Edward Garnett, who had a great reputation for spotting masterpieces by unknown authors, wrote an enthusiastic report on *The Voyage Out* when it was submitted to Duckworth. Yet the idea of having to send her next book to the mild Gerald and the enthusiastic Edward filled her with horror and misery. The idea, which came to us in 1920, that we might publish ourselves the book which she had just begun to write, *Jacob's Room*, filled her with delight, for she would thus avoid the misery of submitting this highly experimental novel to the criticism of Gerald Duckworth and Edward Garnett. So we decided to allow the Press to expand, if it could, into a proper publishing business, to publish a book of short stories by Virginia, *Monday or Tuesday*, in 1921, and to ask Gerald to abandon his option on *Jacob's Room* so that it could be published by the Hogarth Press.[1]

This decision to allow the Press to expand and become professional, respectable, and commercial was bound up with another major decision. Lytton Strachey was considerably intrigued by what he considered to be our eccentric publishing and printing antics. Having, in his usual way,

---

[1] Gerald agreed to this and later we purchased from him the rights in and stock of *The Voyage Out* and *Night and Day* so that all Virginia's books became Hogarth Press publications. The Press also bought from Edward Arnold the rights in my book, *The Village in the Jungle*.

poured a good deal of icy water over the head of the Press and down our backs, he began to warm up a little when we told him that we thought we should have either to kill the Press or expand it into a regular publishing business, which would mean employing someone to work with us. He suggested and was soon urging that we should take Ralph Partridge into the Press. In 1920 Ralph was a unit in a strange *ménage à trois* which inhabited a very pleasant old mill-house in Tidmarsh. It belonged to Lytton, who had just become famous by the publication of his *Eminent Victorians* in 1918. With him lived Carrington, a young woman with one of those mysterious, inordinately female characters made up of an infinite series of contradictory characteristics, one inside the other like Chinese boxes. She was the apotheosis of the lovely milkmaid who is the heroine of the song: 'Where are you going to, my pretty maid?' She had a head of the thickest yellow hair that I have ever seen, and as, according to the fashion of the time among art students at the Slade, it was cut short round the bottom of her neck, it stood out like a solid, perfectly grown and clipped, yew hedge. She had the roundest, softest, pinkest damask cheeks and large, China blue eyes through which one was disconcerted to glimpse an innocence which one could not possibly believe really to exist this side of the Garden of Eden—in 1920 in the Berkshire house of the author of *Eminent Victorians*. She was a painter, having studied at the Slade, and she habitually wore the rather sacklike dresses which in the early 1920s were worn by artistic young women and can still be seen in the works of Augustus John. For some reason unknown to me she was universally called Carrington, which was her surname; I never heard anyone call her by her Christian name and I am not quite certain whether it was or was not Doris. I liked her very much, for she was charming when we stayed at Tidmarsh or when she came to us, and always very affectionate. But she was a silent woman and rarely took part in any general conversation. It was impossible to know whether the Chinese boxes were full of intricate psychological mysteries or whether in fact they were all empty. Carrington was devoted to Lytton, running his house for him and waiting hand and foot upon him and everyone staying in the house, like a perfect housekeeper and a dedicated cook, parlourmaid, and housemaid.

Ralph Partridge was the third member of the trinity living in Lytton's house in Tidmarsh. He was a very large, very good-looking, enormously strong young man. At Oxford he had been a first-class oar and would have got his Blue if he had not suddenly taken against rowing. He fought as a commissioned officer through the 1914 war. I am not quite sure how he got to know Lytton; I think it was through Carrington with whom in 1920 he was very much in love. Ralph was an interesting character; on the surface he was typical public schoolboy, Oxford rowing Blue, tough, young blood, and on the top of this he was a great he-man, a very English Don Juan. But behind this façade of the calm unemotional public school athlete there was an extraordinary childlike emotional vulnerability. An incident made me think that Ralph's emotionalism was in part hereditary.

He once asked us whether he could bring his father to dinner with us, as he was much concerned about him and thought that conversation with us might take his mind off his worries. His worries were curious. He was, like his son, a very large man, with a surface of rugged imperturbability. He was a retired Indian civil servant. He lived in the country and Ralph from time to time went down and spent a weekend with him. Some weeks before, Ralph in his father's study had casually opened the door of a small safe and found lying in it a loaded revolver. Thinking this very strange, he asked his father why he kept a loaded revolver in an unlocked safe. At first his father tried to shrug the whole thing off, but eventually admitted that he was desperately worried. His story was this. When in India, he had bought a considerable number of shares in an Indian company. After his retirement, when he had to make out his income tax returns, for some reason or other, he had got it into his head that he was not liable to pay income tax on the dividends paid in India by an Indian company and he had not included them in his returns for many years. Then suddenly he became aware that the dividends had always been part of his income liable to income tax. He had defrauded the revenue! He wrote to the Commissioners of Inland Revenue explaining what he had done and asking them to let him know what he should now do. His letter was acknowledged and then silence from the Commissioners. He wrote again with the same result, and then a third time with the same result. He then loaded his revolver and decided that, if he did not hear from the Commissioners in ten days' time, he would commit suicide. Ralph, having induced him to hand over the revolver, wrote to the Commissioners of Inland Revenue to inform them that, if they did not reply to his father's letters, his father would shoot himself. Almost by return came a letter informing him of the total tax he must pay on the undeclared dividends. Poor Mr Partridge was saved from self-slaughter and some years later died from natural causes.

I do not think that Ralph, in a fairly long and certainly happy life, probably ever came near to suicide or even to the contemplation of it. But beneath the rather ebullient, hail-fellow-well-met, man of the world façade there was a curious stratum of emotionalism not unlike Mr Partridge's. He was easily moved to tears. He was, as I said, very much in love with Carrington. She was the classic female, if there has ever been a classic female—if the male pursued, she ran away; if the male ran away, she pursued. These tactics, applied to

Ralph, drove him into almost hysterical craziness. We decided that drastic steps must be taken. We asked Ralph whether he really, seriously wanted to marry Carrington, and he said that he did. I explained to him the phenomenon of the classic female, and told him that he must go to Carrington and put a pistol at her, not his head; he must say to her that she must marry him at once or let him go—if she said no, he would go off altogether. She gave in and married him.

Lytton, as I said, was eager that we should take Ralph into the Hogarth Press, first as an employee on trial, and with the prospect of ultimately becoming a partner. Eventually we agreed, and on August 31, 1920, the Press acquired its first paid employee. Ralph was not a full-time employee; he came and worked two or three days a week; he was paid a salary of £100 and 50 per cent. of the net profits. For the year 1920 his earnings were £56, 6s. 1d., and for 1921, £125. The first thing we had to do was to teach him to print, for his main work, at the start, was to help us with the printing. As soon as he was able to set up a page of type and machine it, we decided to develop that side of our activities: in November 1921, I bought a Minerva printing machine for £70, 10s. 0d. and 77 lb. of Caslon Old Face 12 pt. type for £18, 9s. 5d. By 1923, i.e. exactly five years after its birth, the total capital invested in the Press was £135, 2s. 3d.—all of it for printing machines, type, and materials. The Minerva machine was a formidable monster, a very heavy, treadle, platen machine, and, after treadling away at it for four hours at a stretch, from 2 to 6 in the afternoon, as I often did, I felt as if I had taken a great deal of exercise.

When the printing machine was delivered, we had it put in the corner of the dining-room, but, when McDermott saw it there, he shook his head and said it was much too dangerous—the machine was so heavy that if we worked it there, it would probably go through the floor on to the cook's head

Virginia and Dadie Rylands at Monks House

Virginia and Lytton Strachey

Mitz at Monks House

Mitz in Rome

Mitz and Pinka

in the kitchen. So we had to have it all dismantled again and erected in a small larder at the back of the house in the basement. The invasion of the larder was not popular with Nellie and Lottie, the cook and house-parlourmaid, but at least it was safer for them to have it there than over their heads in the dining-room.

The effect of Ralph's joining the Hogarth Press can be seen in the rapid expansion of our list to six books in 1922 and thirteen in 1923. Four in the 1922 lists were printed for us commercially. Virginia's *Jacob's Room* was our first major work, a full-length novel. 1,200 copies of it were printed for us by R. & R. Clark Ltd. of Edinburgh. This was the beginning of our long connection with one of the biggest and best of British printers and with their remarkable managing director, William Maxwell. Willie Maxwell was inside and outside a Scot of the Scots; he was a dedicated printer and a first-class business man. The moment he saw our strange, unorthodox venture into publishing, he became personally interested in it, and he took as much trouble over printing 1,000 copies for us as he did in later times over printing 20,000. When he came on his periodical business visits to the London publishers, busy though he was, he would usually find time to come out and see the Hogarth Press in Richmond. *Jacob's Room* was published in October 1922 and began at once to sell fairly briskly, and I had a second impression of 1,000 copies printed by Clark. By the end of 1923 we had sold 1,413 copies; the cost of printing and publishing up to that date had been £276, 1s. 6d. and the receipts had been £318, 6s. od., so that our publisher's profit was £42, 4s. 6d. We thought that we had done extremely well. It is true that Virginia Woolf, the publisher, had to some extent swindled Virginia Woolf, the author. As the whole thing was an experiment, a leap into the darkness of publishing in which we had practically no experience, and

73

as Ralph had just come into the Press with a half share of the profits, we agreed that Virginia should not be paid a royalty, but should be paid one-third share of the profits. On the 1,413 copies sold she was paid £14, 1s. 6d.

The three other commercially printed books which we published in 1922 were Russian; they came to us through Kot, and either Virginia or I collaborated with him in the translation of them. All three were remarkable. Two of them had just been published in Russia by the Soviet Government and came to Kot through Gorky: *Stavrogin's Confession* contained unpublished chapters of Dostoevsky's novel *The Possessed* and *The Autobiography of Countess Sophie Tolstoi* had been written in 1913 by Tolstoy's wife. The other book, Bunin's *Gentleman from San Francisco*, is one of the greatest of short stories. These books, which I still think to be beautifully printed and bound, were very carefully designed by Virginia and me, and they were unlike the books published by other publishers in those days. They were bound in paper over boards and we took an immense amount of trouble to find gay, striking, and beautiful papers. The Dostoevsky and the Bunin were bound in very gay patterned paper which we got from Czechoslovakia, and the Tolstoy book in a very good mottled paper. We printed, I think, 1,000 of each of the three books and published the Bunin and Tolstoy at 4s. and the Dostoevsky at 6s. Each of them sold between 500 and 700 copies in twelve months and made us a small profit, and they went on selling until we reprinted or they went out of print.

The big expansion of the Press took place in 1923, in which year we published seven books printed by ourselves and six printed for us. *Pharos and Pharillon* by E. M. Forster, which we printed ourselves, was a terrific undertaking. It was an 80-page demy octavo volume and we printed between 800 and 900 copies. Virginia, Ralph, and I set it up, and Ralph and I machined it. It was only just possible to print four pages at a time on the Minerva printing machine, so that Ralph and I between us had to treadle 22 runs of over 800 pages a run. The first edition sold out in less than a year; the receipts, at a published price of 5s., were £135, 10s. 11d., and our expenditure £90, 19s. 0d., so that the book showed a profit for the Press of £44, 11s. 11d. We at once had a second edition reprinted for us, crown octavo, and published it in paper covers at 3s.

The three of us must have done a tremendous amount of printing in the years 1921 and 1922 in order to produce the crop of our hand-printed books published in 1923. For they included *The Waste Land*, 37 pages, and Robert Graves's *The Feather Bed*, 28 pages crown quarto; a large book of Roger Fry's woodcuts, which was not easy printing for amateur novices; two crown quarto books of poetry by Herbert Read and Clive Bell, the latter being illustrated and decorated by Duncan Grant; and a small book of poems by Ena Limebeer. We bound the woodcuts and Ena Limebeer's poems ourselves, but the other books were too large for us to tackle ourselves and we had them bound for us by a commercial bookbinder.

The Hogarth Press, in these early years, met with a rather chilly welcome, or rather cold shoulder, from the booksellers. If you compare the thirteen books which we published in that year with any thirteen similar books from other publishers, you will find that all of ours have something more or less unorthodox in their appearance. They are either not the orthodox size or not the orthodox shape, or their binding is not orthodox; and even worse, what was inside the book, what the author said, was in many cases unfamiliar and therefore ridiculous and reprehensible, for it must be remembered that, if you published 42 years ago poetry by T. S. Eliot, Robert Graves, and Herbert Read and a novel by Virginia Woolf, you were publishing four books which the vast majority of people, including booksellers and the literary 'establishment', condemned as unintelligible and absurd. Conservatism is the occupational disease in all trades and professions, and booksellers suffer from it like everyone else. In 1923 we had no travellers and in a very desultory way we took our books round to the more important booksellers ourselves in order to get subscription orders before publication. It was a depressing business, though no doubt salutary and educative for an embryonic publisher. There were a few booksellers, like the great Mr Wilson of Bumpus, James Bain of King William Street, Lamley of South Kensington, Goulden and Curry in Tunbridge Wells, the Reigate bookshop, who were immediately interested in what we were trying to do and did everything to help and encourage us. But they were the exception. The reception of *Jacob's Room* was characteristic. It was the first book for which we had a jacket designed by Vanessa. It is, I think, a very good jacket and today no bookseller would feel his hackles or his temperature rise at sight of it. But it did not represent a desirable female or even Jacob or his room, and it was what in 1923 many people would have called reproachfully post-impressionist. It was almost universally condemned by the booksellers, and several of the buyers laughed at it.

Most human beings will never move unless a carrot is dangled in front of their noses, and, like the donkey, they must have precisely that kind of carrot which they and their fathers and fathers' fathers back to the primal ass have always recognized as the only true, good, and respectable carrot. Our books 42 years ago were not recognized by the trade as the right kind of carrot, either internally or externally. But looking at them today any bookseller would admit that they are extremely well-produced books and that their jackets are admirable. Within ten or twelve years the binding of books in gay, pretty, or beautiful papers over boards was widely adopted for all kinds of books, particularly poetry. Time or the rise and fall of reputations have justified our judgment of the inside of these books. Only three out of the thirteen, Ena Limebeer's *Poems*, Mrs Lowther, and Reynolds's letters, would not be recognized today as important books by important writers, and even for these there is still something to be said. As for the other ten, there are few publishers who in 1965 would not be very glad to have them on their lists.

In 1922 a storm blew up in the Hogarth Press, the kind of crisis which, during the next 20 years, was to recur with depressing regularity. After two years' experience it was clear to us that our arrangement with Ralph was not turning out successfully. He worked only two or three days a week, and that rather erratically. It was an impossible arrangement if we were to publish, as we did in 1923, twelve books in the year, and ourselves print half of them. We wanted Ralph to become full time, a professional publisher. This he would not do, though he was enthusiastic about the Press and, with tears in his eyes and voice, maintained that nothing would induce him to give it up.

The truth was—as I suspected at the time and now see clearly looking back to 1923—that we were trying to do what is practically impossible, enjoy the best of two contradictory worlds. The success of the Press was forcing it to become a commercial publishing business. My experience in Ceylon had taught me (I think immodestly) to be a first-class business man, but I was not prepared to become a professional publisher. The Press was therefore a mongrel in the business world. We ran it in our spare time on lines invented by myself without staff and without premises; we printed in the larder, bound books in the dining-room, interviewed printers, binders, and authors in a sitting-room.

I kept the accounts, records of sales, etc., myself in my own way, which was from the chartered accountant's view unorthodox, but when it was challenged by the Inland Revenue and I took my books to the Inspector of Taxes, he agreed that they showed accurately the profit or loss on each book published, the revenue and expenditure of the business, and the annual profit or loss, and for many years the Commissioners accepted my accounts for the purpose of assessing income tax.

The organization and machinery of the Press were amateurish; it was, so far as Virginia and I were concerned, a hobby which we carried on in afternoons, when we were not writing books and articles or editing papers. We did not expect to make money out of it. But at the same time we were already committed to publish full-length, important books, not only for Virginia herself, but also for writers whom we considered important. We felt to these writers and their books the responsibility of the commercial publisher to the author, we had to publish their books professionally and competently. Our idea in 1922 was to get someone like Ralph who would work full time in the Press under me and earn his living from it, while Virginia and I would continue to work at it in our spare time as a by-product of our life and energies.

The last sentence shows what a very curious type of business we were trying to create and that the position of the young man who was to work under me would not be easy— nor would it be easy to find the right young man. I have never been an easy person to work with. I emphasize the words 'work with'. My experience in the Ceylon Civil Service proved that I get on much better with subordinates than with equals or superiors in business. In practical affairs I am in many ways a perfectionist—a character for which in the abstract, or when I see it in other people, I have no great admiration. I have a kind of itch or passion for finding the 'right' way of doing things, and by 'right' I mean the quickest and most accurate and simplest way. In 1923 I was still young enough to be hot tempered and allergic to fools.

By the middle of 1922 it was clear to us that Ralph, from our point of view, would not do. As it was, I was becoming a full-timer and he a part-timer, whereas we wanted the exact opposite. We found ourselves sitting uncomfortably on the horns of a dilemma—and the same situation would build itself up again and again from time to time over the following years. Shall we give up the Press altogether or shall we make one more attempt to find a manager or a partner who will help us to run this commercial hippogriff on the lines on which we want it to develop? We were then (and more than once again in the future) very much inclined to give the whole thing up and leave ourselves free of responsibility to pursue our other activities. On the other hand, we were urged from the outside to develop the Press and naturally were rather flattered by this. James Whittall, a cultured American, put out feelers and we considered him as a possible partner. But more surprising was a direct offer from the great publishing house of Heinemann to take us into a kind of partnership or 'association'. We had several talks with Whittall and, invited by the managing director of Heinemann, I went and had an interview with him on November 27, 1922. He offered to take over the whole business management of the Hogarth Press, distribution, accounting, advertising, and, if we wanted it, printing and binding. We should be left complete autonomy to publish or not to publish any book we liked.

We turned down Whittall and we turned down Heinemann. We liked Whittall very much personally, but we came to the conclusion that he was too cultured for us and for the Press. We did not want the Press to become one of those (admirable in their way) 'private' or semi-private

Presses the object of which is finely produced books, books which are meant not to be read, but to be looked at. We were interested primarily in the immaterial inside of a book, what the author had to say and how he said it; we had drifted into the business with the idea of publishing things which the commercial publisher could not or would not publish. We wanted our books to 'look nice' and we had our own views of what nice looks in a book would be, but neither of us was interested in fine printing and fine binding. We also disliked the refinement and preciosity which are too often a kind of fungoid growth which culture breeds upon art and literature; they are not unknown in Britain and are often to be found in cultivated Americans. It was because Whittall seemed to us too cultured and might want to turn the Hogarth Press into a kind of Kelmscott Press or Nonesuch Press that we turned him down. I am, of course, aware that many people would have thought—and some would still think—it ludicrous for us, and particularly Virginia, to talk of anyone being too cultured. The myth of Virginia as queen of Bloomsbury and culture, living in an ivory drawing-room or literary and aesthetic hothouse, still persists to some extent. I think that there is no truth in this myth. Her most obvious fault, as a person and as a writer, was a kind of intellectual and social snobbery—and she admitted it herself. There is also sometimes a streak of incongruous archness in her humour which is almost ladylike and very disconcerting. But her novels, and still more her literary criticism, show that she had not a trace of the aesthete or hypercultured. One has only to compare her attitude towards life and letters, towards art and people, with that of writers like George Meredith or Henry James or Max Beerbohm, to see that, although she was a cultured woman, the roots of her personality and her art were not in culture and that she had a streak of the common-sense, down to earth, granitic quality of mind and soul characteristic in many generations of her father's family.

We turned down Heinemann for the simple reason: *timeo Danaos et dona ferentes*, I fear the Greeks, especially when they offer me gifts. We felt that we were really much too small a fly to enter safely into such a very large web. So there we were with two pretty heavy albatrosses hanging round our necks—the Hogarth Press and Ralph Partridge. Lytton and Ralph put forward various proposals which we could not agree to, and sometime in 1922 we more or less agreed to part. Then a curious thing happened. In November 1922 we were in the midst of our negotiations and conversations and hesitations, and on the 17th of that month we met Whittall in the 1917 Club to discuss Heinemann's offer with him. While waiting for him, a young woman came in and began talking to a man who was sitting near us. She is described in Virginia's diary as 'one of those usual shabby, loose, cropheaded, smallfaced bright eyed young women'. It was impossible not to overhear the conversation. She told the man (who, I think, was Cyril Scott, the composer) that she was sick of teaching and had decided to become a printer. 'They tell me,' she said, 'that there's never been a woman printer, but I mean to be one. No, I don't know anything about it, but I mean to be one.' Virginia and I 'looked at each other with a wild surmise', and when the young woman went out, Virginia followed her and brought her back to our table. There we told her what we were doing with the Press and arranged that she should come and see it for herself and discuss possibilities.

Some days later on a Sunday afternoon the young woman, whose name was Marjorie Thomson, accompanied by a friend, came and had tea with us at Richmond in order to see what we were doing and discuss her possible employment. This was the first time I met Cyril Joad, for the friend

F   81

was Joad, who was to become famous later as Professor C. E. M. Joad, the highbrow radio star. Cyril was a curious character; high minded, loose living and loose thinking, he inhabited a kind of Platonic or Aristotelian underworld. He was one of those people whom I dislike when I do not see them and *rather* like when I do see them. He was in fact a selfish, quick-witted, amusing, intellectual scallywag. He told us that he was going to marry Marjorie in a few months' time, and in a few months' time Marjorie told us that she had married him. They lived together for some time, not I think very happily, in the Vale of Health, but the marriage was one of the many figments of Professor Joad's fertile imagination.

Marjorie had a nice face and a nice character. She belonged to what Virginia called the underworld, and it was, I suppose, looked at from certain altitudes, both socially and intellectually an underworld, a twentieth-century mixture of Bohemia and Grubb Street; a certain number of its inhabitants could always be met in the 1917 Club in Gerrard Street. Marjorie had a bright, if somewhat shallow, mind, and as soon as she saw what we were doing in the Press, was anxious to join us. With Professor Joad's benediction, it was agreed that she should come to us on January 1, 1923, on a salary of £100 and a half share of the profits, Ralph leaving the Press finally in March. This, then, was the position of the Press when in March 1924 we moved from Hogarth House, Richmond, to Tavistock Square in Bloomsbury, and a new phase with rapid development began for our publishing. I will deal with this in the next chapter.

Our energy in the last four years of our life in Richmond was considerable. With no staff, to publish thirteen books (seven printed by ourselves) in a year would, I think, have been considered by many people a full-time job. I kept all the accounts myself and did a good deal of the invoicing. This in itself was no light labour. For instance, *Jacob's Room* was published on October 27, 1922, and by the end of 1923 it had sold 1,182 copies on over 200 orders. Each of these orders was entered by me in a serial number book and in a ledger; the invoices were made out either by me or by Ralph; and the books were packed and despatched by Virginia, Ralph, and me. This was our spare-time occupation almost always confined to the afternoon. During the same twelve months of 1923 Virginia was writing *Mrs Dalloway*, preparing *The Common Reader*, and earning £158 by reviewing. My own major occupation or occupations had become more complicated and variegated.

I wrote *Empire and Commerce in Africa* in 1918 for the Fabian Society. It is a formidable book of 374 pages and I did a great deal of intensive reading for it. It is, I think, one of the earliest studies of the operations of imperialism in Africa. In 1920 Philip Snowden asked me to contribute a volume to the Independent Labour Party's 'Social Studies Series'. In the early 1920s there was a triumvirate of Labour Party leaders, Ramsay MacDonald, Arthur Henderson, and Philip Snowden. Snowden, whom I never knew as well as I knew the other two, was a curious man. He was lame and gave one the impression of being embittered by pain, though in ordinary conversation it was a rather gentle embitterment. I was an active member of the I.L.P., which in those days was the left wing of the Labour Party, and we were inclined to believe that Snowden was the most advanced or progressive of the triumvirate. In this we were very much mistaken. In *Beginning Again* (pp. 217-226) I have dealt with Ramsay; he was an opportunist who genuinely confused the highest political principles with the personal interests of James Ramsay MacDonald; he was neither on the Left nor on the Right, he was always bang on the Centre, and the Centre was James Ramsay MacDonald. In those early days I underestimated Henderson, thinking him to be what he looked like and what his political petname of Uncle Arthur seemed to indicate—a rather stuffy, slow-going and slow-thinking professional politician. He was something more and a good deal better than that. He was a man of some political principle and political understanding, a rare phenomenon among Cabinet Ministers anywhere. He was still capable of genuine and generous feelings for what he thought politically or socially right, and the desiccation of years in the trade union movement and the Labour Party had not dimmed or dulled these feelings. On the surface these were concealed behind a slow, watchful, slightly suspicious stare from hooded eyes, not uncharacteristic in those days of the British working man. Henderson's calibre was shown by his work as President of the League of Nations Disarmament Conference in 1932 and his behaviour to the great rat race of 1931 when Ramsay and Snowden temporarily destroyed the Labour Party. He had been himself chairman of the Labour Party before 1919, and the history of the party, Britain, and even Europe might well have been different and less catastrophic if he and not Ramsay had been leader and Prime Minister in the 1920s.

Snowden, the third member of the triumvirate, was quite unlike Henderson—and indeed quite unlike Ramsay. He came, I think, from the lower middle class and had been a subordinate civil servant and journalist. He was really an old-fashioned Liberal, which meant that by the time that I knew him he was in most things, from my point of view, about as progressive as a member of the Junior Carlton Club whose political faith was limited to support of the Crown, the Church, and free trade. He was one of those very honest, unimaginative, conservative—fundamentally reactionary—politicians who drift into a left wing, progressive, or even revolutionary party, and do a good deal of harm politically. That he and Ramsay were leaders of the Labour Party in the crucial years from 1919 to 1931 was a disaster not only for the party but also for Britain, for their leadership inevitably landed them and all of us in the barren wilderness of the 1930s and the howling wilderness of the war. The most dangerous thing for a boat in a stormy sea is to find herself with no rudder; thanks to Ramsay and Snowden, that was the condition of the Labour Party in the years which followed the 1914 war. Though the upper ranks of the party have always been full of intellectuals, Labour has always shared the general British suspicion and misprision of the intellect and of those who use it in everyday life. As an unredeemed and unrepentant intellectual I was only too well aware of the widespread feeling that intelligence, unless camouflaged by silliness or stupidity, is dangerous and discreditable, and I never felt comfortable with Snowden who was a very British Briton and did not, it seemed to me, like me or my intellect. I was surprised when he asked me to write a volume for the I.L.P. series. I wrote a short book with the title *Socialism and Co-operation*, for which I was paid £25.

I have always been a heretical socialist, and, since very few heresies ever become orthodoxies, this book was even more futile than most of my books. Yet I still think that what the book said is both true and important, though neither the true-blue capitalist nor the true-red socialist nor even the pinkish trade unionist will have anything to do with it. The gist of my argument was that, in the modern world, socialism, i.e. the ownership or control of the means of production by the community, is not an end in itself, but an essential means to a prosperous and civilized society, and that the ownership and control should be based not on the state or the organized producers, but on the organized consumers. The curse of the capitalist system is that it produces states of mind in individuals and classes which contaminate society by inducing a profound, instinctive conviction that the object and justification of everyone's work, trade, profession, in fact of nine-tenths of a person's conscious existence from youth to senility, are and should be money, i.e. the personal interests of the individual. The machinery of communal economics and production is organized not to produce what the community wants or needs to consume but in order to provide either profit or a salary or wage or just 'work' for individuals. Marxist socialists and all those variegated 'packs and sets' of communists and socialists who, since Marx, 'ebb and flow by the moon', because they start from the exploitation of the worker, have unconsciously accepted the psychology of capitalism; both in theory and, where they have the opportunity, in practice, they organize society in the interest of the producers, not the consumers, the economic system being geared to and judged by its ability to provide work, wages, and salaries, competition for the profits between different classes of worker being substituted for competition between capitalists. This process has, of course, been enormously encouraged because in Europe trade unionists and trade unionism have been a dominating influence in all socialist parties, and the trade unionist, as a trade unionist, is concerned not with what he produces and its consumption but with 'work', which the production provides for him, and the amount of money which he can make out of it.

The importance of the British co-operative movement and system is that they have proved that efficient control of large-scale production and distribution by consumers is possible. I argued that it was possible and desirable to develop and extend this system into consumers' socialism, i.e. the control of the industrial system by the community organized as consumers, and that this would not only revolutionize the whole economic system but also the social psychology of capitalism and of socialism based upon production and the interests of the producers.

I think that the nature of social or economic organization has an immense effect upon social psychology for good or ill. I will give a trivial example which, nevertheless, always seems to me to throw light upon our civilization and upon the barbarous psychology which it has bred in us. If you stand at any bus stop in London and observe what happens to the queue of consumers, i.e. of the people who wish to use the bus to get from one place to another in London, you will note a strange thing about this simple industrial or economic operation. The buses drive up very often in conglomerations of three, four, or even five, all of the same number, i.e. all going to the same place—the first bus being full, the second half-full, and the two or three others empty. They dash off almost immediately and the slightest hesitation on the part of anyone in the queue will leave him behind to wait a long wait for another conglomeration of buses. The explanation of this is that the system of transport by bus in London is not organized primarily with the object of transporting the public as rapidly and comfortably and efficiently as possible from one place to another, i.e. in the interests of consumers, but for three entirely different objects: first, for what is known as a schedule, i.e. the timetable which says that the bus must leave a particular garage at a particular time and arrive at another garage at a particular time; secondly, to provide work for the drivers and conductors, i.e. to provide the highest possible wage under the best possible working conditions for the producer; thirdly, to obtain from the public the maximum amount in fares so that, while paying the highest possible wages, the whole business can be run at a profit, or at least not a loss. The interesting fact is that this barbarous system is accepted as rational, inevitable, and civilized, not only by the management, the major and minor bureaucrats who direct London Transport, not only by the workers and employees, but even by the underdogs in the queue, the cringing consumers. And members of the Labour Party and the trade unions will welcome this system as socialism, provided that it is controlled at the top by a Transport Board instead of a Board of Directors.

The psychology of trade unionism and the psychology of capitalism, which spring from the same social postulates, and are complementary like the positive and negative in electricity, are so firmly established in modern society that to most people the idea that the object of industry should be consumption, not production or profit, seems Utopian and even immoral. I never imagined, therefore, that my argument in favour of socialism controlled by consumers would cut any ice in the Labour movement. But even in politics, where reason is so suspect and so unwelcome, I have an absurd, pig-headed feeling that one ought to use one's reason. However, I propose to leave the account of my political activities to the next chapter and to return now to my other occupations in the years 1919 to 1924.

Between 1921, when *Socialism and Co-operation* was published, and 1931, when *After the Deluge*, Vol. I, was published, I did not produce any book, partly because I was so much occupied by journalism, publishing, and politics, and partly because I was ruminating and slowly writing *After the Deluge*. But in 1921 I had one incident connected with my writing which amused Virginia and me. In that year we published in the Hogarth Press a book of three short stories by me, *Stories from the East*, and one of them, 'Pearls and Swine', said Hamilton Fyfe in a review in the *Daily Mail*, 'will rank with the great stories of the world'. Mr Henry Holt, a literary agent, on the strength of this review wrote and asked me whether I would let him have the story for America. I did not do so, and months later in 1922 he wrote to me again, asking whether I would let him deal with the story, which 'ought to have netted you anything up to a couple of hundred pounds for serial rights. Possibly more'.

This time I sent him the book—I don't think that up to this time he had read the story—and told him that he could try his hand. When he read the story, it was obviously a bit of a shock to him, being a good deal too plain spoken for the two hundred pound bracket in the United States of America. He wanted me to tone it down a bit—he called this euphemistically 'a few artistic alterations'—and send it to the great American literary agent, Ann Watkins, who had already expressed an interest in it. I replied that I 'cannot bear to contemplate rewriting anything which I wrote a long time ago', but that he could deal with the story and Ann Watkins himself. This he did. Ann Watkins also thought the story a masterpiece, but was also obviously horrified by it and the idea of offering it to the American market. 'The realism, the vivid picture quality of "Pearls and Swine",' she wrote, 'is so great as to be terrific. It is as powerful a story as I have read in a long time. . . . But there are only about two magazines in America that I think would touch it. You see, we here in the States are still provincial enough to want the sugar-coated pill; we don't like facts, we don't like to have to face them. It seems to be a characteristic of the American people. And where we won't face them in our politics, in our domestic problems, in our personal lives—why in the devil should we be forced to face them in fiction? I think, fundamentally, our demand of the author is that he entertain us with his wares. We veer from the shocking, the revolting— the truth. But holy, suffering cats! how Woolf can write! I should like nothing better than to represent him in the American market. But I should like to represent him only if in so doing I can be of profit to both him and myself.'

Mr Holt was much impressed and wrote to me: 'I wish I could make you realize the tremendous commercial significance of this'. He wanted me to settle down to writing something suitable for the great American market—'I may never again.' he said, 'have patience to bully a man into making several thousand a year, so, for the last time, *do think it over*'. I do not think that I answered this letter, and then one afternoon a car stopped at the gate of Monks House, and out of it stepped Mr and Mrs Holt. He said that he wished to talk to me alone while Mrs Holt would talk to Virginia. It took me the better part of an hour to get rid of him. He said that I must devote myself to writing stories with him as my literary agent, and that, if I did, he would guarantee that I should make £3,000 a year. I said that I didn't want to write stories and in any case I could never think of plots for them. Eventually we went in and joined the ladies over a cup of tea. Virginia recorded the following conversation: ' "He sells everything—he'll be selling me next," she says, very arch. Mr Holt half winked and cocked his head. "Little woman, little woman," said Mr Holt. "He's the straightest boy that ever lived," said Mrs Holt, not without emotion.' At last they drove away, and some days later I got a letter from Mr Holt in which he gave me the outline of a plot for a short story which I should write, and he assured me that, if I would do so and send it to him, he would get me a large sum of money for it. I did not write Mr Holt's story and I do not think that I ever heard from him again.

I have told in *Beginning Again* how it came about that I started and edited the *International Review* for the Rowntrees. It did not last very long, for Arnold Rowntree had, I think, underestimated the costs and loss involved in financing a monthly review dealing with international affairs. When it came to an end, Rowntree asked me to write regularly 16 pages on international affairs for the *Contemporary Review*, which was also a Rowntree paper. I did this in 1920 and 1921 for the noble fee of £250 per annum. From the great newspaper proprietors, like Lord Northcliffe and Lord Beaverbrook, down to the humble sub-editor or reporter, and the still more humble writer for the highbrow weeklies, monthlies, and quarterlies, it is almost impossible for the journalist and the owners of journalists not to believe that what they write or what they hire other people to write has great influence and importance. In general, the bigger the journalistic bug, the bigger his delusion about his influence and importance. I have no doubt that no one who writes for papers ever completely sheds this delusion and that I myself still nourish in my unconscious a secret and sheepish hope, if not belief, that a few people will be influenced by what I write. But I think that my early journalism—writing for the *New Statesman* and for the *Nation* and editing the *International Review*—rapidly disillusioned me. In writing, it seems to me, one just has to cast one's bread upon the waters, resigning oneself to the fact that nothing will ever return to you except so many pounds per thousand words,[1] and the soggy bread will sink without a trace. Certainly one would have had to be very artless or very sanguine to think that many people read or anyone minded 16 pages on international affairs in the *Contemporary Review*. I found it a depressing job, and was not sorry to hand it over to George Glasgow in 1921.

In 1920 and 1921 I still did quite a lot of reviewing and article writing for the *New Statesman* and the *Nation*, earning from the *New Statesman* £65, 7s. 0d. in 1920 and £44, 4s. 0d. in 1921, and from the *Nation* £81, 8s. 0d. in 1920 and £40, 14s. 0d. in 1921. The large sum of £81 which I earned from the *Nation* in 1920 was due to the fact that, as I recorded in *Beginning Again* (p. 185), for three months during that year I temporarily took H. N. Brailsford's place as leader writer on the paper. The *Nation* was owned by the Rowntrees, the Quaker chocolate and cocoa kings of York,

[1] 'No man but a blockhead ever wrote except for money,' said Johnson.

and was edited by H. W. Massingham, one of the most famous editors of his time. In 1922 Brailsford became editor of the *New Leader* and Massingham asked me to take his place on the staff of the *Nation*. I accepted and landed myself in a tangle of events and a journalistic career which lasted for eight years. Initially my duties when I took over Brailsford's job were to go to the *Nation* office in Adelphi Terrace every Monday morning and arrange with Massingham what I should write for next Saturday's paper. Practically always it consisted of the first leader on some political subject, three or four notes on political subjects, and occasionally a review. Massingham was a strange, rather disquieting person. He was a small, neatly dressed, quiet-spoken man whose face had the look of one of those small, brindled, reserved mongrels who eye one with motionless suspicion—the expression of eye and mouth always fills me with apprehension. In 1922 he was 62 years old and had edited the *Nation* for 15 years. All his life he had been a pillar of both liberalism and Liberalism and his whole journalistic career had been on Liberal papers; before editing the *Nation* he had been editor of the *Daily Chronicle*. The *Nation* was supposed to be, and had been, a Liberal weekly supporting the Liberal Party, and Arnold Rowntree, the head of the Rowntree clan, was a Liberal M.P. These facts are important for an understanding of what happened in the next twelve months and of the entanglements in which to my surprise I found myself. For Massingham had in the years just before 1922 drifted further and further from the Liberal Party and had become gradually a supporter of the Labour Party whereas the Rowntrees remained Liberals.

I did not realize any of this when I first stepped into Brailsford's shoes. It was a peaceful office with the gentle, deaf H. M. Tomlinson as literary editor and Miss Crosse one of those highly geared, super-efficient secretaries who are themselves capable of editing and often, *de facto* but not *de jure*, do edit the paper. Then there was a band of very distinguished, veteran Liberals, old friends of Massingham's, who formed the staff of the paper, J. A. Hobson, J. L. Hammond, and H. W. Nevinson. In their company I felt very much the new boy and they were so high-minded—the particular brand of high-mindedness seemed to be peculiar in those days to Liberals who lived in Hampstead and Golders Green—that I always felt myself to be a bit of a fraud in their company. Hammond and Hobson were two charming men; I liked them very much and I became a friend of both; to many people Nevinson was a great charmer, but he was altogether too noble for my tastes. I don't like knights *sans peur et sans reproche*—they, like mongrels, make me uneasy. These three with Massingham and Tomlinson used to lunch together on Mondays and I often used to join them.

Before the lunch I had had my talk with Massingham and decided with him what I was to write. I never felt that I really understood Massingham. He was always extremely nice to me and I got on with him very well, both in work and over the lunch table, but I do not think that I ever got more than a fraction of an inch below the surface. The routine of Monday morning was that he invariably asked me to suggest the subject of my article and notes and left it to me to tell him what I proposed to say. I do not remember him ever not accepting my subject or line of policy, and his comments and suggestions were always very few. But though he said very little when we were talking as professionals on the week's job, there is no doubt that he was a first-class editor in that somehow or other he impressed his personality on those who wrote for him and what they wrote. The consequence was that the paper too had a personality, a flavour, a smell of its own, and this got into what one wrote when one was writing for it. I was never conscious of writing differently in the *Nation* and the *New Statesman* and in my own books—I never felt Massingham looking over my shoulder or breathing down my journalistic back—but if I reread what I had written for him, I was startled to get a faint whiff of Massingham and Massingham's *Nation*.

His editorial and political personality and odour or aura were complex and fascinating. First, he was extremely high-minded; the political aura of the *Nation* in 1922 was still that of Gladstonian liberalism impregnated with sophisticated or civilized non-conformity. Secondly, he was a gentle man, on the side of culture and quiet, of sentiment, if not sentimentality; the *Nation* again reflected this, being pacific, humane, with occasionally a tear—some people said a crocodile's tear—in its eyes and voice. Thirdly, he was a bitter and violent man, with a peculiar bitterness of which I will say more in a moment; the *Nation* had an undercurrent of aggressive acerbity and sudden bursts of intemperance.

I found the study of his public and private character and its extraordinary contradictions absorbing. After we had decided what I should write, we nearly always had for ten minutes or more a general conversation on the political situation. It was a time of continual crisis: Lloyd George's fatal adventure in the Middle East, the Conservative revolt against him, and the break up of the coalition government. I suppose that Massingham must have been in pre-war years a fervid supporter of Lloyd George's, but when I knew him, he hated him with an almost crazy violence and bitterness. He was, as I said, a gentle, quiet-spoken man, but nine Mondays out of ten he would begin a tirade against L. G. He never raised his voice, but out of his mouth poured a kind of commination recital against L. G. and, frequently linked to him, J. P. Scott, editor of the *Manchester Guardian*. I do not know why he had conceived such violent hatred of the immaculate Scott, the journalistic pillar of liberalism, but he astonished me by his venomous and grotesque accusations. I could scarcely believe that I was not dreaming a mad dream when I heard him more than once accuse these two spotless Liberals of a homosexual passion for each other.

Not much has been written about the psychology or psychopathology of political beliefs and emotions. I can remember only two books of any importance. The distinguished psycho-analyst Edward Glover in *War, Sadism and Pacifism* maintained that one had to be peculiarly sadistic and bloody-minded to be a pacifist or even a supporter of the League of Nations, and *Personal Aggressiveness and War* by Evan Durbin and John Bowlby was another original book on more or less the same subject. When I first read Dr Glover's book, I thought that his own unconsciousness was not altogether unconcerned with his finding such very discreditable motives for pacifism in the unconscious of the pacifist, but I have no doubt that there was a good deal of truth in his main thesis. I am sure that if one could look deep into the minds of those who are on the Left in politics (including myself), Liberals, revolutionaries, socialists, communists, pacifists, and humanitarians, one would find that their political beliefs and desires were connected with some very strange goings on down among their ids in their unconscious.

At any rate, watching and listening to Massingham on a Monday morning, I often felt that something like this could only explain the conflict in his character, his gentle high-mindedness and absurd verbal violence. Down below he was, I think, a man of strong feelings which might range from the milk of human kindness to hatred and bitterness. It is also possible that he had the diffused dissatisfaction and grudge against the universe that small men often have, though I may be wrong about this and indeed about his stature. At any rate, as Freud insisted in *Civilization and its*

Discontents, to be even a moderately civilized man is not only difficult but also extremely painful. If you have to be as high-minded all the time as a Liberal of Golders Green or Welwyn Garden City, editing or writing for the *Nation*, in 1922, you had to be suppressing all the time some very violent and curious instincts which might, I think, have surprised and shocked even the editor of the *Nation* had he found them in his unconscious mind. Nineteen hundred years before Freud wrote *Civilization and its Discontents* Horace said *naturam expellas furca, tamen usque recurret* (you may drive nature out with a fork, but she will always return) —and we now know that she returns in strange and very different forms. I have no doubt that the strain of being so civilized caused the explosions of Massingham's verbal violence.

His queer, secretive, complex character had, I am sure, much to do with causing the curious situation in which I found myself involved about a year after I joined his staff. The Rowntrees, proprietors of the paper, were, as I said, Liberals and the *Nation* had been, and was still supposed to be, a Liberal paper. But in fact, when I joined it, it was to all intents and purposes a Labour paper. Massingham had become bitterly hostile to the Liberals and Hammond, Hobson, Nevinson, like Brailsford, Noel and Charles Buxton, who before the war had been active and distinguished Liberal intellectuals, had all drifted into the Labour Party. Massingham never told us exactly what happened behind the scenes between him and the Rowntrees. I am inclined, knowing him and them, to believe that Arnold Rowntree treated him very well, allowing him a great deal of latitude, but warning him that the Rowntrees could not agree to the paper becoming a mere Labour Party organ. All through 1923 the divergence between their political views increased and suddenly there was an explosion or showdown.

I had been told nothing of what was going on, and I was astonished when one morning Massingham told me that the Rowntrees had decided that they could not go on financing the paper as it was, and that they had decided to sell it, but would give him first option to buy it. Massingham said that he knew someone who would put up the money, and he asked me whether I would agree to continue on the staff under a new proprietorship; Hammond, Hobson, Nevinson, and Tomlinson had all agreed to stand by him. I said I would.

There followed weeks of unpleasant doubt and mystery. He was understood to be hard at work raising the money, but he told us nothing. At one moment he went off to the South of France to deal with the man who was to supply most of the money, and we were left to carry on with the editing of the paper. We met for dejected lunches and speculated gloomily on what could be happening. Then Massingham returned, but told me nothing definite. I was astonished when Maynard Keynes in March 1923 told me that he and some others had acquired an interest in the *Nation*, the Rowntrees also still retaining an interest. Hubert Henderson was to be editor and Maynard asked me to become the literary editor. I went to Massingham and explained to him what had happened. I said that if he was going to acquire the *Nation* or was going to be editor of a new weekly, I would continue with him, but, if there was to be no weekly edited by him, I would accept Maynard's offer, provided that he had no objection to my doing so. He said that he had failed to raise the money to purchase the *Nation* and there was no immediate prospect of his editing a new weekly so that I had no longer an obligation to him and I must be free to accept Maynard's offer. This I did, but I insisted upon the following two conditions, which were accepted by Maynard and by Hubert: (1) I would do the work in my own time, though I would normally come to the office on Mondays,

Tuesdays, and the morning of Wednesdays; (2) I should be autonomous in my part of the paper, though the editor would have the right to object to and require the removal of anything which I had passed, but, if he did, I would then have the right to insist that Maynard should arbitrate between us. Maynard only once had to arbitrate between us during the seven years in which I was literary editor. I had given a book to review to David Garnett, then at the beginning of a distinguished literary career, but not yet, I must admit, a very skilful reviewer. When Hubert read his review in proof, he said that it was not good enough and required me not to print it. I insisted that Maynard should arbitrate, as the review, though not very good, did not merit rejection. Maynard agreed with me and the review was published.

The events, such as they were, of my seven years' work on the new *Nation*—which became, of course, a Liberal paper, for Maynard and Hubert were both Liberals—belong to the next chapter and I will leave to that chapter too my political activities on the Labour Party committees and the Fabian Society. In the four years 1920 to 1923, as Virginia's health grew more stable, our social life increased and became more and more of a problem. Our taste in human beings was pretty much the same, but we did not always agree about the best way of seeing them. Virginia loved 'Society', its functions and parties, the bigger the better; but she also liked—at any rate in prospect—any party. Her attitude to this, as to most things, was by no means simple. The idea of a party always excited her, and in practice she was very sensitive to the actual mental and physical excitement of the party itself, the rise of temperature of mind and body, the ferment and fountain of noise. Sometimes she enjoyed it as much in the event as in anticipation, and sometimes, of course, owing to her peculiar vulnerability to the mildest slings and arrows of (not very) outrageous fortune, she would leave a boring party in despair as if it were the last scene of Wagner's Götterdämmerung with Hogarth House and the universe falling in flames and ruin about her ears. Of one of these catastrophic depressions in August 1922 she wrote in her diary: 'No one ever suffered more acutely from atmosphere as I do; and my leaves drooped one by one; though heaven knows my root is firm enough. As L. very truly says, there is too much ego in my cosmos'.

She not only enjoyed society, the kaleidoscope of human beings, conversation, the excitement of parties, she was through and through a professional novelist, and all this was the raw material of her trade. This dual sensitivity to the most trivial meetings with her fellow human beings meant that society and parties were a great strain on her mental health and she herself was well aware of this. The following is another extract from her diary in the summer of 1922: 'Clive came to tea yesterday and offered me only the faded and fly blown remnants of his mind. He had been up late. So had I—at the pictures. For my own part, all my strings are jangled by a night out. Dissipation would rot my writing (such as it is, I put in, modestly). Words next day dance patterns in my mind. It takes me a week to recover from Lady Colefax—who by the way invites me for Friday'.

Virginia always thought she was going to enjoy a party enormously before she went to it and quite often she did. I did not share her optimism, nor, therefore, ever quite so keenly her disappointments, and, though I sometimes enjoyed parties, I never felt the exhilaration which they sometimes gave to her. When we were still living in Richmond, she wrote in her diary that she and I were becoming celebrities and that I denied this, but then I had not, as she had, gone to Logan Pearsall Smith's tea-party in Chelsea or to the week-end with Ottoline Morrell at Garsington. I did occasionally go to Logan's tea-parties where one drank

Earl Grey's china tea amid china, furniture, pictures, books, and human beings, not easily distinguishable from one another or from the tea with its delicate taste and aroma, for they were all made, fabricated, collected in accordance with society's standards of sophisticated culture and good taste. Earl Grey has never been my cup of tea, nor was Logan.

I occasionally went to Garsington, but not as often as Virginia. Garsington, its week-ends and Ottoline and Philip, have been described, with or without venom, in many memoirs and novels, and I have myself had something of a say in *Beginning Again* (pp. 198-203), and I do not propose to say much more about this interesting phenomenon. It was an interesting phenomenon, both from a human and from a social point of view. The ingredients and therefore the flavour and taste of Garsington altered a little when peace came. The C.O.s—Conscientious Objectors—whom Philip and Ottoline had so generously harboured during the war, of course, drifted away. The C.O.s, being pacifists, were, for the reasons which I have explained above in dealing with Massingham's virulence, more quarrelsome and cantankerous than the average man or woman. At week-ends they formed an unquiet, disquieting, turgid sediment beneath the brilliant surface of very important people, the distinguished writers, cabinet ministers, and aristocrats who sat down to breakfast, lunch, and dinner.

Ottoline is almost always described in the setting of Garsington, but she functioned just as characteristically in the large house in Bedford Square. In the 1920s there were three great London hostesses with would-be salons to which the literary gents and ladies were admitted and, if distinguished, welcomed—Lady Colefax, Lady Cunard, and Lady Ottoline Morrell. The social historian of the period could have studied in these salons the antics of some limited and not uninfluential sections of British society—a way of life, a collection of human subspecies, and even a form of influence which have, I suppose, completely died out of London and Britain. The three salons differed a good deal from one another. Of Lady Cunard's I could only speak second-hand, from Virginia, for I never went there myself. Sibyl Colefax was the most professional of the three, an unabashed hunter of lions.

Ottoline's Bedford Square was even more a salon than her Garsington. It existed in four forms: you might be invited to a lunch, a tea, a dinner, or to an evening party after dinner, and the last might be very large or fairly small. At all of them the pudding would certainly contain plums, distinguished or very distinguished persons, and the point of the pudding was, it seemed to me, not so much in the eating as in the plums—the bigger the better. In the pudding of society I am not too fond of plums. Nothing is more enjoyable than 'society', if by the word one means the gathering together round a table or a fire or in a garden of congenial, intelligent, and amusing people, and the enjoyment comes from the play and interplay of character and the congenial, intelligent, and amusing conversation, and is enhanced by pleasant or beautiful rooms and houses, good food, and good wine, This kind of society and its enjoyment is only possible if the number of people gathered together—the party—is strictly limited, indeed small enough to make it possible for the conversation to become at any moment general. Both Virginia and I were very fond of this kind of society and party, and we always contrived to get a good deal of it in Richmond, Rodmell, and later in London.

The society of the professional hostess, of Ottoline in Bedford Square, is entirely different. As a study of human behaviour, both of hostess and guests, it always fascinated me. The psychology of the hostess may contain all or any of the following ingredients: enjoyment of the enjoyment of her guests; a kind of artistic creativeness—the art of hostess-ship; the love of the exercise of power and prestige; the passion of the collector of anything from stamps to human beings. The ingredients in the hospitality of Lady Colefax in Argyll House were quite different from those of Lady Ottoline Morrell in Bedford Square. Sibyl gave me the impression of an armour-plated, electroplated, or enamelled woman, physically and mentally. The range of her feelings behind this metallic façade seemed to be extremely limited; but façades are façades, and behind hers there may, of course, have been a tremulous sensitiveness. Indeed I was often startled and shocked to observe the expression of the eyes in that mask of her hostess face; far behind and deep down below they gave one a glimpse of misery, anguish. But the surface was always hard, polished, plated, professional. Every morning Sibyl wrote her illegible notes or sat at her telephone collecting men and women, ranked solely for their fame or footing, their power or prestige. Her main motives were, I think, pleasure in power and prestige and the delights of collecting—'I must add Walter Lippmann and André Gide to my collection'.

The hostess psychology of Ottoline was quite different. I do not think that she had a very strong passion for collecting, although, as with all professional hostesses, it did exist in her. She was, too, not very much moved by power and prestige; as a Cavendish-Bentinck and sister of the Duke of Portland, she assumed unconsciously, like all aristocrats, that she had a peculiar right and relation to both, and therefore need not trouble about them. She was highly sexed and got some sexual satisfaction as a by-product of the art of hostess-ship. She also got aesthetic satisfaction from the practice of the art, for her aesthetic emotions were strong and persistent, if erratic and sometimes deplorable. The house and garden at Garsington were lovely, and Ottoline gave both an artistic finish, and she gave the same to the rooms in Bedford Square. Her own taste was for disorderly flamboyance, as her dress and hair showed, but she knew and respected what the world and the élite thought to be the right thing in books, pictures, music, houses, rooms, furniture, and persons. The compromise between good taste and her own tastes gave a peculiar and sometimes incongruous aspect to her rooms and a strange and sometimes ludicrous flavour to her parties. Her reactions to what is great in art were strong, untrustworthy, and embarrassing; for instance, I have heard her gush over the beauties of Keats at the breakfast table of a Garsington week-end to five or six silent, gloomy, cynical, sophisticated members of the literary élite. But she had a real gift for and pleasure in the art of hostessship which was unknown to Sibyl. She wanted to know, to have intimate relations with intelligent, imaginative, creative people, and to create herself the best possible surroundings in which these strange men (with an occasional woman) might flourish socially and enjoy one another's society and conversation. There is no doubt that in this she was to some extent successful.

If you want to know what a particular period was like, the nature of its society and classes, the kind of people who lived in it, you can learn something from the way in which the people met and entertained one another formally. The *Symposium* gives one a vivid and startling glimpse, not only of Athens in the fifth century, but of Socrates, Alcibiades, and Aristophanes, just as Petronius makes one suddenly see through Trimalchio's dinner-party a glimpse of what it meant to be a vulgar rich man or a slave girl in the time of Nero. Most of those whom I met in Ottoline's Garsington and Bedford Square or Sibyl's Argyll House are as dead as Socrates and Trimalchio, and the society of the 1920s is almost as dead as that of Athens in the fifth century B.C. or of Rome in the first century A.D. If I describe one or two parties at Sibyl's and Ottoline's, it may give a glimpse of what they and we and a section of London society were like in the third decade of the twentieth century.

First a trivial picture of Sibyl, the insensitive professional hostess, and the failure of her art. In *Beginning Again* (p. 167) I described how, just before the 1914 war, I met for the first time the famous Walter Lippmann, then unknown, how we travelled down from Keswick to London talking intimately the whole time, and how much I liked him. Not long before the 1939 war Sibyl came to see us and for some reason which I have forgotten I must have mentioned this. I also said that in the intervening 25 years I had hardly seen Lippmann. Lady Colefax, the pro, jumped on me. Walter Lippmann would be in London next week; would I come and dine and meet him on Thursday? I knew that at a dinner in Argyll House I should have no chance of the only kind of conversation which I wanted to have with Lippmann, and I therefore refused. But Sibyl, as a hostess, was a ruthless Lady Bountiful, and I was not allowed to get off. She would get Lippmann to come and meet me at six one evening, if I would not come to a meal, and she would ask no one else. I foolishly agreed. We met unhappily and, under the inhibiting eye of Sibyl, had nothing to say to each other.

The second picture was at a top-notch, grand evening party at Argyll House. It was a fine, warm summer evening; the large room was full of Sibyl's top-notch lions, political and literary mainly, together with a sprinkling of lesser lights and the stage army of well-fed and well-dressed men and women whose only distinction was that they were habitually asked to this kind of London party. The doors which led from the large room into the garden were open, and the guests strolled about the garden, which was lit by garlands of fairy lamps. There is a certain beauty in this kind of scene, en-

hanced by the fact that among the strollers under the fairy
lamps are the Prime Minister and half the Cabinet, Mary
Pritchard, Margot Asquith, the editor of *The Times*, Max
Beerbohm, and Augustus John. Everything seemed to be
going as it should, when suddenly there came a social catastrophe of the kind which often happened in Argyll House.
We were all summoned into the large room and seated down
to hear a recital by a distinguished French pianist. She was
led up to the piano by Sibyl and began to play. She had played
only a few bars when two or three people came in from the
garden talking loudly, obviously unaware of what was happening in the room. The pianist crashed her hands on the
notes, got up, and walked to the end of the room, where she
sat down, saying in a loud voice and a thick foreign accent:
'I do not play to accompany people talking'. It is a queer
sensation to sit in such a company of 100 to 150 persons,
in full evening-dress, all in awkward silence and all obviously
feeling rather uncomfortable. No one moved, no one talked.
After what seemed a long time Sibyl got up and walked over
to where Arthur Balfour was sitting and had a longish conversation with him. Then he got up, went to the irate pianist,
bent over her, and obviously pleaded with her. He was
successful and led her gracefully amid applause to the piano.

Ottoline, as I said, treated her lions differently, and the
atmosphere of her Bedford Square zoo was much more ramshackle and informal than that at Argyll House. I can,
perhaps, best give its flavour by describing a tea-party there.
I did not often go to these parties, and it was characteristic of
Ottoline that she insisted that I should come to this one,
because, she said, one of the Georgian poets whom I had
never met was coming and she was quite sure I would like
him. His name, I think, was Ralph Hodgson and Ottoline
thought I would like him because he was a strong silent
man who had written a poem about a bulldog and also a

poem about a bull. When Virginia and I arrived, the poet of the bull and the bulldog was there, strong and silent, together with Yeats and James Stephens, who had written a very successful book, *The Crock of Gold*. It was an uneasy party. Yeats sat in the place of honour, but was grumpy and silent, and Virginia was commandeered, much too obviously, by Ottoline to go over and sit next to him and talk him, if possible, into a better mood. James Stephens was one of those Irish Irishmen, the stage Irishman who never stops talking with the soft brogue which makes one think despairingly of the indomitable soft rain falling upon the lakes of Killarney. Being also what I call a literary gent, he used to fill me alternately with depression and irritation, and I think that he probably had much the same effect upon Yeats. On this occasion he was in full spate, with a whimsical, poeticised fantasy about insects, whom he continually referred to as 'the little craytures'. When he made a more than usually absurd statement about 'the little craytures', before I could stop myself, I said in a loud voice: 'Nonsense'. Ottoline frowned upon me and the party became still stickier. However, nothing stopped Stephens talking, and the other Irishman, the great man, thawed bit by bit under the skilful and soothing ministrations of Ottoline and Virginia. The party began to go in the way in which Ottoline liked parties to go—intimate, intense, and rather intensive talk about books and writers and the arts generally. It was this kind of conversation which made Bedford Square so different from Argyll House. And it was characteristic of a Bedford Square party that it was suddenly deflated, broken up, exploded. For the door opened and in came the Duchess of Portland. She was obviously not expected by Ottoline and she looked upon us all as if we were 'the little craytures'. She sat down on a sofa next to Ottoline and began to talk to her about something which only concerned herself. Silence fell upon

us little craytures; even Stephens was left without a drone or
a buzz, for a Duchess of Portland is capable of silencing the
voice even of the cicada. After a minute or two Ottoline got
up and took her sister-in-law out of the room. They stood
outside the door and the sound of their voices in inaudible
conversation seemed to be going on interminably. When at
last we heard the front door close behind the Duchess, the
party rather despondently broke up.

The kind of party which I have just been describing,
presided over by a professional hostess, is formal, public
entertainment in which social pleasure is very deliberately
offered and pursued. I have never found that kind of pleasure
very pleasurable. On the other hand, as I have said, both
Virginia and I enjoyed society, if private, informal, intimate.
As Virginia's health improved and civilization began to
penetrate to Rodmell in the form of a bus and other ameni-
ties, we became more and more social in that kind of way, and
the number of our friends and acquaintances grew rapidly.
We saw them at Richmond, but we also had them for week-
ends to Monks House. Our week-ends at Monks House
were the antithesis of week-ends at Garsington. We had
room for only one guest, and it was still pretty primitive and
uncomfortable, so that one could only have those with whom
one was already very intimate or with whom one could soon
become very intimate. Among the former were Lytton
Strachey and Morgan Forster, and among the latter T. S.
Eliot.

In the years 1920 to 1923 Tom Eliot stayed with us
several times in Rodmell and he used to come and dine with
us at Richmond. It was in these years that our relations
with him changed deeply, from extreme formality to the
beginning of a real intimacy. But I do not think it was
merely that we got to know him better. I think that Tom
himself changed inside himself to some extent—to the extent

perhaps that anyone ever can change inside himself after his first good cry on leaving his mother's womb and seeing the cruel light of day and the face of nurse and doctor. There was from the first a dichotomy in Tom, which, when he stayed with us on September 19, 1920, Virginia noted in his face; 'The odd thing about Eliot,' she wrote, 'is that his eyes are lively and youthful when the cast of his face and the shape of his sentences are formal and even heavy. Rather like a sculpted face—no upper lip; formidable, powerful; pale. Then those hazel eyes, seeming to escape from the rest of him.' He was so inhibited, those sentences were so formal and heavy that, although—or rather because—I had seen so much in his poetry and in those eyes which seemed to escape from him, the week-end left me with a feeling of disappointment. In conversation it was his brain that was disappointing, so much more rigid and less powerful than I had expected from the poems, and with so little play of mind. He was himself aware of this and disappointed in himself, for, in describing a week-end with Ottoline in Garsington, he said: 'And I behaved like a priggish pompous little ass'. I do not think that it was just conceit that made us think that we had something to do with changing Tom, with loosening up the pomposity and priggishness which constricted him, with thawing out the essential warmth of his nature which, when we first knew him, seemed to be enclosed in an envelope of frozen formality. How inhibited he was then can be seen from an absurd incident which happened at one of his very early visits to Monks House and in which I remember for the first time breaking the ice. He was walking with Virginia and me across the fields down to the river. I suddenly wanted to make water and fell behind to do so. Neither of my companions saw what I was doing, but I suppose it was very obvious what I was doing. Anyhow, when I caught them up again, I felt that Tom was uncomfortable, even shocked.

I asked him whether he was and he said yes, and we then had what gradually became a perfectly frank conversation about conventions and formality. Tom said that he not only could not possibly have done what I did, that he would never dream of shaving in the presence even of his wife.

About literature, even about his own writing, even in those early days of knowing him, he was easy and unreticent —and always very interesting. During this visit Virginia one evening tackled him about his poetry and told him that 'he wilfully concealed his transitions'. He admitted this, but said that it was unnecessary to explain; explanation diluted facts. He intended to write a verse play in which the four characters of Sweeney would appear. What he wanted to do was to 'disturb externals'; he had had a kind of personal upheaval after writing *Prufrock*, and this altered his inclinations, which had been to 'develop in the manner of Henry James'.[1]

Tom had a great opinion of Virginia as a critic. Some ten years after this early visit to Rodmell, he came to us one day and said that he had just written some poetry which he would very much like us to criticize seriously. What he would like would be to send us each a typescript of the poems; we should read them and then come in after dinner one evening and each in turn criticize them—and he might ask one or two other people—Mary Hutchinson, for instance—to come as well. We agreed, and he sent us a typescript of what eventually was published as *Ash-Wednesday*. Then one summer evening we went round to his house after dinner and found Mary Hutchinson and McKnight Kauffer there. We all sat solemnly on chairs round the room and Tom began the proceedings by reading the poem aloud in that curious monotonous sing-song in which all poets from Homer downwards have recited their poetry. Then each in turn was called upon

[1] Some of the above is recorded in Virginia's diary.

to criticize. The order was, I think, Mary, I, Virginia, Kauffer. It was rather like an examination, not of the examinee, but of the examiners, and Mary, Kauffer, and I didn't do any too well—in fact Tom dismissed rather severely some of the things that some of us said. Virginia passed with flying colours. She told Tom that he had got into the habit of ending lines with a present participle; he had done it with great effect at the beginning of *The Waste Land*, and he was doing it again in this poem. She thought he should beware of it becoming a habit. Tom said that she was quite right and that what she said was very useful. I still have the original typescript copy which he gave to me and I have compared it with *Ash-Wednesday* as published. The two versions are not the same, but the present participles remain in the lines. The printed version is:

> *Here are the years that walk between, bearing*
> *Away the fiddles and the flutes, restoring*
> *One who moves in the time between sleep and*
> *waking, wearing . . .*

In the original typescript the three lines read:

> *Here are the years that walk between, bearing*
> *Away the fiddles and the flutes, restoring*
> *One who walks between season and season, wearing . . .*

In the book as published, there are six sections, in the typescript there are only five; presumably section VI was written after our critical seance. Tom did not alter very much in the first five sections; there are two main differences between the two versions. In the typescript each section has a title which is not in the printed book and the final version of section V is much longer than the original. The following are the titles of the sections:

PEACE IN OUR TIME, O LORD

I. PERCH'IO NON SPERO; II. JAUSEN LO JORN; III. SOM DE
L'ESCALINA; IV. VESTITA DI COLOR DI FIAMMA; V. LA SUA
VOLUNTADE.

The gradual growth of our intimacy with Tom can be traced in Virginia's diary. In February 1921 he dined with us at The Cock in Fleet Street and Virginia wrote: 'pale, marmoreal Eliot was there last week, like a chapped office boy on a high stool, with a cold in his head, until he warms a little, which he did. We walked back along the Strand. "The critics say I am learned and cold," he said. "The truth is I am neither." As he said this, I think coldness at least must be a sore point with him.' A month later she was wondering whether we would ever get to the stage of Christian names: 'But what about Eliot? Will he become Tom? What happens with friendships undertaken at the age of 40? Do they flourish and live long? I suppose a good mind endures, and one is drawn to it and sticks to it, owing to having a good mind myself. Not that Tom endures my writing, damn him.' By the end of the year we were calling him Tom and Virginia noted with regret that she was no longer frightened of him.

The first time Virginia met Vita Sackville-West (Mrs Harold Nicolson) was in December 1922, and the first entry in her diary describing Vita is rather critical. We saw something of Harold and her during the next year, but it was not until 1924 that we got to know them well. At that time they lived partly in London and partly in a very pleasant house, Long Barn, near Sevenoaks, and not far from her ancestral home, Knole. We stayed with them there, and Virginia began to see a great deal of Vita. There was a curious and very attractive contradiction in Vita's character. She was then literally—and so few people ever are literally—in the prime of life, an animal at the height of its powers, a beautiful flower in full bloom. She was very handsome, dashing, aristocratic, lordly, almost arrogant. In novels people often 'stride' in or out of rooms; until I saw Vita, I was inclined to think that they did this only in the unreal, romantic drawing-rooms of the novelist—but Vita really did stride or seem to stride.

To be driven by Vita on a summer's afternoon at the height of the season through the London traffic—she was a very good, but rather flamboyant driver—and to hear her put an aggressive taxi driver in his place, even when she was in the wrong, made one recognize a note in her voice that Sackvilles and Buckhursts were using to serfs in Kent 600 years ago, or even in Normandy 300 years before that. She belonged indeed to a world which was completely different from ours, and the long line of Sackvilles, Dorsets, De La Warrs, and Knole with its 365 rooms had put into her mind and heart an ingredient which was alien to us and at first made intimacy difficult.

Vita was, as we used to say to her, only really comfortable in a castle, whereas a castle is almost the only place in which I could not under any circumstances be comfortable. When compared to the ramshackle informality of our life and rooms in Hogarth House and Monks House, Vita's Long Barn, with its butler, silver, Persian rugs, Italian cabinets, and all other modern conveniences, seemed to us a house and a way of life of opulence and grandeur. In their own way—which happens not to be my way[1]—both the house and the way of life had considerable charm and beauty. Later Vita's passion

[1] Virginia, on the whole, liked rather more than I did the conventional opulence of the life and habitations of the wealthy English upper classes. But returning from a week-end at Long Barn, after describing the 'opulence', she added: 'Yet I like this room better perhaps; more effort and life in it, to my mind, unless this is the prejudice one has naturally in favour of the display of one's own character'.

T. S. Eliot at Monks House

The author, Sally, and Virginia in Tavistock Square

for castles led her to buy the great tower and ruined buildings of Sissinghurst. As the thousands of people who every year visit Sissinghurst know, she restored a good deal of the castle and created a garden of very great beauty.

In the creation of Sissinghurst and its garden she was, I think, one of the happiest people I have ever known, for she loved them and they gave her complete satisfaction in the long years between middle age and death in which for so many people when they look out of the windows there is only darkness and desire fails. But there was another facet in her character; she was, in many ways, a very simple person, and it was this side of her which emerged both in her poem, *The Land,* and in her passion for gardening, though combined with the opulent magnificence of the Sackvilles and Knole it produced something at Sissinghurst which could not exactly be called simple. It was this simplicity, when combined with other things in her character, which made one fond of her, the other things her own affectionate nature and her honesty and generosity. The scale of Sackville generosity in those days was to some extent, I think, influenced by the crazy munificence of Vita's mother (described in her book *Pepita*) who in her life had dissipated several million pounds without leaving herself anything to show for it. Lady Sackville lived eccentrically at Rottingdean and Vita used from time to time to drive over to see her. On the way back she used to look in upon us at Monks House and we always went out to her car to see the presents which Lady Sackville had showered on her. The scale of her munificence can be seen in the fact that one day on the back seat of the car was a gigantic porcelain sink in which were piled about 150 green figs. I don't know why Lady Sackville had given Vita a porcelain sink, but the figs came about in this way. She took Vita for a drive to the famous fig garden in Worthing; she asked Vita whether she would like to take back some figs, and, when she said yes, insisted upon buying for her the entire crop of ripe figs.

I find some difficulty in determining exactly when what is called Bloomsbury came into existence. In *Beginning Again* (pp. 21-26) I treated it as having come into existence in the three years 1912 to 1914. I should now prefer to say that in those three years a kind of ur-Bloomsbury came into existence. Of the thirteen members of Old Bloomsbury, as we came to call it, only eight at that time actually lived in Bloomsbury: Clive and Vanessa in Gordon Square and Virginia, Adrian, Duncan Grant, Maynard Keynes, and myself in Brunswick Square, with Saxon Sydney Turner in Great Ormond Street. It was not until Lytton Strachey, Roger Fry, and Morgan Forster came into the locality, so that we were all continually meeting one another, that our society became complete, and that did not happen until some years after the war. First the war scattered us completely and then Virginia's illness, by banishing us to the outer suburb of Richmond, made any return to our day-to-day intimacy impossible. But as Virginia's health improved and it became possible for us to go up to London more often to parties and other meetings, what archaeologists might call a second period of ur-Bloomsbury began. For instance, in March 1920 we started the Memoir Club and on March 6 we met in Gordon Square, dined together, and listened to or read our memoirs.

The original thirteen members of the Memoir Club, identical with the original thirteen members of old Bloomsbury, were all intimate friends, and it was agreed that we should be absolutely frank in what we wrote and read. Absolute frankness, even among the most intimate, tends to be relative frankness; I think that in our reminiscences what we said was absolutely true, but absolute truth was sometimes filtered through some discretion and reticence. At first the memoirs were fairly short; at the first meeting seven people read. But as time went on, what people read became longer and, in a sense, more serious, so that after a few years normally only two memoirs were read in an evening. They were usually very amusing, but they were sometimes something more. Two by Maynard were as brilliant and highly polished as anything he wrote—one describing his negotiations with the German delegates and, in particular, Dr Melchior, in the railway carriage at Tréves after the 1914 war, and the other about Moore's influence upon us and our early beliefs at Cambridge—and these were after his death published, exactly as they were originally read to us, under the title *Two Memoirs*. Some of Virginia's were also brilliant, and Vanessa developed a remarkable talent in a fantastic narrative of a labyrinthine domestic crisis. The years went by and the Club changed as the old inhabitants died and the younger generation were elected. The last meeting took place, I think, in 1956, 36 years after the first meeting. Only four of the original thirteen members were left, though in all ten members came to the meeting.

These meetings meant for us going up to Bloomsbury from Richmond, with late nights, staying in London or midnight train journeys back to Richmond. And we were sucked into other parties both in and outside Bloomsbury. In order to give a more concrete idea of one of these parties in ur-Bloomsbury and of Virginia's social excitement which I have referred to when she found herself at one, I will quote from Virginia's diary the description of a fancy-dress party to which we went in Gordon Square in the first week of January 1923:

Let the scene open on the doorstep of number 50 Gordon Square. We went up last night, carrying our bags and a Cingalese sword. There was Mary H. in lemon coloured trousers with green ribbons, and so we sat down to dinner; off cold chicken. In came Roger and Adrian and Karin; and very slowly we coloured our faces and made ready for number 46. It was the proudest moment of Clive's life when he led Mary on one arm and Virginia on the other into the drawingroom, which was full, miscellaneous, and oriental for the most part. Suppose one's normal pulse to be 70: in five minutes it was 120: and the blood, not the sticky whitish fluid of daytime but brilliant and prickly like champagne. This was my state and most people's. We collided, when we met; went pop, used Christian names, flattered, praised, and thought (or I did) of Shakespeare. At any rate I thought of him when the singing was doing. Shakespeare I thought would have liked us all tonight....My luck was in though and I found good quarters with Frankie [Francis Birrell] and Sheppard and Bunny [David Garnett] and Lydia [Lopokova]—all my friends in short. But what we talked about I hardly know. Bunny asked me to be his child's godmother. And a Belgian wants to translate me. Arnold Bennett thinks me wonderful and ... and ... (these, no doubt, were elements in my hilarity). Jumbo [Marjorie Strachey] distorted nursery rhymes: Lydia danced: there were charades: Sickert acted Hamlet. We were all easy and gifted and friendly and like good children rewarded by having the capacity for enjoying ourselves thus. Could our fathers? I wearing my mother's laces, looked at X's Jerboa face in the old looking glass—and wondered, I daresay no one said anything very brilliant. I sat by Sickert and liked him, talking, in his very workmanlike but not at all society manner, of printing and Whistler; of an operation he saw at Dieppe. But can life be worth so much pain, he asked. 'Pour respirer,' said the doctor. 'That is everything.' 'But for two years "after my wife's death" I did not wish to live,' said Sickert. There is something indescribably congenial to me in this easy artists'

talk: the values the same as my own and therefore right:
no impediments: life charming, good and interesting: no
effort: art brooding calmly over it all: and none of this
attachment to mundane things, which I find in Chelsea.
For Sickert said, why should one be attached to one's body
and breakfast? Why not be satisfied to let others have the
use of one's life and live it over again, being dead oneself? No mysticism, and therefore a great relish for the
actual things—whatever they may be—old plays, girls,
boys, Proust, Handel sung by Oliver [Strachey], the turn
of a head and so on. As parties do, this one began to
dwindle, until a few persistent talkers were left by themselves sitting in such odd positions. . . . And so, at 3, I
suppose, back to No. 50 to which Clive had gone previously.

It was parties like this and our increasing sociability in
London which made the question of whether we should stay
on in Richmond or immigrate to Bloomsbury more and more
urgent. Already in 1922 Virginia was eager for the move.
She had begun to feel imprisoned, secluded and excluded,
in Richmond. If she lived in London, she said, 'I might go
and hear a tune, or have a look at a picture, or find out something at the British Museum, or go adventuring among
human beings. Sometimes I should merely walk down
Cheapside. But now I'm tied, imprisoned, inhibited.' This
was, of course, true, but I had been against a move, solely
because I feared the result on Virginia's health, It had become much more stable, but it could never be neglected or
ignored, and nothing was more dangerous for it than the
mental fatigue produced by society and its social pleasures.
She was one of those people who drained herself, exhausted
herself mentally, both passively and actively, not only at a
party but in any kind of conversation or social intercourse.

In Richmond it was possible to keep some control over our social life and, at a danger signal, to shut ourselves off from it for a time. I feared that this would prove impossible in London.

However, in the middle of 1923 I became converted to the idea, for the disadvantages of staying on in Richmond seemed to outweigh the dangers of moving to Bloomsbury. I had to count the cost both of Virginia's growing feeling of being cabined and confined and, as our engagements in London increased, the increasing strain and fatigue of catching crowded trains or buses in order to keep them. So I gave way and in November we began to search Bloomsbury for a house. The usual alternation of joy and disappointment and despair in house hunting lasted for two months, but on January 9, 1924, we acquired from the Bedford Estate a ten-year lease of 52 Tavistock Square. On March 13 following, we moved into it.

Chapter Two

DOWNHILL TO HITLER

52 Tavistock Square, eventually destroyed in 1940 by one of Hitler's earliest bombs, was a very pleasant house, built, I suppose, by a Duke of Bedford, as speculative builder, early in the nineteenth century. It had four storeys and a basement. We put the Hogarth Press into the basement and ourselves occupied the flat on the second and third floors; the ground and first floors were already let to a firm of solicitors, Dollman and Pritchard. The firm actually consisted of old Mr Pritchard and his son, young Mr George, and a strange staff. First there was old Mr Pritchard's sister, who had, I believe, been matron in a large London hospital but now acted with immense efficiency as a kind of head clerk. Then sitting by himself in a room on the first floor was a most sophisticated Irishman, who had lived a good deal of his life in Paris and spoke perfect French. Finally there were two or three girl clerks. One would have to live many lives and travel a long way to find again as good tenants as the firm of Dollman & Pritchard; we got so friendly with the partners and all the staff that when we moved in 1939 from Tavistock to Mecklenburgh Square, we took the firm with us. Old Mr Pritchard, in looks, in speech, and in character, came straight out of Dickens, belonging to the year 1850 rather than 1924 and to the long line of angelic old men in the great Victorian's novels. The Pritchards were so absurdly generous that, when I employed them as solicitors, I found the greatest difficulty in persuading them to charge me anything.

I have lived practically all my life in London, but I am again and again surprised by its curious, contradictory character, its huge, anonymous, metropolitan size and its pockets of provincial, almost village life—also the congenital conservatism of Londoners, so that if you scratch the surface of their lives in 1924 you find yourself straight back in 1850 or even 1750 and 1650. In the 15 years I lived in Tavistock Square I got to know a gallery of London characters who themselves lived in a kind of timeless London and in a society as different from that of Fleet Street, Westminster, Kensington, or Putney—all of which I have known—as Sir Thomas Bertram's in Mansfield Park must have been from Agamemnon's behind the Lion Gate in Mycenae. There was still in it a strong element of Dickensian London. There was a perfect Dickens character not only at the top, but also at the bottom of Dollman & Pritchard, solicitors. When at 5 or 6 o'clock the business closed its doors and their rooms were empty, the front door was pushed open and in sidled Mrs Giles. She wore, as Kot would have said, a haggish look; indeed, she always reminded me of one of those wizened, skinny, downtrodden, grimy women of the Dickensian underworld. She was the Platonic image of the London char laid up, not in heaven, but in an attic in Marchmont Street, London, W.C. 1. She spoke the language of the Dickensian cockney. And when she was in a room by herself, she talked as, I am quite sure, Dickens's gaunt old women spoke when they were outside his novels—a language which would have been quite impossible in a Victorian novel. It was terrifying. When just before dinner I used to take my dog out into the Square garden for a run, as I passed through the hall, I used to hear Mrs Giles talking to herself as she cleaned Mr Pritchard's front room. It was a monotonous stream of the foulest language which I have ever heard. Some of it was just pure, disinterested swearing for the sake of swearing, but every now and again it turned into a particularized hymn of hate, the most horrible, obscene accusations against the various mem-

bers of the firm. I cannot attempt to explain this strange
phenomenon. There was little or no bitterness in Mrs Giles's
voice—it was not so much vituperation as a monotonous
threnody, a lament for the horrors of Mrs Giles's life—and
all the Mrs Giles's lives—in Marchmont Street.

I used to take my dog for a run in the Square three or four
times a day and I therefore walked in it far more often than
any other resident, and I soon got to know the Square keeper
very well. After a year or two I was elected to the Square
Committee. We were a statutory body, and here again I
found myself back in the London of Dickens. The use and
government of Tavistock Square were regulated by by-laws
which dated, I think, from about 1840. The Square Committee, which administered the bylaws, consisted of three
persons annually elected by householders resident in the
Square and each householder was entitled to a key admitting
him into the garden. One by-law laid it down that no man-
servant or maidservant should be allowed in the Square and
another prescribed what games children should be permitted
to play there. The Square keeper was another type of nineteenth-century cockney. The square was for him the centre
of a large village, bounded on the north by the Euston Road,
on the east by the Grays Inn Road, on the south by Russell
Square, and on the west by Tottenham Court Road. Within
those boundaries few things happened, at any rate of a
discreditable nature, which he did not learn, and, when I got
to know him well, which he did not recount to me at great
length. He knew by sight almost all those whom he counted
to be true inhabitants of this Bloomsbury village and he had
an extraordinary knowledge of the private lives of very many
of them. Many of his stories were libellous and most of them
were, I think, true. He was a sardonic, poker-faced, disillusioned man who noted and described, without heat or
any sign of moral indignation, the frailties and rascalities of

human nature in the rich, the poor, and the police between Tottenham Court Road and Grays Inn Road.

The police were not popular either with my friend or with the poor in Bloomsbury. Their chief victims, according to the Square keeper, were prostitutes, barrow-boys, and eating-house keepers. There was a regular tariff which the first two paid in order to pursue their business in peace. It was almost impossible for restaurant keepers not to break the law occasionally, and many of them insured against the consequences by providing free meals for any policeman from whom trouble might be expected.

I had one absurd brush with a policeman which at the time seemed to me to confirm my friend's view of the force. One Sunday night about 11 Virginia and I were walking down Francis Street towards Tavistock Square, returning from an evening with Vanessa in Fitzroy Street. Towards us came a large woman about 30 to 35 years old, rather drunk and staggery. Some way behind her also walking towards us came a policeman. Two men on the opposite side of the road began to jeer at her. She stopped and let loose a volley of abuse about 'bullocks' balls' across the road at them. They replied, but, catching sight of the approaching policeman, bolted down a side street, dropping in their haste a bottle of beer with a crash on the pavement. The policeman came up to the woman and began to hector her. She was in no yielding mood, and it seemed to me that he was deliberately trying to goad her into doing something which would justify an arrest for being drunk and disorderly. I suddenly lost my temper and dashed in between them, telling her to stop talking and to leave things to me. I told the policeman that he must have seen that it was the two men who had started the whole thing—why had he done nothing to them and begun to hector the woman? An argument began and I suddenly realized that we were already surrounded by a small crowd which murmured its support of me and the woman against the policeman. I gave my name and address to the policeman and told him that, if he prosecuted the woman, he would have to call me as a witness. The woman, finding that she was supported, then turned on the policeman and began to abuse him. The delighted crowd increased and things began to look rather unpleasant, so I turned to a rather sensible looking man who had been standing by my side and asked him to take the woman away before she got into more trouble. He and I induced her to go and I then had once more to face the policeman. Finding that everyone was against him, he was suddenly deflated and apologetic, assuring me that he never meant to charge the woman. We parted almost amicably and, as the crowd broke up, I saw Lydia standing on the outskirts under a gas lamp, gazing with amazement at me and the policeman.

52 Tavistock Square was, as I have said, divided into three parts: the top inhabited by Virginia and me, the middle by Dollman & Pritchard, and the basement by the Hogarth Press. There were four rooms in the basement. The Press used the large room, which had once been the kitchen, as its office, occupied, when we moved in, by our only employee, Marjorie Joad. We printed in what had been the ancient scullery. Then there was a small room at the back, and behind that the old billiard room, which I have described on page 53.

Virginia was such a bad sleeper and so disturbed by noise that, although she habitually used earstoppers, when we first came to Tavistock Square, she thought that, if she slept upstairs in the flat, the noise of the traffic would keep her awake. The first night, therefore, we had her bed put in the small room at the back of the basement and she started to sleep there. But in the middle of the night she was awakened by several rats scampering round her bed on the floor, and she had to retreat up to the flat for good.

The rats were the harbingers of much trouble and of a legal case which I had to bring in the High Court of Justice. The rats came from a large open space, full of old bricks and rubble, which fronted Woburn Place and stretched from the back of Tavistock Square to Russell Square. The Imperial Hotel Company had acquired this site and were clearing it in preparation for building what was eventually the Royal Hotel. The result was a vast number of displaced refugee rats who could be seen in the middle of the day searching the dustbins in the area and who invaded the basement of nights. With the help of a London County Council inspector who looked after vermin, we got rid of the rats, but the building of the hotel caused us a great deal of trouble. While the building operations were actually going on, the noise during the day was pretty bad, and we had double windows put into our main sitting-room, which looked straight into the area of devastation and the scaffolding, in order to keep out the creaking of the cranes, the clanking of lorries, the cries and curses of the builders.

But our troubles really began only after the vast hotel was finished. At the back was a long ballroom the windows of which were immediately below the windows of our sitting-room. When in the evening these windows were open and a jazz band was playing full blast from 8 to 12, the Bedlam of noise, funnelled into our room even with the double windows closed, made life impossible. I wrote to the Imperial Hotel Company complaining, and got back a sympathetic letter from the secretary, promising steps to mitigate the noise. The only possible mitigation was by closing the hotel windows and I think they gave orders that this should be done, but even if their dance began with closed windows, someone always opened them half-way through the evening, letting Bedlam loose into our sitting-room. I went round to see the secretary, who was very friendly, especially when he found that I had known his famous brother, E. C. Bentley, the author of *Trent's Last Case*. (E. C. Bentley and G. K. Chesterton had been members of a debating society to which I belonged, when a boy at St Paul's, as I related in *Sowing*, p. 91.) But in the end I had to take legal action, which turned out to be an interesting experience.

I employed Mr Pritchard as my solicitor. We eventually won our case, and it is, I think, the only serious case which, in my experience, has been taken to court, has been won, and has cost the plaintiff not one single halfpenny—we recovered all our costs. But the proceedings made me realize, as I had not before, the precariousness and helplessness of the individual in modern life. It was essential to prove that the noise was legally 'a nuisance', a nuisance which anyone or everyone would find intolerable, not just a noise which some hypersensitive person would object to. So I went round and canvassed all the residents whose rooms in Tavistock Square and Upper Bedford Place looked on to the back of the hotel, to get them to come and give evidence that the noise was a nuisance to them. Every man and woman whose windows were near the hotel windows said that the noise made life intolerable to them in the evenings when there was a dance band playing, and that they would give evidence, but in the end, when it came to the point, not one single person would do so—they all cried off. The reason was that they all had short leases and were frightened of their land-lord. The rumour was that their landlord, the Bedford Estate, was in some way interested in the hotel operations and was going to sell more property to the hotel company, and that, if any one took action against the company, he would probably find that he could not get a renewal of his lease.

Whether there was any ground for the rumour or for their fears, I do not know. The important point was that these people believed the rumour and, because of their fear, were prepared without resistance to allow 'them'—an impersonal company and an impersonal landlord—to make their lives a burden to them. The tyranny of these impersonal or personal 'thems' has of course always been a terrifying menace hanging over the lives of ordinary people. 'They' used to be kings, aristocrats, classes, and churches, and it was thought at one time that liberty, equality, and fraternity would abolish them, but 'they' have continued to exist and flourish under other names. In 1965 in a Sussex village a man, with a wife and three children, who has worked all his life until the age of 40 on a farm in the village in which he was born, becomes ill and unable to do heavy farm work. He receives legal notice to leave the house, which is required for the man who is to take his place on the farm. There is no other house available for him, but the Rural District Council will find him lodgings, separating him from his wife and family, who will be 'accommodated temporarily in an institution'. In the country, of course, the working classes have always lived in tied cottages and, completely in the power of 'them', in the shadow of fate and eviction. But here in Tavistock Square in the 1920s were middle-class people living under the same kind of menace.

Despite the fact that it became clear that no one would give evidence on my side, I decided to go it alone, for I knew that I had a very strong, if not impregnable, case. For I had up my sleeve a sentence in one of the Company's letters to me which in fact admitted that the noise was legally a nuisance. I was convinced that, when they were confronted in court with that letter, they would be unable to plead that the noise was not a nuisance, and that the only question would be what steps we could force them to take in order to 'abate' the nuisance. We were encouraged by the fact that, when the case was put down for hearing, they more than once applied for an adjournment. Eventually they came to us and asked us to agree to a settlement out of court. After some haggling it was settled that judgment should be entered against them, the terms being that the offending windows would always be screwed up if a band was playing and that all our costs would be paid by the Company. Mr Pritchard managed to get from them every penny of our costs. On the whole the nuisance was satisfactorily abated, though every now and again someone would forget to screw up the windows and our room and ears would be filled with din of jazz music. An irate telephone message from me to the hotel would then be required in order to get the nuisance once more abated.

Throughout my life I have always said to myself—and often to other people—that one should change one's occupation every seven years. The first person to discover this important truth appears to have been an ancestor of mine some thousands of years ago, for it is recorded in the 29th chapter of the book of Genesis that Jacob agreed to serve Laban for seven years for his daughter Rachel, and when Laban swindled him with Leah instead of Rachel, he agreed to work another seven years for Rachel. The number seven has, of course, for ages had some mystical attraction for human beings, connected perhaps with the seven days of the week and the seven stars of the Pleiades. It is possible that the mystical nature of the number had something to do with Jacob's offer to serve seven years for a wife and twice seven years for two, though his fiddling with the ringstraked and speckled goats, so practical and ingenious, showed that he was a pretty tough and hardheaded man. I do not think that I am much influenced by the mysticism of numbers or anything else. My feeling about what should be the length of time of an occupation is based on observation of myself and other people: no matter how interesting and complicated a

DOWNHILL ALL THE WAY

profession or business or occupation may be, after about five years 90 per cent. of it tends to become stereotyped and automatic, and after another two years 99 per cent. is performed with skill and efficiency, but as routine and habit and with about as much thought and originality as the spider has in the last 700,000 years given to its occupation of spinning, with great skill and efficiency, its web. And when that happens, it is time, I (unlike the spider) think, to make a change.

Throughout my life, to quite a considerable extent, I have taken my own advice and septennially changed my occupation. I began with the Ceylon Civil Service in 1904 and resigned from it in 1911 after seven years. From 1915 to 1923—about eight years—I earned a living mainly by journalism, writing for the *New Statesman*, editing the *International Review*, on the staff of the *Nation*. When the *Nation* changed hands in 1923 I was offered and accepted the post of literary editor. At the end of 1930, after rather over seven and a half years, I resigned. As I explained in *Beginning Again* (p. 132) my work as literary editor revealed to me the corroding and eroding effect of journalism upon the human mind, and I have never after 1930 taken a paid job—I have earned my living from the Hogarth Press, from my books, and from occasionally writing articles or reviews.

But for the first seven years in Tavistock Square the diurnal pattern of our lives was in the main drawn for us by my job on the *Nation*. Our offices were in Great James Street, a pleasant building dating from 1720. Every week I spent two or two and a half days in the office, but I also did a considerable amount of work at home, for I wrote a weekly article of about 1,200 words, called 'the World of Books'. For this article I had to read, on an average, two or three books, and I also had to read a rain of articles and poems with which journals like the *Nation* are perpetually deluged. No

The author and John Lehmann
at Monks House

Monks House, Rodmell

Monks House, Rodmell

Rodmell Village

one who has not been an editor and/or a publisher can have any idea of how badly how many people can write—and what is even more astonishing than the number and badness of the writers and writings is the belief or even hope that such lamentable stuff could be accepted and printed. It was just the same in the Hogarth Press as it was on the *Nation*: manuscripts poured in upon us and quite a number of them were fatuous and sometimes ludicrously fatuous. Indeed, when they were sufficiently fatuous, they sometimes acquired a quality of such sublime craziness or profound stupidity that we seriously considered starting a 'Hogarth Worst Books of the Year Series' in which we could publish some of them. The number of people who today 'seriously' write books, articles, and poems must be colossal, and I doubt whether one in a hundred thousand of the manuscripts which they produce is ever published. Certainly it was extraordinarily rare to get an unsolicited manuscript which one could accept for the *Nation* or the Hogarth Press. One is inclined to believe that this universal itch of writing is a disease of universal education and the twentieth century—until one remembers that nearly two thousand years ago Juvenal noted it in its Roman form, *cacoethes scribendi*.

As literary editor I was responsible for getting the 'middles', which was the name given to the two or three articles of a literary or general non-political nature, the reviews of books, and regular articles on plays, pictures, music, and science. I doubt whether any weekly paper has ever had such a constellation of stars shining in it as I got for the *Nation*. Here are some of the writers who wrote articles or reviews for me in the first few months of my editorship: Bertrand Russell, G. Lowes Dickinson, Gorky, Augustine Birrell, Roger Fry, E. J. Dent, Walter Sickert, T. S. Eliot, Virginia Woolf, E. M. Forster, Lytton Strachey, Osbert Sitwell, Richard Hughes, Stella Benson, Robert Graves,

V. Sackville-West, Arnold Toynbee. Many of these were in 1923 and 1924 unknown young men and women. In the last year of my editorship most of them were still writing for me and they had been joined by other writers, e.g. Aldous Huxley, L. B. Namier, and Raymond Mortimer.

The literary side of the *Nation* benefited by my running the Hogarth Press, and the Hogarth Press benefited by my being literary editor of the *Nation*. In the Press we were interested in young, unknown writers whose work might not attract the publishing establishment. A journal like the *Nation* puts into one's hand a very wide net and all sorts of literary fishes, large and small, swim into it. All sorts of literary fish, some the same as and some different from the *Nation's* shoals, swam in and out of the Hogarth Press in Tavistock Square. It was possible to help the budding (and sometimes impecunious) Hogarth author by giving him books to review and articles to write; and, if one came across something by a completely unknown writer which seemed to have something in it, one could try him out with articles and reviews before encouraging him to write a book. Thus Tom Eliot, Virginia, E. M. Forster, Robert Graves, Vita Sackville-West, William Plomer came to the *Nation* via the Press, while Edwin Muir was an example of the reverse process in this shuttle service. Somewhere or other I saw a poem of Muir's which I thought very good, so I wrote and asked him to let me see some more. He sent me a few and I published one of them. I got him to come and see me and this began a friendship which lasted to his death. I offered to give him regular reviewing, and from the middle of 1924 for a long time almost every week he had a review in the *Nation*. In 1925 the Hogarth Press published his *First Poems*, in 1926 *Chorus of the Newly Dead*, in 1926 his first book of criticism *Transition*, and in 1927 his novel *The Marionette*. Nearly forty years later we published his autobiography (originally published by Harrap, but considerably enlarged for us) and his last book, *The Estate of Poetry*, was published by us posthumously in 1962.

I look back on this forty years' connection with Edwin Muir with great pleasure and some sadness. We printed his poems in 1925 with our own hands and he was the kind of author and they were the kind of poems for whom and which we wanted the Press to exist. *Chorus of the Newly Dead* was not a book which in 1926 an ordinary publisher would have looked at. We made it a 16-page book, bound in a stiff paper cover, for which we charged 2s. 6d. As we printed and bound the edition of 315 copies ourselves, the actual cost was negligible, i.e. £6, 4s. 7½d. In the first year we sold 215 copies, and after paying the author £3, 18s. 11d., the Hogarth Press had made a profit of £7, 17s. 0d. Muir was a real, a natural poet; he did not just 'write poetry', the sap of poetry was in his bones and veins, in his heart and brain; that is why, as with practically all real poets, the form and substance of his poetry changed and developed all through his life as he and his mind changed, hammered upon by the grim reality of living. The form and substance of *First Poems* and *Chorus of the Newly Dead* are tremendously different from those of his later poems—so different that, as he tells us in his autobiography, when he reread *Chorus of the Newly Dead* thirty years after he had written the book, the Edwin Muir of 1926 seemed quite strange to the Edwin Muir of 1954. When he reread, he says, the three lines

> *that ghostly eternity*
> *Cut by the bridge where journeys Christ*
> *On endless arcs pacing the sea.*

they seemed 'so strange to me that I almost feel it was someone else who wrote them; yet that someone was myself'. He was an admirable critic. He was so sensitive, intelligent, and honest minded that, as a serious critic, he always had something of his own worth saying even about masterpieces buried long ago under mountains and monuments of criticism. But even in the ephemeral and debased form of criticism, reviewing, he was remarkable. For a long time he used to review novels for me in the *Nation*, a mechanized, mind-destroying occupation for most people. For him it never became mechanical and his mind's eye was as clear and lively after a year of it as when he began.

Edwin's wife, Willa, was also what Koteliansky called a real person and an original writer whose books the Hogarth Press published. They both came from Orkney. An aura of gentleness, soft sea air, the melancholy of remote islands set in turbulent seas surrounded them. All this is too in Edwin's autobiography which we published in 1954. He was the most uncomplaining and unselfpitying of men. I said that I looked back upon my friendship with him with some sadness —the sadness comes from a feeling that life dealt rather hardly with him.

The main interest of my work on the *Nation* came from the people with whom my work brought me into contact. Many of them became my friends. But they were often merely strange adventures, the absurd comedies or tragi-comedies of real life which always astonish and fascinate me. I will give some examples. One afternoon there walked into my room at the *Nation*, Roy Campbell, whose poetry at that time was creating something of a stir. I knew him only slightly. He was dressed in or swathed in one of those great black cloaks which conspirators wear in operas and melodramas and he had a large black sombrero. He sat down, scowled at me, and then said in the peculiar voice which the villain always used in old-fashioned melodramas: 'I want to ask you whether you think I ought to challenge Robert Graves to a duel'. Experience as editor or publisher soon

teaches one that authors, like Habbakuk, are capable of
anything, but I was so astonished by what I heard that I
could only gasp: 'But why?' 'Why?' he said, 'Why? Don't
you remember the review he wrote of my book, the review
you yourself published two weeks ago?' It was true that
Robert had reviewed Campbell's book, but it had never
struck me that there was anything in it to drive the most
hypersensitive writer into lunacy. For the next quarter of
an hour I had a lunatic conversation persuading Campbell
that the laws of honour and chivalry obtaining in Great
James Street in 1926 did not require him to fight Robert
Graves.

Not long after this business I had trouble with another
reviewer, Richard Aldington. I do not remember how I came
across this disgruntled man, who was almost as prickly as
Roy Campbell. He became a regular reviewer for me, the
kind of reviewer who is a godsend to literary editors. He
could and would write me a good review of almost any book
which I sent him—never a very good and never a bad,
always a good review. One day he came to me with a face
almost as gloomy and threatening as Campbell's. He said
that in the last issue of the *Nation* I had had a review by a
Mr X—did I know that Mr X had run off with his (Aldington's) wife? I said that I did not know this and mumbled that
I was sorry to hear it. 'And are you going to employ Mr X as
a reviewer?' said Aldington louringly. I said that Mr X had
written quite a fairly good review and that I would certainly
send him more books from time to time if he continued to
do well. I was immediately presented with a formal ulti-
matum. Unless I gave an undertaking never to employ Mr
X again, Aldington would never again write a review for
me—he could not write in the same paper as the man who
had run off with his wife. I said that I did not think this
reasonable; as a matter of editorial principle, I did not think

133

it right to give an undertaking to A not to send books to X to review merely because in a private capacity X had run off with A's wife. A angrily left me and I do not think that I ever saw him again.

The strangest of all the incidents which came out of the *Nation* was the case of Mr Y. It began one morning when I was working at home and I received a telephone message from the office saying that a Mr X had called and wanted urgently to see me—he could disclose his business only to me. I told them to tell him that, if he came round to Tavistock Square at once, I would see him for a few moments. Twenty minutes later there appeared a small gentle-voiced man in sandals. He told me the following story. He was a New Zealander and when a youth had become a great friend of another youth, Mr Y. Mr Y had been a good deal more affluent and of a higher class in their native land than Mr X —his father was an architect. As young men, the two of them acquired a passion for the works of Samuel Butler, who from 1859 to 1864 had owned and run a sheep farm in the province of Canterbury, New Zealand. They conceived the idea of starting a Samuel Butler museum and they wrote to Festing Jones, Butler's friend and the high priest of his memory, asking whether he would send them some relics of Butler. He sent them a few things which became the nucleus of their museum.

Some time before his call on me Mr X came to England and became a shop assistant in John Barker in High Street, Kensington. After a bit Mr Y followed him and they set up house together in Kensington. They wrote to Festing Jones and he asked the two young men to dinner. Mr Y decided that he must have a dress suit for the occasion and Mr X got into some trouble by borrowing one from John Barker. After this their financial position was precarious and Mr X earned a living by going abroad from time to time to Belgium and Holland, where, walking from small town to small town, he gave readings or recitations of English prose and poetry. Then another catastrophe befell them. Mr Y wrote some extremely indecent poems which he wanted to get printed in order to send them, as Christmas cards, to his friends. So he went to the policeman who stands at the gates of the House of Commons and asked him whether he could recommend him a printer. The policeman gave him an address of a printer in Whitechapel. Mr Y handed the printer the manuscript and asked him whether he would give him an estimate for printing a small number of copies. This printer, I discovered later, had been fined for printing the indecent poems of D. H. Lawrence, and, presumably on the principle of once bitten twice shy, he handed the poems over to the police. The police prosecuted Mr Y for publishing obscene poems and he was convicted and given three months.

Mr X wanted to appeal against the conviction and sentence, but had no money; he had been told by someone that I might be sympathetic and help him to raise the money for solicitor's and counsel's fees. I went into the whole thing carefully and came to the conclusion that it was a monstrous business. I do not think that Mr Y had ever intended to publish these poems in the usual sense of publication; to send them to his friends for Christmas was to be more or less of a joke; but the magistrate held that his handing the manuscript to the printer was technically and legally 'publication'. But to give a first offender three months' imprisonment for this seemed to me gross injustice. I knew Mr Y by sight, for he was a well-known figure in the streets of London, and as soon as I realized from Mr X's description who he was, I saw how prejudice would corrupt the incorruptible British magistrate or judge before whom he might appear. For Mr Y dressed himself in a long robe with skirts to the ground and he wore his hair so long that it hung beneath his shoulders.

I had a talk with Jack Hutchinson, the K.C., about it; he too thought the sentence to be monstrous and was willing to appear in the Appeal Court for a very moderate fee. So I went to a solicitor who lodged an appeal and I began the dreary business of sending round the hat to possible sympathizers. I got donations from seven publishers and more than 20 writers. In the end the solicitor's bill was £91, 7s. 0d. and Mr X spent £12, 4s. 0d. so that I had to raise rather more than £100—it cost me personally over £50. The result was extremely unsatisfactory.

The appeal was heard by Lord Chief Justice Hewart and two other judges. In *Sowing* I wrote the following sentences, to which some people have taken exception, but which I still stand by:

> I have always felt that the occupational disease of judges is cruelty, sadistic self-righteousness, and the higher the judge the more criminal he tends to become. It is one more example of the absolute corruption of absolute power. One rarely sees in the faces of less exalted persons the sullen savagery of so many High Court judges' faces. Their judgments, *obiter dicta*, and sentences too often show that the cruel arrogance of the face only reflects the pitiless malevolence of the soul.

I dare say that in private life Gordon Hewart, 1st Baron Hewart, Lord Chief Justice of England, was a nice man, a good husband and father, a good club man,[1] a pleasant man to play a round of golf with. I watched him 'doing justice'

[1]. It is worth recording that in *Who's Who* the late Lord Hewart used to list his clubs as follows: Athenaeum, Beefsteak, Garrick, Reform, Savage, United Service, Hadley, Littlestone, Moor Park, South Herts, and Woking Golf

in the Appeal Court for the better part of a day and he
seemed to me—and still seems to me—a typical example of
a High Court judge suffering from the occupational disease
of sadistic, vindictive self-righteousness. His treatment of
the unfortunate Mr Y was disgraceful. One side of his
judicial behaviour interested me greatly. In Ceylon for three
years I had to do a considerable amount of work as judge and
police magistrate and I noticed in myself a curious psychological phenomenon against which one had to be on one's
guard if one wanted to be absolutely unprejudiced and just.
If one had tried three or four cases one after the other in
which one had found the accused guilty, one tended to be
overlenient to the next case, particularly if one had had a
moment of slight hesitation in finding the last man guilty.
And vice versa, if one had found four accused in four cases
not guilty one after the other, one had to be very much on
one's guard against being unconsciously over-severe to or
prejudiced against the accused in the next case.

I was interested to detect the same mental process in the
Lord Chief Justice, who, however, took no steps to counteract his bias. In the case which he tried before Mr Y's the
accused had been convicted of housebreaking. You only had
to look at him to see that he was an old lag. The evidence
against him was overwhelming; he had many previous
convictions. He appealed upon a tenuous technical point and
his counsel made a very clever speech. Hewart set aside the
conviction, smacking his judicial lips over the absolute
justice of British justice—'the appellant has been extremely
lucky in having a counsel to put a difficult case so ably. We
are giving the accused, whose record is a bad one, another
chance and we hope that he will take it in order to amend his
ways. . . .' When I heard this, I felt in my bones that British
justice having been so magnanimous to the old burglar
would probably take it out on Mr Y. It did. Jack Hutchin-

son made a good speech and showed to any unbiased person that the sentence was monstrously excessive in relation to the offence. But Hewart made it pretty obvious that he was against Jack and did not like Mr Y. As soon as the case was closed he turned to the judge on his right and to the judge on his left and muttered something to each in turn. The judge on his right was the equivalent on the bench to the old lag, the burglar, whom we had seen in the dock. He had sat on the bench for so long that he administered justice like a machine and therefore mechanically agreed with the Lord Chief Justice. The other on the left was sitting for the first time in the Court of Appeal; I cannot remember his name, but he was a comparatively young man and I knew him to have a reputation for being civilized. He was obviously arguing with Hewart. The three went into a huddle and after a bit the young judge got up and walked round to stand between Hewart and the old judge so that he could put his view more audibly to the old man, as it seemed to me. It was fascinating to watch the, to me, of course, inaudible judicial argument. Hewart was obviously determined and impatient, and at last the young judge with what seemed to me a shrug walked back to his seat. Hewart rejected the appeal with the same self-righteous self-satisfaction with which he had allowed the appeal of the burglar.

Not all the work on the *Nation* was as interesting as this. In fact, after about five years of it, I began to grow rather restive. To be on the editorial side of a journal like the *Nation* is a curious occupation. There is first one's relations with one's immediate equals and superiors. The editorial staff in Great James Street consisted of Hubert Henderson, the editor, Harold Wright, assistant editor, and myself, literary editor. As I have already explained I had made it a condition that within the literary half of the paper I should enjoy practical autonomy. But of course autonomy in that kind of occupation must be relative and limited. I knew Hubert Henderson and liked him. I suppose that in politics in the broadest sense our outlook had a good deal in common. The world is still deeply divided between those who in the depths of their brain, heart, and intestines agree with Pericles and the French revolution and those who consciously or unconsciously accept the political postulates of Xerxes, Sparta, Louis XIV, Charles I, Queen Victoria, and all modern authoritarians. Hubert and I were both on the side of Pericles, but in our interpretation of what liberty, equality, and fraternity meant, or ought to mean, we differed pretty deeply and pretty often. That he voted for the Liberal and I for the Labour Party was in the 1920s not without significance. I thought, and still think, that Liberals after 1914 ought to have realized that Liberalism, like patriotism, is not enough, and that the great problem was to develop an economic liberalism and liberal socialism.

Hubert's articles in the first part of the paper naturally, therefore, often seemed to me extremely able, but conscientiously to hit the bull's-eye on the wrong target. He, on the other hand, regarded a good deal of what I was doing in the other half of the paper with some misprision. Like many liberal intellectuals, he mistakenly prided himself on being culturally an 'ordinary person', a good philistine, with no use for highbrows. This was an amiable delusion, but the result of it was that he had to convince himself that what he called Bloomsbury was impossibly highbrow and that there was far too much Bloomsbury in the literary section of his paper. This worried him more than it did me, for temperamentally, particularly in business and practical affairs, I tend to go my own way and do not worry. Moreover, in my experience there was almost always a pretty deep gulf between the political and literary editors of left-wing weekly papers, like the *Nation* and the *New Statesman*. The cultural

scission or schism which, rather to my amusement, I found
every now and again opening on a Wednesday morning
between me on the one side and Hubert and Harold Wright
on the other seemed to me no wider or more catastrophic than
that which I had observed between the literary editor of the
New Statesman, Jack Squire or Desmond MacCarthy, and
the editor, Clifford Sharp.

Though this kind of thing did not worry me, it was one
example of a good deal of work on the *Nation* which I found
more and more boring. In the editorial rooms of weekly
newspapers there is or was an unending struggle for space.
As soon as the number of pages or columns in the next issue
has been settled, the number of pages or columns to be
assigned to the editor, the literary editor, and the assistant
editor has to be settled. This too often led to a violent struggle
for space between politics and literature. Whether the editor
should sacrifice a page in which he wanted an article on the
Revolution in Bulgaria by Arnold Toynbee to me for an
article on John Donne by T. S. Eliot, or vice versa, might
well entail a stubborn conflict. This kind of thing is bound
up with one side of journalism which, as I have said before,
corrodes and erodes the editorial mind. The moment you as
editor send back to the printer, say on Wednesday afternoon,
the last page proof corrected for the issue of January 1, you
have to begin to think of what you are going to put in the
issue of January 8, and you have to get that question practically settled by next Monday morning. You are perpetually
thinking in terms of articles, notes, reviews, authors, and
titles in relation to pages, columns, lines, and words, and the
scale of time against which you think of a revolution in
Bulgaria or John Donne, of Hitler's Nuremberg Laws or
the behaviour of the crowd at the Derby, is five, or at most
seven days. The editorial mind thinks kaleidoscopically in a
framework of a few hours or days, but the human mind

should, I think, every now and again think steadily *sub specie aeternitatis*. But eternity to the editor of *The Times* is 24 hours and to the editor (and literary editor) of the *Nation* seven days.

Every now and again I have an intense desire for solitude, to shut the door, pull down the blinds, and to be entirely alone for a day or two. When the desire comes upon me, even if Shakespeare or Montaigne knocked at the door, I should pretend to be out. The frame of mind is connected, I think, with a desire occasionally to think of things *sub specie aeternitatis*, the eternal frame of eternity, not the eternity of 24 hours or seven days. To live perpetually in a kaleidoscope of which the kaleidoscopic changes are always more or less the same bores and depresses me. After four years as literary editor of the *Nation* I already began to feel that I had had enough of this kind of journalism and talked to Maynard about giving it up. He wanted me to stay on and eventually I agreed provided that it was arranged that I spent less time in the office, my salary being reduced from £400 to £250. I went to the office only on Tuesdays and Fridays; in fact, I did practically the same work as I had done before—I do not know how I contrived to get through it in less than two full days at the office. But I continued to do this for another three years. In 1929 I told Maynard that I could not stand any more of it and resigned early in 1930.

My resignation from the *Nation* was made possible by our financial situation which was revolutionized in the years 1928 to 1931. From 1924 to 1928 our income only just covered our expenditure and we had to be very careful about both. I propose to give some exact and detailed figures; the private finances of people seem to me always interesting; indeed they have so great an effect upon people's lives that, if one is writing a truthful autobiography, it is essential to reveal them. Here, at any rate are a few figures:

Income in £'s

	LW	Hogarth Press	VW	Other	Gross Income	Tax	Net Income	Expend- iture
1924	569	3	165	310	1,047	126	921	826
1925	565	73	223	404	1,265	114	1,151	846
1926	499	27	713	419	1,658	144	1,514	962
1927	352	27	748	369	1,496	183	1,313	1,193
1928	394	64	1,540	347	2,345	268	2,077	1,117
1929	357	380	2,936	323	3,996	859	3,137	1,120
1930	383	530	1,617	345	2,875	796	2,079	1,158
1931	258	2,373	1,326	411	4,368	1,376	2,992	1,224
1932	270	2,209	2,531	321	5,331	1,278	4,053	1,153
1933	263	1,693	1,916	327	4,199	1,262	2,937	1,187
1934	202	930	2,130	353	3,615	1,086	2,529	1,192
1935	208	741	801	458	2,208	683	1,525	1,253
1936	263	637	721	477	2,098	683	1,415	1,230
1937	271	77	2,466	524	3,184	315	2,869	1,122
1938	365	2,442	2,972	570	6,349	2,462	3,887	1,116
1939	778	350	891	802	2,821	974	1,849	1,069

Some explanation of these figures is necessary. First as regards expenditure. At the end of the 1914 war I invented a system with regard to our finances which we found both useful and amusing and which we kept going until Virginia's death. At the end of each year I worked out in detail an estimate of expenditure for the coming year. This was to provide for only the bare joint expenses of our common life together; it therefore covered rents, rates, upkeep of houses, fuel and lighting, food, servants, garden, upkeep of car (when we got one), doctors and medicine, an allowance to each for clothes. At the end of the year I worked out what the actual expenditure had been and also the total actual combined income, and then the excess of income over expenditure was divided equally between us and became a personal 'hoard', as we called it, which we could spend in any way we liked. For instance, when we decided to have a car, I bought it out of my 'hoard', and if Virginia wanted a new dress which she could not pay for out of her allowance, she paid for it out of her hoard. The amount of our hoards varied enormously as time went on. To take an example, the above figures show that at the end of 1927 we each got £60, but at the end of 1929 we each got £1,008.

The revolutionary increase in our income was due first to the sudden success of Virginia's books and secondarily to the Hogarth Press. In January 1925 Virginia was 42 years old. She had already published three novels (*The Voyage Out*, *Night and Day*, and *Jacob's Room*) and a book of short stories (*Monday or Tuesday*). In 1924 her income from her books was £37, £21 from her English and £16 from her American publishers; she earned £128 by journalism, so that her total earnings for 1924 were £165. In 1925 she published *Mrs Dalloway* and *The Common Reader* with the Hogarth Press in England and Harcourt, Brace in America. These two books brought her in during the two years 1925 and 1926 £162 in England and £358 in America. In England *Mrs Dalloway* sold 2,236 copies and *The Common Reader* 1,434 copies in the first twelve months. In 1927 *To the Lighthouse* was published and was distinctly more successful than any of her previous books, at any rate in England, where the Hogarth Press sold 3,873 copies in the first year, and she earned from her books in that year £270 in England and £275 in America. That meant that at the age of 47, having written for at least 27 years and having produced five novels, Virginia for the first time succeeded in earning as much as £545 from her books in a year—the most that she had ever made before was £356 in 1926.

The turning-point in Virginia's career as a successful novelist came in 1928 with the publication of *Orlando*. In the first six months the Hogarth Press sold 8,104 copies, over twice as many as *To the Lighthouse* had sold in its first 12 months, and Harcourt, Brace sold 13,031 copies in the first six months. In America Mr Crosby Gaige published a limited edition of 872 copies about a week before the

Harcourt, Brace edition was published. The effect upon
Virginia's earnings as a novelist was immediate. In 1928
she earned from her books £1,434 (£556 in England and
£878 in America) and in 1929 £2,306 (£761 in England
and £1,545 in America). In 1929 *A Room of One's Own* was
published and in 1931 *The Waves*. In the first six months
A Room of One's Own sold 12,443 copies in England and
10,926 in America and *The Waves* sold 10,117 copies in
England and 10,380 in America. Virginia's earnings from
her books were in 1930 £1,294 (£546 in England and £748
in America), in 1931 £1,266 (£798 in England and £468
in America), and in 1932 £1,795 (£554 in England and
£1,241 in America). In 1932 *The Common Reader Second
Series* was published and in the first six months sold 3,373
copies in England and 3,271 in America. Then in 1933
came *Flush*. This was a great success. The Hogarth Press
sold 18,739 copies in the first six months and Harcourt,
Brace 14,081 in America, where it was an alternative selection
of The Book of the Month Club.

Virginia finished writing *Flush* in January 1933 and immediately began to work seriously on *The Years*, which she
first called *The Pargiters*. It took her four years to write *The
Years*, and no major book of hers was published between
1933 and 1937. Her earnings from books during those four
years were as follows:

	England	America	Total
1933	£1,193	£1,253	£2,446
1934	301	778	1,079
1935	214	297	511
1936	158	476	634

The Years was published in March 1937 and was much the
most successful of all Virginia's books. It was the only one
which was a best-seller in America. Harcourt, Brace sold
30,904 copies and in the Hogarth Press we sold 13,005

in the first six months. Virginia's earnings from books for the years 1937, 1938, and 1939 were as follows:

	England	America	Total
1937	£1,355	£2,071	£3,426
1938	1,697	1,275	2,972
1939	193	254	447

These figures may seem too dull and detailed to many people, but autobiographically and biographically they are important. The facts behind them had economically a considerable effect upon our lives. After 1928 we were always very well off. In the next ten years our income was anything from twice to six times what it had been in 1924. Neither of us was extravagant or had any desire for conspicuous extravagance; we did not alter fundamentally our way of life, because on £1,000 a year we already lived the kind of life we wished to live, and we were not going to alter the chosen pattern of our life because we made £6,000 in the year instead of £1,000. But life is easier on £3,000 a year than it is on £1,000. Within the material framework which we had chosen for our existence we got more of the things which we liked to possess—books, pictures, a garden, a car—and we did more of the things we wanted to do, for instance travel, and less in the occupations which we did not want to do, for instance journalism.

But the statistics of Virginia's earnings as a writer of books have from another point of view still greater interest and importance. They throw a curious light on the economics of a literary profession and on the economic effect of popular taste on a serious writer. *Orlando*, *Flush*, and *The Years* were immeasurably more successful than any of Virginia's other novels. *The Years*, much the most successful of them all, was, in my opinion, the worst book she ever wrote—at any rate, it cannot compare, as a work of art or a work of genius, with

The Waves, To the Lighthouse, or *Between the Acts. Orlando* is a highly original and amusing book and has some beautiful things in it, but it is a *jeu d'esprit,* and so is *Flush,* a work of even lighter weight; these two books again cannot seriously be compared with her major novels. The corollary of all this is strange. Up to 1928, when Virginia was 46, she had published five novels; she had in the narrow circle of people who value great works of literature a high reputation as one of the most original contemporary novelists. Thus her books were always reviewed with the greatest seriousness in all papers which treat contemporary literature seriously. But no one would have called her a popular or even a successful novelist, and she could not possibly have lived upon the earnings from her books. In 1932 Mrs Leavis, rather a hostile critic, wrote:

> The novels are in fact highbrow art. The reader who is not alive to the fact that *To the Lighthouse* is a beautifully constructed work of art will make nothing of the book. . . . *To the Lighthouse* is not a popular novel (though it has already taken its place as an important one), and it is necessary to enquire why the conditions of the age have made it inaccessible to a public whose ancestors have been competent readers of Sterne and Nashe.[1]

Mrs Leavis exaggerates. It is not true, as the subsequent history of *To the Lighthouse* shows, that the 'common reader' who does not bother his head about 'beautiful construction' or indeed works of art, can make nothing of the book. There is no reason to think that *Tristram Shandy* was more 'accessible' to the eighteenth-century common reader than *To the Lighthouse* is to the twentieth-century common reader. Mrs Leavis in another passage even more strangely asserts that *To the Lighthouse* is more highbrow art and less accessible to the

[1] *Fiction and the Reading Public,* by Q. D. Leavis, p. 223.

ordinary person than Henry James's *Awkward Age* and *The Ambassadors*. But it is, of course, true, as I have shown above by the statistics that up to 1928 Virginia, although widely recognized as an important novelist, was read by a small public. The fate of her books after 1928, however, points to a conclusion quite different from, and more interesting than, Mrs Leavis's. Take, for instance, the sales of *To the Lighthouse* after 1928 and up to the present date. By 1964 the book had sold 113,829 copies in Britain and 139,644 copies in America. It is selling more today than it has ever sold since its publication in 1927. For instance, in 1964 it sold 10,142 copies in Britain and 13,060 in America, and in 1965 22,340 in Britain and 21,309 in America. A book which sells 43,649 copies a year 39 years after publication cannot be said to be unpopular or un-understandable by ordinary people.

A graph of the sales of Virginia's books and of her reputation since 1920 suggests that, so far as original writing is concerned, the law with regard to literature is the exact opposite of Gresham's law by which bad money drives out good. Nearly all artists, from Beethoven downward, who have had something highly original to say and have been forced to find a new form in which to say it, have had to pass through a period in which the ordinary person has found him unintelligible or 'inaccessible', but eventually, in some cases suddenly, in others gradually, he becomes intelligible and is everywhere accepted as a good or a great artist. In Virginia's case she had to write a bad book and two not very serious books before her best serious novels were widely understood and appreciated. And in her case the good drove out the bad. In the years 1963 and 1964, when *To the Lighthouse* sold annually 23,000, the sales of *The Years* and *Orlando* were negligible. In America they were out of print, and in Britain *Orlando* sold 641 in 1963 and 509 in 1964, *The Years* 213 in 1963 and 470 in 1964. But *The Waves*, the most difficult and the best of all her books, sold 906 in 1963 and 1,336 in 1964, and *Mrs Dalloway*, another difficult and the most 'highbrow' of her books, sold 8,242 copies in 1963 (2,306 in Britain and 5,936 in America) and 10,791 in 1964 (2,098 in Britain and 8,693 in America).

In *A Writer's Diary* I published extracts from Virginia's diary which show her engrossed in the day-to-day work of writing these books. She uses these pages as Beethoven used his Notebooks to jot down an idea or partially work out a theme to be used months or years later in a novel or a symphony. While writing a book, in the diary she communes with herself about it and its meaning and object, its scenes and characters. She reveals, more nakedly perhaps than any other writer has done, the exquisite pleasure and pains, the splendours and miseries, of artistic creation, the relation of the creator both to his creation and his creatures and also to his critics and his public. Her hypersensitivity—the fact that criticism tortured her mind like the dentist's drill on an exposed nerve—has seemed to many of her posthumous critics extraordinary and highly discreditable. She herself agreed with her critics that it was highly discreditable.[1] No

[1] On May 17, 1932, Virginia wrote in her diary: 'What is the right attitude towards criticism? What ought I to feel and say when Miss B. devotes an article in *Scrutiny* to attacking me? She is young, Cambridge, ardent. And she says I'm a very bad writer. Now I think the thing to do is to note the pith of what is said—that I don't think—then to use the little kick of energy which opposition supplies to be more vigorously oneself. It is perhaps true that my reputation will now decline. I shall be laughed at, pointed at. What should be my attitude—clearly Arnold Bennett and Wells took the criticism of their youngers in the wrong way. The right way is not to resent; not to be longsuffering and Christian and submissive either. Of course, with my odd mixture of rashness and modesty (to analyse roughly) I very soon recover from praise and blame. But I want to find out an attitude. The most important thing is not to think very much about oneself. To investigate candidly the charge; but not fussily, not very

doubt it was partly due to the fact, which I have noted before, that 'there was too much ego in her cosmos', and an excess of egoism is discreditable. It was also partly due to her attitude to her work, her art, her books. The vast majority of people work for about eight hours a day, and during those eight hours apply less than 50 per cent. of their attention or concentration to the work. Out of the 16 hours of her waking day I should reckon that Virginia normally 'worked' 15 hours and I should guess that she dreamed about it most of the time when she was asleep. Her work was her writing, and when she was actually writing, her concentration was 100, not 50, per cent. But unlike most people, she was almost always at her work even when she was not working. Practically every afternoon, when at Rodmell, she would walk for an hour, two hours, or even more. All the time on the downs, across the water-meadows, or along the river bank, in the front or at the back of her mind was the book or article she was writing or the embryo of a book or story to be written. It was not that she did not see or feel her surroundings, the kaleidoscope of fields, downs, river, birds, a fox or a hare—she saw and felt them with intensity, as her conversation and the extraordinarily visual imagery of her writing show; but at the same time, at the back or just below the surface of her mind there seemed to be a simmering of thoughts, feelings, images connected with her writing and every now and again this simmering would rise to the surface or boil over in the form of a conscious consideration of

---

anxiously. On no account to retaliate by going to the other extreme—thinking too much. And now that thorn is out—perhaps too easily.' The word 'thorn' here has a kind of special meaning. We used to say that Virginia was continually picking up mental thorns—worries which she could not get rid of—particularly from criticism. She would come to me and say: 'I've got a thorn', and we would discuss the thing until we had got the thorn out.

a problem in her book or the making of a phrase or the outline of a scene to be written next morning.

Moreover, though she enjoyed intensely for their own sake the sights and sounds of her walk, these too were, I think, almost always registered as to some extent the raw material of her art. The same is true of all the activities of her life. For instance, as I have said before, no one could possibly have enjoyed society or parties more than she did; on the surface she was carried away by them and so more often than not was a great 'social success'. And yet I do not think that that second sight, that second layer in her mind, was ever entirely quiescent; there the scene, the dinner-party, the conversation, her own feelings were continually registered and remembered as the raw material of her art. This is shown by the fact that she so often described parties in considerable detail in her diary.[1]

[1] The following is an example written on May 26, 1932: 'Last night at Adrian's party. Zuckerman on apes. Dora Chapman sitting on the floor. I afraid of Eddy (Eddy Sackville-West) coming in—I wrote him a sharp but well earned letter. Adrian so curiously reminiscent—will talk of his school, of Greece, of his past as if nothing had happened in between: a queer psychological fact in him—this dwelling on the past, when there's his present and his future all round him: D. C. to wit and Karin coming in late, predacious, struggling, never amenable or comforting as, poor woman, no doubt she knows: deaf, twisted, gnarled, short, stockish, baffled, still she comes. Dick Strachey. All these old elements of a party not mingling. L. and I talk with some effort. Duncan wanders off. Nessa gone to Tarzan. We meet James and Alix on the door. Come and dine, says James with the desire strong in him I think to keep hold of Lytton. Monkeys can discriminate between light and dark: dogs can't. Tarzan is made largely of human apes. . . . Talk of Greece. Talk of Spain. Dick was taken for a ghost. A feeling of distance and remoteness. Adrian sepulchral, polite, emaciated, elongated, scientific, called Adrian by Solly; then in come rapid small women, Hughes and I think his wife. We evaporate at 11.20: courteously thanked for coming by Adrian. Question what pleasure these parties give. Some, presumably, or these singular figures wouldn't coagulate.'

This unremitting intensity with which she worked upon whatever she was writing, when combined with her sensitiveness to all sensations and impressions, was perhaps to some extent a cause of her vulnerability, the intensity of her feeling about criticism of it. Even when she had reached the dangerous pinnacle of success, established as an important writer, she never showed the slightest sign of that fatal occupational disease of the successful writer, the feeling of being a very important person. On the contrary, the more successful she became, the more vulnerable she seemed to become, with a kind of humility and uncertainty which were the exact opposite of the assurance and importance which one felt in the great men of their day, like Wells, Bennett, Galsworthy, and Shaw,[1] and even in many of the smaller fry.

The implacable intensity of concentration upon her writing and her almost pathological fear of the exposure of publication combined to produce the exhaustion and despair which assailed her in the interval between finishing a book and publishing it. All the books, from *Jacob's Room* to *The Years*, induced one of these dangerous crises. I have already referred to them and I do not propose to record in any detail the effect of each, great though it was, upon Virginia herself and upon our day-to-day life. The exact nature of them can perhaps best be seen in what she wrote on December 23, 1932, when she had just finished *Flush*, a book which she wrote very easily and never took too seriously:

I must write off my dejected rambling misery—having just read over the 30,000 words of *Flush* and come to the conclusion that they won't do. Oh what a waste—what a bore! Four months of work and heaven knows how much reading—not of an exalted kind either—and I can't see how to make anything of it. It's not the right subject for

[1] But characteristically not in Hardy.

that length: it's too slight and too serious. Much good in it but would have to be much better. So here I am two days before Christmas pitched into one of my grey welters.

Her major works, by increasing the strain, only increased that 'dejected rambling misery' and the 'grey welter'. The moment she sent back the corrected proofs of *The Waves* to the printer she had to go to bed with a dangerous headache. When the book was published and before she had any criticism of it, whether from Hugh Walpole, John Lehmann, or anyone else, she wrote in her diary: 'I have come up here, trembling under the sense of complete failure—I mean *The Waves*—I mean Hugh Walpole[1] does not like it—I mean John L. is about to write to say he thinks it bad—I mean L. accuses me of sensibility verging on insanity'. And months later she said that she still felt her brain numb from the strain of writing *The Waves*.

How near these strains from writing and publishing brought her at any moment to breakdown and suicide is shown frequently in her diary. For instance, early in July 1933 the worry over revising *Flush* and her excitement over beginning to write *The Years* brought on a headache, and she recorded on July 10: 'And then I was in "one of my states" —how violent, how acute—and walked in Regents Park in black misery and had to summon my cohorts in the old way to see me through, which they have done more or less. A note made to testify to my own ups and downs: many of which go unrecorded though they are less violent I think than they used to be. But how familiar it was—stamping

---

[1] She noted herself later that, though Hugh said that it was 'unreal' and that it beat him, John 'loved it, truly loved it, and was deeply impressed and amazed'. And she adds about herself: 'My brain is flushed and flooded. . . . Lord what a weathercock—not a wave of emotion is in me.'

along the road, with gloom and pain constricting my heart: and the desire for death, in the old way, all for two I dare say careless words.'

Although her day-to-day mental health in general became stronger and more stable through the 1920s and 1930s, the crises of exhaustion and black despair when she had finished a book seemed each time to become deeper and more dangerous. We had a terrifying time with *The Years* in 1936; she was much nearer a complete breakdown than she had ever been since 1913. There are two gaps in her 1936 diary, one of two months between April 9 and June 11 and another of four months between June 23 and October 30. They were filled with an unending nightmare. For the first three months of the year Virginia was revising the book and, as she revised it, we sent it to the printer to be put into galley proofs. We did this—getting galley instead of page proofs— because Virginia was in despair about the book and wanted galleys so that she would be free to make any alterations she wished in proof. But at the beginning of May she was in such a state that I insisted that she should break off and take a complete holiday for a fortnight. We drove down into the west country by slow stages, stopping in Weymouth, Lyme Regis, and Beckey Falls on Dartmoor, until we reached Budock Vean in that strange primordial somnolent Cornish peninsula between Falmouth and Helford Passage, where the names of the villages soothe one by their strangeness—Gweek and Constantine and Mawnan Smith. As a child Virginia had spent summer after summer in Leslie Stephen's house at St Ives in Cornwall—the scene of *To the Lighthouse* is St Ives and the lighthouse in the book is the Godrevy light which she saw night by night shine across the bay into the windows of Talland House. No casements are so magic, no faery lands so forlorn as those which all our lives we treasure in our memory of the summer holidays of our childhood.

Cornwall never failed to fill Virginia with this delicious feeling of nostalgia and romance.

I thought that for Virginia's jangled nerves I might find in Cornwall the balm which the unfortunate Jeremiah thought—mistakenly—he might find in Gilead to salve the 'hurt of the daughter of my people'. That was why I drove west and stayed in Budock Vean, and revisited Coverack and the Lizard and Penzance, and went on to stay with Will and Ka Arnold-Forster in that strange house, Eagle's Nest, perched high up on the rock at Zennor a few miles from St Ives. As the final cure, we wandered round St Ives and crept into the garden of Talland House and in the dusk Virginia peered through the ground-floor windows to see the ghosts of her childhood. I do not know whether, like Heine, she saw the Doppelgänger and heard the mournful echo of Schubert's song: 'Heart, do you remember that empty house? Do you remember who used to live there? Ah, someone comes! Wringing her hands! Terrible! It is myself. I can see my own face. Hi, Ghost! What does it mean? What are you doing, mocking what I went through here all those years ago'.

I drove back by easy stages to Rodmell and then to London. Virginia seemed to be a good deal better, and, as a further precaution, she took another twelve days' complete holiday at Rodmell. She started to work on the proofs again on June 12, but almost at once it became clear that she had not really recovered. After nine or ten days we decided that she must break off altogether and take a complete rest. In fact, on July 9 we went down to Rodmell and stayed there for three and a half months. Virginia did not write at all, did not look at her proofs, and hardly ever moved out of Rodmell. Once a week I drove up to London for the day and it was a pretty strenuous day. I used to leave Rodmell at 8 and get to Tavistock Square about 10, where I dealt with the Hogarth

Press business. In the afternoon I went to the House of Commons for a meeting of the Labour Party Advisory Committee. That meant that quite often I did not leave London until nearly 7 so that I did not get back to Rodmell until close on 9. Virginia did not accompany me on these weekly expeditions. She spent her time reading, drowsing, walking. Towards the end of October she seemed very much better and we decided that I should read the proofs of *The Years* and that she would accept my verdict of its merits and defects and whether it should or should not be published. It was for me a difficult and dangerous task. I knew that unless I could give a completely favourable verdict she would be in despair and would have a very serious breakdown. On the other hand, I had always read her books immediately after she had written the last word and always given an absolutely honest opinion. The verdict on *The Years* which I now gave her was not absolutely and completely what I thought about it. As I read it I was greatly relieved. It was obviously not in any way as bad as she thought it to be; it was in many ways a remarkable book and many authors and most publishers would have been glad to publish it as it stood. I thought it a good deal too long, particularly in the middle, and not really as good as *The Waves*, *To the Lighthouse*, and *Mrs Dalloway*.

To Virginia I praised the book more than I should have done if she had been well, but I told her exactly what I thought about its length. This gave her enormous relief and, for the moment, exhilaration, and she began to revise the proofs in order to send them back to the printer. She worked at them on and off from November 10 until the end of the year, sometimes fairly happy about the book and sometimes in despair. 'I wonder', she wrote in her diary, 'whether anyone has ever suffered so much from a book as I have suffered from *The Years*'; I doubt whether anyone ever has.

But—how often in my life I have gratefully murmured Swinburne's lines—'even the weariest river winds somewhere safe to sea'. She revised the book in the most ruthless and drastic way. I have compared the galley proofs with the published version and the work which she did on the galleys is astonishing. She cut out bodily two enormous chunks, and there is hardly a single page on which there are not considerable rewritings or verbal alterations. At last on December 31 the proofs were returned to the printer. The book was published in March of the following year, and, as I have said, at once proved to be the greatest success of all the novels which she had written.

Virginia was a slow writer. It took her four years to write *The Years* and there was an interval of six years between *The Waves* and *The Years*. Yet she was comparatively a prolific writer. She wrote nine full-length novels, two biographies, and there are seven volumes of literary criticism; in addition to this there must be at least 500,000 words of her unpublished diaries. As a novelist her output was greater than that of Fanny Burney, Jane Austen, the Brontës, George Eliot, Thackeray, or in modern times Joyce and E. M. Forster. This is a remarkable fact when one thinks of the psychological handicaps and difficulties which I have described in the previous pages. It was to a great extent due to her professional, dedicated, industriousness. Neither of us ever took a day's holiday unless we were too ill to work or unless we went away on a regular and, as it were, authorized holiday. We should have felt it to be not merely wrong but unpleasant not to work every morning for seven days a week and for about eleven months a year. Every morning, therefore, at about 9.30 after breakfast each of us, as if moved by a law of unquestioned nature, went off and 'worked' until lunch at 1. It is surprising how much one can produce in a year, whether of buns or books or pots or pictures, if one works hard and professionally for three and a half hours every day for 330 days. That was why, despite her disabilities, Virginia was able to produce so much.

Thus, although she was in such a desperate state about *The Years* all through the last six months of 1936, she already had simmering in her mind *Three Guineas* and the biography of Roger Fry. Indeed on January 28, 1937, exactly one month after sending back the proofs of *The Years* to the printer, she began to write *Three Guineas*; she finished the first draft on October 12, 1937, and began to write *Roger Fry* on April 1, 1938. But already in August 1937 a new novel, which was to become *Between the Acts*, was simmering in her mind and she began to write it, under its first title *Poyntz Hall*, in the first half of 1938. In 1938 we published *Three Guineas* and in 1940 *Roger Fry*. On February 26, 1941, she finished *Between the Acts* and, as had happened four years before, she fell into the depths of despair. On March 28 she drowned herself in the Ouse.

I must return to the subject of our income. I said that the sudden, large jump upwards in our income which began in 1928 was primarily due to the sudden success of Virginia's books. But I also said that it was due secondarily to the Hogarth Press and I will deal now with the development of this curious publishing business. When we moved from Richmond to Tavistock Square in March 1924, the Press, though it had published 13 books in the previous 12 months, was still a very amateurish affair. It had one employee, Marjorie Joad. 1924 was again a year of considerable expansion and we had three publications which in particular were to have a great influence upon our future as publishers.

In 1924 Vita asked us whether we would like to publish a longish short story which she had written, *Seducers in Ecuador*. At that time she had already published some poems and two or three novels with Collins and Heinemann.

Seducers was a curious little story which no ordinary publisher would have looked at. We made a very pretty little book out of it and published it at 4s. 6d. just before Christmas. When we sold out the edition of 1,500 copies we did not reprint. At that time Harold was still in the diplomatic service and in 1925 he was appointed to the British Legation in Tehran. Vita went with him and she wrote a good travel book about Persia, *Passenger to Teheran*, which we published in 1926. She followed this up with *Twelve Days* in which she described an adventurous journey across the Bakhtiari mountains to the Persian oil-fields, and we published this book in 1928. Next year she brought us the manuscript of *The Edwardians*. This was a novel about Knole, the Sackvilles, and Edwardian Society with the most aristocratic capital S, written from the inside of not only Knole, but also Vita. Inside Vita was an honest, simple, sentimental, romantic, naïve, and competent writer. When she let all this go off altogether in a novel about high life, she produced in *The Edwardians* a kind of period piece and a real best-seller. Both Virginia and Vita had been warned by friends and friendly publishers that it was madness to have their books published by such an amateurish, ramshackle concern as the Hogarth Press, which had not the machinery to deal with a best-seller or even a seller. I have always been doubtful about this 'machinery' of publishing and was pleased to find that the machinery of the Press stood up to the strain of a best-seller. We sold nearly 30,000 copies of *The Edwardians* in the first six months, and by the end of a year the Press had made a profit of nearly £2,000 on it. It has gone on selling for years.

Novels by serious writers of genius often eventually become best-sellers, but most contemporary best-sellers are written by second-class writers whose psychological brew contains a touch of naïvety, a touch of sentimentality, the story-telling gift, and a mysterious sympathy with the day-dreams of ordinary people. Vita was very nearly a best-seller of this kind. She only just missed being one because she did not have quite enough of the third and fourth element in the best-selling brew. We published *The Edwardians* in 1930 and *All Passion Spent*, which she wrote in less than a year, in 1931. This was, I think, the best novel which she ever wrote, though there was rather more than a touch of sentimentality in it. It did very well, though not as well as *The Edwardians*, selling about 15,000 copies in the first year —it still sells 35 years after it was first published—and showing a profit of about £1,200. After this book the springs of Vita's invention and imagination which she required for novel writing began to run dry. She produced a fascinating and very amusing book, *Pepita*, a biography of her terrible mother and extraordinary grandmother, which we published with great success in 1937. But I had grave doubts about her two novels, *Family History* and *The Dark Island*, and then she brought us the manuscript of a novel which we felt we could not publish.

The relation of author and publisher is never an easy one. The publisher is, at the best of times, an ambivalent and often not very competent business man, wobbling between profits and art for art's sake; the writer has something of the same kind of wobble and is often convinced that the reason why his book is not a best-seller is because his publisher is an incompetent, profit-making shark. Vita was an ideal author from the publisher's point of view; she never complained when things went wrong and was extraordinarily appreciative of the publisher if they went right. This made it all the more unpleasant to have to tell her that we thought her novel not good enough for us to publish. We knew, too, that we should lose her as an author, because there were many reputable publishers who would publish this novel in order to get her 'on their list'. It was characteristic of her that she was not in the least bit hurt or resentful and the whole thing made no difference to her relationship with us.

By 1924, seven years after it started, the Hogarth Press, still with practically no employees, no capital invested, and no overheads, had on its general list already two potentially best-sellers, Vita and Virginia. But we were not merely a one- or two-horse shay. With courageous wisdom or reckless folly, we took on a considerable number of new authors and new books. There were 34 books announced in our 1925 lists and we had published all of them by 1926. In the next five years we published novels by William Plomer, Edwin Muir, F. L. Lucas, C. H. B. Kitchin, Alice Ritchie, F. M. Mayor, Svevo, and Rilke. The first six of these were first novels. Two of the six, which did quite well when published, are now forgotten, but are, I still think, remarkable, *The Rector's Daughter* by F. M. Mayor and *The Peacemakers* by Alice Ritchie. A little later, in the early 1930s we published Christopher Isherwood's *Mr Norris Changes Trains*, new novels by Ivan Bunin, and Laurens van der Post's first novel *In a Province*. In general publishing we also branched out into art with a classic, *Cézanne* by Roger Fry, in 1926, and very strongly into politics, economics, history, and sociology. This last category was directly connected with my own activities. In the 1920s I wrote *After the Deluge*, Vol. I, and *Imperialism and Civilization*. But I also became more and more occupied with practical politics in the Labour Party and Fabian Society and this is reflected in the large number of political books which we published, among which some of the most important were *The End of Laissez-Faire* (1926) and *The Economic Consequences of Mr Churchill* (1925) by Maynard Keynes, the remarkable books on imperialism in Africa by Norman Leys, and Lord Olivier's *White Capital and Coloured Labour*.

I said above that there were three publications in 1924
which had a considerable influence on the development of
the Press. The first was Vita's book. The second was a series,
the Hogarth Essays, which we started in 1924 with three
volumes, *Mr Bennett and Mrs Brown* by Virginia, *The Artist
and Psycho-Analysis* by Roger Fry, and *Henry James at Work*
by Theodora Bosanquet. This series consisted of pamphlets,
a form of publication which nearly all publishers fought
(still fight) shy of because they always involve a good deal of
work and a loss of money. I was eager to have a series of
pamphlets in which one could have essays on contemporary
political and social problems as well as on art and criticism.
These essays, published at between 1s. 6d. and 3s. 6d., were
surprisingly successful. In the first series in 1924, 1925, and
1926, we published 19 essays, bound in stiff paper with a
cover design by Vanessa, and among the authors were T. S.
Eliot, Robert Graves, Edith Sitwell, J. M. Keynes, E. M.
Forster, J. A. Hobson, Vernon Lee, Bonamy Dobrée, and
Herbert Read. None of them sold a large number of copies,
but every one of them, when they went out of print, had
made a profit. This encouraged me to start in 1930 another
series, Day to Day Pamphlets, devoted entirely to politics,
bound in paper, and published at 1s. or 1s. 6d. In the nine
years between 1930 and 1939 we published 40 pamphlets,
and among the authors were Harold Laski, H. N. Brailsford,
W. H. Auden, H. G. Wells, Sir Arthur Salter, C. Day Lewis,
A. L. Rowse, and Mussolini. This series also paid its way.
It was significant of the political climate in the 1930s that
the two best-sellers were Mussolini's *The Political and Social
Doctrine of Fascism* and Maurice Dobb's *Russia Today and
Tomorrow*, an excellent, though rather rosy, view of Soviet
Russia and communism by a Cambridge don.

The pamphlet is not a commodity which it is easy to sell
in Britain. Every now and again if you publish one by the

right person at the right moment on some controversial subject, it will be a best-seller. We printed 7,000 copies of *The Economic Consequences of Mr Churchill* by Maynard and they sold out at once, but in the general run when we were publishing regularly four or five every year, we did well if we sold over 2,000 copies. Societies like the Fabians which regularly published pamphlets found the same difficulties in selling them. The principal obstruction is the trade. The pamphlet is an awkward and troublesome kind of book to sell, and most bookshops will not look at them. The railway bookstall, which is the right place to market them, also dislikes them, not without reason, as they are not nearly as lucrative as newspapers or that vast range of lurid or alluring publications on whose covers are portrayed murder and rape or the superfeminized female form in every stage of dress or nudity. The result is that the British have never acquired the habit of reading pamphlets. This is a great pity. The pamphlet is potentially an extraordinarily good literary form from both the artistic and the social or political point of view. Those which we published by T. S. Eliot, Roger Fry, Virginia, Maynard Keynes, J. A. Hobson, were remarkable and would never have been written if we had not had this series. All the others were, I think, well worth publishing. Our experience showed us that there is a potential market for the pamphlet. The potentiality never becomes actuality because all avenues of sale between publisher and purchaser are closed or obstructed. And so the habit of writing and reading pamphlets cannot establish itself.

However, these pamphlet series were sufficiently successful to pay their way. They showed us how valuable from the business point of view a series is to a publisher. If one gets a series started successfully with good books, it makes it possible subsequently to publish in the series successfully other books which, if published on their own, however good they might be, would almost certainly have made a substantial loss. In the next few years we started four other series: Hogarth Lectures on Literature, Hogarth Sixpenny Pamphlets, Hogarth Living Poets, and Hogarth Letters. The Living Poets and the Lectures were highly successful. I was over-optimistic about the other two. They contained some interesting and amusing essays, for instance, *A Letter to Madan Blanchard* by E. M. Forster, *A Letter to a Sister* by Rosamond Lehmann, *A Letter to a Grandfather* by Rebecca West. But it was impossible to sell enough of them at 6d. and 1s. to make both ends meet.

The third publication of the Press in 1924 which was to have a considerable effect on its future was a strange one. The publication was announced in our autumn list as follows:

COLLECTED PAPERS. By Sigmund Freud, M.D.
Vol. I. Early Papers and the History of the Psycho-Analytical Movement.
Vol. II. Clinical Papers and Papers on Instinct and the Unconscious.

The Hogarth Press has taken over the publications of the International Psycho-Analytical Library, and will in future continue the series for the International Psycho-Analytical Press. It has obtained the right to publish a complete authorized English translation of Professor Freud's collected papers. These papers are of the highest importance for the study of Psycho-Analysis; they have been translated into English by experts under the supervision of Dr Ernest Jones. The Collected Papers will be published in four volumes. Vol. III, containing 'Five Case Histories', and Vol. IV, containing 'Metapsychology. Dreams', will be published in the course of next year.

The price of Vols. I, II, and IV will be 21s. each, of Vol. III 30s., and of the complete set four guineas.

That was the beginning of our connection with Freud and the Institute of Psycho-Analysis which has lasted until the present day. It came about in the following way. In the decade before 1924 in the so-called Bloomsbury circle there was great interest in Freud and psycho-analysis, and the interest was extremely serious. Adrian Stephen, Virginia's brother, who worked with Sir Paul Vinogradoff on mediaeval law, suddenly threw the Middle Ages and law out of the window, and, with his wife Karin, became a qualified doctor and professional psycho-analyst. James Strachey, Lytton's youngest brother, and his wife also became professional psycho-analysts. James went to Vienna and was analysed by Freud, and he played an active part in the Institute of Psycho-Analysis, which, largely through Ernest Jones, had been founded in London and was in intimate relations with Freud and the Mecca of psycho-analysis in Vienna, being itself a branch of the International Association of Psycho-Analysis.

Some time early in 1924 James asked me whether I thought the Hogarth Press could publish for the London Institute. The Institute, he said, had begun the publication of the International Psycho-Analytical Library in 1921 and had already published six volumes, which included two of Freud's works, *Beyond the Pleasure Principle* and *Group Psychology and the Analysis of the Ego*. They had also signed an agreement with Freud under which they would publish his *Collected Papers* in four volumes. The Institute had hitherto been their own publisher, printing and binding their books in Vienna and having them 'distributed' by a large London publishing firm. They did not find this system satisfactory and they wished to hand over to a publisher the entire business of publishing the International Psycho-Analytical Library in which they hoped regularly to publish a considerable number of important books by Freud and other analysts.

The idea seemed to me very attractive and I drew up an

agreement which the Institute accepted. It was agreed that we should take over the books which they had already published, and publish all future books in the Library. For a fledgling inexperienced publisher this was a bold undertaking. The four volumes of Freud's *Collected Papers* were a formidable work, for each of them ran to over 300 pages and it meant putting a good deal of capital into them. In fact, one of the most distinguished of the large London publishers, who heard what I was about to undertake, gave me a friendly warning that I should be risking too much. The *Collected Papers* was from the start one of the most successful of our publications. I circularized a large number of universities, libraries, and individuals in the United States and had almost at once a good sale in America as well as in Britain. The Institute had bought outright from Freud the rights for £50 for each volume and we bought the rights in the four volumes from the Institute for £200, but as soon as the books began to make a profit, we began to pay a royalty to Freud. The sale of these four fat volumes (we added a fifth later) has gone on steadily for over 40 years. The fact that it was started successfully by a publisher with no staff and no 'machine' throws a curious light upon the business of publishing. The longer my experience of the business, the more convinced I have become that the ideas of most authors and indeed many publishers with regard to the efficacy or necessity of what is called the publisher's 'machinery' for selling books is largely delusion, though this applies only to 'serious' books, not to that branch of large-scale industry and mass production, the bestseller racket, in which books have to be sold by the same methods as beers. You may be able to sell a million copies of Mr X's *Women and Wine* or Miss Y's *Wine and Women* by the pressure cooker of large-scale advertising and the mysterious machinery of the colossal publisher, but it is doubtful whether you will sell ten copies of Freud's *Collected Papers*,

T. S. Eliot's *The Waste Land*, or Virginia Woolf's *The Waves* by these methods.

Publishing the Psycho-Analytical Library for the Institute was always a very pleasant and very interesting experience. In the next 40 years we published nearly 70 volumes in it. In the process I learnt a good many curious things about the art of publishing. For instance, we had in the Library a book by Professor Flügel called *The Psycho-Analytic Study of the Family*. I do not believe that any publisher who saw this book in manuscript or in print or in our list in 1924 would have thought that it had the slightest chance of being a best-seller, and I feel sure that very few of my readers in 1967 have ever heard of it. Yet this book has been a steady seller for over 40 years, selling hundreds of copies yearly. It has practically never been advertised and no advertising would have materially influenced its sale. Its aggregate sale must be considerably greater than that of nine out of ten of the much advertised best-sellers that it has long outlived. It is an original book, an almost unknown classic in its own peculiar field, a publisher's dream. It sold steadily in Britain year after year, and year after year twice a year there came a large order from an American bookseller, because it was a 'set book' in an American college.

The greatest pleasure that I got from publishing the Psycho-Analytical Library was the relationship which it established between us and Freud. Between 1924 when we took over the Library and his death in 1939 we published an English translation of every book which he wrote, and after his death we published his complete works, 24 volumes, in the Standard Edition. He was not only a genius, but also, unlike many geniuses, an extraordinarily nice man. The business connected with his books, when we first began to publish them, was managed by his son Martin, and later after his death by his son Ernst and daughter Anna. They all seemed to have inherited the extraordinarily civilized temperament of their father which made every kind of relationship with him so pleasant.

The publication of the Standard Edition of the Complete Psychological Works of Freud, which we began in 1953, was one of the most difficult and delicate business operations which I have ever put through. The Internationaler Psychoanalytischer Verlag had already in the 1920s published the *Gesammelte Schriften* of Freud in Germany, Austria, and Switzerland, and after the war in 1942 the complete works in German (*Gesammelte Werke*) were published in London. I was most anxious to publish a complete edition in English and in the 1940s discussed the possibility several times with Ernst Freud. There seemed to be insuperable difficulties. Financially an English edition was not feasible unless it could be sold in the United States as well as in the British Commonwealth, but Freud's American copyrights were in such a tangled and chaotic condition that the moment we began definitely to face the problem there seemed to be no way of acquiring all the rights or even of being quite sure of who controlled them. Freud had been incredibly generous and casual with his copyrights. The outright sale of his English rights in the four volumes of *Collected Papers* for £200 was a good example of his generosity; his casualness is shown by the fact that he once simultaneously sold the American rights in one of his books both to the Hogarth Press and to another publisher. In America he had given the copyright in many of his books to his translator and friend, Dr Brill. This—quite apart from the difficulty of discovering who owned the American rights in several of the other books—presented us with an extremely delicate problem. We had been lucky enough to be able to arrange that, if we did ever succeed in publishing the complete works, the edition would be edited and translated by James Strachey, assisted by his wife, Alix. James has, in fact, accomplished this colossal task in 13 years, and the 24 volumes are a monument to his extraordinary combination of psycho-analytical knowledge, brilliance, and accuracy as a writer and translator, and indomitable severity both to himself and to his publisher. I doubt whether there is any edition of technical scientific works, comparable to this one in size, which can compare with it in the high standard of translation and editing.

What made the task of our approach to Dr Brill, and after his death to his heirs and executors, doubly delicate was that we had to obtain their consent first to our publishing in America translations of the works in which they held the American rights, and second to our using not Dr Brill's translations but James's. For a long time every attempt to find a way through the maze of copyrights and overcome the other difficulties failed, but eventually, largely owing to Ernst Freud's tact and perseverance, an agreement with the Brill executors made publication in America possible.

I only once met Freud in person. The Nazis invaded Austria on March 11, 1938, and it took three months to get Freud out of their clutches. He arrived in London in the first week in June and three months later moved into a house in Maresfield Gardens which was to be his permanent home. When he and his family had had time to settle down there, I made discreet enquiries to see whether he would like Virginia and me to come and see him. The answer was yes, and in the afternoon of Saturday, January 28, 1939, we went and had tea with him. I feel no call to praise the famous men whom I have known. Nearly all famous men are disappointing or bores, or both. Freud was neither; he had an aura, not of fame, but of greatness. The terrible cancer of the mouth which killed him only eight months later had already attacked him. It was not an easy interview. He was

extraordinarily courteous in a formal, old-fashioned way—
for instance, almost ceremoniously he presented Virginia
with a flower. There was something about him as of a half-
extinct volcano, something sombre, suppressed, reserved.
He gave me the feeling which only a very few people whom
I have met gave me, a feeling of great gentleness, but behind
the gentleness, great strength. The room in which he sat
seemed very light, shining, clean, with a pleasant, open view
through the windows into a garden. His study was almost a
museum, for there were all round him a number of Egyptian
antiquities which he had collected. He spoke about the
Nazis. When Virginia said that we felt some guilt, that
perhaps if we had not won the 1914 war there would have
been no Nazis and no Hitler, he said, no, that was wrong;
Hitler and the Nazis would have come and would have been
much worse if Germany had won the war.

A few days before we visited him I had read the report of
a case in which a man had been charged with stealing books
from Foyle's shop, and among them one of Freud's; the
magistrate fined him and said that he wished he could sentence him to read all Freud's works as a punishment. I told
Freud about this and he was amused and, in a queer way,
also deprecatory about it. His books, he said, had made him
infamous, not famous. A formidable man.

I must return now to the Hogarth Press and its fortunes.
The figures of our income which I have given above on page
142 show that from 1929 to 1939 the Press contributed on
an average £1,100 to our income. During those eleven years
I had to revolutionize the organization of the business. By
1930 we had a clerical staff of three bookkeepers and shorthand typists. We had a representative who travelled our
books: Alice Ritchie was, I think, the first woman to travel
for a publisher and some booksellers did not like the innovation. She was not only a very good traveller, but also a very

good and a serious novelist. The question of the higher command continued to cause us great difficulty and we never found a satisfactory solution. I was determined not to treat publishing as a means of making a living and I was determined not to become a full-time publisher. The choice, therefore, lay between taking a partner or employing a manager competent enough to be responsible for the everyday running of the business so that I could treat it as a part-time occupation.

We started off with the first alternative. From 1924 to 1932 there entered and left the Press a succession of brilliant and not quite so brilliant young men. They entered as managers and potential partners. As I have already said, I think we were trying to get the best of two contradictory worlds and were asking these brilliant young men to perform an impossible feat, namely to publish best-sellers with the greatest professional efficiency for an amateur publisher in a basement kitchen. I still think that the technical efficiency of the Hogarth Press in the years 1924 to 1939 was extremely high, much higher in matters of importance than that of many—I almost wrote most—large and small publishing firms. For instance, for all those years, when we were publishing from 20 to 30 books a year, selling in the first six months of their existence anything from 150 to 30,000 copies, we practically never—I think that I could truthfully say never, but no one would believe me—ran out of bound copies and were unable to supply an order. This was the result of meticulous daily, sometimes hourly, supervision, checking, organization. Professional publishers will probably politely disbelieve me or at any rate will say (privately) that such a record is impossible for any large publishing business. I am sure that they are mistaken. In a previous volume of my autobiography (*Growing*, pp. 107-109) I related my experience with regard to business organization in the govern-

ment offices of Ceylon. Every head clerk in every kachcheri
to which I was appointed, when on my first day in the office,
I told him that 'every letter received in this kachcheri after
this week must be answered on the day of its receipt unless
it is waiting for an order from me or from the G.A.', threw
up his hands in horror and despair, and said that this was
much too big a kachcheri and received daily far too many
letters to make this possible. The head clerk was mistaken
and after six months he had to admit it. Whether ten letters
or 100 or 1,000 are received daily, they can all be answered
on the day of receipt, provided that there is an automatic
routine and meticulous checking. It is the same with books.
For the efficiency of publishing it is most important that the
decision to reprint or rebind for every book on the list
should be made at the right moment and for the right
quantity so that there is always in stock an adequate number
of bound copies to supply the demand (while, at the same
time, the publisher, for his own sake, does not print or
bind more copies than he can sell). This may seem a fatu-
ously simple and self-evident truism. But a very little knowledge of what goes on behind the scenes will prove how often
in practice the truism is neglected. But in 99 cases out of a
hundred in which a bookseller has to be told that a book
cannot be supplied because it is 'printing' or 'binding', the
failure was avoidable and was due to bad organization and
slovenly supervision. I should perhaps add that all this,
including the truism, often overlooked even by publishers,
is that a publisher cannot have an efficient publishing business unless the business has an efficient publisher.

The Hogarth Press was from 1924 to 1939, I repeat, an
extremely efficient publishing business, though its methods
were in most ways unorthodox. The business side during
those years was managed by me and the succession of young
men. The first young man to enter and leave the basement in

Tavistock Square—and by no means the least brilliant—was G. W. H. Rylands, universally known as Dadie. We were aiming very high when we took Dadie into the Press and began to turn him into a publisher. Not unnaturally he did not stay long in the basement. When he came to us he was only 22; a scholar of Eton and King's, he had just taken a degree and had written a fellowship dissertation. It was from the first understood that, if he got his fellowship at King's, we should lose him, for he would return to Cambridge to become a don. We treated him rather badly, for almost at once we went off for a week or two, leaving him alone in charge of the Press and of a strange, elderly shorthand typist, who, seeing that he was out of his depth and not very happy, tried to cheer him up by feeding him on sandwiches. Dadie, of course, got his fellowship and, much to our regret, left us for a distinguished career in the university, the arts, and the theatre. We published two books of poetry by him, *Russet and Taffeta* (1925) and *Poems* (1931), and *Words and Poetry* (1927), a very original book of literary criticism based on the dissertation which won him his fellowship.

Dadie was followed by Angus Davidson, who stayed with us from 1924 to 1929; he is now very well known as a translator of Italian books. He was followed by a very young man, Richard Kennedy, a nephew of Kennedy, the architect. Richard was too young to be a manager, and we now had, in addition to the clerical staff, a general manager. In 1931 he left us and John Lehmann entered the Press. His appearance on the scene was to have a considerable effect upon the Press and its fortunes. Unlike the other young men, he took publishing very seriously and became a highly efficient professional publisher. His first term of work with us was short and not very successful, largely owing to my fault. Poor John, like Dadie a product of Eton and Cambridge, only 24 years old when he came to us, was put into a small, dark, basement room, from which he was expected, under my supervision, to 'manage' the publication of 22 books to be published by us in the spring of 1931. These 22 books included Vita's *All Passion Spent* (selling 14,000 copies in the first six months, Virginia's *The Waves* (selling 10,000), a first novel *Saturday Night at the Greyhound* by John Hampson (selling 3,000), and two masterpieces by Rainer Maria Rilke, very difficult publishing propositions 30 years ago, the *Dunio Elegies* and *The Notebook of Malte Laurids Brigge*. We published these 22 books—and another 18 in the autumn season of 1931—with a staff consisting of one traveller and four or five in the office. John, Virginia, and I, as well as the 'staff', were expected to be able to take a hand at any and everything, including packing—indeed, we all became expert packers. To pack and despatch 4,000 or 5,000 copies of a book before publication, as we did in the case of *All Passion Spent* or *The Waves*, is a very formidable business, but I do not think that in those days we ever failed to have all our books delivered on subscription orders in the shops well before the publication date. On the top of this John began to help us with the printing. I am not a person who bears even wise men gladly (sometimes and in some ways I bear fools more gladly), and it is not surprising that John soon found the Hogarth Press too much of a good or a bad thing, and left us in September 1932. He returned to us six years later and was Partner and General Manager in the Press until 1946. But that is part of a different story, a different world and phase of my life from that of 1930; it cannot be dealt with here, for it is part of the story of the war years.

John was a young man of 24 when he came to the Press in 1931; I was 51 and Virginia 49. We were well aware that the worst menace of middle age is emotional and mental sclerosis which makes one insensitive to anything in any generation later than one's own. Both as publishers and private persons we wanted, if possible, to keep in touch with the younger generation or generations. In taking John into the Press we had had great hopes that he would help us to do this. A scholar of Eton and Trinity College, Cambridge, a poet himself and the friend of Virginia's nephew, Julian Bell, and the younger generation of Cambridge poets and writers, he seemed to have all the qualities and contacts which we were looking for. In this respect he did not disappoint us and in the two years during which he was with us he helped us to bring into the Hogarth Press some of the best writers of his generation.

The younger generation of the late 1920s and early 1930s was remarkable in quality and quantity. As is usual with the young who have something of their own to say, they were in revolt against their fathers (and mothers, uncles, and aunts). In *New Signatures*, which we published in 1932 and which was and still is regarded as that generation's manifesto,[1] Stephen Spender wrote in his poem 'Oh Young Men':

Oh young men oh comrades
it is too late now to stay in those houses
your fathers built where they built you to build to breed
money on money . . .
Oh comrades step beautifully from the solid wall
advance to rebuild, and sleep with friend on hill
advance to rebel . . .

[1] 'The little book was like a searchlight switched on to reveal that, without anyone noticing it, a group of skirmishers had been creeping up in a concerted movement of attack' (*The Whispering Gallery* by John Lehmann, p. 182). 'The slim blue volume, No. 24 in the Hogarth Living Poets Series, which had caused so much fuss to assemble, came out in the spring of 1932, created a mild sensation then, and has since been taken to mark the beginning, the formal opening, of the poetic movement of the 1930s' (*Journey to the Frontier* by Peter Stansky and William Abrahams, p. 77).

The rebellious youth of the 1930s were nearly all poets, and their knock on the door in *New Signatures* was poetic. Of the nine poets, five were at Cambridge, Richard Eberhart, William Empson, Julian Bell, A. S. J. Tessimond, and John Lehmann; three at Oxford, W. H. Auden, C. Day Lewis, and Stephen Spender; the ninth was William Plomer. Like most young poets, they took a pretty black view of the past, the present, and the future; it might be said of them, to quote Empson, that they 'learnt a style from a despair' (though every now and again, particularly with Julian, in the best tradition cheerfulness would break through). Despair has always been the occupational disease of young poets, but the nine poets of *New Signatures*, it must be admitted, had more reason than most for gloom and foreboding. They looked out upon a world which had been first devastated by war and was now being economically devastated by peace. What could be more grey and grim than the dole and unemployment; the communism of Stalin, the purges, the kulaks, and the Iron Curtain; the tawdry fascism of Mussolini and the murderous nastiness of Hitler and his Nazi thugs? And when they looked from the present toward the future, they could only look forward to dying in another inevitable and futile war. 'Who live under the shadow of a war,' sang Stephen, 'What can I do that matters?' 'A cold wind blows round the corners of the world,' sang William Plomer; 'it blew upon the corpse of a young man, Lying in the street with his head in the gutter Where he fell shot by a revolutionary sniper. . . . He was rash enough to go out for a breath of fresh air. . . . Shot through the stomach he took time to die.'

It was John who brought *New Signatures* to us. Through his sister Rosamond he had got to know Stephen Spender and the Oxford poets. Then through his first book of poems, *A Garden Revisited*, which we had published in 1931, he got to know Michael Roberts, who had been a scholar at

Trinity senior to John. He and John devised *New Signatures* and Roberts edited it. In fact, before John came to the Press, we had already published a good deal of work by the rebellious poets of *New Signatures*. Five years before, in 1926, we had published William Plomer's remarkable first novel, *Turbott Wolfe*. In 1929 and 1930 we had published two anthologies, *Cambridge Poetry 1929* and *Cambridge Poetry 1930*. They were anthologies of poetry written, selected, and edited by Cambridge undergraduates. Four of the five Cambridge poets of *New Signatures*—Julian, John, Eberhart, and Empson—were included in these two volumes. We had even penetrated into Oxford, for already in 1929 we had published Cecil Day Lewis's first book of poems, *Transitional Poem*. However, it was not only the emergent poets whom John helped us to keep in touch with. It was through him, via Stephen Spender, that one of the most remarkable and strange of the emergent novelists came to the Hogarth Press, Christopher Isherwood. In 1932 we published *The Memorial*, in some ways his best novel, and in 1935 the brilliant *Mr Norris Changes Trains*.

After John left us and until he returned to us in 1938, I tried the other alternative. We made no further attempt to find a partner, I ran the Press by myself in my own way, with a woman manager. In many ways this worked very well, but it had, from our point of view, great disadvantages. It meant a tremendous amount of work and much more time devoted to the business of publishing than I wanted to devote to it. It also meant that we were closely bound to the business in Tavistock Square and it was impossible to get right away from it for any length of time. Virginia felt this tie to be very irksome, and we were always on the point of throwing the whole thing up or of trying once more to find the ideal partner. But we drifted on, as one does, when something which one has oneself started in life without much

Man Ray

Virginia

Maynard Keynes and Kingsley Martin at Rodmell

The author and Nehru

thought of the future or of the consequences takes control of one. That did not mean that we let the actual business of the Press drift; we took it very seriously and energetically, and we continued to publish a considerable number of books of every sort and kind. For instance, in 1935, three years after John left us, we published 25 books. These included *Mr Norris Changes Trains* by Christopher Isherwood, *Grammar of Love* by Ivan Bunin, *An Autobiographical Study* by Freud, *Requiem* by Rilke, *A Time to Dance* and *Collected Poems* by C. Day Lewis, together with a great variety of books on politics, education, literature, biography, and travel.

I will leave the Hogarth Press now in its basement in Tavistock Square in our own hands and with us in its hands until the year 1938. It had, as I have said, materially added to our income. We were now very comfortably off, for in the ten years from 1930 to 1939 our average annual income was over three times what it had been when we came to Tavistock Square in 1924. And, as I have also said before, we did not alter the framework of our lives. We lived in the same houses—in Tavistock Square and Rodmell—with the same servants and in the same 'style'. This is shown by the fact that what we spent on that day-to-day framework of living, on house, food, servants, etc., hardly altered—for instance, whereas in 1924 our income was £1,047 and our expenditure £826, in 1934 our income was £3,615 and our expenditure £1,192.

Yet there was one thing which, as Virginia often remarks at the time in her diary, had a great and immediate effect upon the quality and tempo of our life, and the change was directly due to our being able to spend money. In July 1927 we bought a second-hand Singer car for £275. I suppose that the nineteenth-century scientific revolution—in particular electricity and the internal combustion engine—have changed the world—one will probably soon have to say the

niverse—much more profoundly than anything else which
.s happened since God rather foolishly said: 'Let there be
ght'. That God's remark about the light has been the primal
.use of infinitely more evil and misery than of good and
appiness is certainly true. When one thinks of the two world
ars and the destruction of Hiroshima, or even when one
ompares the car-infested streets of London in 1966 with
s humanly inhabited streets which I remember in 1886,
he has to say the same about science and the inventions
hich have given us a Singer car and an aeroplane. Certainly
othing ever changed so profoundly my material existence,
he mechanism and range of my every-day life, as the posses-
on of a motor car. Even as an individual, I sometimes think
ow pleasant the tempo of life and movement was when the
peed limit was about eight miles an hour, and I curse the
ay when I acquired a licence to drive motor vehicles of all
roups. But those moments of nostalgic pessimism are rare
nd unreasonable. There is no doubt whatever that, as an
ndividual, purely as an individual, I have enormously
ncreased the scope and pleasures of living by the six cars
·hich I have owned and driven in the last 40 years.

The most important change and the greatest pleasure
ame, and still comes, from a holiday 'touring' on the Con-
nent—I do not think that anything gave Virginia more
leasure than this. She had a passion for travelling, and travel
ad a curious and deep effect upon her. When she was abroad,
he fell into a strange state of passive alertness. She allowed
ll these foreign sounds and sights to stream through her
nind; I used to say rather like a whale lets the seawater
tream through its mouth, straining from it for its use the
dible flora and fauna of the seas. Virginia strained off and
tored in her mind those sounds and sights, echoes and
isions, which months afterwards would become food for her
magination and her art. This and the mere mechanism and

kaleidoscope of travel gave her intense pleasure, a mixture of exhilaration and relaxation.

Before 1928 and the Singer car we used to go abroad, travelling as English people had done for the last hundred years, comparatively slowly, by boat and rail to some place where one would probably settle down for a week or two. Like so much of life before the motor car and the aeroplane, the tempo was slow. One got into the train at Victoria in the afternoon, crossed Paris from the Gare du Nord to the Gare de Lyon in the evening, and woke up to the entrancing moment when one saw the dawn over the Rhône valley and ate one's first *petit déjeuner*. A few years after the end of the 1914 war, when it again became possible to visit France as a civilian, we saw once more out of the carriage window the dawn break over the Rhône valley, for we were on our way to Cassis. In those days Cassis was a small fishing-village between Marseille and Toulon; it had one small hotel, the Cendrillon, at which we stayed. It is almost impossible to believe today that places like Cassis really did exist 40 years ago on any European coast, warmed by the sun and looking upon the blue waters of the Mediterranean or other oarless sea. For it was a pretty, quiet village lying along a restful bay. There was a small resident colony of multi-racial artists, the ominous harbingers of civilization who could already be found infecting the Mediterranean from Almeria to Rapallo. You would usually find three or four visitors, most probably English, at the Cendrillon. Otherwise Cassis still belonged to the people of Cassis. Looking back upon it today, its chief characteristic seems to have been its quiet. It was indeed so quiet that men might have risen up at the voice of a bird. The voice of the motor car was rarely heard in it. People sat in the café and talked or were silent for many hours; or down by the water they leaned against a boat and talked or just looked out across the bay. In the evening the men played boules.

The first time we went to Cassis was, I think, in March. In the mornings we used to go out and sit on the rocks in the sun and read or write. You were alone, the only sounds the water lapping on the rocks or the gulls crying. If you walked up through the wood over the headland to the east, when you came out of the wood on the other side, you had a view of the long line of sandy coast all the way to La Ciotat, Sanary, and Toulon. It was open, flat country, with scarcely a house to be seen until you got to Sanary. Twenty-six years later I was staying in Sanary and visited this stretch of country again, but the country itself had disappeared—it had disappeared under an unending sea of houses and villas, those hideous little villas which the French build all along the Mediterranean coast. I drove from Sanary to Cassis. A stream of perpetual motion, of moving cars nose to tail and tail to nose, ran on both sides of the dusty road between the unending sea of villas. Cassis itself was submerged in cars and villas. Down by the bay the earth was black with human beings; one's ears were deafened by the voice of the loudspeaker and innumerable transistors. The rocks were littered with bottles and paper bags. The scene is the same from Torremolinos to Rapallo, from Ostende to Brest, and from Deal to Land's End.

In the 1920s, as I said, Cassis was a quiet place and, liking quiet, we returned to it. In those days there lived in Cassis one of those curious Englishmen whose complicated characters seem so English and so un-English. Colonel Teed had been Colonel of the Bengal Lancers. When I first met him, I thought: what a perfect Colonel of the Bengal Lancers! A great horseman, the perfect English cavalry officer! I was quite right, but he was also something entirely different, something which one would not have expected to find in the perfect cavalry officer, for beneath the immaculate surface of the colonel of a crack Indian regiment Teed was funda-

mentally an intellectual who liked artists and intellectuals.
He was also a charming man. When he retired from the
Bengal Lancers, he bought Fontcreuse, a vineyard, with a
lovely house a mile or two from the centre of Cassis. There
he made excellent wine. We got to know him, and when
Vanessa followed us to Cassis, she liked the place so much
that she entered into an agreement with Teed which allowed
her to build a villa on his land free of charge and live in it
rent-free for ten or twenty years (I forget the exact figure),
after which the villa would become Teed's property.

Vanessa and Clive and Duncan Grant used to spend much
of their time in the Cassis villa, and this was an added in-
ducement for us to return there. Teed let us have a room in
Fontcreuse and we usually had our meals with the Bells at
the villa. It was a pleasant way of life, so pleasant that at one
moment we began to buy a villa for ourselves near Fontcreuse; it was called a villa, but was in fact a small, rather
tumbled-down whitewashed house. But we did not complete
the purchase. The procedure for an Englishman at that time
to buy a house in Provence was an unending labyrinth;
weary of the interminable business, we began to realize that
our commitments in England, the Hogarth Press, writing,
politics, made it extremely improbable that we should ever
be able to spend much time in Cassis. So the project lapsed.

I am telling this because it explains why we tended, when
we could snatch a few weeks from London and Rodmell, to
make for Cassis. And in March 1928, under the new dis-
pensation, we set out in our old Singer car to drive there. It
opened to one a new way of life. In the old way of travel one
was tied to the railway; as one moved through a country,
one followed the straight steel parallel lines, one had no
contact with the life of the road, the village, and the town.
In Ceylon I had become accustomed to travel freely and
lightly, on a horse or on foot, along empty roads, paths or

me-tracks. I know nothing more exhilarating than starting
t in the early morning, just before sunrise, through the
ngle or along the straight empty road or the village path for
me distant village, an all-day journey with all the day
fore one. Something of that wonderful feeling of libera-
n comes—or came—to one when one drove out of Dieppe
d saw the long, white, empty road— roads in France, even
e *routes nationales*, were in those days empty—stretching
fore one all the way to the Mediterranean. It is only of this
nd of travel, the travel by road, that Montaigne's saying,
hich I have quoted so often, is really true—it is not the
rival, but the journey which matters.

Our first journey by road on the Continent to the Mediter-
nean and back was in parts an adventure. It was in 1928
d we crossed from Newhaven to Dieppe on March 26 and
r the next six days we rattled along at about 100 miles a
ay in the old Singer car through Burgundy, and then down
e Rhône valley through Vienne, Valence, Montélimar,
d so to Provence, through Carpentras and Aix to Cassis.
 is the journey, not the arrival, that matters! There are few
ings in life pleasanter than this long journey south along
e white roads through the great avenues of trees and the
illages and towns. The slower the better—it is the journey
at matters. Even to recall and repeat the names of the
wns through which we passed gives me—writing today in
 grim grey February day in Sussex—intense pleasure. It is
xtraordinary how vividly the name of a place will recall to
ne from years ago the vision of it. I have only to murmur
 myself Angunakolapelessa and it brings to me from 50
ears ago quite clearly the vision of that small Sinhalese
illage; I can feel again the whip of heat across my face from
he village path; I can hear again the hum of insects across
he scrub jungle; I can smell again the acrid smell of smoke
nd shrubs. So with the names of those towns upon the road

to Provence; each recalls the continual change of sound a
sights and smells as one journeys south. And there are t
particular moments in this journey. The first is at a bend
the road near Montélimar where you suddenly see that t
country before you has changed completely—you have l
northern Europe and central Europe for the south, you a
in Mediterranean Europe. The second is when, after 7
miles of straight Roman roads, your road climbs a hill a
from the top of it you see the Mediterranean sea, and at t
sight of it I shout, like Xenophon's Greeks: 'Thalass
Thalassa!'

We stayed for a week in Cassis at Fontcreuse, the B
family being now established in their villa, and then we s
off for Dieppe. I still in those days regarded travel much
I did in my district in Ceylon; I assumed that one could g
on in a leisurely way anywhere, knowing one's eventual de
tination, but not thinking very much of what from day
day lay before one. I therefore mapped out what I thoug
would be a pleasant route through the centre of Franc
country which I had never been through. In fact, bein
fairly ignorant of geography, a subject which as a classic
scholar I was never taught at school, I was completely u
aware that the centre of France consisted of the mass
central, the very formidable mountains of the Cévennes an
Auvergne. I was also unaware that in early April one mig
run into heavy snowstorms on the top of these mountain
So I drove to Tarascon and, after sleeping there, started
drive through Alais and Florac to St Flour and Aurillac.
was rather dismayed later on in the morning to find myse
confronted by a formidable, black mountain up which th
road began to climb. We climbed and climbed; it gre
blacker and blacker both on the earth and in the sky. Th
clouds seemed to descend upon our heads and we ran into
tremendous snowstorm. The scenery, such as one could se

of it, reminded me of Wagner and Covent Garden, those absurdly melodramatic Valkyries' Rocks and Brünnhilde's cave. So Wagnerian was everything that I was hardly surprised when, driving at about 15 miles an hour and peering through the snowstorm, I saw ahead of me suddenly the side of the mountain open into a long tunnel lit by electric lamps. So we passed through the Massif du Cantal, and, when we issued from the tunnel on the other side, it was into bright sunshine. Despite the sun, our troubles had not ended, and my drive from the Cantal to Dieppe was rather a nightmare. I had really only just learned to drive a car and knew very little about either its inside or its outside. I had not realized that the tyres were very worn and the roads very bad. In the 500 miles from the Cantal to Dreux, where at last I succeeded in buying new tyres, we punctured on an average every 25 miles. It seemed to me that there was hardly any road in France on which I had not grovelled in the mud changing wheels.

Such hazards of travel do, however, bring their compensations in curious meetings. On the day we passed through the Cantal in a grim, black, Wagnerian Auvergne hamlet of a few cottages I punctured immediately outside a cottage from which a man came out and offered to repair a tyre. It was raining hard and we went into the cottage and sat talking to the family. A girl of sixteen was sitting at a table writing a letter. The letter was to a 'pen-friend' in Brighton. The girl had never been more than 20 miles from her home, but there is an international organization that organizes these international pen-friends—and there she sat perched on the top of the mountain in the centre of France writing to a girl, whom she had never seen and never would see, who lived ten miles from us in Sussex. She showed us a photograph and the letters of her Sussex pen-friend, the daughter of an omnibus driver in Brighton. In half an hour we were on terms of warm friendship with the whole family. The internationalism of the savagely nationalistic world of the 1920s was remarkable.

To drive in a leisurely way through a foreign country, keeping one's ears and eyes open, is one of the best ways of getting a vision of both international politics and human nature. I had a curious example of this in 1935. Vanessa was in Rome where she had taken a house and studio for six months. We planned to spend the whole of May abroad, our idea being to drive through Holland, Germany, and Austria to Rome and to stay there for ten days or so. In 1935 people were just beginning to understand something of what Hitler and the Nazis were doing in Germany. I had only once been to that country: Virginia and I had stayed for a week in Berlin with the Nicolsons when Harold was still in the Diplomatic Service and in the Berlin Embassy. By 1935 Harold had abandoned diplomacy for politics—he was an M.P.—and journalism, but when I told him my plans for driving to Italy by way of Germany, he said that he had heard that the Foreign Office had advised Cecil Kisch of the India Office that it was inadvisable for Jews to travel in Germany. He thought it would be as well for me to consult someone in the F.O. It seemed to me absurd that any Englishman, whether Jew or Gentile, should hesitate to enter a European country. I remembered Palmerston's famous speech: '*Civis Romanus sum* . . . ' and how he mobilized the British fleet and blockaded Greek ports on behalf of the British subject Don Pacifico, a Jew born in Gibraltar, in order to recover £150 damages done to this British subject's house in Piraeus. Surely, I thought, the British Government in 1935 would insist that the Nazis and Hitler treat an English Jew as they would any other British subject. However, at that time I knew Ralph Wigram of the F.O.; he lived in Southease, the next village to Rodmell; so when we went down to

Monks House, I rang him up and told him what H
said. Wigram said that he would rather not discuss
over the telephone and would come round and see

When Wigram appeared, I found his attitude ra
He said that it was quite true that the F.O. advised
to go to Germany, and officially he had to give me th
But privately and as a friend, he could say that he
nonsense, and that I should not hesitate to go to
The only thing which I ought to be careful abou
to get mixed up in any Nazi procession or public
He also gave me a letter to Prince Bismarck, Cou
the German Embassy, and advised me to go and
So off I went to see Bismarck in the rather oppres
sion in Carlton House Terrace. Bismarck was
affable—of course, my distinguished wife and I m
Germany. There would be no difficulty of any sor
would give me an official letter which would ensur
government servants would give me assistance if I
He gave me a most impressive document in whic
Bismarck called upon all German officials to show t
tinguished Englishman, Leonard Woolf, and h
guished wife, Virginia Woolf, every courtesy an
them any assistance which they might require.

The sequel was amusing, for a marmoset mad
unnecessary for me to use Bismarck's letter to pr
from the Nazis' anti-Semitism. At that time I had
set called Mitz which accompanied me almost eve
sitting on my shoulder or inside my waistcoat. I had
her from Victor Rothschild. Victor and Barbara w
living in Cambridge. One hot summer afternoon
to Cambridge, dined with them and drove back to
after dinner. We dined in the garden and a rathe
marmoset which Victor had bought in a junk shop a
to Barbara was hobbling about on the lawn. She cli

y lap and remained with me the whole evening. A
ater Victor wrote to me saying that they were going
for some time, and, as the marmoset seemed to have
me and I to the marmoset, would I look after her
ey were away? I agreed and Mitz arrived in Rodmell.
in very bad condition and I gradually got her fit.
ame very fond of me and I of her, and when the
ilds returned to Cambridge I refused—much to
ief—to hand Mitz back to them.

was a curious character. I kept her alive for five
hich was a year longer, the marmoset keeper at the
d me, than the Zoo had ever been able to keep a
et. She was eventually killed by a terrible cold snap
tmas when the electricity failed for the whole of a
ld night at Rodmell. During the day she was always
, but the moment it became dark in the evening she
scuttled across the room into a large birdcage which
ull of scraps of silk. She rolled herself into a ball in
lle of the silk and slept until the next morning—the
the sun rose, she left the cage and came over to me.
extremely jealous, a trait which I on occasions took
ge of to outwit her. She was always quite free in the
ut I had to be careful not to let her get out into the
t Rodmell by herself, for, if she did, she would climb
e and refuse to come down. When this happened,
succeeded in getting her back by climbing a ladder
ling out to her a butterfly net in which I had put the
in with a little honey on it. She was so fond of honey
ally she could not resist it and then I caught her in

one summer afternoon on a Sunday, when we were
ig to get into the car to drive back to London, she
into the garden at Rodmell and climbed about 30
a lime-tree at the gate. When I called to her to come

down, I could see her small head among the leaves watching me, but she would not budge. I tried the butterfly net trick, but not even the honey would tempt her. So I got Virginia to stand with me under the tree and I kissed her. Mitz came down as fast as she could and jumped on my shoulder chattering with anger. We successfully played the same trick on her another time when she got away into a large fig-tree and I could not dislodge her. She was rather fond of a spaniel which I had at the time and in cold weather liked to snuggle up against the dog in front of a hot fire. She would eat almost anything. Meal-worms and fruit were regular articles of her diet. She once caught and ate a lizard and the Zoo keeper told me that in the open-air cage their marmosets would sometimes catch and eat sparrows. Mitz had a passion for macaroons and tapioca pudding. When given tapioca, she seized it in both hands and stuffed her mouth so full that large blobs of tapioca oozed out at both sides of her face.

I took Mitz with me when on May 1, 1935, we crossed from Harwich to the Hook of Holland. At that time I had a Lanchester 18 car with a Tickford hood so that, by winding the hood back, one could convert it from a closed-in saloon to a completely open car. Most of the day Mitz used to sit on my shoulder, but she would sometimes curl up and go to sleep among the luggage and coats on the back seat. For eight days we toured about all over Holland. Whenever I go to Holland, I feel at once that I have reached the apotheosis of bourgeois society. The food, the comfort, the cleanliness, the kindliness, the sense of age and stability, the curious mixture of beauty and bad taste, the orderliness of everything including even nature and the sea—all this makes one realize that here on the shores of the dyke-controlled Zuider Zee one has found the highest manifestation of the complacent civilization of the middle classes. I have felt something of the same thing in Sweden and Denmark, but I do not think that the Scandinavians have ever reached quite the heights of domestication and complacency attained by the Dutch. It is, of course, easy and, particularly since 1847 and the Communist Manifesto, fashionable to pick holes in bourgeois civilization or savagery, and I am sure that I should soon feel suffocated if I had to live my life in the featherbed civilization of Delft or The Hague. Yet there is in fact a great deal to be said for it and for a short time it is very pleasant to feel that one is in a really civilized country from which nature has been expelled by something more efficacious than a fork. At any rate I prefer the tradition of comfortable civilization in the Netherlands to that of Teutonic sentimental savagery across the border.

Mitz was a great success with the Dutch; wherever we went little groups of people would surround the car and go into ecstasies about 'the dear little creature'. On May 9 we crossed the frontier from Roermond into Germany near Jülich. Immediately I had my first distasteful taste of Nazism. When I went into the Customs office there was a peasant just ahead of me who had a loaded farm-cart. The Customs officer was sitting at a desk and behind him, on the wall was a large portrait of Hitler. The peasant did not take his cap off and the officer worked himself up into a violent tirade against the insolence of a swine who kept his cap on in front of the Führer's image. I do not know whether this exhibition was mainly for my benefit, but I felt with some disquiet that I had passed in a few yards from civilization to savagery, and that perhaps it was just as well that I had Prince Bismarck's letter in my pocket.

The Customs man passed me through without abuse and I drove on to Cologne and from Cologne to Bonn. On the autobahn between these two towns I became more and more uneasy. We seemed to be the only car on the road, and all

the way on both sides of it at intervals of 20 yards o⟩
a soldier with a rifle. When I reached what must h⟩
more or less the centre of Bonn, I turned a corner a⟩
myself confronted by an excited German policer⟩
waved me back, shouting that the road was closed⟩
as the Herr Präsident was coming. I tried to find⟩
him whether there was any road open on which⟩
drive to Mainz, but he was too excited to do anyt⟩
shout that the Herr Präsident was coming.

I turned back and parked the car and we we⟩
Beethoven's house in order to revive our droopin⟩
Then we had a cup of tea and considered the situa⟩
were on the right bank of the Rhine and it seemed t⟩
if the Herr Präsident—whom I wrongly thought wa⟩
he was in fact Goering—was coming to Bonn on t⟩
then the road to Mainz on the left bank must be⟩
traffic. What I had to do was to find a bridge over⟩
could drive to the left bank. Leaving the tea shop, I⟩
a man and asked him how I could do this. He⟩
extremely kindly German, and he got into the car an⟩
me across the river. There we were faced by an ine⟩
and disturbing sight. On each side of it the main ⟩
lined with uniformed Nazis and at intervals with⟩
schoolchildren carrying flags. There were flags ev⟩
and the singing of Nazi songs. One had to drive e⟩
slowly as the Nazis were drawn up so as to leav⟩
narrow strip for traffic. It seemed to me that these reg⟩
crowds were obviously waiting for the Herr Präsid⟩
if so, what on earth did it mean? Why were the roac⟩
right bank closed to traffic so that he could con⟩
to Bonn by them, if in fact these stormtroopers anc⟩
children were waiting to greet him on the main ro⟩
to traffic, on the left bank?

At any rate, we had run straight into the kind of⟩

gram had warned us to avoid. Here we were closely
by what, looking down the road ahead, seemed to
ending procession of enthusiastic Nazis. But we
d that there was no need for us to worry. It was a
a day and I was driving with the car open; on my
at Mitz. I had to drive at about 15 miles an hour.
y saw Mitz, the crowd shrieked with delight. Mile
I drove between the two lines of corybantic
and the whole way they shouted 'Heil Hitler!
er!' to Mitz and gave her (and secondarily Virginia
he Hitler salute with outstretched arm.

ent on, as I have said, for mile after mile, and
I could stand it no longer. I decided to turn off the
own to the river, and find an hotel where we could
ight. On the bank of the Rhine, which seems to me
few really ugly rivers in the world, at a place called
we found a very large hotel. We were the only
d we had a curious experience there which threw
ting light on the view which some Germans took
and the Nazis in 1935. We dined in an immense,
ng-room. We sat at a table at one end and at the
the proprietor and his wife had their dinner. There
ther diner and a solitary waiter waited upon us.
the end of dinner the proprietor came over and
whether we had been satisfied. After some desul-
ersation, I asked him whether he knew what the
on was of the Herr Präsident, the closed and open
d the lines of expectant Nazis. He immediately
nd said that he knew nothing about that, but he
eave us and, after some rambling conversation,
where we came from. When I said from Tavistock
London, he suddenly changed into a completely
person: he saw that to an Englishman who lived
ock Square it was safe for him to say anything.

His lamentable tale came pouring out of him. He had been a waiter for many years on the banks of the Thames at Richmond. Then he had returned to Germany in order to marry; he himself would have liked to go back to England, but his wife could not speak English, so he became manager of the Unckel hotel. Before the Nazis appeared on the scene, it was a pleasant and prosperous place; it was always full of young people, for students used to come up the river from Bonn and enjoy themselves. A short time before Hitler began to dominate the scene, our melancholy host had been offered the managership of a London hotel, actually in Tavistock Square itself—there were tears in his eyes as he told us this. He wanted to accept, but his wife could not face a great foreign city in which she would not be able to speak a word of the language. So he refused. Then the Nazis came into power and life in Unckel became hell. 'If one says a word of criticism,' he said, 'one is in danger of being beaten up. It is all processions and marching and drilling. And my business is ruined, for the students in Bonn are kept so busy marching and drilling that they hardly ever now come up the river from Bonn. *Und nun bin ich ins Gefängnis* (and now I'm in prison). They will never let me out; it's impossible to get out of this country.' Here the waiter, who had been standing and silently listening, burst out: 'I'm going to get out. It's terrible here—I'm going to get out—Oh, yes, one can— I shall go to America—that's the place to live in.'

Next day we left the manager, his wife, and the waiter in tears, and drove through Mainz and Darmstadt to Heidelberg, and from Heidelberg through Stuttgart and Ulm to Augsburg, and from Augsburg through Munich to the Austrian frontier, and so to Innsbruck, where on May 12 snow was falling. We did not enjoy this; there was something sinister and menacing in the Germany of 1935. There is a crude and savage silliness in the German tradition which,

The author at Monks House

Group at Sissinghurst

Ben, Virginia, Vita, Nigel

as one drove through the sunny Bavarian countryside, one felt beneath the surface and saw, above it, in the gigantic notices outside the villages informing us that Jews were not wanted.

Not that we had any difficulty anywhere. We forgot about Bismarck's letter, for Mitz carried us through triumphantly in all situations. Pig-tailed schoolchildren, yellow-haired Aryan Fräuleins, blonde blowy Fraus, grim stormtroopers went into ecstasies over *das liebe, kleine Ding*. What was it? Where did it come from? What did it eat? No one ever said a sensible word about Mitz, but, thanks to her, our popularity was immense. In Augsburg in a traffic jam a smiling policeman made cars get out of the way for her and for us. It was obvious to the most anti-Semitic stormtrooper that no one who had on his shoulder such a 'dear little thing' could be a Jew.

As we approached the Austrian frontier, I told Virginia that I proposed to show Bismarck's letter to the Customs officers in order to see what effect it would have. When I drew up at the barrier, the usual scene took place. As soon as the officer saw Mitz on my shoulder, he shouted to his wife and children to come out and see '*das liebe kleine Ding*'. We were soon surrounded by two or three women, four or five children, and several uniformed men. The usual '*Achs!*' and '*Os!*', the usual gush of gush and imbecile questions. I thought that we would never get away, but eventually they calmed down and passed us through without any examination of anything. At the last moment, shaking hands all round, I presented Prince Bismarck's letter. The effect was instantaneous and quite different from that of Mitz, the marmoset. The chief officer drew himself up, bowed, saluted, clicked his heels together, drew all the uniformed men up in line, and, as we drove away, they all saluted us.

Next day we crossed the Brenner and drove down through Italy to Rome, staying a night at Verona, at Bologna, and at

Perugia. How different in those menacing days was the Fascism of the Italians from the Nazism of the Germans! Beneath the surface of Italian life the vulgar savagery of Mussolini and his thugs who murdered Rosselli was, no doubt, much the same as that of Hitler and Goering; but whereas German history has never allowed civilization to penetrate for any length of time, either widely or deeply, into the German people, Italian history has been civilizing the inhabitants of Italy so deeply and so perpetually for over 2,000 years that no savages, from Alaric and his Germanic hordes to Mussolini and his native Fascists, have ever been able to make the Italians as uncivilized as the Germans. In 1935, therefore, whether Jew or Gentile, you did not require either a marmoset or a Prince Bismarck to protect you from the native savages.

The native savages of Italy delighted in Mitz in the same childish way as those of Holland, Germany, and Austria. It is perhaps interesting, from the anthropological and histori- cal angles, to recall the reactions of the people of Holland, Germany, Austria, Italy, and France to Mitz in 1935. In 25 days I spent in the first four countries dozens of Dutch, Germans, Austrians, and Italians spoke to me about Mitz. They all made one or two of five or six standard remarks or asked one or two of five or six standard questions. The remarks and questions were banal, childish, or sometimes incredibly silly. Mitz was mistaken for practically every existing small animal including a rat and a bat. On Sunday, May 26, I crossed the frontier into France at Ventimiglia and had *déjeuner* at Menton, intending to drive on and spend the night at Aix. The Sunday traffic along the Riviera road was so abominable that after Nice I decided to turn north and drive by the unfrequented minor roads to Draguignan and so to Aix. When we got to Draguignan, we had had enough of it, and we decided to stay there for the night.

The stretch of country which runs north of the Riviera road from Grasse to Draguignan is grey and grim; Draguignan itself and its inhabitants are rather grey, grim, and chilly. The woman in the hotel, when she saw Mitz, gave her a chilly reception and refused to allow me to bring her into the hotel. We had at last, after travelling 2,469 miles on the continent of Europe, reached a country in which a marmoset was not a dear, little thing. I left Mitz for the night locked up in the car on the road in front of the hotel. Next morning, as soon as I got up, I went out to see that she was all right. She was sitting on the steering wheel and a soldier was standing on the pavement watching her through the window. I took her out and fed her and the soldier watched and talked to me about her. He was an ordinary soldier, and he talked about her in an adult, intelligent way—he was the first man, woman, or child who had done so in 2,469 miles and he was also the first Frenchman who had talked to me about Mitz. The reaction of the man in the street to a marmoset sitting on the steering wheel of a car teaches one something, I think, about the intellectual tradition, even the civilization, of the country to which he belongs. There are a good many things which I do not like in the French tradition, but its scepticism and respect for intelligence seem to me admirable.

I must now say something about my writing and my political activities in the years between the wars; the two occupations were closely connected; they were complementary attempts, the one theoretical and the other practical, to understand and to help to solve what seemed to me the most menacing problems left to us by the war in a devastated and distracted world. There were in fact two vast, oecumenical problems which threatened, and still threaten, mankind and are interrelated: first, the prevention of war and the development of international government; secondly, the dissolution of the empires of European states in Asia and Africa which seemed to me inevitable and which would cause as much misery to the world as war unless the Governments of the great imperial powers recognized the inevitability, and deliberately worked for an orderly transference of power to the native populations, educated for self-government by their rulers. I had already begun to think and write about these two questions before 1920. In *International Government* I had shown that in fact the relations of states had for long been regulated or not regulated by a system partly of complete anarchy and partly of rudimentary international government, and I had argued that war could not be prevented in the complicated modern world unless some kind of League of Nations system could be established under which the relations of sovereign states would to some extent be controlled by law and order, by international government. I continued to write about this, editing for instance *The Intelligent Man's Way to Prevent War* in 1933, but, as I shall explain more fully in a moment, between 1920 and 1939 I became engrossed in a much wider and more fundamental subject of which the problem of preventing war was only a part. As regards imperialism, I lectured on this subject and I wrote two things specifically about it: *Imperialism and Civilization* in 1928 and *The League and Abyssinia* in 1936.

But as a writer, during the 20 years between the wars, and even beyond that for another 14 years until 1953, I devoted myself to a single subject, doing a great deal of work upon it and writing three books, *After the Deluge* Vol. I (1931), *After the Deluge* Vol. II (1939), and *Principia Politica* (1953) which was really intended to be the third volume of *After the Deluge*. There are 1,000 pages in these books and, I suppose, about 300,000 words. To all intents and purposes they have been a complete failure, but, though like most people I would rather succeed than fail—whether in a game of chess or bowls or in one's life work—in many ways I do not regret them. No doubt owing to the delusion of parentage, I see in my offspring merits invisible to other people. I still think that the subject of these volumes is of immense importance to the historian, the philosopher, the psychologist, and the politician, and that it has very rarely been posed and faced in the way I tried to pose and face it, and I still think that there are a certain number of words out of the 300,000 written by me which contribute something of truth and importance to the subject. As this is an autobiography of my mind as well as of my body, I propose to say something about this.

A good deal of mythological nonsense has been written about the impact of the 1914 war upon left-wing intellectuals, a pack or sect to which, I suppose, I have always belonged. The myth is that pre-war liberals all over Europe believed in the inevitability of progress and the complete rationality of man, the political animal, and that, as the war destroyed the foundations of their political beliefs, they became completely disorientated and exploded. Most intellectuals, dead or living, about whom I have known anything, have resembled Diogenes and the author of *Ecclesiastes* rather than Mr Chasuble, Tom Pinch, and Mr Micawber rolled into one innocent and imbecile optimist. I, like nearly all of them, have never believed that progress is inevitable or that man is politically rational. I was born, as I have recorded, in 1880 into a comfortable, professional middle-class family in Kensington. We had been affluent while my father was alive; his death made the position of the family for many years economically precarious. But in Kensington and Putney, at St Paul's School and Trinity College, Cambridge, life was lived in an atmosphere of social stability and security. The battle of Waterloo was fought 85 years before I went up to Cambridge; the Crimean war had been fought nearly 30 and the Franco-German war nearly 10 years before I was born. There were some signs that European civilization might develop more widely and quickly on the basis of liberty, equality, and fraternity in the twentieth century. Despite colonial wars and rivalry, and despite the endemic danger to Europe from the confrontation of the Triple and the Dual Alliance, to be moderately optimistic about the social and political future of the world was in 1900 not unreasonable.

Moderate optimism was, I think, the attitude of most intellectuals and intelligent people—not of course synonymous —during my lifetime up to the year 1914. The war was a tremendous shock to intellectuals, as it was to the world and all its inhabitants. When Austria invaded Serbia and Germany Belgium, it was one of the great turning-points in human history. There was no longer any place for 'moderate optimism'; as far as I was concerned, it seemed to me that events had proved that in the modern world war and civilization were incompatible, and that, when the war ended the supreme political problem was to find means, if possible, for preventing war. That meant that one must find the chief causes of war and one must discover methods to destroy or counteract those causes. As in all cases of political action, to do this required the use of reason. To find the causes of social or political phenomena you have to use your reason to analyse a series of complicated situations or events; to find means of influencing or altering the series of events requires a constructive use of reason. To say this does not mean that one believes that human beings always act rationally. If you say to a man: 'If you walk over that precipice, you will fall 300 feet on to a hard rock and almost certainly kill yourself', you are using reason analytically and constructively to explain the truth about a situation, cause and effect and the result of future action, to an individual. You do not imply any belief that *he will* use his reason and so avoid falling over the precipice. The problems of history and society are subject to precisely the same laws of reason and unreason, cause and effect. It is as simple as that, though unfortunately in history, the simplicity is delusive because of the immense complication of historical situations and events, and therefore of their causes and effects. Moreover, individuals are rather more rational about walking over precipices than states and governments.

When I began to consider the history of war in Europe in the light of analytic reason, it seemed to me, as it did to many other people, that war would sooner or later be inevitable unless there was at least a rudimentary system of international law and order which would provide for the peaceful settlement of international disputes. That was the theme of my book *International Government,* in which I drew the outline of the structure and functions of a League of Nations. But I never thought or said that a League of Nations, even an effective League, was the only thing necessary to prevent war. No large conglomeration of civilized human beings has ever been able to exist anywhere in comparative peace and prosperity without a system of law and order, without some kind of government whose power to enforce the law against the individual law-breaker rests ultimately upon some kind of force. To say that does not mean that one believes that one only had to have laws, courts, and police to produce law-abiding individuals and a peaceful and civilized government and state. All this is also true of international society in which the units are independent sovereign states.

Ruminating on these matters I had come to three conclusions: first, that in the twentieth century science and industry made war and civilization incompatible; secondly, that without some kind of League system war would be practically and eventually inevitable; thirdly, that war was part of a much wider social phenomenon and problem, namely the government of human beings and what I call communal psychology. It was this third conclusion which led me into spending the next 20 years in writing three books. My mind led me down this path in the following way. When I wrote *International Government,* I did a good deal of reading and thinking about the wars of the eighteenth and nineteenth centuries and about the development of international relations and international government. The more I read and thought, the more interested I became in certain historical facts.

I found that historians accepted it as a fact that the principalities and powers, the captains and the kings, the governments and statesmen who 'made war' on one another had always done so for certain 'objects', and apparently the common people who fought and died in the armies of these rulers accepted these objects until the moment of either final victory or final defeat. It seemed to me curious that, when one examined and analysed these 'objects' for which wars had been fought in Europe ever since the revolutionary and Napoleonic wars, one found that they consisted apparently of beliefs and desires, and that the objects, the beliefs and desires, for which we fought the 1914 war appeared to be precisely the same as those for which our ancestors had fought in 1815 at Waterloo—indeed, they were not very different from those for which, according to Herodotus, the soldiers and sailors of Sparta and Athens fought against Xerxes at Marathon, Thermopylae, and Salamis 2,400 years ago. The revolutionary armies towards the end of the eighteenth century fought for liberty, equality, and fraternity and went into battle singing the Marseillaise; the Napoleonic army fought its way to the walls of Moscow for the same objects and, according to Schubert's famous song, in defeat struggled back to France through the snows of Russia and Poland still singing the Marseillaise. If you open the pages of Herodotus, written, I repeat, over 2,000 years before, and read the wonderful speech in which the Greek unsuccessfully tries to explain to Xerxes—sitting on the shores of the Hellespont and reviewing his mighty fleet—tries unsuccessfully to explain to him what it means to be a Greek and a free man and why one Greek will beat three Persians because he is fighting for—you will find that to all intents and purposes the Greek is saying that he is fighting for liberty, equality, and fraternity. And when in August 1914 the British Government, through the voices of the Prime Minister, Henry Asquith, and the Foreign Secretary, Sir Edward Grey, good liberals echoing the voices of Themistocles and Leonidas, Mirabeau and Lafayette, told us that we were fighting to protect the rights of small nations, the freedom of Serbia and Belgium, from aggression by the Great Powers Germany and Austria, were not statesmen and history once more proclaiming that governments and individuals were fighting a war for liberty, equality, and fraternity?

It seemed to me that, if one wanted to understand the causes of war and perhaps discover some means of preventing it, one must investigate more closely these statements of historians, generals, and prime ministers that wars are fought by nations for objects like liberty, equality, and fraternity. If the statements are true, wars are fought for beliefs and desires, for, if you are called upon and agree to fight for liberty, it means that you believe liberty to be so good and you desire it so deeply that you are prepared to fight and die for it. Moreover, if these beliefs and desires really do influence or cause communal actions like war, then they can accurately be described as communal beliefs and desires. If in 1914 the British answered Kitchener's appeal and joined up because they believed Asquith's appeal to fight for liberty, then it is true that there was a general acceptance in the community of the belief about and the desire for liberty and also a general agreement that these communal beliefs and desires should lead to communal action in war.

Such communal beliefs and desires connected with war seemed to me part of something much wider which I called communal psychology. For according to historians and statesmen communal action is almost always influenced or determined by communal beliefs and desires. For instance, they would hold that the communal belief that political equality was desirable and that it was unattainable unless every adult male had a vote determined the communal action in Britain which produced the Reform Acts of 1832, 1867, and 1884. Again, according to history, the political and economic beliefs and desires of a German Jew enunciated in his book *Das Kapital* in 1867 and in the Communist Manifesto became 50 years later the communal beliefs and desires which caused the Bolshevik revolution and has subsequently led to the spread of communism and the emergence of communist governments all over the world. Again, the paranoid beliefs and desires of a disgruntled Austrian corporal about Germans and Jews became the communal beliefs and desires of Nazism and the Third Reich which produced the second great war and the murder of over five million Jews in concentration camps and gas chambers.

I thought, and still think, that there are some very important and very strange things implied in these beliefs of historians and politicians regarding communal psychology. In every case they imply that some social end or situation is desirable or not desirable and that it can be attained or prevented by certain communal action. If this be true, it means that communal action or the events of history can be and are determined partly by emotional judgments of value —this or that is desirable or not desirable—and partly by reason, the convincing of large numbers of people that something, which is communally desirable, can only be attained by some specific communal action.

Though this is always assumed to be true both in theory or in practice—whether in Thucydides's history of the Peloponnesian war, Gibbon's *Decline and Fall*, a meeting of the Cabinet in 10 Downing Street, or of the Praesidium in the Kremlin—there are practically no serious studies by sociologists, psychologists, or historians of how this process of interaction between communal beliefs and desires and communal actions works or indeed of whether in fact it does work. I decided that, though I was not a professional sociologist, historian, or psychologist, I would try to do as an amateur what the professionals had left undone. In 1920 I had finished and published my book *Empire and Commerce in Africa* and in that year I began to read for and study this problem of communal psychology. Though the subject was vast and complicated, my object could be stated clearly and simply. I proposed to study intensively the years 1789 to 1914 and to try to discover what the relation between the communal beliefs and desires regarding liberty, equality, and fraternity and communal action had been during those years, i.e. what, if any, had been the effect of those communal beliefs and desires not merely upon war and peace but upon historical events generally. I had no idea in 1920 that I should be working and writing on this subject for the next 33 years.

I worked at it, it is true, continually for those 33 years, but I had so many other occupations that I spent a good deal less than half my time upon these books. It was not until 1931 that I published the first volume of *After the Deluge*; it was concerned with democracy and democratic psychology as they developed in the eighteenth century and in the American and French revolutions. Eight years later I published *After the Deluge*, Vol. II, which dealt with the communal psychology of the years 1830-1832, the effect of the communal beliefs and desires regarding liberty, equality, and fraternity on the historical events of those years. 1939, year of its publication, brought down upon Europe and the world the second great war. The years in which the first two volumes had been published had turned out to be between the deluges. I intended to write a third volume, but obviously it could not be entitled *After the Deluge*, Vol. III. It was Maynard Keynes who said to me that what I was really trying to do in these volumes was to analyse the principles of politics and I ought to call the third volume *Principia Politica*. I followed his advice, but it took me a long time to write the book, and *Principia Politica* was not published until 1953.

These three volumes have been, as I have said, to all intents and purposes a failure. The first of the three was published as a Penguin and I occasionally still get a letter of appreciation from some unknown person which faintly stirs in me the pleasure of authorship. All three on the whole had an unfavourable press, and *Principia Politica* was received with derision by the Oxford professional historians who do so much reviewing and who rapped me over the knuckles for having the effrontery to be a member of 'Bloomsbury' and use a title which recalled the works of Newton, Bertrand Russell, and G. E. Moore.

I find it quite difficult to be certain in my own mind as to what 'in the bottom of my heart' is my real attitude towards my own books and criticism of them. My disappointment at the reception and fate of these books has been fairly deep, though not very prolonged. No doubt I was considerably annoyed by reviews which dealt at length with 'Bloomsbury' and the title of the book but never so much as mentioned what the book was attempting to do. No one likes to spend

23 years of his life and nearly 300,000 words on something which is invisible to a Fellow of All Souls or Magdalen. I still think that what I was attempting to do is of immense importance to history and sociology, and that professional historians and sociologists have never attempted to do it.

I am a highly prejudiced reader of these three volumes, but I still think that there is a little more in them than was seen by the professional historians who reviewed them. In 1953 at the age of 73, however, I had to make up my mind whether I should carry on with my original intention and plan to write a fourth and even a fifth volume. I decided not to do so. The three volumes were a failure and I was not prepared to spend another five or ten years and another 200,000 words with the same result. I was, as I say, disappointed, but I do not think that the hurt went very deep or was prolonged. It is interesting, I think, to observe the attitude of different writers (and of oneself) to their writings. I have produced about 20 books, and, like most writers, I probably have, in the pit of my stomach, a better opinion of them than other people. But I am not really much concerned about them and people's opinion of them, once they have been published, and I do not feel the slightest interest in their fate after my death. It is here that I find the attitude of so many writers, good or bad, very strange. They seem to regard the fate of their books as if it were the fate of themselves and they seem to see in the book shops and libraries an unending struggle between mortality and immortality. I could never quite understand Virginia's feeling about her books and their reputation in the world. She seemed to feel their fate to be almost physically and mentally part of her fate. I do not think that she had any belief in life after death, but she appeared to feel that somehow or other she was involved in their life after her death. Being so intimately a part of herself, a hurt to them was felt as a hurt to her, and her mortality or immortality was a part of their mortality or immortality.

The crux of the matter is perhaps there, in the immortality of the soul! The difference in the attitude of different writers to their work probably depends upon whether or not deep within them, even unconsciously, they still believe that they may be immortal. I suspect that Virginia, though she did not believe in life after death, did believe in her life after death in *The Waves*, and not merely in the life of *The Waves* after her death. Even if I had written *The Waves* or *Hamlet*, I do not think I could possibly have felt like that. I cannot believe that death is anything but complete personal annihilation. I cannot, therefore, feel any *personal* interest or involvement in anything of mine after I have been annihilated. I should like to know what happens on the day after my death, e.g. what horse wins the Derby if I die the day before Derby day, and I should like to know what happens to my books after my death, but as I shall never know either, annihilation makes it all one for me. The fate of my books, even before my death, loses some of its importance for me, and this in turn diminishes both the pleasure in success or the pain of failure.

And now I must leave books and theory, and say something of the practice of politics. As a practical politician, I worked mainly in the Labour Party and the Fabian Society, but before I deal with that side of my life, I must mention two other political activities. The first was journalistic. In 1930 I helped to start the *Political Quarterly*. The main credit for successfully launching this journal and for its still being successfully published today, 36 years later, must go to Professor William A. Robson. Willie Robson's enthusiasm and pertinacity succeeded in getting enough capital to start the journal—by no means an easy task—and an admirable group of writers to write for it. He and Kingsley Martin were the first joint-editors, and the Editorial Board consisted of A. M. Carr-Saunders, T. E. Gregory, Harold Laski, Maynard Keynes, Sir Arthur (later Lord) Salter, Sir E. D. (later Lord) Simon, and myself. It was, as the names show, Left Wing politically, but of irreproachable respectability. It proclaimed its object as 'to discuss social and political questions from a progressive point of view; to act as a clearing-house of ideas and a medium of constructive thought'. Its standard was from the beginning extremely high and has remained so for 36 years. A journal of this kind cannot be popular; it is written very largely by experts for an elite, for Members of Parliament and civil servants in the arena of practical politics, and in the academic arena by experts for experts in sociology, politics, law, and history. It can only succeed, indeed it can only justify its existence, by providing ideas for or influencing the ideas of a comparatively small number of 'men at the top'.

When Kingsley became editor of the *New Statesman*, I took his place as joint editor with Willie Robson on the *Political Quarterly*, and for some time during the war I was sole editor and even to some extent its publisher. I continued to be an editor until 1959 and remained on as literary editor until 1962. Having been for over 30 years editorially responsible for it, I am necessarily not an unprejudiced witness regarding its merits and influence. Practically all journalists, from the great Press Lords down to the humblest reporter, suffer from the grossest delusions about the 'influence' of the newspaper which they own, edit, or write for. The megalomania probably increases as you go up from the humble reporter through the pompous editor to the paranoiac owner. I am not sure that the evidence, such as it is, does not point to the fact that the larger the circulation of a paper, the less influence it has upon the opinions of its readers, or even that the influence of every paper is in inverse proportion to the number of copies sold or to the number of people who buy or read it. Certainly the millions who read the popular press seem to be singularly impervious to its propaganda, particularly political propaganda, for vast numbers must vote Labour who habitually read anti-Labour dailies. I do not know whether this should be a subject for rejoicing among the angels in heaven or the Left Wing intellectuals on earth. It depends upon what is the explanation of this curious phenomenon. If the millions who read the popular dailies are interested only in sport, battle, murder, and sex, and therefore are inoculated against the opinions of the proprietor and editor, there is not much reason for rejoicing; but if large numbers have learnt to doubt whether the Northcliffes and Beaverbrooks of the twentieth century are good political advisers to follow, I should feel faintly encouraged.

I feel some encouragement too when I contemplate the other end of the scale where are journals of small circulation like the *Political Quarterly*. There is no doubt that, if their standards, both journalistic and intellectual, are high, they can have considerable influence. The reason is that they are, as I have said, written by experts for experts, or, from another point of view, they are professional or trade papers. The *Political Quarterly* is partly a technical paper in which the professional politician, the administrator, or the civil servant can find information and ideas of the greatest importance to his work and unobtainable elsewhere. No one reads the popular dailies for serious ideas, and practically no one takes their ideas seriously; their main function is entertainment, to titillate the universal desire for sex, violence, gambling, and the royal family. No one reads an article by Professor Robson on local government or by Sir Sydney Caine on the common market for entertainment or for any form of sexual or monarchical titillation, but they may be absorbed and fascinated by the ideas. That is why we were able to start the journal with a capital of a few hundred pounds and we have been able to go on for 36 years without having to raise any more capital. It is perhaps also the reason why its influence has been much larger than its circulation.

I have said that I dislike journalism and editorship, because as soon as one has finished off one number, one has to begin to think about the next. This applied to the editorship of the *Political Quarterly*, but as there were three months instead of seven days, as with the *Nation* and *New Statesman*, between each issue, the perpetual turning of the wheel was longer and slower. On the whole I enjoyed my work on it, because I was extremely interested in the ideas with which it dealt and was working with people pursuing the same objects. I also enjoyed the second by-product of my political activities. In 1938 I was appointed a Member of the National Whitley Council for Administrative and Legal Departments of the Civil Service, and I remained a member for the next 17 years.

The nature of the work of the Whitley Council for the Civil Service is not widely known. It consisted, so far as I was concerned, of sitting three or four times a year on arbitration cases. I found the work extremely interesting and even sometimes amusing, and also exasperating. The British Civil Service does not strike, and an elaborate procedure has been devised in the Whitley Council system for the peaceful settlement of economic disputes, i.e. for determining scales of payment and conditions of employment without resort to strikes or lock-outs. In 1938 the staff side of the Civil Service was organized in the Civil Service Clerical Association, which was in fact the civil servant's trade union. Any claim by a class or section of the Service for higher pay or improved conditions was made to the Treasury through the Clerical Association and negotiations then began between the Treasury and the Association. If agreement was reached, well and good, but if, after a time, the two sides could not agree, the claim was remitted to arbitration. The arbitration tribunal consisted of a permanent chairman, who was a lawyer appointed by the government, and two other arbitrators drawn from two panels. One panel was appointed by the Treasury, and consisted mainly of Directors of banks or railway companies; the other consisted of persons nominated by the staff side, by the Clerical Association. The Association had asked me to agree to serve and had nominated me for their panel.

As Assistant Government Agent in the Hambantota District of Ceylon for nearly three years, I had had a fair amount of judicial experience, for as Police Magistrate and District Judge I had had to try both criminal and civil cases. To try any kind of case in a judicial capacity I find extraordinarily fascinating. The fascination to me consists largely in the curiously complicated state of mind into which you, as a judge, have to get, if you are to be a good judge. Your mind, like Caesar's Gaul, has to be divided into three parts, and yet, like Gaul, maintain its unity. First, your mind must work intellectually with great quickness and concentration upon the facts, for the first essential is that the judge should understand and interpret the facts, which are often connected with spheres of life and activities of which the judge has no previous experience. (In Civil Service arbitration cases one was continually having to understand and interpret very complicated facts about the details of work or occupations of which one was quite ignorant before one began to try the case.) I thoroughly enjoy this kind of intellectual problem. Secondly, no one can be a good judge unless he can combine, with this quick intellectual understanding of facts, an intuitive sensitiveness to human witnesses and their evidence. Often it is only by hearing and, as it were, feeling a witness that you can accurately interpret and assess the value of his evidence.[1] The third requisite of a good judge is, perhaps, in some ways the most difficult—it is complete and unfailing impartiality. Complacent prejudice is the occupational disease of judges. It can make the judge incapable of understanding and interpreting the facts or of judging the character of a witness and the value of his evidence. On the bench one has to be perpetually on one's guard against oneself, to prevent one's previous beliefs and prejudices interfering with one's acceptance or rejection of facts and arguments. But still more necessary is it consciously to watch and thwart one's own instinctive prejudices for and against persons. A woman enters the box oozing feminine charm—how difficult it is to regard her and her evidence exactly as one does the next witness who fills one with physical repulsion. And it requires an even more ruthless act of will against oneself to force oneself to judge with complete impartiality the value of the evidence of a man whose appearance you dislike.

[1] This is well understood and theoretically admitted in British Courts of Appeal, though not always honoured in practice by Appeal Court judges. In Ceylon I learned by experience that, where there was a direct conflict of evidence, often suddenly some small thing, almost impossible to describe accurately—a gesture or movement of the witness perhaps—would reveal to one where the truth lay. Of course, one may have deluded oneself, though there were cases in which I would have staked my life on the accuracy of my judgment. The Appeal Court judge did not always agree. I still remember after 50 years a case in which a villager suddenly appeared in the kachcheri hauling along a man and a cow, claiming loudly and passionately that it was his cow and that the man had stolen it. There was a complete conflict of evidence and suddenly one of the witnesses said something in such a way that I was absolutely convinced that the cow had been stolen. I gave my verdict accordingly and it was set aside in appeal. I am certain that thus the thief obtained the cow, and after my death, if I find myself in heaven, the first thing I shall do is to ask Saint Peter whether my judgment was correct. I am sure that he will answer: 'Yes'.

This last point is to me so interesting that I cannot resist saying a word or two more about it. The behaviour of Lord Hewart in the Court of Appeal, described by me on page 137, is a good example of judicial injustice caused, in part, by the judge allowing his prejudice against a man's appearance to make him give a grossly inequitable judgment. I once watched an even worse exhibition of prejudice by Mr Justice Avory at the Old Bailey. I had been summoned as a juror and was waiting in court for the next case while Avory tried a working-class woman for stealing a piece of luggage at Victoria Station. There was no doubt about the facts. She had been convicted several times of the same offence: she loitered on a railway station platform and walked off with the most likely looking suitcase of some first-class passenger. There was nothing against her character except this inveterate habit of pinching first-class passengers' luggage. She was not attractive to look at, but I was convinced by everything she did and said that, apart from this habit, she was an exceptionally nice person. If ever there was a case of a criminal whose crime was in the eyes of God and medical science not a crime, but a symptom of mental or emotional disorder which might well be curable, there it stood in the dock facing us all in the dingy court, including Mr Justice Avory and the jury. I say that it might well have been curable because I happened to have had personal knowledge of a similar case in a very different walk of life from that of the North Country working-class woman being tried by Avory. I knew a young man, born into a highly respectable professional family, himself in a first-class professional post after a successful university career. Suddenly he was arrested for precisely the same offence as this woman, and it was discovered that he had habitually for some time stolen luggage at railway stations. Like her, normal and law abiding in every other way, he had this uncontrollable compulsion to steal suitcases from railway station platforms. He had the good fortune to be tried by an intelligent and sympathetic judge and he was discharged on condition that he took psychiatric treatment. He did so and was completely cured, ending his life as a respected member of a learned profession.

Very different was the treatment which the working-class woman received from Mr Justice Avory. The indignation which I felt while I watched and listened to him as he summed up rises again in me today. He was an exquisitely elegant man in his wig and gown and immaculate lace, and behind the icy ruthlessness of his pitiless summing up against her I felt the righteous indignation of the first-class passenger confronting the thief who had stolen his suitcase. The jury rightly found her guilty and Avory gave her the maximum sentence. Justice had been done, but—

A man may see how this world goes with no eyes. Look with thine ears: see how yond justice rails upon yond simple thief. Hark in thine ear: change places; and, handy-dandy, which is the justice, which is the thief?

But I must return to the Civil Service Arbitration Tribunal. There, of course, there was no 'simple thief' before us, but, handy-dandy, much the same attitude was required, if one was to be a good arbitrator, as was necessary if one was to be a good High Court judge in the Old Bailey. The procedure was that, when one was chosen from the panel to try some case, one received the detailed claim by the Association or, in some cases, a trade union, and the answer by the Treasury, both in writing. Then on the day fixed for the hearing the three arbitrators heard both sides and any witnesses that they wished to call. When I first became an arbitrator, the case for the staff side was almost always conducted by W. J. Brown, Secretary of the Civil Service Clerical Association. A very able and rather flamboyant man, he was a first-class advocate, and, as he had considerable experience and was meticulous in mastering every detail in the most complicated claim, the case of the staff side was always admirably presented to the court whenever he appeared. I was often greatly interested and amused by the psychological display when William John Brown, who had been educated in the Salmestone Elementary School, Margate, and the Sandwich Grammar School, and had begun his career as a boy clerk in the Civil Service, on one side, confronted a young Treasury official in the Administrative Class, educated at Winchester and New College, Oxford, on the other. Winchester and Oxford were often no match for Margate and Sandwich.

The work was often very interesting. The occupational diversity of the hundreds of thousands of persons—or is it millions?—employed by the state is amazing, and the arbitrators almost always had to get a detailed knowledge of the work of claimants in order to determine what should be a fair wage or salary for the work which they did. In the course of my service on the Tribunal I learned all about the hourly work of the cohort of women who clean out the government offices in Whitehall, foresters in the north of Scotland, the men who talk down aeroplanes at certain airports in fog, and a small and peculiar class of men in the secret service. In order to try the last case, the Tribunal had to be indoctrinated and de-indoctrinated (if that was the correct word) by an army officer. Though this infinite variety made the whole business much more interesting for the arbitrator, the longer I served on the Arbitration Tribunal, the more crazily irrational the whole industrial structure of the Civil Service appeared to me. The Service was divided into classes, e.g. administrative, executive, clerical, and there were a certain number of subclasses and grades. But throughout this enormous business each of the hundreds of government occupations had, on the face of it, a scale of pay and conditions of employment peculiar to itself. On the other hand, the Civil Service Clerical Association, the organized scientific workers, and the trade unions claimed that throughout government employment similar work should entitle the worker to similar pay, and the Treasury agreed. The consequence is that, if 502 workers in occupation A receive a 5 per cent. increase in the scale of their pay, 5,003 workers in occupation B, 47 in occupation C, and 50,004 in occupation D will probably claim a similar increase on the ground that their work is similar to that of occupation A. I should guess that about 80 per cent. of the claims which I had to try in my 17 years on the Tribunal were of this kind. This meant that one had to listen to a detailed exposition of the exact nature of the work in each occupation and then judge whether they were sufficiently similar to justify a similar scale of pay. And one knew that if one assimilated the scale of, say, D to that of A, it was quite probable that the increase of the scale of D would provoke a claim from occupation E and occupation F to a similar increase.

The inevitable result of this system is an unending chain reaction of claims, a successful claim in one part of the Service setting off one or more claims somewhere else. The amount of wasted time and money in negotiations and arbitrations must be considerable. I am sure that much could be done to rationalize the structure of the Civil Service in this respect, though to do so would require courage and determination. If, as was proved again and again on the Tribunal, the work and conditions of occupations A to E, for instance, are so similar that the Tribunal has to give them the same scale of pay and conditions of employment, then those who work in the five occupations should all be recruited into one large government service Division, divided into Classes, each with its fixed scale of pay. This rationalization and reclassification of government employment ought to be done by a Special Commission. It might not be possible to apply the new classification and pay structure to people already in government employ, but it could be applied to all recruits after a certain date. I do not suppose that it would ever be possible to rationalize the whole government service, from top to bottom, in this way; there would always be some occupations so peculiar that their pay and conditions could not be assimilated to any other. But there would not be a great number, and the vast majority of government employees could equitably and efficiently be recruited as, say, a member of Class IV of Division X in the Civil Service. If they were, the work of the Civil Service Arbitration Tribunal would dwindle.

My exit from the Tribunal after 17 years amused me. Though I was on the panel nominated by the staff, I always considered that, as a member of the Tribunal, I had to be completely impartial. And on the whole, I think, we all of us were pretty impartial. Our decisions were nearly always unanimous. On two or three occasions only I found myself in a minority of one; once the chairman and I were on one side, and the Treasury arbitrator on the other. The written statements of the Treasury case were nearly always admirable and the statement of claims by the Civil Service Clerical Association were usually good, but the claims from other bodies were sometimes set out badly. In 1954 one of the big unions put in a claim for a large number of government employees; the statement of claim put in by them seemed to me perfunctory, slovenly; it asked for an increase in the scale of wages, but did not even take the trouble to give the existing scale. When we three arbitrators met before going into the court room, I said that I thought the statement extremely bad and I suggested that the chairman might gently draw the attention of the claimants to the deficiencies.

The other two agreed and the chairman made the mildest of protests. The secretary of the union, who had come to conduct the case, was enraged and refused to continue before us —so we all trooped out astonished rather than dismayed. Arbitrators were appointed to the panels for four years, and hitherto when my four years' term had come to an end, I had always been renominated and reappointed. When shortly after this incident my four-year term came to an end, I was not renominated.

When one comes to the practice of politics, anyone writing about his life in the years 1924-1939 must answer the crucial question: 'What did you do in the General Strike?' Of all public events in home politics during my lifetime, the General Strike was the most painful, the most horrifying. The treatment of the miners by the government after the Sankey Commission was disgracefully dishonest. If ever there has been right on the side of the workers in an industrial dispute, it was on the side of the miners in the years after the war; if ever a strike and a general strike were justified, it was in 1926. The actions of the mine-owners and of the government seemed to me appalling and when the General Strike came, I was entirely on the side of the workers. There was, of course, really nothing one could do, and one watched appalled the incompetence of those who had called and were conducting the strike. Then when the failure of the strike was inevitable, I was rung up one morning by R. H. Tawney, who asked me to come round and see him in Mecklenburgh Square. When I got there, he told me that he was going to try to get as many well-known people as possible to sign a statement publicly calling upon the government to see that there was no victimization when the strike was over. He asked me whether I would be responsible for collecting the signatures of as many prominent writers and artists as possible. I agreed and for the next few days organized a company of young people who bicycled round London collecting signatures. It was the kind of job which I find depressing, because I cannot really believe in the efficacy of what I am doing. However, we worked hectically, and only one person refused when asked to sign. This was Sir John Galsworthy. The young woman who bicycled up to Hampstead and received a pretty curt refusal became Principal of Somerville College and a D.B.E.

In the general practice of politics my main activities were in the Fabian Society and the Labour Party. For many years I was elected a member of the Executive Committee of the Fabian Society, for ten years I was chairman of the Fabian International Bureau, and for even longer was a member of the Colonial Bureau. I do not like to think of the innumerable hours of my life which I have spent on this kind of work. It was mainly committee work. I do not enjoy committees and I am not a good committee man unless I am chairman or secretary; as an ordinary member, I tend either to become exasperated by what seems to me inefficiency and waste of time or to sink into a coma from which at long intervals I rouse myself to sudden, irritated energy. My attitude to the Fabian Society was, I think, always slightly ambivalent. When I first knew it, it was pre-eminently a creation of Sidney and Beatrice Webb. They meant it to be and they made it an instrument for the political education of the labour movement and ultimately of the Labour Party. By what they understood as 'research', by committees, reports, pamphlets, books, and conferences, the Society fed the labour movement with facts and theories, with ideas and policies. I was mainly interested politically in international affairs and in colonial and imperial problems. When, at the end of the 1914 war, Asquith, Lloyd George, and the ruthless logic of history had sterilized and emasculated liberalism and had irrevocably destroyed the Liberal Party, and when

Labour was just emerging as the only political alternative to conservatism and the Tory Party, both among the leaders and the rank and file of the labour movement there was a profound and almost universal ignorance of international and imperial facts and problems. The rank and file were predominantly working class and trade unionist, and were naturally concerned with the industrial and economic aspects of politics of which their knowledge and interests alone made them acutely aware. Even their middle-class leaders and instructors, like the Webbs, before the 1914 war ignored and were ignorant of international and imperial problems. As I have recorded elsewhere, when I first knew Sidney, if an international question cropped up, he would say: 'It's not my subject', and that seemed to mean that it was no business of his and could be left to some other expert. After I had written *International Government* and *Empire and Commerce in Africa* for the Fabian Society, the Webbs treated me more or less as the Fabian and Labour Party 'expert' in international and imperial questions. In the Society Sidney turned over to me or consulted me about such questions and he had me appointed secretary of the Labour Party Advisory Committees on International and Imperial Affairs.

My work in the Society helped my work in the Labour Party and vice versa, though I always felt that the Advisory Committee work was potentially the more important, since it brought one directly in contact with the Executive Committee of the Labour Party and the Parliamentary Party. During the 1920s I did a good deal of work for the Fabian Society, but I did not take much part in its internal politics, though I watched them from a distance with some amusement. At the beginning of the decade, as I have said, the Society was still mainly the creation of the Webbs, who still, spiritually and materially, moved on the face of its waters. But the younger generation, in the person of G. D. H. Cole

and his wife Margaret, were already knocking at the door—
and there was no gentleness or consideration when Douglas
and Margaret Cole knocked on any door. I have always
thought that the way in which Sidney and Beatrice behaved
when they heard that ominous knocking was a perfect
example of how age should face with understanding and
dignity the menace of the younger generation. When Douglas married Margaret in 1918, they were both 30 years of
age; he was an extraordinarily able product of Oxford University and she of Cambridge University. They did not
suffer either fools or the opposite of fools gladly; they knew
exactly what they wanted in life and in the Fabian Society,
and they were determined to get it with the ruthlessness and
arrogance of vigorous youth confronted by distinguished
and static age. There was no gentleness in their opposition
to the Webbs, but Sidney and Beatrice treated them and
their views with the greatest consideration and never showed
the slightest sign of resentment.

But this kind of thing was not very good for the work of
the Fabian Society and between 1920 and 1930 it gradually
went downhill. Indeed, it had got into such a miserable state
that in 1931 the more active members hived off and started
the New Fabian Research Bureau. Douglas Cole was honorary secretary, Clem Attlee, chairman, and Hugh Gaitskell,
assistant secretary. I was a member of the Executive Committee and ran the International Section. We did a considerable amount of work, producing pamphlets and reports. But
after nine years, negotiations opened with the Fabian Society
and we hived back again. The hiving back really meant
that we, the New Fabian Researchers, took control of the
Fabian Society. As far as I was concerned, I was elected a
member of the Executive Committee and served on it for
many years and I was also chairman of the International
Bureau.

I did a good deal of work for the Fabian Society, but much more for the Labour Party. For nearly 30 years I was secretary of the two Advisory Committees each of which met in the House of Commons on alternate Wednesdays. The present General Secretary of the Labour Party (1966) has given me an opportunity of examining the reports which these two committees made to the Executive Committee and the Parliamentary Party. I knew that we had done a great deal, but I must say that I was amazed at the quantity and scope of our work. We simply bombarded the leaders of the Party and the active politicians with reports, briefs, recommendations, policies covering every aspect, question, or problem of international and imperial politics. As a civil servant, an editor of journals dealing with the theory and practice of politics, and a publisher who specialized to some extent in the publication of political books, I have learned—at the cost of infinite boredom and much mental torture—a great deal about political writers and historians, and how they deal with their subjects. Nearly everyone thinks that he can think, and most people today think that they can write what they think; in fact, the ability to think even among professional thinkers, and to write even among professional writers, is extremely rare; and I should put most political writers and historians at the bottom of the class. It is therefore extraordinary to find that the quality of the reports of these committees is in general extremely high; most of them are succinct and to the point, written clearly by experts for ordinary people, full of facts, expressing views and proposing policies with a sense of sober responsibility.

I will deal first with the imperial committee. Today, in the year 1966, imperialism and colonialism are among the dirtiest of all dirty political words. That was not the case 47 years ago at the end of the 1914 war. The British and French Empires were still going strong and still adding to their territories, either unashamedly or, rather shamefacedly and dishonestly, by the newly invented Mandate system, which some people recognized as a euphemism for imperialism. The vast majority of Frenchmen and Britons were extremely proud of their empires and considered that it was self-evident that it was for the benefit of the world as well as in their own interests that they ruled directly or dominated indirectly the greater part of Asia and Africa. It was still widely accepted that God had so ordered the world that both individuals and states benefited everyone, including their victims, by making the maximum profit for themselves in every way, everywhere and everywhen. In the second volume of my autobiography, *Growing*, I recorded my experience as an imperialist empire builder for seven years in the Ceylon Civil Service and how gradually it made me dislike imperialism with its relation of dominant to subject peoples.[1] It was one of the main reasons why in 1911 I decided to resign from the Civil Service. The 1914 war and my work on *International Government* and *Empire and Commerce in Africa* increased my dislike of the imperialist system. It seemed to me certain that the revolt of the subject peoples— 'peoples not yet able to stand by themselves under the strenuous conditions of the modern world', as the Covenant of the League describes them—which had begun in Japan and was now rumbling in China, India, Ceylon, and the Near East, would spread through Asia and would soon reach Africa. In the modern world this was one of the most menacing political problems, and the world's peace and prosperity in the future depended upon accelerating the transfer of power from the imperialist states to their subject peoples in the ramshackle territories called colonies, dependencies, protectorates, and spheres of influence throughout Asia and Africa.

[1] *Growing*, pp. 158, 247-248, 251.

The importance of the Labour Party Advisory Committee on Imperial Affairs consisted for me in the fact that it enabled me, as secretary, to try to get the party and its leaders to understand the complications and urgency of what was happening in remote places and among strange peoples about whom they were profoundly and complacently ignorant. When it came down to day-to-day practical politics in the 'twenties and 'thirties of the twentieth century, there were in this field two main questions which it was essential to deal with: first, the demand for self-government in India and its repercussions in Burma and Ceylon; secondly, the methods of government and economic exploitation in the British African 'possessions'. Between 1918 and 1939 the Advisory Committee did an immense amount of work upon these two questions and I was very lucky to have several members who not only agreed with my view of their importance but had a profound and practical knowledge of them. I propose to say something about what we aimed at and accomplished in each case.

First as regards India. Between 1924 and 1931 we sent 23 reports and recommendations on India to the Executive Committee and Parliamentary Party. We had on our committee four members with a wide and detailed knowledge of India, Major Graham Pole, H. S. L. Polak, G. T. Garratt, and above all Sir John Maynard. They closely followed events and we relied greatly upon them and their intimate knowledge of Indian conditions. John Maynard, who became chairman of the committee, was as I wrote in *Sowing* (p. 228), a very remarkable man. After a distinguished career in the Indian Civil Service he retired in 1927. He was for five years Member of the Executive Council of Governor Punjab. When he joined the Labour Party and the Advisory Committee he was well over 60; at that age most people have lost any ability, if they ever had it, of admitting into their

mind even the shadow of a new idea, and, after over 40 years
as a civil servant in India, he ought to have developed a sun-
baked shell of impermeable conservatism. When one first
met him, one might easily mistake him for the typical top-
grade British civil servant, neat, precise, reserved, reticent,
with an observant, suspicious, and slightly ironical gleam in
his eye. He may have been to some extent all of this, and
yet at the same time he was the exact opposite. For he was one
of the most open-minded and liberal-minded men I have ever
known—he was also personally one of the nicest—and to
add to all his other gifts, after a life spent in administration,
at the age of 75 he wrote one of the best books on Soviet
Russia ever published, *The Russian Peasant and Other
Studies*. Graham Pole, a Labour M.P. from 1929 to 1931,
had a considerable knowledge of India and was an indefatig-
able member of the Advisory Committee; he was convinced
that immediate steps should be taken to give self-government to India. Polak had the same equipment and outlook
as Graham Pole, and he was an intimate friend of Gandhi.

Among the Labour leaders inside and outside Parliament
there was very little knowledge or understanding of the
Indian situation. In the highest regions Ramsay MacDonald
posed as the expert in chief, having been a member of the
Royal Commission on Indian Public Services in 1912 and
having written two books on the 'awakening' and government of India. He was not entirely ignorant of the situation
and took an interest in what we were doing on the committee,
occasionally speaking to me or writing to me about our
memoranda and recommendations. He professed to be, as
usual, upon what I considered to be the side of the angels—
in favour of self-government, but, as usual, he was entirely
untrustworthy—I always mistrusted Ramsay, and particularly when he brought me the gift of agreeing with me. It was
almost the inevitable sign that he would find some reason

for doing the opposite of what he had agreed with you ought to be done. The only other front rank Labour leader who knew anything about India was Clem Attlee, but his interest in and knowledge of it only began in 1927, when he was a member of the Indian Statutory Commission. After becoming Secretary of State for the Dominions in 1942 and Prime Minister in 1945, he played a prominent part in the final events which brought independence and Dominion status to India and Pakistan in 1947.

The perpetual tragedy of history is that things are perpetually being done ten or twenty years too late. When in the last days and hours before the outbreak of the 1914 war, that monstrously unnecessary war, Grey and some of the other European statesmen were trying frantically to put forward proposals to stop it and the general staffs were taking frantic measures to make it inevitable, one of the Foreign Secretaries—I think it was the Austrian—to whom Grey had desperately telegraphed one more proposal which would have involved stopping Austrian mobilization, plaintively replied that events had once more outstripped and outdated the proposal. This outstripping and outdating of the proposals, policies, and acts of governments and statesmen by events is the perpetual story of human history. Over and over again the oncoming of some horrible and unnecessary historic catastrophe—some war or revolution or Hitlerian savagery —is visible and a voice is heard in the wilderness saying to the kings and presidents and prime ministers: 'If you want to prevent this catastrophe you must do X'. Then all the kings, presidents, and prime ministers, the governments, establishments, powers, and principalities shout in unison: 'This is the voice of Thersites, and Jack Cade, and Jacques Bonhomme, of Danton and Marat, of Bakunin and Karl Marx, of bloody revolutionaries, Bolsheviks, Left Wing intellectuals, and Utopians. We conservatives are the only realists—it is fatal to alter anything except the buttons on a uniform or what makes no matter—but to do X would be the end of civilization.' Ten, twenty, fifty years later, when it is ten years, twenty years, fifty years too late, when events have outstripped and outdated X which would have saved civilization, then at last with civilization falling about their ears, the realists grant X. This was the history of the French revolution, of Home Rule and Ireland, of war and the League of Nations.

It was also the history of British governments and India between 1920 and 1947. During the 1914 war the British government had declared that it would co-operate with Indians in order to establish self-government in India. The White Paper, the Round Table Conference, and the India Act of 1935 were the steps by which British conservative and imperialist patriots sought honourably to dishonour this promise. What they gave with one hand—niggardly reforms—they took away with the other—the massacre at Amritsar, the Rowlatt ordinances, the cat-and-mouse imprisonments and releases of Gandhi and Congress leaders. The vicious circle of repression and sedition, sedition and repression—the implacable legal violence of an alien government and the murderous, illegal violence of native terrorists —established itself. At each stage the demands of Congress for self-government and Dominion status were met by such grudging and contemptible dollops of self-government that any politically conscious Indian could only conclude that once more the tragedy of freedom would have to be acted out in India—the alien rulers would release their hold on the subject people only if forced to do so by bloody violence.

Of course, no one can be sure of any What Might Have Been in history. But I have no doubt that if British governments had been prepared in India to grant in 1900 what they refused in 1900 but granted in 1920; or to grant in 1920 what they refused in 1920 but granted in 1940; or to grant

in 1940 what they refused in 1940 but granted in 1947—
then nine-tenths of the misery, hatred, and violence, the
imprisonings and terrorism, the murders, floggings, shoot-
ings, assassinations, even the racial massacres would have
been avoided; the transference of power might well have
been accomplished peacefully, even possibly without partition. At any rate all through the crucial years between 1920
and 1940 the Advisory Committee urged the Executive
Committee and the Parliamentary Party, and the Labour
Governments of 1924 and 1929, to do everything in their
power to meet the demands in India for self-government and
Dominion status. Our memoranda, written by Maynard,
Graham Pole, and Polak, continually explained to the Executive and Parliamentary Party the complicated and fluctuat-
ing situation, and the bewildering kaleidoscope of demands,
proposals, reports, White Papers, negotiations, Bills and
Acts. If we accomplished nothing else, we at least for the
first time did something to educate our masters; we got a
few Labour leaders to take an interest in and understand
what was happening in India. Our recommendations were
clear and consistent: at the crucial moments of the White
Paper, the Round Table Conference, and the Act of 1935,
we insisted that the government's offers or concessions were
totally inadequate. The Party accepted our recommendations
and came out publicly in favour of immediate steps to establish Dominion status.

All political parties make promises or announce policies
generously when they are not in power which they regret,
ignore, and repudiate when they obtain the power to carry
them out. In my 25 years' service as secretary of the Imperial
Advisory Committee I had splendid opportunities of often
seeing that Labour governments and politicians were not
immune from this change of heart or mind; in my own personal
involvement with the Indian question, I have three vivid re-

collections of particular incidents, and one is closely connected
with such a change of mind. It was during the war, when
Attlee was Deputy Prime Minister and Secretary of State
for Dominion Affairs in the Churchill Government. Something had occurred with regard to India which the Advisory
Committee considered of immense importance. The exact
point I do not now remember, but the Committee felt that
something should be done which the Labour Party by its
declared policy was morally and politically bound to stand
for. In view of Attlee's position and his knowledge of the
Indian problem and of the Party's declared policy since 1927,
the committee decided that Charles Buxton and I should go
and see him and put the case as the committee saw it and the
desirability of doing everything possible in this case to follow the lines of our declared policy. Attlee gave us an interview in No. 11 Downing Street. Charles and I sat on one
side of a table and the Deputy Prime Minister on the other
side. I was not an intimate friend of his, but I had worked
with him quite a bit, particularly on the New Fabian Research Bureau; Charles Buxton knew him much better. But
we had a very frigid reception. He listened to what we had
to say and then dismissed us. I felt that somehow we had
committed or were thought to have committed something
rather worse than a political indiscretion by bringing this
inconvenient reminder into the Holy of Holies of power. I
almost felt a slight sense of guilt as I slunk out of Downing
Street past the policeman who during the war examined your
credentials before allowing you to enter it.

My second vision of an incident with regard to the long-
drawn-out tragedy of India is very different. It was in 1931,
just after the Round Table Conference had ended. A Labour
M.P., James Horrabin, said that Gandhi wanted to meet a
few Labour people and discuss with them what his future
action should be; Horrabin asked me to come in the evening

of December 3 to his flat for this purpose. It was a curious
party, consisting of Gandhi and some ten or fifteen Labour
people—who we all were, I cannot now remember, but my
recollection is that we were nearly all of us 'intellectuals', not
first-line politicians. Everyone has seen photographs of that
strange little figure, the Mahatma Gandhi, and he has been
described again and again; what seemed to me remarkable
about him was that, unlike most people, he was in life almost
exactly like the photographs of him. He was, I suppose, one
of the few 'great men'—if there are such people—that I have
met. I do not think that, if I had met him in Piccadilly or
Calcutta or Colombo, I would have recognized his greatness;
but sitting with him in Horrabin's room, I could not fail to
feel that he was a remarkable man. At first sight he presented
to one a body which was slightly inhuman, slightly ridiculous. But the moment he began to talk, I got the impression
of great complexity—strength, subtlety, humour, and at the
same time an extraordinary sweetness of disposition.

Gandhi said that he was not going to talk much himself.
He had asked us to come because he felt that the end of the
Round Table Conference had left him personally in a difficult position and he was not at all clear what line he should
follow when he got back to India. He wanted us each in
turn to tell him how we saw the situation and what we
thought his immediate course of action should be. Then one
after the other round the room each said his piece—I cannot
say that I found my piece very easy or illuminating. When
we had all said our say, there followed one of the most brilliant intellectual pyrotechnic displays which I have ever
listened to. Gandhi thanked us and said that it would greatly
help him if his friend Harold Laski, who was one of us,
would try to sum up the various lines of judgment and advice
which had emerged. Harold then stood up in front of the
fireplace and gave the most lucid, faultless summary of the

complicated, diverse expositions of ten or fifteen people to which he had been listening in the previous hour and a half. He spoke for about 20 minutes; he gave a perfect sketch of the pattern into which the various statements and opinions logically composed themselves; he never hesitated for a word or a thought, and, as far as I could see, he never missed a point. There was a kind of beauty in his exposition, a flawless certainty and simplicity which one feels in some works of art. Harold's mind, when properly used, was a wonderful intellectual instrument, though as years went by he was inclined to take the easy way and misuse it both for thinking and writing.

My third vision connected with India is in Artillery Mansions in Victoria Street and another famous Indian, Shri Jawaharlal Nehru. It was in February 1936 that I received a letter from Nehru saying that he would very much like to have a talk with me: would I come in the afternoon of Monday and see him in Artillery Mansions, where he was staying? He had just been elected President of the All India Congress. I went to keep my appointment on a cold, grey, foggy, dripping, London February afternoon. I knew Artillery Mansions well, for at one time my sister, Bella, had a flat there. It fills me with despair whenever I see it—even on a bright spring day. It must rank among the greatest masterpieces of Victorian architectural ugliness; but it is not only horribly ugly, it is a monument of dark, gloomy inconvenience. It is one of the many human habitations over which I have always felt the inscription should be: 'Abandon hope all ye who enter here'.

It was no bright spring day when I went to see the future Prime Minister of India; it was, as I said, one of those dirty yellow, pea-soup, dripping London February days which make the heart sink. My heart sank as I climbed the dark staircase to Nehru's flat. The door of the flat was open, and, as nothing happened when I rang the bell, I walked in. The doors of all the rooms were open and the rooms were barely furnished. Hesitatingly I looked into a room from which came the sound of conversation; in it were three chairs and a table, Nehru, and another Indian. Nehru told me to come in and sit down, and the quite private conversation between the two went on for five or ten minutes as if I had not been there. My experience in Ceylon had taught me that the European custom of domestic privacy is unknown to Asiatics. In Asia houses and rooms often have no doors, and, no matter what may be happening in a room, all kinds of extraneous people will probably be wandering aimlessly in and out of it.[1] Eventually the Indian left and I had a conversation for about half an hour with Nehru. We talked in the bare room with the door of the room open and the door of the flat open and, as it seemed to me, all the doors in the world open. This is not calculated to give one a sense of privacy and comfort on a cold February afternoon in London. I liked Nehru very much as a man; he was an intellectual of the intellectuals, on the surface gentle and sad. He

[1] I saw a curious example of this when I revisited Ceylon in 1960. I was taken by Mr Fernando, the head of the Civil Service, to see the Prime Minister, Mr Dahanayake. The previous Prime Minister had only a short time before been assassinated. Mr Dahanayake was living in a large house, the gates of which were guarded by two soldiers carrying rifles who stopped us and examined our papers and credentials with the greatest care before admitting us. But the large compound at the back of the house was separated from other compounds only by a low unguarded fence through which any would-be assassin could easily have come unseen. And I had a long conversation with the Prime Minister in an open, unguarded room and, while we talked, all kinds of people wandered vaguely in and out of it. I remember thinking at the time how very different the precautions would have been if I had gone to see the Prime Minister in Downing Street although it was nearly 150 years since a Prime Minister had been assassinated in England.

had great charm, and, though there was a congenital aloofness about him, I had no difficulty in talking to him. It was a rather strange and inconclusive conversation. I had thought and still think that he had intended to discuss politics and, in particular, imperial politics from the Labour angle with me. And in a vague way we did talk politics, the problems of India and Ceylon; but it was pretty vague and somehow or other we slipped into talking about life and books rather than the fall of empire and empires. After about half an hour I got up to go and Nehru asked me where I was going. I said that I was going to walk to the House of Commons to attend a Labour Party Advisory Committee there and he said that he would walk with me as he would like to go on with our conversation. When we got down into the extraordinary sort of gloomy well outside the front door of the Mansions, we found waiting a press photographer who wanted to take a photograph of Nehru. Nehru insisted upon my being included in the photograph, which is reproduced here opposite page 177. The gloom of Artillery Mansions, of London on a February afternoon, of life in the middle of the twentieth century, as it weighed upon the future Prime Minister of India and the Honorary Secretary of the Labour Party Advisory Committee on Imperial Affairs, and on their dingy hats and overcoats, is observable in the photograph. We then walked on up Victoria Street to the House of Commons, talking about life and literature on the way. We parted at the door to the central lobby and I never saw Nehru again.

There was another subject which the Imperial Advisory Committee spent even more time on than that of India—imperialism in Africa, the government of British colonial territories and the treatment of their native inhabitants in Africa. In knowledge and experience of this kind of imperial question the committee was exceptionally strong. In Norman

Leys and MacGregor Ross we had two men who had spent many years of their lives as government servants in Kenya. Among other members were W. M. Macmillan, Director of Colonial Studies in the University of St Andrews, who had been educated and was subsequently a Professor in South Africa; Norman Bentwich, who had been in the Palestine Government and was Professor in Jerusalem; Lord Olivier, who had been in the Colonial Office, a colonial governor, and Secretary of State for India; T. Reid, who had been 26 years in the Ceylon Civil Service; Arthur Creech Jones, M.P., who became Secretary of State for the Colonies in 1946; Drummond Shiels, M.P., who was Parliamentary Under-Secretary of State for India in 1929 and Parliamentary Under-Secretary of State for the Colonies 1929-31. And in the chair we had Charles Roden Buxton, who came of a family which, ever since the abolition of the slave trade, had a hereditary interest and concern in the protection of the rights of subject peoples in the colonial empires.

As soon as the committee got to work I began to put before it memoranda on the government of the colonial empire and on its future. It was soon decided that we should produce for the Executive Committee a detailed report on the political and economic conditions and government in the British African colonial territories, together with, if possible, a detailed long-term policy which we could recommend for adoption by the party. In the next few years we spent a great deal of time and thought on this. As we gradually worked out a policy, the drafting of it was left to Buxton and me. The final report was a formidable document, but it was adopted in its entirety by the Executive Committee and published in a pamphlet under the title *The Empire in Africa: Labour's Policy*.

Rereading the pamphlet today, it seems to me remarkable that such a document should have been produced over 40 years ago and that the principles and policy in it should have been adopted by a political party which was on the point of being returned to power and therefore responsible for the government of the empire. The pamphlet dealt in detail with three subjects: (1) land and labour in our African possessions, (2) government and self-government, (3) education. It pointed out that Britain was pursuing two completely different and contradictory administrative policies in her east- and west-coast African possessions. On the west coast the policy was to preserve native rights in land, prevent its sale to Europeans, and promote a native community of agriculturalists and the growth of native industries; on the east coast the policy was to sell or lease immense areas of land to European syndicates or individuals, to help them to develop the country through 'hired' or forced native labour, and to confine the native population not working for Europeans to 'reserves'. Labour maintained that the east-coast system had deplorable results and that the right policy for the future was to treat land as the property of native communities so that there should be no economic exploitation of the native by the European, and the native should be given the opportunity of developing the economic resources of the land as a free man and for the benefit of the native community. As regards self-government, the declared policy was ultimately the establishment of native representation on Legislative Councils and the gradual transfer of responsible government to these Councils. In order to train Africans to govern themselves, the government must educate them for self-government by making primary education accessible for all African children, by the provision of training colleges for teachers, technical colleges, universities, and experimental and model farms.

When our private or public world is overwhelmed by deserved or undeserved misfortune, no one is more silly or enfuriating than the self-satisfied person who says to us: 'I told you so'. I do not wish to seem to be saying here: 'We told you so'. But nothing is more important than that people should realize that the inveterate political conservatism of human beings—and pre-eminently of the ruling castes and classes—has produced an unending series of unnecessary historical horrors and disasters, ever since the Lord began it by trying to prevent Adam and Eve from learning the truth about the badly devised universe and world which He ill-advisedly had just created. I have lived nearly half a century since the end of the 1914 war, watching go by what must have been probably the most senselessly horrible 50 years in human history. When a hundred years hence the historian can calmly and objectively survey what we have seen and suffered, he will almost certainly conclude that fundamentally the most crucial events of the period were the revolt in Asia and Africa against European imperialism and the liquidation of empires. It has been a process of slow torture to millions of ignorant and innocent human beings— misery and massacre in Asia from India to China, Indo-China, Korea, Vietnam, and Indonesia; anarchy, massacre, and misery in Africa from Algiers and Mau Mau in Kenya to the Congo and Rhodesia. And the objective historian in 2066 will also, I feel sure, conclude that a very great deal of this misery and massacre would have been avoided if the imperialist powers had not blindly and doggedly resisted the demands of the subject peoples, but had carried out their own principles and promises by educating and leading them to independence.

At any rate for 20 years the Advisory Committee persistently pressed upon the Labour Party Executive the necessity for forestalling events by preparing and promoting self-government throughout Britain's colonial empire. We were not concerned with pious promises or generalizations.

We continually put before the Executive detailed practical proposals to meet the actual situation throughout Asia and Africa, whether in India or the Far East, in Kenya or Rhodesia. Again and again the Executive accepted our recommendations and publicly announced them to be the Party's policy either in official pamphlets, drafted by us, or by resolutions passed at annual conferences.

I have said above that it is characteristic of politicians and political parties to announce policies and make promises when in opposition and to forget or repudiate them when in power. Between 1919 and 1939 there were two Labour governments; the first lasted nine months, the second two years, and neither commanded a majority in the House of Commons. Obviously this meant that the time was too short, the programme too crowded, and the voting strength in the House too small for the government to take any major steps in the carrying out of Labour's colonial policy. Nevertheless, the record of Ramsay MacDonald's government in Asia and Africa seemed to me and a good many other people very disappointing by failing to carry out its promises in cases where it could and should have done so. An incident connected with the Advisory Committee, which I have already referred to, will show what I mean. In 1930 in Ramsay's second government Sidney Webb was Secretary of State for the Colonies and Drummond Shiels, a Scottish Labour M.P., was Under-Secretary. Sidney was in politics curiously ambivalent; he must have been born half a little conservative and half a little liberal. He was a progressive, even a revolutionary, in some economic and social spheres; where the British Empire was concerned, he was a common or garden imperialist conservative. Shiels, a medical man by profession, had been an assiduous member of the Advisory Committee and had, I think, learnt a great deal from it. There was nothing of the wild revolutionary about him; he was a hardheaded, liberal-minded, unsentimental Scot, and he was a convinced believer in the necessity for putting into practice the colonial policies worked out by the Advisory Committee and adopted by the Party. He used from time to time to ask me to come to the Colonial Office and discuss things with him. He was dismayed by Sidney's conservatism and his masterly inactivity whenever an opportunity arose to do something different from what Conservative governments and the Colonial Office Civil Servants had endorsed as safe, sound, and 'progressive' for the last half-century.

Towards the end of 1930 the Advisory Committee decided that an opportunity had occurred for trying to get Sidney to implement a small part of the Labour Party's policy. In those days the budgets of Crown Colonies had to be 'laid on the table' of the House of Commons and approved by the Secretary of State. I kept my eye on them so that any important point with regard to a budget might be discussed by the Advisory Committee. I brought the Kenya 1930 budget before the Committee when it was laid on the table of the House. The Committee considered that the proposed expenditure on education and communications was grossly unfair to the natives. The amount to be voted for the education of white children was enormously higher per head than that for the education of African children; the proposed expenditure on roads to serve the white settlers' estates was far higher than that proposed for roads serving the native reserves. On the other hand, the taxation of Africans was proportionally much more severe than that of the settlers.

The Committee decided that Charles Buxton and I should ask Sidney Webb to see us, and that we should point out to him that this discrimination against the African was absolutely opposed to the Labour Government's policy with regard to the education of Africans and promotion of African agriculture, and that the Secretary of State for the Colonies should insist upon a revision of the budget. Sidney, who was now Lord Passfield, for some strange reason asked us to meet him at the House of Lords instead of at the Colonial Office. We had an absurd meeting with Sidney in the red and gold Chamber of the House of Lords, which was, of course, completely empty except for the tiny Secretary of State for the Colonies and the humble chairman and secretary of the Advisory Committee sitting one on either side of him. We got, as I had expected, nothing out of Sidney, who was an expert negotiator and had at his fingers' ends all the arguments of all the men of action for always doing nothing.

This kind of thing, which often happened, made one wonder whether the immense amount of work which these Advisory Committees did was of any use at all. From time to time, off and on, one or other of the most active members would come to me and say that they had had enough of it, that we did an immense amount of work, pouring out reports and memoranda which the Executive Committee accepted, which became 'Party policy', and were then never heard of again. I tried to mollify and console them by recommending to them the rule by which I regulated my life and its hopes and fears: 'Blessed is he who expects nothing, for unexpectedly he may somewhere, some time achieve something'. The two Advisory Committees of which I was secretary did occasionally achieve something, though nothing commensurate with the amount of work we did. We spread through the Labour Party, and to some extent beyond it, some knowledge of the relations between the imperialist powers and the subject peoples of Asia and Africa, and even some realization of the urgent need for revolutionary reform so that there would be a rapid and orderly transition from imperialist rule to self-government. And within the Labour Party— particularly in the Parliamentary Party—the committees did a useful educational job. When Drummond Shiels became Under-Secretary of State for the Colonies in 1929 and Arthur Creech Jones became Secretary of State for the Colonies in 1946, they were far better equipped for their jobs than most M.P.s who get ministerial office, and they both of them did very good work in the Colonial Office. They would, I am sure, have agreed that they had learnt a great deal from the Advisory Committee; the same is true of many rank and file Labour M.P.s who never reached the rank of Minister.

Much of what I have said about the Imperial Advisory Committee applied to the International Advisory Committee. As I have said before, in 1919 the ignorance of foreign affairs in the Labour movement was almost as deep and widespread as the ignorance of imperial affairs. Like its sister committee, the International Committee performed a useful educational function in the Parliamentary Party, and even outside it. It was, perhaps, in membership rather stronger than the Imperial Committee. Until 1937 Charles Buxton was chairman, and two 'experts' in foreign affairs, Philip Noel-Baker and Will Arnold-Forster, did a great deal of work on it. In the 1920s both Ramsay MacDonald and Arthur Henderson kept in close touch with our work and the upper political stratum in the Party always treated the International Committee with rather more respect than the Imperial Committee. For instance, in June 1937, Ernest Bevin attended a meeting and developed to us the points which he had made in an important speech at Southport. There were 23 members present, and all, including Bevin, agreed that a memorandum should be sent to the Executive urging that a constructive peace policy should be put forward in the House of Commons by the front bench. The policy should be that the muddled pacts against aggression recently made by the government should be brought together into a uniform system, and it should be made clear that there would be an instant retort in event of any further act of flagrant aggression by Hitler.

In the terrible years between 1919 and 1939 everything in international affairs was dominated by the emergence of fascism in Europe and the menace of another war. To make up one's mind what seemed to be the right foreign policy and, where passions and prejudices became more and more violent, to keep cool and have the courage of one's convictions was a difficult, often an agonizing business. Even today it is difficult to write truthfully and objectively about those years and the part which one played in them, for the passions and prejudices persist and distort history.

I propose first to give an account of my own attitude during those 20 years and then describe the trend of opinion and policy, as I saw it, in the Advisory Committee and the Labour Party. Like most people on the Left who had some knowledge of European history and of international affairs, I thought that the Versailles Treaty, particularly in the reparation clauses, was punitively unjust to the German people, that it would therefore encourage militarism and desire for revenge in Germany. In this way it had sown the seeds of a second world war. I accepted Maynard's arguments in *The Economic Consequences of the Peace*. It seemed to me disastrous that, instead of supporting and encouraging a pacific, democratic Social-Democratic German government, France and to a lesser extent Britain did everything calculated to weaken and discredit it. The final folly, which played into the hands of the German nationalists and militarists, was the occupation of the Ruhr.

This attitude towards Germany and France was condemned at the time by many people as pro-German. It is still today condemned by some as pro-German and short-sighted; the subsequent history of Hitler, the Nazis, and the 1939 war shows, they say, that the Versailles Treaty was far from being too harsh; it was too mild; the Allies should have made a recrudescence of German militarism impossible by subjecting Germany to a modern version of the treatment by which 2,000 years ago Rome settled Carthage. The real question in this dispute and argument is: which was the cart and which the horse in the years 1919 to 1924? What we said was that, if you demand impossible sums in reparations and unjustly penalize Germany, you will cause economic chaos, you will get no reparations, you will encourage the revival of German militarism and a demand for a revision of the treaty. Here you have sown the seeds of a future war. At least the course of history followed exactly as we had prophesied.

From 1920 to about 1935 I thought that the international policy of the British Government, and therefore of the Labour Party, should be based on the League of Nations; the aim should be to build it up into a really efficient instrument of international government, a system for developing co-operation between states, the peaceful settlement of disputes, and collective security and defence against aggression. At every opportunity I put before the Advisory Committee proposals for implementing this policy. In 1927 Will Arnold-Forster and I drafted a Convention for Pacific Settlement which I put before the Advisory Committee; it was intended to close a gap in the League system as laid down in the Covenant. I received the following characteristic letter from Ramsay MacDonald:

House of Commons   January 17th, 1927
My dear Woolf,

I have been reading a very admirable memorandum put up by you and Arnold Forster regarding a Convention for Pacific Settlement. I think it is really a good piece of work, although one may see the possibility of filling certain detailed proposals, the idea and the general line laid down, seem to me to be excellent. I hope something will be done with it.

Yours very sincerely,

J. Ramsay MacDonald

The cryptic and ungrammatical second sentence is, I think, one of Ramsay's usual backdoors of escape which would enable him, if necessary, when the time came, to sabotage the damned thing with a clear conscience. I rather think that in fact that was precisely what he did do later on when Henderson put our draft before the League of Nations.[1]

All through the 1920s the Labour Party maintained this policy that the strengthening of the League and the collective security system was the only effective way of preventing another war. For 17 out of those 20 years a Conservative government was in power, first under Baldwin and then under Neville Chamberlain; neither of these statesmen believed in a League policy or attempted to use or develop the League as an instrument of peace as between the major powers. In this they were supported by the great majority of conservative politicians, though the curious incident of the Peace Ballot and the Hoare-Laval abortive agreement in 1935 makes it probable that a considerable majority of the rank and file conservatives disagreed with their leaders and would have supported a League policy. The two crucial tests of the League and collective security came in 1932 when Japan attacked China and in 1935 when Italy attacked Abyssinia. In both cases Baldwin with his Foreign Secretaries, Sir John Simon and Sir Samuel Hoare, contrived that the

---

[1] I think this document was what was called 'The General Act', that it was put by Henderson before the General Assembly of the League of Nations and adopted; and then Ramsay refused to allow Henderson to ratify it. Mr Philip Noel-Baker confirms this.

League's collective security system with full sanctions against the aggressors should not be operated.

By 1935 I had personally become convinced that Baldwin and the French statesmen who thought and acted as he did had finally destroyed the League as an instrument for deterring aggression and preventing war. The rise of Hitler to power, his withdrawal from the League, his adoption of compulsory military service, followed by his reoccupation of the demilitarized Rhineland showed the precariousness of the international situation and the necessity to take steps to meet the menace of war from Nazi Germany. I wrote several memoranda to the Advisory Committee urging that the new situation required a new policy: the League was to all intents and purposes dead and it was fatal to go on using it as a mumbled incantation against war; the only possibility of deterring Hitler and preventing war was for Britain and France to unite with those powers, including the U.S.S.R. if possible, who would be prepared to guarantee the small powers against attack by Hitler. I also pointed out that, if the Labour Party was going to support new security agreements against fascist or nazi aggression in place of the obligations under the League Covenant, 'mere negative opposition to a policy of rearmament would be sterile and ineffective'; if the Party really meant to commit itself to a policy of resisting any further acts of aggression by Hitler, then it committed itself to the corollary that Britain must make itself strong enough on land and sea and in the air to defeat Hitler.

These memoranda for the first time provoked a deep division of opinion in the Advisory Committee. But this was only part of a widespread disagreement, a profound, uneasy, often concealed ambivalence which for many years had permeated the Labour movement. There was within it a very strong pacifist element, derived in part from the tradi-

tional internationalism of the Labour and Socialist movements of the nineteenth century, and in part from the strong
Liberal contingent which, with the break up of the Liberal
Party after the war, had joined the Labour Party. To oppose
armaments in general and to vote against the Service esti-
mates in particular was traditional policy. This may or may
not have made sense when the pacifists and their parties were
opposing the jingo or imperialist policies of Conservative
governments which made the armaments necessary. But
when the pacifist Labour people (and surviving Liberals)
accepted the obligations of the League Covenant and its
collective security system, they were faced by an entirely
different situation. How could they agree to commit Britain
to join with other members of the League in resisting any act
of aggression by military means, if necessary, and at the same
time refuse to provide the armaments which alone could make
such military resistance feasible? There were some Labour
pacifists who, when confronted with this dilemma, logically
took the view that the obligation under the Covenant to use
force to resist aggression could only lead to world wars and
should be repudiated. But there was a far larger number who
never faced the dilemma and whose policy therefore contained a profound and dangerous inconsistency. The
dilemma and the disagreement were for years habitually and
discreetly ignored or glossed over. But as the menace of
Hitler and another war became more manifest, the divergence
of view within the Party rose to the surface. The show-down
came at the Labour Party Conference in Brighton in 1935.
George Lansbury had been Leader of the Parliamentary
Party since 1931; he was one of those sentimental, muddle-
headed, slightly Pecksniffian good men who mean so well in
theory and do so much harm in practice. He was a convinced
believer in the desirability of having the best of two contradictory worlds, of undertaking the obligation under the

League to resist aggression without providing the arms which would be required for the resistance. At the Conference Ernest Bevin, who took the view—with which I agreed—that, if you were going to fight against Hitler or any other aggressor, you must have arms with which to fight—rose in the pretty Regency Pavilion and made the most devastating attack upon the unfortunate Lansbury that I have ever listened to in a public meeting. As I said in *Beginning Again* (p. 221), he battered the poor man to political death—Lansbury afterwards resigned the leadership—and, although I was politically entirely on the side of Bevin in this controversy, I could not help shrinking from the almost indecent cruelty with which he destroyed the slightly lachrymose, self-righteous Lansbury.

The Advisory Committee was, as I said, divided, like the Party, on this question. There was a majority in favour of the League system of collective security and armaments adequate for resisting aggression. But there was a minority consisting of some who took the pacifist view and, with their eyes open, opposed rearmament and of some who, as it seemed to me, shut their eyes to the dilemma, inconsistently combining support of resistance to aggression with opposition to rearmament. In consequence there was never unanimity on the Committee for my memoranda; the Committee always decided to forward them to the Executive Committee without any positive recommendation. A (to me) sad result of this disagreement was Charles Buxton's resignation of the chairmanship of the Advisory Committee. He was essentially what Pericles, Aristotle, and Theophrastus would have called a 'good man' both in public and in private life. He was really mentally and emotionally a nineteenth-century non-conformist Liberal of the best type and therefore never completely at home in the twentieth-century Labour Party. A gentle man, he was on the side of civilization, hating violence of

all kinds, regarding it as a first duty to devote oneself un-
selfishly to the public good. It was characteristic of him that
he joined the Quakers and tried to translate the ethics of
the Friends into political terms. It was a curious trait in this
kind of nineteenth-century Liberal often to develop a not
altogether rational attachment to some foreign nation,
nationality, or race. There were pro-Turks, pro-Americans,
pro-Boers, pro-Bulgarians, and in the twentieth century pro-
Germans. In the Balkan wars of 1912 and 1913 Charles
became a pro-Bulgarian, and in 1914 he and his brother
Noel went to the Balkans on a mission the object of which was
to keep Bulgaria out of the war. A Turk tried to assassinate
them and shot Charles through the lung. The Versailles
Treaty made him what was called a pro-German in the grim
years of peace, and I do not think that in the 1930s, when
Hitler and the Nazis came to power, he could bring himself
to face the facts and the terrible menace of war and barbarism from Germany. He necessarily took the extreme pacifist
view, and, as the majority on the committee held the views
which I did, he resigned the chairmanship. He and I had
worked closely together on both Advisory Committees for
many years, and it was sad to see him go, though our political disagreement made no difference to our personal
friendship.

My views on this subject involved me in a curious incident
in 1938. When Hitler invaded Austria in March, I was convinced that the last glimmer of hope of preventing war was
drastic action on the part of Britain and France, and that
this would require a dramatic change of policy by the Labour
Party. The evening after the invasion I was at a meeting or
party at which several Labour people were present—inevitably discussing the situation. I said that I thought that the
Executive Committee and the Parliamentary Party ought
to have a joint meeting and instruct the Leader of the

Parliamentary Party to make a formal public statement on their behalf as follows: The danger of further aggression by Germany and of war was so acute that the Labour Party considered that drastic action was necessary on the part of Britain and France to warn Hitler that any further aggression would be resisted; with a view to this the Party would be willing to enter a coalition government under Mr Winston Churchill pledged to forward this policy and would agree to an immediate introduction of conscription and rearmament. Over the week-end I was rung up by someone who had heard what I said; he told me that my arguments had convinced him and some others and they thought it important to try to get the Labour leaders to take action along the line which I had suggested—would I come and discuss what we might do with a few people on Tuesday? I was dining out on the Tuesday, but after dinner I left my party and went round to Wansborough's flat in Russell Square. There I found Douglas Jay, Tommy Balogh, and, I think, Hugh Gaitskell and Evan Durbin; there may have been one or two others. After some discussion it was decided that we should try to get hold of one or two of the leaders and induce them to put my proposition before a joint meeting of the Labour Party and T.U.C. which was to be held later in the week. One of us—I forget who it was—undertook to see A. V. Alexander, who seemed to be one of the most likely leaders to put forward the policy, and I agreed to talk to Phil Noel-Baker. Alexander agreed with our arguments and proposal and half promised to come out publicly in favour of it at the conference if he could get support beforehand within the Parliamentary Party. I could not get hold of Phil, because he was at a meeting of the International in Paris. The whole thing fizzled out: Alexander could get little or no support and drew back. Nothing was done—and the herd, Europe and the world, continued downhill all the way under Hitler's direction and 'ran violently down a steep place' into war.

I must leave the subject of politics. The years 1930 to 1939 were horrible both publicly and privately. If one was middle aged or old and so had known at least a 'sort of a kind' of civilization, it was appalling impotently to watch the destruction of civilization by a powerful nation completely subservient to a gang of squalid, murderous hooligans. My nephew, Quentin Bell, who was 20 years old in 1930, has recently described what it felt like to be a young man alive in those years:

> Who but we can recall the horror of that period? Of course, it was not continuous: we had our gaieties, our moments of hope, of exhilaration, of triumph even. Nevertheless, they were years of mounting despair: unable to compound our internecine quarrels, unable to shake the complacency of a torpid nation, we saw the champions of tyranny, war and racial persecution winning a succession of ever easier victories. In those twilight days it was bloody to be alive and to be young was very hell.

To the middle aged, i.e. to those who were already going downhill all the way to old age or death, it was also often in those twilight days bloody to be alive and very hell to be no longer young. In 1938 I wrote a play, *The Hotel*, about the horrors of the twilight age of Europe, the kind of hush that fell upon us before the final catastrophe. It was published in 1939 and was republished by the Dial Press in America in 1963. I can best explain how I came to write it by quoting the introduction which I wrote for the American edition of 1963:

> It is a long time since I wrote this play, *The Hotel*, and it seems even longer. It was written and published in England just before the 1939 war, and Hitler and Stalin

and Mussolini—the nazis, communists, and fascists—finally destroyed the world in which it was written. That, after all, is what the play is about; what it prophesied has happened. Looking about us today, we can say with Stanovich: 'The ceiling's down; the clock's smashed; and there's no door. There's no back to the hotel and no boiler room, and the wind coming through is fair cruel. . . . What a place! What a place!'

That, perhaps, is all that the author can say about the play in an introduction to its publication, after more than twenty years, in America. It was written in the tension of those horrible years of Hitler's domination and of the feeling that he would inevitably destroy civilization. There is, however, one small point which I can add as author; I had never written a play before I wrote *The Hotel*. But for a long time I had wanted to write one in which the scene would be the entrance hall of a hotel, with the revolving door through which a string of heterogeneous characters would have their entrances and their exits. It is a scene in real life which always seems to me infinitely dramatic. And then one day in 1938 I suddenly saw that my hotel on the stage might be both realistic and symbolic, the *Grand Hôtel du Paradis* which had become the *Grand Hôtel de l'Univers et du Commerce*, with Peter Vajoff, the proprietor, standing in front of the fire—and with bugs in the beds.

I was 40 in 1920 and 60 in 1940. The twilight was in one's private as well as in public life. Death is, according to Swinburne, one of the three things which 'make barren our lives'; 'death', said Virginia in the last paragraph of *The Waves*, 'death is the enemy'. If one does not oneself die young, the moment comes in one's life when death begins permanently to loom in the background of life. Parents, brothers, and sisters, who were parts of one's unconscious mind and memories, die; the intimate friends of one's youth die; our loves die. Each death as it comes, so inevitable of course, but always so unexpected and so outrageous, is like a blow on the head or the heart. Into each grave goes some tiny portion of oneself.

This erosion of life by death began for Virginia and me in the early 1930s and gathered momentum as we went downhill to war and her own death. It began on 21 January 1932 when Lytton Strachey died of cancer. This was the beginning of the end of what we used to call Old Bloomsbury. Lytton was perhaps the most individual person whom I have ever known. His father was a Strachey and his mother a Grant; he came, therefore, on both sides from one of those distinguished upper middle-class families of country gentlemen who in the nineteenth century found their professional and economic home in India or the army. The mixture of Strachey and Grant blood in Lytton's family produced remarkable results; I gave some account of it in *Sowing* (pp. 186-192). It consisted of ten sons and daughters, all of whom were extremely intelligent and many of them intellectually remarkable. Lytton was unquestionably the most brilliant. He had an extremely subtle and supple mind, with a tremendously quick flicker of wit and humour continually playing through his thought. Everything about him—his mind, body, voice, thought, wit, and humour—was individually his own, unlike that of anyone else. His conversation was entrancing, for his talk was profounder, wittier, more interesting, and original than his writing. This was one of the reasons why his books, brilliant and successful though they were, slightly disappointed the expectations of many who had known him as a young man of 20. He had a tremendous reputation among the intellectuals as an undergraduate at Cambridge and we thought that he might well become a great Voltairian historian or biographer. He never achieved that, though *Eminent Victorians* and *Queen Victoria* are much more remarkable than they are currently and momentarily judged to be, and they obviously had a considerable influence on biography and history in the 20 years which followed their publication.

Lytton's personal influence on his own generation and those which immediately followed it at Cambridge was also very great. His personality was so strong that he imposed it, intellectually and even physically, upon people, especially the young. You could tell who saw much of him, for they almost inevitably acquired the peculiar Strachey voice which had a marked rhythm and, in his case, a habit of rising from the depths in the bass to a falsetto squeak. Lytton repelled and exasperated some people, particularly the dyed in the wool, athletic, public school Englishman, with no (but O so much) nonsense about him. By public school standards he did not look right, speak right, or even act right, and, apart from such major vices, he had the lesser faults of arrogance and selfishness. He would therefore often exasperate even his most intimate friends—but only momentarily and superficially. Fundamentally he was an extremely affectionate person and had (in life and conversation, though not always in his books) a great purity of intellectual honesty and curiosity. That was why his death shocked and saddened us so painfully: it was the beginning of the end, for it meant that the spring had finally died out of our lives.

After Lytton's death Carrington tried unsuccessfully to commit suicide. It was clear that sooner or later she would try again. Ralph asked us to come down to Ham Spray and see her; he thought we might be able to do some good. On March 10 I drove down with Virginia in the morning. It was one of the most painful days I have ever slowly suffered. The day itself was incongruously lovely, sunny, sparkling.

I remember most vividly Carrington's great pale blue eyes and the look of dead pain in them. The house was very cold; she gave us lunch and tea and we talked and she talked quite frankly about Lytton and his ways and his friends. At first she seemed calm and cowed—'helpless, deserted', as Virginia said, 'like some small animal left'. There was a moment when she kissed Virginia and burst into tears, and said: 'There is nothing left for me to do. I did everything for Lytton. But I've failed in everything else. People say he was very selfish to me. But he gave me everything else. I was devoted to my father. I hated my mother. Lytton was like a father to me. He taught me everything I know. He read poetry and French to me.' We left after tea, and just before we got into the car Virginia said to her: 'Then you will come and see us next week—or not—just as you like?' And Carrington said: 'Yes, I will come, or not'. Next morning she shot herself.

Two years later Roger Fry died, as the result of a fall in his room. Roger belonged, of course, to an earlier Cambridge generation than we did—he was 14 years my elder, but he was an integral part of Old Bloomsbury and of our lives. I have tried to describe his character in *Beginning Again* (pp. 93-98) and I will not repeat myself here. From 1920 until his death 14 years later he was indeed, as I have said, part of our lives. Living in Bernard Street, just round the corner from Gordon Square where the Bells lived and Tavistock Square where we lived, he was in and of Bloomsbury. With his death again something was torn out of our lives.

On July 18, 1937, death struck again when Vanessa's son, Julian, was killed driving an ambulance in the Spanish civil war. The story of Julian's life and death has been told at length, and with great skill, sympathy, and understanding, by two Americans, Peter Stansky and William Abrahams, in their book *Journey to the Frontier*. It would be silly of me to try to do in a page what they have done so well and fully in so many. I saw him at close quarters grow from a rampageous, riproaring child into a very large, serious, gay, rampageous youth and finally man—he was 29 when he was killed. His mother and father, Vanessa Stephen and Clive Bell, were extraordinarily dissimilar in mind, temperament, and looks, and there was, I think, an unresolved discord in Julian's genes the effect of which could be traced in his character, mind, and life. I have never known any child make so much noise so cheerfully, and he never quite grew up: there was still something of the child, riproaring round the sitting-room in Gordon Square, in the young man of 25 driving a car or having a love affair. He was an extremely attractive and lovable person and highly intelligent, but, like all ebullient and erratic people, he could at moments be exasperating. Virginia was devoted to him and so was I. His death and the manner of it, a sign and symptom of the 1930s, made another terrible hole in our lives.

Finally—a very different death—just before the war, on July 2, 1939, my mother died. She was then an old woman of 87 or 88; but in many ways she never grew old. She still retained an intense interest and curiosity in all sorts of things and persons, and was physically very active. Being short and fat and impulsive, and unwilling to accommodate herself to the limitations and infirmities of old age, she was always tripping over a footstool in her room or the curb in the street and ending with a broken arm or leg. At the age of 87 she did this once too often, for the broken limb this time led to complications and she died in the London Clinic. I described her character at some length in *Sowing* (pp. 31-35); of her nine surviving children, four, in mind and body, were predominantly Woolfs, my father's family; two were predominantly de Jonghs, my mother's family; and two were half and half. I was very much my father's and very little my mother's son, and there were many sides of my character and mind which were unsympathetic to my mother; I had no patience with her invincible, optimistic sentimentality, and my un-sentimentality, which seemed to her hardness and harshness, distressed her. There was no quarrel or rift between us, and I always went to see her once a week or once a fortnight up to the day of her death—but, though she would never have admitted it even to herself, I was, I think, her least-loved child. But there is some primitive valve in our hearts, some primeval cell in our brains—handed down to us from our reptilian, piscine, or simian ancestors, perhaps—which makes us peculiarly, primordially sensitive to the mother's death. As the coffin is lowered into the grave, there is a second severance of the umbilical chord.

With my mother's death we reached the beginning of the second war and, therefore, the end of this volume. I will actually end it with a little scene which took place in the last months of peace. They were the most terrible months of my life, for, helplessly and hopelessly, one watched the inevit-able approach of war. One of the most horrible things at that time was to listen on the wireless to the speeches of Hitler, the savage and insane ravings of a vindictive underdog who suddenly saw himself to be all-powerful. We were in Rodmell during the late summer of 1939, and I used to listen to those ranting, raving speeches. One afternoon I was planting in the orchard under an apple-tree iris reticulata, those lovely violet flowers which, like the daffodils, 'come before the swallow dares and take the winds of March with beauty'. Suddenly I heard Virginia's voice calling to me from the sitting-room window: 'Hitler is making a speech'. I shouted back: 'I shan't come. I'm planting iris and they will be flowering long after he is dead.' Last March, 21 years after Hitler committed suicide in the bunker, a few of those violet flowers still flowered under the apple-tree in the orchard.

INDEX

INDEX

INDEX

INDEX

Tawney, R. H., 217-18
Teed, Colonel, 180-81
Tessimond, A. S. J., 175
Three Guineas, 27, 157
Times Literary Supplement, 17, 61
To the Lighthouse, 64, 143, 146-47, 153, 155
Tomlinson, H. M., 92, 93, 97
Two Stories, 59, 66n, 68

Unwritten Novel, An, 60, 61

Verrall, Jacob, 12, 13, 15
Versailles, Treaty of, 28, 38, 240-41
Village in the Jungle, The, 47, 68n
Voyage Out, The, 16, 55, 58, 63, 68, 143

Walpole, Hugh, 152
war, history and prevention of, 195-205; 1914-1918 war, 9, 13, 40, 169, 197-98, 200, 218, 221, 226, 235; 1939-1945 war, 13, 22, 48, 202, 248, 254; *see also* Spanish civil war
Watkins, Ann (agent), 89
Waves, The, 53-54, 59, 60, 144, 146, 147-48, 152, 155, 156, 173, 206, 249
Webb, Beatrice, 218-20
Webb, Sidney (later Lord Passfield), 218-20, 236-38
Whitley Council for the Civil Service, 209-10; *see also* Civil Service Arbitration Tribunal
Whittall, James, 79-80, 81
Wigram, Ralph, 185-86, 191
Woolf, Leonard, at Hogarth House, Richmond, 9-14; buys Monks House, Rodmell, 14-15; edits *International Review*, 17-21; attitude towards communism, 19-27, 28-33; stands for Parliament, 33-42, 46; defeated, 46; and operation of Hogarth Press, 66-69, 73-83, 158-63, 169-73, 176-77; helps to translate Russian books, 67, 74; writes *Socialism and Co-operation*, 83-88; 'Pearls and Swine' and America, 88-90; writes for *Contemporary Review*, 90-91; on *Nation*, as leader writer, 91-96; as literary editor, 97-98, 128-41, 130-34; resigns, 141; attitude towards 'society', and hostesses, 101-107; and T. S. Eliot, 107-

111; and Bloomsbury group, 111-18; decision to move to London, 118; at Tavistock Square, 119-22, 124-127; friendship with Edwin Muir, 130-32; views on judicial injustice, 136-38, 212-13; finances, 142-45; trip to Cornwall, 153-54; gives verdict on *The Years*, 155; publishes Freud and the International Psycho-Analytical Library, 163-68; meeting with Freud, 168-69; takes John Lehmann into the Hogarth Press, 172; publishes *New Signatures*, 173-176; purchases first car, 177; stays at Cassis, 179-83; tours France, 181-85; acquires marmoset, Mitz, 186-88; travels with Mitz in Holland, Germany, Italy, and France, 188-95; writes *After the Deluge*, Vols. I and II, 196-97, 203-204; and *Principia Politica*, 204; attitude towards fate of his work after his death, 205-206; edits *Political Quarterly*, 206-209; serves on Civil Service Arbitration Tribunal, 209-212, 213-17; and General Strike, 217-18; work for Fabian Society, 218-20; as secretary of Labour Party Imperial Advisory Committee, 221-239; meeting with Gandhi, 228-30; with Nehru, 230-32; as secretary of Labour Party International Advisory Committee, 239-48; writes *The Hotel*, 248; death of friends and family, 250-54
Woolf, Marie (author's mother), 253-54
Woolf, Virginia, *Night and Day* and *Kew Gardens* published, 16-17, 59-60; attitude towards political issues, 27, 41-42; illness and threatened illness, 49-51; routine and accoutrements of writing, 52-53, 54n; intensity of concentration while writing, and emotional reaction upon completion of each work, 54-55, 148-53; sensitivity to criticism, 56-58, 148-49, 151-52; publishes *Monday or Tuesday*, 59; writes *Jacob's Room*, 60-61; *Mrs Dalloway*, 61, 83; journalism, and attitude towards reviewing, 61-62; earnings from her writing, 1919-1924, 63-64; decision

to have her books published by Hogarth Press, 68; earnings from *Jacob's Room*, 73-74; and culture, 80-81; love of 'society', and parties, 98-101, 107, 115-18; friendship with T. S. Eliot, 107-11; with V. Sackville-West, 111-12; and Bloomsbury group, 114-17; desire to live in London, 117-18; at Tavistock Square, 53, 123; increased income from writing, 143; success of *Orlando, Flush,* and *The Years*, 144-45; near-breakdown while revising proofs of *The Years*, 153-56; productivity, 156-57; writes *Between the Acts*, 157; meeting with Freud, 168-69; passion for travelling, 178; attitude towards fate of her work after her death, 205-206

Wright, Harold, 138, 140

Writer's Diary, A, 148; and quoted *passim*

Years, The, 55, 144, 145-46, 147, 151, 152, 153-57

Yeats, W. B., 106

zoos, 42-46

Zuckerman, Solly, 150n

5002   £8 – 157

WILLIAM HUDSPETH-LAMB
F.C.S.D.
NOTTINGHAM COLLEGE OF
ART & CRAFTS.

Historic
Ornament

PATTERN WITHOUT PAIN

By Allen W. Seaby

A series of concise, informative talks on design and its treatment, written for students by the former Professor of Art in the University of Reading. It deals with elements, repeated ornament, the drop pattern, distribution, the use of plant and other natural forms, colour arrangements and contrasts, etc. Containing 128 pages of text, nearly 100 line illustrations from drawings by the Author, and 8 plates in colour.

Demy 8vo

COMPOSITION

By Cyril C. Pearce, R.B.A.

An Introductory Analysis of the Principles of Pictorial Design. With chapters on Tone, Distribution, Graduation, Scale, Perspective, Rhythm, Harmony and Balance of Colour. Illustrated by 130 comparative and analytical sketches and diagrams, 7 plates in colour and 28 full-page illustrations from paintings by Turner, Goya, Whistler, Rembrandt and many other masters.

Demy 8vo   *Second Edition*

BATSFORD BOOKS

CHINESE PAINTED SILKS, 18TH CENTURY.

A Manual of
HISTORIC
ORNAMENT

TREATING UPON THE EVOLUTION, TRADITION, AND DEVELOPMENT OF ARCHITECTURE & THE APPLIED ARTS

PREPARED FOR THE USE OF STUDENTS AND CRAFTSMEN

BY RICHARD GLAZIER

HON. ASSOCIATE OF THE ROYAL COLLEGE OF ART
ASSOCIATE OF THE ROYAL INSTITUTE OF BRITISH ARCHITECTS
LATE HEAD MASTER OF THE MUNICIPAL SCHOOL OF ART, MANCHESTER

SIXTH EDITION, REVISED AND ENLARGED
WITH 700 ILLUSTRATIONS BY THE AUTHOR
AND FROM PHOTOGRAPHS, ETC.

B. T. BATSFORD LTD.
LONDON ● NEW YORK
TORONTO ● SYDNEY

First Published	.	.	.	.	.	1899
Second Edition	.	.	.	.	.	1906
Third Edition	.	.	.	.	.	1914
Fourth Edition	.	.	.	.	.	1926
Fifth Edition	.	.	.	.	.	1933
Sixth Edition	.	.	.	.	.	1948

MADE AND PRINTED IN GREAT BRITAIN AT
THE UNIVERSITY PRESS, LTD., ABERDEEN, FOR
THE PUBLISHERS B. T. BATSFORD, LTD.
LONDON: 15 NORTH AUDLEY STREET, W.1
AND MALVERN WELLS, WORCESTERSHIRE.
NEW YORK: 122 EAST 55TH STREET
TORONTO: 480-6 UNIVERSITY AVENUE
SYDNEY: 156 CASTLEREAGH STREET

NOTE TO THE FIFTH EDITION

After the thorough revision of the previous edition it has not been thought necessary to make many additions, but some plates in colour have been included, for the blocks of which we have to thank Herr Jacobs of the well-known firm of Julius Hoffmann, Stuttgart. In addition a number of line and half-tone illustrations have been added, and the whole work thoroughly overhauled and rearranged. The correction of a number of minor errors and misprints has also been carried out, and in this connection the co-operation of Mr. Percy L. Marks is gratefully appreciated.

To the Board of Education thanks are due for the photograph of a Louis XIV. cabinet, and to the British Museum for permission to reproduce Figs. 2, 3, 4, 6 and 8, Plate 1, from their "Handbook to the Ethnographical Collections."

THE PUBLISHERS.

August, 1933.

PREFACE TO FOURTH EDITION

When the time came for the third edition of this work to go out of print, the late Mr. Richard Glazier had passed away. Nothing, of course, could be done to alter his drawings except to reproduce afresh some plates where the engraving was defective. In regard to enlargement and revision, after the benefit of consultation with Mr. Henry Cadness, Mr. Glazier's friend and colleague for many years, it was decided to add a series of 16 photographic plates, with descriptive accounts where required, to supplement the extant series, and call further attention to certain aspects of art attracting prominent notice at the present time. The research in connection with this project has been confided to Mr. Francis M. Kelly, the author of "Historic Costume," and after a number of difficulties in obtaining suitable material, plates have been prepared of Illuminated Manuscripts, Engraved Ornament, late Gothic and Renascence Wood and Metal work, and similar subjects. The plates devoted to the work of the late 17th and 18th centuries are included in view of the present interest in that period; in the same way it has been thought advantageous to supplement the sections on Architectural Art and Textile Fabrics, and to include some examples of Peasant Art. For these Mr. Kelly has contributed the descriptions and has selected the examples illustrated from a very large number of experimental photographs. In addition, the text has been carefully revised by expert advisers, and a number of further text illustrations added from various sources.

While attempting to broaden its scope and increase its usefulness, the object of the book, to give a concise general view of Historic Ornament, and to supply a handy manual for students and schools, has been kept in mind, and, it is hoped, maintained. Hence much revision, rearrangement and addition which was possible and indeed advantageous, in regard to both text and illustrations, has been abstained from, to keep the work an inexpensive and simple text-book.

Thanks are due to various experts who have revised the text and advised on the selection and grouping of new illustrations.

THE PUBLISHERS.

October, 1926.

REFACE

This manual has been prepared with the three-fold object of giving an elementary knowledge of Architecture and Historic Ornament, of awakening a responsive and sympathetic feeling for the many beautiful and interesting remains of ancient and mediæval civilization, and lastly, of directing the attention of students and craftsmen to the beauty, suggestiveness, and vitality of the Industrial arts of the past, and their intimate relation to the social and religious life of the people.

The advantages to be derived by students and craftsmen from such a study are manifold, for, by careful study of these arts we may see the capabilities and limitations of material, the appropriateness and application of ornament, the continuity of line and form—yet with a marked diversity of enrichment and treatment—the interest and significance of detail, and the customs, myths, and traditions of the past, with their range of thought and expression.

The illustrations, which have been chosen expressly for this work, are typical examples of each period or style, and are produced in line as being the method best suited to the requirements of students, giving definition, emphasis, and constructive qualities of design rather than pictorial effect.

In the appendix will be found a list of text-books and works of reference, which may be studied with considerable advantage by students desiring further information upon this important subject.

RICHARD GLAZIER.

MANCHESTER,
1899.

CONTENTS

ALPHABETICAL LIST OF PLATES

ALPHABETICAL LIST OF PLATES—*cont.*

ILLUSTRATIONS IN THE TEXT

Part I
The History and
Development of
Architecture & Ornament

1. Eskimo engraving on bone.
*2. Ornament with fish hawks, Solomon Islands.
*3. Basketwork hat, with whaling scene, N.W. America.
*4. Ornament derived from creeper shoots, Iban, Borneo.
5. Painted earthenware, Ica, Peru.
*6. Dragonfly diaper, Bushongo pipe, Congo.
7. Bird ornament, textile, Pachacamac, Peru.
*8. Shale pipe, with totemic carvings, Queen Charlotte Islands.
9. Vase from Knossos, Crete.

British Museum Ethnographical Collection.

# PRIMITIVE ORNAMENT

The ornament of primitive races presents a vast field for study, which it is difficult to focus adequately, and which has not yet been fully investigated. It is only possible here to note a few isolated instances. Some of its manifestations have a distinct degree of kinship to the scanty remains which have survived of the work of the long prehistoric eras, and also show similarities with departments of decorative art in such highly-developed yet self-contained civilizations as Crete and Peru. Examples of the work of these two latter styles are here included for comparison, figs. 5, 7 and 9. The first patterns were probably the simple rows of roughly incised diagonal lines on early vessels such as the beakers. Geometrical patterning on pottery naturally originates readily and spontaneously, and is found with a considerable degree of similarity in many parts of the world. These naturally develop after ages into chevrons, frets, scrolls and wave-like forms, which can be effectively combined, distributed and coloured, as in vases from Istria, and Cypriote work. One mask from Benin has interlacements markedly reminiscent of Celtic ornament. Geometrical design is used with much effectiveness by the Indians of the Americas, as in wampum beadwork, basketry, and blankets, and also in the leather-work and palm-cloth of Central Africa. In metal and ceramic work of the Iron Age abstract design is found with naturalistic or conventional figures, which are used in panel or frieze form. But widely distant peoples have sometimes succeeded in the effective conventionalization of animal and plant forms, as in a dragonfly diaper wood-carving on a Congo pipe (fig. 6), and the hawk-ornament from the Solomon Islands (fig. 2). The sea forms of Cretan pottery are vigorous if naturalistic. From Borneo comes some effective floral ornament derived from the shoots of a creeper (fig. 4), and the Kenyak-Kayan tribes have mixed with the scrolls of their carved houseboards humanistic figures and dog-like forms. The Eskimo have graphically and ingeniously represented the activities of a whole settlement by engraving in narrow strips on ivory or bone (fig. 1). The Indians of North-west America have inserted a version of a whale hunt on a hat of basketwork (fig. 3), and like many other peoples, can turn the human face to account by varied repetition. The totem poles of British Columbia are crowded with figures and other devices, in a style which is applied to various objects, and often rises, as in a shale pipe of the Haida of Queen Charlotte Island, to a Breughel-like grotesqueness (fig. 8). Tribal ornament ranges from a few casual scrappy patterns, like those of peoples of such low type as the aboriginal Australians, to vigorous pattern, well distributed, and carried out with feeling for the character of the material. The craftsman has generally made use of his chances, and produced achievements among races of widely differing culture and many periods all over the globe.

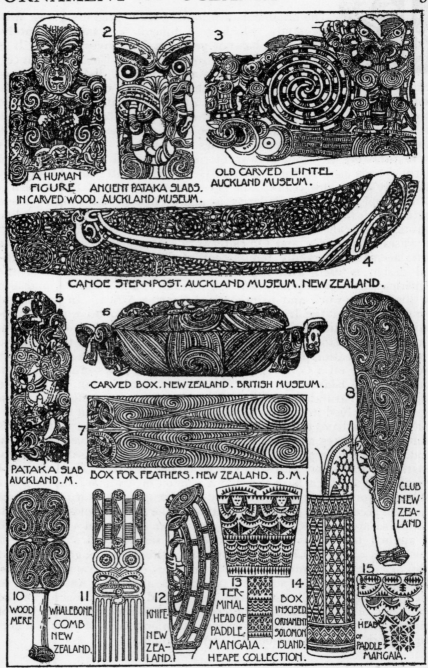

1. A HUMAN FIGURE IN CARVED WOOD. AUCKLAND MUSEUM.

2. ANCIENT PATAKA SLABS.

3. OLD CARVED LINTEL AUCKLAND MUSEUM.

4. CANOE STERNPOST. AUCKLAND MUSEUM. NEW ZEALAND.

5. PATAKA SLAB AUCKLAND. M.

6. CARVED BOX. NEW ZEALAND. BRITISH MUSEUM.

7. BOX FOR FEATHERS. NEW ZEALAND. B.M.

8. CLUB NEW ZEALAND

10. WOOD MERE

11. WHALEBONE. COMB NEW ZEALAND.

12. KNIFE. NEW ZEA-LAND.

13. TERMINAL HEAD OF PADDLE. MANGAIA. HEAPE COLLECTION.

14. BOX INCISED ORNAMENT SOLOMON ISLAND.

15. HEAD OF PADDLE MANGAIA.

ORNAMENT OF OCEANIA

The ornamentation of the people of the Pacific Isles is full of interest, and is remarkable for the evolution and perfecting of an ornamental style by a primitive people, with myths and traditions purely local, and in no way influenced by other nations. It is a style of ornament full of meaning and symbolism, yet simple in detail and arrangement, not founded upon the beautiful vegetation and flora of their islands, but upon abstract forms derived from the human figure, and arranged with a pleasing geometrical precision remarkable for a primitive people.

The ornamental art of these people may be broadly divided into provinces, each with its distinct ornamental characteristics and traditions, New Zealand showing the highest development and Australia the lowest in the ornament of Polynesia and Melanesia.

Much of the ornament is purely linear, consisting of parallel and zig-zag lines; that of Australia consists almost entirely of these lines incised in the ground and occasionally filled in with colour. In New Guinea a higher development is reached, the ornament, of straight and curved lines, being carved in flat relief. In the pro-

ORNAMENT FROM A CLUB. SAMOA.

NEW GUINEA SHIELD

vince of Tonga-Samoa, the surface is divided into small fields, and the linear ornament runs in a different direction on each of the fields. The Hervey and Austral Islands are distinguished by their remarkable adaptations of the human female figure, the illustrations given here showing the original type and its ornamental development. These examples, together with the circular eye pattern, form the elements of the Hervey province, of which the Heape collection contains many fine examples. In the Solomon Islands the

linear ornament is occasionally interspersed with an inlay of angular pieces of mother of pearl. The New Zealand province is distinguished by its skilful pierced carving, the beauty of its spiral forms adapted from the human figure (figs. 1-12), and the constant use of the border here given. No preliminary design was used, nor was the pattern outlined upon the object of the decoration. It was, so to speak, evolved from the artist's head as he worked, much as a musician improvises at the piano. This art, once general, now appears to be falling rapidly into oblivion.

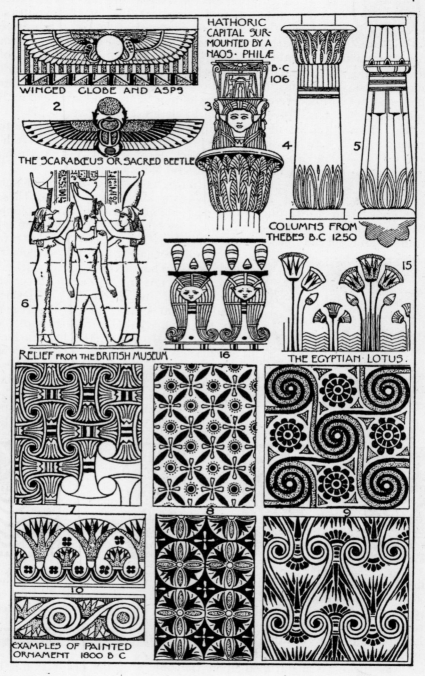

WINGED GLOBE AND ASPS

2

THE SCARABÆUS OR SACRED BEETLE

HATHORIC CAPITAL SUR-MOUNTED BY A NAOS · PHILÆ

B.C 106

3

4   5

COLUMNS FROM THEBES B.C 1250

6

RELIEF FROM THE BRITISH MUSEUM

16

15

THE EGYPTIAN LOTUS.

7   8   9

10

EXAMPLES OF PAINTED ORNAMENT 1800 B C

EGYPTIAN ORNAMENT

The history of Egypt extends from nearly 4000 B.C. to 340 B.C.

The capitals of the Ancient Empire comprised Memphis and Abydos ; of the Middle Empire, Thebes, Luxor and Tanis ; and of the New Empire, Sais and Bubastes. The remarkable civilization of these early dynasties is attested by the many fine remains of architecture, sculpture, and decorative arts that enrich our national museums. The three great periods of Egyptian art are *Memphite* (fourth, fifth, and sixth dynasties) in which figure sculpture appears somewhat heavy, but accurate ; the *Theban* Age (from the eleventh to the twenty-first dynasty) ; and the *Sait* or Neo-Memphite Age. The sculptures of the second Theban Empire are important and numerous.

The Sphinx, half animal and half human, is probably of the VI. dynasty, yet it is singular that all the earliest sculptures of the III. and IV. dynasties with which we are acquainted were realistic portraiture, remarkable for fidelity to nature. Kings, queens, and individuals of note were finely sculptured, frequently of a colossal size. But the Deities, Amen Sekhet, Horus, Hathor, Isis, and Osiris were represented in the later dynasties by small votive statuettes, noticeable for their number rather than for their artistic qualities, never reaching the excellence or vitality of the earlier period. Much of the architectural enrichment was in *Cavo Relievo*, a peculiarly Egyptian mode of ornamentation, the outline of the figures, birds, or flowers being sunk into the surface of the granite or basalt, and then carved within this sunk outline, leaving the ground or bed raised, these reliefs being invariably painted red, blue, green, and yellow. The frieze, which in the hands of the Greeks, at a later period, became their principal ornamental field, was used by the Egyptians in superposed bands, showing, in *cavo relievo*, the industrial arts and pursuits—weaving, glass blowing, and the making of pottery ; ploughing, sowing, and reaping ; also hunting and fishing. The composition and sculpture of these incidents was simple, refined, and purely decorative, with a *naïveté* and unaffectedness appropriate to the architectonic conditions. Mingled with these incidents were the beautiful hieroglyphs, or picture writing of the Egyptians. Figs. 7-13 are examples of painted decorations showing the spiral construction of lines, together with the symbolic treatment of the Lotus, the latter being regarded by the Egyptians as a symbol of fertility and of a new life, hence the profusion with which it was used in their decorative work. Great fertility of invention was displayed in enriching their architectural capitals with the Lotus, the Papyrus, and the Palm. A singular feature introduced during the XVIII. dynasty was the Hathor Capital, surmounted by a small Naos. During the Ptolemaic period— 300 B.C.—the Hathor Capital was placed upon the vertical bell-shaped capital (fig. 3).

7

BAS-RELIEF.
BRITISH MUSEUM.
1

COLUMN
FROM
PERSE-
POLIS
4

2

3

ORNAMENT FROM NIMROUD

5

SCULPTURED PAVEMENT
FROM KOUJUNJIK.
BRITISH MUSEUM.

7

ORNAMENT FROM PERSEPOLIS.

6

AN ASSYRIAN
PATERA.

8

BAS-RELIEF
IN ALABASTER
BRITISH
MUSEUM.

SSYRIAN ORNAMENT

The early history of Babylonia and Assyria is one long series of wars and conquests. Originally one nation, they became divided, and the younger Assyria in the north became the most powerful empire of that period, under Tiglath-Phalasar I., 1100 B.C., Ashur-nasir-pal, 885-60 B.C., Shalmaneser II., 860-25 B.C., Tiglath-Phalasar III., 745-27 B.C., the Great Sargon, 722-705 B.C., Senna-cherib, 705-681 B.C., Esarhaddon, 681-668 B.C, and Ashur-ban-pal, 668-626 B.C. In 609 B.C.. the Capital, Nineveh, was destroyed by Cyaxares the Mede, and Babylon arose again to power under Nebuchadnezzar, 604-562 B.C. : this city was destroyed by Cyrus the Persian, 539 B.C.

Assyrian art, with its racial influences, religious beliefs, and climatic conditions, differs in a remarkable degree from Egyptian art. Though stone is found is Assyria, the great cities were built of brick, no doubt owing to the fact of the arts and civilization coming from Chaldea, where stone was scarce and clay plentiful. Both at Babylon in Chaldea and Nineveh in Assyria the traditional type of building was rectangular, with arched openings and vaults, built of sun-dried bricks. The lower part of the wall was covered with large alabaster slabs, carved in low relief with scenes representing the king and his warriors engaged in hunting or fighting (fig. 1). The upper part of the wall was in enamelled brick, or in coloured stucco, with details of the Lotus and the bud, together with the rosette, which was often carried round the archivolt. The representation of the industrial arts and the pursuits of agriculture, which is so admirably illustrated upon the Egyptian reliefs, is entirely absent in Assyria. The enamelled bricks of Chaldea were modelled in low relief, with enamels of turquoise blue, yellow, white, and black, of fine quality and colour—one splendid example of enamel on beton is the Frieze of Archers from the Palace of Susa (p. 19). The enamelled bricks of Assyria were usually flat, or modelled but slightly, and the enamels were less pure. The external walls were similar to the internal ones, but with larger friezes and bolder reliefs, and usually with religious subjects (fig. 9). The portals were enriched with colossal winged and human-headed bulls, of alabaster, finely carved in relief. Typical examples of Assyrian ornament are the Lotus and the bud (figs. 2 and 3), the Patera or Rosette (figs. 6 and 7), and the Hom, or Tree of Life (fig. 8). The Lotus enrichment shows Egyptian influence, and only came into use during the 7th century B.C., when intercourse between the two nations was established. It is differentiated from the Egyptian Lotus by its vigorous growth and curved profile, and the geometrical form of the calyx of the flower and bud (fig. 2).

The type of Anthemion or *Hom*, with its alternate bud and fir-cone, and with strong lateral markings, is beautiful in line and proportion of mass (fig. 3). The *Hom* is frequently used as a flower on the sacred tree, a form of enrichment that influenced much of the later Persian and Sicilian textile fabrics.

9

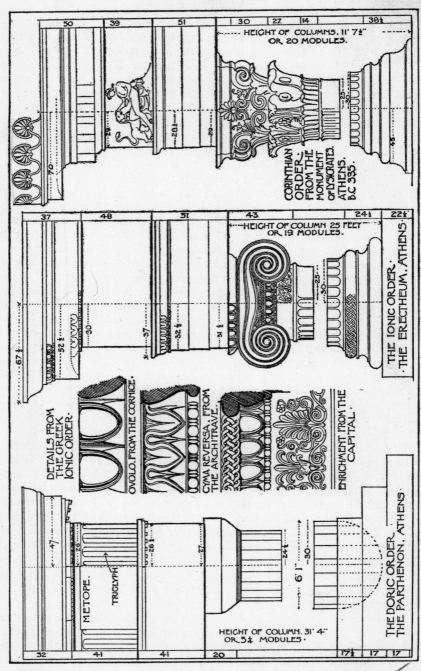

HEIGHT OF COLUMNS. 11' 7½"
OR 20 MODULES.

CORINTHIAN
ORDER.
FROM THE
MONUMENT
OF LYSICRATES.
ATHENS.
B.C. 335.

THE IONIC ORDER.
THE ERECTHEUM, ATHENS.

HEIGHT OF COLUMN 25 FEET
OR 19 MODULES.

DETAILS FROM
THE GREEK
IONIC ORDER.

OVOLO. FROM THE CORNICE.

CYMA REVERSA. FROM
THE ARCHITRAVE.

ENRICHMENT FROM THE
CAPITAL.

METOPE.

TRIGLYPH.

THE DORIC ORDER.
THE PARTHENON. ATHENS.

HEIGHT OF COLUMN. 31' 4"
OR 5¼ MODULES.

10

GREEK ARCHITECTURE

Classic or columnar architecture is divided into the Greek and Roman styles, and each style comprises several orders of architecture : the Grecian orders are the Doric, the Ionic, and the Corinthian, and many examples of each of these orders are still extant in Greece and her colonies—Asia Minor, Southern Italy, and Sicily. From a comparison of these buildings, certain constructive and decorative features are observed to be present, and thence they are considered as the characteristics of the style or order, which comprises the Base (except in the Grecian Doric, which has no base), Column and Capital, and the Entablature, which consists of the Architrave, Frieze and Cornice. The proportions of these orders are generally determined by the lower diameter of the column, which is divided into 2 modules or 60 parts, the height of the column always including the base and capital. The DORIC order was used for the early Greek temples from 650 B.C., and culminated in the Parthenon, 438 B.C. The COLUMNS in this order are $4\frac{1}{2}$ to 6 diameters in height, with 20 shallow flutings with intermediate sharp arrises ; the CAPITAL is half a diameter in height, and is composed of an echinus or ovolo moulding with annulets or deep channellings below, and a large square abacus above. The ARCHITRAVE is plain ; the FRIEZE is enriched by rectangular blocks, with 3 vertical channellings in the face, termed triglyphs, alternately with square metopes which were frequently sculptured. The CORNICE, composed of simple mouldings, projects considerably beyond the face of the frieze.

CARYATIDE, ERECHTHEUM.

The IONIC order has COLUMNS of from 9 to $9\frac{1}{2}$ diameters in height, with 24 flutings divided by narrow fillets ; the BASE is half a diameter in height, and composed of a plinth, torus, fillet, cavetto, fillet, torus, and fillet. The CAPITAL is $\frac{7}{10}$ of a diameter high, and consists of a pair of double scrolls or volutes, supported by an echinus moulding enriched with the egg and tongue, with an astragal below.

The ENTABLATURE is one quarter the height of the columns, the ARCHITRAVE of one or more fascias, the FRIEZE continuous and frequently enriched with sculpture in low relief ; the CORNICE has simple and compound mouldings supported by a dentil band. Caryatides were occasionally introduced into this order ; they were female figures clad in drapery having vertical folds which re-echoed the flutings of the Ionic column. These Caryatides supported the entablature in place of the columns ; a beautiful example is in the south portico of the Erechtheum at Athens.

The CORINTHIAN order was not much used by the Greeks; the examples, however, show considerable refinement and delicacy of details. The COLUMNS are 10 diameters in height, with 24 flutings; the BASE is half a diameter high; the CAPITAL is a little greater than a diameter in height, and is enriched with acanthus foliated leaves and spiral volutes. The ENTABLATURE is richer and the CORNICE deeper and more elaborate than those of the other orders.

The principal Doric buildings in Greece are:—The Temples at Corinth[2, 8], 650 B.C., Ægina[2, 8], 550 B.C., the Parthenon[2, 9], and the Theseum[2, 8], 438 B.C., the Temples of Jupiter at Olympia[2, 8], 436 B.C., Apollo Epicurius at Bassæ[2, 8], 430 B.C., Propylæa at Athens, 431 B.C. and the Minerva at Sunium, 420 B.C. Ionic buildings are:—Temples at Ilyssus[1, 7], 484 B.C., Nike Apteros[1, 7], 420 B.C., and the Erechtheum, *ca.* 420 B.C. (see plan, plate 85), North Portico[7], East Portico[8], at Athens. In Asia Minor there are the Temples of Samos[8], Priene[8], Teos[8], Diana at Ephesus[9], (with 36 of its columns sculptured), and of Apollo at Miletos. Corinthian buildings are:—The Monument of Lysicrates, 335 B.C., the Tower of the Winds (octagonal in plan), and Jupiter Olympius[2, 8], 200 B.C.

During the 5th century B.C., the Doric order was extensively used in the Greek colonies at Sicily. At Agrigentum there are the remains of six fine Doric temples, of which the Temple of Zeus[2], 450 B.C., is the largest, being 354 by 175 feet. In this Temple were found the *Telemones*, or *Atlantes*, male figures, 25 feet in height, with their arms raised probably supporting the roof. This Temple is also remarkable for its portico of seven columns, 60 feet in height, and having the peristyle walled up.

At Selinus there are five large Doric temples[2, 8], and one[5, 9] with columns 57 feet in height, with an entablature of 19 feet. At Segesta there is a Doric temple[2, 8] with only the peristyle complete and the columns unfluted, and at Pæstum, in Southern Italy, there are two Doric temples[2, 8] and a basilica[5] with its porticos of nine columns each.

All these buildings in Sicily and Pæstum date between 500 and 430 B.C.

CLASSIFICATION OF CLASSIC TEMPLES.

ARRANGEMENT OF COLUMNS AND WALLS.

[1] *Apteral* .	When the side walls have no colonnade.
[2] *Peripteral* .	When there is a colonnade standing apart from the side walls.
[3] *Pseudo-peripteral*	When the colonnade is attached to the side walls.
[4] *Dipteral* .	When there is a double colonnade standing out from the walls.
[5] *Pseudo-dipteral* .	When the inner row of columns is attached to the side walls.

THE RELATION OF THE ENDS OF THE TEMPLE.

In Antis .	When the columns do not project beyond the ends of the side walls.
Prostyle .	When a portico stands in front of the temple.
[6] *Amphi-prostyle* .	When there is a portico at each end.
Mono-prostyle .	If the portico is one column in depth.
Di-prostyle .	If the portico is two columns in depth.

THE NUMBER OF COLUMNS IN THE PORTICO.

[7] *Tetrastyle* .	If of four columns.
[8] *Hexastyle* .	If of six columns.
[9] *Octastyle* .	If of eight columns.

12

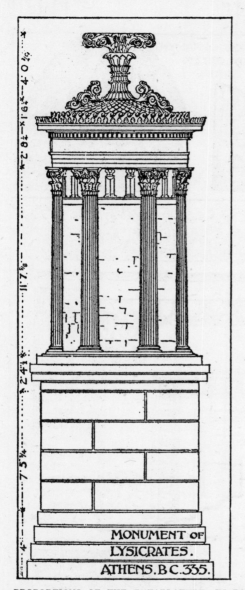

MONUMENT of
LYSICRATES.
ATHENS.B C.335.

PROPORTIONS OF THE ENTABLATURE, IN PARTS.

		Archi-trave.	Frieze.	Cor-nice.	Total Entab-lature.
DORIC -	Parthenon -	44½	40½	26	111
	Theseus -	50	55½	25½	131
IONIC -	Erechtheum	51½	48½	37½	137½
	Priene	46⅝	29	55⅞	131½
CORINTHIAN	Lysicrates-	51	39½	50	140½
	Jupiter Olympius	41¾	27½	48	117

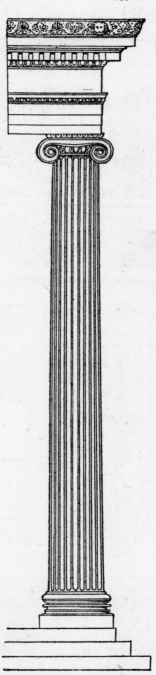

IONIC ORDER, TEMPLE OF
ILYSSUS.

ANTHEMION ORNAMENT.
FROM GREEK
TOMBS.

SIDE
ELEVATION
OF CONSOLE.
A

SIZE OF
OPENING.
HEIGHT 16'. 8".
WIDTH, (LOWER diameter 7'.10"
— " Upper · · 7'.4"

1' 7"

A

3 FEET

DETAIL of THE
ARCHITRAVE of
NORTH DOOR,
ERECHTHEUM,
ATHENS.
409 B.C.

REEK ORNAMENT

Greece, or Hellas, consisted of a number of small states, speaking the same language, and worshipping the same gods. Almost the whole of the Ægean coast of Asia Minor was occupied in early times by Greek Colonies, which supplanted those of the Phœnicians of Tyre and Sidon. The southern portion of this seaboard was occupied by the Dorians, and the northern by Ionians. In the course of time other Greek settlements were made on the Black Sea and Mediterranean coast of Asia Minor, as well as at Syracuse, Gela and Agrigentum in Sicily, and in Etruria and Magna Grecia in Italy. These colonies appear to have reached a higher state of art at an earlier period than Greece itself. The ascendancy in art in Greece was enjoyed by the Dorians circa 800 B.C. ; after which Sparta took the lead but was in turn excelled by the Ionians, when Athens became the focus of Greek art, and attained a degree of perfection in that respect that has remained unequalled to this day. Athens was destroyed by the Persians under Xerxes, 480 B.C. ; but under Pericles (470-429 B.C.) Greek art reached its culmination.

The abundant, although fragmentary, remains of Grecian architecture, sculpture, and the industrial arts show most vividly the artistic feeling and culture of the early Greeks, with their great personality and religious sentiment, in which the personal interest of the gods and goddesses was brought into relation with the life and customs of the people. Their myths and traditions, their worship of legendary heroes, the perfection of their physical nature, and their intense love of the beautiful, were characteristic of the Greek people, from the siege of Troy to their subjection by Rome, 140 B.C. The almost inexhaustible store of Greek art, now gathered in the British and in other European museums, furnishes one of the most valuable illustrations of the many glorious traditions of the past. The vitality of conception, the dignity and noble grace of the gods, the consummate knowledge of the human figure, and the exquisite skill of craftsmanship, are here seen in the greatest diversity of treatment and incident.

The work of Phidias, the most renowned of Greek sculptors, is largely represented in the British Museum by noble examples, showing his great personality, wonderful power, and his remarkable influence upon contemporary and later plastic art.

The Parthenon, or temple of the goddess Athene (plan, plate 85), which was built upon the Acropolis at Athens by Ictinus and Callicrates, 454-438 B.C., was enriched with splendid works of sculpture by Phidias. Many of the originals are now in the British Museum forming part of the Elgin Marbles, which were purchased from the Earl of Elgin in 1815. The two pediments of the temple contained figure sculpture in the round, larger than life size. The Eastern group represents the birth of Athene, and the western group the contest of Athene and Poseidon

15

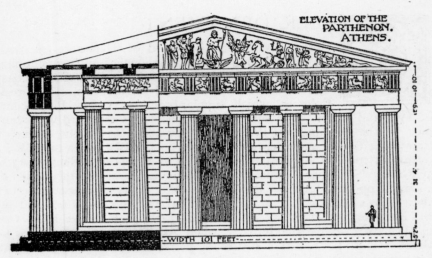

ELEVATION OF THE
PARTHENON.
ATHENS.

WIDTH 101 FEET

for the soil of Attica. The fragments of these pedimental groups are now in the British Museum, and though sadly mutilated, show the perfection of sculpture during the Phidian age. Of the 92 square metopes sculptured in high relief that enriched the Doric frieze, 15 are included in the Elgin Marbles. The subject represented on these metopes was the battle between the Centaurs and Lapithæ—a fine example of composition of line and mass, and dramatic power of expression.

DORIC FRIEZE: FROM THE PARTHENON. ATHENS.

The continuous frieze upon the upper part of the cella wall, under the colonnade or Peristyle, was 40 feet from the ground, 40 inches in height, and 523 feet in length. It was carved in low relief, the subject being the Panathenæic procession, the most sacred and splendid of the religious festivals of the Ancient Greeks. This frieze, with its rhythm of movement and unity of composition, its groups of beautiful youths and maidens, sons and daughters of noble citizens, its heroes

16

and deities, heralds and magistrates ; its sacrificial oxen, and its horses and riders is doubtless a most perfect production of the sculptors' art. Each figure is full of life and motion, admirable in detail, having an individuality of action and expression, yet with a unity of composition, appropriate to its architectural purpose as a frieze or band.

NORTH FRIEZE FROM THE PARTHENON ATHENS

The Parthenon, however, was but the shrine of the standing figure or statue of the goddess Athene, which was 37 feet high, and formed of plates of gold and ivory, termed *Chryselephantine* sculpture. Probably owing to the intrinsic value of the material, this work of Phidias disappeared at an early date.

Among the examples of sculptured marbles in the British Museum is the beautiful frieze from the interior of the Temple of Apollo at Bassæ or Phigaleia erected by Ictinus, 430 B.C. This frieze, which shows an extraordinary vitality and movement, is 101 feet long and consists of 23 slabs 25½ inches in width, the incidents depicted being the battle of the Greeks and the Amazons, and the contest between the Centaurs and the Lapithæ. The dignity and reserve of the Parthenon frieze is here replaced by activity and energy of line and an exuberance of modelling.

BATTLE OF THE AMAZONS, FROM THE FRIEZE AT PHIGALEIA

Some of the marbles in the British Museum are from the Nereid Monument of Xanthos, 327 B.C., so called because the female figures display moist clinging garments, and have fishes and seabirds between their feet. These sculptures show a high degree of perfection, and were probably the work of the Athenian sculptor, Bryaxis.

Among other examples of the Greek treatment of the frieze, is that of the Erechtheum, 409 B.C., with its black Eleusinian stone background, and white marble reliefs. The Temple of Nike Apteros, of about the same date, is noted for the beautiful reliefs from the balustrade which crowned the lofty bastion on which the temple stands. An example of Nike or victory, adjusting her sandal is here given. These reliefs are remarkable for their delicacy and refinement of treatment, and the exquisite rendering of the draped female figure. Other friezes now in the British Museum are from the Mausoleum erected by Artemisia to her husband, Mausolus, 357-348 B.C. This tomb consisted of a solid basement of masonry, supporting a cella surrounded by a colonnade of 36 columns. The upper part of the basement was enriched with a frieze illustrating the battle of the Centaurs and Lapithæ ; the frieze of the cella was illustrated with funeral games in honour of Mausolus. Seventeen slabs of the frieze of the order from the colonnade are in the British Museum ; they represent the battle of the Greeks and Amazons.

BAS-RELIEF FROM NIKE APTEROS.

In their composition these slabs show extraordinary energy of movement and richness of invention. This frieze differs absolutely from the Parthenon frieze in its fertility of incident and intensity of action. Bryaxis, the sculptor of the Nereid monument executed the north frieze, while the south was by Timotheus, the east by Scopas, and the west by Leochares.

A remarkable building, where again the frieze was an important feature, was the great altar at Pergamos, erected by Eumenes II., 168 B.C. This had a basement of masonry 160 feet by 160 feet, and 16 feet high, enriched with a sculptured frieze 7½ feet high. The subject is the *Gigantomachia*, or battle of the gods and giants ; the treatment being characterized by passionate energy and expression, and daring skill in grouping and technique. Ninety-four of the original slabs of this frieze are now in the Berlin Museum.

The frieze was an important decorative feature with the Assyrians and Greeks. The continuity of incident and rhythm of movement that was possible with the continuous frieze, together with its functional use of banding, no doubt tended to preserve its traditional form, hence we have many remains from antiquity of this beautiful decorative treatment. An early and fine example is the frieze of Archers from the palace of Susa, 485 B.C., now in the Louvre. This frieze, of which an illustration is here given, was executed in enamel on beton. A dignity of conception and unity of composition were here combined with skilful modelling of relief work, and fine colouring of blue, turquoise and yellow. This treatment of the frieze no doubt influenced the later work of the Greeks, who so nobly carried on this tradition of the frieze.

Greek ornament is distinguished by simplicity of line, refinement of detail, radiation of parts, unity of composition, and perfect symmetry. The anthemion, which is the typical form, differs from the earlier Lotus type in its more abstract rendering and its absence of symbolism; it has a charm of composition and a unity and balance of parts.

FRIEZE IN ENAMELLED BRICKS FROM THE PALACE OF SUSA 485 B.C. LOUVRE

The anthemion was sculptured upon the top of the funeral stele (figs. 1, 2, and 5, plate 8), upon the architrave of doorways (fig. 6), and above the necking of the Ionic columns (plate 6), or painted upon the panels of the deep coffered ceilings. It was also used in a thousand ways upon the many fine vases and other ceramic wares of that period. The simplicity and beauty of the anthemion and its ready adaptability, has doubtless rendered it one of the best known types of ornament. Like the Egyptian and Assyrian prototypes the Greek anthemion is usually arranged with alternate flower and bud, connected by a curved line or more frequently by a double spiral. Illustrations are given on plates 8 and 9 of a few typical examples, where the rhythm and beauty of composition are indicative of the culture and perfection of Greek craftsmanship.

Another feature, which at a later period received considerable development, was the scroll given on plate 9, which is a fine example from the roof of the monument to Lysicrates. The scrolls, cut with V-shaped sections, spring from a nest of sharp acanthus foliage. This

EXAMPLES OF BANDS FROM GREEK VASES. OWEN JONES.

FROM THE MUSEUM NAPLES

ORNAMENT IN MARBLE. FROM THE ROOF APEX, MONUMENT
OF LYSICRATES. ATHENS. B.C. 335

scroll is formed of a series of spirals springing from each other, the junction of the spiral being covered by a sheath or flower ; the spiral itself being often broken by a similar sheath.

This spiral form, with its sheathing, is the basis of the Roman and Italian Renascence styles, and sharply differentiates them from the Gothic ornament, in which the construction line is continuous and unbroken.

The rosette, a survival of the early Greek form, found at Crete, (1600 B.C.) was frequently used upon the funeral stele and the Architrave (plate 8) where its circular and radiating form contrasts beautifully with the functional straight lines of architectural design. The extraordinary vitality and versatility of the Greek craftsman may be traced through a magnificent series of coins dating from 700 B.C. to 280 B.C. The interest of subject, beauty of composition and largeness of style, combined with the utmost delicacy of technique, of these gold, silver, and electrum coins, are a reflex of the artistic feeling for beauty of the early Greeks.

GREEK VASE OF THE STYLE OF NICOSTHENES (*v.* p. 107).

Colour, as well as form, was a great factor in the art of the Greeks ; their architecture and sculpture were enriched and accentuated by the judicious use of beautiful colour. The Parthenon, with its simple and refined Doric architecture and magnificent sculpture by Phidias, was enhanced by colour, which was introduced in the background of the pediment and the frieze, and also upon the borders and accessories of the draperies. The " Lacunaria," or sunk panels of the ceilings, were frequently enhanced with blue, having rosettes or stars in gold or colour. A frank use of pure colour was almost universal in early Egyptian and Assyrian art, and the Greeks were not slow to avail themselves of any art that was beautiful.

COIN OF PHILIP II B.C. 339-336.

COIN OF TERINA B.C. 412.

COIN OF AGRIGENTUM B.C. 412-406

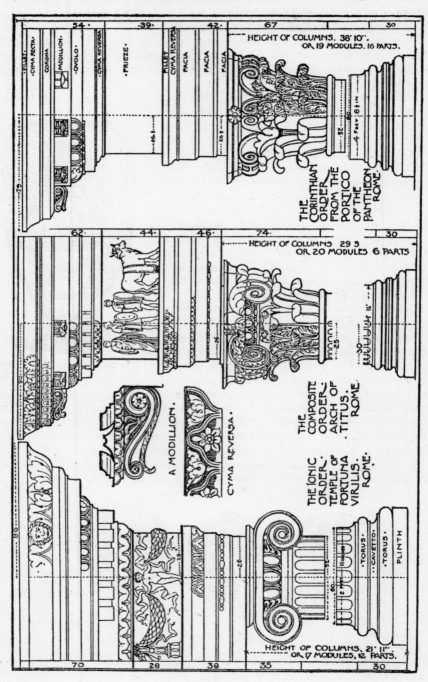

THE CORINTHIAN ORDER FROM THE PORTICO OF THE PANTHEON. ROME.

HEIGHT OF COLUMNS. 38' 10". OR 19 MODULES. 16 PARTS.

THE COMPOSITE ORDER. ARCH OF TITUS. ROME.

HEIGHT OF COLUMNS 29' 5" OR 20 MODULES 6 PARTS

A MODILLION.

CYMA REVERSA.

THE IONIC ORDER. TEMPLE OF FORTUNA VIRILIS. ROME.

HEIGHT OF COLUMNS. 21' 11" OR 17 MODULES. 12 PARTS.

ROMAN ARCHITECTURE

Is differentiated from that of Greece by the extensive use of the arch and of superposed orders. The many fine remains of Roman temples and public buildings show the extraordinary versatility and conception of the Roman architects, their constructive skill, and their remarkable power of assimilating the arts of other nations. The Roman temples were somewhat similar in plan to their Greek prototypes, but usually without the side colonnade, larger in scale, and with an ostentatious display of mouldings and ornaments, less refined in contour and detail.

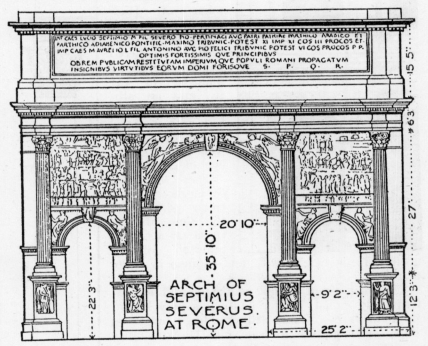

IMP CAES LVCIO SEPTIMIO M FIL SEVERO PIO PERTINACI AVG PATRI PATRIAE PARTHICO ARABICO ET PARTHICO ADIABENICO PONTIFIC MAXIMO TRIBVNIC POTEST XI IMP XI COS III PROCOS ET IMP CAES M AVRELIO L FIL ANTONINO AVG PIO FELICI TRIBVNIC POTEST VI COS PROCOS P P. OPTIMIS FORTISSIMIS QVE PRINCIPIBVS OB REM PVBLICAM RESTITVTAM IMPERIVM QVE POPVLI ROMANI PROPAGATVM INSIGNIBVS VIRTVTIBVS EORVM DOMI FORISQVE S. P. Q. R.

ARCH OF SEPTIMIUS SEVERUS. AT ROME.

A typical example is given here of a triumphal arch, namely, that of Septimius Severus, A.D. 203. Other examples are the Arch of Titus, A.D. 81, and the Arch of Constantine, A.D. 326, all near the Forum at Rome. Trajan's Arch, A.D. 114, was destroyed by Constantine, who used many of the reliefs for the building of his own arch.

The superposition of columns and arches is seen in the Theatre of Marcellus, 20 B.C., where the lower order is of the Doric and the upper of the Ionic; this, like the early Greek Theatre, was semi-circular in plan.

The Colosseum, commenced by Vespasian, A.D. 72, and completed by

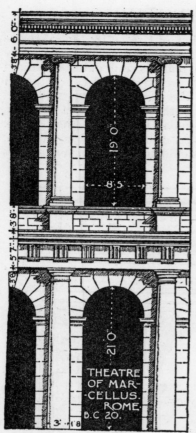

THEATRE OF MAR-CELLUS. ROME. B.C 20.

Domitian, A.D. 82, has a third storey, having the Corinthian order, and an attic storey with Corinthian pilasters, the whole reaching to a height of 157 ft. The diameters of the amphitheatre were 584 and 468 ft.

One of the best preserved buildings of the early Roman period is the Pantheon (plan, plate 85), built during the reign of Hadrian, A.D. 117-38. This has a fine dome of coffered panels, having a diameter of 142 ft., and an altitude of 71 ft. 6 in., with a total height of 143 ft. from the floor to eye of dome.

The beautiful octastyle Corinthian portico, of the time of Agrippa, 27 B.C., has granite columns 46 ft. 6 in. in height, with fine capitals in white marble.

The magnificent temple of Castor and Pollux, frequently called Jupiter Stator, is only known from the three columns still standing ; but these show the magnitude of scale and the exuberance of detail that characterized the finest period of Roman architecture. The proportions of this order are columns, 45 ft. 3 in. in height and the entablature 11 ft. 7 in.

The Tuscan and Composite orders were added to the Doric, Ionic, and Corinthian orders, thus forming the five orders of architecture.

The Romans rarely used the peristyle temple, consequently the cella was of the same width as the portico. In the civic buildings and palaces, the Romans show the greatest constructive skill

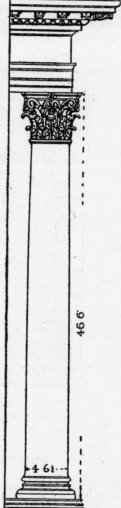

THE CORINTHIAN ORDER FROM THE PANTHEON.

24

and splendour of embellishment. The skilful planning and appropriateness of decorative treatment in their basilicas and amphitheatres are evidences of the practical nature of the Romans.

The Basilica or Hall of Justice was an important architectural feature, rectangular in plan, with a semi-circular apse at one end, where the tribunal was placed; roofed with timber framing, or vaulted with concrete, and supported with rows of columns or piers. The remains of two typical Roman basilicas are still in existence: the Basilica of Trajan, A.D. 114, rectangular, 180 by 160 ft., five aisles, the centre aisle with a semi-circular wooden roof, and enriched with bronze plates is typical of one class; and the Basilica of Maxentius, A.D. 310, with a width of 195 ft., and a length of 260 ft., is typical of a vaulted basilica, the two side aisles with barrel-vaults, and the centre aisle with an intersecting vaulted roof.

The form of these Roman basilicas was adapted by the early Christians to their service, and the basilica church became the typical form used up to the 12th century in the former Roman provinces.

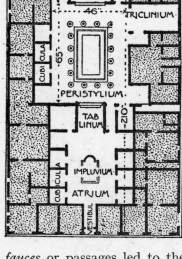

The Roman houses were of two types: the *Domus*, or houses clustered together, and the houses which were surrounded by streets. Most of the finest Pompeian houses were of the *Insular* type.

The usual plan of a Roman house consisted of the *Ostium*, an entrance or *Vestibule*, which opened into the *Atrium*, a large room or court partly roofed over, with an opening in the centre called the *Compluvium*, under which was the *Impluvium*, or cistern of water, placed below the level of the ground. Small Chambers surrounded the *Atrium*, and at the further end was the *Tablinum* or private room, frequently leading to the *Peristylium* or private part of the house, an open court with a colonnade surrounding a marble fountain, with flowers, shrubs, and trees forming a *Viridarium*. Surrounding the *Peristylium* were private rooms, one of which was the *Triclinium*, or dining room. From the *Peristylium*,

fauces or passages led to the *Porticus*, a colonnade which overlooked the garden.

25

FIG 1

42 INCHES

FRIEZE. FORUM OF TRAJAN. LATERAN MUSEUM.

2

26 INCHES

ONE SIDE OF A SQUARE
SEPULCHRAL CIPPUS

3

15 INCHES

ROMAN SCROLL

4 & 5
MARBLE
PANELS
BRITISH
MUSEUM

14½

6

PANEL OF VOTIVE CIPPIUS

7

32 INCHES

TRIANGULAR BASE OF A MARBLE
CANDELABRUM. BRITISH MUSEUM.

8

38 INCHES

FRIEZE. FORUM OF TRAJAN. ROME 110 AD

ROMAN ORNAMENT

Rome became, by successive wars and conquests, the mistress of the world, absorbing successively the arts and the architecture of the Etruscans, the Samnites, and of Corinth and Carthage. From these varied sources arose the style termed Roman, assimilating and adopting the column and the horizontal entablature of the Greeks ; the arch, the vault, the mural paintings, and the decorative use of bronze and terra-cotta of the Etruscans, with the sculpture, ornament, mosaics and coinage of the Greeks and Carthaginians. These varied arts were assimilated and perfected by the Romans during the period 100 B.C. to A.D. 337.

Roman ornament is the continuity of the Greek and Etruscan styles, consisting of the acanthus, the scroll and the anthemion ; the Romans using these forms with greater exuberance and elaboration, together with bold and vigorous carving, yet lacking the simplicity, refinement and graceful contour of the Greek and Etruscan forms.

Roman ornament consists largely of continuous spiral lines, clothed with cups and sheaths of acanthus foliage, the various spirals terminating in a rosette. These main spirals are frequently interwoven with fine curved or spiral lines, clothed with acanthus or other foliation such as the vine, olive, and ivy. Birds and reptiles and cupids, and the chimera or griffin (fig. 1) are often interspersed with the ornament, thus giving that largeness of mass, and contrast of form, which is so characteristic of Roman art. The Thermæ or baths, and public buildings, displayed decorative ceilings, having deep sunk panels called Lacunaria, or coffers ; square, hexagonal or octagonal in form, with a centre rosette in high relief and the border mouldings of the coffers being enriched with the egg and dart, or the water leaf.

COFFERED CEILING, BASILICA OF MAXENTIUS.

These exhibit an effective treatment of moulded surfaces. The ceilings of the tombs and palaces were in many cases ornamented with circular

FIG 1

3 MARBLE RELIEF IN THE UFFIZI GALLERY.
FLORENCE

STUCCO
DECORATION IN LOW RELIEF.
REPRESENTING NYMPHS RIDING ON WINGED
& SEA MONSTERS & NEREIDS SURROUNDED
WITH ORNAMENT FROM A TOMB ON THE
VIA LATINA, ROME A.D. 160. DISCOVERED IN 1860.
THE CEILING IS BARREL-VAULTED & ORNAMENTED.
SEE FIG. 2.

2

5 FEET 9

STUCCO ORNAMENT IN LOW RELIEF UPON A CEILING IN TOMB VIA LATINA
ROME

4

5

RELIEF PANEL FROM THE INSIDE OF THE PORTICO OF THE
PANTHEON. ROME. A.D. 125

6

CINERARY URN BRITISH MUSEUM

MARBLE URN BRITISH MUSEUM

and square panels, richly decorated with arabesques or mythical figures, and cupids in low relief of fine stucco ; the mouldings or divisions in higher relief, and having the water leaf or the egg and dart enrichment (plate 12).

The architectural frieze and the sepulchral urn and sarcophagi of this period were often decorated with festoons (figs. 4 and 5, plate 12), which were supported by cupids or by candelabra (plate 12), or by the skulls of oxen, as on the frieze from the Temple of Vesta at Tivoli, here given.

FRIEZE. TEMPLE OF VESTA TIVOLI.

The architectural basilica and forum of Trajan, erected A.D. 114, by Apollodorus, a Greek of Damascus, was of the utmost magnificence, the remains attesting to the skill and artistic craftsmanship of the Romans. Apollodorus also erected the marble column of Trajan, having a rectangular pedestal 18 ft. high, and richly sculptured with the dresses, armour and standards of the Roman army. This pedestal supports a column of the Tuscan order of architecture 97¼ ft. high, and 12 ft. in diameter, enriched with a series of spiral bands, having bas-reliefs representing the successive events of the Dacian War by the Emperor Trajan. This magnificent and well preserved relic of antiquity furnishes a complete epitome of the costumes and the arms and armour of that period. Another well preserved column, similar to that of Trajan, was erected in Rome by Marcus Aurelius, A.D. 174, the subjects of its reliefs being the war with the Marcomans. Large marble urns, or tazze, enriched with Bacchanalian figures, surrounded with foliage and birds and animals ; magnificent tables, chairs, couches, and candelabra, of bronze, enriched with silver damascening, together with the choice remains of sculpture and mosaics, all indicate the luxuriousness and love of magnificence of the wealthy Roman citizens.

In Roman architectural ornament we see the most powerful modelling combined with the use of the continuous scroll growing from a nest of foliage, repeated in their painted decorations (see Pompeian). This elaboration of typical ornamentation shows the rounded serrations of the Acanthus (see plate 11) and forms the chief characteristic of Roman ornament, which is wonderfully bold and vigorous in conception and execution, but deficient in the refinement and delicacy of Greek art.

There is a considerable difference in the foliations of the various capitals. The Corinthian capital of the Parthenon has foliage of the simple olive leaf type. In the composite capital of the Arch of Septimius Severus the foliage is serrated like fig. 8, plate 11, while that of the Corinthian Capital of the Temple of Vesta, Tivoli, is more of the parsley leaf type, and each leaf is folded forward at the terminations.

29

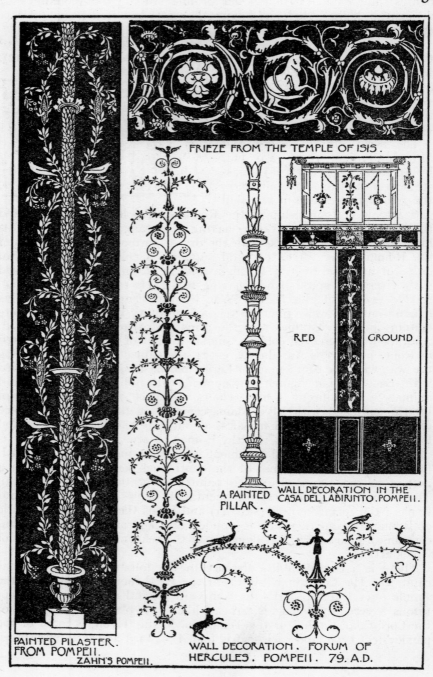

FRIEZE FROM THE TEMPLE OF ISIS.

RED   GROUND.

A PAINTED
PILLAR.

WALL DECORATION IN THE
CASA DEL LABIRINTO. POMPEII.

PAINTED PILASTER.
FROM POMPEII.
            ZAHN'S POMPEII.

WALL DECORATION. FORUM OF
HERCULES. POMPEII. 79. A.D.

CAPITAL. SANTA SOPHIA,
CONSTANTINOPLE.

"WINDBLOWN" CAPITAL. ST. MARK'S,
VENICE.

SCULPTURED FRIEZE. SARCOPHAGUS OF THE ARCHBISHOP THEODORE, RAVENNA.

SCULPTURED SLAB, TORCELLO.

FROM ST MARKS, VENICE.

LILY CAPITAL. ST MARKS.

CAPITAL FROM SAN VITALE. RAVENNA

PIERCED MARBLE SCREEN. ST MARKS.

SARCOPHAGI OF THEODSIUS. 7TH CENTURY. S. APOLLINARE. RAVENNA.

PIERCED MARBLE SCREEN. ST MARKS.

FROM ST MARKS.

ANCIENT PIER. VENICE.

CARVED PANELS IN ALABASTER FROM ST MARKS. VENICE. 1071.

OMPEIAN ORNAMENT

Pompeii, Herculaneum and Stabia, Roman cities, were buried by an eruption of Vesuvius, A.D. 79. These cities had already suffered from an earthquake, A.D. 63, and were being rapidly rebuilt when they were finally destroyed by the eruption. The Younger Pliny, the historian, was a spectator of the event at Pompeii, and wrote two letters to his friend Tacitus, describing the event and his flight from the doomed city, which remained buried for seventeen centuries, with the treasures of gold and silver, bronzes of rare workmanship, mural paintings on a most magnificent scale, and floors of mosaics of marvellous execution and design ; everything affording a vivid glimpse of the domestic and public life of the Romans of the 1st century A.D. Herculaneum was discovered in 1709, and Pompeii 1748, and from these cities many valuable remains of art have been taken. In the museum at Naples there are over 1,000 mural paintings, some 13,000 small bronzes, over 150 large bronzes of figures and busts, and 70 fine large mosaics.

A plan of a Roman house is given on page 25 showing the arrangement and use of the rooms. The floors were covered with mosaics (see plate 54), those of the vestibule, corridors and small rooms having simple patterns enclosed with borders of the key pattern, or the guilloche in black, red, grey and white tesseræ. The floor of the triclinium, or dining-room, was often a magnificent mosaic representing some mythological or classical subject. The walls were painted in colour, usually with a dado one-sixth the height of the wall, with pilasters dividing the wall into rectangular panels and a frieze above (plate 13). The general scheme of colour was, the dado and pilasters black, the panels red, and the frieze white ; or black dado, red pilasters and frieze, with white or yellow panels. The decoration upon these various coloured grounds was light and fanciful, and painted with great delicacy. Representations of architectural forms, such as columns and entablatures, are often rendered in perspective upon the painted walls.

The painted ornament has somewhat the same characteristics as the Roman relief work, but is usually much more delicate in treatment. The spiral form and the sheath are always prevalent, and from these sheaths and cups grow the finer tendrils or delicately painted spray of foliage, upon which birds are placed.

Stucco enrichments, such as ornamental string courses and mouldings, were frequently combined with the painted ornament ; they consist of small details, such as the water leaf, the egg and dart, and the anthemion, and are repeated in a regular series.

Herculaneum differed considerably from Pompeii, for here the finest works of art and innumerable MSS. have been found, showing that a higher intellectual life existed than that at Pompeii, where not a single MS. has been found.

YZANTINE ORNAMENT

The decline of the Roman empire, in the 3rd and 4th centuries A.D., had its inevitable influence upon contemporary art, but perhaps a more potent influence was that of Christianity, which, in the reign of Constantine, received State recognition and support ; and when this Emperor removed the seat of government from Rome to Byzantium, the traditional Greek and Roman arts were assimilated with those of Persia and Syria, but moulded and influenced by the new religion, giving that strong vitality, deep significance, and symbolism which is so remarkable a feature of the Byzantine style.

The change of style did not take place immediately, for most of the buildings erected by Constantine were in the traditional Roman style, but the arts were gradually perfected until they culminated in the building of S. Sophia, by Anthemius of Tralles and Isidorus of Miletus, during the reign of Justinian, A.D. 538. This building is remarkable for its splendid dome, supported by semi-domes and pendentives on a square plan (see plate 85), its embellishment with mosaics of glorious colours, and the great inventiveness and symbolism of the detail. The traditional sharp acanthus foliage of the Greeks was united with the emblems of Christianity, such as the circle, the cross, the vine, and the dove ; the peacock also is frequently seen. Figure sculpture was rarely used, but groups of figures were used in great profusion in the gold-ground mosaics that covered the upper part of the walls and the vaults and domes of the magnificent Byzantine buildings. The churches of Ravenna, in Italy, have somewhat similar characteristics : S. Vitale, A.D. 535, the basilica churches of S. Apollinare Nuovo, A.D. 493-525, S. Apollinare in Classe, A.D. 535-45, together with the Baptisteries, are rich in mosaics and sculptured capitals of the 6th and 7th centuries. In the cathedrals of Torcello, A.D. 670, and Murano, and the beautiful S. Mark's at Venice, marbles and mosaics were used in great profusion to enhance the architecture. The sketch plans given on plate 85 are typical of Byzantine planning, in which the symbolism of the circle and cross are used as constructive features. This symbolism is a marked feature in Byzantine ornament ; interlacing circles and crosses mingle with the acanthus or the vine, and are cut with a peculiar V-shaped section. The circular drill is largely used at the sinking of the leaves, and but little of the background is visible in the sculptured ornament of this period.

Pierced marble screens of interlaced foliage, or the fret in combination with the circle, were frequently used (see plate 84). A large number of pierced parapets in S. Mark's are carved in low relief, with various modifications of the interlacing guilloche, or circles.

FRIEZE FROM THE CHURCH OF SAINT-GILLES. PROVENCE.

PORTION OF ENGLISH MS.
A D 1020 BRITISH MUSEUM.

DETAIL FROM DOORWAY.
S? AGOSTINA.

CAPITAL
FROM
LAON

BASE OF COLUMNS
MODENA
CATHEDRAL.

BASE OF COLUMNS. WEST
DOOR. VERONA CATHEDRAL

PORTAL
FROM
SAINT-
-GILLES
PROVENCE

ROMANESQUE ARCHITECTURE & ORNAMENT

Romanesque architecture is characterized chiefly by the universal use of the arch, the absence of the classic entablature, and in the imagery and symbolism of its sculpture and ornament, doubtless due to Northern influence. One of the earliest existing buildings of this style is the church of S. Ambrogio, Milan (11th century), which has a nave and aisles, three eastern apses, and a western atrium, surrounded by an open arcade, enriched with vigorous reliefs of interlaced ornament and animals. Contemporary in date is S. Michele, Pavia, with a nave and transepts and central cupola: there is a single eastern apse, having an open external gallery and bands of sculptured ornament. This and the frequent use of the lion or griffin as a support for pillars, are characteristic of the Lombardic style, and are seen at S. Michele, Lucca, and the Cathedral, Baptistery, and the Campanile of Pisa, and the Cathedral at Trogir, Dalmatia.

It was, however, in France and Germany that the Romanesque reached its highest development, principally in the south and south-west of France, where the churches are distinguished for the richness of the west fronts.

S. Trophime, Arles (12th century), has a fine low semi-circular projecting porch, resting upon a sculptured frieze and pillars. A cloister, with arcading of coupled columns richly sculptured, is attached to this church; while S. Gilles (1076) has a low projecting porch of three arches, enriched with vigorous sculpture and ornament (plate 16).

The Cathedral at Angoulême has a vaulted nave, with three cupolas, and a west front with recessed arcading and figures : two square towers, with open arcading and conical spires, rise from the angles of the façade. Notre Dame, Poitiers, is even more rich in its gabled west front having a fine doorway with two tiers of arcading above. The façade is flanked by two circular turrets, with massive columns attached, having an open arcade above, with a conical spire ; enriched corbel tables are carried across the front, over the door, the upper arcade and window, and round the turrets.

Saint-Front, Périgueux, has a richly sculptured west front and nave of the 11th century, to which was added, in 1150, a larger church similar in plan to S. Mark's at Venice (a Greek cross, see plate 85), and roofed with five cupolas in stone. In central France there was the magnificent Abbey Church of Cluny, with its range of six towers ; and in Germany this number of towers is found at the great Romanesque churches at Speyer, Worms, and Laach, with their singular western apse and external clearstory gallery.

Plate 16 illustrates a few of the chief features of Romanesque ornament. The upper frieze is similar to the Roman Scroll, but less vigorous in modelling, and with a rounder form of serration of leaf form. The Laon capital has rich interlacing ornament and animals that suggest Scandinavian influence. The portal of Saint-Gilles shows the exuberant carving and storiation that characterized many of the churches of south-west France.

A CELTIC INITIAL
1

2 INITIAL

FROM THE GOSPELS OF
LINDISFARNE.
END OF 7TH CENTURY.
BRITISH MUSEUM.

CELTIC INTERLACEING FRET.
3

4 INTERLACED ANIMALS. FROM THE BOOK
OF KELLS. 8TH CENTY. BRITISH MUSEUM.

5 CAREW CROSS.

6 BRONZE
SHIELD. ENRICHED WITH RED
ENAMELS. BRITISH MUSEUM.

7 PORTION OF THE
TRUMPET PATTERN.
OR DIVERGENT
SPIRAL FROM
THE BOOK OF
DURROW. TRINITY COLLEGE. DUBLIN.

CELTIC ORNAMENT

No period in the history of art is more remarkable than the Celtic. The carved stone architecture and crosses, the bronzes, enamels, and silversmith's work, the splendid illuminated books and manuscripts with capitals and borders full of imagery and intricacy of detail, and the clear and accurate writing of the text are all indications of the culture and love of ornament of the early Irish people, showing a remarkable preference for the spiral and interlacing forms. The bronze shield (fig. 6), with its spirals and bosses of enamel enriched with the northern " Fylfot " is a typical example of the 2nd or 3rd century, A.D. Then comes the trumpet pattern or divergent spiral, which, seen in its infancy on the bronze shield, reached a great degree of elaboration in the 8th and 9th centuries, A.D. (figs. 2 to 7), being typical of Celtic work up to the

middle of the 11th century when all trace of this spiral is lost. The interlacing bird and animal forms used from the 8th to the 14th centuries are doubtless derived from Byzantine and Lombardic sources. The serpent or dragon, which is such a marked feature from the 7th to 15th century must have been borrowed from the north, as Ireland had no traditions of snakes or dragons, and it is to Scandinavia, with its legend of Fafni, that we must look for the origin of the dracontine treatment. It is this Zoomorphic character that distinguishes the Celtic from all other styles of ornament except Scandinavian. The obverse of the magnificent processional Cross of Cong (A.D. 1123), is divided into 46 panels of decorations, and convoluted snakes occupy 38 of them.

The illustration given here of the Irton Cross is a typical example of the Celtic ornamentation. The early or Pagan period is noted for its bronze work, cast and wrought, and enriched with Champlevé enamels. The fine chalice of Ardagh (page 133) and the Tara Brooch (plate 60) 7th century, are splendid examples of the Christian period dating from St. Patrick, A.D. 440-460. The beautiful Book of Kells, the Book of Armagh, the Book of Durrow, manuscripts of the early part of the 9th century (Trinity College, Dublin), and the Book of Durham, called the Lindisfarne Gospels, A.D. 689-721, written by Eadfrith, and illuminated by Ethelwald, are a tribute to the vitality, assimilation of ideas, and the culture and wonderful craftsmanship of the early Irish people. In Irish manuscripts gold is not used, except in the Lindisfarne Gospels, where a minute quantity is used.

CELTIC CROSS AT
IRTON, CUMBERLAND.

37

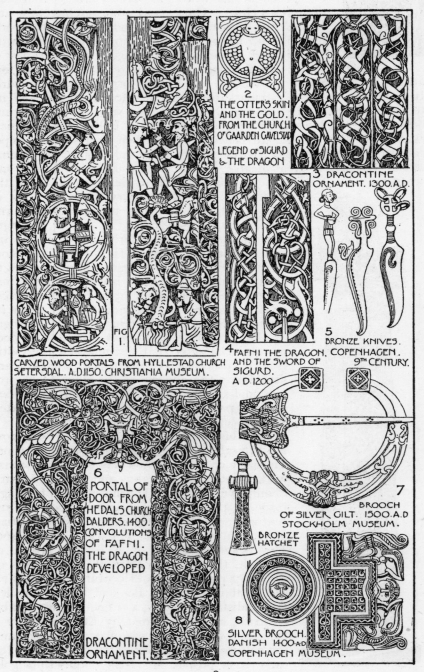

2
THE OTTERS SKIN
AND THE GOLD.
FROM THE CHURCH
OF GAARDEN GAVELSTAD
LEGEND of SIGURD
& THE DRAGON

3 DRACONTINE
ORNAMENT. 1300. A.D.

5
BRONZE KNIVES.
COPENHAGEN.
9TH CENTURY.

FIG 1.

CARVED WOOD PORTALS FROM HYLLESTAD CHURCH
SÆTERSDAL. A.D.1150. CHRISTIANIA MUSEUM.

4 FAFNI THE DRAGON
AND THE SWORD OF
SIGURD.
A D 1200

6
PORTAL OF
DOOR FROM
HEDALS CHURCH
BALDERS. 1400.
CONVOLUTIONS
OF FAFNI.
THE DRAGON
DEVELOPED

DRACONTINE
ORNAMENT.

7
BROOCH
OF SILVER GILT. 1500.A.D
STOCKHOLM MUSEUM.

BRONZE
HATCHET

8
SILVER BROOCH.
DANISH 1400·A·D
COPENHAGEN MUSEUM.

CANDINAVIAN ORNAMENT

The beautiful bronze and silver jewellery and implements of war of the early Viking period, found in Norway, Sweden, and Denmark, display no trace of plant forms in their ornamentation, the latter consisting wholly of interlacing animal forms—chiefly the dragon. The Viking ship found at Sandifiord in 1880, although destitute of ornament, shows traces of the "Bronze Dragon Prow," referred to in the early Scandinavian Sagas. At the commencement of the 12th century, plant forms are found mingled with the dragons, and figure sculpture became important in treating of the myths of the gods ; Frey, Woden, Thor, and Tyr, of the pagan period, being influenced by the newer cult in religion. This is shown by the Sigurd Overlap, and the story of Sigurd the Volsung.[1]

The farmer Hreithmar had three sons—Otter, Fafni, and Regin the smith ; and three of the Scandinavian gods—Woden, Hœni, and Loki—wandered towards the farm, and, through misunderstanding, Loki killed Otter. For this the three gods were seized, and released only on payment of enough gold to cover the skin of Otter (fig. 2) when hung up by the nose. This price was procured by Loki, who compelled the dwarf Andwari to surrender all the gold he possessed, as well as a magic ring, which carried with it a curse that for eight lives the gold should be fatal to its owner. Then Hreithmar was slain by his surviving sons for the treasure, which was carried off to a great mound on Gnita Heath by Fafni, who lay round his plunder in the form of a dragon. Regin, his brother, in order to obtain the treasure, prompted Sigurd, his foster son, to slay the dragon. Sigurd, in testing his sword, broke it in twain ; thereupon Regin made him a magic sword, with which he lay in the trail of the dragon, and pierced it through (figs. 1-4). Then Regin took out the heart of the dragon, which Sigurd cut into pieces and toasted while Regin slept. Sigurd, burning his fingers, placed them in his mouth, and tasted the blood of Fafni, the dragon (fig. 1), and lo ! he heard the voice of birds saying that Regin was plotting to kill him. Then Sigurd killed Regin, ate the heart of Fafni, placed the treasure on the back of the noble horse Grani, and departed, only to be slain for the gold by Gunnar, who for this crime was cast into the pit of serpents (fig. 1).

This myth explains much of the Scandinavian ornament, for in figs. 1 and 2 the story is told in a series of incidents remarkable for the fertility of invention and dracontine ornamentation. Halton Cross in Lancashire, and a slab at Kirk Andreas, Isle of Man, illustrate the same subjects, dating from the 11th century. In later times, the dragon becomes more pronounced in character, until in the 14th century it fills the whole portal with the beautiful interlacing ornament (fig. 6).

[1] " The Pagan-Christian Overlap in the North," by H. Colley March, M.D. (Lond.).
" Sigurd the Volsung," by William Morris.

NORMAN & GOTHIC ARCHITECTURE

English architecture has been broadly divided into periods for the purpose of classifying the styles, the following being the most generally accepted :—

By Sharpe.[1]		A.D.	By Rickman.[2]		A.D.
Roman-esque	Saxon .	1066	Norman . . .		1066-1189
	Norman .	1066-1145	Early English . .		1189-1307
Gothic	Transitional .	1145-1190	Decorated . . .		1307-1379
	Lancet . .	1190-1245	Perpendicular . .		1379-1483
	Curvilinear .	1245-1360	Tudor. . . .		1483-1546
	Rectilinear .	1360-1550			

Most of our magnificent cathedrals were founded, A.D. 1066-1170, by Norman bishops, some upon the old Saxon foundations, such as Canterbury and York, or near the original Saxon buildings, as at Winchester, or upon new sites, such as Norwich and Peterborough ; and were without exceptions more magnificent erections than those of the anterior period, portions of the older style still existing in many cathedrals, showing the fusion of Roman and Byzantine architecture with the more personal and vigorous art of the Celtic, Saxon, and Scandinavian peoples.

Lincoln is a typical English plan, showing no trace of the semicircular apsidal arrangement so universal in Norman and French cathedrals. Each vertical division in the nave, the choir, and transept is termed a bay. On plate 19 is an illustration of four typical bays of English cathedrals, showing the development of style from the 12th to the 15th century. The general characteristic of each bay is given separately, but obviously it can only be approximate, as the building of each cathedral was influenced by local considerations, each period necessarily overlapping its predecessor, thus forming a transitional style. For instance, in the choir of Ripon Cathedral the aisle and clearstory have semi-circular Norman windows, and the nave arcading has pointed arches. In the triforium and clearstory arcading, round arches are seen side by side with the pointed arch.

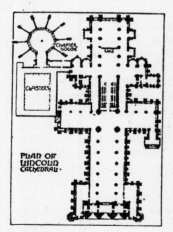

PLAN OF LINCOLN CATHEDRAL.

The PIERS—sometimes termed columns—of these bays have

[1] " The Seven Periods of Church Architecture," by Edmund Sharpe.
[2] " Gothic Architecture," by Thomas Rickman.

distinctive features which are characteristic of each period of the Gothic development.

Sketch plans are here given showing the changes that took place in the section of the pier from 1066 to 1500. The same general characteristics are observed in the arch mouldings and string courses.

CHARACTERISTICS OF THE NORMAN PERIOD

NAVE ARCADING.—The universal use of the round arch, cylindrical or rectangular piers, with semi-circular shafts attached to each face.

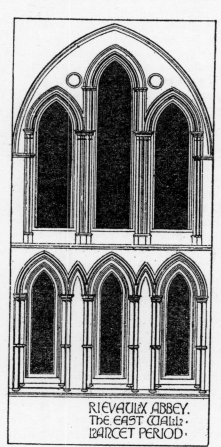

RIEVAULX ABBEY.
ThE EAST WALL·
LANCET PERIOD·

Capitals cubical and cushion-shaped. Arch mouldings enriched with concentric rows of Chevron and Billet ornament.

TRIFORIUM.—In early work, of one arch. In later work, two or four small arches carried on single shafts under one large semi-circular arch.

CLEARSTORY. — One window, with an open arcading in front, of three arches, the centre one larger and often stilted. This arcade forms a narrow gallery in the thickness of the clearstory wall. The roof of the nave of wood, flat and panelled, roof of the aisles semi-circular quadripartite vaulting. An arcading of semi-circular arches was usually placed upon the wall, under the aisle windows. Early windows are narrow, flush with the external wall, and deeply splayed on the inside. Later windows are recessed externally, with jamb-shafts and capitals supporting an enriched moulded arch. A few circular rose windows still remain, of which a fine example is to be found in Barfreston Church, Kent.

41

EARLY ENGLISH OR LANCET PERIOD

The Lancet or pointed arch universal.

CAPITALS, of three lobed foliage and circular abacus. The pier arch mouldings, alternate rounds and hollows deeply cut and enriched with the characteristic dog's tooth ornament. A hood moulding which terminates in bosses of foliage or sculptured heads invariably surrounds the arch mouldings. This moulded hood when used externally is termed a "Dripstone," and when used horizontally over a square headed window, a "Label."

The TRIFORIUM has a single or double arch, which covers the smaller or subordinate arches, the spandrels being enriched with a sunk or pierced trefoil or quatrefoil. The Triforium piers are solid, having delicate shafts attached to them, carrying arch mouldings of three orders, and enriched with the dog's tooth ornament or trefoil foliage.

The CLEARSTORY lancet windows are in triplets, with an arcading on the inner face of the wall. The vaulting shaft occasionally springs from the floor, but more usually from a corbel above the nave capitals, and finishes under the clearstory string with an enriched capital, from which springs the simple vaulting usually quadripartite or hexapartite in form. Early windows in small churches were arranged in couplets, and at the east end, usually in triplets, with grisaille stained glass.

The example given on the previous page from the east end of Rievaulx Abbey shows a finely proportioned window and its arrangement. Figure sculpture, beautiful and refined in treatment, was frequently used upon external walls.

The figures of Saints and Bishops were placed singly under triangular pediments and cusped arches, of which there are fine examples at Wells, Lichfield, Exeter, and Salisbury (fig. 5, plate 19). Splendid examples of circular rose windows are to be seen in the north and south transepts of Lincoln Cathedral, also at York, but they are comparatively rare in England, while France possesses over 100 of the finest and most important examples of this type. They are to be seen in the Cathedrals of Notre Dame, Paris ; Rouen ; Chartres ; and Rheims.

DECORATED OR GEOMETRIC PERIOD

In this, the piers have engaged shafts, with capitals having plain mouldings, or enriched with finely carved foliage of the oak, maple, or mallow, seen in perfection at Southwell Minster, which contains the finest carving of this period—1280-1315 (plate 22). The pier arches have mouldings of three orders, also enriched, usually with the characteristic ball flower, or foliage similar to that upon the capitals.

The TRIFORIUM consists of double arches, with subordinate cusped arches adorned with geometric tracery. The inner arcading of the clearstory is absent, the one large window being divided by mullions

42

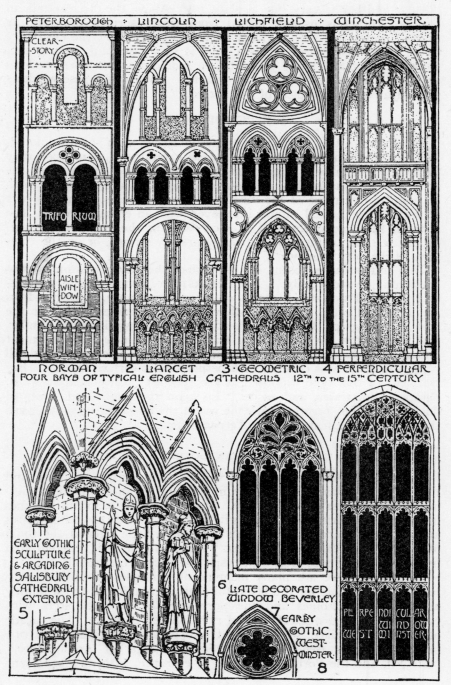

PETERBOROUGH · LINCOLN · LICHFIELD · WINCHESTER

CLEAR-STORY

TRIFORIUM

AISLE WINDOW

1 NORMAN   2 · LANCET   3 · GEOMETRIC   4 PERPENDICULAR
FOUR BAYS OF TYPICAL ENGLISH CATHEDRALS 12TH TO THE 15TH CENTURY

EARLY GOTHIC SCULPTURE & ARCADING. SALISBURY CATHEDRAL EXTERIOR
5

6 LATE DECORATED WINDOW BEVERLEY

7 EARLY GOTHIC. WEST-MINSTER

PERPENDICULAR WINDOW WINCHESTER

8

1 NORTH WEST DOOR. LINCOLN CATHEDRAL.

3 BILLET MOULDING

4 ZIGZAG & BALL LINCOLN.

5 BEAK HEADS. IFFEY CHURCH

2 SOUTH DOOR KILPECK CHURCH. HEREFORD-SHIRE.

6 ORNAMENT UPON ARCH. ST PETERS. NORTHHAMPTON.

7 CHEVRON & KEY PATTERN. DURHAM CATHEDRAL.

8 FRENCH CAPITAL

9 CAPITAL & COLUMN AT WOOTTON

10 ENRICHMENT FROM THE JEWS HOUSE LINCOLN

11 FRENCH CAPITAL.

NORMAN ORNAMENT

Norman architecture was distinguished by the use of the traditional semi-circular arch, superseded by the pointed arch of the early Gothic period. These semi-circular arches in the earlier dates were decorated with rudely executed carvings, cut or worked with the axe. Later Norman work is very rich, the mouldings being well carved with enrichments of the Chevron, the Cable, Billet, Star, Fret, or Key Patterns ; the Lozenge and the Beading or Pearling. Characteristic features of this period also are the Beakhead (fig. 5), and the Corbel-table, which was a series of heads of men or animals, from which spring small arches supporting the parapet. Many rich examples of Norman surface ornament are still extant ; at Christchurch, Hants, a beautiful intersecting arcading of semi-circular arches occurs, the enrichment above being a scale or imbricated pattern ; at St. Peter's, Northampton, a very rich example of surface ornamentation may be seen (fig. 6).

Floral forms are but rarely used in Norman ornament ; instances are known of the use of the rose and the fir-apple, but they are the exception and not the rule.

Early doorways usually have a square head recessed under semi-circular arch mouldings, decorated with the Chevron, Key, or Beakhead. The semi-circular Tympanum over the door was plain or enriched with rude sculpture in low relief. Later doors show a great profusion of ornament in the archivolt and arch mouldings, which are often carried down the jamb mouldings. The recessed columns are also enriched with the Chevron, or diagonal lines of pearling (fig. 1), and have sculptured capitals showing a classical tendency in the arrangement of acanthus foliage and the volute. Fine examples of this period may be seen in the west front of Lincoln Cathedral (fig. 1), the Galilee porch at Durham, and the west door of Iffley Church, Oxfordshire. A fine, deeply recessed semi-circular Norman doorway is at Tutbury Church, having a richly recessed window over, now filled with flamboyant tracery.

Early Norman capitals are usually cubical or cushion-shaped, with a square or cruciform abacus, or occasionally octagonal as at Durham, or circular as at Gloucester, and enriched with the Chevron, Star, or Anthemion, the Capitals being escalloped with segments of circles, or enriched with Volutes or the Anthemion. Early examples are in the White Tower and St. Bartholomew, London. Later Capitals, usually rich in ornamentation, are found at St. Peter's, Northampton, and at Wootton, more frequently they have interlacing bands of ornament and animals ; there are others with figures, or " Storied Capitals," as in the North Porch, Wells.

In the transition period—end of 12th century—Capitals were concave or bell-shaped, with foliage of the serrated water-leaf type clinging to the bell and turning up under the abacus, forming a Volute. This foliage was varied in type and vigorous in technique. Fine examples are at Christ Church, Oxford, and at Canterbury Cathedral.

2 · STONE BOSS ·

STONE: SPANDRIL FROM CHANCEL ARCADE & STONE CHURCH. KENT

4 · CROCKET YORK CATHEDRAL ·

3 · EARLY GOTHIC GLASS · SALISBURY

5 · FROM SALISBURY CATHEDRAL ·

6 · FROM ELY CATHEDRAL ·

8 · TOOTH ORNAMENT.

9 · PETERBOROUGH

ELY CATHEDRAL ·

DIAPER WESTMINSTER.

10 · EARLY ENGLISH CLUSTERED CAPITAL · LINCOLN CATHEDRAL ·

11 · EARLY FRENCH GOTHIC. NOTRE DAME ·

12 · EARLY FRENCH CAPITAL. RHEIMS CATHEDRAL ·

EARLY GOTHIC ORNAMENT

The NORMAN style was succeeded by the pointed, or GOTHIC style, remarkable for its variety, its beauty of proportion, and the singular grace and vigour of its ornament. Showing no traditions, beyond Sicilian and Arabian influence, it grew rapidly, and reached a high degree of perfection in France and England. The massive and barbaric character of the Norman style gave place to the light clustered shafts and well-proportioned mouldings of the early English Gothic with its capitals characterized by a circular abacus, and the typical three-lobed foliage growing upwards from the necking of the shafts, thence spreading out in beautiful curves and spirals under the abacus. This tendency to the spiral line is peculiar to the early Gothic, and differentiates it from the Decorated and Perpendicular Period. The diagrams of the three crockets here given show the distinctive character of English Gothic ornament.

Early Gothic, three-lobed leaves arranged in spiral lines. Decorated Gothic, with natural types of foliage, such as the oak and maple, with a flowing undulating line. Perpendicular Gothic, showing the vine and leaves as elements, and arranged in a square and angular manner. The same features and characteristics are observed in the borders here given. The carved spandril from the Chancel Arcade, Stone Church, Kent (fig. 1), is one of the most beautiful examples of English ornament, remarkable for the vigour and flexibility of curve, its recurring forms of ornamentation, and admirable spacing, typical of much of our early English foliage from about 1170-1280.

The type of foliage in early English stained glass is somewhat similar to contemporary carved work, but showing more of the profile of the leaf; it has a geometric or radiating arrangement in addition to the spiral forms of foliage (plate 59), and the admirable spacing of the ornament shows the skill in design that the mediæval craftsman possessed.

CAPITALS FROM CHAPTER HOUSE. SOUTHWELL.

FROM THE TRIFORIUM OF NAVE. St. ALBANS.

A MISERERE.

PARAPET. BEVERLEY MINSTER.

THE BALL-FLOWER.

ALTERNATE BALL-FLOWER.

FINIAL & CROCKETS. LINCOLN.

CORBEL OF VAULTING SHAFT. EXETER.

FOUR-LEAVED-FLOWER.

DECORATED GOTHIC ORNAMENT

Decorated Gothic is remarkable for its geometric or curving tracery, its natural types of foliage, and the undulating character of line and form in its ornamental details. The foliage of the oak, the vine, the maple, the rose, and the ivy were introduced in much luxuriance and profusion, being carved with great delicacy and accuracy. Lacking the dignity and architectonic qualities of the early Gothic foliage, it surpassed it in brilliancy and inventiveness of detail. The capitals, enriched with adaptations from nature, carved with admirable precision, were simply attached round the bell (page 102), giving variety and charm of modelling, but lacking that unity which was so characteristic of early work.

FINIAL & CROCKETS. EXETER CATHE-DRAL.

The illustrations from Southwell are characteristic examples of the richly-carved clustered capitals of this period. The arch mouldings were also enriched with foliage of a similar type, and at the springing of the vaulting shaft of the nave, beautiful carved corbels, such as those at Exeter, were used, while the walls, screens, and parapets, were diapered with low relief carving.

Crockets and finials, which were introduced in the early Gothic period, were now treated with exceeding richness and used in the greatest profusion. A characteristic example is given here from Exeter Cathedral.

The three surviving Queen Eleanor Crosses (erected 1291-4), at Geddington, Northampton, and Waltham, are perhaps the richest examples of the Decorated period, showing the exuberance of modelling and the versatility and skill of the English craftsman in the finest period of Naturalistic foliage (1280-1315). The statues of Queen Eleanor are by William of Ireland, "imaginator."

The "Ball Flower" so characteristic of the decorated period, replaced the equally characteristic "Tooth Ornament" of the preceding style, and was much used in some buildings, even to excess—as in the south

WALL DIAPER. WEST-MINSTER.

aisle of Gloucester Cathedral. It is found in the hollows round doorways, windows, arches, and canopies, and it has been known to alternate with the "Four-petalled Flower."

51

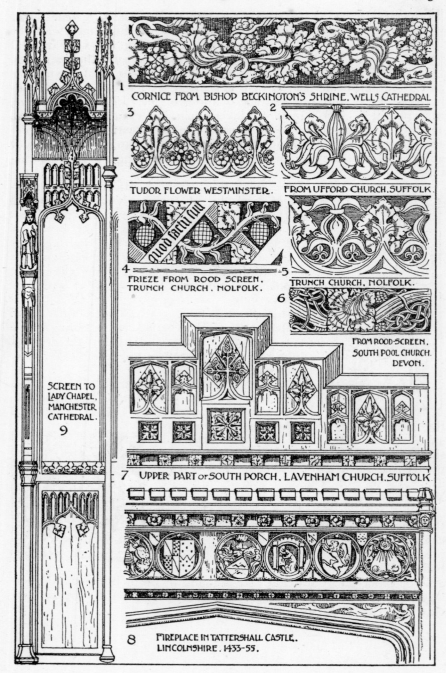

1 CORNICE FROM BISHOP BECKINGTON'S SHRINE, WELLS CATHEDRAL

3 TUDOR FLOWER WESTMINSTER.

2 FROM UFFORD CHURCH, SUFFOLK

4 FRIEZE FROM ROOD SCREEN, TRUNCH CHURCH, NOLFOLK.

5 TRUNCH CHURCH, NOLFOLK.

6 FROM ROOD-SCREEN, SOUTH POOL CHURCH, DEVON.

9 SCREEN TO LADY CHAPEL, MANCHESTER CATHEDRAL.

7 UPPER PART OF SOUTH PORCH, LAVENHAM CHURCH, SUFFOLK.

8 FIREPLACE IN TATTERSHALL CASTLE, LINCOLNSHIRE. 1433-55.

52

SCREEN DETAIL, EDINGTON CHURCH, WILTSHIRE.

SCREEN CARVING, NORTON FITZWARREN, SOMERSET.

PERPENDICULAR GOTHIC

The latest Gothic style in England is characterized by a verticality of line in construction and ornament. One of several exceptions is the beautiful fan-vaulting, such as that in the cloisters at Gloucester Cathedral, and in Henry VII.'s Chapel at Westminster, which are not approached by any Continental example for beauty of craftsmanship or scientific precision of masonry. The many splendid towers, having elaborate panelled tracery, and capped with pinnacles, open parapets and battlements, such as those at Wrexham and S. Mary's, Taunton, are also characteristic of this period. The windows, with vertical mullions running to the window-head, which is frequently a four-centred arch, have, in large examples, one or more transoms, enriched with battlements or Tudor flowers, to divide the lofty windows horizontally (plate 19). The 15th century carving and detail, especially in woodwork, is gloriously rich and varied, vigorous in design, and of consummate craftsmanship. Local schools of marked individuality occur ; thus an East Anglian screen is entirely different to one in Devon. The great mass of fine work extant in cathedrals and churches : screens, pulpits, stalls, font-covers, etc., is a great heritage from mediæval times, of which all should be proud, and learn to explore and appreciate. The many choir screens and stalls, with their canopies, have panels, friezes, crestings, and finials, and are frequently carved with treatment of the vine (figs. 1-7), the Tudor flower being prevalent.

The terminals of the ends of stalls were frequently enriched with foliated "Poppy-heads," often of great beauty.

Heraldic forms, such as shields, with their supporters, together with badges and crests, were largely associated with the ornament in the richer buildings of this period, such as King's College Chapel at Cambridge, and Henry VII.'s Chapel at Westminster.

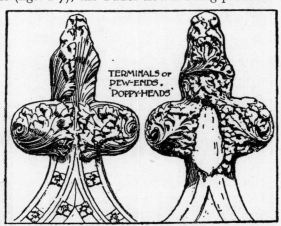

TERMINALS OF PEW-ENDS. "POPPY-HEADS"

Nave piers are usually rectangular or lozenge in section, consisting of a few rounds and double ogee moulds, and an octagonal capital is typically carried by some of the round members of the pier. A common enrichment in the hollows of the strings and arch mouldings is a four-petalled flower, alternate square and circular (figs. 7 and 8).

EARLY GOTHIC STONE CARVING. NOTRE DAME. PARIS.

1

3
13ᵀᴴ CENTURY CAPITAL.

4
14ᵀᴴ CENTURY CARVINGS.

5

WOOD CARVING.

CANOPY OF
STALLS IN
CATHEDRAL,
AMIENS.
LATE GOTHIC.

2

FRENCH GOTHIC ORNAMENT

French cathedrals show a marked contrast in scale and enrichment to those of England, being wider, shorter, and higher in proportion, and the sculpture bolder, more profuse, and larger in scale than in contemporary English cathedrals. The principal doorways are also on a large scale and are usually enriched with numerous statues, placed under canopies, which cover the whole of the recessed arch; whilst the central pier of the door, carrying the figure of the Madonna or a bishop, supports the tympanum (the space within the arch), which is also covered with horizontal bands of sculpture. The figure sculpture of the late 13th and early 14th centuries has considerable skill of composition, and well arranged draperies; broad and simple in mass, and vigorous in execution (page 56).

The gables of the doors are frequently enriched with crockets and finials, or with beautiful open tracery —as in the west doors of Rouen Cathedral. The Cathedral of Amiens has a delightful series of sculptured reliefs of Biblical subjects, called the Bible of Amiens, enclosed within quatre-foil panels, which extends across the lower part of the façade.

The early relief ornament of the 13th century is remarkable for its vigorous carving and boldness of relief. It differs from contemporary English work in having a rounder form of leaf, divided into lobes, with strongly marked radiating mid-ribs (compare fig. 1, plate 25, with fig. 1, plate 21). The capitals, with the foliage clinging closely to the bell (fig. 3) have not the spiral tendency which characterized English ornament of the same period. The abacus is generally square (page 102), and the clustered pillars and the bell-shaped moulded capitals, without foliage, which are typical of English work, are almost unknown in France. In the 14th century, the foliage, like contemporary carving in England, is naturalistic (figs. 4 and 5, plate 25, and page 102), with a ribbed tool-mark following the direction of the leaf.

Among the many splendid examples of the 15th century, or flamboyant period, are the stalls of Amiens (fig. 2), where flowing tracery is intermingled with rich cusped-arches, open gables, and crocketed pinnacles.

Plate 26

FRENCH GOTHIC SCULPTURE

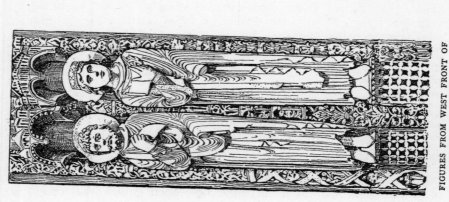

CENTRAL PIER AND PART OF TYMPANUM, SOUTH DOOR,
AMIENS CATHEDRAL, XIII. CENTURY.

PIER FROM WEST DOOR,
AMIENS.

FIGURES FROM WEST FRONT OF
CHARTRES CATHEDRAL,
XII. CENTURY.

ENASCENCE ARCHITECTURE & ORNAMENT IN ITALY

Lombardy, in the north of Italy, had witnessed a singular blending of the old classic art with the vigorous traditions and myths of the Longobards, and the symbolisms of Byzantium ; thus producing the architecture known as Lombardic, with its multiplicity of small columns and arches, quaint imagery of sculpture, and the frequent use of a lion or dragon as a support for the columns. These are features of the early art at Lucca, Bergamo, Padua, Verona, and other towns in Lombardy (see Romanesque, page 35) ; a beautiful illustration from Lucca is given in the appendix to Ruskin's " Stones of Venice," Vol. I. Contemporary with this period came the Gothic influence, with its clustered columns, pointed arches, its cusps and crockets, and its strong vitality, impressing the arts and architecture with a lasting influence ; hence during the 12th and 13th centuries in Italy, this intermingling of styles, traditions, religious beliefs and myths, produced an art barbaric and vigorous in character, the imagery full of suggestiveness, and the detail rich and varied in conception. Yet it was but the herald of a style which culminated in the epoch of the Renascence, a style where symmetry was to play an important part as in classic art, where refinement of line and detail, of culture and craftsmanship, are found ; and which, though beautiful in proportion, unity of parts, and perfect adaptability, yet lacked that symbolism, suggestiveness, inventiveness and rugged strength of the early Byzantine, Lombardic, and Gothic styles.

The earlier Italian Renascence is broadly divided into three periods, viz. : The Tre-Cento, A.D. 1300-1400 ; the Quattro-Cento, 1400-1500 ; and the Cinque-Cento, 1500-1600.

In the Tre-Cento period the sculpture and decorative arts are marked by dignity of conception, and a mingling of Gothic and Classic traditions. Two of the earliest examples showing Renascence influence are the hexagonal pulpits in the Baptistery at Pisa and the Cathedral at Siena by Niccolo Pisano. These are transitional in style, having sculptured panels distinctly classical in treatment, associated with cusped Gothic arches. Niccolo also executed the beautiful octagonal fountain at Perugia and was assisted in much of his work by his son Giovanni Pisano, who was the author of the beautiful pulpit in the Cathedral at Pisa. A fine monumental work showing these characteristics is the tomb of S. Peter the martyr in the Church of S. Eustorgio at Milan.

In the architecture, Gothic forms prevail, together with panelling of white and grey marble, lofty pilasters, pinnacles, and gables, enriched with a geometric patterning of marbles or mosaic, and also a frequent use of the twisted pillar.

The Cathedral at Florence (plan, p. 176), with its panelling, pointed arches, and rich tracery, was by Arnolfo di Cambio (died 1300) and

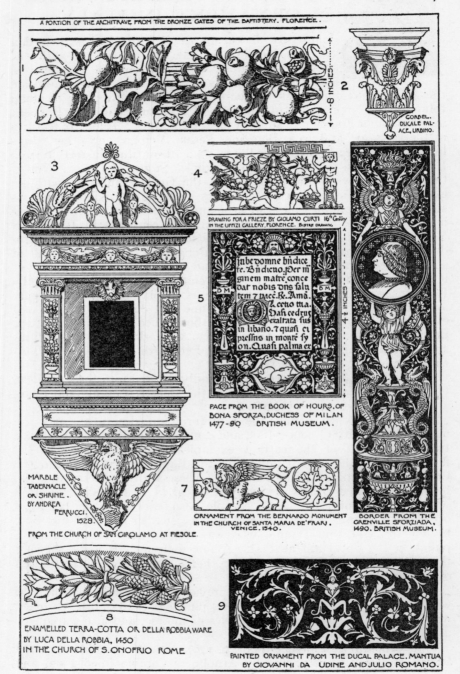

A PORTION OF THE ARCHITRAVE FROM THE BRONZE GATES OF THE BAPTISTERY. FLORENCE.

1

2   CORBEL.
DUCALE PAL-
ACE, URBINO.

3

4   DRAWING FOR A FRIEZE BY GIOLAMO CURTI   16th Century
IN THE UFFIZI GALLERY, FLORENCE. Bistre drawing.

5   PAGE FROM THE BOOK OF HOURS, OF
BONA SFORZA, DUCHESS OF MILAN
1477-90   BRITISH MUSEUM.

MARBLE
TABERNACLE
OR SHRINE.
BY ANDREA
FERRUCCI
1528.
FROM THE CHURCH OF SAN GIROLAMO AT FIESOLE.

7   ORNAMENT FROM THE BERNARDO MONUMENT
IN THE CHURCH OF SANTA MARIA DE' FRARI.
VENICE. 1540.

BORDER FROM THE
GRENVILLE SFORZIADA,
1490. BRITISH MUSEUM.

8
ENAMELLED TERRA-COTTA OR DELLA ROBBIA WARE
BY LUCA DELLA ROBBIA, 1450
IN THE CHURCH OF S. ONOFRIO ROME

9   PAINTED ORNAMENT FROM THE DUCAL PALACE. MANTUA
BY GIOVANNI DA UDINE AND JULIO ROMANO.

Francesco Talenti, who completed the nave, choir, and apses in 1321. Arnolfo and Talenti were also the architects for the Church of Santa Croce and the Palazzo Vecchio, Florence (1290), where, in 1434, Michelozzo added the beautiful cortile, and C. Salviati and De Faenze, pupils of Vasari, enriched the circular and octagonal pillars with beautiful stucco ornamentation (plate 28), in 1565.

The fine campanile by Giotto (1336), Andrea Pisano, and Francesco Talenti, who introduced the upper Gothic windows, is a noble accessory to the Cathedral of Florence.

In 1293 Arnolfo introduced some Prato marble pilasters at the angles of " San Giovanni," the octagonal Florentine Baptistery, an ancient building where many of the great citizens of the Republic received their baptism ; it was here that Dante was baptised in May, 1265.

The last of the Tre-Cento masters was Andrea Pisano, who made the first bronze gate of " San Giovanni," or the Baptistery of Florence. This gate has 28 quatre-foil panels in relief, and bears the inscription " ANDREAS UGOLINI NINI PISIS ME FECIT, A.D. MCCCXXX."

The true Renascence or Quattro-Cento period is remarkable for the vitality of the arts, and the vigour and versatility of its craftsmen. Brunelleschi is the earliest architect (page 68), and Lorenzo Ghiberti the first ornamentist and sculptor, whose chief works are the two bronze gates for the Florentine Baptistery. The first gate (1403-24), has 28 quatre-foil panels similar to the earlier one by

MONUMENT TO ILARIA DEL CARRETTO,
BY JACOPO DELLA QUERCIA.

Andrea Pisano, and the last gate (1425-59), has 10 rectangular panels with incidents from the Old Testament in high relief (plate 65).

The styles or framework of these gates, have a series of single figures in niches with circular medallions between them.

The bronze architrave round each of the Ghiberti gates and the earlier gate by Andrea Pisano, are rich examples of Quattro-Cento design. The details are natural fruits, flowers and foliage, banded together with ribbons, with the introduction of birds, squirrels, etc. The egg-plant and pomegranate portion (fig. 1) is a familiar example.

Other masters of this period were Jacopo della Quercia, who, in 1406, executed the beautiful monument shown on the previous page to Ilaria di Carretto, in the Cathedral at Lucca. The recumbent figure of Ilaria is sculptured in white marble with perfect simplicity and beauty ; another famous work of Jacopo was the fountain at Siena.

Luca della Robbia executed a beautiful organ gallery in marble for the Cathedral at Florence (1431), now in the museum of the Opera del Duomo, Florence, with admirable singing and dancing figures, in relief. Donatello was remarkable for the singular grace and sincerity of his portraiture, especially of children. The dancing figures in

THE "CANTORIA," OR SINGING GALLERY, BY DONATELLO (1435).

relief on the panels of the singing gallery of the Cathedral of Florence with which he was commissioned in 1443 are perfect examples of his art.

This frieze of children is a delightful example of one phase of Donatello's craftsmanship, showing the vitality and exuberance of his conception. The peculiar relief, called " *stacciato*," of the figures which shows a series of almost flat surfaces, upon which is carved exquisitely delicate reliefs, contrasted with an abrupt contour giving strongly-marked shadows, is typical of much of Donatello's relief-

60

S. GEORGE, BY DONATELLO.

work. An illustration is also given of the famous S. George, from the Gothic Church or oratory of Or San Michele, Florence. This church has niches and canopies on the external walls, each with its statue by great Quattro-Cento masters. Three statues in marble of S. Peter (1412), S. Mark (1412), and S. George (1415), are by Donatello; three in marble, S. Philip (1408), Four Crowned Martyrs, and S. Eligius (1415), by Nanni di Banco; S. John (1415), S. Matthew (1422), and S. Stephen (1428), in bronze by Ghiberti; Christ and S. Thomas (1483), bronze, by Verrochio; and S. Luke (1601), in bronze, by Giovanni da Bologna.

The Monastery of San Marco is one of the remarkable buildings in Florence. Built in 1437-50 by Michelozzo for Cosimo de Medici, it was enriched with the most beautiful frescoes by Fra Angelico.

The art of the medallist, which had declined since the time of the Roman Empire, now took its position among the arts of the Quattro-Cento period, under Vittore Pisano, called Pisanello. The vigour of his modelling and the individuality of his medals of the contemporary princes of Italy, are exceedingly fine. Among other remarkable medallists, were Sperandio of Verona, Caradossa of Milan, Vincentine of Vicenza, Benvenuto Cellini of Florence, Lione Leoni, Pompeoni Leoni, and Pastorino of Siena.

Other names of this period were Desiderio da Settignano, his master-

RELIEFS FROM THE SINGING GALLERY, BY DONATELLO, IN THE MUSEUM OF THE OPERA DEL DUOMO, FLORENCE.

piece being the tomb of Carlo Marsuppini, in the Church of Santa Croce, Florence ; Mino da Fiesole ; Andrea Verrochio, the author of the fine equestrian statue of Bartolomeo Colleone at Venice (see Bronzes, plate 65) ; Matteo Civitali ; and the Rossellini, a remarkable family of five brothers, of which the most famous was Antonio Rossellino, who executed a charming tomb to Cardinal Jacopo di Portogallo, in the Church of the Nunziata, Florence.

The Cinque-Cento period was the culmination of the Renascence, when architecture, sculpture, painting, and the decorative arts, were under the munificent patronage of the popes and princes of Italy. Palaces, churches, and public buildings were completed (see Renascence Architecture, pages 68-70), and embellished with beautiful sculptures and decorations ; hung with the most sumptuous fabrics of the Venetian, Florentine, and Genoese looms ; decorated with altar paintings and mural decorations by the most renowned of painters ; and enriched with the magnificent productions of the gold and silversmiths' art, and the loveliest of intarsia, or inlaid woodwork.

THE CUMÆAN SIBYL BY MICHEL ANGELO

The Sistine Chapel, built for Sixtus IV., in 1473, by Baccio Pintelli, is decorated with fresco paintings on the walls by the great Cinque-Cento masters, Luca Signorelli, Sandro Botticelli, Cosimo Rosselli, Perugino, the master of Raphael, Domenico Ghirlandajo, and Michel Angelo, who painted " The Last Judgment " on the end wall, and the famous ceiling with incidents from the Old Testament, and with the prophets Joel, Ezekiel, Jeremiah, Jonah, Daniel, Isaiah, and Zechariah, and the sibyls Erithræa, Perscia, Lybica, Cumæa, and Delphica. These are splendid examples of decorative painting, where unity and dignity of conception, powerful draughtsmanship, and marvellous execution are shown in a remarkable degree.

The New Sacristy of San Lorenzo, Florence, designed and executed by Michel Angelo, having the tombs of Lorenzo and Giuliano de Medici, with the reclining figures of Dawn and Twilight, Day and Night, shows his remarkable versatility, power, and conception of art.

The art of mural decoration reached its highest degree of achievement during this period in the hands of Raffaele and his contemporaries. The earliest fresco paintings by the Quattro-Cento masters, such as those in the Arena Chapel at Padua and the Church of San

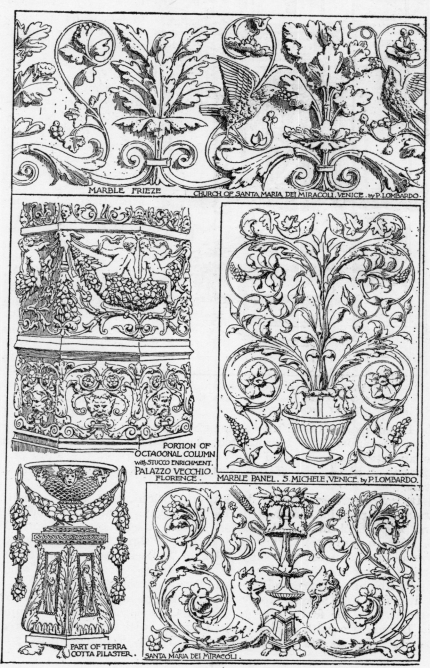

MARBLE FRIEZE   CHURCH OF SANTA MARIA DEI MIRACOLI, VENICE . by P. LOMBARDO.

PORTION OF OCTAGONAL COLUMN with STUCCO ENRICHMENT. PALAZZO VECCHIO. FLORENCE.

MARBLE PANEL . S. MICHELE . VENICE . by P. LOMBARDO.

PART OF TERRA COTTA PILASTER.

SANTA MARIA DEI MIRACOLI.

TOMB OF LORENZO DE MEDICI,
SACRISTY OF SAN LORENZO, FLORENCE,
BY MICHEL ANGELO.

Francesco at Assisi by Giotto, and the series of panels by Benozzo Gozzoli in the Chapel of the Riccardi Palace at Florence undoubtedly exercised a stimulating influence upon the Cinque-Cento masters, but a more potent influence was the discovery of the ancient baths of Titus, and the house of Livia with their arabesques and mural paintings.

These antique painted arabesques, or, as they were termed, *Grotteschi*, were now utilized and developed to an extraordinary degree of richness and diversity of type. Pinturicchio was probably one of the first masters to use this arabesque type in the decoration of the Papal apartments in the Castle of Sant Angelo at Rome (1494) for Pope Alexander VI. Pinturicchio, doubtless with other artists in collaboration, also carried out the decoration of the Cathedral Library at Siena, one of the most complete decorative schemes in Italy.

It was, however, at the Vatican that decorative art, especially arabesque painting, reached its highest development under Raffaele and his school in the decoration of the Loggia of the Court of S. Damaso (1515-20). This open Loggia of three storeys (plate 29) was decorated under the supervision of Raffaele, with whom many artists collaborated, chief among them being Giovanni da Udine, Giulio Romano, Francesco Penni, and Perino del Vaga.

The first and second storeys of this Loggia are roofed with low cupolas. In the first storey the cupolas are decorated by Giovanni da Udine, two with trellis work alternate with one with coffered panels. The second storey is the most richly decorated (plate 29), the walls, piers, pilasters, and ceilings being covered with arabesques. In the cupolas of the ceiling are small rectangular panels painted by Raffaele with Scriptural subjects, and called Raffaele's Bible. The arabesques are painted in polychrome, chiefly in the secondary colours, on a light ground, with panels painted with festoons of fruit on a dark blue ground by Giovanni da Udine.

The third storey was also largely the work of Da Udine (1520-30), but in 1580 Padre I. Danti painted upon the walls maps of ancient and modern Italy, and Tempesta and Paul Briel, towns and landscapes.

Modelled stucco work took a most important part in framing the pilasters and panels of this loggia, doubtless under the direction of Giovanni da Udine, for Giorgio Vasari writes :—" One Pietro Lorenzo Luzzi, a youth from Feltri, studied many of the graves and grottos, and earned for himself the name of Morto di Feltri. He re-introduced into ornamental art Stucco and Sgraffito, for although it may have been by Giovanni da Udine and other artists who are now distinguishing themselves, that these decorations have been brought to their ultimate perfection, yet it is not to be forgotten that our first thanks and commendations are due to Morto di Feltri, who was the first to discover and restore the kind of painting we call ' grotesque,' seeing that they were for the most part hidden among the subterranean portions of the ruins of Rome whence he brought them."

Morto went to Florence and with Andrea di Cosimo executed at the Gondi Palace the first *sgraffito* decorations.

Contemporaneously with the Loggie of the Vatican, the Stanze, a series of four rooms, was enriched with mural paintings by Raffaele. His first mural painting here was the " Disputa " (1508) in the Camera della Segnatura, followed by the " Poetry, Philosophy, or School of Athens " and " Jurisprudence," the ceiling being painted with figures and arabesques by Sodoma (Bazzi). The Stanze of Heliodorus (1514) has the " Expulsion of Heliodorus from the Temple," " Miracle of Bolsena," " Leo I. and Attila," and the " Deliverance of S. Peter." In the Stanze Incendio del Borgo (1517), are the " Incendio del Borgo Vecchio," the " Justification of Leo III., before Charlemagne," the " Coronation of Charlemagne by Leo III.," and the " Victory of Leo IV. over the Saracens." Perino del Vaga and Giovanni da Udine assisted Raffaele in the last two paintings. The mural paintings for the Sala of Constantine were designed by Raffaele, but were carried out by his pupils, Giulio Romano, Francesco Penni, and Raffaele del Colle.

With the death of Raffaele in 1520 and the completion of the decorations, the Vatican School with its splendid tradition of artistic resource and skill was largely requisitioned by the nobles of Rome and North Italy for the embellishment of their palaces, the most important example of civic patronage being the decoration of the Farnesina Palace (1510-24) by Baldassare Peruzzi, Giulio Romano, Giovanni

E

ARABESQUES FROM THE SECOND FLOOR.

LEO·X·PONT·M·

PAVLVS III PONT MAX

ELEVATION
TO COURT

LOGGIA
OF THE
VATICAN

SECTION
THROUGH
LOGGIA.

da Udine, and G. Razzi.   The upper storey of the palace was decorated by Romano, and Da Udine with the story of Psyche designed by Raffaele.   Da Udine also carried out the magnificent decorations of the Villa Madama (1520-4), where there are some of the finest stucco enrichments of this period.   The best example of decorative painting by Peruzzi is the Villa Belearo, Siena (1535).

Giulio Romano entered the service of Federigo Gonzaga, Duke of Mantua.   He enriched with paintings and arabesques the Palazzo Ducale and the Palazzo del Tè.   Perino del Vaga carried the art to Genoa, decorating with arabesques and medallions the Palazzo Andrea Doria.

Francesco Primaticcio, who for six years was Giulio Romano's chief assistant at Mantua, was in 1531 invited by Francis I. to Fontainebleau, where he decorated the Great Gallery, or the Gallery of Ulysses, with the subjects from the " Odyssey," together with many delicate reliefs.

All these Italian painted arabesques show a great inventiveness and skilful combination of parts, but they are not to be compared with the refined and beautiful modelling, and harmonious composition of the contemporary carved reliefs by Andrea Sansovino, Jacopo Sansovino, Agostino Busti, Pietro Lombardo, and his sons Tullio and Antonio.   These delicate reliefs have the traditional Roman acanthus, but treated with a refined feeling for modelling, and beauty and symmetry of line and mass.

In many examples, vases, masks, shields, and similar accessories are found in profusion (plate 28).   The composition of the Cinque-Cento ornament is usually symmetrical, the details being varied and interesting in the best examples.

Andrea Mantegna (*circ.* 1430—*d.* 1506), who possessed a romantic passion for the antique, executed nine paintings or cartoons in tempera upon linen, representing the triumphs of Julius Cæsar, which are a portion of a frieze 9 ft. high. and 80 ft. long, painted for Lodovico Gonzaga's Palace of S. Sebastian at Mantua. They were purchased by Charles I. and are now at Hampton Court. An illustration of this frieze, from an engraving upon copper in the British Museum, is given here.   It was also engraved on wood by Andrea Andreani in 1599.

The study of classical architecture was stimulated by the publication at Rome, in 1486, of the treatise by Vitruvius, an architect of the time of Augustus ; an edition was also published at Florence in 1496, and at Venice in 1511.   In 1570, Fra Giocondo, at Venice, published " The Five Books of Architecture," by Andrea Palladio.

Another treatise upon architecture, by Serlio, was also published at Venice in 1537 and 1540.

Beautiful types of the Renascence decorative art were the Venetian well-heads, situated in most of the public squares of Venice, and in many of the courtyards of her princely palaces. Designed with details of the most varied and beautiful character by such artists as Andrea Sansovino, Pietro Lombardo, and his sons Tullio and Antonio, the Venetian well-head became a type of beauty, diversified in its treatment, but never losing its characteristics or its usefulness.

MARBLE WELL-HEAD FROM S S BARNABA   IN THE MUSEUM VENICE

The earlier examples are square or circular, with enrichments of Byzantine character, consisting largely of interlacing, circular, and angular lines, enclosing quaint bird and animal forms. In the later examples the Renascence treatment is used with singular richness and appropriateness, the grace, delicacy and diversity of detail being a tribute to the vivacity and artistic feeling of the Venetian Republic. These well-heads, worked mostly in white marble and evincing good judgment in the quality of relief, now show comparatively little injury after centuries of usefulness. Occasionally they were of bronze, like the two fine examples still in position in the courtyard of the Doge's Palace.

Many of these well-heads are carefully treasured in our European Museums, teaching us that beauty of form, and perfection and delicacy of ornament are quite compatible with usefulness, when used by an artistic people.

RENASCENCE ARCHITECTURE IN ITALY

The Renascence in Italy was distinguished by the many magnificent ecclesiastical and secular buildings erected during the 15th and 16th centuries in the chief cities in Italy. Florence was the first to show activity, and with Brunelleschi the history of Renascence architecture commences. The great dome of the Cathedral (1420-34), the Pazzi Chapel (with a fine frieze of cherubs' heads by Donatello and Settignano) at S. Croce (1420), and the Church of S. Lorenzo (1425), were his first works, and were followed by S. Spirito (1433) and the Pitti Palace.

The severe dignity of the bold rusticated stone work, which was usually varied in each storey, the circular-headed windows, and cornices of great depth and projection, became the type of the early palaces of Florence and Siena.

The first Renascence palace was the Riccardi, built for Cosimo de Medici, in 1430, by Michelozzi; and it was followed by the Pitti

(1435) and the Quaratesi (1442), by Brunelleschi; the Rucellai (1451), by Leon Battista Alberti, where pilasters with their entablature were used for the first time in a Renascence façade; the Strozzi (1489), by B. da Majano and Cronaca; the Gondi (1490), by G. da San Gallo; the Guadagni (1490), with *sgraffito* decorations in grey and white plaster; and the Nicolini, by Bramante, the Pandolfini (1520), by Raphael; and the Bartolini (1520), by Baccio d'Agnolo. The plan of these palaces was usually a rectangle, having an internal cortile, with open arcades on the ground floor, the next floor having windows, while the upper storey was sometimes open.

In Rome the palaces were characterized by largeness of scale, the frequent use of the pilaster or attached super-imposed columns, and square-headed windows, with triangular or segmental pediments. The plan is rectangular, with a cortile of one or more storeys of open arcades of semi-circular arches, springing direct from the capital, as in the Cancelleria Palace.

The chief palaces are the Cancelleria (1495) and the Giraud (1503), by Bramante, the Farnesina (1511), the Massimi (1529), and the Villa Ossoli (1525), by Baldassare Peruzzi; the Farnese (1517), by Antonio da San Gallo; the Villa Madama (1516), by Raffaele and Giulio Romano; the Borghese (1590), by Martino Lunghi; the Laterano (1586), by Fontana; and the Barberini (1626), by Maderna, Borromini, and Bernini.

The chief ecclesiastical building is S. Peter's (plan, plate 85), commenced in 1450 by Alberti and Rossellino for Pope Nicholas V.; then carried on by Bramante and San Gallo (1503), Raphael and Peruzzi (1514-20), Antonio da San Gallo (1534), Michel Angelo (1546), Vignola (1556), Giacomo della Porta (1590), and Carlo Maderna (1608). In 1627 S. Peter's was dedicated by Urban VIII., and in 1667 the colonnade in the piazza was erected by Bernini.

The architecture of Venice is rich and varied in style, and the great *palazzi* of the Byzantine, Gothic, and Renascence periods bear tribute to the versatility and skill of the Venetian architects and craftsmen.

The Renascence period may be said to commence with Pietro Lombardo, who built Santa Maria dei Miracoli (1480), a building remarkable for the singular grace and refinement of the internal carved enrichments (plate 28). Another work by Lombardo was the Spinelli Palace (1480), which has mullioned windows, grouped centrally as in the Gothic palace. This feature, together with the use of pilasters or attached columns, became the type of the later Renascence palaces, such as the Palazzo Vendramini, also by Pietro Lombardo. Then followed the rebuilding of the courtyard of the Ducal Palace by Antonio-Bregni (1485), which was completed in 1550 by Scarpagnino; the Scuola di San Marco (1485) by Martino Lombardo; the Palazzo Cornaro (1532), La Zecca (1536), the Loggetta of the Campanile (1540), destroyed by the falling of the Campanile in 1905, but rebuilt, and the Library of S. Mark (1536), by Jacopo

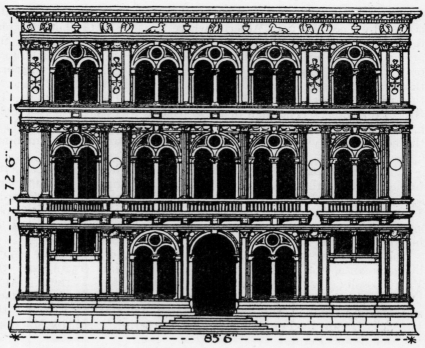

THE PALAZZO VENDRAMINI, VENICE, BY PIETRO LOMBARDO.

Sansovino ; the Grimani Palace (1549) by San Michele ; the Pesaro Palace (1650) and the Church of Santa Maria della Salute (1631) by Baldassare Longhena.

Andrea Palladio of Vicenza was the most famous of the later architects of the Renascence. His chief works are the Basilica Vicenza (1549), which has a fine elevation of two super-imposed orders of attached columns, with arched openings and coupled columns in each storey ; the Valmarana (1556), the Chiericati (1560), and the Tiene (1565) palaces ; and the Teatro Olimpico (1580) ; all of which are in Vicenza

In his later work, which is frequently built of brick and stucco, he adopted the device occasionally used by Peruzzi and San Michele, of an attached column, with or without pedestal, reaching throughout the two storeys of the full height of the building, as in the Casa del Diavolo, Vicenza.

Scamozzi, of Vicenza, succeeded Palladio. He built the Trissino at Vicenza (1588), the Procuratie Nuove (1584), at Venice, and completed Palladio's Church of San Giorgio Maggiore at Venice.

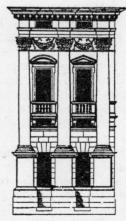

CASA DEL DIAVOLO
VICENZA (PALLADIO).

PALAZZO VERZI, VERONA.

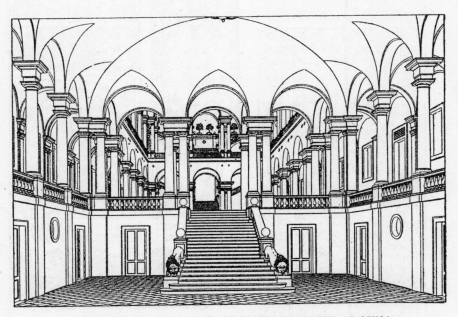

ENTRANCE HALL TO THE PALACE OF THE UNIVERSITY AT GENOA.

EARLY RENASCENCE SCREEN. CLUNY MUSEUM.

FRONT OF COFFER. PERIOD OF LOUIS XII. CLUNY MUSEUM.

CARVED WOOD PANEL. CLUNY MUSEUM.

PANEL OF DOOR. ST. MACLOU. ROUEN. BY JEAN GOUJON.

PANELS FROM LIMOOES CATHEDRAL.

FRENCH RENASCENCE

At the close of the 15th century the Italian Renascence began to exert its influence upon the vigorous and beautiful Gothic art of France, Charles VIII. (1483-89) inviting the Italians, Fra Gioconda, Paganino, Boccador, and various Italian craftsmen to assist in building the castle at Amboise.

At first the influence of the Italian Amboise School was confined to the smaller architectural features, but at the commencement of the 16th century, the classic orders of architecture and the delicate arabesques of Italy, were incorporated with the high-pitched roofs, mullioned windows, dormers, crocketed gables and pinnacles of the beautiful flamboyant Gothic, and fused into the style known as the French Renascence, which is usually divided into distinct characteristic periods, viz. :— I., François Premier, 1515-47 ; II., Henri Deux and Henri Quatre, 1547-1610 ; III., Louis Treize, 1610-43 ; IV., Louis Quatorze, 1643-1715 ; V., Louis Quinze, 1710-70 ; VII., Louis Seize, 1774-89 ; and VIII., The Empire, 1790-1830.

Typical examples of the early Renascence architecture are seen in the numerous châteaux planned upon the earlier type of fortified house, that of Chambord (1526), which is singularly flamboyant in style, has circular towers at the angles

ANCIEN HÔTEL D'ECOVILLE CAEN.

and flanking the entrance, with a roof of cones and cupolas having high dormer windows and chimneys.

The Italian influence received a stimulus from François I., who in 1530 invited Il Rosso to the Palace of Fontainebleau, and Rosso was followed in 1531, by the painter Francesco Primaticcio. The decoration of " Galerie de François Ier " in this palace by these Italians consists of figure subjects in fresco, surrounded with cartouches, and figures in stucco. A panel (fig. 1, plate 32) is a representative example of this period, showing the emblem of the King, a salamander, in a cartouche. Emblems of the various kings and queens are important decorative features in French Ornamental Art.

73

FRANCIS
CVS

FRANCORVM
REX

CARVED PANEL BY F. SIEBECQI.
GALERIE DE FRANCOIS 1er. FONTAINEBLEAU.

SILK BORDER . THE EMPIRE PERIOD . 1805 .

PAINTED PANEL BY JEAN BÉRAIN.
GALERIE D'APOLLON. LOUVRE
LOUIS XIV.

PANEL.
HOTEL DE VILLE.
BORDEAUX.
LOUIS XVI.

DESIGN FOR A PAINTED CEILING, WITH THE MONOGRAM OF WILLIAM III.
BY DANIEL MAROT, *ca.* 1700.

DETAIL OF ROCOCO WOOD-CARVING ROUND A MIRROR IN THE MINISTRY OF PUBLIC
WORKS, PARIS.

Plate 35

FRENCH SILK TEXTILES, LOUIS XVI PERIOD.
USED AS WALL COVERINGS.

In 1541 the architect Sebastiano Serlio, and the goldsmith Benvenuto Cellini, joined the "School of Fontainebleau," which undoubtedly exercised a controlling influence upon the contemporary French architects, Jacques Androuet du Cerceau, Pierre Lescot, Philibert de l'Orme, and Jean Bullant, and the sculptor Jean Goujon.

The Louvre was commenced by Lescot, who built the south-west angle, which was enriched with sculpture by Goujon. These two also collaborated in the building of the beautiful Fontaine des Innocents at Paris (1550), with its fine low relief panels of draped figures.

The reign of Henri II. was a period of remarkable activity in the Arts ; during this reign and that of Henri IV., the prevalence of interlaced strap-work, delicate reliefs, and the liberal use of the cartouche are the characteristic features. These are seen in the Oiron or Henry Deux pottery (plate 56), the geometrical interlacings of the Grolier bindings (plate 73), and the book illustrations of Orance Fine and Jean Cousin.

The Ballroom or "Galerie de Henri II." at Fontainebleau has a richly coffered ceiling of wood by de l'Orme, and the wall painted in fresco by Primaticcio (1564). P. de l'Orme commenced the Tuileries, and Du Cerceau and Duperiac continued the building of the Louvre.

During the Louis Treize period, the tradition of fine architecture and ornament continued, but was considerably influenced by the Spanish and Flemish barocco. The Luxembourg Palace was built by Salomon de Brosse in 1615-24. Other architects of this period were Jacques le Mercier, who continued the Louvre, and François Mansart, who built the new wing at Blois.

The decorative work was chiefly under the control of Simon Vouet, a prolific painter and designer who largely used the "barocco" style characterized by a twisted and broken cartouche, together with masks and a massive type of arabesque. The beautiful book-bindings by the brothers Eve (plate 73) are fine examples of the more delicate ornamentation of this period.

Louis le Vau, the architect, and Charles le Brun, the painter, were the chief men who controlled the arts during the early period of the long reign of Louis Quatorze, Jules Hardouin Mansard, Jean le Pautre, and Jean Berain during the later period. Le Vau continued the building of the Louvre, the Tuileries, and Versailles, and Le Brun painted his finest decorative work in the "Galerie d'Apollon" at the Louvre, and the "Galerie des Glaces" at Versailles (1662-84), which was re-modelled by Mansart in 1680.

The voluminous festoons and arabesques of Le Pautre and Jean Bérain (plates 32 and 74), the beautiful Rouen pottery by Louis Poterat, and the inlaid furniture by André Boulle, are representative of the decorative arts during the latter part of the reign of Louis Quatorze, one of the most important architectural works being the colonnade and east front of the Louvre by Claude Perrault.

77

1

ROCOCO OR LOUIS QUINZE.
WOOD CARVING. NOTRE DAME.

2

3

PANEL IN CARVED WOOD.

4 TROPHIES OF ARMS BY GIRARDON.   VERSAILLES.

(1) DETAIL OF STUCCO ORNAMENTAL PANEL, FROM THE HÔTEL
DE LA BOURSE AT NANTES.

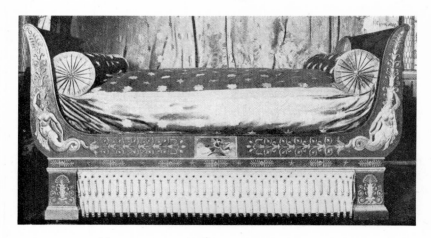

(2) DETAIL OF PLASTER FRIEZE, FROM THE CHAMBRE DES NOTAIRES
AT NANTES.

(3) BED, FROM THE HÔTEL BEAUHARNAIS, PARIS.

The REGENCY, under the Duke of Orleans, was a period remarkable for the development of the " Rocaille," or Rococo, type of ornament in the hands of Just Aurèle Meissonier and Gilles Marie Oppenord. In this *rocaille*, or scroll and shell work, symmetry was systematically avoided, the ornament showing no restraint or reticence of line or detail, reliance being placed upon the brilliancy and playfulness of modelling and design for effect.

The "rocaille" of the Regency continued to be the chief decorative feature of the LOUIS QUINZE. Rooms had shallow vertical panelling, the lines formed of broken curves and scrolls terminating in shell forms and ribbons (plate 34). The acanthus is replaced by the palm as the chief element in the ornamentation, which in spite of its shallow pretence, is attractive, and was in keeping with the social and civic life of the period. J. Verberckt, Nicolas Pineau, and Jules-Antoine Rousseau are the chief carvers associated with the decorative work of the Louis Quinze.

The architecture, unlike the ornamentation, had a greater severity and dignity of style in the hands of Robert de Cotte, Germain Boffrand, and Ange Jacques Gabriel, the latter being the architect of the Place Louis XV. and of the Petit Trianon (1762-68), one of the most perfect small houses of this period.

Under LOUIS SEIZE, insistence is laid upon symmetry in the arrangement of the ornament, and reticence and delicacy of treatment in the details, which consist of the olive, myrtle, and the lily, with swags and garlands and flowers interwoven with ribbons. The cartouche is eliminated, and the oval medallion or tablet takes its place. Room decorations were frequently in pale colours or white and gold, with delicate stucco or painted ornament and panels. Distinguished ornamentists of this period were Delafosse, Cauvet, Salembier, Lalonde, with the *ebenistes* Riesener and David Roentgen and Gouthière, the worker in metal. Representative architects are Jules Nicolas Servandony, and Soufflot, the architect of S. Geneviève (Panthéon).

The period known as the EMPIRE was one of artistic activity characterized by a cold classic formalism founded upon Greek and Roman models. The elements of the ornamentation were the anthemion, acanthus (plate 37), pateræ, urns, and cornucopias, intermingled with the palm and olive symmetrically arranged, frequently arranged upon diagonal lines, with circular medallions and lozenge shapes.

The chief artists of this period were Charles Normand the architect, and Charles Percier, who in collaboration with P. L. Fontaine, controlled the principal decorative work.

AN ANTHEMION FRIEZE BY P. N. BEAUVALLET, 1820.

DESIGN FOR A TIME-METRE. BY HOLBEIN. 1544.

CANOPY TO STALLS. ST. CROSS. WINCHESTER. 1528.

WOODCARVING. ASTON HALL

PORTION OF CEILING AT ASTON HALL, BIRMINGHAM.

PORTION OF HENRY VII TOMB BY TORRIGIANO. WESTMINSTER ABBEY.

PANEL FROM THE CHICHESTER TOMB, PILTON CHURCH, DEVON. 1566.

STONE CARVING, CREWE HALL. CHESHIRE.

(1) PLASTER CEILING FROM THE STAR HOTEL, GREAT YARMOUTH.

(2) PLASTER CEILING FROM THE REINDEER HOTEL, BANBURY, OXON.

[Both now removed to America.

ENGLISH RENASCENCE

The Renascence commenced in England in the early part of the 16th century, about a hundred years later than that in Florence. The first important work was the tomb of John Young, in terra cotta, originally in the Rolls' Chapel, now in the Record Office Museum, Chancery Lane, completed in 1516 by Pietro Torrigiano, who also executed the fine tomb of Henry VII. (1512-18) in Westminster Abbey. This consists of a rectangular sarcophagus of black marble, on which rest the bronze effigies of the king and his consort. On the sarcophagus are gilded bronze pilasters and circular panels in relief, surrounded with wreaths of black marble (plate 38). The tomb of Margaret, Countess of Richmond, and the high altar and baldachino of black and white marble in the Abbey are also by Torrigiano.

Contemporary with Torrigiano was Benedetto da Rovezzano, of Florence, who was commissioned by Cardinal Wolsey, in 1520, to make a sarcophagus of black touchstone, with a recumbent figure of Wolsey in bronze. On the Cardinal's fall, Henry VIII. commissioned Rovezzano to alter and elaborate the work ; but it was left incomplete, and in 1646 the bronze was sold, and the sarcophagus became the resting-place of Nelson in 1806, and is now in S. Paul's Cathedral. Another Florentine, Giovanni di Majano, modelled some terra-cotta medallions for Wolsey at Hampton Court (1521).

In the work of Hans Holbein (plate 38) the Italian feeling is still retained, showing but little of the Gothic tradition ; but in the middle of the century there came a marked change in the ornamental details, the cartouche and strap work, features common to the developed French, Flemish, and German Renascence becoming a pronounced feature of the English Renascence (plate 38).

A typical early Tudor house consisted of a series of rooms placed irregularly round an open court having an entrance gateway flanked by octagonal towers ; the principal room was the lofty hall with its screen and traceried windows. Oxburgh Hall, Norfolk (1482) and Hengrave Hall, Suffolk (1538), are representative of these Tudor houses.

The famous Elizabethan and Jacobean manor-houses are characterized by regularity and symmetry in plan and elevation. The chief buildings of the Elizabethan period are Charlecote (1558), Longleat (1567), Kirby Hall (1570-75), Montacute House (1580), Wollaton Hall (1580-88), and Hardwick Hall (1597). Of the Jacobean period there are Holland House (1607), Hatfield (1611), Audley End (1615), Aston Hall (1620), and Blickling Hall (1620), with their long galleries and rectangular mullioned windows—characteristic features of the Elizabethan and Jacobean period. There are magnificent circular bay windows at Kirby Hall, Burton Agnes (1602-10), and Lilford Hall (1635), and fine octagonal bays at Astley Hall.

CARVED PANEL FROM THE CHURCH OF ST. MARY, BUILT BY WREN, 1695. SOUTH KENSINGTON MUSEUM.

FRIEZE FROM THE CHOIR STALLS, ST. PAUL'S.

PANEL IN STONE. NORTH PORCH. ST. PAUL'S CATHEDRAL.

DOOR·HEAD CLIFFORDS INN.

DOOR·HEAD FROM CLIFFORDS INN.

FRIEZE OF THE UPPER ORDER OF THE BANQUETING HOUSE, WHITEHALL, BY INIGO JONES. 1622.

CARVED FIRE·PLACE IN OAK & CEDAR, FROM A ROOM AT CLIFFORDS INN. LONDON. 1686. NOW IN THE SOUTH KENSINGTON MUSEUM.

The top panel is from ST. MARY, SOMERSET, Upper Thames Street, London, now pulled down except the Tower.

(1) FROM THE WHITE ROOM, WESTWOOD PARK, WORCESTERSHIRE.

(2) FROM HOLYROOD PALACE, EDINBURGH.

(3) FROM THE CHAPEL GALLERY, BELTON HOUSE, LINCOLNSHIRE.

John Thorpe, whose drawings are dated 1570-1621, and Robert Smithson with drawings 1599-1631, are the chief names associated with architectural documents of this period.

Some beautiful ceilings, consisting of geometrical panelling fan-tracery, and pendentives, were similar to wood and stone ceilings of the late Gothic period. These richly-moulded pendentives were connected together with moulded ribs. The ribs frequently had a repeating pattern impressed while the plaster was soft (plate 39). Occasionally a double frieze was used, the lower having delicate arabesques and strap-work, while the upper one had boldly-marked cartouches and arabesques. One of the most important examples of early Renascence plaster is the frieze in the presence chamber, Hardwick Hall. It is decorated with hunting subjects, as Diana and her train, surrounded with forest foliage. This frieze is 11 ft. in height, modelled in low relief, and coloured in tempera.

Inigo Jones introduced the purely Italian Renascence. He was known from 1604-30 as the designer for the elaborate scenery for the brilliant masques by Ben Johnson that were performed by the nobles and court of that period. In 1622 Inigo Jones completed the Banqueting House, Whitehall, the only portion of his great design which was carried out. He also designed the Water Gate, York House, executed by his favourite carver, Nicholas Stone ; the Queen's House, Greenwich ; and the great room at Wilton, with its fine mantelpiece and panelling.

The ornament of Inigo Jones is excellent in proportion, and Italian in type. The decoration of the panels and friezes consisted of boldly designed festoons, masks, and shields. The plaster ceilings have large rectangular, circular, or oval panels, with massive moulded ribs enriched with classical detail or with fruit or flowers in relief.

In the work of Wren, which followed, the details are less refined in type, being largely under the influence of realistic ornament and the Dutch School (plate 41).

The era of church building began with Sir Christopher Wren in 1666, after the great fire of London, in which old S. Paul's, ninety-three parish churches and chapels, the Exchange, the Guildhall, and fifty of the City Companies' halls were destroyed. S. Mary le Bow (1680), S. Bride's (1680), S. Clement Dane (1684), and S. Stephen's, Walbrook, illustrate some of the typical features of the fifty-one parochial churches that he designed, and his masterpiece, S. Paul's (1675-1710), is a noble example of English Renascence (plan, plate 85). Wren also built portions of Hampton Court and Greenwich Hospital. Nicholas Hawksmoor, a pupil of Wren, built S. George's-in-the-East (1723), Spitalfields Church (1729), and S. George's, Bloomsbury (1730). Castle Howard (1714) and Blenheim Palace are by Sir John Vanbrugh; S. Philip, Birmingham (1710), by Archer ; Burlington House (1717) by Campbell, who also brought out his great work on English architecture, " Vitruvius Britannicus " (Vol. I., 1715, Vol. II., 1717, Vol.

LIBRARY CEILING BY THE BROTHERS ADAM.

SPANDRIL OF BRONZE STOVE-GRATE BY ALFRED STEVENS.

DOOR PANEL BY ROBERT ADAM.

BORDERS BY GODFREY SYKES.

DESIGN FOR A POMPEIAN CEILING (V. & A.M.).

ADAM'S DESIGN FOR A CEILING AT CULZEAN CASTLE, SCOTLAND.

A LONDON CEILING OF ADAM TYPE.

III., 1725, while Vols. IV. and V. were issued by Woolfe and Gandon in 1767). This book gives introductory descriptions, with plans, elevations, and sections of the chief English buildings erected between 1600-1750. The Horse Guards (1742), Holkham (1734), and Devonshire House (1734) were designed by William Kent. S. Mary-le-Strand (1717), S. Martin's (1721), The Senate House, Cambridge (1730), and the Radcliffe Library, Oxford (1747) were by James Gibbs.

Somerset House (1776), by Sir William Chambers, is a typical example of late 18th century classic; accurate in proportion, with refined details and excellent workmanship and materials. Chambers published his " Decorative Part of Civil Architecture " in 1759.

Other architects of this period were George Dance, the elder, who built the Mansion House, completed in 1753 ; Paine, Carr of York, Gandon, Dance the younger, and Robert and James Adam, who designed and built the Adelphi (1768) and many streets and mansions in London and Edinburgh. Robert Adam also designed many accessories, such as console tables and candelabra, and on the ceilings, pilasters, and panels were composition enrichments (plates 42 and 43).

Of modern Renascence, the Wellington Monument in S. Paul's Cathedral, by Alfred Stevens, is distinguished by its strong personality and architectonic treatment of composition, and the beauty and singular grace of its details.

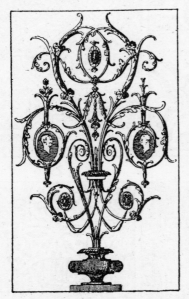 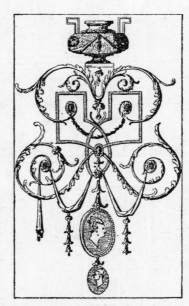

TWO ORNAMENTAL PANELS FOR PAINTING, STUCCO, OR CARVING,
BY MATTHEW DARLY.

85

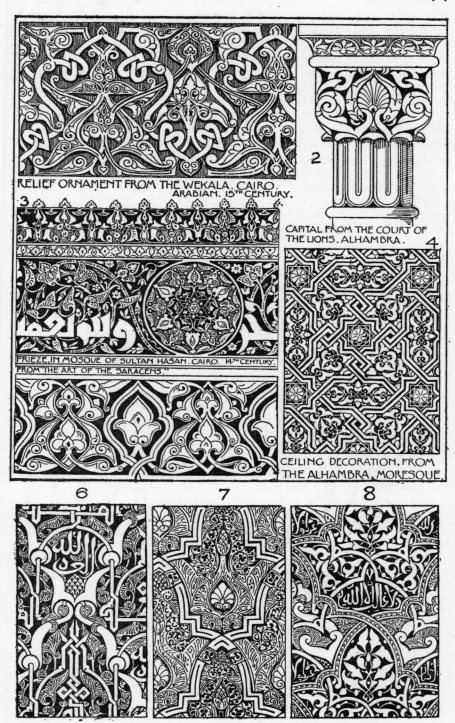

RELIEF ORNAMENT FROM THE WEKALA. CAIRO.
ARABIAN. 15ᵀᴴ CENTURY.

CAPITAL FROM THE COURT OF
THE LIONS. ALHAMBRA.

FRIEZE, IN MOSQUE OF SULTAN HASAN. CAIRO. 14ᵀᴴ CENTURY.
FROM "THE ART OF THE SARACENS."

CEILING DECORATION, FROM
THE ALHAMBRA, MORESQUE.

WALL DECORATION FROM THE ALHAMBRA, SPAIN.   MORESQUE.

# OHAMMEDAN ORNAMENT

The rise and development of the Arabs is most remarkable : the wide appreciation and liberal patronage of the arts by the Khalifs ; the influence of the Mohammedan religion and precepts upon contemporary and later periods of art ; the distinct individuality and geometrical arrangement of their ornamentation ; all had a most marked effect upon tradition and craftsmanship.

The history commences with Mohammed, A.D. 569-683, who founded and consolidated the empire, of which, under Omar, A.D. 635, Damascus became the capital ; in A.D. 638 Kufa and Bassora were founded in Persia. In A.D. 641 Egypt was conquered, and the Mohammedan capital, Fustât, founded. Persia was conquered in A.D. 632, Spain invaded in A.D. 711, Bagdad in Persia became the capital of the Arabian Khalifs in A.D. 762, and in A.D. 827 Sicily was conquered ; but it was not until the dynasty of Ibn-Tulun, A.D. 878-914, that the history of Cairene art begins, of which the mosque of Ibn-Tulun in Fustât, or old Cairo, is the earliest example. Under the Fatima dynasty, A.D. 867-1171, Cairo was founded, and the arts, receiving further encouragement, were now introduced into Sicily and Europe. In A.D. 711 the Mohammedan invasion of India took place. In A.D. 796-965 the mosque of Cordova was built, and in A.D. 1236 the kingdom of Granada was founded and the Alhambra was built, by Mohammed ben Alhamar, A.D. 1248, and Mohammedan art, as exemplified in architectural decorations, arms and armour, woodwork, ivory, textile fabrics, and illuminated books, reached its culmination under the Mamluk dynasty, A.D. 1250-1516.

Thus the Arabs, from a roving tribe, became, by religious zeal and conquests, the most powerful and the wealthiest nation of mediæval times, assimilating and influencing the customs and the arts of the different nations and provinces.

The term MOHAMMEDAN ART includes ARABIAN, MORESQUE, PERSIAN, INDIAN, and SICILIAN, all having the same characteristics, yet distinguished by the racial influence and custom. The Arabian is marked by its flowing, interlacing, and symmetrical lines, geometrical arrangement (doubtless derived from Byzantine sources), and its prevalence of inscriptions or texts from the Koran. In Spain a more complex geometrical arrangement is found, intermingled with a flowing foliage or arabesque of a purely conventional type. This style is noticeable for its entire absence of any natural forms and its abundant use of inscriptions and glazed enamelled tiles, distinctly influenced by Persian tradition, though purely geometric and formal. These tiles cover the lower part of the wall, the upper portion, as also the ceiling, being decorated with arabesques of modelled plaster in flat relief, of two or more planes, enriched with red, blue, white, and gold ; this is typical of the Moresque style. The Sicilian work is remarkable for its beautiful fabrics of silk and the prevalence in its ornament of birds, animals, and heraldic forms, showing the continuity of the traditions of Persia (plate 75 and page 160).

87

PLATE
SILICEOUS GLAZED EARTHENWARE. RHODIAN. 15 or 16ᵗʰ Century
WHITE GROUND. RED FLOWERS. BLUE & GREEN FOLIAGE.

HOOKER BASE. GLAZED EARTHENWARE WITH
ARABESQUE ORNAMENT. 16ᵗʰ OR 17ᵗʰ CENTURY.

EARTHENWARE PLATE. 16ᵗʰ CENTURY
BLUE GROUND. WHITE & GREEN FLOWERS & FOLIAGE.

BLUE, WHITE & GREEN WALL TILES.

RHODIAN TILE. WHITE ORNAMENT ON RED GROUND. THE DARK PART DEEP BLUE.
15ᵗʰ OR 16ᵗʰ CENTURY.

TILE FROM CAIRO. RHODIAN. 16ᵗʰ CENTURY. BLUE GROUND.

BLUE AND GREEN TILE FROM DAMASCUS.

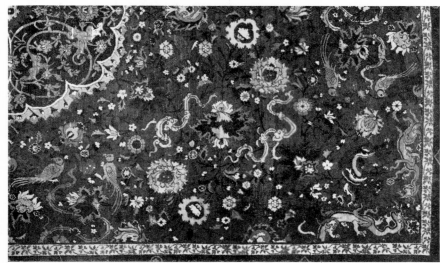

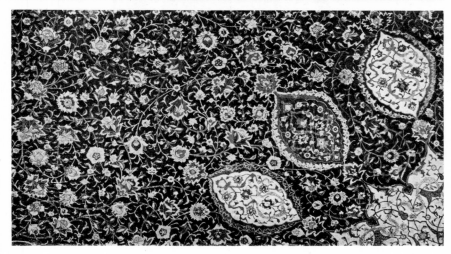

(3) PORTION OF EMBROIDERED BEDSPREAD, SOUTH INDIAN, EARLY 18TH CENTURY.

(2) PORTION OF A 16TH CENTURY PERSIAN CARPET.

(1) PORTION OF A CARPET FROM THE MOSQUE AT ARDEBIL, PERSIA. 1540 A.D.

PERSIAN ORNAMENT

PERSIAN ORNAMENT
The early art of Persia was similar to that of Assyria and Babylon, having the same forms, materials, and traditions. With the accession of the Sassanides, A.D. 223, came the introduction of the elliptical dome, so typical of eastern architecture. This dome rested on pendentives, which occupied the angles of the square base. These pendentives and the elliptical dome are distinctive features in Mohammedan architecture.

The industrial arts of Persia were largely influenced by the traditional arts of Assyria and Chaldea. This tradition was carried on with rare skill and selective power by the Persians, culminating in the splendid period of Shah Abbas, A.D. 1586-1625. The vitality, beauty, and interest of detail, combined with perfect decorative adaptation to material, are characteristic of the textiles, pottery, metal work, and illuminated manuscripts of the 15th, 16th, and 17th centuries.

The Mohammedan conquest of Persia, A.D. 632-637, by Abu Bekr, the successor of Mohammed, largely influenced the development of the arts of the Persians, who adopted the customs and habits of contemporary races, yet preserved all the characteristics of their art; and there is no doubt that the art of the Arabs was founded upon the traditional arts of Persia.

Persian decoration is characterized by a fine feeling for form and colour, and for the singularly frank renderings of natural plants, such as the pink, hyacinth, tulip, rose, iris, and the pine and date. These are used with perfect sincerity and frankness, and are essentially

PERSIAN PLATE. 16TH CENTURY. S.K.M.

decorative in treatment, combining harmony of composition of mass, beauty of form, and purity of colour. It was doubtless owing to these qualities, together with the perfect adaptation of ornament to material, that the Persian style so largely influenced contemporary work, and especially the European textile fabrics of the 16th and 17th centuries. The illustrations given are of some familiar types of Persian adaptations of natural flowers, doubtless chosen for their significance, beauty of growth and form, and appropriateness of decorative treatment. Purely Arabian forms, as given in plate 44, are frequently associated with the Persian floral treatment, showing the influence of the artists of Damascus. Many fine examples of lustred wall tiles, dating from the 10th and 11th centuries, are in the Victoria and Albert Museum, South Kensington, of which the blue, brown, and turquoise colouring is of a splendid quality. They often have Arabic inscriptions interspersed with the floral enrichments, as in plate 48 (5). Examples of wall tiles of the 8th century have been found in the ruins of Rhages.

These lustred tiles (*v.* below) are a remarkable instance of tradition or hereditary proclivity. This art, beginning with the enamelled bricks of Babylon, and the later frieze of Susa (page 19) with its brilliant enamel and fine colour, was continued by the Persians, and, passing to the Arabs, the tradition was carried to Cairo, Spain, and Majorca ; thence into Italy, where enamelled lustre ware was made, differing from the original Persian in its frequent absence of utility, which was fundamental to the art of the Persians.

While Indian ornament has a conventional rendering of plants, and the introduction of the lion, tiger, and the elephant (fig. 2, plate 49), in Persian work there is a still less formal constructive arrangement, with floral forms clearly defined in line and mass, and the introduction of the human figure with the horse, the lion, the tiger, and birds (plate 46 (2)). In Persian carpets, animal forms, chosen with rare selective power and judgment, are combined with the typical floral enrichment of Persia, with a wealth of colour, admirable detail of spacing and mass, beauty of incident and vigour, and appropriateness of treatment (plate 46 (1), 47, 48, figs. 1 and 4). These are features that distinguish the industrial designs of Persia, and it is doubtless due to the interest and vitality of their ornament that we owe the remarkable influence of Persian art upon the contemporary and later craftsmanship of Europe.

STAR-SHAPED PERSIAN LUSTRED TILES.

Plate 47

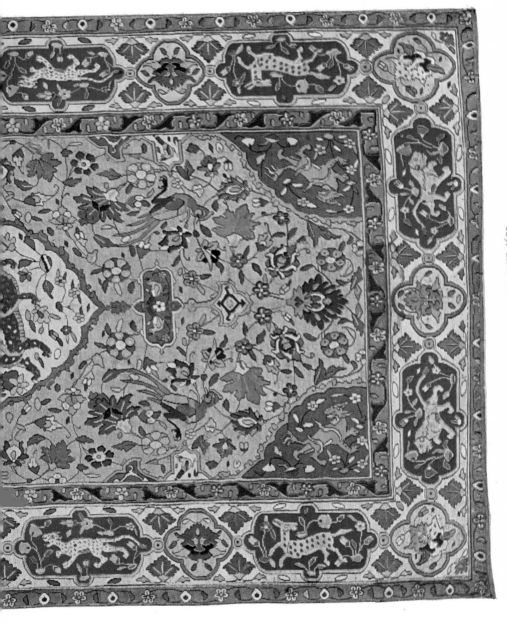

A PERSIAN RUG, OF ABOUT 1600.

12 INCHES

k---12 INCHES-------k

2

3

WHITE PATTERN ON RED GROUND.
GENOSE FROM A PERSIAN DESIGN. S.K.M

4

FROM A PERSIAN DRAWING
SOUTH KENSINGTON MUSEUM.

VELVET STUFF WITH
RAISED PATTERN OF VASES,
FLOWERS & FIR CONES IN
CRIMSON & GREEN, ON A
WHITE GROUND
   ITALIAN (GENOSE)
FROM A PERSIAN
DESIGN 16 TH Century
SOUTH KENSINGTON
MUSEUM

PORTION OF PERSIAN
CARPET
SOUTH KENSINGTON
MUSEUM

5

PANEL OF TILES FROM THE SENARIYEH MOSQUE AT DAMASCUS. 1580   SOUTH KENSINGTON MUSEUM.
TILES 6¼ INCHES SQUARE.

1

2 WOVEN FABRIC
BENARES. S K.M.

COLUMN FROM
TEMPLE OF VISHA
BENARES.

3 PRINTED COTTON BOCK COLLECTION.
MANCHESTER.

4 SILK BROCADE, WITH PINE SHAPED
FLOWERS. BENARES. S.K.M.

5 COTTON PRINT WITH FLOWERS IN
THE FORM OF A LEAF. S.K.M.

6 CASHMERE SCARF WITH THE PATTERN
FORMED OF PINES SCARLET GROUND. S K M.

Plate 50

INDIAN RUGS OF GEOMETRICAL DESIGN.

INDIAN ORNAMENT

The civilization of India dates from the remote past, but the oldest remains of its art and architecture are connected with the Buddhist religion, introduced by the prophet Sakya Muni (638 B.C.). This influenced the arts of India till A.D. 250, when the Jaina style was adopted. The examples of Buddhist architecture consist of Topes (which were sacred or monumental temples, either detached or rock-cut), and monasteries. The rock-cut temples usually consist of a nave and aisles, and a semi-circular recess containing a statue of the seated Buddha. The hall has square or octagonal columns, with bracket capitals (fig. 1). The finest examples of these temples are those at Ajanta, which are richly decorated in colour with incidents of Hindoo mythology. The fine temples at Ellora, which are cut entirely out from the rock, are of the Jaina period (A.D. 250). The pagodas at Chedombaram are of the Brahmin period, as is also the great hall of 1,000 pillars, which is 190 by 340 ft., containing the sacred image of the god Siva.

Alexander the Great conquered India 327 B.C., and doubtless left the influence of the Persian tradition in India. This influence was still further developed by the commercial intercourse of Persia and India, and by the Arabian invasion of India in A.D. 711, when a Mohammedan dynasty was established (711-1152). This largely controlled and influenced the arts under the Mogul dynasty (1525-1857), when the decorative arts and the manufacture of the beautiful woven brocades and silks were fully developed. The splendid carpets and rugs, printed cottons, metal work, and fine enamels of this dynasty bear a remarkable tribute to the vitality, originality of ideas, and the practical utility of the industrial arts of India.

Indian ornament has the typical Mohammedan division of spaces, but is more flowing and graceful than the pure Arabian style. These divisions are filled with fine conventional floral forms, such as the lotus, the date or hom, the iris, the rosette, and the pine. This pine is treated occasionally as a single flower but more frequently as a cluster of flowers, which still retains the distinctive form of the pine (plate 49, figs. 2, 4, and 6).

Typical also of this period is the judicious treatment of the elephant, lion, tiger, peacock, and the human figure, as accessories in the decorative arts of India. They were applied with rare knowledge and skill, combined with an artistic perception of applied art, and show a very strong affinity with contemporary Persian ornament (plate 46 (3)).

Indian ornament has a more conventional rendering of natural forms than the frank treatment of Persian ornament. Block printing upon silk and cotton fabrics reached a high degree of perfection during the last century. The inventiveness and significance of detail, the charm of composition of line and mass, and the beautiful colour of these printed fabrics, are a reflex of the decorative feeling for beauty by the people of India.

1. WOVEN SILK. CHINESE 18TH CENTURY. BOCK COLLECTION. MANCHESTER

2. WOVEN SILK. CHINESE 18TH CENTURY. BOCK COLLECTION. MANCHESTER

4. CHINESE DRAGON

3. CHINESE DRAGON EMBROIDERY

PAINTED BORDERS. MING DYNASTY. A.D.1538.

PAINTED PORCELAIN. 15TH CENTURY

94

(3) PRINTED COTTON HANGING, EARLY 19TH CENT. JAVANESE, SHOWING CHINESE INFLUENCE.

(2) EMBROIDERED WALL HANGING, 16TH CENTURY.

(1) PART OF EMBROIDERED SILK COVERLET, 19TH CENTURY.

CHINESE ORNAMENT

The early bronzes, enamels, porcelain, and textile fabrics of China are indicative of the perfection and luxuriance of the decorative arts of that ancient empire. This perfection is shown by a splendid technique and a fine appreciation of colour and ornamentation, differentiated from the western nations by myths, traditions, and the remarkable persistency of a few typical forms through many centuries, doubtless owing to the profound ancestral worship and veneration for the past. The dragon was represented under many aspects, frequently forming vigorous lines of composition (plate 51, figs. 3, 4). The beautiful flora of the country largely influenced Chinese art. The peony and chrysanthemum (frequently highly conventionalized) are typical examples, forming the elements of decorative design. Geometric forms, such as the hexagon, octagon, and the circle, enriched with flowers or the fret, are largely used. The many splendid examples of bells, gongs, and incense-burners in bronze and iron; the carvings in wood, ivory, and jade; the beautiful woven silks, richly patterned with the conventional chrysanthemum, the peony (fig. 2), or with geometrical forms, filled with the fret or rosettes (fig. 1); the magnificent fabrics, designed with dragons, birds, and conventional flowers, excellent in technique and colour (frontispiece); and the richness and purity of their porcelain, more especially the old blue and white of the Ming dynasty, A.D. 1568-1640 (plate 56, fig. 4), all testify to the versatility and vitality of the Chinese decorative arts in the past.

Their architecture was distinguished by complexity and quaintness of form, rather than beauty of proportion and detail. Their pagodas and temples, of which numerous examples are still extant, were of wood, iron, brick, or marble; and one, the Nanking Pagoda, A.D. 1412-31, destroyed in 1854, was encased with yellow and green porcelain tiles, and had 150 bells pendant from the roof. Pagodas are from 3 to 13 storeys in height; that at Peking has 13 storeys and is 275 ft. high, the Nanking porcelain pagoda was 250 ft. high, and a fine brick one of 7 storeys on the River Yangtsze is 140 ft. in height. The roof of each storey curves outwards and upwards, and usually supports a balcony.

Colour symbolism is an important feature of all Chinese art, especially that associated with their religious rites.

In the Temple of Heaven during the religious ceremonies blue is the prevailing colour; blue light is transmitted into the building, the sacrificial vessels are of blue porcelain, the robes of the priests are of blue brocades, and the exterior is covered with tiles of a deep cobalt blue. Yellow porcelain and brocades are used in the Temple of Earth, red in the Temple of the Sun, and white in that of the Moon.

95

CRANES.
PAINTED BY MORI IPPŌ,
1840. BRITISH MUSEUM.

THE QUICK POSTMAN, FROM THE MANGWA,
OR ROUGH SKETCHES, BY HOKUSAI. 1760-1849

WOVEN SILKS.

THE KIRI-MON & KIRU IMPERIAL CRESTS.

JAPANESE ORNAMENT

The arts of Japan, though doubtless owing their origin to China, are differentiated by a keener observation of nature and a more literal treatment of landscape, bird and animal life, and the beautiful flora of the country— the " kiku " or chrysanthemum, the " botan " or peony, the " kosai " or iris, the " yuri " or lily, the " kiri " or paulawina imperialis (somewhat resembling our horse chestnut), the " matsu " or fir, and the " take " or bamboo—likewise the peacock, the crane, the duck, the pheasant, and many smaller beautiful birds, together with reptiles, insects, and fishes ; all are elements in the decorative arts, being rendered with remarkable fidelity and delicacy of touch, united with a fine feeling for composition of line.

Physical phenomena, such as the snow-clad mountain, Fujiyama, have always exercised considerable influence upon the Japanese mind. This may be readily seen in the thirty colour prints by Hiroshige, and the hundred views of this mountain by Hokusai. The cherry and plum blossoms, emblems of the beauty and purity of spring, are also intimately associated with the life and the ornament of the people. It is this literal treatment of natural types, the marvellous technique, and especially the significance of the forms chosen, that constitutes the charm of the earlier Japanese art. It is singular that the materials used by the Japanese should be of little intrinsic value. Having no jewellery, they use little of the precious metals ; iron, bronze, enamels, clay, wood, and lac being the chief materials utilized in the decorative arts of Japan. Bronze is one of the earliest materials used in the arts of Japan, and their large statue of Buddha at Kamakura, cast in A.D. 748, rests upon a lotus flower with fifty-six petals, 10 ft. by 6 ft., and the height from base to top of figure is 63 ft.

Pottery made but little development until the 13th century, when a coloured earthenware, having but little decoration, was produced at Seto, in Owari, and it was not until 1513 that porcelain was introduced from China into Arita, by Shondzui ; and at the commencement of the 17th century a fine porcelain, decorated with birds and flowers in blue, red, and gold, now known as " Old Japan " or " Old Hizen," was produced. Kioto, Seto, and Arita were also noted for the production of a fine blue-and-white porcelain.

Cloisonné enamels, introduced in the 17th century, reached a high degree of technical excellence, but never quite reached the beauty, purity, and harmony of colour that characterized the old Chinese cloisonné.

Lacquer developed in Japan during the Heian period (A.D. 782-1192). The Ashikaga period (A.D. 1336-1573) saw the rise and progress of lacquer decoration in relief ; and in the Tokugarva period (1615-1867) the technical skill of the craftsmen reached a high water mark. Towards the middle years of the 18th century an abundance of detail overwhelmed the old simplicity of motif.

97   G

THE ARCHITECTURAL CAPITAL

The form and enrichment of the Architectural Capital offer one of the most interesting and instructive fields of study in the history and evolution of architecture and ornament. The remarkable persistency of the capital as a distinctive feature in architecture may be traced through many centuries, though differentiated by climatic conditions and racial influences, yet still preserving a remarkable similarity of form and enrichment among the various nations of the earth.

The function of the capital is to sustain and transmit to the columns the weight of the entablature or archivolt, and the beauty and appropriateness of the capital depends (1) upon this functional treatment of strength; (2) upon the beauty of profile or mass; (3) upon the enrichment and proportion of the capital.

The dignified Doric capital of the Greeks illustrates these functions and conditions by its perfect adaptability, simple functional strength, beauty of profile, appropriateness of enrichment and proportion and harmony of parts, qualities which are essential to beauty of architecture. In the Parthenon (438 B.C.), we have the finest treatment of this capital—a treatment full of dignity, reserve, and unison of profile (plate 6). The many examples of the Doric Order in Greece and her colonies attest to the esteem in which this order was held by the Greeks. The Indian capital (plate 49) exhibits the same functional treatment by the use of brackets or modillions, which undoubtedly are a survival of a wooden construction, and which are typical of Eastern architecture.

The remarkable persistency of the profile and enrichment of the capital extending through a period of 4,000 years may be illustrated by a series of diagrams of typical examples. The profile of the capital has not varied to any appreciable extent in the examples here given, and the enrichment of the bell is remarkable for its persistency, though differentiated by racial influences. The Corinthian capital, with its volutes and acanthus foliage, is but the architectural continuity of the Egyptian capital. The only pure Greek example of this order is from the monument of Lysicrates, but the Romans continued the tradition, assimilating and elaborating until they produced the magnificent capitals of the portico of the Pantheon and the temple of Castor and Pollux. In these examples the leaves are arranged in series of two rows of eight leaves each, the volutes springing from sheaths and stems between the leaves which support the angle of the volutes. The

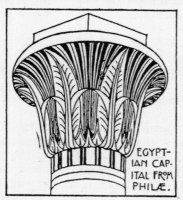

EGYPTIAN CAPITAL FROM PHILÆ.

example of early French Gothic has similar characteristics and illustrates the continuity of style.

The Ionic capital (page 13), though one of the most persistent in the history of architecture, never reached the architectonic perfection of other capitals. There is a want of unity between the volutes and ovolo of the capital; in brief, it has neither coherence nor harmony of parts. The exquisite craftsmanship of the capitals of the Erechtheum, with their anthemion enrichment of the greatest purity, the beauty of the ovolo and the subtility of the volutes compensates to some extent for the lack of unison (plate 6). The enrichment of the architectural capital is no doubt a survival of the primitive custom of binding floral forms round the simple functional capital, these forms being afterwards perpetuated in stone or marble.

In early Corinthian examples these floral forms were frequently of beaten metal, which, in turn, gave place to the beautiful marble foliage of the Greeks and Romans.

That the ancients used metal work in their capitals we have abundant proof.

The Composite capital is deficient in coherence and unity of parts,

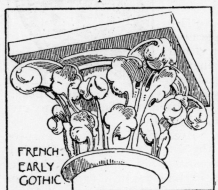

having the same defects as its prototype the Ionic. The annexed illustration gives an unusual treatment by the introduction of the human figure in the centre of the face of the capital.

The Byzantine capital differs from those of the Greeks and Romans in its marked symbolism of detail and the prevalence of the cushion form. Functionally, this type of capital is admirable, yet it lacks the vigorous upward growth of the Egyptian and early Gothic capitals.

99

The Byzantine capitals have a wonderful complexity and variety of detail, such as interlacing circles and crosses with their symbolism, basket work, chequered details, and the traditional sharp acanthus foliage of the Greeks.

These features are seen in the greatest profusion at S. Sofia at Constantinople; S. Apollinare and S. Vitale at Ravenna, and S. Marco at Venice. These splendid capitals of a splendid period are exceedingly beautiful in fertile inventiveness of enrichment, and show the assimilative power of the Byzantine craftsmen. The abundant use of chequer work, wreaths of chain work and of lily work in Byzantine capitals, many of which are figured in Ruskin's "Stones of Venice," show the continuity of style and tradition in architecture.

The Byzantine capitals have the square abacus, usually consisting of a simple fillet and chamfer enriched with the billet, dentil or star pattern. The Dosseret, a singular adjunct to the capital, was introduced during this period; it was a cushion-shaped or cubical stone placed upon the abacus of the capital to give additional height.

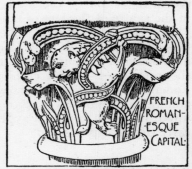

The Byzantine influence is seen upon the Norman capitals with their square abacus of fillet and chamfer and the cushion profile of capital. Some remarkable Siculo-Norman capitals are in the cloisters of the Benedictine Monastery of Monreale in Sicily (A.D. 1174-1184). The great fertility of inventiveness in the 200 capitals, their storiation, the intermingling of figures, birds, and animals with the classic and Byzantine foliage makes this cloister one of the most remarkable in the history of the world. The Arabian capital, which frequently shows the traditional volute, differs from the typical bell-shaped form in its marked squareness of profile with flat or low reliefs enriched with colour.

The early Gothic capital is one of the most vigorous and beautiful.

The perfect adaptability of its foliage to stone carving, the richness of its detail, the spiral growth of its foliage, and the vigorous contrast of light and shade are the chief characteristics of this period. Lacking, perhaps, the delicacy or variety of detail of the Byzantine period, or the later Gothic work, it excelled them in the appropriateness of its enrichment, which is more beautiful in the early English examples with their circular abacus than in contemporary French capitals where the square abacus was prevalent. The transition from the circular column to the square abacus was always felt to be a difficulty, and was rarely overcome, but in the circular abacus of the early English capitals we have a break in the continuity of the style of the capital.

The English foliage of this period differs from the French in the use of a deep mid-rib and simple trefoil leaf. The French

examples have a less pronounced mid-rib, and the leaf is convex in form and divided into three lobes, and the foliage adheres more closely to the bell, consequently the brilliant play of light and shade which is so characteristic of early English work, is generally absent from French examples (fig. 12, plate 21).

The decorated Gothic capitals differ essentially from those of the early Gothic period, a more natural type of foliage being used, consisting of the briony, maple, mallow, and oak. This foliage was

carved with singular delicacy of touch and grace of profile, and is beautiful in its modelling and play of light and shade, yet frequently the capitals are trivial in conception and arrangement, lacking that architectonic character which is so essential to all architectural constructive features.

The perpendicular, or late Gothic capital, was usually octagonal in form with square conventional foliage of the vine, showing a marked decadence in tradition and craftsmanship.

SOUTH-WELL MINSTER DECORATED CAPITAL

14ᵀᴴ CENTURY CAPITAL. CHARTRES.

The Renascence capital was frequently marked by a fine feeling for profile, splendid craftsmanship, diversity of enrichment, and vitality of conception, more especially in Italy.

RENASCENCE CAPITAL. VENICE.

102

ART II

The Applied Arts

WOODCUT FROM THE GROTESQUE ALPHABET OF 1464
(FLEMISH), BRITISH MUSEUM.

ENGRAVED PANEL BY HEINRICH ALDEGREVER, ONE OF THE
LITTLE MASTERS OF GERMANY.

BYZANTINE WALL MOSAIC COLOURED ORNAMENT ON GOLD GROUND. ST MARKS VENICE.

ROMAN PAVEMENT. 2ND CENTURY. VATICAN ROME

WALL MOSAIC OF COLOURED MARBLES. ARABIAN. 14TH CENTURY. S.K.M.

MOSAIC FLOOR. ROMAN. FOUND AT ROME.

MARBLE INLAY ITALIAN. 15TH CENTURY CHURCH OF ST JACOPO. FLORENCE

ROMAN PAVEMENT IN RED, WHITE & BLACK MARBLE FOUND IN 1795 NEAR LINCOLN.

MOSAICS

Mosaic is the art of forming patterns by means of pieces of variously-coloured materials fitted together, and is broadly divided into *Opus Tesselatum*, of small cubes, like dice; *Opus Sectile*, of slices of marble; and *Opus Musivum*, or glass mosaic: and may be divided into *Opus Figinum*, or ceramic mosaic; *Opus Vermiculatum*, with (*a*) *majus*, black and white marble; (*b*) *medium*, all materials and colours; and (*c*) *minus*, of minute tesseræ, used for furniture inlay. *Opus Alexandrinum* is an inlay of porphyry and serpentine on white marble.

It was in Rome that the art of mosaic was brought to its greatest perfection. The finest example is from the House of the Faun, Pompeii, and represents the battle of Issus, between Alexander and Darius. This mosaic, of the 3rd century B.C., is probably a copy of a Greek painting. A good example of this period is the so-called " Pliny's Doves," a representation of four doves upon a basin.

Many fine Roman mosaics have been found in England, at Cirencester, London, Lincoln (*v.* plate), Leicester, and at Brading.

Magnificent examples of mosaic are found at Ravenna and Constantinople, reaching a culmination at Venice. Of the Ravenna mosaics (page 33), those of the Baptistery, A.D. 450, S. Apollinare and S. Vitale are typical examples of the earlier Byzantine mosaics, having dark green and blue backgrounds, with tesseræ about $\frac{3}{8}$ in. square. The beautiful frieze of male and female saints in S. Apollinare extends along both sides of the nave, and is 10 ft. high. The vaulting and domes of S. Mark are entirely covered with the characteristic 11th century Byzantine gold ground mosaic, formed by fusing two pieces of glass together with gold leaf between. At Santa Sophia, Constantinople, and in the Capella Palatina, Palermo, are other fine mosaics.

Splendid examples of *Opus Alexandrinum* are found on the pavement of the Pantheon, Rome (A.D. 118-38). Other examples, dating from the 8th century, are in Rome, in the nave of the Basilica of San Lorenzo fuori le Mure, having interlacing circular bands of geometrical mosaic on white marble. In Santa Maria in Trastevere, the pattern is formed of hexagons and stars of six or eight points. A beautiful design of a large eight-pointed star of porphyry, with the triangles between the points of the star filled with small geometric mosaic, is in the Church of SS. Giovanni e Paolo.

In the 13th and 14th centuries in Italy, the Cosmati (a family of mosaicists) produced some geometrical inlaid mosaics upon the vertical and twisted pillars in the cloisters of San Giovanni Laterano and on the splendid " Ambone," or pulpit, in Santa Maria in Araceli, Rome. On the tombs of Edward (A.D. 1270) and Henry III. (1280), in Westminster Abbey, are some good examples of this " Cosmati " mosaic.

TYPICAL FORMS OF GREEK VASES

HYDRIA. FOR CARRYING WATER.

CRATER. FOR MIXING WINE AND WATER.

CANTHAROS. WINE CUP.

AMPHORA. FOR CARRYING WINE

OINOCHOE. FOR POURING WINE.

LEKYTHOS. FOR POURING OIL

KYLIX. WINE CUP.

Nº 2.3.4 5.6 & 7 FROM THE MANCHESTER COLLECTION.

DANCING FIGURES FROM an AMPHORA. B.C. 400.

2 — OINOCHOE B.C. 600.

3 — TWO-HANDLED VASE. OEDIPUS. JOCASTA. AND THE SPHINX. B.C. 400. RED FIGURED PERIOD

4 — OINOCHOE, OR WATER JUG B.C. 500.

5 — AMPHORA BLACK FIGURED PERIOD. B.C. 500

6 — LEKYTHOS RED FIGURED PERIOD.

7 — RED FIGURED PERIOD.

KYLIX B.C. 400.

GREEK CERAMICS

It is difficult in modern times to realise the importance of vases in ancient times. To the Greeks a vase was a receptacle for food or liquid, and was used for the adornment of the home; it was used in the daily life of the living, and buried with the dead. Most of the finer vases found in Etruscan tombs are of Greek workmanship, imported from Greece or Grecian colonies; some black unglazed Etruscan vases have been found, but painted vases of Etruscan origin are rare.

Early Greek pottery, dating probably from the 10th century, B.C., has been found in Greece, the colonies of Rhodes, Cyrene in Africa, and Naucratis in the delta of Egypt. These, showing a historic development, are arranged in groups, each with its distinctive characteristic. (1st) PRIMITIVE VASES, simple in shape, handles small or absent, decorations in simple line, punctured or incised, or in raised slip. (2nd) MYCENÆ or COLONIAL (900-700 B.C.) vases, often covered with a creamy slip, the designs, painted in brown and black, being derived from geometric patterns with marine and animal forms. (3rd) DIPYLON or GEOMETRIC (700 B.C.), with fret pattern enrichment, and panels with rude figures of men and animals in black and brown. (4th) PHALERON WARE (700-550 B.C.), with continuous bands of animals, probably derived from Phœnicia or Assyria (fig. 4). Among the animals depicted, are placed portions of the fret pattern, a survival of the previous style. The details are incised through the black or brown figure, showing the colour of the clay body. A development of this Phaleron ware was the introduction of the rosette, taking the place of the fret pattern between the figures or the animals. (5th) BLACK FIGURE PERIOD (600-480 B.C.) vases, fine in profile, and with good handles, the body of the vase, in red ware, being painted with subjects of Grecian mythology in black, and the details incised; the faces, arms, and legs of the female figures were afterwards painted in white or red slip and fired at a lower heat. The AMPHORA (fig. 5) was the chief form of this black figure period. Some fine examples are signed by Exekias and Amasis. (6th) THE TRANSITIONAL PERIOD (500-470 B.C.), when the black silhouette figures on a red ground gave way to the RED FIGURE PERIOD on a black ground. Artists of this style were Epiktetos, Pamphæios, Nicosthenes (page 21), and Pythos. Many of the vases by Nicosthenes resemble contemporary metal work in their shape and handles. The 7th group (525-400 B.C.) was the culminating period of Greek vase painting, the chief form employed being the KYLIX. A fine series of these *Kylikes*, with red figures on a black ground, signed by Cachrylion, Euphronios, Duris, Pethenos, and Hieron are in the British Museum.

The later vases (400-200 B.C.), are the polychrome sepulchral " Lekythi,"covered with white slip, and enriched with paintings, and the elaborate vases, decorated with subjects from the Greek drama, which were produced in the Greek cities of southern Italy.

1 ROMAN: RED LUSTROUS, OR SAMIAN WARE: WITH ENRICHMENTS

2 IN RELIEF, OBTAINED BY PRESS-ING INTO MOULDS & BY THE USE OF DIES. MUSEUM OF GEOLOGY.

3 ROMAN. ORNAMENTED WITH PIPECLAY SLIP, ON BLACK GROUND. MUSEUM OF GEOLOGY.

5 A PORTION OF OIRON POTTERY. INLAY OF COLOURED CLAYS, ON THE WHITE BODY OF THE WARE.

4 CHINESE VASE PAINTED WITH CHRYSANTHEMUMS & FOLIAGE IN BLUE. MING DYNASTY. SOUTH KENSINGTON MUSEUM.

6 CANDLESTICK. OIRON. OR "HENRI-DEUX" WARE. A.D. 1524-40. S.K.M.

7 JARDINIÈRE. ROUEN WARE. 1720. A.D. S.K.M.

8 PORCELAIN VASE. SÈVRES. PERIOD OF LOUIS XVI. S.K.M.

9 THOMAS TOFT

10 DISH OF SLIP WARE. BY THOMAS TOFT. 1660. M of G.

WHITE, GREEN & LILAC JASPER. WEDGWOOD WARE. S.K.M.

11 MELEAGER. FULHAM STONEWARE BY DWIGHT. 1671-1700. BRITISH MUSEUM.

CERAMICS

The antiquity of ceramic art and its scientific and artistic qualities, render this subject one of considerable interest to art students.

The plasticity of clay and its hardening qualities under the influence of intense heat, its adaptability to the most refined forms, its affinity for the beautiful glazes and enamels so often associated with pottery, and its splendid traditions of craftsmanship, of colour, form, and decorations, so beautiful and varied in character, all combine to invest the subject with a charm and fascination of its own. Intrinsically valueless in its natural state, it is capable of being rendered almost priceless by scientific workmanship and artistic skill. The history of this material, and of its easy adaptation to the most refined and intricate, as well as the simplest of forms, affords invaluable lessons for present-day students.

Pottery clay may be classified under three divisions or headings :— (1) EARTHENWARE, (2) STONEWARE, (3) PORCELAIN. Under the first are grouped the largest number of ceramic wares. The pottery of Egypt, the faïence of Assyria and Persia, the Greek and Etruscan vases, the famous red ware from the Isle of Samoa, and its counterpart the Roman Samian ware, the beautiful Maiolica of Spain and Italy, and the Rouen, S. Porchaire, Delft, and most of our English pottery are earthenwares ; the paste or body consists of natural clays selected for their plasticity, their hardening qualities, their fusibility or their colour, which when burnt have a porous opaque body, usually dull in colour. This dulness was usually overcome by coating the ware with a slip of fine white clay, which, whilst not possessing inherent qualities to form pottery by itself, would adhere to the coarser coloured body of the earthenware, thereby forming a smooth white ground. The early Greek vases of Naucratis, the later Lekythos of the Greeks, the faïence of Persia, the Mezza Maiolica and the Sgraffito of the early Italian Renascence, and our English slip ware are examples of this method of giving a smooth white surface to coarse coloured earthenware. A similar result to the slip covering was also produced by the use of a silicious glaze, rendered white and opaque by the addition of oxide of tin. Early Assyrian faïence, Della Robbia ware, the Maiolica of Spain and Italy, and the wares of Delft and Rouen are earthenwares coated with a tin enamel.

The silicious glaze here referred to is prepared by fusing silicious materials with soda or potash, and is known as Vitreous, or glass glaze. Plumbeous, or lead glaze, is produced by the addition of oxide of lead to the silicious glaze, rendering it more fusible, and still transparent. A white opaque enamel formed by using oxide of tin with the vitreous glaze is termed Stanniferous, or tin enamel. These different processes of covering the porous body of the earthenware largely influenced the decorations and scheme of colouring. The beautiful faïence of Damascus and Rhodes is covered with the silicious slip or glaze, and painted with rich blues produced by cobalt, turquoise and green by cobalt and copper, and purple by the use of manganese, and then covered with an alkaline glaze.

In the Rhodian ware the same scheme of colour prevails, except that the purple is replaced by a fine opaque red of great body, called Rhodian red, produced from Armenian bole.   On the Italian Maiolica, with its tin enamel and plumbeous glaze, there are fine blue, turquoise and green, but red is very poor in colour, and is generally replaced by rich yellow from antimony, and orange from iron.   This white tin enamel was undoubtedly introduced into Europe by the Moors, as some tiles in the Alhambra date from 1273-1302.

A large number of bowls and dishes, known as Samian ware, but now called *Terra Sigillata* (seal clay), of Roman importation have been found in England.   The paste is usually of a fine sealing-wax red, with a good glaze.   These bowls are enriched with a series of horizontal bands, containing the festoon, the scroll, birds, animals, and figures.   The bands, or friezes, are often divided by the traditional egg and tongue moulding (fig. 2).   Clay moulds, impressed with stamps, were made and then fired.   The red paste having been pressed into the mould, the interior was smoothly turned in the lathe.   A mould of this character was found at York in 1874, so it is possible that some of this ware was made in England, by Roman potters.   Roman pottery has also been found at Castor, near Peterborough, doubtless made at the former place, kilns for firing having been found on the same site.   This Castor ware is usually brown, with a black glaze being ornamented with indented tool marks and raised slip patterns of pipe-clay (fig. 3).   Many Roman dishes and vases of a dark grey colour, ornamented with incised lines and raised bosses of clay have been found in the Upchurch Marshes in Kent.   Little artistic pottery of the mediæval period, however, is known to exist. Early in the 13th century beautiful encaustic tiles were made for the great monasteries, abbeys, and cathedrals.

About 1500, the production of tiles was introduced into Holland, quantities of small blue and white ones, decorated with scriptural subjects, being made at Delft, and thence exported to England for the lining of fireplaces, etc.   Some fine painted tiles or *Azulejos* were made at Valencia about the 17th century.

In the 16th century, the porcelain of China was introduced into Europe by the Dutch and Portuguese traders, and much of the Delft and Rouen ware subsequently produced was in imitation of this oriental porcelain.   " Delft " ware, which takes its name from the small town of that name in Holland, dates from A.D. 1500, and is a ceramic coated with stanniferous enamel, decorated with a full and liquid brush upon the absorbent enamel ground, and then glazed with a plumbeous glaze. Some of this Delft ware is very fine in quality, the cobalt blues under the glaze being remarkably soft and rich in colour. Early examples were decorated with historical subjects often containing numerous figures, the middle period being notable for its imitation of Chinese porcelain, and the application of coloured enamels on coloured grounds. Vast quantities of this kind of ware were manufactured up to 1760, and exported to all parts of Europe. The production of Delft ware was first introduced into England at Lambeth by some Dutch potters in 1676, being subsequently extended to Fulham, Bristol, and Liverpool.

The use of stanniferous enamel was introduced into France by Girolama della Robbia, son of Andrea della Robbia, during the reign of Francis I., and in the second half of the 16th century several Italian potters followed in his track. Enamelled ware similar to the later productions of Urbino was made at Nevers, where also was produced a fine ware decorated with Persian *motifs* in yellow and blue. At Rouen, also, a fine earthenware covered with a tin enamel was manufactured, the decorations consisting of the lambrequins or scallop pattern, symmetrical in arrangement, and converging to the centre of the plate or

SÈVRES PORCELAIN VASE OF LOUIS XV. PERIOD. BRONZE MOUNTS BY THOMIRE.

dish. The ornament was based upon Chinese examples, influenced by the contemporary woven fabrics of France. The decorations were usually in blue, and with overglaze painting, *i.e.*, after the white enamel was fired, finer and more delicate detail being obtained by this process, but at the cost of the purity and liquid softness of colour which is so characteristic of Delft and oriental underglaze painting.

III

In Rouen ware, the ground is generally white, but some fine examples at the Victoria and Albert Museum have a soft yellow ground, a rich Indian yellow being sometimes introduced with the blue decoration. It was under the directions of Louis Poterat (1673) that this most beautiful faïence was perfected.

Bernard Palissy (d. 1590), by repeated experiments, discovered the stanniferous or tin enamel. His first productions were rustic dishes, elaborately decorated with carefully modelled fishes, reptiles, and plants or natural foliage, covered with an enamel of great brilliancy and purity, were the chief productions. The later pottery of Palissy consisted of saltcellars, inkstands, ewers, with elaborate figure decorations. An example of his work is seen on page 114.

Henri-Deux or S. Porchaire's ware (formerly described as Oiron ware) is of a pale straw colour, enriched with inlays of yellow, blue green, and brown coloured clays, the interlacing and arabesque ornamentation being similar in type to the contemporary bookbinding of Maioli and Grolier.

Many early examples of Staffordshire slip ware are to be found in England, consisting chiefly of candlesticks, cups, tygs, posset pots, piggins and plates, the slip decorations being in yellow, white, and brown. This ware was made at Wrotham as early as 1649, and by Thomas Toft, at Shilton, about 1660 (fig. 9). Marbled, combed, and tortoise-shell ware were formed by using colour slips or clays. Agate and onyx ware were formed by layers of different coloured clays, crossed, cut, and pressed into moulds. These methods were perfected by Thomas Wheildon and Josiah Wedgwood, who perfected both the Queen's and the variegated ware. Queen's ware of a creamy colour was made chiefly for dinner and dessert services, being decorated with painted flowers in enamel.

In 1775, Wedgwood introduced his famous Jasper ware, and Jasper dip or washed Jasper. This latter ware was dipped into admixtures of metallic oxides, producing blue, lilac, pink, sage green, olive, yellow, and black as desired. The decorations in low relief are of the purest white (fig. 10), and in the traditional classic style, the figures being arranged as cameo medallions, or in bands with the scroll, the festoon and the vine in delicate relief (v. figure, page 115). Many of these beautiful cameos were designed or modelled by Flaxman, Pacetti and Angelini, Bacon, Hackwood, Stothard, Tassie, and Webber.

STONEWARE differs from earthenware, owing to the presence of a larger percentage of silica in the plastic material, which, being fired at a greater degree of heat, vitrifies the body or paste into a kind of glass, thus ensuring a closeness and hardness of material not possessed by ordinary earthenware. Stoneware is usually glazed during the firing by throwing common salt into the kiln, which being volatilized, re-acts upon the silica in the body, forming with it a silicate of soda or glass, having a minute granular texture. The usefulness and the artistic character of stoneware were perfected by the Flemish and German potters of the 16th century.

The principal varieties of this ware are the grey and white " Canette " of Siegburg, near Bonn (see annexed fig. and plate 66), and the pale brown or grey ware of Raeren, near Aix-la-Chapelle, with its incised and stamped enrichments, sometimes with blue decoration. Frechen, near Cologne, probably supplied the " Bellarmines " or " Grey beards," largely imported into England under the name of " Cologne Pots." Examples of this Frechen ware were frequently ornamented with a raised scroll of oak leaves. Grenzhausen, in Nassau, produced a beautiful grey ware, having delicately moulded reliefs filled in with blue and purple. Many grey jugs ornamented with the initials of William III., Queen Anne, and George I., were imported into England from the Nassau kilns.

A stoneware similar to Rhenish stoneware, also termed by him " Cologne ware," was produced at Fulham by John Dwight, about 1685. Some fine jugs and a few cleverly modelled unglazed statuettes, believed to have been made at this place, are to be seen in the British Museum (fig. 11).

Another peculiar red stoneware, porcelain (or Red China as it was called) was made near Burslem by the brothers Elers (1688-1710), the ornamentation being obtained by pressing sharp intaglio copper moulds upon pieces of clay attached to the shaped ware. Astbury (1710-39), continued the traditions of Elers, producing a fine white stoneware, which largely influenced the Staffordshire pottery of that period. A stoneware was also made at Nottingham from 1700-1750.

PORCELAIN is technically known under the terms " hard paste " (" pâte dure ") and " soft " (" pâte tendre "). Hard porcelain is made from clays containing much alumina and felspar or decomposed granite, having but little plasticity, which necessarily influenced the shape or profile of the vessel. The beauty of form which is so typical of the Greek earthenware vase, is absent in porcelain, where the cylindrical or octagonal form is principally used. " Pâte tendre " is a soft and vitreous porcelain, having a great affinity for the beautiful coloured glazes and enamels used in the early examples of Sèvres.

During the Ming dynasty in China (1568-1640), porcelain reached its highest development in the perfection of its body, ornamentation colour and glazes, blue and turquoise being the chief colours of this period ; this limited range of colour was owing to the intense heat required to fuse the felspar glaze upon the hard porcelain.

Amongst the earliest known pieces brought from China to England are a couple of bowls given by Philip of Austria to Sir Thomas Trenchard in 1506. But whatever the date, it was inevitable that attempts should be made to imitate this beautiful ceramic. Florentine or Medician porcelain was made in 1575-80. It was not, however, until 1690 or 1700, that a similar manufacture was established at Rouen and S. Cloud. In 1709 Böttger commenced making hard porcelain at Meissen, in Saxony, subsequently producing some excellent examples about 1715. This was the commencement of the well-known Dresden china. In 1768, the manufacture of hard porcelain was adopted at Sèvres, replacing that of " pâte tendre " which had been in use from 1670. Both " pâte dure " and " pâte tendre " were made at Buen Retiro in Madrid (A.D. 1759), all the porcelain manufactured for the first twenty years being kept for the exclusive use of the Royal family. There are some finely modelled Buen Retiro tiles in the Royal Palace at Madrid.

About the middle of the 18th century the manufacture of porcelain was established in England. A factory at Bow dates from at least 1744, and in 1750 there was a factory working at Bristol.

PLATE WITH THE CHILDHOOD OF BACCHUS, BY BERNARD PALISSY.

That of Worcester dates from the following year, while those of Derby, Longton Hall, and Lowestoft are more or less contemporary. The best examples of English porcelain of this period are copies of oriental porcelain, chiefly Persian and Chinese. A great advance in the technique of the porcelain produced in this country took place after the discovery of Kaolin in Cornwall by William Cookworthy (1755).

Of early English porcelains, those of Derby are, perhaps, the most refined in form and in treatment of decoration, the plates, cups, and saucers having borders of blue or turquoise, with enrichments of festoons, leaves, and flowers ; many of the cups were pressed with fluted, ribbed, or imbricated patterns. The Derby works were in existence in 1750 ; in 1756 they were owned by William Duesbury and John Healy. In 1769 Duesbury purchased the Chelsea works and carried on the two simultaneously until 1784, when the Chelsea plant was transferred to Derby. From 1770-84 the ware called " Chelsea Derby " was produced, and between 1773-82 " Crown Derby " was introduced.

Porcelain of an excellent quality was made at Nantgarw between 1811-14, and at Swansea 1814-17, the decorations in enamel colours consisting of a natural rendering of flowers, birds, butterflies, and shells, chiefly painted by Richard Billingsley.

In some of the earlier Rockingham ware the outlines of the flowers and butterflies were in transfer printing, and the colouring was added by hand.

The earliest Worcester porcelain is often moulded with rococo reliefs, and painted within panels; and there are also a number of excellent pieces decorated in the Japanese style. About 1768 the factory engaged the best Chelsea painters and flourished until about 1780.

A WEDGWOOD TEAPOT.

Transfer printing over the glaze was adopted at Worcester about 1757, the transfers being taken from copper plates engraved by Robert Hancock, a pupil of Ravenet, who was employed at the Battersea enamel works about 1750. Sadler and Green in 1756 also adopted over-glaze printing on the Liverpool delft. About 1770 under-glaze printing on the biscuit ware superseded the over-glaze process.

The Hispano-Moresque and Italian Maiolica (plate 57) are remarkable for the technical excellence of their white enamel, rich, blue, yellow, and orange, the iridescence of their gold and ruby lustre, and their high technical skill in painting.

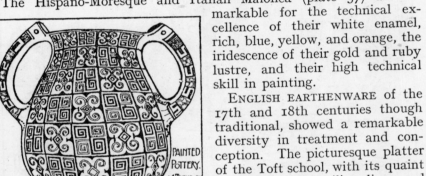

ENGLISH EARTHENWARE of the 17th and 18th centuries though traditional, showed a remarkable diversity in treatment and conception. The picturesque platter of the Toft school, with its quaint enrichment of trailing lines and heraldic forms in coloured slip, the fine red stoneware of Elers, with its graceful enrichments in delicate relief, and the varied and beautiful jasper ware of Wedgwood mark a distinct phase of the potter's art, and bear a tribute to the vitality and personality of the founders of the " *Potteries*."

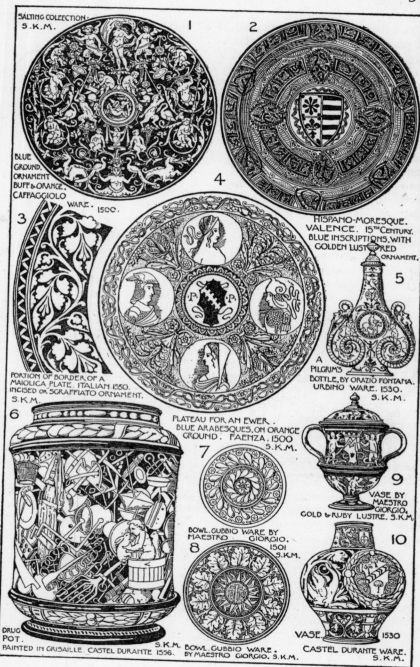

SALTING COLLECTION.
S.K.M.

1

2

BLUE
GROUND.
ORNAMENT
BUFF & ORANGE.
CAFFAGGIOLO
WARE. 1500.

3

HISPANO-MORESQUE.
VALENCE. 15TH CENTURY.
BLUE INSCRIPTIONS, WITH
GOLDEN LUSTRE RED
ORNAMENT.

4

5

PORTION OF BORDER OF A
MAIOLICA PLATE. ITALIAN. 1550.
INCISED OR SGRAFFIATO ORNAMENT.
S.K.M.

A
PILGRIM'S
BOTTLE, BY ORAZIO FONTANA.
URBINO WARE. 1530.
S.K.M.

6

PLATEAU FOR AN EWER.
BLUE ARABESQUES, ON ORANGE
GROUND. FAENZA. 1500
S.K.M.

7

9

VASE BY
MAESTRO
GIORGIO.
GOLD & RUBY LUSTRE. S.K.M.

BOWL. GUBBIO WARE BY
MAESTRO GIORGIO.
1501
S.K.M.

8

10

DRUG
POT.
PAINTED IN GRISAILLE. CASTEL DURANTE 1556.

S.K.M. BOWL. GUBBIO WARE.
BY MAESTRO GIORGIO. S.K.M.

VASE. 1530
CASTEL DURANTE WARE.
S.K.M.

MAIOLICA

Maiolica or Italian faïence is an earthenware, coated with a stanniferous or tin glaze, termed enamel. This is formed by the addition of oxide of tin to a silicious glaze or slip, thus rendering it white and opaque, hence its name, enamel.

The origin of this beautiful ceramic art may be traced to Chaldea and Persia, with their magnificent enamelled bricks, such as the " Frieze of Archers " from the Palace of Susa (485 B.C.), and now in the Louvre (page 19). From Persia the art was carried by the Arabians to Fustat, or old Cairo, which was destroyed A.D. 1168, and amongst the ruins many fragments of gold or copper lustred ware have been found. This enamelled ware was introduced into Spain in the 13th century, and perfected there by the Moors, giving rise to the Hispano-Moresque ware. This ware was enriched with central heraldic arms, surrounded by concentric bands of foliage, arabesques, or inscriptions in blue with a copper lustre. This Hispano-Moresque ware was manufactured chiefly at Malaga, Talavera, Triana, and Valencia, and dates from the Moorish occupation of Granada (A.D. 1235-1492).

In the Island of Majorca, from which this beautiful ware derives its name, fine examples were manufactured at an early date by Persian and Arabian potters. After the conquest of Majorca by the Pisans (A.D. 1115), many of these examples were introduced into Italy, the art being subsequently cultivated in some of the smaller central states.

The early Italian Maiolica was usually covered with a thin white " slip " or engobe of clay, which served as a ground for the coloured patterns. It was then coated with a lead glaze, and was known as mezza or mixed Maiolica. In some examples the design was scratched or engraved through the upper layer or white engobe, showing the darker body underneath. This type of ware, known as *sgraffito*, was also glazed with the lead glaze, forming, when fired, the beautiful iridescent lustre.

Few remains of a tin enamel of Italian workmanship have been found in Italy prior to the time of Lucca della Robbia, who discovered an enamel of peculiar whiteness and excellence. The secret of its composition was kept by him, his nephew Andrea, and his great-nephews, Giovanni, Luca, and Girolamo, until 1507. The mezza Maiolica was then superseded by the true Maiolica, or the tin enamelled wares of Caffaggiolo, Castel Durante, Urbino, Pesaro. Faenza, Forli, Diruta, Siena, and Gubbio—cities all within a limited district, lying towards the east coast of Italy, and renowned centres of the Maiolica fabrication.

The Gubbio ware is noted for its metallic ruby and golden lustre, and was sometimes signed by Maestro Giorgio (Giorgio Andreoli), the finest period of this master was about 1525. The same artist also lustred many wares made by the potters of Urbino and Castel Durante. Other examples of Urbino ware are signed by Niccola da Urbino (1530); Orazio Fontana, the head of a noted family of potters, consisting of father, son, and grandson (1510-1600); Francesco Xanto Avelli (1530-40). Faenza ware was produced at the Casa Pirota Botega, and Siena ware was signed by Maestro Benedetto.

The chief characteristics of Caffaggiolo ware are arabesques and figures in white, grey, or yellow on a rich dark-blue ground. Urbino has small medallions with figures and blue and yellow arabesques on a white ground, called Raffaelesque, being from designs by Raffaelle del Colle. Faenza has a yellow ground with blue arabesques.

In brief, the number of colours that could be used on the absorbent tin enamelled ground with its lead glaze was somewhat limited, consisting of blue, turquoise, yellow, and orange. These colours are of great depth and translucency, and are only equalled by the blues and turquoise of China, Persia, and India.

MAIOLICA FRUIT-DISH, ORNAMENTED WITH "AMORINI" TROPHIES AND ARABESQUES, ITALIAN, c. 1560.

Gubbio ware is frequently enriched with a raised curved fluting called *gadroons*, a most effective method of enhancing the beautiful ruby lustre of Maestro Giorgio. This Gubbio tradition was continued by Giorgio's son, Vicentio, called Maestro Cencio, and many beautiful works are signed by him.

This lustre was produced by exposing the ware to the action of smoke during the firing in the kiln; the smoke, being carbon in a highly-divided state, reduces the metallic salts of the pigment or glaze, forming a thin film of metal upon the surface, the beautiful iridescent lustre resulting from the relative thickness of the film.

Castel Durante was frequently enriched, on white or grey borders, with delicate raised scroll-work in white slip or enamel, a process called *Lavoro di sopra bianco* or *bianco sopra bianco*.

Faenza Maiolica has, frequently, the whole surface of the ground covered with a dark-blue enamel, enriched with dancing amorini and arabesques in blue, heightened with white *Sopra Azzurro*.

A frequent form of enrichment upon plates was to have small medallions painted with portraits and appropriate inscriptions, and doubtless intended as lovers' presents. They are known as *Amatorii Maiolica*.

TERRA COTTA

Terra cotta is usually made from pure clay, which will burn to a white or yellow colour, or from impure, which will burn to a red colour owing to the presence of oxide of iron. Pure clay is a hydrous silicate of alumina, containing 47 parts per cent. of silica, 40 of alumina, and 13 of water. Clay in this proportion is the Kaolin or china clay.

Fire clay, which is found in the coal measures, has a larger proportion of silica than Kaolin, and from it much of the terra cotta is made. When first dug out, it is hard and compact, and of a greenish-grey colour, deepening to black. It is often weathered before using; this causes it to "fall," and facilitates grinding. Old fire-clay, previously burnt ("grog" as it is called), is added to the new clay to counteract the excessive shrinking to which all close-grained clays are liable.

The coarser the clay, the less the shrinkage. Pure clay contracts as much as one-eighth from the size of the mould: one-half of this contraction takes place in drying, the other half in burning.

The colour of the clay varies according to the quantity of lime, iron or bitumen it contains.

The moulds for terra cotta are usu-

GREEK TERRA-COTTA. SELENE & PAN.

ally piece-moulds, made of plaster of Paris, which absorbs much of the moisture of the clay. Sheet clay about 2 in. thick is used. This is carefully pressed into the mould, and supported by webs of clay of the same thickness. It is essential that the clay be uniform throughout, or the shrinkage would be unequal. It is then placed upon a flue to dry, for from two to six hours, when the clay will have contracted sufficiently to allow the mould to be taken off. It is then dried for a further period, and burnt in a kiln. For fine work, the kiln is "muffled"—the "muffle" being a lining of bricks to keep the clay from actual contact with fire and smoke. The dry or semi-dry process is the pressing of clay-powder into metal moulds, which obviates the excessive shrinkage of the wet process. Encaustic tiles are made in this way, the ornament being run into the incised pattern with "slip." Many tiles are decorated in the same way as ordinary earthenware, that is, painted and glazed.

Terra cotta was largely used by the nations of antiquity, especially  by the Assyrians, whose clay tablets or books throw so much light upon Assyrian history. With the Greeks, terra cotta was extensively used for antefixæ, and the many beautiful Tanagra figures now treasured in our museums show the exquisite modelling by the Greeks in this material.

GREEK TERRA-COTTA

This material was used by the Etruscans for their sarcophagi and recumbent figures. The Pompeians tiled their roofs with terra cotta. It was used for votive statues and offerings, and for lamps, some of which were dipped in molten glass.

During the revival of art in Italy in the 15th and 16th centuries, terra cotta was extensively used by the della Robbia family. Lucca della Robbia produced many beautiful terra cotta reliefs, coated with the white tin enamel and enriched with coloured enamels. Among his numerous works was the marble "Cantoria" or Singing Gallery (1431-40), with its ten panels of sing-  ing and dancing figures in relief, which was placed by the organ of S. Maria del Fiore, or Cathedral of Florence. Lucca also executed five marble reliefs, in 1437, for the Campanile, from designs by Giotto, and the two kneeling angels holding candelabra, in the Sacristy of the Cathedral, Florence, are the only figures in the round by this master.

A BAMBINO BY LUCCA & ANDREA DELLA ROBBIA

Among his many beautiful examples of terra cotta are the "Resurrection" and the "Ascension," over the doors of the Sacristy in the Cathedral; the splendid monument to Bishop Federighi, with its beautiful recumbent figure of marble, in the Church of S. Trinita, Florence ; the Tabernacle of Peretola ; the Madonna of Or San Michele, and the many fine heraldic medallions, with the arms or emblems of the various Guilds, that enrich this beautiful Oratory of Florence (see page 61).

Other heraldic medallions in Florence are the Pazzi and Serristori arms for the Quaratesi Palace, and in the Victoria and Albert Museum are some fine medallions with the arms of King Renè d'Anjou, and twelve medallions representing the months. Most of these examples have the typical quattrocento borders of fruit, flowers, and foliage or fir-cones (fig. 8, plate 27), and are enamelled in brilliant colours.

Ottaviano and Agostino Duccio, contemporary sculptors of repute also collaborated with Lucca in the production of this ware. Andrea della Robbia, the nephew of

TERRA COTTA RELIEF BY ANDREA DELLA ROBBIA.

Lucca, carried on the traditions with rare selective power and artistic skill. Among his early works are the medallions with the *bambini*, for the Loggia of the Spedale degli Innocenti, or Foundling Hospital, at Florence, in collaboration with his uncle, Lucca, and Brunelleschi, the architect. The Adoration and the Annunciation were familiar subjects with Andrea. There is a splendid "Adoration" in the Victoria and Albert Museum.

121

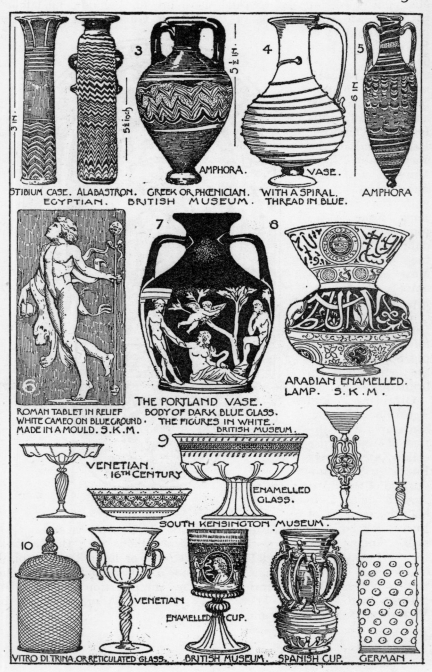

STIBIUM CASE. ALABASTRON. GREEK OR PHŒNICIAN. WITH A SPIRAL. AMPHORA
     EGYPTIAN. BRITISH   MUSEUM. THREAD IN BLUE.

3
4 VASE.
5 AMPHORA.
AMPHORA.

6 ROMAN TABLET IN RELIEF
WHITE CAMEO ON BLUE GROUND.
MADE IN A MOULD. S.K.M.

7 THE PORTLAND VASE.
BODY OF DARK BLUE GLASS.
THE FIGURES IN WHITE.
BRITISH MUSEUM.

8 ARABIAN ENAMELLED.
LAMP. S.K.M.

9 VENETIAN.
16TH CENTURY
ENAMELLED
GLASS.
SOUTH KENSINGTON MUSEUM.

10 VITRO DI TRINA, OR RETICULATED GLASS.
VENETIAN
ENAMELLED CUP.
BRITISH MUSEUM.
SPANISH CUP.
GERMAN.

122

LASS

The purity of glass, its adaptability to colour, and its remarkable ductility while hot for blowing, twisting, or drawing into threads, differentiates it from all other materials and methods of treatment. Its tradition dates from the remote past, for glass-blowing is represented on the tombs at Thebes (2500 B.C.). It was also used in Egypt for vitreous pastes for bronze and gold cloisonné jewellery, and for the small bottles or Stibium, with chevron patterns, in yellow, turquoise, and white on a coloured ground. Similar patterns, colours, and forms were used by Phœnicia and her colonies. Many remains of bowls were found in Assyria, one of transparent green glass having the name of Sargon (722 B.C.). Greece seems to have imported most of her glass from Phœnicia, but the Romans carried on the tradition, producing fine MOSAIC or MILLEFIORI. This was made by fusing rods of white and coloured glass together, then drawing it out to fine threads, and slicing it transversely ; the section is then placed in a mould and a bubble blown, uniting the mosaic, which is then blown into various shapes. The Romans also used the interlacing of white and coloured rods, called LATICINIO, but they excelled in the CAMEO GLASS, of which the Portland vase is the finest known example. This vase is of dark blue glass, covered with white opaque glass, which was ground away with the wheel, leaving the figures in delicate relief. It was found in 1644 in the sarcophagus of Alexander Severus (A.D. 235), the subject of its relief being the myth of Peleus and Thetis. Another Roman example of cameo glass in the British Museum is the Auldjo vase or Oinochoé, with beautiful reliefs of vine leaves. Frequently these reliefs were blown or pressed into moulds (fig. 6). The tradition then declined until the 14th century, when the Venetians in the Island of Murano perfected the art of glass-making.

The earliest examples of VENETIAN GLASS were massive, richly-gilt, and enamelled in colours. One fine example in the British Museum is signed by its maker, "Magister Aldrevandini." In the 15th and 16th centuries, the most delicate and beautiful blown glass was made, often uncoloured, and with enrichments of knots and wings in blown and shaped blue glass. The Venetians used with equal skill all the old methods of glass-making—the MILLEFIORI ; the LATICINIO, or threads of opaque white enclosing pattern ; RETICELLI, a network of white lines enclosing at the intersections a bubble of air ; and the beautiful VITRO DI TRINA, filigree or lace glass, formed by canes or threads of white or coloured glass being placed in a mould, a bubble being then blown in, and the glass afterwards taken from the mould and blown or twisted to the shape required. The artistic bronze mirrors of ancient and mediæval times now give way to the glass mirrors of the Venetians (A.D. 1500).

HERALDIC GLASS FROM OCKWELLS HOUSE. BERKS. 1422-6

EARLY GRISAILLE GLASS SALISBURY CATHEDRAL

EARLY GOTHIC BORDER FROM BOURGES CATHEDRAL

DECORATED GLASS FROM ST MARY'S TRURO.

13TH CENTURY MEDALLIAN GLASS. SAINT CHAPELLE. PARIS.

TAINED GLASS

With its depth and translucency, owes its intrinsic qualities to metallic oxides, such as cobalt, giving fine blues, silver, pale and deep yellows, pink from iron and antimony, and ruby from gold and copper, which also yields fine greens. When these oxides are mixed with the glass in its fused state, it is termed "pot-metal," but if the coloured oxides are applied to the surface of the glass only, it is termed "flashed" or "cased glass." Ruby, owing to its depth of colour, is usually cased glass. Fine blues are often flashed, and splendid effects are produced by flashing ruby over yellow or blue pot-metal glass. Cased glass is of the greatest value, owing to the variety of tint that can be produced on a single sheet of glass, and also because the colour may be removed by grinding or by the use of fluoric acid.

The rationale of the glass painter is :—(1) The scheme of composition and colour shown on a small scale ; (2) a full-sized cartoon in charcoal or monochrome, with all the details carefully drawn, and showing the lead lines and positions of the iron stanchions for strengthening the window ; (3) a tracing on cloth showing the lead lines only, called the cut line, on which are cut the selected pieces of glass ; (4) a tracing of the details from the cartoon, with brown enamel, on each piece of glass, the pieces after firing being then fixed in the leading, and kept together with H-shaped leads.

The brown enamel, which is used entirely for outline, detail, or shading, is a fusible glass in combination with opaque manganic or ferric oxide and tar oil. With this enamel, smear shading or stipple shading is worked. This may be removed

PORTION OF A "JESSE" WINDOW, CANTERBURY CATHEDRAL.

as required, before firing, by means of a pointed stick or quill, so as to give the details of embroidery or of heraldic forms.

Silver stain (oxide of silver), introduced at the beginning of the

14th century, is largely used in stained glass, and usually on the back of it. According to the different degrees of heat in the firing, a pale yellow or deep orange of great transparency is produced.

Coloured glass was made by the Egyptians 4,000 years ago, but

14ᵀᴴ CENTURY HERALDIC GLASS

the earliest stained glass windows recorded were those at Brionde (A.D. 525). None, however, are known to be still in existence prior to those of S. Denis (A.D. 1108). The early examples found in Norman windows have small medallions of figures and ornament of a decided Byzantine type, extremely deep in colour, being, by their style of treatment, termed mosaic glass. The 13th century, or early Gothic period, has single lancet lights, with medallions containing small figures surrounded by the typical 13th century foliage; or the windows were entirely of ornament in *grisaille*, arranged symmetrically—or with a flowing treatment of the vine growing from the recumbent figure of Jesse, and called the " Tree of Jesse "—with narrow bands of ruby or blue, and wide borders. These *grisaille* windows are of a greenish-white glass, with the ornament in outline, and the ground hatched with brown enamel in fine cross lines (figs. 1 and 2). The north transept window at York Cathedral, called the " Five Sisters," is typical of this *grisaille* glass. The finest examples, however, are at Salisbury, Canterbury, and Chartres Cathedrals. Later in the period, single figures were introduced under a simple canopy or gable, plain or crocketed, with an ordinary trefoil arch.

" Quarry " glass, square or diamond in shape, with brown enamel details, was frequently used where simple masses were desired.

"QUARRIES," ENGLISH EARLY 16TH CENTURY. (V. & A.M.)

In the 14th century, the figures were larger and placed under canopies in each light of the mullioned windows; such figures in rich colours form a bright belt across the window, surmounted by the canopies, cusped and crocketed, and in strong yellow pot metal, or yellow-cased glass. The borders were narrow, with a somewhat natural rendering of the rose, the maple, and the oak.

In the 15th century a further change took place, figures became more numerous, and the canopy or shrine larger, and chiefly in white glass, with the crockets and finials tipped with yellow stain ; a good illustration is that given from All Saints' Church, York. The coloured border of the earlier glass is entirely absent, its place being taken by the shaft of the canopy, and the crockets, finials, and ornaments are square in treatment, and based chiefly on the vine leaf.

Fairford Church perhaps contains the finest series of late Gothic glass (A.D. 1500-30). Like the contemporary architecture of the 16th century, stained glass was now influenced by the Renascence. The canopy still survived, but was horizontal or pedimental in form, with purely classical columns and details. Good examples of this period are the windows of King's College Chapel, Cambridge (1520), where rich Renascence work is introduced into late Gothic mullioned windows. These windows are probably similar to those by Barnard Flower, glazier, placed in Henry the Seventh's Chapel at Westminster Abbey, as in Henry the Seventh's will it was expressly provided that "the walles, doores, windows, archies, and vaults and ymagies of the same, of our said chapell, within and without be painted, garnisshed, and adorned with our armes, bagies, cognoisaunts, and other convenient painteng, in so goodly and riche manner as suche a werk requireth, and to a King's werk apperteigneth " :—" that the windows of our said chapell be glased with stores [? stories], ymagies, armes, bagies, and cognoisaunts."

Of this glass little remains, but we know that a contract was made in the time of Henry the Eighth to complete the windows of King's College Chapel, Cambridge, "with good, clene, sure, and perfyte glasse, and oryent colors and imagery of

LATE GOTHIC WINDOW, NORTH AISLE, ALL SAINTS' CHURCH YORK.

the story of the old lawe and of the new lawe, after the forme, maner, goodenes, curiousytie, and clenelynes, in every poynt of the glasse windowes of the Kynge's new Chapell at Westminster." This glass was by Francis Williamson and Simon Symonds, glaziers, of London, and its cost was to be sixteen pence per foot. Galyen

Hoon, Richard Bownde, Thomas Reve, and James Nicholson also agreed to execute eighteen windows of the upper storey of King's College Chapel, similar to those at Westminster by Barnard Flower, six of the windows to be set up within twelve months, and the bands of leads to be at the rate of twopence per foot.

At Warwick, the windows of the Beauchamp Chapel were glazed by John Pruddle, of Westminster, "with the best, cleanest, and strongest glasse of beyond the sea that may be had in England, and of the finest colours of blew, yellow, red, purpure, sanguine, and violet, and all other colours that shall be most necessary and best to make and embellish the matters, images, and stories that shall be delivered and appointed by the said executors by patterns in paper, afterwards to be traced and pictured by another painter, in rich colours, at the charges of the said glazier."

About 1540, transparent enamels were introduced with skill and reticence, but gradually glass painters began to vie with pictorial oil painting in effects of light and shade, the ground work or material losing that beautiful translucent or transmitted colour which is the chief glory of stained glass. An example showing the degradation of this art is the west window of New College, Oxford, painted by Jervas, in 1777, from designs by Sir Joshua Reynolds.

In the 14th century, the English craftsman attained a thorough mastery over his materials, and consequently the type of ornament followed English contemporary architecture more closely.

To sum up, stained glass changed through the different periods from the rich coloured mosaic of the Normans, the equally rich coloured medallions and *grisaille* glass of the early Gothic, the decorated Gothic, with glass in lighter colours and a prevalence of yellow stain, culminating in the later Gothic period, when largeness of mass, lightness, and silvery colour were the characteristics.

ST. ELIZABETH OF HUNGARY, GERMAN, 15TH CENT.

A beautiful treatment of stained glass, dating from the 15th century, was used by the Arabians. This glass, which has a singular gem-like quality, and is without enamel or stain, was let into a framework of plaster, which had been cut and pierced with geometrical or floral patterns.

NAMELS

Of the many decorative arts, enamelling is one of the most beautiful, having a singular charm of limpid or opalescent colour of great purity, richness, and durability, and being capable of a most refined and varied treatment for the enrichment of metals.

Enamel is a vitreous or glass compound, translucent or opaque, owing its colouring properties to mineral oxides, or sulphides, a fine opaque white being produced by oxide of tin. These enamels require different degrees of heat in order to fuse them and to cause their adhesion to the metal. Enamels are divided into three classes :—CLOISONNÉ, CHAMPLEVÉ, and PAINTED ENAMELS.

CLOISONNÉ enamel is that in which the cloisons or cells are formed by soldering thin, flat wire of metal upon a plate of copper, the cloisons being filled with the various enamels, in powder or in paste ; then, in order to vitrify the enamel, it is heated in a kiln, if upon a flat surface, or by the aid of a blow-pipe if upon a curved surface.

Cloisonné was in use from the early dynasties in Egypt, many fine large pectorals having been found in the tombs. These usually have the form of a hawk and are of gold or bronze with well-defined cloisons, which were filled with carefully fitted coloured paste or glass, and this undoubtedly was the origin of the true or vitreous cloisonné enamel. Byzantine enamel is invariably cloisonné, and one of the most beautiful examples of this period is the Pala d'Oro of S. Mark's at Venice (A.D. 976, see page 135). Perhaps the Chinese and Japanese have carried this cloisonné to its greatest perfection in softness of colour and beauty of technique. The earliest Chinese cloisonné such as that deposited at Nara is of the 8th century ; after a considerable lapse of time it reappears in the 13th and 14th centuries.

Early Japanese cloisonné was doubtless derived from Chinese sources, and it is characterized by extremely thin beaten copper grounds and the frequent use of a dark green ground in place of the dark blue of the Chinese cloisonné.

The Japanese cloisonné reached its culmination during the last century, when many splendid examples of refined and delicate enamels were produced, remarkable for their beautiful opalescent and translucent colour. Gold cloisons with opaque and translucent enamels were frequently inserted in iron or silver objects by the Japanese of this period.

An early example of English cloisonné is the jewel of King Alfred (page 133). A fine Celtic cloisonné treatment may be seen in the Ardagh chalice (page 133), where the cloisons were cut out of a plate of silver and embedded in the enamel while soft. The Celtic craftsmen also had a beautiful treatment of enamelling by engraving or pressing a pattern in intaglio or sunk relief, on an enamelled ground, and then filling these intaglios with other enamels.

A most exquisite kind of enamel called " *Plique à Jour* " was used by the Byzantines : this was composed of open filigree cloisons, filled with translucent enamels.

CHAMPLEVÉ enamel is formed by engraving, casting or scooping out the cloisons from a metal plate, leaving a thin wall or boundary between each cloison, which is then filled with the various enamels as in the cloisonné method. This Champlevé method was practised in Britain before the Roman Conquest, and was probably derived from the Phœnicians, who, centuries before the Romans came to England, had traded with Cornwall for tin. The beauty of colour and perfect adaptability of these early enamelled brooches, fibulæ and trappings of horses of the early Britons and Celts, are remarkable, showing a fine sense of colour and a harmony of line and mass. A splendid bronze Celtic shield (fig. 6, plate 17), now in the British Museum, is enriched with fine bosses of red enamel. These Champlevé enamels upon bronze have usually an opalescent or cloudy appearance caused by the fusion of the tin in the bronze alloy during firing. Champlevé enamels were used with rare skill and refinement to enhance the beautiful art of the goldsmith during the Middle Ages ; the Chalice, the Paten, the Reliquary, the Thurible, the Crozier, and the bookcovers of the Churches especially, were enriched with beautiful enamels. Classed among the Champlevé enamels is that method called JEWELLER's ENAMEL or "Baisse Taille," in which the plate is engraved in low relief or beaten up in repoussé and then flooded with translucent enamel. The Lynn cup of the time of Richard II. is one of the oldest pieces of corporation plate and is covered with fine translucent blue and green enamels (plate 60).

In India, where fine colour is a splendid tradition, Champlevé enamel soon attained a remarkable perfection of technique and purity and brilliance of colour almost unknown to the Western nations. The Champlevé enamels of JAIPUR have most beautiful lustrous and transparent blues, greens, and reds laid on a pure gold ground. PERTUBGHUR is renowned for the fine green or turquoise enamel fired upon a plate of gold ; while the enamel was still soft a plate of pierced gold was pressed into the enamel. This pierced plate was afterwards engraved with incidents of history or hunting. In RATAIN, in Central India, a similar enamel is made having a fine blue in place of the Pertubghur green.

The fine monumental brasses, of which many still remain in our English cathedrals and churches, are a survival of the Champlevé process, the cloisons being usually filled with a black NIELLO, but occasionally the heraldic shields are enriched with coloured enamels. During the 11th and 12th centuries, LIMOGES was renowned for its Champlevé enamels, but early in the 15th century PAINTED ENAMELS were introduced, and Limoges became the centre of this art, called late Limoges or GRISAILLE ENAMEL.

The enamel colours were now used as a pigment, and were painted and fired upon a copper plate. The enrichments in grisaille, or grey and white were used upon a black, violet or dark blue ground, the grisaille afterwards being enriched with details of fine gold lines. These Limoges enamels have a splendid technique, but they lack the charms of the luminous colour and judicious use of enamels of the early Champlevé period. The most renowned masters of the painted enamels of Limoges were the Penicaud family, Courtois, Pierre Raymond, and Leonard Limousin. About 1600-1650 Jean Toutin and his pupil Petitot produced some fine painted miniatures in opaque enamels upon gold, remarkable for delicacy and perfection of enamelling. About 1750 painted enamel was introduced into England, and produced at Battersea later, and in

LIMOGES ENAMELLED DISH BY PIERRE RAYMOND.

Bilston and Wednesbury in South Staffordshire. The enrichment consisted of ornaments painted in natural colours on a white ground.

The finest enamels undoubtedly are those in which the enamel is used in small quantities, such as in the Celtic jewellery, the bookcovers, and the Church and Corporation plate of the Gothic and early Renascence period, and the early Byzantine cloisonné, such as the Hamilton brooch in the British Museum, and the Pala d'Oro of S. Mark's, Venice, which was made at Constantinople for the Doge Orseolo in A.D. 976, and has 83 panels of fine cloisonné enamel set in a framework of gold.

BATTERSEA ENAMEL

The " *Plique à jour*," the " *Baisse taille* " and the Pertubghur enamels are fine examples of appropriateness of treatment with translucency or opalescence and richness of colour.

The Japanese cloisonné with its literal treatment of natural forms, and the painted enamel portraits of Francis I. and contemporary princes by Leonard Limousin, clever as they undoubtedly are, lack the depth and purity of colour obtained by the early methods. Frequently, however, the Penicauds, Nardou and Jean I., and II., obtained some richness in the painted enamels by the use of " *Paillons* " or pieces of metallic foil which were afterwards flooded with translucent enamel. Although pictorial rather than purely ornamental in treatment, the work of Henry Bone (1755-1834) deserves mention here, as an English achievement unique of its kind.

131

ROMAN
SILVER CUPS,
FROM THE TREASURE-TROVE
OF HILDESHEIM. BERLIN.

OCTAGONAL
GOLD VESSEL. PART
OF THE TREASURE OF PETROSSA.
BUKAREST MUSEUM.

THE TARA
BROOCH.
10TH CENTURY.
DUBLIN.

THE
LIMERICK
CROSIER.
SILVER GILT
PASTORAL
STAFF,
ENRICHED WITH
TRANSLUCENT
ENAMELS.
IRISH.
EARLY
15TH CENTURY.

THE LYNN CUP.
SILVER GILT
& ENAMELLED.
ENGLISH
14TH CENTURY.
CORPORATION OF
KING'S LYNN.

DESIGN FOR
QUEEN JANE
SEYMOUR'S
GOLD CUP
BY HOLBEIN.
1536.
BODLEIAN
LIBRARY,
OXFORD.

GOLD AND SILVER

With their intrinsic value, ductility, and beauty of colour, Gold and Silver have long been associated with the decorative arts of the past, and the many splendid examples still in existence are a tribute to the culture and personality of the craftsman.

Beautiful early examples were found in 1859 with the mummy of Queen Aah-Hotep (1800 B.C., Cairo Museum), and consisted of bracelets, armlets, rings, chains, a diadem, a small model of a war galley, and a poniard, all of exquisite workmanship and of pure gold, enriched with jasper and turquoise vitreous pastes. At Petrossa, in 1837 (Bukharest Museum), some splendid gold objects of Byzantine workmanship were found, consisting of two neck-rings or Torques, a large salver, hammered and chased, a ewer, a bowl with figures in repoussé, four fibulæ enriched with precious stones, a gorget, and two double-handled cups (plate 60). At Guarrazar, in Spain, ten gold votive crowns of Gothic workmanship were found : one inscribed with the name of King Suintila (A.D. 630) is now in the Museum at Madrid ; the others are in the Hotel Cluny, Paris, the largest having the name of King Rescesvinthus (A.D. 670) in pendive letters.

Of silversmiths' work, the most important is the " Treasure of Hildesheim," found in 1868 (Berlin Museum), consisting of thirty objects, cups, vases, and dishes, beautiful in contour and admirably enriched with delicate repoussé work of the Greco-Roman period (plate 60).

GOLDEN CANDLESTICK FROM THE ARCH OF TITUS. ROME.

THE ARDAGH CHALICE. CELTIC. Xᵗʰ Century.

Of the gold and silver vessels used by Solomon in the temple, we have only a representation of the seven-branched golden candlestick on the arch of Titus, at Rome.

English work of an early date is rare, but there are two very beautiful examples, one, the gold ring of Ethelwulf, enriched with blue Champlevé enamel, now in the British Museum, and Alfred's jewel of gold, with cloisonné, opaque, and translucent enamels, with the inscription : " Alfred me has worked " : this is, with the single exception of the S. Ambrose altar-frontal, the oldest signed enamel extant (871-901, Ashmolean Museum, Oxford).

Contemporary Irish work was even more skilful, and the Ardagh chalice of silver, with gold filigree and enamel enrichments, and the Tara brooch (plate 60) are fine examples.

133

ENGLISH SILVER-WORK.

1 GRACE CUP, SILVER-GILT & ENAMELLED MERCERS COMPANY. 1500.

2 SALT-CELLAR SILVER GILT NEW COLLEGE OXFORD 1490.

3 SILVER-GILT SALT-CELLAR CORPUS CHRISTI COLLEGE, CAMBRIDGE 1560.

4 SILVER-GILT STANDING CUP, ST JOHN'S COLLEGE, CAMBRIDGE 1615-6.

5 CHALICE. CORPUS CHRISTI COLLEGE 1507. CAMBRIDGE.

6 CHALICE. S.K.M. 15TH CENTURY.

7 PIX. A VESSEL TO CONTAIN THE CONSECRATED WAFER. 14TH CENTURY ST MARKS VENICE.

8 THURIBLE OR INCENSE BURNER. 14TH CENT. CLUNY MUSEUM.

9 GOLD CUP, EXETER COLLEGE. OXFORD. 1660-70.

10 SILVER BOWL 1685. AT KNOLL.

11 SILVER VASE BY R. ADAMS. 1772. S.K.M.

12 THE RICH CUP. SADDLERS HALL, 1681.

13 SILVER CANDELABRUM. S.K.M. 1714.

14 SILVER PUNCH-BOWL. VINTNERS HALL. 1702.

15 SILVER VASE. 1770. S.K.M.

The wealth and elaborate ritual of the mediæval church called forth the finest effort of the craftsman, more especially the gold and silversmiths, who in England, perhaps more than in other countries, produced abundant examples of ecclesiastical plate. Altar-frontals of gold, used only on rare festivals, are some of the richest relics of the past. An early example (11th century) was given by the Emperor Henry II. to the Cathedral of Basle (Cluny Museum). It is of gold, 3 ft. high and 5 ft. 6 in. wide, and has many figures in relief. At S. Ambrose, Milan, is an altar-frontal of silver-gilt, set with precious stones and enamels, and signed by " Wolvinus," an Anglo-Saxon, and dated A.D. 838. The great altar-frontal or Pala d'Oro of S. Mark's, Venice, was commenced in 976 at Constantinople. It is 9 ft. 9 in. wide and 6 ft. 6 in. high, consisting of 83 plaques of gold, on which are figures of our Saviour, angels, and saints in cloisonné enamels, and set with precious stones.

The early two-handled chalices were frequently very large, and it is recorded that Charlemagne gave one of pure gold, set with precious stones, and weighing 53 lbs., to S. Peter's at Rome. From the 12th century the chalice became smaller and without handles, and the bowl semi-ovoid or conical. The knob or boss on the stem, together with the base, are usually lobed or hexafoil, and enriched with repoussé work and enamels (plate 61).

The pax, introduced in the 13th century, was a small rectangular plaque, used in the celebration of the Mass to convey the kiss of peace. The cross, the shrine, the reliquary, the pix, the ciborium, the monstrance, the thurible or censer were of gold and silver, enriched with jewels and enamels or delicate repoussé work.

The pastoral staff, or crosier, was first a staff of wood, capped by a ball or knob with a simple volute ; then later the knob developed into tabernacle work, with canopies and figures, and the volute or crook, enriched with crockets, frequently enclosed the *Agnus Dei* (Lamb of God) or other sacred group. The early crosiers (12th or 13th centuries) were usually of copper, gilt and enamelled, and of Limoges workmanship. From the 14th century, gold, silver, and ivory were the materials generally used. The Limerick crosier is a good illustration of this period (plate 60).

Contemporary with this splendid ecclesiastical work was the college and corporation plate, of which the Lynn Cup (plate 60) is perhaps one of the most beautiful among many magnificent examples extant. The Leigh Cup (plate 61, fig. 1) and salt-cellar (fig. 2) are also of the Gothic period, but with the first half of the 16th century the Renascence appears in the works of the great goldsmiths, such as Benvenuto Cellini, of Italy ; Etienne de Laune, of France ; and Jamnitzer, of Germany. With Holbein's design for a gold cup (plate 60) the English Renascence appears, and civic plate was enriched with strap-work and cartouches, with foliated pendants of fruit and flowers (figs. 3 and 4, plate 61). In the 17th century, the acanthus foliage, with delicate chasing and relief, is the chief feature.

135

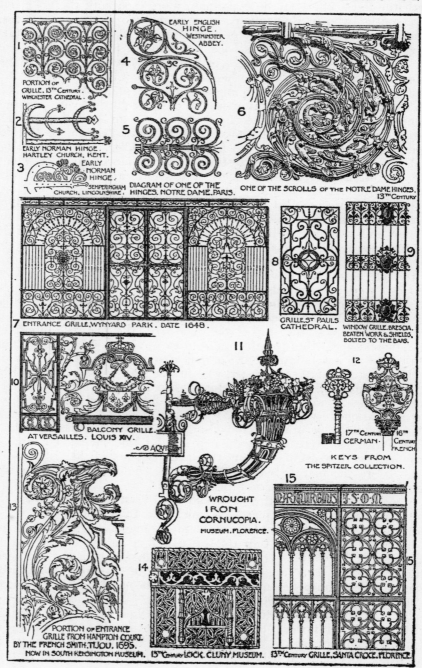

1. PORTION OF GRILLE. 13TH CENTURY. WINCHESTER CATHEDRAL.

2. EARLY NORMAN HINGE. HARTLEY CHURCH. KENT.

3. EARLY NORMAN HINGE. SEMPERINGHAM CHURCH, LINCOLNSHIRE.

4. EARLY ENGLISH HINGE. WESTMINSTER ABBEY.

5. DIAGRAM OF ONE OF THE HINGES. NOTRE DAME. PARIS.

6. ONE OF THE SCROLLS OF THE NOTRE DAME HINGES. 13TH CENTURY.

7. ENTRANCE GRILLE. WYNYARD PARK. DATE 1648.

8. GRILLE. ST PAULS CATHEDRAL.

9. WINDOW GRILLE. BRESCIA. BEATEN WORK & SHIELDS. BOLTED TO THE BARS.

10. BALCONY GRILLE. AT VERSAILLES. LOUIS XIV.

11. WROUGHT IRON CORNUCOPIA. MUSEUM. FLORENCE.

12. KEYS FROM THE SPITZER COLLECTION. 17TH CENTURY GERMAN. 16TH CENTURY FRENCH.

13. PORTION OF ENTRANCE GRILLE FROM HAMPTON COURT. BY THE FRENCH SMITH. TIJOU. 1695. NOW IN SOUTH KENSINGTON MUSEUM.

14. 15TH CENTURY LOCK. CLUNY MUSEUM.

15. 13TH CENTURY GRILLE. SANTA CROCE. FLORENCE.

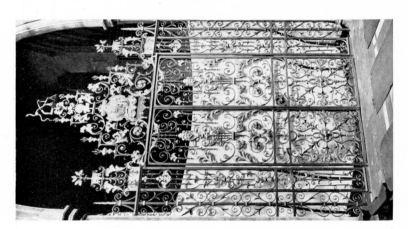

(3) MIDDLE GATES, S. PAUL'S CATHEDRAL. BY JEAN TIJOU.

(2) GATES AT ST. MARY'S, REDCLIFFE, BRISTOL. BY WILLIAM EDNEY, 1710.

(1) "OVERTHROW" OR CRESTING OF GATES, S. PAUL'S CATHEDRAL. BY JEAN TIJOU.

ROUGHT IRON-WORK

The decorative qualities of iron, with its strength, durability, and comparative cheapness, have rendered it one of the most useful metals in the applied arts. Many fine Norman hinges of wrought iron are still in existence, having a straight central bar or strap, with small scroll terminations ; these central straps were strengthened with crescent-shaped pieces, terminating in small serpent forms, probably a survival of the Viking traditions. This form of hinge was succeeded by the early Gothic hinge, which was a series of spirals springing from the straight bar or strap, the spiral being welded or fastened with collars ; these spirals were enriched with a three-lobed foliage, or trefoil, typical of the early Gothic period ; fine examples of this hinge occur on the west door of Notre Dame, Paris, where this typical spiral has the trefoil leaf, with birds, dragons, and small rosettes in stamped iron. This stamped characteristic may be seen, but in a less degree, in the fine hinges of Leighton Buzzard Church, Eaton Bray Church, Bedfordshire, and the Eleanor grill in Westminster Abbey, by Thomas de Leghton, in 1294. In the 14th and 15th centuries, when panelled doors took the place of the earlier doors, this early Gothic style of hinge was not needed (fig. 5), so that we find no trace of it in that period, but the art of wrought iron was continued with the hammered and chiselled hinges and lock plates of the most varied and delicate workmanship, which enriched the beautiful Gothic chests of the 14th and 15th centuries. The simple wrought screen, which was so largely used in the 13th century, was now elaborated, especially in Italy, and fine examples of quatre-foil grilles with massive wrought framing and a rich frieze of foliage, cupids, and animals in pierced and hammered iron are to be seen at the cathedrals of Orvieto, Prato, and Siena, dating from about 1337 to 1350, and at Santa Croce, Florence (1371) ; but it was in Spain and France that the screen reached its culmination. The Spanish screens or "Réjas" in the cathedrals of Seville, Toledo, and Granada have a fine range of turned and chiselled vertical bars, some 30 to 50 ft. high, with an elaborate frieze and cresting.

The wrought iron gate piers in St. George's Chapel, Windsor, with their architectural treatment of open panelling, cresting, and massive buttresses, are filed, bolted, and riveted, and are splendid examples of Flemish workmanship, probably by Quentin Matsys.

In England, after a period of decided eclipse during the 17th century, many fine examples of wrought iron gates and grilles were produced during the early part of the 18th century ; Jean Tijou, whose chief works are at Hampton Court and S. Paul's Cathedral (1690-1710), (plate 63, figs. 1 and 3), was followed by Robert Bateman, of Derby, the brothers Roberts, of North Wales, William Edney, of Bristol (plate 63, fig. 2), and the London smiths, Robinson, Warren, and Buncker whose skilful and artistic work, produced from 1707-20, is still extant in many parts of the country.

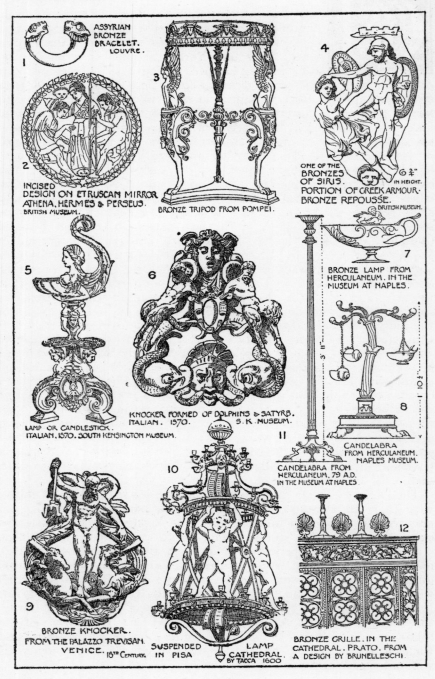

1. ASSYRIAN BRONZE BRACELET. LOUVRE.

2. INCISED DESIGN ON ETRUSCAN MIRROR. ATHENA, HERMES & PERSEUS. BRITISH MUSEUM.

3. BRONZE TRIPOD FROM POMPEI.

4. ONE OF THE BRONZES OF SIRIS. PORTION OF GREEK ARMOUR. BRONZE REPOUSSÉ. 6¾" IN HEIGHT. BRITISH MUSEUM.

5. LAMP OR CANDLESTICK. ITALIAN. 1570. SOUTH KENSINGTON MUSEUM.

6. KNOCKER FORMED OF DOLPHINS & SATYRS. ITALIAN. 1570. S. K. MUSEUM.

7. BRONZE LAMP FROM HERCULANEUM. IN THE MUSEUM AT NAPLES.

8. CANDELABRA FROM HERCULANEUM. NAPLES MUSEUM.

9. BRONZE KNOCKER. FROM THE PALAZZO TREVISAN. VENICE. 16TH CENTURY.

10. SUSPENDED IN PISA CATHEDRAL. LAMP BY TACCA 1600.

11. CANDELABRA FROM HERCULANEUM, 79 A.D. IN THE MUSEUM AT NAPLES.

12. BRONZE GRILLE. IN THE CATHEDRAL. PRATO. FROM A DESIGN BY BRUNELLESCHI.

BRONZES

Bronze, an alloy of copper and tin, has been in use from a remote period ; its adaptability for casting, its durability and colour, to say nothing of the fine green patûre, render this material one of extreme beauty and usefulness. Among the many examples of antiquity are the 1,000 statues of Osiris, found in the temple of Rameses III., and the bands of figure subjects in relief from the Assyrian Balawat gates, now in the British Museum. In Greece, bronze was wrought with exquisite skill and refinement, and the name of Lysippos (340 B.C.) is usually associated with the finest statues.

Two beautiful repoussé bronzes (fig. 4) probably by Lysippos, found in 1820 near the river Siris, in Italy, are admirable examples of this period. Many Greek statues have been found in Pompeii and Herculaneum, of which the beautiful statuette of Narcissus is the best known, and many bronze heads are still extant with the eyes formed of ivory or beautiful stones and jewels.

Etruscan bronzes have a most expressive treatment of incised lines, which differentiates them from the repoussé work of the Greeks. The bronze mirrors with an incised treatment of classic mythology (fig. 2), and the cistæ, or toilet caskets, all found, with but few exceptions, at Palestrina, are typical of Etruscan bronzes. Of small decorative bronzes, Naples Museum alone has over 14,000 examples. consisting of candelabra, tripods (figs. 3, 5, 8, and 11), tables, chairs, and couches, which eighteen centuries ago were used by wealthy Roman citizens. The well-known winged " Victory " of Brescia is a beautiful example, reminiscent of a Greek statue.

Early bronze equestrian statues are the " Nero " found at Pompeii (Naples Museum), and the " Marcus Aurelius " at Rome (A.D. 175, plate 65). The four bronze horses, now in front of S. Mark's, at Venice, are probably of the time of Nero. Many fine mediæval English bronze effigies are still extant, replacing earlier effigies of Purbeck marble, such as the Earl of Salisbury at Salisbury (1227), and the earliest recumbent figures in gilded bronze are those of Henry III. (1272), and Queen Eleanor (1291), in Westminster Abbey, by William Torell, goldsmith of London. In Canterbury Cathedral is the fine effigy of the Black Prince (1376). The Richard II. and his Queen, in Westminster Abbey, are by Nicholas Broker and Geoffrey Prest (1395), and at Warwick is the magnificent Earl of Warwick, by William Austin and Thomas Stevens (1453). Later examples are the " Gattamelata " at Padua, by Donatello (1453), the magnificent " Colleone " at Venice (plate 65), by Verrochio and Leopardi, and the " Louis XIV." by Girardon, cast by Jean Baltazar Keller in 1699, and destroyed in the French Revolution.

The Florentine Torregiano in 1512, made the beautiful recumbent effigies of Henry VII. and his Queen (see page 81), and also the Countess of Richmond, which are in Westminster Abbey, where there are also the gilded bronzes of the Duke of Buckingham (1628), and the

EQUESTRIAN STATUE OF MARCUS AURELIUS. ROME. A.D.175.

EQUESTRIAN STATUE OF BARTOLOMEO COLEONE. BY ANDREA VERROCCHIO & ALESSANDRO LEOPARDO. A.D. 1488. VENICE.

1554.

ONE GATE OF BAPTISTERY AT FLORENCE, BY LORENZO GHIBERTI.

STATUE OF PERSEUS BY CELLINI. FLORENCE.

Duke and Duchess of Richmond (1623), by an unknown artist. The statue of Charles I. by Le Sueur, and the Charles II. at Chelsea, and the James II. at Whitehall, by Grinling Gibbons, are later English examples of bronzes.

In Rome, the recumbent effigies of Sixtus IV. (1493), and Innocent VIII. which are the finest of Renascence bronzes, were by Antonio Pollajuolo. In 1508 Michel Angelo made the colossal seated statue of Pope Julius II., which was over the door of S. Petronio at Bologna. Benvenuto Cellini was the great Florentine goldsmith ; his " Nymph of Fontainebleau," a relief in bronze for the lunette over the door of the Palace, is now in the Louvre, but his masterpiece is the " Perseus " (plate 65), in the Loggia dei Lanzi, at Florence, where the " Judith and Holofernes " by Donatello is also placed. Another eminent master was Giovanni da Bologna, who executed the beautiful fountain with the figure of Neptune, at Bologna.

BRONZE CLOCK, FRENCH EMPIRE.
circa 1800.

The shrine of S. Sebald at Nuremberg, by Peter Vischer (1508-9), and the figure of the Emperor Maximilian at Innsbruck, by Lodovico Scalza, of Milan, which is enclosed by an elaborate grille, and surrounded by twenty-eight large bronze statues of men in armour, are excellent examples of German Renascence.

Many of the early historical buildings still retain their original bronze gates. Those of the Pantheon (A.D. 118-38), are still in position, also those of the cathedral at Hildesheim, with the panels of scriptural subjects in high relief, and the name and date of Bishop Bernward (1015). Early Byzantine gates cast at Constantinople by Staurachios, are at Amalfi (1066), and at S. Salvator, Atrani (1087), enriched with figures in silver damascening.

The west door of San Zeno, Verona (12th century), is of wood, covered with panels of repoussé work. Early cast bronze gates in Italy are those of S. Ambrogio, Milan (1170), and at Trani, Ravello, and Monreale Cathedral (by Bonanno, 1186), having relief panels and bosses upon the styles of the door. In 1150, Bonanno cast some gates for the Cathedral at Pisa, which were destroyed, with the exception of one, by fire in 1596, the west door being replaced in 1600 by a fine work by Giovanni da Bologna.

The noble gates to Henry VII.'s Chapel at Westminster, dating from the commencement of the 16th century, are of bronze. With their fine panels and well-executed heraldic devices and animals they represent the highest type of Gothic design.

141

IERCED, CHASED, & ENGRAVED METAL-WORK

Apart from screens, balconies, door-mounts, and the like, there were—more especially from *c.* A.D. 1500—endless varieties of applied metal-work, of which our limits only permit a casual mention.

Down to the 16th century, armour, whether for the field or the lists had been, on the whole, sparing of ornamentation. Weapons, too, other than mere " processional " pieces, never sacrificed practical considerations to display. But after 1500 a more florid style of decoration intrudes itself increasingly, even into military and tournament equipment ; engraving, etching, embossing, and inlays of gold and silver. Highly ornate work of this kind is associated with the greatest armourers of the age, such as the Negroli brothers, and Lucio Piccinino of Milan, or the Colman family, and Anton Peffenhauser of Augsburg. Pierced chiselled work also occurs, but mainly restricted to the guards and mounts of sword, dagger, or to ceremonial "hafted weapons" (halberds, partisans, glaves,

ITALIAN 16TH CENTURY RICHLY ORNAMENTED BREASTPLATE.

etc.). Especially beautiful examples are the Italian and Spanish cup-hilted rapiers (with their daggers) of the 17th century, the pierced design resembling fine point lace.

Clasps, hinges, and mounts for various purposes, and outer cases for books also illustrate the engraving, piercing, and chasing of metal. Heraldic motives (*cf.* plate 66 (2)) are frequently introduced. Another fruitful field for fine work was provided by locks and keys, while the 17th and 18th century clocks and watches are extensively adorned with fine engraved and saw-cut metal, and metal mounts for furniture provide a fruitful field for study.

WATCH FACE, SILVER AND
ENGRAVED COPPER.
FRENCH, EARLY 17TH CENT.

WATCHCOCK PATTERNS, BY DANIEL MAROT, *circa* 1700.

(1) SILVER BOOK-COVER IN CHASED OPENWORK, GERMAN, LATE 17TH OR EARLY
18TH CENTURY.

(2) PIERCED COVER FOR A BIBLE, WITH ARMS OF SAXONY,
ETC. WURTEMBERG, 1575.

(3) A STONEWARE MUG, SIEGBURG,
PRUSSIA, 1589.

ERALDIC ORNAMENT

Heraldry was, in its origin, severely practical. As during the course of the 12th century, the knight grew to be " sheathed in complete steel," it became important for him to bear distinctive and conspicuous marks by which he might be known to friend and foe alike. The earliest traces of Heraldry thus date from the 12th century, though the science was probably not reduced to a regular code till well into the 13th. The knight's colours and armorial bearings were originally displayed upon his shield, surcoat, and horse's trappings, and his crest above his helmet ; but the men of the Middle Ages, quick to perceive the decorative possibilities of their devices, soon applied them to architectural ornament, furniture, books, plate, and even to garments.

Whereas the spirit of heraldry declined with the Middle Ages, its ingenious adaptation to the most varied objects throughout the 16th century, and even later, continually provoke our admiration. Heraldry, applied as an engraved, stamped, cut, or modelled decoration is, as countless examples go to prove, a genuine embellishment in its fit place. The skill with which Dürer has worked heraldic designs into his engraved compositions is especially noteworthy, and his contemporaries, Beham, Burgkmair, Weiditz, and many others, produced a volume of fine work in decorative heraldry.

It should be noticed that, down to the 17th century, when it was not feasible to render appropriate " tinctures " and " metals " by means of paints or enamels, colours were simply ignored. Various systems of hatching and cross-hatching were then introduced to express colour by black and white.

HERALDIC PANELS FROM THE BRASS OF JOHN I., DUKE OF CLEVES, *circa* 1481.

143

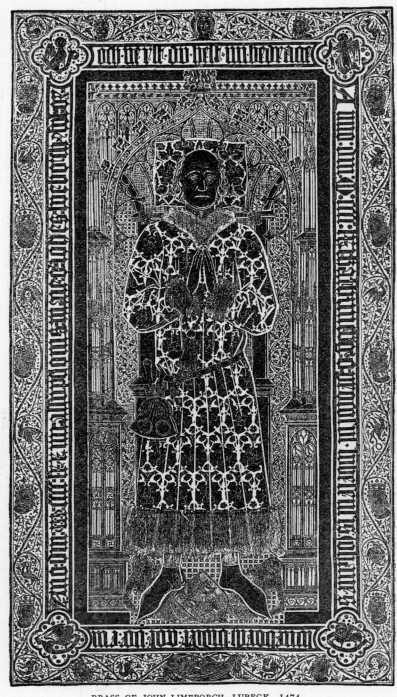

BRASS OF JOHN LIMEBORCH, LUBECK, 1474.
FROM AN ORIGINAL RUBBING. SCALE ·8″ — I FOOT.

RASSES AND INCISED SLABS

A form of art much associated with England is the monumental brass. It appears to derive, on the one hand, from the kindred incised stone slab, on the other from Limoges enamel work. In general treatment it is but an improvement of the former, while from the latter it borrows the occasional introduction of enamel, or some coloured substitute, into the heraldic motives.

Although brasses were at one time in common use in France, Belgium, and Germany, it would appear that England at all times held premier place for the number of such memorials. At the Dissolution of the Monasteries there were in existence about 150,000 such brasses, of which only a fortieth part remains to-day. But though various causes have reduced our heritage, the religious and other wars abroad have wrought far greater havoc.

Though the earlier brasses contain little but the figure of the deceased and an appropriate inscription, from about 1320 we meet with the ornamental canopy, often embellished with heraldic or symbolic motives. The Continental brass in particular, whose background was of *solid* brass,[1] admitted of very lavish decoration. Architectural and heraldic motives and rich diapers cover the whole field, adding immensely to the effect. It may be worth while to remark that whereas in England the earliest brasses (1277-1400) are undoubtedly the finest, a rapid decline being noticeable after 1500, the Continental brasses of the 15th and 16th centuries are often full of technical skill and vigour. Such fine examples as those at Meissen, Lubeck (see plate 67), Bruges, and elsewhere, show a remarkable mastery over the material, and great minuteness of detail. The cross-hatching and shading, however reprehensible in principle, is at least the work of firm and practised hands, and very different to the meaningless scratches that often pass for shading with our own craftsmen.

PORTION OF A BORDER ILLUSTRATING THE AGES OF MAN. BRASS OF PIETER LANSAME AND WIFE, YPRES, 1487-89.

[1] The English brass was cut out and laid upon a stone matrix.

1 RENASCENCE TABLE.
BARDINI COLLECTION LATE 16TH CENTURY.

2 BY DE CERCEAU.

3 GRÆCO-ROMAN MARBLE TABLE. POMPEII.

4 TWO LATE RENASCENCE TABLES, CLUNY MUSEUM. 5

6 CARVED CASSONE, ITALIAN, 16TH CENTURY. SOUTH KENSINGTON MUSEUM.

CORONATION CHAIR.
WESTMINSTER ABBEY, EDWARD 1

RENASCENCE CHAIRS, CLUNY MUSEUM.

7   8   9   10

DECORATIVE FURNITURE

Caskets, chests, and cabinets, chairs, tables, couches, and bedsteads have been of universal use during many ages, differentiated in design and craftsmanship according to the culture, wealth, and customs of the people, and the versatility, inventiveness, and skill of the craftsman. Many materials have been used for furniture, the chief being wood of various kinds, which was selected for its constructive qualities, beautiful texture, grain, and colour, and its adaptability to carving and inlay.

The universal use of the chair has doubtless tended to preserve its

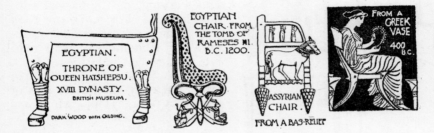

typical form through many centuries, and though undergoing various modifications, it has still retained its essential character as a seat. Numerous illustrations of early chairs are found on the carved reliefs of ancient Egypt and Assyria, and there are in the British Museum some early Egyptian chairs, one of which is of ebony, with uprights turned in the lathe, and inlaid with ivory. Many Greek chairs, remarkable for their simple and beautiful form, are shown upon the early Greek vases ; and the Roman " Sella Curulis," or chair of senators and consuls, is represented on the Byzantine ivories (plate 72, fig. 9).

The Chair of S. Peter, of the 1st century A.D., which has enrichments of ivory and gold, is purely architectonic in form, and the same may be said of the coronation chair (fig. 7), which is the earliest example extant in England. The Gothic chairs, few of which remain, were of the box form, with carved linen-fold panels. During the age of Elizabeth, chairs were of oak, with turned supports, the back having an arcade in low relief or in open work. This form of chair was continued during the reign of James I., when the " Farthingale Chair " was introduced. In the middle years of the 17th century the chairs had twisted supports and rails, the back and seat being covered with hide or with stamped and coloured leather. In

VENETIAN CHAIR.
XVI. CENTURY.

the reign of Charles II. and James II. the twisted or carved and scrolled forms of legs were common, with the seat and portion of back in cane, and the back, cresting, and rails in richly-carved open work, similar to fig. 10. In the time of William and Mary, the long supports were turned, and the front supports and arms turned and scrolled, the back of the chair being either of open work, or upholstered and stuffed. The chairs with simple curved or cabriole front legs, the arms, seat, and back upholstered with cut velvets, are characteristic of the early 18th century.

With George II. and III. we come to the use of mahogany and the work of Thomas Chippendale, who published a work on furniture

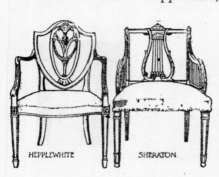

HEPPLEWHITE   SHERATON.

in 1754. His chairs have frequently straight legs, with shallow sunk carving, or the carved cabriole leg and claw foot ; the back is of open work of scrolls, strapwork, or ribbon-work, with delicate carving. Mathias Lock issued a book on furniture in 1765. In 1789, the *Guide*, a set of designs by George Hepplewhite, was published. Much of his work is refined and delicate in treatment and distinctive in form, such as his chairs with the shield-shaped backs. Excellent chairs were made by Thomas Sheraton, with straight legs, turned, fluted, or enriched with delicate carving, or an inlay of coloured woods, and having a delightful reticence of form and treatment.

Early Gothic tables were of the trestle form, the ends being of two pieces, connected by the upper frame and a lower stretcher. The Renascence table retained this form (figs. 1, 2, 4, and 5), which was but a survival of the Greek and Roman marble table (fig. 3). The Elizabethan table had legs of a bulbous form, gadrooned or carved, with upper and lower rails. The Gate-leg table, with spiral or turned legs, is characteristic of the second half of the 17th century. Chippendale frequently used the straight legs and carved or open rails, with a raised fret-work edge round the edge of the table. Side open tables of the late 18th century were frequently inlaid with different coloured woods, or of satin-wood veneer, painted with flowers or wreaths.

Early cupboards were of oak, with pierced and carved tracery panels, which were followed by the linen-fold panel, a favourite mode of enrichment from 1480 to 1560. In the early Renascence (plate 31), the Gothic and classic styles were intermingled, but a little later the panels were carved with medallion-heads and wreaths. This was followed by the classic furniture designed by the French architects Philibert de l'Orme and Du Cerceau, who published a book on

(1) LOUIS XIV. TABLE, MARQUETRY OF BRASS AND TORTOISE-SHELL, WITH ORMOLU MOUNTS ; PROBABLY BY BÉRAIN. (2) LOUIS XV. COMMODE BY JACQUES CAFFIERI, WALLACE COLLECTION. (3) LOUIS XVI. SIDE TABLE BY J. F. SELEN ; PAINTINGS ON GLASS BY DEGAULT.

furniture in 1550 (fig. 2), and the famous master *ébénistes* of the Renascence, of whom the best known is André Boulle, who used a fine inlay of tortoise-shell and brass (" Boulle work "), also ebony, enhanced with gilded bronze mounts.

In Louis XV.'s reign, Charles Cressent (1685-1768), produced fine examples of furniture with *appliqué ormolu* enrichments. Another great craftsman of this period was Jacques Caffieri, an artist of extraordinary dexterity and caprice in metal mountings for furniture, as may be seen in plate 69 (2). Some beautiful furniture was lacquered with a transparent Vernis Martin.

CONSOLE TABLE CARVED & GILT: PERIOD OF LOUIS SEIZE · 1774 ·89. 5 K M ·

With Louis XVI. and Marie Antoinette, a reaction set in for more restraint in ornament and severity of line and form, and the beautiful cabinets by Reisener, David Roentgen, and Weisweiter were remarkable for refined craftsmanship and beauty of ornamentation, with a marquetry of flowers, festoons, and diaper borders of rosewood, tulip, pear, and lime upon mahogany and ebony ; they were enhanced with bronze mountings by Gouthière, who was a renowned and skilful craftsman.

The Elizabethan and Jacobean periods were famous for their tester bedsteads, which have richly-carved panelled or arcaded backs, the tester also having elaborate panelling and carving. The baluster pillars at the foot usually have square bases, with pierced or open arcadings, and the slender pillars above have wide bulbous divisions, gadrooned or carved.

In Italy, during the 16th century, many beautiful *cassone*, or chests, were produced, enriched with carving (fig. 6), gesso, and gilding, or painted by the great masters of the Renascence. In-tarsia (an inlay of wood) was practised in Italy for the enrichment of the beautiful choir stalls, etc., of the 15th and 16th centuries.

ELIZABETHAN BED PILLAR.

SOFA OF CLASSICAL TYPE, BY THOMAS HOPE, 1807.

149

1

CARVED FRAME IN
WALNUT, BY
ANTONIO BARILI.
Late 15TH Century.
SIENA.

2

CENTRE OF CARVED TRIPTYCH BY VEIT STOSS.
SOUTH KENSINGTON MUSEUM.

3

A MISERERE. WESTMINSTER ABBEY.

4

CARVED MIRROR FRAME.
GRINLING GIBBONS. 1648-1721.
SOUTH KENSINGTON MUSEUM.

5

CARVED AND
GILT WOOD
PEDESTAL FOR A
CANDELABRUM
OR "GUERIDON".
PERIOD OF
LOUIS XIV.
S.K.M.

(1) AND (2) PANELS FROM THE CHOIR STALLS, S. PIETRO, PERUGIA.

(3) AND (4) CHOIR-STALL PANELS, PERUGIA : (3) FROM S. PIETRO, (4) FROM THE COLLEGIO DEL CAMBIO.

CARVED FRIEZE FROM THE ALTAR, S. MARTINO MAGGIORE, BOLOGNA.

OOD CARVING

Wood carving is perhaps one of the earliest and most universal of the industrial arts. The splendid carved statues and statuettes found in the early tombs of Egypt, the vigorous reliefs of the spiral and dragon from the Scandinavian churches (plate 18), the intricate spirals of New Zealand (plate 3), the pierced and carved screens of India, the beautiful carving on the furniture of the Renascence (plate 68), and the delicate and skilful work of Grinling Gibbons (plate 70 (4)) bear tribute to the universal skill of craftsmanship, which reached its highest point of excellence in the later Gothic and Renascence period.

The choir stalls of Amiens Cathedral (plate 25) by Arnold Boulin, Alexander Huet, and Jean Turpin (1508-22), are magnificent examples of the versatility and skill of the flamboyant carver. But France was not alone in the excellence of this craft, for almost contemporaneous are the beautiful doors of the Stanza della Incendio and the Stanza della Eliodoro in the Vatican at Rome (see page 65), by Giovanni Barili, and the choir stalls in S. Pietro, Perugia (plate 71), and in the Cathedral at Siena by Antonio and Giovanni Barili. The magnificent candelabra and the delicate carvings and intarsia in the choir of Santa Maria in Organo, at Verona, by Fra Giovanni da Verona, and the stalls and screen in Santa Maggiore, Bergamo, by Stephano da Bergamo, are some of the finest examples of wood carving in Italy. The richly carved oak stalls by Jörg Syrlin (1464-74) in the Cathedral at Ulm, indicate the beginning of the intricate and florid scroll-work, which became the type of the later German Renascence. The hanging screen and crucifix of S. Lawrence, and the crucifix at S. Sebald's, at Nuremberg (1518), by Veit Stoss (plate 70, fig. 2), are admirable examples of the skilful and florid carving of the German school during the early part of the 16th century.

In Flanders, the splendid chimney-piece in the Palais de Justice, Bruges, with carvings of Charles V. and his ancestors, by Guyot de Beaugrant, from designs by Blondell (1529-31), is rich, yet restrained in treatment, but in the pulpit of the Cathedral at Brussels, by Verbrüggen (1699), carved with figures and foliage, representing the expulsion from Paradise, and in the pulpit by Van de Voort in the Cathedral of Antwerp, carved with naturalistic birds, trees, and figures, extraordinary technical skill is attained, but with a loss of dignity and appropriateness of treatment.

Admirable examples, good in design and technique, abound in English cathedrals, in the screens, canopies, and misereres of the choir stalls (plates 23, 24, 40) of the 14th and 15th centuries, and later.

With Grinling Gibbons wood carving reached its culmination in delicacy and skilful craftsmanship, though too naturalistic and imitative in design (plate 70, fig. 4). His principal works, consisting of flowers, festoons, and birds, are carved chiefly in lime; fine examples are at Belton House and Petworth; and in collaboration with Sir Christopher Wren he executed splendid carvings in the library at Trinity College, Cambridge; S. Paul's Cathedral; S. James's, Piccadilly; the vestry of S. Lawrence, Jewry; and at Hampton Court Palace. Much work attributed to him is, however, by other hands.

FIG I

TRIPTYCH. FRENCH. 14TH CENTURY.
SOUTH KENSINGTON MUSEUM.

ASSYRIAN PANEL WITH INCISED
ORNAMENT BRITISH MUSEUM.

TANKARD & COVER. IVORY BODY
IN HIGH RELIEF. ITALIAN 16TH Century

HEAD OF A PASTORAL
STAFF. FRENCH. 14TH Cent
SOUTH KENSINGTON
MUSEUM.

TOP OF MIRROR CASE THE ELOPEMENT OF QUEEN
GUINEVER & SIR LAUNCELOT. FRENCH. 14TH Century.
SOUTH KENSINGTON MUSEUM.

CENTRE OF BOOK COVER.
BYZANTINE 6TH Century.
IN MILAN CATHEDRAL.

SVMMACHORVM

ΗΛΕΝΟ ΥΙΤΑΡΟΝΤΑ
ΡΑΙΜΑΟ ΟΝΤΗΝΛΗΑΝ

VINL COM DOMEST EQVIT
ΕΤ CONS ORD

10

HANDLE OF KNIFE

ONE LEAF OF A ROMAN DIPTYCH. 5TH CENTURY.
SOUTH KENSINGTON MUSEUM.
THE COMPANION LEAF IN THE CLUNY MUSEUM.

BYZANTINE DIPTYCH. 4TH CENT.
BRITISH MUSEUM.
THE LARGEST KNOWN
IVORY PLAQUE.

LEAF OF
A CONSULAR
DIPTYCH.
OF THE CONSUL ANASTASIUS.
BYZANTINE. 6TH CENTURY.
SOUTH KENSINGTON MUSEUM.

FORK FROM
NURNBERG
MUSEUM.
17 CENTURY.

VORIES

Doubtless owing to the beautiful texture, colour and adaptability for delicate carving, ivory has been in use from a remote period. Egypt, Assyria, and India have each contributed many beautiful examples of fine craftsmanship, indicative of the artistic culture of the centuries preceding the Christian Era.

In the Periclean age of Greece, ivory was used for the figure of Athene Parthenos by Pheidias, placed inside the Parthenon. This statue of the standing goddess, 40 ft. high, was of gold and ivory (called *chryselephantine sculpture*), the drapery being of beaten gold and the exposed parts of the figure of carefully-fitted pieces of ivory. A seated *chryselephantine* figure of Jupiter, about 58 ft. high, in the temple of Olympia, was also by Pheidias. Pausanias, the Roman traveller, enumerates some ten *chryselephantine* statues which he saw in his travels (A.D. 140).

The Roman period is noted for the many beautiful Consular diptychs, which may now be seen in our national museums. They consist of two ivory leaves usually 12 by 5 in., the inside having a slightly sunk plane covered with wax for writing upon, the outside being enriched with delicate carved reliefs (figs. 7, 8, and 9). These diptychs were given by new consuls on their appointment, to their friends and officers of the state. The consul is usually represented seated on the cushioned curule chair, or chair of state, and his name is generally written across the top of one leaf.

The Byzantines enriched the covers of their manuscripts with ivory, of which an illustration is given in fig. 6 ; the ivory throne of Maximian, Archbishop of Ravenna (A.D. 546-556), is also of this period. A beautiful treatment of ivory was used in the 13th and 14th centuries by the Saracens of Egypt ; they frequently worked a fine geometric inlay of ivory upon ebony ; in other examples ivory panels were pentagonal, hexagonal, or star-shaped, and carved with delicate arabesques, the framing of the panels being of cedar or ebony. In India ivory carving reached a high degree of perfection, especially in the many ivory combs, with pierced and relief work representing the figure of Buddha surrounded with foliage and richly caparisoned elephants.

In the Carlovingian period, 8th to 10th centuries, ivory was largely used for coffers or small chests. During the early Gothic period in Italy and France, ivory crucifixes, pastoral staffs, croziers, statuettes, and triptychs were made in large numbers ; and the ivory combs and mirror cases of the Renascence period have fine reliefs of legendary or allegorical subjects. Of pictorial ivories the modern Japanese craftsmen show the highest technical skill, combined with a keen perception of nature and movement, yet their ivories lack the beauty and dignity of composition and the decorative treatment of the early and mediæval ivories.

1. IVORY BOOK COVER. IX Century. NORTH ITALY.

2. PORTION OF A DURHAM BINDING IN BROWN LEATHER. BENEDICTINE MONASTERY, DURHAM.

3. STAMPED PANEL BY JEHAN NORINS. 1528.

4. STAMPED LEATHER BINDING. S. GEORGE. BY JOHN REYNES. 1520. ENGLISH.

5. RED MOROCCO BINDING WITH GOLD TOOLING. Q. CVRTIVS. THO MAIOLI. ET AMICOR. BOUND FOR TOMMASO MAIOLI.

6. CORYCIANA. IO·GROLIERII· ET AMICO RVM. BINDING IN YELLOW MOROCCO TOOLED IN GOLD. GROLIER BINDING.

7. RED MOROCCO BINDING. TOOLED IN GOLD BY NICHOLAS EVE.

8. RED MOROCCO BINDING. TOOLED WITH THE ARMS 6 CYPHER. OF LOUIS XIII.

9. PORTION OF BLUE MOROCCO. BINDING. BOUND AND TOOLED IN GOLD BY ROGER PAYNE. 1795.

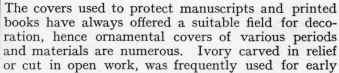

OOKBINDINGS

The covers used to protect manuscripts and printed books have always offered a suitable field for decoration, hence ornamental covers of various periods and materials are numerous. Ivory carved in relief or cut in open work, was frequently used for early Byzantine MSS. (fig. 1). The chief material in use since the 10th century is leather, stamped with dies or tools. An early example dating from the 10th century is of red leather, with a raised interlacing Celtic design, and is now at Stonyhurst. Four remarkable leather bindings were executed at Durham for Bishop Pudsey (1153-95), stamped with small dies, of which there are over 50 varieties. Contemporaneous with these were similar stamped covers of the Winchester Domesday Book, produced at Winchester, and the Liber Sapientiae, at London. The tradition was continued in the 15th century at Oxford, and by Caxton (1477-91), who frequently used intersecting diagonal lines, between which small dies were placed. In the Low Countries and in Germany many beautiful bindings were produced by the panel stamp. The earliest English example has the Arms of Edward IV. impressed. Other fine examples are by F. Egmondt (1493), Richard Pynson (1520), and Jean Norris (1528), who used the acorn panel (fig. 3), and the S. George by John Reynes (fig. 4), who was binder with Thomas Berthelet (1542) to Henry VIII. The introduction of the *roll* in 1530 superseded the panel, and with the exception of those by Nicholas Spering, of Cambridge, these designs with Renascence figures and arcades are not to be compared for vitality and beauty of detail with those of the earlier period.

The gold tooling, which superseded the " blind tooling," was introduced from Saracenic sources into Europe at Venice, where, in 1488, Aldus Manutius commenced his fine series of printed books, and his early bindings (1500-10) had parallel lines and slight Arabic enrichments at the corners. Then followed the beautiful interlacing patterns that were executed for the famous book collectors, Tommaso Maioli and Count Grolier (figs. 5, 6). The Royal bindings for Francois I. and Henry II. were by Peter Roffet, Philip le Noir, and Geoffrey Tory, who probably was also responsible for the Grolier bindings. The 17th century famous French binders were Nicholas and Clovis Eve (fig. 7), Macé Ruette, and Le Gascon, famous for his *pointillé* work. The 18th century binders were N. Boyet, and A. Padeloup, and the Deromes, while the bindings of red morocco with broad tooled borders, executed for the Earl of Oxford (1710-41), known as the Harleian style, and the beautiful and refined bindings by Roger Payne (1795, fig. 9) are of contemporary English work.

The early Grolier tools were distinctly Arabian and solid or barred, while the bindings of "Eve" have interlacing circular and square panels with sprays of foliage. Some French bindings for Henry IV. are tooled with a *semis* of monograms on flowers.

Examples 5 to 9 are in the John Rylands Library, Manchester.

155

ENGRAVED & PRINTED ORNAMENT

The earliest printed Books of Hours, of the later 15th and early 16th centuries, retained in a large measure the borders, storiated initials, and allied page ornaments of their illuminated MSS. prototypes. Towards the same period the engraved tokens—often highly decorative—of printers and publishers appear on the title-pages or at the close of books. Slightly later, woodcut or copper-plate head or tail-pieces come into vogue. We are however, less concerned with work of type than with the drawings and engravings of pure ornament freely published from the 16th century onward. These are often explicitly designed for the use of jewellers, architects, intarsia workers, etc., but are none the less adaptable to a variety of crafts. Many noted artists and engravers from Holbein downwards were not above executing such designs singly or in a series. One of the most curious examples, resembling rather an elementary drawing-book was published in 1540 by Heinrich Vogtherr. More noteworthy executants in the 16th century are Aldegrever, H. S. Beham, Androuet du Cerceau the elder, Etienne de Laune, Woeriot, Flötner, Daniel Mignot, Hans Mielick, Virgil Solis, and Vredeman de Vries. In the 17th century we may note Pierre Le Pautre, Le Brun, Jean Marot, and Simon Gribelin.[1]

JEWELLERY ORNAMENTED BY COLLAERT (16TH CENTURY).

FROM A BOOK OF HOURS. (T. KERVER, PARIS, 1505.)

DESIGNS FOR SILVERSMITHS BY PIERRE BOURDON, PARIS (LATE 17TH CENTURY).

[1] This artist, French by origin (*b.* 1662, *d.* in London, 1733), produced a book of ornament (published 1682, revised 1710) and an album of Cyphers published in 1697. He designed the

(2) THREE ORNAMENTAL PANELS BY LE PAUTRE, FRENCH, LATE 17TH CENTURY.

(1) FROM SIMON GRIBELIN'S "NEW BOOK OF ORNAMENT," 1710.

The Louis XIV. style finds its principal exponents in Jean Le Pautre, Berain, Daniel Marot, Durant, Bourgnet; and that of Louis XV. in

TWO DESIGNS FROM SIMON GRIBELIN'S "BOOK OF ORNAMENTS," 1682.

Ranson, Meissonnier, Watteau, François Boucher and Pillement; while Salembier, Cauvet, Delafosse, Choffart, Neufforge, Eisen and de Fontanien represent the Louis XVI. period, and Percier and Fontaine the "Empire."

This engraved ornament of the three Renaissance centuries covers a very wide field, and comprises a number of manners and styles. In addition to the numerous pattern books which present designs for jewellers, watch and clock-makers, etc., there are series which claim to be prepared for printers, decorators, carvers, and for the stocks and barrels of guns, etc. There are panels and arabesques, friezes, ceilings, altars, little engraved flowers, and many other motives. Often these are of remarkable delicacy and minuteness, though sometimes meretricious, coarse, clumsy, or grotesque. The above names represent the chief innovators or exponents of their contemporary tastes. The Victoria and Albert Museum is very rich in ornamental pattern-books, covering the whole range of periods and styles.

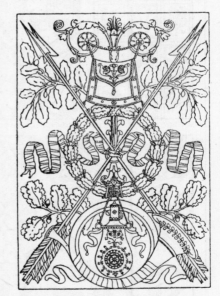

DESIGN FOR AN ORNAMENTAL PANEL FROM HEILIGENTHAL'S CATALOGUE OF ORNAMENT, STUTTGART, 1832.

book-plate for Worcester College, Oxford, and worked mainly in England. His detail is worked out very minutely, with a feeling for delicacy and proportion, and would look well in jeweller's chasing.

EGYPTIAN FABRICS.
FROM AKHMIM. 5TH OR 6TH CENTURY.
MANCHESTER COLLECTION.

EGYPTIAN FABRIC FROM AKHMIM
6TH CENTURY.
SOUTH KENSINGTON MUSEUM.

SICILIAN 13TH CENTURY. S.K.M.   SOUTH ITALIAN. 14TH CENTURY. S.K.M.

SICILIAN. 13TH CENTURY. S.K.M.

SILK DAMASK. SICILIAN. 13TH CENTURY.
SOUTH KENSINGTON MUSEUM.

SICILIAN. 13TH CENTURY.
MANCHESTER COLLECTION.

SICILIAN. 13TH CENTURY.
BOCK COLLECTION. MANCHESTER.

VENETIAN. FROM A PERSIAN DESIGN.
15TH CENTURY.

TEXTILE FABRICS

The utility, universality, construction, texture, ornamentation, and colour of textile fabrics are full of interest and suggestiveness, for in the remarkable development of textile fabrics we may trace the continuity of style and tradition, the intermingling of races and customs, and the grafting of religious ideas with the wealth and luxuriance of the past. All fabrics wrought in the loom are called textiles. They are broadly divided into three classes :—(1) Plain fabrics in which the warp and weft alternate equally ; (2) those fabrics in which a pattern is produced by the warp and weft intermingling in different proportions or colours, figured cloths and tapestries being included in this class ; (3) those fabrics in which the plain textile No. 1 is enriched with the needle, termed embroideries, or by printing, termed printed fabrics.

Owing to their perishable nature, few remains of ancient textile fabrics are in existence. The oldest examples are found in the tombs of Egypt, where, owing to the dryness of the climate, some fabrics of the early dynasties still remain. They are usually of fine linen, and without enrichment, yet upon the same tombs are many painted patterns that undoubtedly show a woven origin. With the exception of a few tapestry fabrics of the XVIII. dynasty, the oldest figured fabrics found in Egypt are of the 6th century A.D., and they show a remarkable similarity to the early patterns of Persia and Byzantium, for it was in India, Persia, and Arabia that textiles reached perfection of workmanship. This splendid tradition was carried from Persia and India to Byzantium in the 5th century, and in the 8th century the Arabians absorbed and assimilated the arts of Persia, India, Egypt, and Spain, and brought the art of weaving to its culmination during the 14th and 15th centuries.

The ornamental designs of textile fabrics of different nations and periods are characterized by well-defined forms, differentiated by racial influence, climatic conditions, and the myths and traditions of the people. Yet the traditional Eastern origin may be traced through many textile designs, for there is no doubt that India, Persia, and Arabia influenced the designs of textile fabrics more than other nations. This was due no doubt partly to the Eastern weavers carrying their art and traditions with them to various parts of Europe, and also to the exportation of their splendid fabrics, but principally to the beautiful and interesting designs, which were perfectly adapted to the process of weaving. It is no doubt this frank adaptation of natural forms and their appropriateness to the technical necessities of woven fabrics, that has rendered this Eastern influence so persistent through many centuries in different parts of Europe. It is remarkable that even in Italy during the whole of the Renascence period, with the characteristic scroll forms and acanthus foliation of its architecture and decorative arts, the textiles are quite distinct in style, having the characteristics of the Sicilian, Persian, and Indian ornament.

In the 12th century, Roger II., the Norman King of Northern Sicily, took Corinth and Argos, and carried many weavers and embroiderers from Greece to Sicily and established them at Palermo, where they quickly assimilated the Sicilian style, and produced many fine fabrics during the 13th and 14th centuries.

SICILIAN FABRIC.

The crusades now began to influence the arts. In 1098, Antioch was taken, and the spoil distributed through Europe. In 1204, Constantinople was taken by Baldwin, Count of Flanders, and the Venetian Doge, Dandolo, and the vast spoil of textiles distributed. It was doubtless under the influence of the crusades that the Sicilian weavers of the 13th and 14th centuries produced the many beautiful fabrics enriched with winged lions, foliated crosses and crowns, rayed stars, harts and birds linked together, and with the introduction of armorial bearings. Early in the 14th century this splendid tradition was introduced into Italy, and at Lucca many beautiful fabrics were produced, having the same characteristics and technique as the Sicilian fabrics. The cloak upon the recumbent bronze figure of Richard II., in Westminster Abbey, has a pattern of foliage, with couchant harts and rayed stars, and was most probably copied from the original silk made for Richard at Lucca or Palermo.

The beautiful materials and designs of Indian textile fabrics are indicative of the love of nature and the splendour of colour of a remote antiquity. Though influenced at various times by Greek, Persian, and Arabian traditions, India still preserved an indigenous ornamental art of remarkable freshness and vitality, the designers choosing their own flora and fauna with rare selective power and adaptive qualities. With an instinctive feeling for ornamental art, aided by the splendid colourings of the native dyes, they produced textile fabrics of silks, brocades, and gold and silver lace remarkable for richness and perfection of material, beauty of design, and harmony of colour.

The Indian pine is a familiar form of enrichment, differentiated

PRINTED COTTON·
INDIAN· 18TH CENTY
S·K·M·

from the cypress of Persia (fig. 1, plate 48) by the spiral at the apex. This typical pine is treated with a wonderful diversity of detail (figs. 4, 5, and 6, plate 49). The splendid carpets of India were doubtless influenced by the Persian tradition, and they follow the same methods and ornamental arrangements, adapting, conventionalizing, and emphasizing plants, flowers, and seeds, and rendering them with a fine feeling for form and colour. Block printing was largely used for silks and cottons, and many splendid examples are now treasured in our museums. An illustration of a printed cotton Palampore from the Victoria and Albert Museum is shown on the previous page, showing the beautiful floral treatment, diversity of detail, and contrast of line and mass. The gold and silver brocades, or " Kincobs," of Ahmedabad and Benares, with patterns of animals, flowers, and foliage richly spangled, the delicate muslins of Dacca, the gold and silver printed muslins of Jaipur, and the woollen shawls of Kashmir with the well-known pine pattern, are splendid examples of richness of material, delicacy and skilfulness of technique, and beauty and appropriateness of ornamentation.

The pile carpets of Persia, especially those of Kurdistan, Khorassan, Kirman, and Ferahan, are the finest in the world, being magnificent in colour and having bold conventional patterns of their beautiful flora, with birds and animals interspersed with the ornament, giving a largeness of mass and interest and vitality of detail. The hyacinth, tulip, iris, and the pink are frequently introduced, together with the hom, or tree of life. An illustration is given (fig. 2, plate 48) of a Genoa fabric, but of Persian design, showing the conventional " pink " with its simplicity and beauty of line. This traditional art of Persia had a most marked influence upon the textile fabrics of Europe from the 12th to the 17th centuries. This was no doubt due to many causes ; but the perfect adaptability to the process of weaving, the interest, inventiveness, and beauty of the ornament, and the singular frank treatment of form and colour, doubtless appealed to the craftsmen of Europe, and hence we find many Persian designs produced in Sicily, Spain, Italy, France, and Flanders.

The finest silk velvets and damasks produced from the looms of Florence show a distinct Persian influence in their bold artichoke and pomegranate patterns. In Genoa, similar patterns in many coloured velvets were produced, and it is singular how largely this persistency of type prevails in all countries.

In 1480, Louis XI. introduced the art into France, when looms were established at Tours, and in 1520 they were established at Lyons by Francois I., and the art of weaving rapidly spread. The earliest fabrics of these looms have patterns similar to the Persian and Italian fabrics ; but soon the vase pattern, which no doubt had its origin in Byzantine textiles and which had been used by the Persians and Italians, began to influence French designs.

However, this rapidly gave place, towards the middle of the 17th century, to the imitation of ribbons and laces in textile fabrics, together with a more naturalistic treatment of floral forms, and the beauty, suggestiveness, and interest of the early patterns now gave way to prettiness, affectation, and a naturalistic treatment which culminated in the period of Madame Pompadour.

The remarkable invention of perforated cards for facilitating the weaving of figured fabrics was introduced by Bonchon (1725), and continued by Falcon in 1728, by Vancanson in 1745, and perfected by Joseph Marie Jacquard in 1804.

The revocation of the Edict of Nantes in 1685 by Louis XIV. caused numbers of weavers to come to England, bringing their art and tradition with them, and many established themselves at Spitalfields.

A representative pattern is given in the annexed cut taken from a Spitalfields pattern book now in the Victoria and Albert Museum in which there are many original designs for silk brocades, some by French and others by English designers dating from 1715 to 1754, which was doubtless the most prosperous period of the Spitalfields industry. The patterns, consisting of natural arrangements of flowers, were necessarily largely influenced by fabrics of Lyons.

The textile fabrics of Flanders reached a high degree of perfection in the 16th and 17th centuries, Bruges being famous for its silk damasks and velvets, the patterns showing the traditional Persian, or the pomegranate and artichoke type of the Florentine textiles.

Block printing had been introduced into Flanders in the 15th century, and many fine patterns with Indian motives were produced up to the 17th century.

At Ypres, fine diapered linen was manufactured, and Ghent was famous for its woollens, but the remarkable prosperity of Flanders was destroyed by the Spanish occupation (1556-1648), when large numbers of Flemish weavers came to England and settled in many parts of the country, bringing their traditions and craftsmanship, which have undoubtedly had a most marked influence upon the production of cotton and woollen textile fabrics in England.

Tapestry, of which many fine examples of the 16th and 17th centuries are treasured in our museums and palaces, differs from most

Plate 78

A DUTCH BOOK END-PAPER OF ABOUT 1800; DESIGN FOUNDED ON
EASTERN STUFFS.

woven fabrics in its method of production, which consists of inter-weaving and knotting short pieces of coloured wefts, which form the pattern, to a strong warp, a ground weft being thrown across each pick to bind the material well together.

This is almost the same method as that used in the manufacture of the Indian and Persian carpets. It was during the 14th and 15th centuries, at Arras in Flanders, that storied tapestries were brought to their culmination, and the tapestry workers became a most power-ful guild. From about 1480, Brussels produced many magnificent hangings from designs by the great masters of the Italian Renascence. Raphael's famous cartoons, which are now in the Victoria and Albert Museum, are the original designs for the ten tapestries manufactured at Brussels for Pope Leo X., for the enrichment of the Sistine Chapel in the Vatican ; the seven cartoons, three being lost, were purchased by Charles I. These cartoons by Raphael were in collaboration with Giovanni da Udine and Francesco Penni, and were in 1515 handed over to the tapestry master, Peter van Aelst, and were completed in 1519.

Many of the great Flemish painters also designed for the Brussels tapestries, such as Van Orley, Van Leyden, and Jan Mabuse.

Francis I. caused tapestry looms to be set up at Fontainebleau in 1539, but it was not until the Gobelin tapestry manufactory was established in 1603 in the Faubourg Saint Marcel by the Fleming, Marc de Comans, and François de la Planche, that French tapestry reached any importance. Under the Minister Colbert in 1667, the Royal Gobelin manufactory produced many fine tapestries designed by the painter, Charles le Brun.

About 1590, some carpets, called Savonnerie, were made in the Louvre, the technique being somewhat similar to the Persian carpets, but the patterns were more pictorial and naturalistic in treatment. Fine tapestries were also produced at Beauvais and Aubusson. It was not until the time of James I. that tapestry weaving assumed any importance, when a tapestry manufactory was established (1619) at Mortlake, under the direction of Francis Crane, with skilled weavers from Bruges and Oudenarde, and the master-weaver Philip de Maecht.

In 1662, the painter Antonio Verrio was engaged to supply designs, but owing to a lack of financial support the Mortlake productions ceased in 1700. Other tapestry works were founded at Lambeth, where in 1670 some large tapestries (now in Haddon Hall) were made for the Countess of Rutland.

Some fine Flemish tapestries are in the Victoria and Albert Museum, and eight large pieces by Bernard Van Orley are in the Great Hall of Hampton Court. The coloured cartoons by Mantegna in Hampton Court, representing the triumph of Cæsar, were to be reproduced in tapestry for the Duke of Mantua. There are some fine Gobelin and Beauvais tapestries in Windsor Castle which were gifts from the Court of France, and they all show the most

1. BROCATELLE ITALIAN 16TH CENTURY. S.K.M

2. SINGLE MULLION PATTERN. FLEMISH 16TH CENTURY

3. FLOWER-VASE PATTERN LATE 16TH CENTURY VENETIAN. BOCK COLLECTION MANCHESTER

4. DOUBLE MULLION PATTERN. ITALIAN 16TH CENTURY. MANCHESTER BOCK COLLECTION

5. VELVET FROM GENOA FROM A PERSIAN DESIGN. 16TH CENTURY. S.K.M

6. VELVET. ITALIAN 16TH CENTURY MUSÉE DES ARTS DÉCORATIFS. PARIS.

7. SILK. ITALIAN. 16TH CENTURY.

8. SILK BROCADE. 18TH CENTURY.

9. FIGD. SATIN. 18TH CENTURY. LYONS.

Plate 80

JAVANESE FABRICS, 19TH CENTURY.
MANUFACTURED BY THE IKAT PROCESS; A COMBINATION OF WEAVING AND DYEING.

consummate technique, beauty of material, and harmony of colour. The so-called Bayeux tapestry is not tapestry but needlework in coloured wools upon a white linen ground. It is 214 ft. in length and 22 in. in width, and divided into 72 compartments, with incidents representing the Norman Invasion of England by William I. Though reputed to be the work of Queen Matilda, the probability is that it is the work of English hands some years after the invasion. This embroidery or tapestry is still preserved in the Cathedral of Bayeux.

The remarkable civilization of the Incas or Peruvians is shown in the many splendid objects of the industrial arts now treasured in our museums. Of these relics of a vanished civilization, the textile fabrics are perhaps the most instructive and interesting. The high technical skill of the craftsmanship, the fine spinning of the wool and cotton, and the perfection of the dyeing of the yarn, together with the skilful weaving of the figured cloths and tapestries, are a tribute to the vitality and civilization of a people remote from all Asiatic or European influences.

These Peruvian textiles are remarkable for the absence of the beautiful flora of Peru as elements for decoration. The fret is a frequent form of enrichment. The wave scroll so typical of Greek work is also a remarkable element in Peruvian ornament, and illustrates the singular development of the same ideas and aspect of form among people so remote from each other as the Greeks and Peruvians. But the patterns that sharply differentiate Peruvian examples from all other styles are the conventional treatments of figures, birds, fishes, and animals. The llama

TAPESTRY IN WHITE & BROWN.

DOUBLE CLOTH IN BROWN & YELLOW.

KEY PATTERN IN BROWN & YELLOW.

is conspicuous in many patterns, but the bird forms are the most remarkable, having many variations of type and treatment.

It is difficult to fix any date for these Peruvian examples, but as it is known that during the reign of Inca Pachacutic (*circa* 1390) the ceramic art was at its best, we may assume that the sister art of weaving reached its perfection about the same period, and continued until the Spanish Conquest in the 16th century. Many of the fabrics are of double cloth, of deep brown and pale straw colour, and show the same colour and pattern on both sides of the cloth. Some of the fabrics are tapestry woven, having short strands of coloured wool inserted into the fabric by the aid of the needle.

167

MBROIDERY & LACE

Needlework ornamentation in textile or other materials goes back to a remote period. Actual fragments of Egyptian decorative stitchwork of the 16th and 15th centuries B.C. are preserved, and its general use in Babylon, Assyria, Persia, and other ancient civilizations, may be inferred from wall-paintings and reliefs. Embroidery was known to the Greeks and Romans and, passing from thence to the Byzantines, became rigidly conventionalized, its richness hardly compensating for its stiff, insensitive treatment. From then onwards, the art of embroidery has flourished, being applied principally to hangings, covers, church vestments and state garments. In the 13th century England was famous for her embroidery (*opus anglicanum*) whose surviving masterpiece is the Syon cope at the Victoria and Albert Museum. From the 15th to the 17th centuries embroidery was exceedingly splendid, especially in the varieties known as " black work " and "petit point," the latter often forming elaborate pictures in needle-work.

BRIDAL BEDCOVER IN FILET-LACE, FLEMISH, 16TH CENTURY.

LACE, a net-like ornamental openwork of thread (flax, cotton, silk, mohair, gold or silver) is peculiar in that the production of ornament and fabric is simultaneous and inseparable. Its main division is into needlepoint lace and pillow lace. Lace work hardly dates further back than the latter part of the 16th century, the art first attaining perfection in North Italy and Flanders. England borrowed the fashion from France, but for a long time failed to make any state provision for the encouragement of the craft. Among early pattern-books of the 16th and 17th centuries are those of Vinciolo (1587), Vecellio (1592), and Isabetta Parasole. The finest work nowadays is produced in Belgium, France, and the British Isles.

LATE EMPIRE ORNAMENT.

(1) SPANISH AND PORTUGUESE WHITE SATIN DALMATIC, *circa* 1600.

(2) SILK HANGING, ITALIAN, 17TH CENTURY.

(3) SILK ALTAR FRONTAL, ITALIAN, 17TH CENTURY.

(4) DETAIL OF EMBROIDERY ON CLOAK, FRENCH, LATE 16TH OR EARLY 17TH CENTURY.

(*a*) PAGE FROM A FRENCH BOOK OF HOURS,
circa 1400.

(*b*) PAGE FROM A FRENCH BOOK OF HOURS,
circa 1480.

(*c*) FROM THE SAME BOOK AS (*b*). (V. & A.M.,
SALTING BEQUEST.)

(*d*) PAGE FROM AN ITALIAN BOOK OF HOURS,
circa 1520.

# ILLUMINATED MSS.

No form of artistic expression is more imbued with the very spirit of the Middle Ages than the illuminated manuscript. Although its origins may be retraced to a remote date—in embryo we find examples among Egyptian papyri and classical MSS.—it is none the less true to describe it in its highest development as a typically mediæval product. An illuminated manuscript usually comprises three elements : *the written text* (often an ornament in itself) ; the *pictures*, or pictorial motives ("histories" as they were termed) ; and the purely decorative *motives* (chiefly borders and large initials). The scribe was invariably distinct from the artist, or artists, we might say, as the pictures and decorative motives were apt to be by different hands, even where the miniatures are the work of a single artist.

In the earlier book of the Byzantine and Frankish periods, richness of effect is often obtained by a background of gold-leaf, or staining with purple, against which pictures, initials, etc., stand out strikingly. The initials to the four gospels are usually treated as full-page ornamental designs, often of great beauty and originality. The decoration of the Celtic MS. of the 7th, 8th, and 9th centuries (*e.g.* the Book of Kells, the Book of Armagh, Lindisfarne Gospels, etc., *cf.* plate 17) are remarkable for their intricate convolutions, largely based on the fret-pattern. Gold is hardly ever used in these, but this is compensated for by brilliancy of colour and design ; animal forms though freely introduced are highly conventionalized and subordinated to the general pattern.

From the 13th to the 15th century there is a steady progression of excellence in the art of illumination in all its branches. The ornamental borders so characteristic of the later period are at first in the nature of ornamental flourishes prolonging the great initials along the margins, which they gradually fill on three, then on all four sides of the text.

In a general way the illuminated MS. may be said to have reached its zenith about 1380-1450. The simple, yet rich and delicate, leaf borders that fill the margins in the earlier part of this period are succeeded by the more pretentious floral designs, relieved with pictorial and animal motives much favoured by the Burgundian school. These again were succeeded by borders of solid brush gold, on which were depicted with scrupulous realism flowers, insects, and fruit (occasionally varied by landscape and architectural borders). The Italians from about 1480 favoured elaborate borders in shaded gold, " camaïeu " and the like, composed of classical columns, urns, shields, acanthus leaves, mascarons, etc., on a ground of crimson or black ; or a characteristic variant of white scroll-work on a blue ground dotted with white. The latest borders are commonly wholly pictorial in treatment ; in other words, the miniature forms a frame for the text.

But from *c.* 1480 the decline is clearly marked, and despite some brilliant exceptions, the art may be considered as dead towards the middle of the 16th century.

Perhaps the highest achievement of the art of illumination is the "Très Riches Heures," once belonging to John, Duke of Berry, and now at Chantilly. Among names of famous miniaturists known to us are : Hubert Van Eyck,[1] Pol de Limburg, and his brothers, Jehan and François Fouquet, Philip de Mazerolles, Simon Marmion, Jean Bourdichon, Gerard of Bruges, Memling, and Simon Bening.

The commonest (and often richest) MSS. were those described as *liturgical*, including antiphonars, bibles, books of hours, breviaries, gospels, graduals, missals, and psalters. The books of hours (intended for private devotion) outnumber the rest by perhaps 10 to 1.

[1] To whom Durrien and Hulin de Lou independently ascribe the exquisite " Heures de Turin," unfortunately burnt in 1904.

ILLUMINATED PAGE FROM FRENCH GOSPELS, LATE 14TH CENTURY.

170

(2)

(1)

(1) CANVAS CUSHION COVER EMBROIDERED IN COLOURED SILKS. 18TH CENT. CRETAN EMBROIDERY (V. & A.M.).
(2) EMBOSSED LEATHER POUCH, NORTH GERMANY, A.D. 1739.

(3) APPLIQUÉ AND EMBROIDERED LEATHER BELT, LINZ, UPPER AUSTRIA.

PEASANT ART

Although characteristic examples of peasant art are to be seen in many museums, in this country, at least, we seem to have no collection of such productions arranged according to district of origin. The productions of the peasantry often vary not only from province to province, but from village to village, and are, generally speaking, influenced by conventions akin to those that obtain in more primitive cultures : *e.g.* the carved wood is not entirely dissimilar to that of Oceania (*cf.* plate 3). These arts are usually characterized by a charming, if sometimes rather casual, naïveté, and often by a native sense of design and colour-distribution. The peasant art of the Balkan States and neighbouring countries is thought to have been materially affected by Oriental influences, whilst the folk embroideries of Spain are reputed to be worked in a technique handed down from the Moors.

These handicrafts flourished most vigorously in the 17th and 18th centuries, but the work was often continued into the 19th century, and is only now actually dying out. There are important schools in Russia, Germany, Scandinavia, Switzerland, the Tyrol, Austria, and Hungary. The Central European countries produce elaborate fretted carvings often applied to furniture and exteriors ; Norway makes carved and gaily painted wooden objects similar to those of the Tyrol ; Germany has distinctive local types in Swabia, Brandenburg, Bavaria, etc., and Czecho-Slovakia is remarkable for embroideries, as are also the Dalmatian districts. In this the design is often highly conventionalized with use of traditional abstract forms (plate 83).

England cannot show much art of this type, but mention should be made of the Sussex ironwork industry which produced wrought or cast firebacks, potcranes, etc. ; of the old samplers and smocks, and the lace of Devonshire and North Buckinghamshire ; the flourishing Buckinghamshire chair-turning, which is more a traditional handicraft than an art.

The rise of modern mechanical mass-production, and improved communications have naturally succeeded in almost obliterating these small native arts and handicrafts, and it would be well if some full museum collection could be made of them, whilst still in existence, to form an epitome of the fresh and instinctive peasant work of the last few centuries.

TRADITIONAL CUT PAPER DESIGNS.

171

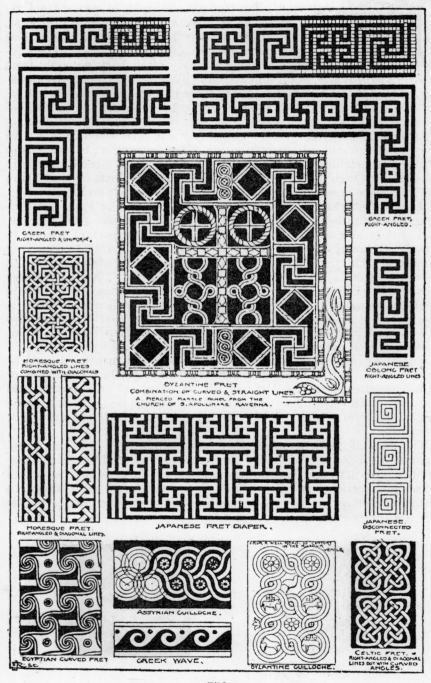

GREEK FRET
RIGHT-ANGLED & UNIFORM.

GREEK FRET,
RIGHT-ANGLED.

MORESQUE FRET
RIGHT-ANGLED LINES
COMBINED WITH DIAGONALS

JAPANESE
OBLONG FRET
RIGHT-ANGLED LINES

BYZANTINE FRET
COMBINATION OF CURVED & STRAIGHT LINES.
A PIERCED MARBLE PANEL FROM THE
CHURCH OF S. APOLLINARE RAVENNA.

MORESQUE FRET.
RIGHT-ANGLED & DIAGONAL LINES.

JAPANESE FRET DIAPER.

JAPANESE
DISCONNECTED
FRET.

EGYPTIAN CURVED FRET.

ASSYRIAN GUILLOCHE.

FROM A WELL HEAD 10 CENTURY
IN THE MUSEUM VENICE.

CELTIC FRET.
RIGHT-ANGLED & DIAGONAL
LINES OUT WITH CURVED
ANGLES.

GREEK WAVE.

BYZANTINE GUILLOCHE.

RETS

The remarkable universality of the fret, the simplicity and rhythm of detail, its adaptability and usefulness for surface enrichment, have made the fret one of the best known forms of ornamentation. It was used in the surface decorations of the tombs of Egypt, the temples of Greece, and the civic and domestic buildings of Rome.

The Greek form with its right-angular and equally-spaced keys, was used on the simple abacus and plain fascias of the Dorian architecture, in bands upon the painted vases, and in a concentric form when used in the interior of the red-figured circular cylix. The Romans, without imparting freshness, used the same right-angled key-pattern, chiefly as borders for mosaic pavements and upon the horizontal soffits of their architecture. The Byzantine, using the same type in conjunction with the cross and circle, gave more significance to the fret.

The Arabian fret differs in the use of the oblique line, together with the right-angled key, obtaining a wonderful degree of complexity and richness.

The Celtic fret is chiefly a diagonal one, but the recurrent angle is rounded to a curve.

Chinese and Japanese frets are usually right-angled, and are used in great profusion, often in a secondary field or background.

WALL-MOSAIC OF COLOURED MARBLES

The Japanese key or "*Fret diaper*" is used in the greatest profusion; it is used alike on silks and brocades, damascened in metal, in cloisonné enamel and in lacquered work, and is frequently arranged in irregular shaped compartments or medallions.

The Greek continuous fret border is rarely used by the Japanese, who generally use the disconnected or irregular fret. A similar irregular fret border was used by the Peruvians (pages 115 and 167), by the Mexicans, and by the natives of Polynesia.

The Assyrian and Byzantine guilloche is but a curved fret, but additional interest is given by the introduction of radiating forms in the principal interstices of the fret.

The simplest form of construction for frets, or key patterns, is to use squared or ruled paper. The Chinese or Japanese key is comparitively simple to construct by making the double T 17 squares in length with arms at each end of 13 squares, and placed alternately at right angles to each other.

173

RINTED INITIAL LETTERS

The initial letter, with its beauty of line and colour, its emphasis and distinctive character, was a frequent form of enrichment to the beautiful early manuscripts, and when, in the latter part of the 15th century, the printed book began to supersede the MS., the " Illuminator," or rubricator, was still called upon to enrich the printed page with his beautiful initials. Frequently, however, the rubricator was not called upon, with the result that many of the early printed books are still without their intended initial letters, as we find in many of the magnificent folios issued from the Aldine Press at Venice about 1500.

When the printed initial first made its appearance, it necessarily followed the type and character of the illuminated examples, as in the fine B (page 33), from the Mainz Psalter[1] in red and black, which is the earliest example known printed with the text (1457), and this initial is distinctly based upon the earlier illuminated capital.

Illustrations are given on pages 7, 9, 11, 23, 89, 105, 119, 147 of eight beautiful printed initials from the " Suetonius " of 1470[1] by the Germans, Conrad Sweynheim and Arnold Pannartz, who in 1456 introduced the art of printing into Italy at the Benedictine Monastery at Subiaco, near Rome. These initials, with their distinctive and refined Roman type, and delicate interlacing scrolls, are admirable examples of the early printed initial. They were afterwards acquired by Riessinger, who used them in 1480-98 for his printed books at Rome. The examples, with well-designed interlacings, given on pages 37, 39, 103, and those on 55 and 81 are taken from the fine " Euclid " by Ratdolt, of Venice, printed in 1481.[1] Three excellent initials from the beautiful printed books by Aldus Manutius, at Venice,[1] are given on pages 7, 95, 125.

Well-designed Gothic initials are given on page 15 from the " Fasciculus Temporum " (1481) by Ratdolt of Venice, the D (page 51) by Antonios Campigollis (1475), and the N from the " Life of Campanus," by M. Feronis, at Milan (1495, page 40). Beautiful Gothic initials given on pages 27, 137, 151, 159, 173, having well-spaced conventional foliage and flowers, are taken from " Froissart's Cronycles," printed in London by Richard Pynson (1523).[1] Other examples are the two from the Golden Bible (pages 35, 103) and the C on page 109 from the " Missale Traijectense " (1515), showing an intricate interlacing of the letter itself, the same characteristic appearing in the Romaunt of the Rose given on pages 73, 123, 129, 155.

Two rich examples of foliated initials by Israel van Meckenen (1500) are given on pages 58 and 87. The P on page 31 is from Venice (1498); the N, page 47, is dated 1510; the G, page 133, is from the Flemish woodcut alphabet of 1464 (British Museum); and the T on page 175 is from the Basle woodcut copy of this alphabet.

The Italian examples on pages 139 and 174 illustrate the decorative use of the figure in the early 16th-century initials.

[1] From the original editions in the John Rylands Library.

ERMS USED IN ORNA-MENTAL ART

Ornament is the means by which Beauty or Significance is imparted to Utility. It is either Symbolical or Æsthetic. Symbolic ornament consists of elements or forms chosen for the sake of their *significance*—Æsthetic ornament consists of forms or elements chosen for their *beauty* alone, or their power of appealing to the senses.

Of the historic styles of ornament, the Egyptian, Assyrian, Byzantine, Scandinavian, Persian, Indian, Gothic, Polynesian, and much of the Chinese and Japanese are symbolical, having elements and ornamental details chosen for their significance ; while in the Greek, Roman, and Renascence ornament the purely æsthetic motive is characteristic.

Ornament, again, may be natural or conventional—Imitative or Inventive. The terms " natural " and " imitative " have the same significance—viz., the exact copying of natural forms, so that they become principal, not secondary as perfect ornament should be. Conventional ornament is the adaptation of natural forms to ornamental and technical requirements, and is seen in its greatest beauty in the frank treatment by the Indians and Persians of their flora and fauna for the decorative enrichment of their textile fabrics, pottery, and jewellery.

Inventive ornament is that which consists of elements not derived from any natural source ; the Moresque style is a good example of this type.

The *elements* of ornament are the details or forms chosen for ornamental motives, and the *principles* of ornament are the arrangement of these forms and details ; they comprise repetition, alternation, symmetry, radiation, balance, proportion, variety, eurythmy, contrast, intersection, complication, fitness, and utility.

Repetition is the use of elements in a continuous series ; *Alternation* is the repetition of an element at intervals, with others intervening ; *Symmetry :* when the leading lines are equal or similar (or reciprocal) on both sides ; *Radiation :* when the lines spring from a centre, for example, a bird's wing and the flower of the daisy ; *Balance* and *Proportion :* when the relation and harmony of parts is based upon natural laws ; *Variety* implies difference in the details, with respect to form or type ; *Eurythmy* signifies rhythms or harmony in ornament ; *Contrast* is the arrangement in close proximity of colours or forms of opposite characters, as the straight line with the curve, or light with dark ; *Intersection* is the crossing of the leading lines, the Arabian, Moresque and Celtic styles are examples of this principle ; *Complication* is the effect produced by elements so arranged as to be more or less difficult to trace with the eye alone : as in the Japanese key and the Moresque star pattern. *Fitness* and *utility* as their names imply are essentials in all good periods of ornamentation.

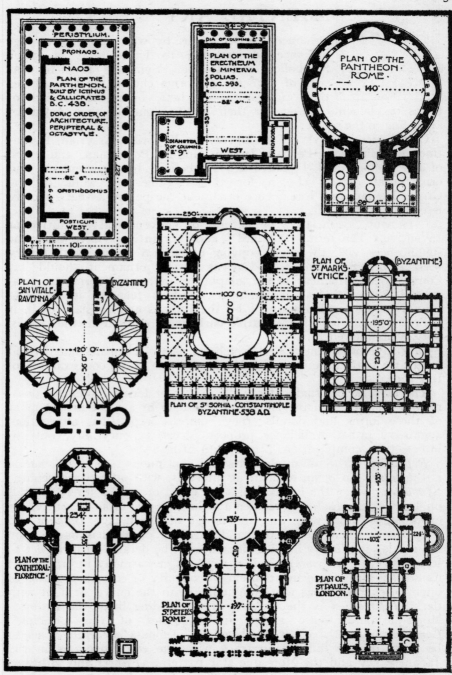

SELECTED TEXT-BOOKS.

ORNAMENT.

Handbook of Ornament. *F. S. Meyer.*
Styles of Ornament. *A. Speltz.*

ARCHITECTURE.

A History of Architecture on the Comparative Method. *Sir Banister Fletcher.*
The Art of Architecture. *A. E. Richardson and H. O. Corfiato.*
English Architecture. *T. D. Atkinson.*
Glossary of Architecture. *T. D. Atkinson.*
Local Style in English Architecture. *T. D. Atkinson.*
Mediæval Architecture, 3 vols. *C. E. Power.*
Outline of English Architecture. *A. H. Gardner.*
The Story of Architecture. *P. L. Waterhouse.*
A Short Critical History of Architecture. *H. H. Statham.*
The Styles of English Architecture, Handbooks, 2 vols.; Lecture Diagrams, 2 series. *A. Stratton.*

SCULPTURE.

Classical Sculpture. *A. W. Lawrence.*
Handbook of Greek Sculpture. *E. A. Gardner.*
History of Sculpture. *G. H. Chase and C. R. Post.*

DESIGN.

The Bases of Design. *Walter Crane.*
Line and Form. *Walter Crane.*
Pattern Design. *Lewis Day.*
The Things Which are Seen. *A. Trystan Edwards.*

HISTORY OF ART.

History of Art, 2 vols. *H. B. Cotterill.*
Outline History of Art, 3 vols. *J. Pijoan.*
Short History of Art. *A. Blum and R. R. Tatlock.*
Art Through the Ages. *H. Gardner.*

SELECTED WORKS OF REFERENCE.

ORNAMENT.

Coloured Ornament of Historic Styles, 3 vols. *A. Speltz.*
Encyclopedia of Colour Decoration. *H. T. Bossert.*
Examples of Chinese Ornaments. *Owen Jones.*
Fifteenth Century Italian Ornament. *S. Vacher.*
Grammar of Ornament. *Owen Jones.*
History of Ornament, 2 vols. *A. D. F. Hamlin.*
Ornament. *H. T. Bossert.*
Pattern in Western Europe. *J. Evans.*
La Peinture Decorative en France du XIe au XVIe Siècle. *P. Gélis-Didot.*
Polychromatic Ornament. *M. A. Racinet.*
Pompeian Ornament. *R. A. Briggs; P. Gusman; A. Noccolini; W. Zahn.*
Specimens of Ornamental Art, 2 vols. *L. Gruner.*

ARCHITECTURE.

Dictionary of Architecture and Building. 3 vols. *R. Sturgis.*
History of Architectural Development, 3 vols. *F. M. Simpson.*
History of Architecture, 5 vols. *J. Fergusson.*
History of Architecture, 4 vols. *R. Sturgis.*
Architecture of Ancient Greece. *W. J. Anderson, R. P. Spiers and W. B. Dinsmoor.*

Architecture of Ancient Rome. *W. J. Anderson, R. P. Spiers and T. Ashby.*
Orders of Architecture. *J. Gibbs; J. M. Mauch; C. Normand; R. P. Spiers; A. Stratton.*
Fragments d'Architecture Antique, 2 vols. *H. D'Espouy.*
Byzantine Architecture and Decoration. *J. A. Hamilton.*
English Romanesque Architecture, 2 vols. *A. W. Clapham.*
Architectural Parallels (English Gothic). *E. Sharpe.*
Gothic Architecture in England. *F. Bond.*
Gothic Architecture, Details of, 2 vols. *J. K. Colling.*
Gothic Ornaments, 2 vols. *J. K. Colling.*
A History of Gothic Art in England. *E. S. Prior.*
English Church Architecture, 2 vols. *F. Bond.*
Mediæval Styles of the English Parish Church. *F. E. Howard.*
Parish Churches of England. *J. C. Cox and C. B. Ford.*
Romanesque Architecture in France. *J. Baum.*
Dictionnaire Raisonnée de L'Architecture Française, 10 vols. *Viollet le Duc.*
Nouvelle Encyclopédie Illustrée de L'Art Française. L'Art Roman. *L. Lefrançois-Pillion.* L'Art Gothique. *L. Réau.* L'Art Renaissance. *P. Du Colombier.* L'Art au XVII Siècle. *C. Mauricheau-Beaupré.*
Fragments d'Architecture du Moyen-âge et de la Renaissance, 2 vols. *H. D'Espouy.*

Gotische Kathedralen in Frankreich. *P. Clemen.*

Architecture of the Renaissance in Italy. *W. J. Anderson and A. Stratton.*

Bankunst der Früh-Renaissance in Italien. *J. Baum.*

Bankunst der Hoch- und Spät-Renaissance in Italien. *C. Ricci.*

Baroque Architecture and Sculpture in Italy. *C. Ricci.*

Renaissance Palaces of Northern Italy, 3 vols. *A. Haupt.*

Renaissance Rome: Edifices de Rome Moderne, 4 vols. *P. M. Letarouilly.*

Roman Baroque Art, 2 vols. *T. H. Fokker.*

Architecture of the Renaissance in France, 2 vols. *W. H. Ward and J. W. Simpson.*

Domestic Architecture of England during the Tudor Period, 2 vols. *T. Garner and A. Stratton.*

Architecture of the Renaissance in England, 2 vols. *J. A. Gotch.*

A History of Renaissance Architecture in England, 2 vols. *R. Blomfield.*

Early Renaissance Architecture in England. *J. A. Gotch.*

Mansions of England in the Olden Time, 4 vols. *J. Nash.*

Old English Mansions, 4 vols. *C. J. Richardson.*

English Home from Charles I to George IV. *J. A. Gotch.*

English Homes, 1066-1820, 9 vols. *A. Tipping.*

Smaller English House, 1660-1830. *A. E. Richardson and H. D. Eberlein.*

Small Houses of the Later Georgian Period, 2 vols. *S. C. Ramsey and J. Harvey.*

Later Renaissance Architecture in England, 2 vols. *J. Belcher and M. Macartney.*

London Churches of the 17th and 18th Centuries. *C. H. Birch.*

Old Churches of London. *G. Cobb and G. Webb.*

Old Colleges of Oxford. *A. Vallance.*

The Age of Adam. *J. Lees-Milne.*

The Architecture of R. and J. Adam, 2 vols. *A. T. Bolton.*

The Regency Style. *D. Pilcher.*

A History of Spanish Architecture. *B. Bevan.*

Renaissance Architecture in Spain. *A. N. Prentice.*

SCULPTURE.

Decorative Sculpture. *G. Kowalczyk.*

Sculpture Through the Ages. *L. Rothschild.*

Sculpture and Sculptors of the Greeks. *G. M. A. Richter.*

Chinese Sculpture from the 5th to the 14th Century, 4 vols. *O. Sirén.*

Carved Ornament from Irish Monuments. *H. S. Crawford.*

English Church Monuments, 1150 to 1550. *F. H. Crossley.*

English Church Monuments, 1510 to 1840. *K. A. Esdaile.*

English Gothic Foliage Sculpture. *S. Gardner.*

English Mediæval Sculpture. *A. Gardner.*

Mediæval Figure Sculpture in England. *E. S. Prior and A. Gardner.*

Mediæval Foliage. *J. K. Colling.*

Florentine Sculptors of the Renaissance. *W. Bode.*

Italian Sculpture of the Renaissance. *E. Maclagan.*

THE APPLIED ARTS.

MOSAICS.

Early Christian Mosaics from the 4th to the 7th Centuries. *R. Huch and W. F. Volbach.*

Mosaici Antichi di San Marco a Venezia. *S. Bettini.*

Mosaici di San Vitale in Ravenna. *S. Muratori.*

Pittura delle Origini Cristiane. *S. Bettini.*

CERAMICS.

The Art of the Potter. *W. B. Honey.*

The Book of Pottery and Porcelain, 2 vols. *W. E. Cox.*

General History of Porcelain, 2 vols. *W. Burton.*

Pottery and Porcelain, 3 vols. *E. Hannover.*

Greek Vase Painting. *E. Buschor.*

History of Ancient Pottery, 2 vols. *H. B. Walters.*

The Art of the Chinese Potter. *R. L. Hobson and A. L. Hetherington.*

The Ceramic Art of China and the Far East. *W. B. Honey.*

Chinese Porcelain, 2 vols. *W. G. Gulland.*

Chinese Pottery and Porcelain, 2 vols. *R. L. Hobson.*

The Early Ceramic Wares of China. *R. L. Hobson.*

The Later Ceramic Wares of China. *R. L. Hobson.*

Corean Pottery. *W. B. Honey.*

Dutch Pottery and Porcelain. *W. P. Knowles.*

Old Dutch Pottery and Tiles. *E. Neurdenburg.*

Early Netherlands Maiolica. *B. Rackman.*

Oud-Nederlandsche Majolica en Delftsch Aardewerk. *C. H. De Jonge.*

Early Islamic Pottery. *A. Lane.*

Islamic Pottery. *A. J. Butler.*

English Pottery and Porcelain. *W. B. Honey.*

English Pottery. *B. Rackham and H. Read.*

Old English Porcelain. *W. B. Honey.*

English Blue and White Porcelain of the 18th century. *S. Fisher.*

French Faience. *A. Lane.*

A History and Description of French Porcelain. *E. S. Auscher.*

Porcelaine Française du XVII au mileau du XIX siècle. *Alfassa and Guérin.*

German Porcelain. *W. B. Honey.*

A History and Description of Italian Majolica. *M. L. Solon.*

Russisches Porzellan, 1744 to 1923. *G. Lukomski.*

Ceramica del Levante Español. *N. G. Marti.*

Catalogues of Ceramics in the following Collections : *Sir Percival David, Eumorfopoulis, Glaisher, Leonard Gow, Leverhulme, Lady Ludlow, W. T. Walters.*

GLASS.

The Art of Glass. *W. Buckley.*

English Glass. *W. A. Thorpe.*

English Table Glass. *P. Bate.*

European Glass. *W. Buckley.*

Gläser der Empire- und Biedermeierzeit. *G. E. Pazaurek.*

Glass. *E. Dillon.*

Glass : A Handbook for the Study of Glass Vessels of all Periods and Countries. *W. B. Honey.*

Glass in Architecture and Decoration. *R. McGrath.*

History of English and Irish Antique Glass, 2 vols. *W. A. Thorpe.*

History of Glass Making in Ireland. *M. S. D. Westropp.*

Old English Glasses. *A. Hartshorne.*

STAINED GLASS.

Adventures in Light and Colour. *C. J. Connick.*

Ancient Painted Glass in England, 1170-1500. *P. Nelson.*

English Mediæval Painted Glass. *J. D. Le Couteur.*

English Stained Glass. *H. Read.*

Gotische Glasmalerei in Österreich bis 1450. *F. Kieslinger.*

History of Design in Painted Glass, 4 vols. *N. H. J. Westlake.*

History of English Glass Painting. *M. Drake.*

Mittelalterliche Bildfenster der Schweiz. *F. Zschokke.*

Stained Glass of the XIIth and XIIIth Centuries from French Cathedrals. *G. C. Coulton and M. Aubert.*

Stained Glass of the Middle Ages in England and France. *L. B. Saint and H. Arnold.*

Vorbildliche Glasmalereien aus dem späten Mittelalter und der Renaissancezeit. *E. Wasmuth.*

Windows : a book about Stained and Painted Glass. *L. F. Day.*

GOLD AND SILVER.

Domestic Silver of Gt. Britain and Ireland. *E. Wenham.*

English Domestic Silver. *C. Oman.*

An Illustrated History of English Plate, 2 vols. *C. J. Jackson.*

Old English Plate. *W. J. Cripps.*

Old English Silver. *W. W. Watts.*

Old Silver Work, Chiefly English. *J. Starkie Gardner.*

Paul de Lamerie, his Life and Work. *P. A. S. Phillips.*

The Goldsmiths of Italy. *C. G. E. Bunt and S. J. A. Churchill.*

Silversmiths' Work of European Origin, 1350-1678. *Burlington Fine Arts Club.*

Old Silver of Europe and America. *E. A. Jones.*

Oriental Silverwork, Malay and Chinese. *H. L. Roth.*

Catalogues of the Plate in the following Collections : Cambridge Colleges, Oxford Colleges, Tower of London, Windsor Castle, Baroness de Rothschild, Emperor of Russia. *E. A. Jones.*

Catálogo de la Exposición de Orfebreria Civil Española. *P. de Artinano.*

WROUGHT IRONWORK.

Decorative Ironwork. *C. Ffoulkes.*

Encyclopedia of Ironwork. *O. Hoever.*

English and Scottish Wrought Ironwork. *B. S. Murphy.*

English Ironwork of the 17th and 18th centuries. *J. Starkie Gardner.*

Ferronerie Ancienne, 2 vols. *H. R. Allemagne.*

Il Ferro Nell'arte Italiana. *G. Ferrari.*

Hierros Artisticos, 2 vols. *L. Labarta.*

Rejeria of the Spanish Renaissance. *A. Byne and M. Stapley.*

A New Book of Drawings containing several sorts of Ironwork. *J. Tijou.*

Wrought Iron and its Decorative Use. *M. Ayrton and A. Silcock.*

Wrought Iron in Architecture. *G. K. Geerlings.*

BRONZES.

Early Chinese Bronzes. *A. J. Koop.*

Bronzi Italiani : Raccolta Alfredo Barsanti. *L. Pollak.*

Il Bronze e il Rame Nell'arte Italiana. *A. Pettorelli.*

Italian Bronze Statuettes of the Renaissance. 6 vols. *W. Bode.*

DECORATIVE FURNITURE AND INTERIORS.

Decorative Furniture. *G. L. Hunter.*

Encyclopedia of Furniture. *J. Aronson.*

Encyclopedia of Furniture. *H. Schmitz.*

Kunstgeschichte des Möbels. *A. Feulner.*
Ancient Furniture. *G. M. A. Richter.*
Chinese Furniture. *H. Cescinsky.*
Gentlemen and Cabinet Maker's Director. *T. Chippendale.*
Cabinet Maker and Upholsterer's Guide. *G. Hepplewhite.*
Cabinet-Maker and Upholsterers' Drawing Book. *T. Sheraton.*
Decorative Work of R. and J. Adam.
Decoration and Furniture in England, 4 vols. *M. Jourdain and F. Lenygon.*
Dictionary of English Furniture, 3 vols. *F. Macquoid and R. Edwards.*
Early English Furniture and Woodwork, 2 vols. *H. Cescinsky and E. R. Gribble.*
Encyclopedia of English Furniture. *O. Brackett.*
English Furniture, Decoration and Woodwork. *T. A. Strange.*
English Furniture from Charles II to George II. *R. W. Symonds.*
English Furniture, Gothic to Sheraton. *H. Cescinsky.*
English Furniture of the 18th Century, 3 vols. *H. Cescinsky.*
The English Interior. *A. Stratton.*
English Interiors from Smaller Houses, 1660-1820. *M. Jourdain.*
History of English Furniture, 4 vols. *P. Macquoid.*
Regency Furniture. *M. Jourdain.*
Holländische Möbel und Raumkunst. *C. H. De Jonge.*
Old Interiors in Holland. *K. Sluyterman.*
Dictionnaire du Mobilier Français de l'Epoque Carlovingienne à la Renaissance, 6 vols. *E. E. Viollet-Le-Duc.*
French Interiors, Furniture, Decoration and Woodwork. *T. A. Strange.*
Louis XIV and Regency Furniture and Decoration. *S. de Ricci.*
Furniture of the Louis XVI Period. *S. de Ricci.*
Empire und Biedermeier. *J. A. Lux.*
Deutsche Möbel des Mittelalters und der Renaissance. *O. Von Falke and H. Schmitz.*
Deutsche Möbel des Barock und Rokoko. *O. Von Falke and H. Schmitz.*
Deutsche Möbel des Klassizismus. *O. Von Falke.*
Furniture and Decoration of the Italian Renaissance. *F. Schottmüller.*
Italian Furniture and Interiors. *G. L. Hunter.*
Die Renaissance in Italien, 4 vols. *A. Schütz.*
Spanish Interiors and Furniture, 3 vols. *A. Byne and M. Stapley.*
Colonial Furniture in America, 2 vols. *L. V. Lockwood.*
Decorative Plasterwork of Great Britain. *L. Turner.*
English Decorative Plasterwork of the Renaissance. *M. Jourdain.*

History of Old English Wallpaper. *A. V. Sugden and J. L. Edmonson.*

WOOD CARVING.

English Church Woodwork and Furniture. *F. E. Howard and F. H. Crossley.*
Bench Ends in English Churches. *J. C. Cox.*
English Church Screens. *A. Vallance.*
Greater English Church Screens. *A. Vallance.*
Pulpits, Lecterns and Organs in English Churches. *F. Bond.*
Woodcarvings in English Churches, 2 vols. *F. Bond.*
English Interior Woodwork of the 16th, 17th and 18th centuries. *H. Tanner.*
English Renaissance Woodwork, 1660-1730. *T. J. Beveridge.*
Grinling Gibbons and the Woodwork of his Age. *A. Tipping.*
French Woodcarvings from the National Museums. *E. Rowe.*
Il Legno nell'arte Italiana. *G. Ferrari.*

IVORIES.

The Book of Ivory. *G. C. Williamson.*
English Ivories. *M. H. Longhurst.*
Ivories. *A. Maskell.*

BOOKBINDINGS.

Bindings in Cambridge Libraries. *G. D. Hobson.*
Bookbinding in France. *W. Y. Fletcher.*
English Bindings before 1500. *G. D. Hobson.*
Gothic and Renaissance Bookbinding, 2 vols. *E. P. Goldschmidt.*
Islamic Bookbindings. *F. Sarre.*
Maoli, Canevari and others. *G. D. Hobson.*

TEXTILE FABRICS.

Decorative Textiles. *J. L. Hunter.*
Encyclopedia of Textiles. *E. Fleming.*
Historic Textile Fabrics. *R. Glazier.*
History of Design in Silk Fabrics. *O. Von Falke.*
Textil-Ornamente. *F. Fischbach.*
Die Gewebe-Sammlung des Königlichen Kunstgewerbe-Museums, Berlin, 11 vols.
Toiles Imprimées de la Perse et de l'Inde. *H. Ernst.*
Chinese Carpets and Rugs. *A. Hackmack.*
Chinese Rugs. *G. B. Leitch.*
Fine Carpets in the Victoria and Albert Museum. *A. F. Kendrick and C. Tattersall.*
Handwoven Carpets, 2 vols. *A. F. Kendrick and C. Tattersall.*
Masterpieces of Oriental Rugs, 3 vols. *W. Grote-Hasenbalg.*
Old Oriental Carpets from the Austrian Museum for Art and Industry, 2 vols. *F. Sarre and H. Tkenkwald.*

Oriental Rugs—Antique and Modern. *W. A. Hawley.*

Oriental Rugs and Carpets. *A. U. Dilley.*

The Ryijy Rugs in Finland. *U. T. Sirelius.*

Tapis de Finlande, Norvège et Suède. *H. Ernst.*

Tapis de Pologne, Lithuanie, Yougoslavie. *H. Ernst.*

Tapis Roumains. *H. Ernst.*

A History of Tapestry. *W. G. Thomson.*

Gestickte Bildteppiche und Decken des Mittelalters, 2 vols. *M. Schuette.*

French Tapestry. *A. Lejard.*

La Tapisserie Française du Moyen-âge à nos Jours. *F. Salet.*

La Tapisserie Gothique. *E. Planès.*

Tapestry Weaving in England. *W. G. Thomson.*

English Decorative Textiles. *W. G. Hunton.*

Kunstgeschichte des Alten Peru. *W. Lehmann and H. U. Doering.*

Kunst und Kultur von Peru. *M. Schmidt.*

Tissus des Indes Néerlandaises. *D. Réal.*

Tissus Nègres. *H. Clouzot.*

EMBROIDERY AND LACE.

Art in Needlework. *L. F. Day.*

Domestic Needlework. *S. Seligman and T. Hughes.*

English Embroidery. *A. F. Kendrick.*

English Mediæval Embroidery. *A. G. L. Christie.*

Ernst Series of Embroidery Portfolios : Chinese, Czech, Indian, Roumanian. Russian, Spanish, 6 vols. *H. Ernst.*

Mediæval und Near Eastern Embroideries, 2 vols. *A. J. B. Wace.*

Needlework through the Ages. *M. Symonds and L. Preece.*

Samplers. *L. Ashton.*

Samplers and Stitches. *Mrs. A. Christie.*

Samplers and Tapestry Embroidery. *M. B. Huish.*

Art and Craft of Old Lace. *A. Von Henneberg.*

History of Lace. *Mr. B. Palliser.*

Old Italian Lace, 2 vols. *E. Ricci.*

Old Lace. *M. Jourdain.*

ILLUMINATED MANUSCRIPTS.

The Book of Kells. *E. Sullivan.*

English Illuminated Manuscripts from the 10th to the 15th Centuries, 2 vols. *E. G. Millar.*

History of English Illumination, 2 vols. *O. E. Saunders.*

History of German Illumination, 2 vols. *A. Goldschmidt.*

History of Spanish Illumination, 2 vols. *J. D. Bordona.*

Illuminated Ornaments Selected from Manuscripts and Early Printed Books. *H. Shaw.*

Les Joyaux de l'Enlumière. *H. Martin.*

La Miniature Flamande au temps de la Cour de Bourgogne. *C. D. Durrieu.*

La Miniature Française aux 15ᵉ et 16ᵉ siècles. *A. Blum and P. Lauer.*

PEASANT ART.

(See also Textile Fabrics and Embroidery)

Peasant Art in Europe. *H. T. Bossert.*

Peasant Art in Austria, Hungary, Italy, Roumania, Russia, 4 vols. *C. Holme.*

Peasant Art in Sweden, Lapland and Iceland. *C. Holme.*

Deutsche Volkskunst, 13 vols. *E. Redslob.*

Folk Art of Rural Pennsylvania. *F. Lichten.*

MISCELLANEOUS.

Les Terres Cuites Grecques. *J. Charbonneaux.*

Terra Cotta of the Italian Renaissance. *The Terra Cotta Association.*

Enamelling. *L. F. Day.*

European Enamels. *H. Cunynghame.*

Mediaeval Spanish Enamels. *W. L. Hildeburgh.*

Battersea Enamels. *E. Mew.*

A Record of European Arms and Armour, 6 vols. *G. G. Laking and F. H. Cripps-Day.*

The Armoury of the Castle of Churburg. *O. Trapp.*

The Art of Heraldry. *A. C. Fox Davies.*

Heraldry and Floral Forms as used in Decoration. *H. Cole.*

Monumental Brasses, 2 vols. *H. Haines.*

Monumental Brasses from the 13th to the 16th Century. *J. G. and L. B. Waller.*

A Book of Facsimiles of Monumental Brasses on the Continent of Europe. *W. F. Creeny.*

Ancient Sepulchral Monuments. *W. Brindley and W. S. Weatherley.*

Monumental Effigies of Great Britain. *C. A. Stothard.*

One Hundred Title-Pages. *A. F. Johnson.*

German Renaissance Title-Borders. *A. F. Johnson.*

Title-Page Borders used in England and Scotland, 1485-1640. *R. B. McKerrow and F. S. Ferguson.*

Propyläen Kunstgeschichte, 16 vols.

Burlington Magazine Monographs on Chinese, Georgian and Spanish Art, 3 vols.

Survey of Persian Art, 6 vols. *A. U. Pope.*

The Decorative Arts in England, 1660-1790. *H. H. Mulliner.*

Church Symbolism. *F. R. Webber.*

Outlines of Chinese Symbolism and Art Motives. *C. William.*

Ko-ji Ho-ten, Objets d'Art Japonais et Chinois, 2 vols. *V. F. Weber.*

Arts of the South Seas. *R. Linton and P. S. Wingert.*

Mediæval American Art, 2 vols. *P. Kelemen.*

La Collection Spitzer, 6 vols.

INDEX

FOR ALL MANKIND

(A l'Echelle Humaine)

FOR ALL MANKIND

(*A l'Echelle Humaine*)

by

LÉON BLUM

Translated by

W. PICKLES

LONDON
VICTOR GOLLANCZ LTD
1946

4180

PRINTED IN GREAT BRITAIN BY RICHARD CLAY AND COMPANY, LTD.
BUNGAY, SUFFOLK.

TRANSLATOR'S PREFACE

WHEN THIS book first appeared, it was like a voice from the dead, for it was published in French in the early months of 1945, while the author and his wife were still prisoners in Germany, and although it was known that the physical conditions of their captivity were better than might have been feared, all their friends knew only too well that Léon Blum and Madame Blum were being kept alive solely to allow their captors to use them as hostages when occasion arose. Chance and German miscalculation sent that plan astray, and Léon Blum returned to France in May 1945 to find his book in print. The manuscript had been smuggled out of prison early in 1942 and preserved by faithful friends during the remaining two years of German occupation. Parts of it, if I am not mistaken, had appeared anonymously in the underground *Populaire*, as early as 1943, and after the liberation of Paris the whole was seen through the Press by Blum's old friend, the G.O.M. of French Socialism and France's greatest authority on Marxism, Bracke, who, under his real name of A.-M. Desrousseaux, is also one of France's greatest Hellenic scholars.

Here is the Preface that Bracke wrote for that first edition:

As you take up this book, try to bear in mind that the author finished writing it in December 1941. Then, whatever you feel about the author, whether you like him or not, you will not fail to recognise the observations and conclusions you find here as those of a

lucid and penetrating mind. As you follow the argument, your mind will go back to the point of time at which Léon Blum turned to look at his country's immediate past, at the degradation of the conqueror's "armistice" and to consider what was to be France's future road and her goal. Try to imagine Léon Blum, in the solitude of his successive prisons, gathering together his memories, sorting them out, questioning them, putting his thoughts into ordered and written form at Bourrasol, revising and rounding them off in the snow-covered fortress of Pourtalet. Do that, and you will not misunderstand, if you meet, here and there, an expression that displeases you, a statement that you would have made more cautiously or would have qualified in the light of what you have learned from the events of 1942, 1943 and 1944. This is 1941, seen through the eyes of a prisoner of Vichy and of Hitlerite Germany, before that Riom Trial, of which ultimately even the pretence was abandoned.

It was, of course, intended that the book should be printed as soon as it was possible for it to be published. A few people read it in typescript. Now it is available to all, exactly as it was written. Not a word has been altered, not even where prudence or experience suggested that this or that should be added or cut out. It bears the imprint of no mind other than that of Léon Blum, and so is entitled to fair consideration on its merits alone. The reader who refuses it that consideration will himself be the loser.

Those who can look back on the changing impressions, on the many different phases of France's great ordeal, who can avoid confusing July 1940 with August 1939 and the last months of 1943 with the spring of 1942, will admire the limpid certainty of judgment that enabled Blum to see future events in the shadows they cast before them.

What is most striking about this book? Is it the respect for truth, so patently shown by a man who analyses the errors and weaknesses of his own party, but sees the behaviour of others only in terms of what conditions

and explains it? Is it the perspicacity that could look behind the picture of a Russia made vulnerable by isolation, to see and almost to predict the acts that placed her on the common road of an expanding human freedom? Or is it the confident serenity which never doubted even in the darkest hours that the Russian army would rise again to contribute to the final defeat of Fascism everywhere—which, indeed, never doubted anything of the international shape of the ultimate victory?

Whatever be the answer to that question, the reader will find only encouragement to work with the author for the achievement of that tremendous task whose scope and goal he measured and traced within his prison walls.

BRACKE

(*A.-M. Desrousseaux*).

It was in these words, then, that Bracke reminded his readers of the date at which *A l'Echelle Humaine* had been written. The reminder was intended, in some sort, as an apology for what might otherwise appear to be lapses from historical accuracy. In fact, to the reader who remembers that the book was written during the blackest period of the war, Léon Blum's serene confidence, explicit and implicit, in Allied victory, his belief in what one may call, with literal accuracy, the *moral* certainty of that victory, will seem to call for anything but apology. What, on the other hand, may appear to require explanation to the English reader not familiar with French history, or who has not been able to follow events in France during the war, are some of the allusions in the first four chapters. The English Socialist reader will find much to profit him in this book, but he may well wonder—brought up, as he has been, under an unchallenged Parliamentary tradition—why it should be considered necessary to devote so much time

and space to a defence of the abstract principle of democracy. To him, then, in particular, a word of explanation. France is a country in which for 150 years no single political system has been taken for granted, as constitutional Monarchy and the parliamentary system have for so long been taken for granted in this country. An absolute Monarchy up to 1789, for two years France tried, and failed, to feel her way towards constitutional Monarchy, and after that was in succession, and leaving out the intermediary forms, Republic, Dictatorship, Empire, semi-constitutional Monarchy, Republic, Dictatorship again, Empire again, and finally Republic for the third time. It is true that when the latest of the world wars broke out, the third Republic was nearly seventy years old, but it is equally true that its constitution had been written by monarchists, for their own purposes, and that its existence had been threatened at least twice in those seventy years, the second time being as late as 1934, when Paris saw the beginnings of a fascist *coup d'état.* That is the much-simplified constitutional history of 150 years, and it is important to readers of this book, because it means that Léon Blum had to address himself to a people whose minds had never been allowed to accustom themselves to the idea of democracy. They lived in a Republic, whose motto was "Liberty, Equality, Fraternity!" but there had always been people around them urging that other systems and other mottoes were better.

At the actual point of time at which Blum wrote, all this anti-democratic propaganda had suddenly found new fields of action. The military collapse of 1940, with all the so-often described and still indescribable material and mental confusion that followed upon it, had been seized upon by the enemies both of the Republic and democracy in a way that was too painfully familiar to the Frenchmen for whom Léon Blum wrote in the first place, but that was

never more than glimpsed in this country, through the occasional allusions of a much-truncated Press.

The men who made up the Government, the administration, and the Press and propaganda machine of Vichy, were, politically speaking, a motley crew. They included Fascists, monarchists, authoritarians of other brands, syndicalists, pacifists, ex-socialist internationalists who really believed in Hitler's "new order", as well as the usual complement of careerists and opportunists. They had in common a dislike, temporary or permanent, of democracy, and they found themselves faced with a population in whom sudden, unexpected and overwhelming defeat had bred despair; despair, both of their country and of its political system.

Almost immediately, this numbed and stunned population was drenched with propaganda—defeatist, anti-democratic and anti-Republican. The defeatist propaganda was stupid and self-destroying—"Every day I say to myself, 'we have been defeated'," proclaimed Pétain in one of his speeches, and this inverted and perverted Couéism, which was typical, did much to promote disgust with Vichy. But the other two forms of propaganda were more skilfully done. The name of the Republic itself was abolished, and France became "the French State", "*l'Etat Français*"; with its motto no longer "Liberty, Equality, Fraternity", but "Labour, Family, Fatherland", and so on. The important thing here is the precise meaning of "and so on". The men of Vichy were too intelligent to try to go the whole way at one step. French experience of democracy was too deep-rooted, after 150 years, for it to be possible to overthrow it at a blow. So the Vichy counter-revolutionaries left much of the framework for the time being. Parliament, the Trade Unions, Municipal Councils were never formally abolished. More important still, many of the men and much of the argument remained

unchanged—and that, indeed, is what, for a time, made
Vichyism seem more dangerous in France than Nazism,
with its new and unknown ideas preached by new and
unknown men, had seemed in Germany. Well-known
Socialists (or recent ex-Socialists) like Déat, Spinasse,
Lafaye; Syndicalists like Lagardelle; Trade-Unionists like
Belin, Dumoulin, Vigne and dozens of others whom one
could name in each of these groups—to say nothing of the
many prominent Radical politicians supporting Vichy—
had a familiar democratic and even a working-class audience ready and waiting for them, and they were careful to
use arguments already in part familiar. Every democrat
had heard criticisms of this or that weakness of the constitution or the parliamentary procedure of the Third
Republic—of the excessive grip of the elector in non-
political matters, of the relative weakness of the executive,
of the absence of party organisation. It was all too easy to
slip out of these familiar ruts into criticism of democracy
as a whole, and the cleverest among them did it with great
skill. In the same way, every Socialist and some of the
Radicals were familiar with criticism of narrow national-
isms, customs barriers, competing standards of living, and
the ingenuity with which a Déat or a Dumoulin, for instance, could enlarge these themes into pleas for Hitler's
new "European order" was worthy of a better cause.
Propaganda for the "National Revolution", which was to
be Vichy's positive contribution, was more difficult, because nobody in the Vichy team agreed with anybody
else, as Léon Blum points out, but this had not always
been as evident as it was soon to become.

The whole had much more than a passing success, and
it was to combat all its dangers, particularly in the minds
of young people, that Léon Blum sat down in his icy prison
cell in those dark days of 1941 to write this book. Since
then, the victory that he anticipated with so much con-

fidence has done much of his work for him. Just as defeat made Frenchmen doubt the value of democracy, so victory helped to bring back their faith. Léon Blum, indeed, says as much, in a new Preface—a Preface that in the circumstances is almost an epilogue—written originally for the first German translation of the book. Here it is:

The first edition of this book appeared early in April, 1945, in Paris. It was preceded, as it is here, by an introduction by an old and dear friend, Bracke-Desrousseaux, who read the proofs and consented to present the work to the public on behalf of his absent friend.

For I was, indeed, still absent, and doubly so; I was both a prisoner and outside France. At the beginning of April, 1945, my wife and I had just left the Buchenwald concentration camp, in which we had been interned for two years. We were finally freed only at the beginning of May, after five weeks of wild wandering across the centre and south of the greater Reich. Yet it was not in a German prison that I wrote *For All Mankind*, but in one of my French prisons. I began it in Bourrasol, near Riom, in February 1941 and had almost finished it by July, when I learned of the murder of my friend Marx Dormoy. The emotions that the news aroused in me were so strong that they interrupted my work for long weeks. Then came my transfer from Bourrasol to the fortress of Pourtalet, the announcement of my coming appearance before the "Supreme Court" of Riom, work on my defence, return to Riom, the trial itself. Finally it was almost the spring of 1942 before I could put the finishing touches to the last part.

The reader will understand, as soon as he begins to read, the kind of preoccupation that led me to undertake this task. Although living in prison conditions, and on the whole severe prison conditions, I was not entirely cut off from reports from the world outside. I saw that

the disasters of 1940, thoroughly exploited by Vichy propaganda, had led a considerable proportion of French opinion to lose faith in democratic ideals. I realised that the infection had spread to great numbers of young people, including some of the best among them. It was these young people that I had in mind as my audience when I decided to write this book. It was, in other words, as a defence of democracy that I saw it, and as a defence that could be effective only if it was sincere. It could justify the hopes I expressed for democracy only if it had the courage to admit also democracy's faults.

Since then, democracy has provided its own justification by its victory. The dictatorships have collapsed in blood and ruin. For the whole French people, the hypocrisy and servility of Vichy are now only memories whose shame they would prefer to forget. Democracy, therefore, no longer needs an advocate; indeed, its greatest difficulty is to choose between its friends and defend itself against their excessive zeal. And so, in the $4\frac{1}{2}$ years that have elapsed between the conception of this book and the writing of this brief introduction, both the facts of the present and the visions of the future have shifted, and I owe it, in honesty, to the reader, to warn him of it.

And yet I have no great fear that my reflections may appear inappropriate or out-of-date. I hope it is not too great a presumption to believe that they remain interesting as glimpses of the past and important as comments on the present. That, at any rate, was my own impression as a reader, when I first saw it in print on my return to France, and I was, I think, an impartial reader, for my memories of it were of the vaguest, and I judged it, page by page, as if it were somebody else's work. It is true, of course, that I found in it passages that I would not write today, or that I would write differently, and others that I would like to strengthen with new arguments. But in general and on balance, I remain faithful to my former views. I regret nothing of what I wrote, and—more important—I withdraw none of it.

I merely ask the reader, if here and there he finds a page that shocks him, to keep a little in mind the date at which I was writing. In particular, I ask him to make friendly allowance for the duty I had imposed upon myself, of being sincere about others and severe towards myself.

L. B.

So much for the time, the place and the circumstances in which this book was written. They have gone out of date, and yet—and this is the justification for the presentation of a work of this kind in another language—the book gains from this very out-of-dateness. From an *œuvre de circonstance*, with the severely limited purpose of correcting the views on some points of current politics of some of the men and women of one country, it becomes a treatise on democracy itself, readable and ponderable with equal profit everywhere.

One comment on the translation. In general, and by agreement with Léon Blum, I have tried to keep both the author's slightly old-fashioned style and his extreme accuracy of thought, but where I have been compelled to choose between mere verbal accuracy and the accurate rendering of an idea, I have, of course, chosen the latter. Two words, however, which occur frequently in *A l'Echelle Humaine*, present serious difficulties to the translator. The words "*bourgeois*" and "*bourgeoisie*" have been taken over into English from French with the meaning, roughly, of "middle-class". In French, they have, in addition to this sociological connotation, a political and an economic one, equivalent respectively to something like "non-socialist" and "capitalist", and where one of these meanings was clearly intended, I have given it the appropriate English equivalent. There are, however, a great many occasions on which every French political writer uses these words with a mixture of two or more of the three

meanings, without himself being clear as to their precise semantic content. This is normal and inevitable, but is a nuisance to the translator. Where it seems to have happened here, I have simply left "bourgeois" and "bourgeoisie", and trust to the reader, after this warning, to supply the rest of the meaning for himself.

W. P.

FOREWORD

AT THE end of the last war, I wrote a little book addressed to young people and, in particular, to my son. Today my son is nearly forty, and is a prisoner of war in Germany. I know enough of his intellectual integrity and his strength of character to be sure that neither he nor his companions in captivity are in need of advice or comfort. But there are other young men, as young as he was then, adolescents who are growing up away from home or whose father is away from home in some prison camp, and these are searching in vain among the ruins of the past for some certainty, for a rule of life, a faith, they are trying vainly to lift the curtain of the future in the hope that they may find behind it some consolatory gleam, some guiding star. Do they not need someone to turn to them and offer help? Is it not the duty of men upon whom life has thrust its accumulated experience to try on their behalf to think honestly, to offer them an honest analysis of the first precepts of wisdom and the first principles of action, and to do so in no spirit of presumption, as an elder, but in affectionate solicitude for their welfare? That is primarily what I have set out to do in the following pages, written in prison. I am still in prison, and have no idea how they will reach any of the unknown readers who have inspired them and whose attentive faces I can picture round me. But I do know that one day they will reach them. It is quite possible to speak and write from within prison walls. Indeed, in a warm-hearted country like our own, the voice that comes from prison carries further and finds more ready listeners. Bolts and bars have not

separated me from France. My heart beats in tune with hers; with every breath I draw, I share her hopes and feel her suffering, and my solitude serves, I hope, only to give my reflections more weight and more independence.

No one knows better than I that my generation failed in its task. Yet I do not propose to defend it, but rather to try to point out to the rising generation—and to those to whom we shall pass on our burdens tomorrow—what can be learnt from our mistakes, our illusions and our misfortunes. That lesson will be of more use to others than to us. That was, at least, the hope that led me to put down on paper the fruit of my solitary reflections. I wanted, above all, to put young people, and adults as well, on their guard against a feeling in which there is perhaps presumption as well as discouragement.

France today is faced, not with a vacuum, but with an interregnum. Not everything has been destroyed, not everything needs to be rebuilt. Defeat revealed the collapse of our military machine and the bankruptcy of our ruling class, it discredited in men's minds the political system which that class had created in its own image, it destroyed human lives and wealth. But it did not destroy France's people, her soil, her nature, all the complex of traditions, convictions and aspirations that we call today the spirit of France. Seen from the angle of our military power, the war is, no doubt, over for us; but in terms of our national existence it goes on. France is not yet beaten; her fate is not yet sealed while the war is fought on elsewhere, without her, but on her behalf. I believe that it is not unreasonable to hope that she may yet emerge from it independent, intact, with her moral stature perhaps increased, in a Europe once more free and at peace.

CHAPTER I

No crisis in a people's history leaves the previous equilibrium undisturbed. That is why a crisis is always something of a revolution, whatever its material consequences may be. At the end of a long war, victory, like defeat, changes everything.

France learnt this from her own experience twenty years ago. All the normal bonds of affection, habit or interest are broken, sometimes permanently. Families are bereaved or dispersed, whole populations are uprooted or transplanted. Occupation, wealth, conditions and the ordinary human contacts of life are subjected to sudden change. Fears, suffering and anxiety of every kind prepare the way for feelings essentially religious, either in form or in content, for disturbing reflections on the destiny of the individual, of the nation, of humanity. The value attached by every individual to his own life, which in normal times is fairly constant, changes with equal suddenness, falling or rising according to whether the shock produces a spirit of self-sacrifice or simply develops egoism and fear. Lastly, all the great crises of history seem to drive into retirement, or even into premature decline, those generations, already decimated, which have played a direct part in them. One or two old men may be kept as mascots or idols—as were Thiers and Clemenceau—though they, too, are soon thrown on the scrap-heap, but for the rest, the storm has always cleared the way for youth. Racing ahead of the normal rate of inheritance or transmission of authority, youth feels itself no longer merely destined to future responsi-

bility, but suddenly and unexpectedly burdened with it now. It becomes in consequence both flattered and hesitant. Everyone who is capable of casting his mind back twenty years will agree that this picture is, in essence, true.

But when war has ended in defeat, and when sudden and total defeat has brought with it humiliation and despair, then a different type of collective feeling appears— a feeling that is probably as old as human society itself, so old certainly that its primitive elements can be found in ancient religions, and especially in Jewish prophecy. When they had lost a battle, the ancient Greeks tried to decide by what negligence they had alienated the protection of their patron deity, and the Jewish people accused themselves, through the voice of their prophets, of having violated their treaty of alliance with the God of Battles. The instinct of a people leads them to believe in justice. When they have been injured, they need to believe that they have not been wrongly injured, and they examine their own hearts to discover the guilt within them. And so, from the beginning of time, national calamities are linked with the idea of sin or guilt, and hence with their natural consequences—contrition, expiation, redemption.

Nations, like men, are always tempted to believe that what happens to them and affects their existence has never happened before or to others. It is true that there are few precedents in history for so deliberate and complacent a cultivation of the idea of sin and redemption as the effort we are witnessing in France today, or for the vitiation of the idea by a mania for self-flagellation carried almost to the point of perversion. Nor has it ever before been exploited with greater subtlety or dishonesty. But it is also true that the world knows no older belief, and that this belief is the most ancient of illusions. For it is absurd to suppose that history

follows the elementary rules of retributive justice. A national catastrophe must inevitably have its causes, but it does not follow that the causes are sin and guilt. If defeat be the deserved punishment of error, ignorance or vice, then we must believe, too, that victory is the legitimate reward of wisdom, merit and virtue. Even those who believe that human affairs are ruled by some providential plan never see it in such simple terms. The ways of God seem to them less direct, more remote, less easily penetrable. Where will you find a people whose changing destinies can reasonably be attributed to the alternate workings of reward and punishment? In 1914 France was victorious. Was she then less frivolous, more moral, more pious than the France of 1939? To what virtues must be attributed the victories of Hitler and Mussolini? To what vices the defeat of Belgium, Holland and Norway?

It is time we stopped beating our breasts so noisily; time we called a halt to this mortification and self-denunciation—or rather to these denunciations of others, for these stern judgments are usually accompanied by a remarkable complacency, not to say a deliberate blindness. The condemnation of a whole people should have as its basis and condition a vigorous self-examination. Yet in fact those who are most arrogantly generous in their dealing out of collective vituperations and maledictions are careful not to begin with a confession of their own sins, a *mea culpa* of their own. But let us not pursue that. What is true and natural is that a nation after a great defeat, like a man after a great failure or a great sorrow, should take conscience as its mirror, look closely and fearlessly into it and check over meticulously all that it finds there. It is proper, too, that the self-examination should be severe, and that it should lead perhaps to stern self-criticism, but not that its course should be determined

in advance by prior admission of personal unworthiness, of a fall from grace. We are in the wrong when we have recognised and understood our own error, not merely because events have proved us wrong. Those are the principles by which we should examine and pronounce judgment on ourselves. The rule of equity applies just as much in this case as when we judge others.

When a whole nation is shaken by catastrophe, the first instinct of its people—first because it is simplest—is to accuse what is nearest to hand: their responsible leaders, their political system, their institutions. It often happens that this reflex movement is sound. The guilt for Waterloo and the capture of Paris was quite properly attributed to Napoleon, that for Sedan and Metz to the Second Empire, and in the same way, after their own recent disaster, some sections of public opinion denounced the Republic and its leaders. That the movement this time was by no means general, and still less spontaneous, is immaterial. What matters is that it did undoubtedly become both deeper and more widespread precisely because of this century-old instinctive trend. But it went far beyond merely placing responsibility for the catastrophe on the country's political system or its recent leaders, it refused to stop at the mere constitution and personnel of the Republic, but went on to accuse in addition the whole complex structure of public life, its form and its content. The net of accusation was cast wide enough to bring in everything that for a century and a half had given life to political doctrine and habit as well as to institutions. Let us not mince words: What was attempted, in addition to a political revolution, was no less than a counter-revolution in social relations and civic obligations. Responsibility for defeat was laid at the door, not only of the Republic, but of democracy, of the idea

of individual liberty, of the principle of the natural equality of all citizens. The seminal conceptions, the motivating ideas which from the time of the Revolution we had thought of as the foundation of society, ideas that even the Monarchist Charter of 1814 and the Imperial Constitution had recognised and proclaimed, had, it seemed, been reduced to dust by the shock of the armies of Hitler. To deny them or to ignore them is not enough; we are assured that they have been destroyed, reduced to nothing by some *reductio ad absurdum* or some evidential proof, and we are invited to look upon their ruin and mock them.

I am aware that exponents of this view make much play of their intention to build afresh from amid the chaos, but I shall waste no time on these attempts at reconstruction, even though they be dignified with the name of National Revolution. Their first inherent vice is their precariousness; they are condemned in advance to survive neither the increasingly probable defeat of Hitler, nor even his final victory. The second is their self-contradiction. The fumbling craftsmen who have taken upon themselves this task of reconstruction are perpetually torn between two patently contradictory concepts—between a return to French traditions and customs of an earlier time and mere imitation of the totalitarian systems built up from nothing by German Nazism and Italian Fascism. The feelings that lie behind these two concepts have in common the proof they offer of the routine thinking, the unimaginative minds, the intellectual poverty of their authors, but beyond that they are in total contradiction with each other. The desire to return to old French traditions is the mark of an overweening nationalistic infatuation with everything that is or was French, while the urge to imitate the totalitarian *régimes* is evidence rather of a spirit of national self-abasement, of submission

to the conqueror, of servility. The two may converge in
their common desire to destroy Republican France, but
there is neither compatibility nor possibility of compromise between them when they turn to the task of construction. There is no comparison possible between
Monarchist France, imbued throughout with abstract
and sentimental beliefs and governed by a King who
represented in his own person a whole hierarchy of classes,
guilds and privileges, and the sinister autocracies in which
idolatrous worship of one man has taken the place of
religious faith or principle, where the bloody caprices of
human brutality have replaced the ordered majesty of
force, and the storied structure of individuals and groups
is reduced to a dead level of fanatical servitude. The
totalitarian dictatorships, selecting among the fruits of
modern civilisation only the material achievements of
progress, would drive our European societies back into a
period of history much more remote than Monarchy as
we knew it. They go back through the centuries of
history to the legends of barbarian kings and elemental
tribal rites. Moreover, besides refusing to mix with each
other, these two conceptions are both in themselves
among the emptiest of intellectual aberrations. Pre-
revolutionary France cannot be restored. We can honour
the dead, find inspiration in their example, but we cannot
resuscitate them. A tradition may persist in men's minds,
but none can mould present reality into dead forms. Or,
to recall a phrase of Jaurès, its flame can be kept burning,
but its dead ashes can never be revived. And if we turn to
the other concept, what reason is there to believe that the
edifices built by Hitler or Mussolini will prove more
durable than those of Napoleon? How can we give a
European basis to a structure that is bound up with
the lives of its founders, even in their own countries?
Scattered elements of it may survive, but the whole,

the essential portion, will not. The truth is that two thousand years of history cannot be reduced to nothing in a decade, for human progress has its own irresistible force. Nothing established by violence and maintained by force, nothing that degrades humanity and is based on contempt for human personality, can endure.

There is no need to insist further on these too evident truths. The constructive work that we are shown or promised is cankered from the start. What is required today is an examination and judgment of the work of destruction. I have said that it satisfies an atavistic instinct, and I am not surprised to find that it has proved attractive to much of our youth. I have not yet forgotten the days when I, too, was young. Youth is enthusiastic, logical, uncompromising; it condemns as easily as it admires. To demolish everything existing and then to throw on to the dust-heap materials still good, or made useless only by the demolition, to clear the ground for a new world made in the image and to the measure of youth—these are projects that must prove tempting.

Is it true, then, that everything in the world of yesterday was false, mediocre, or bad? Let me appeal to the young people to hesitate a moment and to answer me one question, and one only, before they take up the pick. Do you want peace? Do you hate war? If it be admitted that war is not the worst of all evils for a people—for there are times when a nation, like an individual, can save its life only by risking it, and life is not the supreme good for a people any more than for the individual— would you agree that for humanity in general it *is* the worst of all afflictions? Do you agree that without certainty of peace there can be no security for man's labour, nor for his personal happiness, no continuity of progress, no satisfaction of the higher needs of the human soul? Do you accept, as the noblest of man's tasks, the abolition

of even the possibility of war from the new world to be built? If the answer is " Yes "—and I believe it is—then it is not true that everything was deserving of wholesale condemnation in the France of yesterday, in democratic France, in the France of the Third Republic, and you would be wise to hesitate a moment before you destroy indiscriminately everything that made up political, moral and social life. The France of yesterday had at least one virtue: that in general—unanimously even— she wanted peace and was ready for and adapted to peace.

Carry your self-examination a little further. Do you honestly believe that a European war would have been possible if all the countries of Europe had had a political and social system like our own, so much despised *régime* ? Suppose the political system of Germany and Italy had been modelled on our own unhappy democracy, which men denounce today with such arrogant scorn, would not the peace of Europe have been stable and durable? It is true, of course, that the European system contained many absurdities and many iniquities, although, after all, the Europe remoulded by the Treaty of Versailles was less absurd and less iniquitous than at any other known moment of its history. But if all the countries of Europe had had our wretched *régime*, the difficulties would have been resolved little by little by amicable negotiation, or rather they would have disappeared slowly under the gently healing hand of time. Ask yourselves exactly when, and under what impulse, the possibility of war appeared once more in Europe. Is it not clear that it was precisely when Hitler seized power, and under the impulsion of Hitlerian race-theories? On the very eve of that event, with democracy as its guiding spirit, Europe was organising for peace. General disarmament was no mere chimæra, but a real hope. The risk of war

grew in Europe as the despotic power of Hitler grew in Germany. It could not have been otherwise; tyrannies are by nature aggressive, just as democracy is pacific. At the very time at which I write, President Roosevelt and Mr. Churchill have just published their eight-point Charter of the peace which the Anglo-Saxon democracies propose to set up after the defeat of Hitler. To this, the official spokesmen of the French Government have replied with mocking contempt, "This is an old story. The eight points of Roosevelt and Churchill are the fourteen points of President Wilson. Twenty-five years ago this pose of high-minded frankness may have taken people in; today we have learnt to our cost what it means and we know that it offers no assurance of peace and justice." What in fact we know is that the failure of the League of Nations after the last war was the result, first, of the spirit of embittered and mistrustful suspicion in which it was conceived and born, second, of the refusal of the United States to join, and last—and most important—of the appearance in Europe of dictatorial parties and *régimes*. Who would dare to affirm, who could have dared to hope, that it would finally have failed, if the task had been taken up again, boldly and frankly, and with the wholehearted participation of the United States, in a Europe purged of the dictatorships?

Dictatorship and war, democracy and peace—these, then, are the inevitable concomitants. If you do not deny this—and you dare not—you have no right to throw democracy so casually on to the scrap-heap. You have no right to condemn out of hand, as tainted with error and fraud, the work of the men who have been trying for one hundred and fifty years to establish it in the world. You have one right and one duty only: to seek to know why our effort failed, in order the better to carry it on after us.

You will reply, no doubt, that your generation has no

intention of wasting time on the Utopian schemes to which you attribute some of our misfortunes. Indeed, I understand the reflex that was, for so many of you, the first product of defeat. Along with a general disgust at all present reality, you felt a need for reflection, for withdrawal into yourself, that you then extended from yourself to your country. You want to isolate France as penitents or the sick are isolated. You think of her as needing a period of retreat, of prolonged and deep self-examination, a withdrawal to a convent or a sanatorium. In what remains of the war, you think, France no longer has any duties and almost no interests. Henceforward, she must take part in European affairs only insofar as is absolutely necessary to her continued material existence. Above all, she must watch over herself, nurse herself, find new inspiration and new strength, and when she is strong again, we shall see. You were not the first to recommend that line of conduct to a defeated nation. Fichte spoke in the same way; so did Stein in the Prussia that survived Jena and Tilsit; that was, in the main, the theme of Nazi propaganda in Germany after Versailles, it was the attitude of Thiers, and still more of Gambetta, after the Treaty of Frankfurt. But what do you intend to do with the France you have rebuilt in her solitude? How is she to use her strength, once it has been recovered? For revenge, always dreamed of in secret, but never mentioned openly? Do you want France to be strong so that she can profit fully from what opportunities may be offered by the immanent justice of history—or perhaps even seek to provoke them? In that case, revenge will call for more revenge, and from war to war and from generation to generation—to quote Jaurès once more—the poisoned cup of the Atrides will be passed eternally backwards and forwards between the nations of the earth. Is this, then, the future that you imagine? I do not believe it, and if it is peace you want, then it is no use trying to compress and

accumulate your country's strength, like superheated steam in a boiler. On the contrary, it must spread and expand, it must be used to promote the free co-operation of all peoples, to organise them in equality and fraternity, so that "Liberty, Equality, Fraternity" becomes your international watchword. Proclaim it then, today, after defeat, as we did, a little more deservingly twenty years ago, after victory, and then, whether you know it or not, you will find yourself following once more in the footsteps of the republicans and democrats whom you disowned with such scathing vehemence only a little while ago.

I have tried to use only one argument in my demonstration of the absurdity, indeed, of the impossibility of this attitude of blind condemnation and indiscriminate rejections. I could have found many more; I chose what seemed the weightiest, the least resistible. I hope that none will be surprised at the use I made of the idea and the very name of peace, at a time when we are passing through the most terrible phase of the war, when indeed, whether we like it or not, we are playing our part in its atrocities. A good German enjoys the accounts of a night's bombing of London, and for our part we applaud when our newspapers tell us of the tragic end of the *Bismarck*, sinking with all hands. When we read in an Eastern front *communiqué* that "a division has been destroyed" we make no attempt to imagine the reality that lies behind these words, though it would sicken us if we could see it, and we do no more than express satisfaction or dismay, according as the division annihilated is on our side or the enemy's. Passion has stifled all human feeling, as it did among the spectators at the Circus in Rome. But shall we stay after the war in the state to which, in spite of ourselves, war has brought us? If war did not leave us at least with a determination never

again to accept it as inevitable, we should have to despair of the human race. Our resolve may prove fruitless; we may still fail in our purpose, as we have once before, but it is unthinkable that the resolution should not be made; it is, as it were, obligatory on us. If we did not accept it in complete sincerity, and in complete honesty, if, instead, we acquiesced in the adage, as old as war itself, according to which war is eternal, then we should have no right to talk of building a new world, and the future would become as futile as the present.

I cannot refrain at this point from commenting on one of the peculiarities of these times, though it is perhaps peculiar only in appearance. The men, the parties, the newspapers that preached and made profession of extreme nationalism and distorted to their own uses that grand word "patriotism" all called loudly for the armistice and applauded the capitulation. Today they all advocate collaboration with the conqueror, or, more accurately, with the enemy. And yet, during the early months of the war, when almost all Frenchmen looked forward to slow but certain victory, these same people were anxious to lay down in advance peace terms of inflexible harshness. Many wanted to put an end, once and for all, not only to Hitler and his gang, but to the millions of men, women and children that make up the human reality behind the term "Germany". They demanded not only that Germany should be kept under supervision, but that she be dismembered and large portions of her territory annexed to France, and they were ever ready to accuse socialists and democrats of lack of patriotism, because they asked of victory no other fruit than a "new order", in which the mutual co-operation of peoples would be the guarantee of peace. To-day they worship the force that yesterday they were prepared to misuse, and

tomorrow they will repeat their crimes. In a France once more free and strong, they will become nationalist and jingo again. They will begin all over again their attacks on the treachery of "pacifists", who refuse to abandon the idea of founding a peace based on human liberty and the fraternal equality of nations, and the men whom they denounced yesterday and will denounce again tomorrow as "pacifists" are those whom today they describe as "warmongers". For there is another side to this apparent contradiction. The pacifists of yesterday and tomorrow are calling today for a wholehearted and unrelenting struggle for the independence of France, precisely because they see peace as a compact freely entered into by free peoples. They disavowed the armistice that handed France over to Hitler and risked handing over Europe along with her. They repudiate a "collaboration" which to the Germans means only the exploitation of the whole of French resources in the interests of Germany and the German war machine, while for France it inevitably means servility and abdication, a hypocritical betrayal following on the cynical betrayal of the separate armistice, and offering not the slightest guarantee that the victor, to whom perjury has become second nature, will in any way modify the rigour of his demands when the day of the final peace settlement comes. Even when they were trying desperately, and in all too short a time, to rebuild the military strength that the jingo nationalists had allowed to fall into ruin, even when France had been forced back on to the arbitrage of war by the despotic ambition of Hitler, and they exhorted her people to persist in the struggle to the limit of their strength, they remained in fact consistent with their past selves and true to their former teachings. They were still the champions of peace. They had gone into the war only to preserve the conditions of any peace worthy of the

name, and peace remained their one war-aim. I believe that if the young people to whom this book is chiefly addressed will look into their consciences, they must agree that these men and women were right and doubly right.

CHAPTER II

In the preceding chapter I referred in passing to a historical precedent which merits closer examination, for in the list of our great military defeats the disaster of 1870 precedes immediately the disaster of 1940. It struck France at a time when, even more than in 1940, she was hypnotised by her conviction of her own strength, for in those days the Napoleonic legend was still a living influence in France, and there were few indeed in the country, even among the opponents of the Empire, in whose eyes the invincibility of the French Army was not one of the laws of nature. The collapse, too, was even more violent. A month after the fighting began, the Emperor capitulated at Sedan with our last army but one, the last being encircled in Metz, where it, too, soon surrendered. In 1940 military collapse led to political change. The difference between 1870 and 1940 is that in the former case the revolution took place openly, as a manifestation of the sovereign will of the people, and that the new Republican government was formed, not to plead for an armistice, despite the annihilation of the Emperor's armies, but to continue the war at all costs, by an appeal to French patriotism for a *levée en masse*. There were those, however, then, as in 1940, who believed secretly in immediate peace, peace at any price, and saw in Gambetta, the inspirer and hero of national resistance, only a dangerous lunatic.

It was natural that the political system overthrown by the victory of Prussia should be regarded as responsible for the country's defeat. I have said, and I believe, that the

verdict was a just one. For five or six years prior to the
defeat a series of almost incredible blunders—Poland,
Denmark, Mexico, Prusso-Italian alliance, Luxembourg,
the Rome expedition—had locked France inside an ever-
narrowing circle, from which, inevitably, only failure
or a new adventure could free her. And yet, at
the last moment, a stroke of luck, of the kind he was not
entitled to hope for, offered the Emperor an honourable
and peaceful way out—which he refused to take. The kind
of fatal fascination that seems inherent in autocracies
drove him on into headlong attack on an opponent whose
strength he had no right to under-estimate, especially
after Sadowa. The first incidents of the campaign had
made scandalously clear, not only the inadequacy of our
armament, but the complete lack of competence, order or
any kind of technical preparation. To what inherent vices
of the *régime* were these fatal weaknesses to be attributed?
Even before Sadowa, all contemporary critics gave the
same reply. The vices of the imperial *régime* were personal
power, the concentration of every kind of authority in the
hands of one man, to whom everybody else was in principle
responsible, while he was in fact responsible to nobody, the
suppression of all forms of Parliamentary supervision, of
all free discussion by the Press and public opinion, the
secrecy that marked the conduct of all home and foreign
affairs, both reduced to the level of Cabinet intrigues.
Such was the general diagnosis, and after an unhappy
peace, which nevertheless left a mourning nation with its
honour intact, agreement on the remedy was no less
general. In this respect, the Royalists, including even the
legitimist branch, were in no way different from the republicans; all agreed that what the country needed first of all
was liberty, freedom of speech and of the Press, a Government working in public and responsible to the elected representatives of the country. In other words, what is the

remedy today was the evil yesterday, and what is now the evil was then the remedy.

There were writers, nevertheless, who did not stop at this immediate conclusion, but tried to probe deeper into the reality of the national crisis. Their examination of the problem was the more anxious in that the defeat was scarcely complete before it was followed by a more terrifying upheaval, the revolutionary Commune of Paris, and so their probing went deeper than the political institutions of the State, to the moral constitution of Society. If the organs of government had become vitiated, had not the mind and the will of the individuals and groups that make up the nation become cankered too? Renan, Taine and a few others made up the *élite* of the group that thought in this way. The book published by Renan after the war and the Commune was called *La Réforme Intellectuelle et Morale*— Intellectual and Moral Reform. France had allowed herself to slip into a state of intellectual and moral decline, of which the military defeat and the revolutionary movement that followed it were both the expression and the penalty. The decline could, of course, be regarded as being itself in a sense a consequence of the autocratic *régime*, but it had also developed its own consequences, and required a separate treatment, without which "national renovation" would remain a superficial and empty achievement. It had shown itself in many ways; in frivolity—not to be confused with gaiety, which is an authentic feature of French temperament—in presumptuousness, lack of serious study of serious things, lack of honesty and scrupulousness in public affairs, in greed for money and greed for pleasure, in the spreading love of luxury and ostentation and the consequent spread of corruption and venality, in the loosening of family ties and open contempt for the dignity of home life. And so the collapse of the Empire had been, as it

B

were, the biblical climax of a grand orgy that had dragged the whole of bourgeois society little by little into its infernal whirl.

In earlier days, under the Monarchy, we had seen these periods of public shamelessness—under the Regency, for instance, and at the end of the reign of Louis XV—but on those occasions the corruption had never touched either the intellectual strata or the respect that society, as a whole, owes to them. It was of this perhaps that Renan, Taine and their friends were most keenly aware. The France of the Second Empire had allowed all general culture to fall into decay; she had abandoned the pursuit on any considerable scale of disinterested study and research, and given herself over entirely to two dangerous trends that in her periods of greatness she has always been able to discipline; these were a passion for oratorical rotundity and that mocking curiosity, with its love of wit and wine and women, that we call the "*boulevardier*" spirit. And so, little by little, she had yielded to Germany her primacy in all the higher realms of the intellect: philosophy, pure science, erudition. And at the other end of the scale, she had shown herself unable to organise a sound popular education, as Prussia had already organised it. A saying current at the time put the school teacher on a level with the needle-gun and the Krupp cannon as an agent of the victory of Prussia. The practical conclusion of all this seemed only too evident. There was no point in seeking to whitewash or paint over in new colours a building whose foundations were rotten. The work had to begin again from the bottom. The whole system of public and private education must be reformed, family and social relationships must be rebuilt on sound principles—in a word, all those things must be renewed which influence in turn the mind and character of the individual, the opinion of society and—in a democracy—government itself.

Such were, seventy years ago, the reactions arising and the morals drawn from a national catastrophe, and nothing could be more legitimate than the undertaking of a similar task today. We should all agree on the need for an analysis of our institutions and customs in search of the organic or functional defects to which defeat may have been due; on the submission to our defeated nation of a practical plan of contemplation and construction; on the need for a course of internal effort and external hygiene capable of restoring both her pride and her modesty, her wisdom and her love of labour. What is not legitimate is to push the analogy still further. In 1870 France was entitled and, indeed, obliged to hold the constitution and the *régime* responsible for the ills that had befallen her; she is not so entitled today. The Empire was guilty, but the Republic was only unfortunate. The Empire was evil and destructive in its very principle, which was personal autocracy; the Republic is right and creative in its principle, which is government of the people by the people. Its mistakes were due to defects of organisation or of working, whose origins can easily be traced and for which remedies are easily found. Still less is it legitimate to accuse a system of ideas made almost sacred by so many sacrifices, acknowledged in principle by both French Empires, set down in words in the Declaration of the Rights of Man and solemnly recognised every time we cast a vote. As in 1871, intellectual and moral reform are needed today, but the briefest analysis will show that the faults they are to correct are entirely independent of the constitutional system or the ideology upon which it is based. I have already shown, by a single, but weighty example, how wrong would be any outright and summary condemnation of democratic principles. Let us now look more closely at the reproaches addressed to the *régime* that yesterday had only supporters and flatterers, and that today only the brave will defend.

The Empire wanted war, as all known autocracies have always wanted it in the long run, even when they had promised or solemnly vowed themselves to peace. It wanted war because it needed prestige, and because the interest of the dynasty required it to compensate at one blow for a long series of aberrations themselves rooted in autocratic power, but leaving a humiliated and discontented France with a sense of shame. Republican and democratic France did *not* want war. From the victory of 1918 she hoped for no other conquest than that of lasting, organic peace. It was towards this that her collective will was turned, that all her aspirations converged. There has probably been no example in history of a nation so generally and so consciously peaceful. No painful uphill effort was required of her, because she had emerged triumphantly from the latest European crisis and because she had regarded herself and was regarded by others as the strongest Power. Her internal *régime* required no effort of popularisation or revivification, because up to the time of Hitler's accession to power nobody challenged it, except a few negligible groups of conspirators and theorists. In any case, war could have done nothing to popularise a *régime* in essence pacific. It is, I think, beyond dispute that, when Hitler seized power in Germany, there was in Europe neither the risk nor any reasonable possibility of war, and history will confirm a fact which two years ago every Frenchman regarded as blindingly self-evident—that it was Hitler who brought war back into the European perspective, and Hitler who imposed it on republican France.

I should be the last to deny that from that time onwards mistakes were made. But the worst of these was the failure to appreciate or to foresee the danger; the failure to realise quickly and clearly enough the Hitlerite plan of rearmament, revenge and conquest, the failure to perceive the

inexorability of its unfolding. Because she was in essence pacific, France preferred to believe in the possibility of "peaceful co-existence" of the democracies already installed in Europe and the warlike autocracy growing up. The increasing sacrifices she made for the sake of this possibility—Four-Power Pact, weakening and ultimate abandonment of sanctions against Italy, acceptance of the occupation of the Rhineland, Munich—did no more than weaken her prestige abroad and increase disunity at home, and so aggravate the danger. Today I go so far as to ask myself if France ought not to have used force in 1933 to prevent a still-disarmed Germany from handing over power to Hitler and his party. Nobody in France at that time contemplated so violent an intervention in German affairs; and yet it would have saved Germany and preserved Europe.

I recognise that there were mistakes of the kind I have just described, wrong attitudes that the French shook off only little by little and one by one, and which many had still failed to shake off when the hour of collapse came. I confess to them, without a blush, because they are the right kind of mistakes. They are not so much mistakes as illusions, testimony to a premature faith in the future of peace, in the inherent virtue of peace itself. The French people almost in its entirety professed the idealist belief that no people wants war, and that the general opposition to it would finally get rid of war, by imposing upon Governments the kind of compromise that is, indeed, always possible, and even easily achievable, on the sole condition that it be honestly sought. In any case, if it is possible to reproach republican France with not foreseeing the war quickly and clearly enough, this is at least a sign and a proof that she did not seek war as the Second Empire sought it, and yet war found the Second Empire

completely isolated in Europe and in the world, without an ally, a friend or a sympathiser. One after another, all these had been lost, and had given way to every kind of suspicion in turn, sacrificed to the inconsequent caprices of a *régime* whose ambitions had but little more than the consistency of dreams.

When the war began, the French Republic had friends or allies almost everywhere in Europe and in the world. It is true, of course, that earlier weaknesses and failures had had their effect. The acceptance of the occupation of the Rhineland had lost us the Jugoslavian alliance and alarmed the other two partners of the Little Entente. Munich had made possible the elimination of Czecho-slovakia, and prepared the Russian change of front; the civil war in Spain had thrown that country into the camp of the autocracies, the alliance of Hitler and Mussolini, after being for long in the balance, was finally realised after the occupation of the Rhineland and the Abyssinian War. The irrevocable oaths had been exchanged and Mussolini had sacrificed one victim—Austria—upon their altar. On the other hand, our alliance with England had never been so close and wholehearted, or our friendship with America so warm and cordial, especially before Munich. France was still, in the letter or in the spirit, the centre of the groupings of the smaller States of Europe, and international opinion was with us and our allies. In short, France was revered and liked, instead of envied and suspected, she was bound by intimate ties to all the democratic and pacific Powers of the world, because she had herself remained, or had once more become, the champion of militant democracy.

Perhaps if we turn to the problem of military technique, we shall find more comparable situations. Not, of course, that the army of the Republic was taken by surprise, in the state of internal confusion which had paralysed the Im-

perial armies from the start. Not that it entered the fight with the overwhelming inferiority of armament that has been claimed, with the backing of figures ridiculous to the point of buffoonery: on this matter, truth will come into her own, in a way that will astonish honest men and cover the slanderers with shame. What is true is that, like the Empire, the Republic was slow in getting under way, slow to realise the strength of the force growing up beside her and against her. The Empire had begun rearming only in 1867, on the morrow of Sadowa, the Republic only towards the end of 1936, while Hitler had been master of Germany from 1933 and had not lost a single day. As early as 1934, the Doumergue Cabinet had abandoned the search for a method of "peaceful co-existence" with Hitler along the lines of agreed limitation of armaments, and had begun instead a diplomatic campaign for new or closer alliances, which Germany could with some justice regard as an attempt at encirclement. The obvious counterpart should have been the immediate inauguration of a process of rearmament in France. This, however, the Doumergue–Pétain Cabinet put off, as its predecessor had done and as did its immediate successor, although it boasted of being a strong Government, a Government of Public Safety and even of national "renovation". It is equally true that, like the Imperial army, the armies of the Republic suffered both from a superiority complex and from hidebound thinking. After the victory of 1918, just as on the eve of the defeat of 1870, they had been proclaimed the greatest in the world; for fifteen years they had, indeed, been almost the only armies of any size in the world. The French army had never lost this conviction of its own superiority; it had become an article of faith, and I prefer not to name the men who still accepted it at the beginning of the war. That was no doubt the prime reason, both for the inadequacy of the forces employed and for the out-

of-dateness of the methods used when it was finally decided that the effort must be made. Too few people realised that what was needed was innovation rather than mere addition. An ageing personnel continued to work on obsolete lines, because both dated from the last war and had led us then to victory. They failed to see the completely new character of German rearmament, which had the advantage of starting from scratch and rebuilding from the bottom upwards, in a country organised for that sole purpose. They shut their eyes to the transformation of tactics and strategy that were the inevitable product of technical military progress. As in 1867, they strengthened the old army, instead of boldly building a new one.

I have made this comparison in a spirit of strict impartiality. It reveals clearly that any unqualified condemnation, such as was unanimously pronounced against the Second Empire by its contemporaries, would today be an act of ignorance, injustice and ingratitude. But it does also reveal serious mistakes at the top, such as are almost invariably found if one looks back with a severely critical eye on any sequence of human affairs. I have tried neither to hide these mistakes, nor to excuse them, but I do seriously ask how far they can be traced to Republican institutions or to the principles of democracy that have in great measure inspired them. Like the men of the generation of Taine and Renan, we must examine this question seriously, without any thought, conscious or unconscious, of self-interest, of justification or of revenge. But for myself, I can give my conclusion now. It is that an examination of the mistakes made in the general conduct of affairs, or in military or foreign affairs in particular, shows that these mistakes can plausibly be traced to different features of the republican institutions of France, but not to the essential and universal principles of democracy.

Let us leave aside the failure to look ahead, the mis-judging and under-estimating of what was to come; these are common weaknesses that only the greatest minds escape, and they not always. In logic, converging causes can produce only one effect, but when the human mind looks at them at any given moment of time it may easily see a whole bundle of diverging possible effects. Chance plays its part in all this. The far-seeing man is he whom events have proved right, which often means no more than he who drew the winning number in the lottery. Let us look more closely at one reproach, which by dint of repetition has become almost a truism—namely, the weakness of the *régime*, whose characteristics in the eyes of its detractors were lack of authority, of continuity, of stability. There is in this reproach a kind of residue of truth which it is the duty of the honest student to isolate and measure. But he must first remember that problems of authority are not to be confused with problems of sovereignty. There have been autocracies in which authority remained absolute and yet frequently changed hands, which were at the same time aggressive and weak. France experienced authority of this kind for the last time only three-quarters of a century ago. There have been democracies—the Anglo-Saxon countries today are the living proof—in which authority was strong. Authority is not bound up with any particular form of constitution. A representative parliamentary system, in which sovereignty resides in the people and is delegated to elected representatives, is in principle in no way incompatible with a powerful, stable and continuous authority, as a glance at English history proves. Let us not forget, either, the difficulty of drawing and keeping a line between the authority that in practice is needed by any Government and the liberty properly claimed by nations and individuals. This problem is, indeed, the oldest and most difficult in politics. A Government can

be too strong, just as it can be too weak, and the instinctive reaction of peoples is to rush from one extreme to the other. That is why anarchy always carries the risk of engendering tyranny. But it is in seeking to avoid these violent and absurd reflexes that a nation proves its maturity. For that matter, the progress of civilisation, or, more accurately, the necessities of social life, have already eliminated bit by bit the elementary forms of anarchy, and we were entitled to hope that they had eliminated in the same way the more barbarous forms of tyranny. History will be astonished by their reappearance in our times, and it would indeed be an abdication of the dignity of human reason if we were to yield to their monstrous attraction, on the pretext that the errors or hesitations of democracy have disappointed us.

Finally, I should like to remind my readers that the governmental instability of which so much has been made is by no means peculiar to republican democracy. The Republic today has lasted more than four times as long as any other political *régime* we have had in a century and a half; it was stable for more than sixty years, in the sense that its legality was no longer contested or its existence threatened, and that nobody dared publicly to oppose it. It is still stable today, whatever people may say or do about it, for it is so deeply rooted in popular habit and affection that any effort to get rid of it would be doomed to failure, and if I am asked why so many political systems, each as unstable as the other, including the restored Monarchy and the military Empires, have followed each other in the last hundred and fifty years, why they all collapsed in turn and why the Third Republic itself had to withstand so many of the kind of shocks that would have shaken or destroyed a less popular *régime*, I can only recall what so many statesmen of limited vision and so many second-rate polemists seem to be unaware

of or to lose sight of—that no government can remain stable in an unstable society and an unstable world. A hundred and fifty years ago, France underwent, and slowly transmitted to the rest of the civilised world, the most profound transformation it had known since the spread of Christianity. How many centuries did Europe take, when once its essential principles had been transformed by the Christian revolution, to recover its consistency and the beginnings of stability? Is it, then, surprising that France should need a few decades to achieve her stability? The results of great revolutionary changes are never consolidated all at once. Equilibrium is reestablished bit by bit, and that, indeed, is how nature imposes *a posteriori* upon revolutions the rules that would normally have applied to a more normal evolution. To bring forth specifically new features, societies need the revolutionary method of change, but in the end revolutions do not save time. This is the quite natural explanation of the succession of shocks experienced by the political order in France since the Revolution. The shocks are not attributable to some evil virus introduced into the body of the nation by the democratic Revolution; thay are rather the growing pains that the revivified body had to endure before it reached a full, stable, adult state, and if these pains have again become acute since the 1914–18 war, it is useless to seek the explanation in any particular weakness of French institutions, since the phenomenon can be observed throughout Europe, and indeed throughout the Universe. It is the war itself that is the explanation, together with the wholly new problems—territorial, economic, financial, monetary and social—that it left behind it. If there was perhaps nothing new in the nature of those problems, their extent made them new, and only partial, crude and patently provisional solutions had been found for them when the new war broke out.

CHAPTER III

ALTHOUGH THESE are in my view self-evident and general truths, I would not wish to appear to use them in order to avoid the vital detail of the argument. I admit freely that our system of government had in addition internal weaknesses and contained within itself organic causes of instability, ineffectiveness and lack of continuity. I will agree, even, if pressed, and although the point appears to me to be arguable, that these weaknesses had been aggravated during the twenty-odd year period between the wars. There is no need to go over here the list of clinical symptoms that anybody can read anywhere, and whose colour and detail have been magnified and heightened *ad lib*—the useless din of oratory, the slowness of procedure, the successive encroachments and mutual usurpations of legislative on executive and executive on legislative; the group rivalries and personal quarrels, the weakness and precariousness of Ministries without backing or staying power, imagination or courage or anything that could have given them simple competence. There was no firm direction, and as the engines were not working properly, they gave poor results in proportion to the energy they consumed. This is the picture I painted myself twenty-five years ago, after my first contacts with Cabinets and Assemblies. But the only legitimate conclusion is the one I drew then: that the French system of government, the representative or parliamentary system as practised in France, needs radical modifications. And even if, as is claimed, no modifications adequate to the need can be found, the only conclusion that can properly

be drawn is that the parliamentary or representative *régime* is not the form of democratic government best adapted to French society, and that we must therefore look around for more suitable ones.

What nobody has a right to do is to push the conclusion still further and stretch the verdict to cover the essential principles of democracy itself—sovereignty of the people, government of the nation by itself, supervision by the nation of the executive power, recognition and guarantee of the civil and personal rights of the individual. Let it, therefore, be clearly stated and remembered that the parliamentary system is not the only, exclusive or necessary form of democracy. This, indeed, is one of the vital points of the argument. Democracy and parliamentary systems are in no way synonymous or interchangeable terms. There is, to the best of my knowledge, no country in Europe in which the origin of parliament is linked in history with a democratic movement or with any democratic claim; wherever one looks, the parentage of parliaments is aristocratic or oligarchic, and the parliamentary system began to take on the characteristics and put forward the claims of democracy only bit by bit, as there came to be associated with it two ideas of a quite different order—namely, the responsibility of Ministers to elected assemblies and the universality of the franchise. The parliamentary system, then, is not of necessity democracy. Similarly, democracy does not necessarily imply parliamentary government. There are two democratic republics, one very big and one very small, the United States and the Swiss Confederation, both of which, from the time of their foundation onwards, have had *régimes* that are not parliamentary, in that the sovereignty of the people is not incorporated in and absorbed, so to speak, by parliamentary assemblies. I note in passing that the Swiss and American constitutions have each a federal

basis; in other words, there is in each case a high degree of administrative decentralisation and, more particularly, of "deconcentration", that is, of devolution, of power. They seek, and have achieved, in the one case in a small and in the other in a large country, the maintenance of an active local political life. The excessive centralisation and concentration of power which is a periodic subject of general complaint is therefore in no sense a specifically democratic vice. The advocates of a return to our pre-Revolutionary provinces would be well advised to keep in mind the fact that, although the French Revolution found it necessary—like Lincoln and his friends during the American Civil War—to fight hard for the principle of national unity, in the face of both foreign and civil war, our administrative centralisation was the intentional and tenaciously defended work of absolute monarchy.

I can therefore repeat more firmly what I have already said. Supposing even that there is some basis in fact for the fashionable criticism of the parliamentary system, including even the most far-fetched and those most patently inspired by self-interest, granting even that its functional defects are irremediable, beyond all renovation or reform, there still remains only one sound and logical conclusion, which is to enquire whether some different form of democratic government would not be more suited to the characteristics of French society. In such an enquiry, we should no doubt be wise to look closely at the American and Swiss models. I know, of course, that throughout the nineteenth century politicians and political scientists, from Royer-Collard and Guizot to Gambetta and Jaurès, almost unanimously regarded the representative system as the most perfect form of "free government". Indeed, for a historian like Guizot, the parliamentary system, embodying the primacy of the middle classes, is the end and purpose of civilisation, the final cause towards which

the whole course of modern history has inevitably tended. It is none the less legitimate to refuse to join this almost universal chorus, which incidentally was inspired by the steady progress of parliamentary government in England, and I am, for my part, quite ready to admit that the same success has not been achieved in France, provided only that it be conceded in return that the real moral of the failure is the need to find a different kind of democratic system. It is, then, in this way, and only in this way, that one should welcome the idea of a constitutional change, and it goes without saying that only the people as a whole are entitled to make that decision, that it must be made freely, by an entirely free vote, uninfluenced by any moral or material obstacle and after free and balanced discussion. Let those who so desire try now to convince the nation—provided always that equal freedom of speech is accorded to those holding opposite views—but let nobody claim the right to coerce them. Above all, let nobody try to usurp the place of the people, for they have not resigned the power that is rightly theirs, nor handed it over to anybody.

If any light is to be cast on this controversy, the first task must be to discover why the confidence and hope of the nineteenth century were so bitterly disappointed, what was the determinant cause of the failure in France, and in particular under the Third Republic, of the representative system that succeeded and made progress in England. A fund of historical experience, rich enough by now to yield historical laws, reveals quite clearly that the proper functioning of any representative or parliamentary system requires the existence of political parties. If the parliamentary system has succeeded in England and failed in France, it is essentially because there exists in England a strong and established party system, while in France it has not been possible for a century and a half—

except in rare cases that confirm the rule—to create anything similar. It is easy to condemn parties, or to jibe at
them, especially if one starts from the standpoint of the
totalitarian dictatorships, to whom the very name of party
is a challenge. But it is none the less certain that ministerial instability, the flaccidities and vacillations of
Governments, the slowness and disorder of parliamentary
debates—in short, the failures and the fitfulness of the
French parliamentary machine—are in the first place
the consequences of the absence of disciplined and homogeneous parties. This was true under the Restoration,
under Louis-
Prince-Preside
Neither Thier

to build up a
able Governm
since the beg
"radical spiri
had more tha

ERRATUM

Page 48, lines 12 and 13: for "the Prince-
President" please read "Marshal MacMahon."

forgotten the history of this party since the last war, its
internal divisions, its changes of tune, the open rivalries of
its leaders, its permanent inability to maintain any real
unity of policy or action? The attempt to form a great
Conservative Party immediately after the elections of
November 1919 failed even more lamentably, since by the
end of the 1919 Parliament no trace of it remained. Ten
years later, M. Tardieu tried again and had to give up the
attempt almost before he had begun. When the present
war broke out, there was no Conservative Party in France.
The disparate elements of the Right and Centre were incapable of uniting for any purpose other than that of
systematic opposition. Who was their leader? The political and personal differences between M. Paul Reynaud,
M. Flandin, M. Laval and M. Marin were more marked
and more evident even than those of the Radical leaders.

There is no need to look further for the determinant, and indeed the sufficient cause of the ineffectiveness of the parliamentary *régime* in France. The same congenital inability to create genuine and regular parties explains the distasteful and often revolting character of our parliamentary struggles, the persistence of personal rivalries, the impatient and often dishonest bitterness of the struggle for power. Politics is not a sport, but, like every other kind of struggle, it becomes degraded and is repulsive to the spectator if it is not governed by rules imposing a certain minimum of honesty and propriety. It is clear, I think, that impropriety and dishonesty in politics can be prevented only by stable parties, whose stability itself leads them to respect in opposition the code of behaviour from which they in turn will benefit when they become the Government. Further reflection will reveal no less clearly that it is the lack of organised parties in France that makes the elected representative the agent of his electors, and that it is to the same cause, much more than to the undoubted weaknesses of our electoral system, that we owe the reduction of elected members to the rôle of representatives or custodians of local interests.

Is this lack of proper political parties a permanent feature of French character, or is it characteristic only of French bourgeois society today? What so far has prevented the foundation of parties worthy of the name is intolerance of discipline, addiction to mocking, carping, disparaging criticism, lack of confidence in or of gratitude —or almost even of good feeling—towards the leader whom people make a show of following. It was difficult for a leader to secure recognition for himself, even, or rather especially, if his qualifications for leadership were overwhelming; his authority was never frankly accepted, his followers were incapable of fidelity; the private member was usually too anxious to be in the public eye, his high

opinion of himself made him impatient to leave the ranks and play a more important part. The influence of his surroundings quickly promoted the growth of what was not so much individualism as "personalism", compounded of varying quantities of vanity, suspicion and ambition. It is possible to regard these idiosyncracies as inherent in French character, in the sense that signs of them are to be found in greater or less degree in every period of our history. Yet any honest observer would feel bound to admit that the working-class parties and organisations had a feeling of discipline which, except in the case of the Communists, was not suppression of the individual, but his voluntary subordination, the gift of his person to the public good, to a conviction, to a cause. He will agree that in these parties we did meet obedience to a rule or to a leader, pride in rather than envy of ability, culture and character, and that through all the vicissitudes of parliamentary life they have regularly given proof of a coherence at least as great as that of Anglo-Saxon parties. All this, I know, raises a whole swarm of difficult issues with which I am familiar, and that I shall not seek to avoid, but I am entitled to state as a fact that if around all the other political and social trends—radicalism, pro-capitalist liberalism, catholic democracy, backward-looking conservatism—there had grown up parties whose structure and working resembled that of the Socialist Party, parliamentary government would have been possible in France as in England, and the ideal of the nineteenth-century theorists would have become a reality.

This view will perhaps becomes clearer if I present another aspect of it. The risk of disruption for workers' parties lies especially in stagnation, in marking time, in the commonplace; what most surely keeps them in compact and ordered ranks is movement, advance, creation. For

bourgeois parties, the opposite rule applies. Movement and innovation break up the parties or embryo parties of the bourgeoisie; only resistance can give them a transient cohesion. Since the beginning of the parliamentary system, I can find only three examples of Governments whose longevity was founded on homogeneous majorities that had the appearance of strong parties. These were Villèle and the ultra-royalists under the Restoration, Guizot and the ultra-conservatives under Louis-Philippe, Jules Ferry and the "opportunists" under the Third Republic. In these three cases the coherence of the Governments and of their majorities was due much less to the exceptional qualities of the leaders—practical mind, moral prestige or force of character—than to the special nature of the circumstances. In all three cases the bourgeoisie in power— for Villèle and his friends were landowners rather than aristocrats—were alarmed by the upsurge of hostile forces, and their stiffening and discipline were born of and sustained by fear. It was in precisely the same spirit that the French bourgeoisie handed itself over gagged and bound to the Second Empire, to which it gave an open mandate to manage and defend its affairs.

In none of the three situations I have mentioned was the bond formed by a positive or forward-looking programme, and the stability of the Governments in question was related to no capacity for creation or evolution. Self-preservation and resistance to change are the only motives capable of rallying the French bourgeoisie. The principle of unity, the party rule becomes in their case only a purely negative conception of order, of order seen as the means of destroying or holding in check the threat to private and public privilege; the fear they all shared was the only source of their discipline. Thus, bourgeois political parties in France are compelled to choose between division and decomposition on the one hand,

whenever by chance they take the risk of movement, and, on the other, the effort to hold together by limiting themselves to barren resistance, which in fact means to inertia, in a society evolving with terrifying rapidity and in a universe whose political life is changing at no less a pace. The time soon comes when inert resistance gives way to the pressure from within and without; the edifice that had seemed unshakable collapses with all the noise and tremor of a quasi-revolutionary movement, so that in the long run these episodes are as transient as they are petty. The records of Conservative Governments in France during the last twenty years—that is, of the *bloc national* Governments of Poincaré and Doumergue, of Millerand, Tardieu and Laval—are very little different from the earlier examples I have quoted.

Our political jargon, which is subject to the dictates of a rather vulgar fashion, has today one very fashionable word, *facilité*. It means something between easy-goingness and total lack of principle and is used to try to blacken the democracies' efforts at social reform. But what in fact is better described as facile than the tendency to meet every difficulty of government with precarious expedients requiring the minimum of effort or of sacrifice, or to run away from every radical measure, every bold solution, every great concession, simply because these require firmness of conviction, which means imagination, logic, persistence, which in turn imply courage, audacity and a touch of recklessness for its own sake? Taken all in all, this tendency is simply one aspect of bourgeois conservatism; it is the modern form of what was called "resistance" in Guizot's day and "opportunism" at the time of Jules Ferry. A political body that lives in fear of the risk of action must equally, and for the same reasons, be afraid of making use of youth. A fearful, pusillanimous policy has faith only in experience, and experience invariably has

an element of senility. The aristocratic systems carried youth into high office and gave it wide opportunities of action, and English democracy has been able to keep something of this heritage; popular revolutions have always brought forth and led into action an immense reserve of youthful energy; popular organisations have never been afraid of youthful leaders. But bourgeois prudence has always been afraid of youthful temerity, in public as in private life. It will not take the risk of letting youth work off its high spirits in office; with very rare exceptions, it insists on the slow methods of hierarchical promotion, and carefully preserves the rigid ladder of rank and age. There is a little-read work of Balzac, known only for its peculiar title, that this great visionary wrote very shortly after the July revolution of 1830. In it he foretold the early demise of the bourgeois monarchy and attributed it in advance to its mistrustful neglect of youth, to which it nevertheless owed its rise and its place. In the Third Republic the attitude to youth was only a little more enthusiastic and its consequences only a little less disastrous. But like effects invariably come from like causes. For more than a century everything that has happened in France suggests that the bourgeoisie as a political entity has been using up its sap and expending the creative virtue from which it formed and on which it nourished the new France in the great days of 1789. It would seem that for the French bourgeoisie the Revolution was a crisis in which it exhausted the greater part of its energy, the rest going in the struggle against the restored Monarchy, for from then onwards one finds only intermittent traces which ultimately disappear altogether. That fact settles its fate. A governing class that can maintain its cohesion only at the cost of inaction, that can survive only on condition that it does not change, that is incapable either of adaptation to the course of events or of using the

fresh energies of rising generations is condemned to disappear from history.

I have already set down one firm conclusion—namely, that the arguments advanced against our representative system are not valid against the general principles of democracy. I am now entitled to add a further conclusion —namely, that the evidence provided against the parliamentary system in France proves only that the French bourgeoisie has ceased to have the characteristics of a governing class. The conclusion would be corroborated if, in the footsteps of Taine, Renan and their friends, we were now to probe beneath purely political phenomena, to the moral conditions of society.

Admittedly, the Third Republic in the inter-war period is very far from presenting the same picture as the end of the Second Empire or certain periods of the *ancien régime*. We do not find the same shamelessness, the orgies of riotous living, the fever of speculation and gambling. There had been the beginning of something similar during the two or three years immediately following the victory of 1918, but this was no more than an animal reaction; a whole people had been kept for months at high pitch by restriction and suffering, and now everyone in his own way or according to his own means allowed the nervous tension to relax. There was, no doubt, an element of indiscipline, a fever of spending and pleasure-seeking, an orgy of business enterprise, an intolerance of all bonds, a quest for novelty degenerating even into a craze, a passion for liberty going to the point of licence. Perhaps the most characteristic feature of that time was the collective frenzy of its dances. But the period did not last; as soon as nerves were calmer, life took on its normal aspect. In any case, the illusion of prosperity that victory had left to us was soon dispelled. A series of increasingly severe

slumps swept away one after another the adventurous new enterprises, affected even the oldest and most prudent of them, and made everyday life an ever graver problem in every household.

To present the inter-war period as an age of pleasure-seeking when in fact it was in most cases and for most Frenchmen a period of hard trial, is to travesty history to the point of ridicule. It is no less ridiculous to denounce these twenty-odd years as an example of political corruption. In the main, the Third Republic, like the second and the first, was an honest *régime*. The lives of public men, including their private lives, were watched over by a strict and suspicious public opinion. Republican Members of Parliament were in great majority honest men. Its "scandals" were exploited noisily for party purposes, but in fact were neither frequent nor widespread, and needed only to be revealed in order to provoke what were no less than moral revolts, like the one that, on February 6th, 1934, was finally transformed into an insurrection.

And yet, if we were to seek the source of these scandals, we should find it in the fact that private interests had succeeded in varying ways in getting their own accepted representatives into Parliament, and if we were to look at all the scandals of this type for a century back, we should observe that this collusion of business and politics is precisely one of the characteristics of bourgeois capitalism. The Civil Service had been more deeply affected by the corruption than the politicians. After having for long been justly famed for the irreproachable and almost aggressive severity of its professional virtues, it came during the inter-war years to feel the contamination of business. But let us not forget that, unlike Austria, Germany and England, where the upper and middle ranks of the Civil Service were filled largely from the aristocracy, France was a country in which they were exclusively bourgeois.

It is impossible to look back on the rôle of the national Press in France in the last twenty years without experiencing a sense of shame, and none can honestly deny that its almost universal venality, revealing itself in both moral and technical inadequacy, became a focus of infection for the country as a whole. But our national newspapers were almost entirely dependent on big business; in other words, the Press too had become a bourgeois institution.

As for the state of culture, of science, of education, on which Renan and Taine had thrown the brunt of their criticism, they were satisfactory only at their extremes, research and university education on the one hand, elementary education on the other. In these fields the Third Republic had built edifices that defy its detractors. It was deplorable in the middle parts, in other words in secondary education, to which must be added two branches improperly regarded as higher studies, namely law and medicine, or rather, those parts of the two faculties that are devoted purely to preparation for professional practice. Here, not only had there been no progress, but decadence had become more marked. Secondary education in particular, although it held the eye of public opinion, although it attracted ever increasing numbers of both sexes, nevertheless turned out a steadily worsening product year by year. Now, the *lycée* and the *collège* are bourgeois institutions in France, just as medicine, the bar and the Civil Service are almost exclusively bourgeois professions. What the last century called the enlightened bourgeoisie has disappeared, the ignorant bourgeoisie with which we have to deal today no longer provides a public for any work requiring a certain minimum of knowledge. The kind of review we knew last century, pitching its vulgarisations a little high, would find no readers today, and we know the kind of magazine that has taken its place.

Whichever way we look, then, clinical observation leads

us to the same conclusions. In everything connected with the bourgeoisie, in every proper domain of bourgeois life and power, we find adulteration, senescence, decay. If today all our impressions can be summed up in one, and that one of a general collapse of French society, the ultimate reason is that the framework of that society was bourgeois, and that framework has given way.

CHAPTER IV

IT IS indeed true that, despite all appearances, France really has been ruled for a century and a half by her bourgeoisie. The apparent exceptions presented by the inter-war period are purely illusory. The grouping of forces (rather than of parties) that we called the *Front Populaire* was no more than a defensive coalition, formed spontaneously after February 6th, 1934, by a kind of instinct of self-preservation, for the defence of democratic principles. The Socialist Party was called upon to take its share of the task of government, but it knew perfectly well that it could exercise power only within the framework of bourgeois society. It was, indeed, for this reason that it had avoided power as long as circumstances made this possible. Even when the elected Chamber seemed to be held by a working-class majority, the bourgeoisie kept in its hands methods of resistance which yielded only temporarily to fear, and became effective again as soon as the fears were stilled. It kept its grip on the local Councils, the Civil Service, the Press, finance, big business and most of all on a Senate endowed with powers such as no Second Chamber, in any country or at any time, has had before, and owing its existence to the deliberate intention of the authors of the constitution in 1875 to create within the Republican system an irreducible stronghold of Conservatism. In fact, every time the will of the country, revealed through the ballot-box, had compelled the creation of a Government based upon working-class support and actively reformist in tendency, the ruling bourgeoisie had been quick to expel it, like a foreign body,

from its system. The French bourgeoisie held power, and was unwilling either to abandon or to share it. And, in fact, it kept it intact. When war broke out in 1939, the bourgeoisie was still at the helm. But it no longer had the qualities required to steer the ship.

I am not seeking here to draw up in doctrinal terms the indictment of one class by another. It may be that there was nothing inevitable about this twofold trend that ended in dissonance between French society and its governing class, in the inadequacy of the one to meet the needs of the other. I admit freely that other parts of the world, and even other countries of Europe, present a different picture. But such are in France the reality and truth, as anyone can confirm by looking around him and by examining recent history with an unprejudiced eye. Is it not clear that, for ten years, the bourgeoisie has found no reserves of energy within itself, no source of imagination, no capacity for renewal or revival of its own powers to deal with the economic crises; that it found no other resource than humbly to implore Government help, in flat contradiction of its own principles; and that wherever it has failed to find this help it has dropped its arms helplessly, without even attempting to fight? Is it not clear that in every field of productive activity—industry, agriculture, trade, banking—it had never left the rut of its traditions, and in a France inevitably left behind by more powerful countries in the quantity of its production, had been unable to preserve the prestige of our quality? In every sphere in which initiative and invention had given us something of a lead, it had allowed us to be caught up and left behind. It had allowed the condition of the workers to fall below the poverty line. It had not understood that both its own interests and those of the nation required perpetual modification of the relationship between workers and employers. In 1936, when it had become necessary

to cover in one stride the ground lost by the bourgeoisie, when a *Front Populaire* Government tried to secure general acceptance for the great reforms that had become the one alternative to bloody revolution, the bourgeoisie accepted them only reluctantly, through fear, and then, ashamed and embittered by its own fear, did all it could by violence or by trickery to go back on its word.

The threat of Hitler, nearer and more serious every day, compelled France to rearm at great speed. The world will know, some day, in what state of decomposition the succession of purely bourgeois Governments that ruled France from the beginning of 1934 had left our military apparatus. It will learn, too, of the incompetence shown by French industry—which means the employing class, which means the bourgeoisie—when we were faced with the need for an intensive effort of rapid re-equipment. I am aware of the accusations made against the workers' organisations, and I shall speak on that subject as freely as on all the others. But even if one admits the unhelpfulness of some of the leaders of the working class, it still remains too true that the behaviour of the employers gave them, if not good reasons, at least plausible excuses; it is unfortunately too true that under cover of the national danger, the employers' associations were seeking to go back on the reforms; it is only too true that for lack either of enthusiasm or of energy they failed to reorganise either their working methods or their system of production. The rearmament programme showed the lack of any inventive spirit or boldness of approach on the part of the General Staff, and the beginnings of its application revealed almost immediately that our plant and equipment were miserably inadequate and hopelessly obsolete, and that there was an acute shortage of the skilled workers who ought to have been provided in great numbers, in a country like ours, by vocational training or apprenticeship schemes. And

so the State, called in as it had been during the slump, was compelled to spend milliard after milliard in order to rush up factories and import modern machines from abroad. Everything had to be begun again from scratch under the lash of time and necessity, and in this supreme effort the French employing class showed itself to be a very poor collaborator indeed. No boldness of vision, no great plans, no initiative, no capacity for taking risks, no disinterestedness; instead a petty penny-wise pound-foolishness, a miserable calculation of immediate profit and loss, that reduced industrial policy to the niggling arithmetic of the huckster; finally, and in contrast with what happened in 1914–1918, an almost universal mediocrity among both owners and managers. This time there was no emergence of an *élite* of captains of industry, whose qualities of character were as remarkable as their technical gifts, in whom love of initiative and the will to succeed were greater than the desire for immediate gain. This perhaps, more than anything else, reveals the steady degeneration of the bourgeoisie between the two wars. It is useless to seek to explain or to excuse this degeneration by the increasing bitterness and inconvenience of the claims, or even of the intrusions of the working class, for the challenge to the authority of the employers was scarcely, if at all, less strong before 1914. The growth of working-class strength was an undeniable fact, then as now, and the employers had to make up their minds what was to be their attitude towards it. What sort of employing class is it that can neither fight the working class nor come to terms with it, neither dominate it nor allow it its share of authority, and whose authority is useless without the backing of the law or the help of the police? There is in this age only one way for the employers to preserve their authority, and that is to give it the support of a self-evident superiority, to prove that its exercise brings life

and prosperity. That was precisely what the French bourgeoisie was no longer capable of doing.

It is worth while also going a little deeper, and examining the attitude adopted during the past twenty years by the governing bourgeoisie towards the crucial problem of war and peace. The French bourgeoisie today is both jingo and pacifist, in the sense that it wants peace not so much with honour—that is a phrase that Pétain has made it impossible for us to use any longer—as with pride. When peace was still possible, it was not prepared to pay the price for it, yet it accepted war only when war had become inevitable. President Wilson's "dreams"—the League, mutual assistance, collective security, disarmament, European federation—all these ideas it received with a suspicion and scorn based partly on the precepts of an outmoded prudence and partly on the intoxication of recent victory. At a time when France was in a position to organise peace and dictate it to Europe, the French bourgeoisie disdained to use its opportunity, and so one day without warning it found itself face to face with the danger it had been too incompetent to avoid. The military dictatorship that had been rebuilt in Germany was more alarming than the one the Allies had just defeated, because it no longer appealed only to physical force and intellectual argument, but to the animal instincts and savage bigotries of man. Hitler had moved to power on a new wave of revengeful nationalism; once in power his whole trend was towards universal domination; the independence of Europe as a whole and of France in particular were in danger. There came a time when unflinching acceptance of the need to fight offered the only hope of averting war and the only chance of preserving the integrity and independence of France. Then the bourgeoisie, which had shown itself incapable of welcoming a great hope, proved itself equally incapable of performing a

noble duty; it showed itself as emasculate in the one cir-
cumstance as in the other. I should be justified in con-
trasting the conduct of the bourgeoisie with that of men
who are slandered today and who, too, changed their line
of conduct, but in the opposite direction, who worked with
all their might for peace, so long as there remained a hope
of organising it in Europe, and then tried to kindle the
flame of vital energy in the soul of France, when Hitler's
plan of conquest and domination had been revealed.

It is easy to understand why bourgeois prudence should
have hesitated in the face of new ideas like those of Wilson
and Briand, or of prospects like that of an international
democracy. What seems inconceivable is that the country
should not have been unanimous in the face of danger,
in its determination to meet it, in its acceptance of the
sacrifices that its own defence demanded. Why was there
no upsurge in France after the Anschluss, after the
occupation of Prague, or before or after Munich, of the
spirit of national unity that in England brought together
all sections of society in a common impulse? It was the
duty of the bourgeoisie, as the ruling class, to take charge
of this movement and direct it; in fact, it not only did not
do so, but tried to check it. Its vulgar attachment to what
it thought were its own interests as a possessing class, its
desire, unyielding and yet timid, to preserve its own wealth
and privileges had stifled its sense of patriotism. It
wanted peace at any price and yet was not afraid of Hitler,
because its whole capacity for fear was taken up by its
dread of the Popular Front and more especially of Communism. It saw in Nazism a threat to its wealth and
privileges much less dangerous than Communism, and
may even have nourished a secret hope that the armed
might of Hitler would discipline a too rebellious working
class. And so its class egoism sent it tumbling down the
slopes that led to a desire for reconciliation with Hitler

at any price. I remember a remark, appalling but typical of this spirit, that fell from the lips of the editor of a great bourgeois newspaper at the time of Munich. One of his reporters, just back from one of the Paris stations, was telling how the reservists, called up as a measure of precaution, were entraining without any empty display of enthusiasm, but with every sign of serious resolve. The editor banged the table in anger. "It is easy to see," he said, "that they have nothing to lose." Thus the bourgeoisie of France allowed war to come upon a people upon whom it had impressed neither its causes nor its meaning. Thus it entered upon the war that it only half accepted and in whose justification it only half believed. History will decide how far it was responsible for military defeat, but we do not need to wait for history to proclaim now that if the first shock of military defeat was turned into national disaster, the fault lay in the irresolution of the bourgeoisie.

I hope I have by now brought out with some boldness of outline the deeper reasons for the distress that seized almost the whole nation in those desperate days. The bourgeoisie had exercised in the name of the nation the sovereignty that the Constitution of 1875 had in fact delegated to it. But the bourgeoisie had just collapsed; a dreadful tragedy had revealed its decadence and its poverty. It had shown itself not only incapable of wielding power, but unworthy of holding it, and its incapacity and unworthiness appeared not merely as the cause of the disaster, but as the justification for it. Its final sin, less pardonable than all the others, was to consider its own ruin as that of the whole nation. It had proclaimed and had led public opinion to believe that when it had collapsed, nothing remained. When Bazaine was court-martialled for his surrender at Metz he cried, "What

could I do? There was nothing left", and the President of the Court, the duc d'Aumale, replied, "France was left". The ruling bourgeoisie had forgotten that France was left, and France herself, carried away by the wave of panic and despair, forgot that she remained. She saw what she thought was a gaping abyss at her feet, and was seized with all the vertigo of fear.

Then we saw the spectacle of a nation whose body and soul were on the rack, that felt no solid ground beneath its feet and saw no straw at which it could clutch. In 1870, the Republic, emerging armed and ready from the ruins of the Empire, had immediately revivified France by its appeal to those great passions of the Revolution, the love of fatherland and of liberty. In 1940 this flame could have been rekindled, but the bourgeoisie stifled it in the dust of its collapse, and apart from a few scattered cliques in the shadow of a great name, nothing appeared to fill the vacant place, to stop the yawning gulf. This consciousness of the abyss opening suddenly at one's feet, of vacuum all around one, is as unbearable for nations as it is for individuals, and yet it remains today, a year after the armistice, the dominant element in the nation's distress. Many things and many men have fallen, much material wealth has been lost, many private existences are overwhelmed by anxiety and poverty. But these things there have always been, in all the vicissitudes of history, and no people is broken by its losses if it knows them to be reparable. Today France knows that she has lost—or believes that she has lost—everything that gives guidance to the life of a nation, and she sees no way to make good this loss. A great succession is open and the heirs are not apparent. Such has been the domestic tragedy of France since the armistice, enclosed, as it were, within the universal tragedy. For if France wonders what she is to become tomorrow, and finds no answer, she wonders even more

C

anxiously what is to become of Europe, and what will be her place within this Europe. She does not know what her frontiers will be, or her material conditions. She does not even know whether she will survive as an independent nation.

This vitally important phenomenon, the disappearance of the bourgeoisie as a governing class, has not yet been fully understood in all its reality and consequences. Impartially considered, the adventure that has bestowed upon itself the title of "New Régime" or "National Revolution" will be seen to be in fact a supreme effort to resuscitate and revivify the corpse by a generous transfusion of "young blood", and the young blood, of course, is to be borrowed from the system that defeated our own, from the Nazi ideology, regarded now as a universal donor! Yet it is permissible to ask whether the bourgeois system can assimilate this Nazi blood. It is true that the dictators have borrowed from the bourgeoisie a part of their governing personnel. If one judges only by their social origins, it is clear that their administrative *cadres* are in the main bourgeois rather than proletarian, although they belong in fact to those strata of the bourgeoisie that had fallen in class and been proletarised by a succession of economic crises. It is equally true, though it would appear at first sight a contradiction, that in almost all cases the governing bourgeoisie, the political expression of modern capitalism, entered into alliance with "national socialisms", despite the fact that these latter presented themselves as anti-capitalist. In Italy it was the bourgeoisie that invented and brought forth Fascism as a preliminary to putting it into power; in France it applauds, or pretends to applaud, the "National Revolution". Talk to the bourgeoisie about a classless society, about the abolition of the wage-earning class and the proletariat, about some form of social and professional

unification under a collective authority, and you will find that it cannot contain its applause, for it knows perfectly well exactly how these professions of "socialism" will be translated into action—by the destruction of working-class organisations and institutions, by the suppression or regimentation of Trade Unions, by the abolition of all the rights, laws, liberties and customs in which the workers have found their principal weapons in the century-old struggle against their masters. What does it matter to the bourgeoisie if "National Socialisms" and "National Revolutions" declaim against capital (without in practice doing anything substantial against it), so long as they suppress the only enemy the bourgeoisie really fears? They are convinced that when once Nazism has got rid of working-class socialism for them, the normal movement of history will eliminate Nazism in its turn. Then the bourgeoisie would emerge independent again, all-powerful, re-tempered by the life-giving breath of Nazism, and, with its economic privileges intact, would get back the political power of which, for a time, it had been robbed.

Will the future in fact justify this selfish and simple-minded calculation? No honest observer believes that it can. "National Socialism" and "National Revolutions" can have at best only temporary alliances with the bourgeoisie. It matters little that these new movements preserve for the time being the essence of the social structure of which the bourgeoisie is the expression; they are none the less compelled to proclaim themselves anti-capitalist, or, in other words, anti-bourgeois. Although in political alliance with the bourgeoisie, they usually borrow the current vocabulary of the classes opposed to the bourgeoisie, so that the essential themes of socialist polemic, if not of socialist doctrine, have become a part of their equipment, and the vulgar devices by which they try to use these weapons only on carefully chosen and limited

targets, like freemasonry or the Jews or Anglo-Saxon plutocracy, in no way affect the essentials of the matter. If capitalism is not the target, it none the less feels the blows. So it is foolish to imagine that when the inexorable march of history has swept away the last remnants of totalitarianism, it will leave behind it a refreshed and re-invigorated bourgeoisie. The bourgeois pact with the Nazi devil will not rejuvenate it as it did Faust; rather will it emerge from its partnership more discredited, more debilitated, more suspect than today.

Moreover, I have argued so far on the assumption that the blood-transfusion from Nazism was in truth an infusion of young blood and that the principle of Nazism was a principle of life. In fact, as we all well know, this postulate is an impudent imposture that shocks human reason. Nazism does not give back youth to humanity, it takes it back to the savageries of childhood. Those among its apologists who come nearest to sincerity are perpetually telling us that it "makes men". So did the Napoleonic Empire, and so, under our own eyes, does Bolshevism. Does that mean that humanity is condemned to return to barbarism if it is to escape decrepitude? Is there no force other than brutality, no energy other than primitive ferocity? Who would ever accept so impious a view for its own sake? The problem of civilisation, as it has been seen ever since humanity became conscious of itself, is precisely that of replacing animal energies by disciplined, harmonised and spiritualised forces, of transforming savage idolatries and bigotries into reasoned certainties, or into convictions based on the demands of the individual conscience. Human progress lies in the preservation and development of vital energy, and then in its application to ends that give increasing satisfaction to the imperatives of reason and of the individual conscience, and so to those collective ideals that we call liberty, fraternity, justice.

Whether we speak of Christian civilisation, of classical humanism or of historical materialism, we are thinking in fact only of that evolution, which is the law of humanity itself. But Nazism proposes to turn back this current, to smash all the acquired results of human progress, and so it flouts and denies all the ideals and principles that have been the inspiration of that progress. It is not an elixir of youth, but a deadly poison; it can kill the living flesh, but it cannot resuscitate corpses.

Today, the French bourgeoisie applauds propaganda slogans which, taken literally, would be the death-warrant of capitalism. If only this calculated support had been a real and generous act of self-sacrifice! If only the bourgeoisie had really been resolved, in the interests of national revival, to sacrifice the privileges it gets from the capitalist property system! If only it had laid down, as the condition of this self-immolation, the safeguarding and extension of those principles of political, civil and individual liberty that have been since 1789 its banner and its *raison d'être*! Then, indeed, it could have found a new temper and a new life, not from an injection of Nazi blood, but from a new and all-pervading contact with a wholly French spirit of confidence, humanity and concord. It would have been seized and carried away on a current of creative enthusiasm, such as revolutionary France knew on the night of August 4th, 1789, or on the day of the Federation, and if anyone had failed to respond to their appeal, it would not have been the working masses of France, who, receiving at one and the same time the gifts of justice and liberty, Socialism and Democracy, would have seen the realisation of the "tried and glorious" formula of the Social Democrats, of Marx and, at bottom, of Jaurès too. In the interests of a democratic socialism, at last achieved or on the way to realisation, the workers would have been willing, as they have always been

willing, to make their contribution to the unity of the nation, and they would have had the certainty that the common needs of labour and production and the supreme requirements of peace would bring together in ever closer bonds all the peoples that share their own aspirations. This, indeed, is a wonderful dream, and it required only the willing consent of the governing bourgeoisie to make it a reality. If, then, there remains any spark of life in it, let it use it to set an example of sacrifice. Then it really will rise again, phoenix-like, from its own ashes. But it will never do that. It is less capable even than the aristocracy of 1789 of abdicating its privileges, thought it has long since ceased to regard them as legitimate. To be capable of sacrificing its immediate interests it would need precisely the understanding, the courage, the spirit of abnegation that it has lost, it would mean that the national disaster and the sufferings of France had already brought about, deep in the conscience of the community, that moral revolution of which, in fact, no single symptom is visible.

The term "moral revolution" is used intentionally; it indicates the seat of the infection from which the French bourgeoisie is dying before our eyes. The organ affected, the one from which the disease has spread gradually to all the others, is precisely the moral faculty. To go more closely into the history of the bourgeoisie, taking facts and texts for over a century and a half, is to come only to the same conclusion. That was indeed the source of the evil, the root of the contagion. Not that the French bourgeoisie did not have great virtues. They were upright and honest, patient and prudent, modest and decent, thrifty and reasonable, entirely suited to the conditions of life of an earlier period. Within the narrow limits of family, profession, city or village life, their class had prospered and

multiplied. But it was not made for life under intense, large-scale capitalism, for the phase of accumulation and over-production of wealth. The system that suited it best was one of steady and prudent progress, that of nascent capitalism, with its family concerns, its fortunes slowly accumulated over long periods from modest profits, its perpetual rounding off of income from factory or estate, its almost insensible modification of social conditions. In such an atmosphere, the French bourgeoisie found the circumstances that protected and encouraged it. It was not fitted for a life of frequent shocks, for the sudden ups and downs of the trade cycle. The breakdown of barriers, the inter-mixing of classes, customs and standards of life, weakened and corroded it, as acids corrode metal. Look around, and you will perceive that there are two parts the French bourgeoisie cannot play without losing something of its qualities : they are the rôles of new rich and new poor. The qualities that it has lost are those that the shape of the new age had made unfashionable and almost ridiculous. Its one-time rigid code of honour has weakened and collapsed under the influence of its contacts with modern big business. In the days of Birotteau and the *père* Goriot, even in those of M. Poirier, everyone thought it proper and natural that a bankrupt should blow his brains out. Honour may have been limited to respect for the signature on a contract, but that at least meant that the concept of honour existed. It has been worn out now, under the pressure of the great capitalist crises that have been following each other for nearly a century in an almost regular sequence and with ever-increasing intensity, and so the bourgeoisie has lost its own sense of inward dignity. It has lost, too, that energy and the creative vigour of the mind that presuppose some measure of honour, dignity and self-satisfaction. The decay of its private virtues has led to that of its public virtues too.

Why should the French bourgeoisie have shown this lack of adaptability to a new social climate, and have perished in consequence, whilst other sections of the middle classes, like those of the Anglo-Saxon countries, for instance, have been able without too great difficulty to adjust their moral standards to the progress of economic evolution? The contrast is no doubt explained by differences of national character, and perhaps also by the importance of the religious factor in the education and upbringing of the Anglo-Saxon bourgeoisie, even today. In any case, the facts are there, patent and eloquent. The decline of the bourgeoisie in France kept pace with the transformation and concentration of capitalist production, it became more marked as new external and internal problems inherent in the new world economy arose and took shape. After the collapse of the Second Empire, after the heroic impulse that is forever personified by the name of Gambetta, after the solemn *examen de conscience* that I have attached to the names of Renan and Taine—though in fact many other memories are associated with it—after the prolonged and conscientious effort that led to the passage and coming into force of the Constitution of 1875, it was permissible to believe that the patient was on the road to recovery, the progress of the disease arrested. Instead, there came the inevitable relapse. Ten years later there was the Boulanger escapade, and, five years after that, the Panama scandal. The French bourgeoisie could recover its capacity for political leadership only in the one environment suited to its temperament, which would mean putting back the clock of world economy by more than a century. That, indeed, is precisely what today's "National Revolution", driven by its own internal logic, seems to be seeking to do. Yet it is an enterprise in which even the totalitarian dictatorships must fail. Nazism and Fascism may have been

able to bring about the temporary eclipse of the great
spiritual principles that have guided humanity for centuries, but they cannot annul or obliterate from our
memories the vast scientific and technical discoveries
that have transformed the physical universe. They may
have been able to lead millions of men back to brutal
savagery, but they cannot lead the economic system back
to the era of hand tools and gilt-edged securities, of
the family workshop, the family store and the family
plot.

In this discussion of the rôle of the bourgeoisie, I
have considered it throughout only as the governing
class, the political expression of modern capitalism. I
readily agree that this class has produced many individuals who in the last two years have set an invaluable
example of patriotism and devotion to their country.
War and defeat, like all great collective crises, have been
the testing-bench of character, and among those who have
emerged unscathed and greater in stature from this process of natural selection are bourgeois of every shade,
whose services will be needed in the France of tomorrow.
I will go further, and admit that not only individuals
but whole groups belonging to the more cultured section
of the old liberal and catholic bourgeoisie have formed the
most compact centres of national resistance. Both these
individuals and these groups would no doubt be the first
to agree, in the sincerity of their own consciences, that the
class to which they belong is no longer in a fit state to
maintain its monopoly of property, nor in consequence
to exercise its privilege of government, and that the
historical justification for its existence therefore no longer
exists. France stands today at the end of a second revolution, which in fact has lasted more than a century. The
first revolution had transferred power to a rising class that

C 2

was already to a great extent in control of property. The second threw out a decayed class that had been unable to adjust its rigid temperament either to the necessities of industrial production or to the needs of democratic government.

CHAPTER V

THERE WAS a time when the cry was, "The King is dead; long live the King!" The transmission of royal authority took place automatically, and without a moment's hiatus. In France, the reigning class has passed away, and the nation sees no other to proclaim in its place. She abhors with her whole heart the totalitarian dictatorships, which in any case will disappear even from the countries where they now hold sway, for they will not survive the war, and humanity will root out the cancer that was beginning to eat at its vitals. Shall she go back then to one of the *anciens régimes*, and if so to which—to the one we knew before 1789, or before 1830, or even before 1848? A powerful monarchist party, based on traditions and loyalties still almost intact, and with a majority in the National Assembly, failed in just such an effort after the defeat of 1871. What reasonable man would dream of repeating the experiment today, with the monarchy no longer even a memory for anybody and no more than the obstinate dream of a handful of theorists? The experience of England and Belgium has shown that monarchy is not incompatible with real democracy, but in France it ceased a century ago to be the symbol of national unity, and if it were tried again it would have the backing, neither of a durable aristocracy, nor of a coherent bourgeoisie, nor yet of a loyal populace. If the monarchy were to be reinstated, as part of a representative system and with a liberal trend, it would be no more than a new edition of the parliamentary Republic in all its debility. If it were to return as a counter-revolutionary

Restoration, it would be in violent opposition to the reality of things and to the inevitable trend of the times. The country knows perfectly well that all these chimæra belong to a hopelessly dead past. On the other hand, it has never been deceived by the opportunist adventure, initiated under cover of the national disaster and dignified by the name of National Revolution. Instinctively, it feels in it a crude compromise between the principles of monarchy by divine right, which it rejects with everything in it, and totalitarian discipline, which it finds even more repugnant. It sees in its daily hesitations and aberrations the symptoms of the congenital contradictions that divide it from the start. Who, then, is the heir of the Third Republic? Who will be its successor?

France is conscious of living through an interregnum which will last she knows not how long and lead to she knows not what. These great historic intermissions are always times of tragic anxiety, and today the chasm lies open before a country two-thirds occupied by enemy forces, committed to a war in which she is no longer a participant but which none the less goes on, and in which her own destiny is one of the stakes. Even a France free, and with material conditions stable, would feel the burden of this unexpected hiatus in her sovereignty. How could she be other than overwhelmed by the unprecedented conjuncture in which circumstances have placed her today? It is true that on every occasion in history in which the form of authority has changed, there has occurred what I have described, in a much-misunderstood expression, as "*une vacance de la légalité*", a constitutional holiday. Even when the new authority is installed immediately, it cannot bring with it a ready-made legality; the institutions of the authority overthrown have been destroyed with it, and those of the new authority can be developed only slowly, so there ensues

an interval that of necessity is filled by temporary institutions, in some degree dictatorial in character. The
phenomenon is a normal one and alarms nobody, and a
country like France, which has seen many political revolutions, accepts it as such. What is lacking today, however, is not law or constitution, but sovereign authority
itself, and it is impossible to say when and by whom the
gap will be filled.

There is, indeed, an heir apparent, whose claims can
be said to be still valid, since it is the natural sovereign.
That heir is the people themselves, those whom a Catholic
propagandist in a recent pamphlet called "the multitude".
Why, then, do the parties and organisations most genuinely
representative of the masses not make their presence felt?
Why do they not demand power, as happened in September, 1870, after the collapse of the Empire? Why has
not public opinion in France turned instinctively to
them. Why does it still not turn to them for help? The
people themselves constitute the only legitimate and possible successor; only they are left, and on them converges
every trend of history. By an all-but-unanimous movement, the whole country hopes for the suppression of
monopoly and privilege—which is justice; for the super-
session of a social structure based on artificial and hereditary distinctions by one based on natural and personal
qualities—which is equality; for the subordination of
private interest to public good—which is the collective
organisation of the production and distribution of wealth,
and for peace—which is international order. Socialism
and Trade-Unionism embodied in advance this desire for
a new order. They are in line with the whole trend of
economic evolution, of which, indeed, they are themselves
the product. They are the rising sap of the nation, and
nobody who has lived and worked on familiar terms with
them can have failed to sense the inexhaustible reserve of

new forces that seethes within them. In them are distilled
the essence of all the popular education whose steady progress in France in the last half-century has coincided with
the decay of bourgeois culture. An active Socialist or
Trade Unionist was astonishingly avid for knowledge,
serious in thought and mature in judgment; a working-
class or peasant audience in a public meeting would follow
the most subtle, technical argument with a degree of
attention, of care, of pleasure, at which, for my part, I
have never ceased to wonder. In that, I am a jingo: the
French working class is, I believe, the most intelligent in
the world. The instability of the Governments of the
Third Republic was essentially a product of disorder and
indiscipline, of the lack of the compact, homogeneous
and durable parties on which a representative system
must be based. But I have already pointed out that the
working-class parties in no way shared this purely bourgeois incapacity. They formed compact bodies, united
and disciplined in tactics and in voting, and remained
faithful in action to programmes publicly debated and
defined.

Indeed, they laid themselves open rather to the opposite
reproach, of having sacrificed too much and too readily
to their own rules of order and unanimity. This accusation
has in any case been made against them, and I believe it
to be in part well founded. Discipline is a normal state
for a political party, and its unity should be strictly maintained against selfish defections inspired by personal interest, ambition or other form of temptation. In return,
some relaxation, or even the total suspension of party
bonds, must be boldly accepted whenever some extraordinary crisis turns the problems of public life into
matters of conscience. The real criterion of morality in
the life of political parties, as in most of the incidents of
private life, is disinterestedness. The breaking of party

bonds is immoral and hateful whenever it bears any trace
of what, in the widest sense of the term, I would call
venality. It becomes respectable, and even praiseworthy,
when it is no more than obedience to the imperative demands of conscience, in the face of some crucial problem.
It is, incidentally, by these efforts at discrimination in
particular cases that British parties have been able in
practice to transform and renew themselves along with the
spirit of the times, instead of clinging to immutable programmes and unchanging leadership.

There I must leave this digression, on which I would
not have entered had I not wished to provide proof of my
own sincerity. In tune, then, with the feelings and ideals
of the masses, breathing, as it were, in tune with universal
laws of economic development resting on solid foundations
and tried methods of propaganda, recruitment and organisation, having proved their ability to govern by their
participation in public life and their handling of their
own internal democracy, Socialism and Trade-Unionism
had all the qualities and all the qualifications required to
take over the vacant succession in the name of the workers
of France. And yet, the fact remains that the nation
showed no sign of turning to them. On the contrary, from
all corners there came a hail of sardonic rumours, often
originating in the mouths of men who owed their whole
career to the Socialist movement, announcing that Socialism was dead, evaporated in the heat of catastrophe.
Others noticed, with ill-concealed satisfaction, its "irremediable political and intellectual decline". As for Trade-
Unionism, if it was not yet quite dead, it was at least so
weakened that the National Revolution would have no
difficulty in absorbing it into its own corporatist organisation. There was, undoubtedly, a good deal of reckless and
wishful thinking in these assertions. Is Socialism really
bankrupt or moribund? It was much harder hit by the

repression that followed the revolt of 1848 and the Commune of 1871. The many military executions, with their aftermath of pseudo-judicial repression, were supposed to have uprooted Socialism for ever. To come down to our own times, Socialism was infinitely weaker and more fragile just after the period that covered the Treaty of Versailles, the Victory election of 1919 and the Communist split, that robbed it of its most active members. Yet, on each of these occasions, the party has risen again from its ashes, in the teeth of the prophets of disaster, both stronger and more conscious of its strength. How could it have been otherwise? The Socialist idea is one of the inventions of the human mind, but it feeds on the inevitable nature of things. In the form given to it by the brilliant synthesis of the ideas of Marx and Jaurès, which for thirty years has been its doctrine in France, it is the meeting-place of all the dynamic ideas of our time. What are the essential problems facing, not only our own country, but every other too? The reconciliation of the rights of nations with the need for peace, and of the rights of individuals with the need for order, of planned production and consumption with the free development of the personality of the individual. It was the Socialist movement that stated these problems for the first time in the modern world—or rather, it was they that created Socialism. They are symbolised in the name "Social-Democracy", which was the official title of most of the political organisations of Socialism, and whose full meaning we begin to see today for the first time. That is why it is safe to predict that the Socialist movement will rise again. What does it matter if the silence of oppression has reduced it once again to purely embryonic existence? The nature of things and the power of ideas will do their work; its renaissance cannot be long delayed, and is probably already near.

Nevertheless, I recognise—and I must insist on it once more—that the working people of France have not turned to it in their distress. Its presence was not felt even in the tragic hours of defeat and armistice. At a time when the workers of France saw the bourgeoisie falling into decomposition before their eyes, when they had only to come forward to seize its empty place, the Socialist movement that should have been their natural weapon and their normal instrument was itself absent. Why? To answer that question, we must proceed to a ruthless examination of our own consciences.

When the political framework of bourgeois life fell to pieces under the weight of military disaster, one passion, and one only, was capable of running like an electric current through the French nation; one passion only could pull it together and give it a new and living unity. That passion was patriotism, the instinct of national self-preservation. And no party could carry the people with it, or become the instrument of a spontaneous popular movement, if it failed to embody that passion. The Jacobins in the Committee of Public Safety had personified this "sacred love of country" in 1793, as had Blanqui during the siege of Paris, as Jaurès would have done, if he had lived, during the 1914 war, as his masters and disciples, Guesde, Renaudel, Vaillant, and Albert Thomas personified it when they stepped into his still-bleeding place and led the people of France to the vanguard of the struggle. But in 1940, as we must admit, French Socialism failed to follow in those footsteps.

That was not, as its detractors claim, because it had "forgotten the nation" in the heat of its own long propaganda, or because it felt the accumulated weight of its "anti-militarist and internationalist" campaigns. It had always seen international order as resting upon a founda-

tion of free and independent nations. It had fought against jingo patriotism, but itself remained ardently patriotic. It had worked with its whole being for the building of a just, equitable and stable peace, but it had never cultivated the more cowardly forms of pacifism. It cried shame on any tendencies that may have arisen to confuse love of peace with the acceptance of slavery, and it had never ceased to proclaim that it would be the first to rise in defence of the soil of France if she were attacked. It had mocked at the set and unimaginative routine that kept the sons of working-class homes imprisoned for long periods in dreary barrack-rooms, and its mockery may not always have been in the best of taste. It had quite properly denounced the odious system, less tolerable than ever since every citizen has become a soldier, which makes the army in time of peace the guardian of a capitalist "order", the weapon of a class against the majority of the nation. But it had never ceased its endeavours, never since the unforgettable efforts of Jaurès, to raise the organisation of national defence to the level made possible by scientific, technical and social progress. It is true that, in a spirit of ritual fidelity to a traditional symbol, the Parliamentary Socialist Party continued to vote against military credits, well knowing that its vote could not prevent their passing, and there was no doubt something hypocritical in this attitude. But when, in 1936, it was called upon to take office in a Government of which one of its members was the head, it was the first to propose the supplementary votes that were at last to make possible the replacement of the obsolete equipment of the last war by more modern arms. The first considerable and coherent attempts since the Nazi revolution to place France in a position to resist German aggression bore the signature of the Socialist Party. In the same way, Jaurès, Guesde and Vaillant had themselves not only voted against military credits,

they had led the campaign against them with much greater polemical violence than their successors, but the memory of this agitation did not cut them off from the patriotism of the mass of the people when the 1914 war broke out.

What, then, separated the Socialist movement from the working class in the hour of defeat in 1940 was neither its established doctrine, nor its long-standing propaganda, but something much simpler and much more recent— namely, the constrained and ambiguous attitude it had had from Munich onwards towards the problem of the threatening war. The working population had waited in vain for a clear and inspiring lead from the Socialist Party, which remained incapable of making up its mind one way or the other. It is true that, if one looks only at the documents prepared by Socialist Conferences or the Parliamentary Socialist Party, a clearly defined doctrine emerges. Having been, in most cases, myself responsible for the drafting of these official texts, I am in a position to know what they contained. They maintained rigidly the doctrine that the best guarantee of peace was collective security, based on respect for obligations, and they proclaimed unequivocally the duty of the workers to defend the independence of the country against all danger and all aggression. But the texts of motions and resolutions count for little in the eyes of public opinion, which prefers to judge by actions and public attitudes. And our attitude was ambiguous, hesitant, half ashamed of itself. Opposing the texts officially stating the position of the Party there had always been a minority group within the Party, deriving its importance rather from the position of the men who led it than from its own size, dangerous because of the arguments it concealed rather than of those it expressed. The simple truth is that, from Munich onwards, the French Socialist movement was divided into two parts, in conflict with each other over the fundamental problem

of public life, and varying in their relative strengths as circumstances changed. It was this internal conflict that reduced it to impotence and almost to silence. It was anxious at all costs to maintain an appearance of unity, and any clear line of action, or even any categoric statement, would have revealed the latent dichotomy, and no doubt led to a schism. The opposing forces within it were balanced to the point of mutual cancellation. At the same time, the attacks and slanders from outside, which had broken against it so long as its unity had been a reality, had redoubled in virulence from the moment when internal dissension gave them an echo in its own ranks. And so, for nearly two years, it had dragged on a humiliated and mistrusted existence, until in the end its very presence seemed to go unnoticed. It would surely have been better to allow open rupture to separate the two elements whose attitudes to a vital problem were beyond reconciliation. The outcome would have been the test. The mass of the workers would have re-formed their ranks around those whom events had shown to be right. All this I have confessed before—but the cult of unity had by then prevailed.

I would add, with no less frankness, that the Party had injured, or rather compromised itself, by its still recent collaboration with Communism. There was, of course, nothing to blush for in the alliance it had contracted amid the eddies of the insurrection of February 6th, 1934, and in the face of an immediate threat to the Republic itself, in the "united action" pact that was to become the foundation of the Popular Front. An irresistible and spontaneous popular instinct drove the Socialist Party into an alliance that was seen as, and indeed was, the defender of freedom. Today, we have seen the unfolding, under cover of national disaster, of the adventure of which February

6th was only the first episode, and we can no longer doubt that without the alliance of all the forces of democracy and the Republic, France would have been reduced five or six years ago to the condition of Franco Spain. Was there, then, anything impious or harmful in this alliance? Is "collaboration" forbidden only when it is with fellow Frenchmen? Nor is it possible any longer to complain of the Socialist Party's endorsement of the Franco-Soviet pact, negotiated as early as 1935 by MM. Laval and Flandin, or of the support it gave, during the interval between Munich and the war, to the proposed Treaty of Military Aid with the Soviets. Here again, time has brought proof. A closer understanding between Soviet Russia and the French and Anglo-Saxon democracies, or in other words an international Popular Front, would have saved peace!

But that is precisely what did not happen, because Stalin had evaded the understanding. In the end, it was with Hitler that he made his pact, and it was the bargain struck by those two that made possible the invasion of Poland, and led immediately to war. Then, very properly, public indignation was aroused; Stalin had betrayed peace, and the Communist Party, remaining obstinately loyal to him, was betraying France. It was natural that this tragic reversal of policy should call to mind all the successive recantations of the French Communist Party in recent years. Up to the eve of the 1935 pact, it had advocated and practised "revolutionary defeatism"; immediately after, it had become the most ardent champion of the honour and independence of the motherland. Up to the eve of the Russo-German pact, it had set the tone, and indeed supplied the impetus, of the campaign against Nazism; immediately after, it proclaimed its unchanging submission to Stalin, the ally of Hitler against France. These changes of front had happened without previous

preparation or any attempt to soften the blow, and with no other possible explanation than a change of orders from Moscow, which in turn were explicable only by the successive reversals of Soviet policy. Thus it had become clear that the trend of Communist Party policy was not determined by the Party, but imposed from outside. It owed blind obedience to orders coming, not from an international organisation, but from another Power, a State, which changed the orders of its own accord as its own national interests changed. The Communist Party was thus not an internationalist, but a foreign, nationalist party. The distinction is vital. Internationalism is based on the postulate that, among all nations at the same stage of economic development, there exist a certain number of common ideals and interests. The activity of an internationalist working-class party is based on the conviction that, if one looks far enough below the surface and far enough into the future, the interests of every country will be seen to be inseparable from the deep and long-run interests of the other countries of Europe, and even of humanity itself. It believes that in serving the international cause it is serving the cause of its country : it is national in its internationalism, and because of its internationalism. The Communist Party was quite the contrary. It was a foreign, nationalist party, because it was based on the postulate that the cause of the workers of other countries depends on the particular interests of one single State, the Soviet Republic, and then not on any ideal and permanent interests, but on the changing requirements of its material and political interests.

Now, from August 1939, Stalin had decided that the interests of the Soviet Republic required it to ally itself with Hitler, the enemy of France. It was, therefore, inevitable that, during the war and immediately after the

defeat of June 1940, the submission of the Communists to
Stalin should appear as treachery to the country. It was
no less inevitable that something of the disgust aroused by
this treachery should be felt, with varying degrees of confusion, towards the Socialist Party too, which everyone
thought of as closely related to the Communist Party, as
its sponsor and guarantor, first in the Popular Front, and
then in the Parliamentary majority of 1936. The confusion arose the more easily because a large section of
public opinion has never established in its own mind any
clear distinction between Socialism and Communism—
though these are in fact two completely separate forms of
working-class doctrine and action—and because, in the
current vocabulary of their common detractors, the term
"marxism" is used to cover both. In a situation whose
every element had been transformed, it was hard to
remember, as justice required, that "unity of action" had
been, in the strictest sense, imposed by circumstances, so
that its real authors were none other than the authors of
the plot that had put Republican liberties in danger.
People put Communism and Socialism "in the same
boat", denouncing the one and claiming to condemn the
other to some sort of automatic elimination. Today, fifteen months after the armistice, these unhappy errors
seem to have been corrected, but the problem that
weighed so heavily on the pre-war years remains, as a
burden no less alarming for the future. What can and
should be the place of Communism in French political
life? The question is still open, and we must face it
frankly, the more so since a new change has taken place
in the Soviet position, which has had a repercussion on
French Communism no less immediate than those of the
earlier changes.

Stalin was unexpectedly attacked by Hitler. He has
become the ally of the Anglo-Saxon democracies. Soviet

Russia is fighting today for stakes, among which the liberation of the occupied countries, and therefore of France, has a prominent place. A Popular Front has been formed again among the peoples. In this struggle, Soviet Russia has astonished world opinion and compelled its admiration. Those thinkers who imputed to Bolshevism, as an unforgivable crime, the perversion and degradation of the human race must, if they are honest, now revise their judgment. It is true that Bolshevism destroyed belief in personal liberty, independent criticism and moral and intellectual scruples, insofar as these had existed in Russia, but it has also preserved and even exalted courage and the spirit of sacrifice; it has created a faith. Like the peasants of France under the Terror, the people of Russia are attached to the system that has been imposed upon them, because they remember with horror the *régime* that Bolshevism overthrew, and see only enemies in those who would claim to deliver them. In France, idolatrous submission to Stalin coincides once more with needs of national patriotism, as it did in 1935 and in the days before Munich, and this time it no longer expresses itself in empty words and propaganda campaigns of doubtful purpose. French Communists are risking their lives; they are in the front ranks of the repressed, as in those of resistance. Among them and among the Jews Hitler chooses his hostages and his victims. When victory has been won, it will be clear that the new unity of the nation has been cemented with their blood; how, then, can they be excluded from that unity? Yet the problem will not have been solved; we shall still be confronted by the intolerable anomaly of the intrusion of a foreign, nationalist party into French political life. For all its great record, French Communism can be accepted as an element assimilable by the national organism, it can take its full place in public life, only if a radical change has taken place either

in the nature of the bond that unites it with Soviet Russia, or in the relations between Russia and the rest of the European community. Either French Communism must free itself of its obligations towards Soviet Russia, or Soviet Russia must accept obligations towards Europe, or both.

Without this change, France would inevitably find herself once more a prey to the internal difficulties from which she suffered before. Is it really too much to hope for or to count on? Just as French Communism was rigidly dependent on Russian Bolshevism, so there were people in France linked with German Nazism or Italian Fascism, by ideological bonds almost equally close. Is it fantastic to hope that all these wounds will have been cauterised in the fires of war, of common suffering, of final liberation, so that none but *free* Frenchmen will remain in France? Is it not reasonable to believe that Russia, for her part, may have had to modify her internal *régime* in order to secure unity against German aggression? For my own part, I am counting firmly on a development by which, after the disappearance of the totalitarian dictatorships, after the victory of the Anglo-Saxon democracies—a victory in which she will have taken a heroic part, but to which she will owe her own salvation—Russia will inevitably find herself integrated into a European community, a European federation. A genuine peace treaty will be a Charter of peaceful co-operation and emulation between nations; as that Charter is consolidated, as the ideal and material interests that they have in common are revealed, Soviet Russia will cease to be an extra-European Power, and French Communism will cease to be a foreign sect within the nation.

CHAPTER VI

CONFUSION AND indecision within its own ranks over the problem of war, confusion in the public mind with a Communist Party tainted with treason—these two reasons suffice to explain why the Socialist movement was left out of account in a series of events which should logically have carried it into the vacant seats of power. But there were, in fact, other reasons for the absence of the Socialists and, in consequence, of the people themselves, and the evils that they represent have not yet been fully explored. I have said that the politically active working class, and the Socialist movement which was its natural expression, had provided a model of disciplined organisation, of political maturity, of aptitude and readiness for rational education. This view I still affirm. One accusation, never fully formulated, has been made against both the workers and the Socialist movement, and this I reject, as I deny the right of its authors to make it. It is that they have developed, alongside bourgeois corruption, a different form of corruption of their own; that they have seen human progress in terms of crude material advantages; that, in their impatient search for material well-being, they have cultivated idleness and selfishness—in a word, and in the terms of the most common formulation of the accusation, that they have debased the concept of duty, by placing all their emphasis on the rights they claim. It is constantly said, for example, that the social laws of 1936, the reduction of working hours, the increase of wage-rates, the introduction of the idea and the practice of leisure, led to a debasement of the moral sense of the

working class. It is important to remember that these social laws, which it is so easy to criticise after the event, were the price we paid to avoid civil war. In any case, what in fact lowers working-class morality is not paid holidays, shorter hours or higher wages, but unemployment and poverty. Leisure is not idleness, but rest after labour. The organisation of leisure, increases in the purchasing power of wages, these allow the worker's family to maintain its health by exercise and its spirits by games, to give more time to domestic occupations and affections, and one day they will make it possible for working-class mothers to give up all their time to their homes and families; in other words, they strengthen, in fact, the moral factors of existence. Humorists have found a good deal of material in the "two-Sunday week", and it may well be that æsthetic feelings were not wholly satisfied by the spectacle of the long processions of couples and families with children, whose tandems and motor-cycles and light cars filled the roads around our big towns every week-end. No doubt the campers in the meadow and picnic-parties on the edge of the wood made a less elegant sight than the golf-courses on which the employing classes were gathering at the same time, but the picture was none the less both moral and encouraging. These are the ways in which a nation finds new youth and new strength, for there is no joy in labour without joy in life.

Or, to take the problem on a somewhat higher level, and looking at it within the framework of capitalist society, will anybody deny that the incessant progress of science and technique *must* be accompanied by a regular improvement in the conditions of working-class life? Modern industry makes it possible to produce an ever-increasing quantity of goods in an ever-shorter time. Can we really refuse the wage-earner his modest share of

this general increase in wealth, and what can this share be, if it is not a reduction of previous working hours and an increase of previous wage rates? That is his mite, and only the most iniquitous abuse of force would deprive him of it. When the wage-earner demands it, he is accused of giving way to a depraved spirit of self-seeking. He would not need to demand it if others had thought first to offer it. The bourgeoisie are indeed ill-placed when they profess surprise and indignation at the "incessant demands" of the workers, and the spirit they believe it indicates among workers of all kinds. It was the demands of the workers that marked the first awakening of their class-consciousness; they organised to press their demands, to defend themselves against the iron law that governed their work and wages, and that based them, not on the amount of national wealth, not on the cost of living, but on the law of supply and demand, on the current price of human merchandise in the labour market. How many people really know in detail how the worker in agriculture or industry spends his money? How many can imagine how the smallest reduction in hourly wage rates affects immediately the life of every member of the family? They are accused of forgetting their duties too easily; is it not truer to say that it was the rest of us who began it, by forgetting their rights? For many long centuries the working class has known nothing but duties, as others have thought of nothing but its duties—duties forced upon the worker by the need to live, by all the organs of social coercion and religious persuasion. What they call their emancipation was in fact the laborious conquest of rights already morally theirs, and this conquest is not yet complete. We are told that there can be no rights without duties; no doubt, but it is equally true that there are no duties without rights. Is it surprising that the workers are not always conscious of the interdependence of these two

ideas, when they have suffered so long from its denial? And is their interdependence always present in the minds of those who have never been deprived of the rights—whose rights today look very much like privileges?

All this is indubitable; my arguments are irrefutable . . . and yet some instinct deep within me, some hidden anguish almost, warns me that I am very near one of the deep-lying roots of the evil. In terms of distributive justice, all my evidence and all my arguments are valid. It is still not true that the demoralisation of the bourgeoisie was accompanied by a parallel perversion of the masses. Nobody is entitled to make this grave accusation against the mass of the people, the active workers of the Socialist and Trade-Union movements, or even their responsible leaders. Even if it were possible, in some spheres and in some circumstances, to find instances of exaggerated demands or too embittered protest, they would be a hundred times excusable. Let us accept all that. It is still true that the real problem lies elsewhere. What we are trying to discover is why the working class, acting through its legitimate representatives, did not seize the succession left open by the collapse of the bourgeoisie. And proof of purely negative innocence provides no satisfactory answer to this question. The fact that the working class was not guilty of the charges laid against it was not enough to make it worthy of the mission of sovereignty that lay within its grasp. The bourgeoisie was collapsing, because it had shown itself unworthy of its part; it was all the more important for the working class to prove its worthiness to take the vacant place. Sovereignty implies superiority. The working class should have been able to show, not merely a clean moral record, but an unmistakable moral superiority, and that it did not possess. It lacked precisely the qualities needed to lead a nation—generosity, magnanimity, an ideal bearing, self-evident

disinterestedness, readiness to sacrifice one's own desires to the common good, all that Nietzsche called somewhere "the grand manner in morals", all those qualities that make of morality a religion, and of propaganda an apostolate.

Here again I should like to illustrate my meaning by more detailed examples. The *Front Populaire* Government thrown up by the election of 1936 had introduced laws reducing working hours, consolidated wage increases by the operation of collective agreements, secured recognition for Trade Unions, and legalised the status of shop stewards. At the same time it had inaugurated a vast and methodic programme of rearmament, in view of the threat of German armament and the discovery that nothing had been done, or even seriously attempted, since the end of the last war, to renew our own military equipment. The two operations were to be carried through simultaneously, without either affecting the other adversely; indeed, wherever the requirements of national defence were affected, the 1936 social legislation allowed and provided for every kind of exception. But this did not get rid of the fear in the public mind that the new laws might interfere with the execution of the rearmament programme, and that fear was maliciously encouraged and exaggerated. The proof of the malice and the exaggeration lies in the fact that the 1936 rearmament programme, including the additions made to it later, was carried through on time. Better than that; when France entered the war, and despite all that has been said and is still said to the contrary, inside and outside France, the execution of the programme was considerably in advance of its time-table. The French Army was already in possession of up-to-date equipment which, in quantity at any rate, was enough to place it on a footing of equality with the German Army, and that,

indeed, is why the French Army leaders faced the prospect of war without too great apprehension. Nevertheless, and whatever the final and total result may have been, the man-power problems encountered in the execution of the programme were very real. Overtime was bargained over or refused by the Unions, even for the production of material urgently needed; agitation persisted in a good many factories; production per man-hour fell.

Whenever any attempt was made to explain to the workers that they had not understood the spirit behind the new laws, they invariably replied that they were defending the letter of their rights so tenaciously only because they felt them to be threatened. "The employers", they said, "have not accepted the laws honestly and wholeheartedly; they are using the requirements of national defence to sabotage them. We are being asked to work harder, but have the employers done all that is required of them in the way of systematisation, organisation, capitalisation? Have they built new factories, installed new machinery, started multiple-shift systems, trained skilled workers? No. They have been afraid of expansion, afraid of risk, afraid of earning less from Government orders than from private enterprise. When all this incompetence leads to delay and shortage of equipment, it is always the worker who is asked to make it good, and the concessions we make today will be used against us tomorrow. Why should we be the only ones to make the extra effort and the extra sacrifice?" There is no doubt that this kind of complaint was very largely justified. Nearly everything the worker said was true. Insofar as the problem was purely one of distributive justice, nothing could be said against them; they were in no way guilty. But were they showing themselves worthy of the mission of leadership, to which they laid claim? They were quite right in denouncing the motives of the employers, their profit-seeking, their fear of loss

and—what, more than anything else, corrupts genuinely human feeling—the fear of being the dupe of one's own generosity. But were not the workers, in fact, actuated by the same base motives? Whenever they used bourgeois pettiness as an argument, they put themselves on the level of the bourgeoisie, instead of showing their ability to rise above it. It was pettiness that was killing the bourgeoisie as a governing class: those who wished to replace them should have proved themselves free of it. "Yes, we agree gladly to what is asked of us. We know perfectly well what is happening. We know the kind of failure that our belated sacrifice is to remedy. We know that it will be useless if the employers fail to do more than their duty, as we are doing. But we are not bargaining and not arguing, we are setting the example that the others must be shamed into following. If the bourgeoisie are to rate their petty calculations and manœuvres higher than the common need, let them do so; we shall not follow them." This is the kind of language that would have shown the working class to be worthy of leadership. The nation would have called them to power, or have welcomed their accession to it, if only they had imposed themselves by their own greatness, and crushed bourgeois mediocrity by the sheer force of their own nobility.

What I have said about war production could be applied in exactly the same way to other similar cases. The work on the 1937 Exhibition, for instance, would have provided one, but I prefer to choose my second example in a different field. From the time of the last war and the Treaty of Versailles, the idea of peace had occupied a preponderant place in Socialist and Trade-Union propaganda. It could scarcely have been otherwise. The tragic futility of war had never been more cruelly evident; the heroism, the slaughter and the victory had led only to immeasurable disappointment. But what, in fact, were

the arguments used in the pacifist propaganda of the Teachers' Union and some sections of the Socialist Party? They were based on a belief in the sanctity of individual life. This is undoubtedly a concept of great purity and nobility, which has been and still is the basic principle of whole civilisations, but it is essential that it be read as a precept—"Thou shalt not voluntarily deprive any other man of his life", and not as a commandment—"Thou shalt at all costs save thine own skin". Man must know the value of human life, but he must also know how to subordinate it to ideal ends, or, in other words, to the collective ends of justice, human liberty, national independence, peace itself, for peace is one of the necessary goals of humanity—the most necessary of all, perhaps, in the sense that it is a condition of almost all the others. Subordination of this kind means, in practice, sacrifice, and a revolutionary propaganda that can no longer teach it has allowed itself to become cheapened and debased; it may drag out some kind of existence in normal times, but it fails entirely in times of tension, anxiety or danger.

Experience teaches that in critical times men can save their lives only by risking them. In the same way, a nobler propaganda would have shown that, in the face of the danger that threatened Europe, peace could be preserved only at the cost of deliberately and courageously risking war. The Treaty of Versailles had not disarmed Europe, but the Hitlerite Revolution had re-armed it. Now, in an armed Europe, there was no other way of conquering war than through an armed organisation for mutual assistance, and assistance pacts could be effective only if the peoples of all the signatory countries proved their readiness to honour their signatures with their blood. "We will not die for Danzig", was the cry, but dying for Danzig meant dying for peace, and peace could not be saved unless men were ready to die for it. And so Socialists and Trade

D

Unionists had been more than right in preaching peace, but they had cheapened both their teaching and themselves by their infusion into it of the elements of selfishness and false realism. Courage and the spirit of self-sacrifice are not remnants of barbarism. What *is* barbaric is the purpose to which men still put these qualities. They are great and virile virtues that must still be cultivated, for no future can be built without them, and it is by them that a people recognises its leaders in the critical moments of history.

When a Socialist speaker was addressing a working-class audience, he rarely finished without an exhortation along lines something like these: "Working men, come in and join us! But let me first tell you what you are promising to do, if you do join our Party. You are undertaking to set an example always and everywhere, to be a model to others and to inspire them by the example of your conduct. In the factory, you must set the pace in ability and conscientiousness. The private life and the working life of every member of the Party have a propaganda value in themselves to the Party as a whole. Help us to prove to our enemies that to make men free is to make them live better lives." That is how the Socialist movement interpreted its creed to its own members, but it failed to interpret it in its own corporate life. The Party, too, should have proved itself better, nobler and worthier than all others in public activities, in its political doctrines and in the ethical motives that lay behind them; it, too, should have been a model to other parties and the whole nation; an example of the pride, the complete disinterestedness, the greatness of mind and spirit that are the proper mark of youthful strength. It was our duty to aim always at the highest, and renounce every kind of base or doubtful method, even if such methods were being used against us.

"No aggression merely because others attack us, no insults merely because others insult us", should have been our rule. We were not as other men, not on the same plane or at the same level of human development, and everything we did should have proved this. It was our duty not only to persuade men's minds, necessary though this was, but to go on from there to appeal to their emotions and kindle their imaginations.

There are questions I put to myself, after all the years I have given up to action and the more recent months devoted to scrupulous meditation. I ask myself if these failures are not the fault of the chosen leaders of the working class. Did they fully understand their mission? Did they do their whole duty? Had we grasped clearly enough the significance of Jaurès' attempt to transform Marxian logic. Marx had supplied the most powerful and invigorating stimulus to the working-class struggle, by his teaching that the inevitable evolution of history was on our side. But the inevitable is not necessarily just, and its results may not always be satisfying to reason and conscience. It was Jaurès who added to Marx the demonstration that the Social Revolution is not merely the inexorable consequence of economic evolution, but would satisfy also the eternal demands of man's reason and conscience. So, in his view, Socialism was to become the realisation and the justification of the glorious watchwords of the French revolution, "the Rights of Man and the Citizen" and "Liberty, Equality, Fraternity", and through Socialism the heroism of the fighters for democracy, whose struggles have filled Europe and the world for a century, would find its highest expression and its triumph. Thus Jaurès infused into the materialist conception of history all the idealism of the creeds of democracy and human brotherhood.

Did we make enough of this idealist teaching in our

day-to-day propaganda? Were we emphatic enough in refusing in all circumstances to have recourse to the cruder instincts of the human animal, to brutality, envy and malice? Did we remember always to appeal only to the nobler sentiments of the human mind, to its inborn need of justice, affection and fraternity? It is often argued that it is useless to change social institutions until the mentality of the individual has changed, and the argument has too often been a convenient justification for the indefinite postponement of necessary changes. But have we, in fact, done what lay in our power to change the individual human unit, while we tried to change society? Did we carry on the two tasks together as we should have done, so that they intermingled and supported each other? These are some of the questions I ask myself, and although my own conscience does not reproach me over-violently, I hesitate to give a categoric answer. In the early days of Socialist propaganda, fierce and implacably combative as it was, we reached greater moral heights. We fought together against danger, in a common spirit of self-sacrifice that exalted our faith. Jaurès, too, had lived in permanent danger of prison and assassination. Then the risks grew less, and faith was dulled. We had become too strong and less careful, we had slipped gradually into the mould of ordinary life. We had become too successful, and when the time came, when the nation was waiting for a rallying cry, a call to action, there was none in our ranks great enough to voice it.

An English thinker whose system is not unlike that of Marx has maintained that, in the march of history, moral forces play only a negligible part. In his view, the intellectual forces controlling material progress are the only important factors in evolution. The human race, he claims, has been living for some three thousand years on

the same almost unchanging stock of moral ideas, that appear and reappear in almost the same form in every religion and every philosophy. But humanity itself has changed startlingly during this period, and one must therefore conclude that its variations cannot be related to a practically unvarying cause. I am not setting out to contest this theory, which no doubt contains some element of truth. It may well be that the idea of perpetual progress is as foreign to morals as it is, for instance, to art, while it remains an absolute law for pure thought, science and technical subjects. But, even if their progress is not parallel, it must at least be admitted that the persistence and consistency of what may be called a particular moral atmosphere are among the necessary conditions of intellectual progress. This atmosphere, this set of convictions and beliefs, has, indeed, been the common property of all humanity since the beginning of our civilisation, and it constitutes the moral environment, outside which all intellectual progress—and therefore all material progress, too—would have been impossible. It is easy to believe that intellectual progress does not always keep step with moral progress, but it is difficult to see how moral retrogression can fail to lead to a similar intellectual loss. Nazism in Germany is a proof of this. In a society whose principles have required it to stifle the instincts of justice and charity, break the bonds of family and friendship, and destroy respect for human life, which sees fanaticism, cruelty and denunciation as duties, the permanent moral background that had protected and cherished the forward march of the mind suddenly ceases to exist. The result is an abortion of what had been growing up to that point. Turning back to a barbarian morality means returning slowly to barbarian thought and life. But we never learned, like the Spartans, to watch the "drunken Helot", and profit from his example.

CHAPTER VII

I SHALL CONCLUDE these reflections by trying only to sum up and put in order the conclusions to which they have led me.

A ruling class and a political system have succumbed under the impact of events, as if they had gone down in the upheaval of revolution. That has happened before in French history without the country's being any the worse for it. Feudal aristocracy, monarchy based on divine right, both disappeared. Today, since a country cannot live without laws, France is faced with the immediate task of creating new institutions. There is nothing new about the principles on which these institutions will be based; they are known and laid down in advance. The French people are almost unanimous in their hope that the world war will end in a world-wide victory for democracy. The constitutional problem, therefore, is essentially a simple one. A weak and perverted bourgeois democracy has collapsed, and must be replaced by a true democracy, an energetic and competent democracy, popular instead of capitalist, strong instead of weak.

I am no constitution-maker; that is a task I leave to the specialists. But I have, I think, established two incontrovertible truths in the course of these arguments. The first is that Parliamentary government is by no means necessarily either the only or the purest form of democracy; the second is that the faults for which the French Parliamentary system is so often blamed are in reality the shortcomings and the vices of the French bourgeoisie. I do not intend to try to define what should be the rôle of

the representative or Parliamentary principle in a popular democracy. I claim only that, whatever be the function allotted to the legislative Chambers when the distribution of powers in the future Republic takes place, there can be no question of any attack on the elective principle nor on universal suffrage, which is the very symbol of democracy. To attempt to get rid of them would be to attack the deepest roots of French political tradition. On the other hand, the representative principle, using that term in its narrowest sense—that is, in the sense of the wholesale delegation of popular sovereignty to an elected House, and its expression through the sole medium of legislative assemblies—will, in all probability, not survive the experiment in bourgeois democracy that has now lasted more than a century.

My personal preference is for some system along American or Swiss lines—that is, founded on the separation and balance of powers. This means that sovereignty is divided, and that the executive can exercise within its own sphere an independent and unbroken authority. These systems have given rise to stable Governments and have, in addition, the great advantage of substituting for the somewhat fictitious concept of governmental responsibility, which has always loomed too large in our country, the much more real principle of supervision of the executive by the legislative.

Still following the American and Swiss models, I should like this conception of the functions of a central Government to be allied to a strongly centrifugal development, which I would carry, indeed, to the point at which it becomes federalism. I have never been afraid of federalism. The individual States in America, the Cantons in Switzerland have both retained some share of democratic sovereignty—and they maintain the fires of local political life. They offer the public-spirited citizen adequate oppor-

tunities for a free and useful political life in his own locality. I am reminded, in this context, of life as it was lived in our former provinces. Moreover, I have always been attracted by the ideas put forward by Rathenau after the German collapse of 1918. Functional devolution has always seemed to me as essential as decentralisation. In other words, a single executive authority, a single legislative body can no longer deal adequately with all the aspects of life in a modern State. We are led logically, therefore, to envisage the central authority, whose primary task is one of general direction and co-ordination, as becoming progressively surrounded by smaller satellite authorities with special fields of action, within which they have a limited independence. Totalitarian Germany has in part put this system into practice. There is a German Führer, but each region and each of the main functions of the State have their own führer, each with a very real measure of autonomy. Our problem, therefore, is to reconstruct within the framework of democracy, the institutions that Nazi Germany adapted to a system of personal dictatorship. But I do not want to dwell too long on this kind of problem. It is permissible to argue about the data, but no useful purpose is served by discussions regarding possible solutions of the problem; those France must find for herself.

The second point I want to make is that this popular democracy will be—indeed can only be—a Social Democracy. That is the condition of future stability. There can, in logic, be no divorce between political and economic authority. The political power of the bourgeois class was derived from its economic power. It has now been stripped of that political power, and if economic power—which the bourgeoisie proved no less incapable of using for the good of the community—were to remain in its hands, then

France would be exposed to the most dangerous risks. There would, almost certainly, be a new period of disturbance and impotence, a new series of upheavals, perhaps even of revolutions. Yet, although, up to now, the bourgeoisie has made only fumbling and hesitating attempts to use its economic privileges, it still retains legal and theoretical possession of them. This disequilibrium must be removed. There must be progressive, legal expropriation, carried out by peaceful means, but none the less ruthless in its action. Indeed, it will be, in reality, not expropriation but appropriation. Our task today is to re-write the phrase used by Thiers and Dufaure of the Third Republic, so that it reads, "The people's Republic will be a Social Republic or it will be nothing".

There is, indeed, no way of evading the social problem when the facts themselves render its solution so urgent. How shall we continue to tolerate a system in which men have neither sufficient food, nor healthy houses, nor the wherewithal to protect their families from hunger, cold, illness and vice? Can we tolerate such a system in the future? Will the younger generation be prepared to accept the existence of social scourges as if they were acts of God? Most assuredly they will not. They are resolved to face them, and to master them, though they know that the task is an heroic one. But how can they be got rid of, except within the framework of a Social Democracy? Any system that involves the abolition of the wage-earning class—that is, the disappearance of the worker's dependence on the employer to whom he must sell his labour—is bound to move towards a society in which producers of all kinds work together, in the positions in which they are most useful to the community, for the production and consumption of wealth. The process may or may not be conscious, but it can end only in the creation of a collectivist system. It is easy to talk glibly about the abolition

of the wage-earning class, but it is more important to realise all that the term really implies. Even if the solution that France adopts leaves intact the framework of capitalist society—and consequently preserves a wage-earning class—the worker's absolute right to a wage will still have to be recognised, and by "a wage" I mean a "living wage", the minimum earnings necessary to maintain, not only physical life, but also the full life of a free citizen and of his family. For I maintain that the wages of the working man must be sufficient to maintain himself and his family, and I strongly object to the present position, in which the home is kept going only by the addition of the earnings of his wife and children. That takes us right into State Socialism, for it is obvious that the power of the State will have to be used to define, protect and guarantee the status of the worker. What we shall have to do is to translate into real social conditions the ideals that became current as revolutionary slogans in 1848—"the right to live, the right to work, the organisation of labour". Whichever of these two courses we adopt, the task of organising and regulating production will still fall on the Government. And, whatever form of Government we adopt, it will still be unable to evade the responsibility of organising and planning production, for the result of inadequate or chaotic production will be civil war.

Then there will arise other problems, whose solution will be no less imperative. The march of scientific and technical progress means the production of an ever-increasing amount of wealth in an ever-shorter time. This progress is not the achievement of any one individual. It is the common heritage, and therefore the collective property of humanity, for it embraces and results from the accumulated labour of successive generations of human beings. Bourgeois capitalism was incapable of distributing this abundant wealth among the mass of con-

sumers, and so got rid of it by means of periodic slumps and deliberate deflation. Under capitalism, progress had become a source of excessive profits for the privileged or the lucky few, and of unemployment and poverty for the immense majority of men. Progress belongs to all men, and we must willy-nilly find a way to make it benefit all men. Our present-day rulers have talked a great deal about the desirability of the worker having some share in the profits of the firm that employs him. That means little or nothing, but there is another kind of profit-sharing that must and will come; it is the one that gives to the majority of the nation a share in the benefits for whose creation society as a whole is responsible, each worker receiving his dividends in the form of an increase in his well-being or a reduction of his working hours.

Nor can increased production be reduced purely to a question of industrial research, machine-tools and "rationalisation". The optimum point is reached only when each job is done by the one person whose physical or mental aptitudes are most suited to do it. The organisation of labour implies the greatest possible degree of planned specialisation, and consequently of education and selection. The needs of production will therefore themselves require the democracy of tomorrow to introduce real equality, in the form of those institutions that are, in my view, the be-all and the end-all of Socialism.

This real equality in no way ignores natural inequalities. On the contrary, it takes full account of them, and indeed makes use of them. True equality means the proper utilisation of every human being, carefully fitted into his own appropriate niche in the community. It means rating all functions equally highly, since all are, in a sense, equally useful. Under bourgeois capitalism, it was possible to move from one social class to another, and examples of such transfers were quoted with complacency.

But these interchanges between classes were accidents,
exceptions to the normal working of the rules of society.
For a worker to acquire capitalist property was a miracle;
for a bourgeois to revert to manual wage-labour was a
catastrophe. The democracy of the future must know how
to get the best out of every man by using his natural
aptitudes, without reference to class distinctions—that is,
without taking into consideration the caste, birth, race or
fortune, either of the man himself, or of his parents or ancestors. The son of a blacksmith must be able to become
Prime Minister or an industrial leader, as he can today,
but the son of the industrial leader or Minister must be a
blacksmith, if that is what he is best suited for.

There is nothing new in these ideas; Trade Unions and
Socialist parties preached them before the war. At a given
stage of material evolution, just as at a given stage of
scientific research, the same problems present themselves
to the minds of all. Like Fascism and Nazism before it, the
political system that calls itself the National Revolution
itself declares that they must be solved. But I cannot say
too clearly or too often that France intends to solve them
by herself, and by democratic methods. In France, at
least, political and social democracy are inseparable
terms. Political democracy cannot survive if it does not
develop into social democracy; social democracy would be
neither true nor stable if it were not based on political
democracy. The French people will not consent to sacrifice the great human ideals laid down in 1789 to the
major imperatives that material reality has added to
them since then, or vice versa; they want to combine
economic order and social equality with political, civil
and personal liberty. The task is a difficult one, but they
intend to see it through themselves, using the political
power that they have won in a hard struggle, and that
nothing will induce them to relinquish. They refuse to

accept these things ready-made, from the hands of rulers whom they have not chosen, and whose credentials they do not recognise. They demand justice and do not ask for charity; indeed, they know too well that justice can never be doled out from above, like alms to the poor. They have discovered that in other countries Nazi and Fascist autocracies reduced labour to slavish routine, but did nothing to suppress the privileges of the capitalist property-owner. Even in France, they can see that, if the slogans with which they are bombarded were honestly translated into action, then the whole bourgeois structure would be destroyed, and they know that if it is not, it is because the inventors of the slogans are themselves bourgeois, convinced of the importance of their class and doing all they can to preserve it. The achievement of the political sovereignty of the people is therefore a concept and a task indissolubly allied to the parallel concept of social justice. The foundation of a "Social Democracy" in the full meaning of the term, which was yesterday's hope, has become tomorrow's programme.

That is my second conclusion. Now for the third. Just as political democracy in France must develop into social democracy if it is to survive and be stable, so French social democracy, to survive and be stable, must be integrated in a European order, or rather—since the present war has still further diminished Europe's place on the map of the world—in a human or universal order. Democracy implies social democracy, and social democracy implies internationalism in the noblest sense of that term. Here again we shall find that the conclusion is a logically inescapable and necessary deduction from the facts. The establishment of a social democracy implies, by definition, a number of measures whose effect is to transform either the legal notion of property or, as a minimum, the con-

ditions of working-class life and the control of the nation's economy. Now it is evident that measures of this kind cannot be introduced, within the very limited field of a single country, without disturbance, damage and even the risk of failure. As long as a nation's economy is ruled by the laws of competition and of international trade, as long as it seeks markets and is itself a market, its equilibrium must be that of its environment, and its economic environment is a world economy. It is bound by the laws and customs that bind all others, outside its own boundaries, and if it runs counter too boldly to this universal code, then every infringement will make it liable to severe commercial and financial penalties, and so, in consequence, to political penalties too. A reforming nation can avoid these penalties in only two ways. Either it must cut its communications with the outside world, stop the normal working of competition and international trade, and seal itself hermetically within the framework of a despotic autarky—as Soviet Russia and Nazi Germany did—or it must accept the fact that it is no more than one part of a great whole, and suit its own actions to those dictated by the international community. France dislikes the first solution; she must therefore devote all her energies to securing the triumph of the second.

If we go back a few years, it becomes clear that the Popular Front Government, set up in France in the middle of 1936 under a Socialist Prime Minister, found itself facing precisely these two alternatives, although its programme had not included any very revolutionary social measures. It is, of course, also true that it was the victim of a form of political mendacity—by which I mean that, in spite of appearances, the Government did not in reality possess complete power; its authority was incomplete, so long as the law allowed a hostile bourgeoisie to occupy important and powerful positions. But the fundamental

and almost insoluble difficulty was the fact that the
changes which it made in the condition of the workers
and in the social structure could have been put into effect
with ease and certainty only within the framework either
of an international organisation or of a self-sufficing,
totalitarian system. Alas! The world was not ripe for the
first solution. If only it had been possible to give to the
French example the capacity to inspire, as it had done in
the great days of '89! If only we could have kindled
throughout Europe the flame of enthusiasm, whose contagion Michelet has described with such lyrical reverence!
But the reality was very different; Europe was sceptical
and hostile. Never since the signing of the Treaty of Versailles had she been farther removed from idealistic enthusiasm and, in consequence, from unity. She had neither
coherence nor confidence nor any concord of opinion, and,
as she sullenly prepared for fresh battles, she closed her
mind automatically to all thoughts of collective organisation. As for the second solution, the dictatorial imposition
of a closed economy, that was excluded in advance for a
Government which set out, as a part of the struggle
against Fascism, to re-kindle love of democracy in France
and revive its principles and practice. The Popular Front
Government was thus confronted by an inherent contradiction, which its leaders, indeed, understood and expected, and to which they sacrificed themselves (if the
term is permissible), in order to save the country from
bloodshed. I recall this item of past history only in order
to make my point clearer and to predict more accurately
what is likely to happen in the future. For tomorrow, as
yesterday, policies inspired by the same spirit will encounter similar obstacles. Tomorrow, as yesterday, the
only satisfactory solution, the only one, at any rate, that
is compatible with free institutions and the principles of
liberty, will be to knit national achievements into the

framework of an international organisation, to fit them into a structure covering all those parts of the universal economy that have reached the same stage of evolution.

We must, then, assume as a fact that any social democracy in France will of necessity be based on an international organisation. It would be useless to try to create one except on this basis, and if, by some miracle, it were created, it would not be viable, for it would be swept away the very next time a threat of war tore Europe apart once more. Almost inevitably, as the history of the last twenty-five years proves, it would collapse either under the direct onslaught of war or among its preparations and consequences, and victory, in this respect, would be only a little less pernicious than defeat. And how are we to do away permanently with wars and threats of wars without a solidly established international organisation? How are we to create a lasting spirit of solidarity? How can we arouse the complex feelings which necessarily precede such a state of mind, and which we sum up in the term "security"? The history of the last twenty-five years gives us the answer to those questions too. Immediately after every great world-wide upheaval there comes a brief period of rationality when these great tasks can be accomplished, and it is essential that the opportunity be seized, for it passes quickly, and seized with decision and enthusiasm, with firm hope and faith. After a world war, all mankind is anxious that the scourge whose recent marks it still bears shall vanish from the face of the earth for ever. We have learnt how important it is to encourage this almost unanimous desire, to give it strength, durability, efficacity, and we know what a price we paid for our failure to do so last time. Posterity will never forgive us if we make the same mistake all over again; we must be ready and firmly resolved to act this time.

The war will end one day, and that day may come soon.

It will end inevitably in the overwhelming defeat of the Axis Powers. But that alone will not create the conditions of a lasting peace. Any peace is, to a greater or lesser extent, a *Diktat* imposed by the victor on the vanquished. I have never approved the severity of much of the criticism of the authors of the Treaties of Versailles; never throughout history did representatives of victorous Powers make so great an effort to give a foundation of justice to a new organisation of society which had been created by force. Yet the Treaties of Versailles left a heritage of mistakes, illogicalities and wrongs to be paid for in torrents of blood. I am sure that those who are responsible for the future peace will be imbued, even more than were the statesmen of Versailles, with the spirit of equity, with the will to build a peace on the unshakeable foundations of justice and even—I would add—of human charity. Yet we can be sure, in advance, that this future peace, also, will not be without flaws, that it will not be perfect; that it, too, will leave a heritage of unsolved and recurrent problems, of wrongs unrighted or righted only at the cost of creating fresh injuries. Let us look for a moment at the undertakings entered into during the course of the war, dictated by the necessities of war, and ultimately to be consolidated by victory, at the claims founded on the *status quo ante*, or on strategic needs, or on the need of access to the sea; let us consider all the inextricably intermingled questions of racial and ethnic minorities, which Hitler solved so simply by extermination or forced migration. If the warlike spirit persists, if it is not replaced or mastered by the institutions of peace, then, inevitably, the treaties that end this war will contain in themselves motives—and sometimes even legitimate motives—for acts of reparation or revenge. Territorial claims will inevitably crop up sooner or later, and will be backed by force, if the whole conception of frontiers does not gradually lose caste, does not shed, bit by bit, some

of its present importance, through the close incorporation of nations in an international body, competent, among other things, to undo any obvious mistakes and to make the appropriate legal changes when the *de facto* situation has been too radically altered. On one point my convictions are profound and unshakeable, whatever the world may say. If this war does not at last give rise to fundamentally stable international institutions, to a really effective international power, then it will not be the last war. Europe and the world will again be exposed to this scourge, and the whole structure of political and social democracy, whether on the national or international plane, will be threatened with ruin, and this time perhaps with irrevocable ruin.

International organisation, a European order, these are expressions that today are on everyone's lips. The totalitarian dictators and their followers never make a speech or deliver a message without invoking the European Order. In France, the men of the Armistice, its theorists, executants and apologists, are never tired of explaining to us that they have betrayed France in order to remain faithful to Europe, and thus to International Socialism. It is hardly necessary for me to say once again how utterly I repudiate the abominable abuse of expressions drawn from the vocabulary of our Socialist Movement. When Hitler and Goebbels talk of organising Europe, when the French "collaborators" echo their words, we know what they mean and what they want. In present realities, their European Order is nothing but the utilisation of all European resources, the extraction and extortion of all we have, for the benefit of the Axis, and their so-called "organisation" of Europe is no more than the future total enslavement of Europe by the Nazi *régime*. Thus, the same words are used with diametrically opposite meanings. When *we*

talk of a "European Order", we are thinking, not of war, but of peace; when we talk of "European Organisation", we are thinking, not of a common subjection to the domination of a tyrant, but of the federation of free and equal nations, of a League of Nations! Let us not be afraid to admit that the ideal of 1919 was a fine one. It is cheap and easy today to mock at the League, but if we have the courage to ignore the mockery, we must agree that we shall yet have to return to the same inspiration.

As it was conceived at the end of the last war by all the great democrats of both hemispheres, the League of Nations was a noble and magnificent creation. I believe this to be true, in spite of its failure, which I do not seek in any way to minimise or excuse. I remain convinced, despite its failure, that it would still be sufficient and able to impose respect for international order among those political societies that gave it birth. Its failure, moreover, was something from which the world will have to learn its lesson. The League of Nations, created by the Treaties of Versailles, failed because great Powers like Russia and the U.S.A., whose support was essential, were outside it from the start. It failed because its founders, trying to disarm suspicions here and fears there, did not dare to give it the instruments and the living strength that it needed to function properly. It failed because it was not itself a great sovereign Power, distinct from national sovereign Powers and greater than they; because it had neither the political authority nor the material force to enable it to carry out its decisions and impose its will on national States; because its powers were too restricted and too intermittent to allow it to cover the same fields of activity as national sovereign States. It would be easy to quote arguments and facts in support of each of these reasons. If we take the antithesis of each of them, we shall have outlined the principles which must be applied this time

in order to have a living and effective international organisation. All the Great Powers, and particularly America and Russia, must be parties to the new Covenant. The international body must have the institutions and the powers it needs to do what it is created to do; in other words, it must be boldly and openly set up as a super-State on a level above national sovereignties, and that, in turn, means that the member-States must have accepted in advance as much limitation and subordination of their particular sovereignties as this superior sovereign Power requires. The international body must be in a position to see that refractory nations carry out its decisions, which means that it must have a superiority of force, arising either from the exclusive right to use certain weapons, such as military planes, or from an adequate degree of disarmament by the member States. The super-State must have its own organs of government and a policy of its own, instead of being governed by conferences of delegates, each of whom is still serving the interests and obeying the instructions of the State he represents. It must be kept permanently at work by the multiplicity of its functions, for a real International Community is more than just a Court of Arbitration or a meeting-place for diplomats. It must create an international order, if it intends to preserve peace, and to do so its activity must be continuous, for economic conflicts and crises will threaten its order just as surely as political disagreements.

The founders of the League of Nations, well aware of this need for continuous action, set up the complementary institution known as the International Labour Office. But the I.L.O. had even less power to take and carry out decisions than the League itself. This time the international body must have authority enough to enforce its decisions on all the labour problems which, as I have shown elsewhere, cannot be satisfactorily solved by

nations acting separately. It must be prepared to lay down rules and give decisions on the urgent problems of markets, raw materials, population movements, which lie so dangerously along the frontiers of economics and politics. It must settle customs questions, find a remedy for the general currency crisis, perhaps by introducing an international currency. It must have the means to operate great public-works schemes on an international plane— public health, industrial equipment, transport and colonisation schemes in the widest sense of the term—so that, little by little, nations can be raised to the same level of civilisation. And to this end it must be empowered to issue loans and to have its own budget, derived no longer from the miserable voluntary contributions of member-States, but from low taxes on articles of general consumption, or from its ownership of certain international monopolies. . . . Immediately after the last war a number of Socialists met at Frankfurt. Among them were two now dead —Matteotti, murdered by Mussolini, and Hilferding, handed over to Hitler by the French Government—and the others represented all the belligerent nations. They met to study the problem of reparations, but they produced, and at that date, a plan similar to the one I have just outlined.

All these suggestions could easily be amplified and justified from the most recent textbook of world history. But if we really want to put our finger on the weakness and precariousness of any peace that is not based on a strong international structure, we have only to look at the German and Russian problems. Hitler will be beaten, and what then happens to him is of little importance; but when he has collapsed and disappeared from the scene, what will the victors do with his country? They will find themselves facing a dilemma that is not capable of being

intelligently resolved in the Europe we now know—that is, in a Europe of independent sovereign Powers. On the one hand, the general consensus of opinion, embittered, alas, by hatred and the desire for vengeance, which Hitler has called forth throughout the whole world, will be that Germany must this time be rendered for ever incapable of entering on another terrible adventure, such as we have just experienced. There will be a refusal—legitimate, I agree—to distinguish between the tyrant who has deceived a whole nation and the nation that pitilessly served the tyrant, and men will protest that peace is no more than a lying and cruel simulacrum, if the world is not fully protected against future irruptions of German barbarism. All that will be natural and reasonable. Yet, if we look at the well-worn track of history, and think in terms of independent sovereign nations, then it is surely clear that these natural and reasonable demands can lead only to divisions, dismemberments, annexations, restrictions and indemnities. This, no doubt, is what will be demanded, and the most clamorous voices will be those of some of our present "collaborators". On the other hand, if the men who are responsible for making the peace have the courage to reflect and look back, they must surely realise what the future would hold for a world order founded on force and its abuse. Hatred cannot banish hatred, nor violence put an end to violence. A whole nation cannot simply be annihilated with its language, traditions and legends. Might abused breeds a spirit of revenge that time will not efface, and sooner or later the hazards of history will offer it unexpected opportunities. However harsh the conditions imposed on Hitler's Germany, they can hardly be more so than those that were imposed on Prussia after Jena. Who could have foretold that, after such disaster and such mutilation, Prussia would recover her strength? Yet, only a few years after

Jena came Leipzig, and only a few decades separated Tilsit and Sedan. There is only one way to resolve the contradiction, to make Germany harmless in a peaceful and stable Europe, and that is to incorporate the German nation in an international community powerful enough to re-educate her, discipline her and, if necessary, master her. If it became necessary to use force in order to compel Germany to enter such a community, then the use of force would be as legitimate and as salutary as a paternal rebuke, for it would be used in the service of justice and peace. In those circumstances, time and custom would bring adaptation and co-ordination, and so lead to pacification and reconciliation.

What I have said of Germany is no less patently true of Russia, though for quite different reasons. Already the Russian problem, the Russian enigma, is casting its cloud over the face and the very hope of peace. I have already pointed out that there are countries, chief among which comes France, in which normal government becomes virtually impossible if a section of the working class remains either directly or indirectly dependent on a foreign Power. Similarly, it will be virtually impossible to preserve a stable peace among the nations of Europe and of the world, if they are continually disturbed by risks of an internal revolution, prepared and engineered from outside by the same Power. What future can there be for either democracy or peace if such a serious difficulty cannot be removed? For my part, I do not think that it will be removed as a result of some modification in the Soviet system of government; it is unrealistic to imagine that there is enough contact between Russia and other countries to enable a common level to be established. Russia will, no doubt, retain all the essential characteristics of her present system; she is unlikely to modify either her system of property or her form of government in order to fall into

line with the rest of the world. On the other hand, her outward conduct, her behaviour towards other Powers, will be found to have changed considerably, as a result both of the prestige won in her heroic struggle and of the consolidation and recognition of her strength that victory will bring her. Russia will come out of the war cured of the growing pains from which she has been suffering for the last twenty-five years, confident of her strength, more powerful and less afraid, and in consequence able to make the necessary effort to co-operate in international life without provoking new discords, that are themselves a threat to peace.

What are we entitled to expect of Russia? That she shall no longer maintain alien elements within other nations, and no longer behave towards other nations as if she were herself alien to them—in other words, that she shall give up her provocative policy of ignoring all the traditional concepts of morality and humanity. There can and must be a Concordat covering difficulties of this kind. It should lay down rules for the co-operation of Russia with the rest of the world, and we may perhaps hope that its provisions will be fixed and their observance ensured by the arbitration and persuasive pressure of the international organisation itself, of which Russia will be a member. I use the word Concordat intentionally, and yet with some hesitation. I am, of course, fully aware that it has been used hitherto to describe an agreement between a Government and the Roman Catholic Church, and I do not want the associations which it conjures up to offend any susceptibilities. But if we look at it objectively, it must surely be clear that what I am suggesting here is precisely an agreement between nation-States and a temporal Church, delimiting the respective domains of national sovereignty and of orthodox belief. I think that a Russia that keeps the Soviet system would nevertheless

agree to a compromise of this kind, and I base my confidence on the fact that it is clearly in her interests to do so. She will neither want nor be able to isolate herself from the Anglo-Saxon Powers, without whose assistance she could not have defeated Nazi aggression, and without whose continued co-operation she will be unable to restore her ravaged economy. For the Soviet Union, incorporation in an international body will mean full, unreserved and unqualified recognition of her position as an equal, which is something that her leaders have wanted for a long time and that no country has so far granted her—not even those who have signed treaties and negotiated agreements with her. Finally, Russia will be anxious that none shall outpace her, in the eyes of the workers of the world, in the quest for peace, and she knows that enthusiasm for international organisation will be considered the most visible and certain evidence of her determination to get it. I would add, indeed, that only in this way can Russia counterbalance the weight of responsibility for the war that now lies so heavily upon her. If, by isolationism or intolerance, she were to obstruct the work of building up a lasting peace, she would undo the immense services that her heroism has rendered to humanity, and so would revert to the position that she held in the eyes of the civilised world in September, 1939, on the morrow of that criminal blunder whose very memory must be wiped out. . . .

Both association of ideas and the logic of my argument lead me at this point to consider the desirability of including in the international body another member, the Vatican, the Holy See. The inclusion of the Holy See on exactly the same terms as nation-States would be the most striking indication that in the world of tomorrow, temporal powers will not be the only ones to count. If the

Vatican were to consent to active co-operation, all its disputes with Governments, which now disturb the internal politics of so many countries and lead to intolerable conflicts, could be treated on a higher level and settled by general Concordats. A Church which is pacific both by definition (since it is the incarnation of a religion of peace) and by constitution (since it is organised on an international basis) would surely be suitably employed in this way. Papal influence, as it has always been, is still used on the side of lasting peace, founded on justice, on equality of men and nations and on the sanctity of contract. The first public speech made by Pope Pius XI from the balcony of St. Peter's after the Lateran treaties was a pathetic plea for peace.

The Church needs peace, and the work of organising peace needs, no less, the support of the Church. But if the Catholic Church, alone of all faiths in the regions forming part of the international community, is organised as a centralised and world-wide hierarchy, it is far from being the only one to which many men subscribe. The principle of equality between religions, as between nation-States, must, therefore, be recognised, and all must be invited on an equal footing. It will be difficult to work out a satisfactory method of representation, for other religions are not organised hierarchically like an Empire, as is the Catholic Church. But, assuming that difficulties of this kind can ultimately be overcome, as I believe they can, we are bound logically to conclude that the insuperable obstacle would be the Catholic Church itself. No doubt the Church will be warmly and helpfully sympathetic in its attitude to the international experiment, but will nevertheless in all probability not become an active partner, will not undertake specific obligations, or impose duties upon herself. Is it conceivable that she would

accord equality of rights, or even *de facto* recognition, to other religions that she regards as heretical or pagan? Could she agree to a kind of sharing out of the sum of human faith, when divine revelation has promised her that in the end she shall win over all men's souls, so that to abandon her right to them would be to renounce her divinely appointed mission? Could she accept the supremacy of a super-State, abandon to it some of her sovereignty, when in her own view the mere fact of her existence makes her herself supreme? In a word, could she take her share of responsibility for an international organisation other than one whose principles were laid down by herself?

If we turn from the field of principle to that of practice, if we consider that the day-to-day work of an international community would be to settle disputes, pass judgment, to define, and perhaps apply sanctions, then surely the Church could not consent, even as a member of the international community, to side with one State against another—that is, with some of the faithful against others—when she considers herself to be the mother of all? Both during the last war and this she refused to do so; how, then, could she do so in peace-time?

When I examined the position of the Russians, I assumed that the temporal interests of the Russian State would take precedence over the rigid requirements of Communist doctrine, but I can make no such assumption in the case of the Papacy, for the Papacy no longer has any temporal burdens. A sixteenth-century Pope, who had an army, entered into coalitions, went to war, might perhaps have hesitated between some urgent need of the Papal states and the uncompromising rigours of Catholic doctrine, but today the Papacy can no longer be confronted by any such dilemma and has no need to consider

these compromises. The Church is exclusively a spiritual power. That is precisely why her presence in the international community seems to me pre-eminently desirable, and precisely why I hold also that it would be futile to hope for it.

CHAPTER VIII

I FULLY REALISE that to look forward in this way to an international society ruling the world of tomorrow is to arouse, not only the facile scepticism of those who, at bottom, are only over-credulous (and who can therefore be left out of account), but also the perfectly honourable and legitimate feeling that we call patriotism. Patriotic feeling, always more acute and sensitive after a defeat, becomes, by the same fact of defeat, more touchy and more jealous. I can hear the objections that will be put forward : "What! France has not yet arisen from her ruins, her wounds are not yet healed, and you talk about Europe and the world! You invoke all over again the humanitarian soft-heartedness from which we have suffered so much in the past, and that at a time when our sense of patriotic duty should be our one clear-cut, imperative and exclusive preoccupation. No! France first, France above all! France's only chance of salvation lies in the egoistic devotion of all her children."

It is true that, in our country's misfortune, we become more deeply and clearly conscious of the love we all bear her, even though at other times it may go unrecognised within us. It is true that the history of recent years ought to have taught us how to preserve all the natural dignity and vigour of patriotic feeling. And yet I believe that when I try to show that the Europe and the world of tomorrow must be organised within a larger framework than that of the nation, if they are not once again to revert to chaos and war, I have said nothing that need offend, injure or lessen patriotic feeling. I am not suggesting that patriotism

must go, that it must give way, as if it were an old-fashioned instinct, belonging to a past age, and no longer corresponding to the aspirations of the modern mind. Nor do I think that it must be absorbed—which, in effect, means dissipated—in a more general and, if you like, more noble sentiment, such as faith in human solidarity, love of humanity. Love of country is eternal. It is on the same plane as love of family, love of one's native town or village, of all the fundamental realities that in our heart of hearts we hold nearest and dearest. But I am quite sure that there is nothing incompatible between patriotism and humanism—or, if you like, between national and international loyalties. Love of a nation and love of the human race, as one great man once said, can co-exist in the same conscience, as naturally as patriotism and love of family, or as patriotism and religious belief.

For evidence of this, we need look no further than the citizens and soldiers of the Revolution of '89. It was not only their ideal, but their positive and well-considered intention, to set up one comprehensive human society, founded on universal principles. Yet, never at any period in our history was patriotism more ardent and unyielding. Never was the soil of France defended with more heroic tenacity. The explanation is simple. It is that the irreducible basic element of any international structure must be free peoples, independent nations. The primary objective of every international community is to guarantee the liberty and independence of the separate nations of which it is made up. Nations will join together and organise themselves in communities, while yet remaining themselves, formed by their particular history and traditions, with their own tastes, preferences, national characteristics and peculiarities. National characteristics are the necessary constituents of human harmony; they

will be respected and, indeed, encouraged within the international organisation, just as individual characteristics are preserved within the organisation of society. In neither case does the existence of a community require, or even imply, any kind of official or compulsory uniformity. When I look forward to the future Comity of Nations, I cannot help recalling an expression of Hugo: "I see them", he said, "gathered around the common source of Justice and Peace like sisters round the fireside", sisters of the same blood, but distinguished from each other by their clothes, gestures, accent and facial expressions. Jaurès once said that, while a little internationalism took one farther away from patriotism, much internationalism brought one closer to it again. The real meaning of these words, as I understand them, is that the individuality of nations can flower most freely and luxuriantly in the serene atmosphere of peace and comfort which international solidarity carries with it, that men become conscious of its full value only when they can feel its impact in the deepest fibres of their being. I add, and with some pride, that this harmonising of humanism and patriotism comes more naturally and easily to a Frenchman than to the citizens of any other nation, for it is a French characteristic, as I have already remarked, to understand—as France has always understood and still understands today—the noble urge to think and act for universal causes.

The risk of friction and internal conflict will, no doubt, still exist, and will never be completely eliminated. It is not always an easy matter to order even one's personal life, and place in proper hierarchy the diverse passions that make up a human character. But an effort of integrity and intelligence can usually find some way of harmonising them, and that effort will almost always take the form of freeing either patriotism or humanism from

the natural impurities that had corrupted it. For there is an instinct, as old as the history of men, akin to the spirit of the tribe or of the clan, which leads us to abandon and almost to condemn every attempt at rationality and objectivity, where the relations of our own and other countries are concerned. "I do not need to look farther; my country cannot be wrong, because it is my country." Or again: "My country is the natural and predestined leader of others . . .". This instinct is mistakenly called patriotism, but it can be described accurately only by the pejorative terms of chauvinism and nationalism. It breeds arrogance and hatred, it holds sway in other countries just as it does in our own, and the conflicts between peoples to which it gives rise admit neither of arbitration, nor—more important—of reconciliation. Alongside this instinct there is another sentiment, of much more recent origin, for it has developed only under the impetus of certain forms of revolutionary propaganda, that is the exact opposite of chauvinism. In any international dispute its exponents disavow in advance, on *a priori* principles, the attitude and interests of their country. "My country must be wrong, because it is my country." Those who hold such sentiments become alienated from the national community just as surely as the blind nationalists become imprisoned within it. But it would be wrong to describe it as internationalism; for in reality it is no more than inverted nationalism. Any attempt to distinguish real nationalism from chauvinism and real internationalism from inverted nationalism will reveal that the two authentic sentiments are, not only compatible, but almost always co-existent. Real patriotism and internationalism both imply a readiness to judge international relations and all the problems arising from them by the criteria of reason and moral principle that are common to all men, and to do so, not with absolute

impartiality—for that would be unnatural—but with an effort to achieve as much impartiality as is humanly possible. And, looking at the problem in this way, no honest man can fail to come to the conclusion that, at the present stage of human evolution, the liberty and the prosperity of one nation are virtually inseparable from those of others, and that love of country cannot, either rationally or emotionally, be separated from certain other beliefs which are valid for the whole human race.

The foundations of the new world should therefore be laid in this order ; within the nation, political democracy will prove its worth and strengthen its position by becoming also a social democracy ; together, the national democracies will maintain an international order that completes their structure and keeps a balance between them. When this war has freed humanity from the last convulsions of barbarism and despotism—and that will surely be the meaning and the result of the Allied victory—men will have to turn their efforts towards the construction of some world order of this kind. It is in this sense that I interpret the Atlantic Charter, signed by Mr. Winston Churchill and President Roosevelt, in the names of the two great Anglo-Saxon Powers, and agreed to unreservedly by all the other allied States. The triumph of liberty and justice in war will lead naturally to the organisation of liberty and justice in peace. I can see, indeed, no other road for the world to take, in its search, either for the satisfaction of its immediate needs, or for the attainment of its future security.

I have given careful consideration to the possibility that, in expressing this belief in the logic of history, I have perhaps erred on the side of over-confidence, or have succumbed to the temptation, to which men who have been in public life are peculiarly prone, to cast the present

E

and the future into the mould of the past. It is true that all that I have done, in outlining this picture of the world of the future, is to return to conceptions more than twenty-five years old, and that all my plans and hopes for the post-war years are merely a repetition of the hopes entertained by my contemporaries at the time of the signing of the Treaty of Versailles—hopes which we showed ourselves, later, unable to realise. Why should the picture be original? While problems remain essentially the same, their solutions cannot be expected to undergo any fundamental modifications either. A generation cannot change at will the nature of the problems with which history is to confront it. On the other hand, it is no less true that progress such as I have outlined assumes peaceful labour, friendly understandings between nations and a solidarity which approximates to union, and I am fully aware that, to many minds, the realities of the future appear in a totally different light. "How", I shall be asked, "can you expect the ordered beauty of classical architecture to spring from a soil that will be torn by popular upheavals, once peace has liberated the forces whose expansion has been so long held in check. No doubt, humanity will discover some day an order of its own, but only after an inevitable period of dislocation and chaos, and through means very different from the peaceful and considered will of nations! There has been too much misery and suffering, there will remain too much legitimate anger, and none of those can be appeased by the serene contemplation of an ideal! Then again, we shall certainly have to take account of the force of attraction exercised by the Soviet Union and of the natural prestige of a Power which, if not the sole conqueror, was certainly the first to check the military might of Germany. We shall have to reckon with the work of propaganda and organisation carried out in the face of every kind of danger by the Communist parties of all the

occupied countries. Europe cannot escape a revolutionary crisis after the war, and it is from this crisis alone, and by methods which, like the crisis itself, are essentially revolutionary, that justice and peace can be born. . . ." This is the kind of historical development that my arguments would seem to have left entirely out of account. I understand the views of those who think that this is what is most likely to happen, but I cannot share them.

Nor do I hold that war—and particularly a long war— creates a revolutionary situation, that it brings to victor and vanquished alike the opportunity to make a revolution. Twenty-three years ago, in 1918, I found it difficult to accept this mechanical association of the conclusion of a war and the outbreak of a revolution, and today I have still no hesitation in rejecting it. Not that experience or age have deadened my revolutionary ardour. How, indeed, could a profession of revolutionary principles cause alarm to anyone, in an age when everyone, everywhere, including even the most bare-faced reactionaries, is labelled "revolutionary"? I reject it because I perceive more and more clearly that the essence of all revolutions lies in their aims and achievements, and not in the means by which they obtain their results. Any fundamental change in political structure—and so *a fortiori* in the systems governing production and property—even obtained by eminently legal and peaceful means, is a revolutionary process; violent insurrection, the seizure of power by force of arms, even terror, would be merely unsuccessful attempts at revolution if they did not bring about a clearly marked political or social transformation. Now, war can, in certain circumstances, create conditions favourable to insurrection and to the seizure of power, but it cannot create conditions favourable to revolutionary transformation. This conclusion reinforces my previous arguments,

which gave us grounds for the fear that Allied victory would be followed by a Communist propaganda campaign in France in favour of insurrectional violence. The most forcible and urgent collective feelings throughout Europe at that time will doubtless be much simpler than we tend to assume. Men are the same everywhere, and what they want, first and foremost, is the satisfaction of the elementary human needs, material, emotional and even intellectual, that war does not eliminate, though it makes them seem less important, and for which the coming of peace seems to promise immediate relief. Men have been separated from their families and forced to leave their homes, and they want to see them again. They have been hungry, and they want to eat their fill. They have been bound and gagged by every kind of violence, and they want to live their own lives again and to speak their minds freely. For months and years they suffered from "the world's insomnia", now they want peace and rest. These are the fundamental feelings that will emerge from the froth of demand, anger and reprisal. There is only one collective need that a long war can inflame to the point of transforming it into a revolutionary passion, and that is quite simply the need of peace. It was this need that Communism exploited so efficiently, both inside and outside Russia, during the last stages of the last war and during the early post-war period, and that the leaders of the "National Revolution" did their best to exalt and to exploit before and after the Armistice. It exists, and will continue to exist for some time after victory has been won. Over-taxed and worn out by war, men will want to be sure—as they did in 1918—that their sacrifice is at least of some benefit to their children. Then it will be the duty of those who have some influence over them to take this potential enthusiasm, keep it alive, and so prevent it from exhausting itself in impotent convulsions during the period,

in all probability short, before it is submerged by habit and routine.

It will not be difficult to convince the peoples of the world that true peace can be built up only on the three-fold foundation of political democracy, social democracy and international order. It is, indeed, almost mathematically certain that the work of world reconstruction will move towards that goal, for its starting-point will be the destruction of the totalitarian dictatorships and it will be controlled by the two greatest democracies in the world. Nor do I think that nations will take long, in the face of the overwhelming evidence, to realise that history is offering them a chance of a fresh start. Material obstacles have collapsed, and will crumble at the first onslaught. The political power of the bourgeoisie no longer exists, and its economic power will, in all probability, vanish as soon as it is attacked. In France, and indeed throughout the European continent, the whole bourgeois structure is buried beneath its own ruins. In the great Anglo-Saxon countries the bourgeoisie has already consented to an infusion of new blood that is equivalent to abdication. The winds of history are favourable, and everywhere the workers are conscious of being carried by the tide. But this is where the real difficulty arises. Will they be worthy of their destiny? Will they be able to play the parts for which history has cast them? Will they understand, or can they be made to understand, that favourable material conditions, even if they are overwhelmingly favourable, cannot alone carry them into power, much less keep them there? Can they understand that if, to seize power, they will need both force and the authority that come from being in harmony with the nature and the trend of economic evolution, they will have no less need of dignity, of the ascendancy, in a word, that comes from moral

superiority and efficiency. For a transfer of power to be consolidated and established before history, it must be acceptable to the conscience of mankind no less than to human emotion and to human reason. It must call forth from every sincere man the spontaneous tribute, "It had to be", but not that alone. He must also say, "It is right, it is good and it is beautiful ". Like all other peoples, the French people will fulfil their mission—in other words, they will build the world of their ideals, only if they show themselves able to cultivate and cherish in themselves those virtues that must be present to justify any form of human supremacy, the virtues of courage, generosity of heart, righteousness of mind and conscience, abnegation of self in favour of the good of all.

This is what we should be preaching. This is the task we ought now to be undertaking, and we may have only a short time in which to accomplish it. In human affairs, new roads must be taken boldly and quickly. Otherwise there is always the danger that the attraction of the old ruts will be so strong that men will be pulled back almost automatically into them. There is, therefore, not a moment to lose. Above all, it must be borne in mind that the effort will be incomplete and fruitless if it is limited to the sum of individual *examens de conscience*. The ethics of the group—of political, social and moral groups—are no less real than individual ethics, and it is precisely the organs of collective life that need thorough moral renewal. It is evident, for example, that national democracy would undergo a sea change if the interplay of forces within the nation were not in the future to be judged according to criteria of good faith, integrity and honour. Democracy everywhere presupposes freedom of action and, consequently, political conflict. But it does not follow that there are no rules in this civil conflict, that no holds are barred or that its ends justify any means, and this is as true of parties, social groups

and the Press as it is of individuals. No advantage won, no plea of necessity, can justify lies, slander, dishonesty, the abuse of force, failure to fulfil obligations or to keep one's word. The argument becomes even stronger if we turn to the international order, for its foundations *must* be the belief in the validity and the sacredness of contracts; if that foundation is lacking, it is built on sand, and must collapse. No doubt, contracts will still be violated in the international sphere, just as crimes are still committed in civil society. What is essential is that at least the injured nation shall be able to count with certainty on the support of others against the offender. In other words, morality must remain the law, and the offending nation the exception.

Moreover, at every stage of this collective life subordination of private interests to those of the community must be recognised as an inescapable obligation, and treated as such. Social life would be impossible if the individual did not subordinate his particular and temporary interests to the more general and permanent interests of the group. The difficulty is to secure from political and social groups what is required of the individual—namely, voluntary subordination to the general and permanent interests of humanity. Obstinate partisanship, narrow-minded clannishness and jingo nationalism are essentially the same as the selfishness of the individual. This renunciation of rivalry and of claims arising from the divergence of immediate interests, this spontaneous surrender to a higher will, this consciousness of permanent contact with and dependence on a higher order of reality extending by stages to embrace the broadest of all concepts, is what Socrates and Plato meant by wisdom and what a Christian thinker like Pascal calls humility. But humility of this kind should be a source of strength, and men should be proud to feel it. In the past, men felt that it implied faith

and obedience. We must see that it leads to faith and action.

Can it be a Socialist who is putting forward this view? Indeed it can, and one, moreover, who flatters himself that he is being perfectly consistent. The aim of Socialism is to set up a universal society founded on equal justice for all men and on equal peace for all nations. Many means must work together to this end, but no Socialist worthy of the name would claim that the end could be achieved unless human personality is perfected, enriched and deepened in the process, or unless the spirit of discipline and sacrifice are continually developed and more widely spread. Socialism has never denied either "moral" or "spiritual" values and has never repudiated either the sentiment of virtue or that of honour. All that it has done, like Christianity before it, is to interpret these concepts differently.

Socialism has often been reproached for attracting only the unfortunate multitudes by holding out to them the prospect of what Renan last century called "the satisfaction of their purely material needs" and of what today we call "*jouissances*". The suppression of poverty, of the scourges of cold, hunger and disease, are not "purely material ends". What is there about belief in social justice that could make it more materialist than belief in charity? When a worker demands better wages, he is not thinking only of piling his table a little higher with food, but also of a larger and healthier home, of better-clad and better-educated children. Life, family, home, the healthy growth of children and security in old age are not "material" preoccupations. All the same, if Socialism had restricted itself to demands like these, noble and selfish at the same time, it would not have attracted the mass support it now has. Socialism teaches its followers that

their own individual and selfish needs are inextricably related to those of their fellow men, that their rights and their liberty are inseparable from the rights and the liberty of others. It teaches men that they can satisfy their own needs only together with those of others, by a common effort on the part of all to create a whole as full, coherent and harmonious as that which obtains in the physical realms of the universe. Socialist philosophy is, therefore, inseparable from the most comprehensive of human ideals, the belief in the universality of ordered life and human bonds. Jaurès, for instance, always regarded the concept of Humanity as the essential principle of all human progress. It afforded a new basis for virtually immutable moral precepts, as well as for ever-changing customs and rights, and a new raw material for artists and philosophers. The idea of Humanity, like that of God in the Middle Ages, could inform all the different aspects of individual life, and all forms of social existence. This "complete Socialism" is in no sense of the word a religion, for it has neither dogma nor rites nor priests, but it does appeal to and satisfy the religious urge in men. It teaches its own concepts of what is good and right, encourages the practice of conscientious scruple, and asks its followers to base their conduct on ideals that transcend the sphere of the individual and are their own reward, and it can do so because the assent it receives comes near to the kind of religious faith to which the sacrifice of individual interest is normal and legitimate.

How is it that Socialism has been so misunderstood? How have fair-minded people come so to depreciate ideas that millions of people throughout the world cultivated in their own hearts as the highest of human aspirations? I have already tried to show the extent to which we Socialists must ourselves be held responsible for this misconception which does us so much harm, but I think I can

explain in a few words the real reason for the mistake. The development of great human ideas, and even of religions, is influenced as much by the resistance they encounter as by the nature of their own initial impetus. Socialism had first to survive, then to make a niche for itself and to make its way; in order to establish its right to live, it had first to criticise its opponents, and, to protect its early achievements, it had to struggle. Capitalist society, misled by the instinct of self-preservation, treated Socialism as an implacable enemy with which no compromise was possible and which must be overthrown and destroyed without mercy. Attack was held to be the best form of self-defence, and so the pulpit gave way to the battlefield, and battles inevitably call forth all man's most primitive instincts, including fear—on both sides—greed and intolerance.

This polemical phase now belongs to the past. Socialism can move from the militant to the victorious period. The social system which it attacked and by which it was in turn attacked is now falling into ruin, and even where it still survives does so without belief in itself and in contradiction with its own laws. The men and parties who have most bitterly opposed Socialist assumptions and axioms have now taken them over for their own purposes. Today, whether consciously or not, society is being reconstituted everywhere on principles laid down by Socialists. Even the Catholic Church, although it has never withdrawn its condemnation of the principles of Socialism, has, in the course of the last fifty years, adopted points of view, particularly on the problems of labour and property, that take it along a road parallel with ours and perhaps even converging with ours, in a way that at least rules out all real incompatibility. In such a situation polemics are almost pointless and conflict baseless. The task of the Socialist movement is now only one of preaching and

conversion. Like the Church in those periods of history when its temporal interests had dangerously obscured the real purpose for which it existed, it must now rediscover the purity of its initial inspiration.

Does that mean that religious propaganda is one of the tasks of Socialism? In a sense it does. Spinoza said that "if we have a concept of God, every action that falls within our control must be based on our religion". If for what Spinoza calls "the concept of God", we substitute the concept of Humanity, of all mankind, of the universe seen as a whole, the statement remains true. There is no doubt that in this form it corresponds to the peculiar genius of France, whose people have, throughout their history, from the Crusades to the French Revolution, held that human solidarity and a desire for universalism constituted the highest form of patriotism. This is what men and nations must teach—I am almost tempted to say preach—if they are to be worthy of their historic mission. The aim of their mutual efforts must be to improve man and society, to stimulate and encourage man's potentialities for good, so that he can make his personal contribution towards the creation of the best possible society. Now is the time to undertake these great tasks, when the ground has been prepared by the political crises which shook Europe before the war, by the war itself and by defeat. Hemmed round as we are by day-to-day responsibilities and anxieties, we are never optimistic enough in our outlook, for optimism in world affairs demands appreciation and understanding of the time factor. Who can be sure that a century or two hence, when philosophers can regard the events of our time with complete detachment, they will not conclude that even Nazism and Fascism had some share in the providential march of progress?

Only a short time ago I re-read a work of Renan, published only a few months before the war of 1870, in

which he foretold and seemed to hope for an outbreak of those barbarian forces that he regarded as a kind of latent residue, a dynamic vitality that humanity holds perpetually in reserve. If, he says, these barbarian forces are released, more than that, if they spread widely over highly civilised countries at a time when their vitality is temporarily exhausted, then the effect may very well be one of stimulation and renewal. The flood passes, the barbarian elements are driven back to their Stygian retreats, but the fertility, the renewal, are none the less real and lasting. I have already explained why I cannot admit that totalitarian barbarism possesses this stimulating and fertilising virtue. Renan was thinking of possible historical developments of a totally different kind. He was thinking of the tides of youth and freshness that for thousands of years at periodic intervals have submerged the known forms of civilisation, of the alluvium spread by the German tribes at the time of the Roman Empire and, in modern times, by the spread of the Slav and even of the Oriental races. But he was not thinking, and could never have thought, of looking upon the destruction of civilisation as an ideal, nor of suggesting that one section of civilised humanity might come deliberately to adopt as its own ideal a return to primitive savagery. This kind of development is no river bringing down its fertile mud, but a desert wind that scatters in sterile dust the strata of soil slowly built up through the ages. Some poisons can cure, but others are always fatal. I therefore refuse categorically to apply Renan's argument to totalitarian dictatorships. But let us assume for a moment, even though the assumption is rationally inadmissible, that this barbarian fertiliser has renewed the productive capacity of an exhausted soil. Let us admit that, by some historical accident incomprehensible to contemporary minds, the plunder of the soil of Europe by Nazism and Fascism has made it possible for the Social-

ist way of life to come at last to its full flowering in the lives of all men. What a restitution, what a magnificent revenge that would be! It would point to the existence within the universe of a harmony of design that made the *raison d'être* of the totalitarian dictatorships the ultimate emergence in France of that democratic Socialism which is the living and creative element of international democracy!

In the work of Renan to which I have just referred, after emphasising the "uniqueness" and "decisiveness" of the French Revolution—which he calls "the glory of France, the most French of all epics"—and after claiming that for centuries "the Revolution will divide men and be one of the pretexts of their loves and hates", Renan goes on to add these strangely prophetic words: "Wherever we find, in the history of a nation, some unique event, its cost is almost always a long period of suffering, and sometimes the very eclipse of the nation itself. It was so in the case of Judea, of Greece, of Italy. These nations created something unique, in which the human race itself has found life and profit, but they did so only at the cost of centuries of humiliation, and of eclipse as nations. The nations that created religion, art, science, the Empire, the Papacy— all of which are universal rather than national creations— were more than nations; but they were also, and by virtue of the same fact, less than nations, in the sense that they were the victims of their own achievement." The word expiation has become familiar to us; we are always being told that our country today is expiating the Revolution of 1789 and the train of errors that has followed it for more than a century! But these claims are no more than vulgar polemics; Renan, who is a historian and a philosopher, uses the term in a way that makes it both nobler and more just.

What France is expiating, in his view, is not a false or

evil work, but one which was too fine, too vast and above all too wide in scope for one nation to accomplish alone, and he sees its consequences as a sacrifice rather than an expiation. A nation which was the first to conceive of and to introduce universal truths sacrifices itself to all mankind in so doing. But Renan held that the consequences of this holocaust would not be as lasting in the case of France as they were in those of Judea, Greece and Italy, precisely because France's revolutionary achievement was less significant and less "universal". He thought that the expiation for the French Revolution would last throughout the nineteenth century, after which, having paid for her noble recklessness, France would rise again, younger and stronger, just as Germany recovered after the period of political decline which was her way of expiating the Reformation. Renan's calculations were inaccurate; the expiation lasted half a century longer. Today France has recovered her former status among nations; now it is her turn to receive the deferred reward for the sacrifice from which the whole of humanity had benefited.

All these reflections must surely combine to justify our confidence, to give us comfort and encouragement, and to convince us that justice will be done. If we should ever be tempted to discouragement in face of the miseries and evils of our times, then we have only to look beyond the present brief moment of time towards the past and the future; we must learn to see, beyond the little world of our immediate surroundings, the universe that is a harmonious whole. That does not mean that immediate tasks are to be neglected in favour of empty speculation. We are not dreamers, we cannot afford to dream. But this moment will pass, the dictatorships that now hold Europe in their grip will pass, present sufferings and ills will pass and the eternal truths will remain. There is a human destiny which is linked to the laws of the universe, into which

we must write our own brief fate. We are working *in* the present but not *for* the present. How many times in public meetings have I quoted these words of Nietzsche: "Let the future and what it holds in the far distance be your guide today and every day. My advice to you is to love, not just your neighbour today, but those who will come long after you." Why should the human race, or the French people, prove unworthy in the future of all that they have achieved in the past? Wisdom, science and art are human creations. Why, then, should the human race be incapable of creating justice, fraternity and peace? Humanity produced Plato, Homer, Shakespeare, Hugo, Michael Angelo, Beethoven, Pascal and Newton—all human heroes whose genius lay essentially in their contact with essential truths, with the central reality of the universe. Why should humanity not produce guides who can lead us forward towards those forms of social life most in harmony with universal laws? The social system, like the stellar system, must have its laws of attraction and gravitation. Man is not a dual personality, with one side of his nature that sings and learns while the other acts; one that feels beauty and understands truth and another to feel brotherhood and understand justice. Nobody who sees mankind and the universe in this way can fail to be conscious of an invincible hope. Let man only keep his gaze fixed on his goal, let him keep his faith in his destiny, let him not shrink from using the strength that is his, and in times of anxiety and discouragement, let all his thought be for all mankind.